Handbook of Research on Enterprise 2.0:

Technological, Social, and Organizational Dimensions

Maria Manuela Cruz-Cunha
Polytechnic Insitute of Cavado and Ave, Portugal

Fernando Moreira
Portucalense University, Portugal

João Varajão
Universidade de Trás-os-Montes e Alto Douro, Braga, Portugal

A volume in the Advances in Business Information Systems and Analytics

BUSINESS SCIENCE Reference
An Imprint of IGI Global

Managing Director: Lindsay Johnston
Editorial Director: Joel Gamon
Production Manager: Jennifer Yoder
Publishing Systems Analyst: Adrienne Freeland
Development Editor: Joel Gamon
Assistant Acquisitions Editor: Kayla Wolfe
Typesetter: Lisandro Gonzalez
Cover Design: Jason Mull

Published in the United States of America by
Business Science Reference (an imprint of IGI Global)
701 E. Chocolate Avenue
Hershey PA 17033
Tel: 717-533-8845
Fax: 717-533-8661
E-mail: cust@igi-global.com
Web site: http://www.igi-global.com

Library of Congress Cataloging-in-Publication Data

Handbook of research on enterprise 2.0 : technological, social, and organizational dimensions / Maria Manuela Cruz-Cunha, Fernando Moreira and Joao Varajao, editors.
pages cm
Includes bibliographical references and index.
Summary: "This book collects the most recent developments in evaluating the technological, organizational, and social dimensions of modern business practices in order to better foster advances in information exchange and collaboration among networks of partners and customers"--Provided by publisher.
ISBN 978-1-4666-4373-4 (hardcover) -- ISBN 978-1-4666-4374-1 (ebook) -- ISBN 978-1-4666-4375-8 (print & perpetual access) 1. Information technology--Management. 2. Web 2.0. 3. Communication in organizations--Technological innovations. I. Cruz-Cunha, Maria Manuela, 1964- II. Moreira, Fernando, 1969 August 16- III. Varajao, Joao, 1972-

HD30.2.H36425 2014
658'.05--dc23

2013015165

This book is published in the IGI Global book series Advances in Business Information Systems and Analytics (ISSN: 2327-3275; eISSN: 2327-3283)

British Cataloguing in Publication Data
A Cataloguing in Publication record for this book is available from the British Library.

Advances in Business Information Systems and Analytics (ABISA) Book Series

Madjid Tavana
La Salle University, USA

ISSN: 2327-3275
EISSN: 2327-3283

Mission

The successful development and management of information systems and business analytics is crucial to the success of an organization. New technological developments and methods for data analysis have allowed organizations to not only improve their processes and allow for greater productivity, but have also provided businesses with a venue through which to cut costs, plan for the future, and maintain competitive advantage in the information age.

The **Advances in Business Information Systems and Analytics (ABISA) Book Series** aims to present diverse and timely research in the development, deployment, and management of business information systems and business analytics for continued organizational development and improved business value.

Coverage

- Big Data
- Business Decision Making
- Business Information Security
- Business Process Management
- Business Systems Engineering
- Data Analytics
- Data Management
- Decision Support Systems
- Management Information Systems
- Performance Metrics

IGI Global is currently accepting manuscripts for publication within this series. To submit a proposal for a volume in this series, please contact our Acquisition Editors at Acquisitions@igi-global.com or visit: http://www.igi-global.com/publish/.

The Advances in Business Information Systems and Analytics (ABISA) Book Series (ISSN 2327-3275) is published by IGI Global, 701 E. Chocolate Avenue, Hershey, PA 17033-1240, USA, www.igi-global.com. This series is composed of titles available for purchase individually; each title is edited to be contextually exclusive from any other title within the series. For pricing and ordering information please visit http://www.igi-global.com/book-series/advances-business-information-systems-analytics/37155. Postmaster: Send all address changes to above address.

Titles in this Series

For a list of additional titles in this series, please visit: www.igi-global.com

Uncovering Essential Software Artifacts through Business Process Archeology
Ricardo Perez-Castillo (University of Castilla-La Mancha, Spain) and Mario G. Piattini (University of Castilla - La Mancha, Spain)
Business Science Reference • copyright 2014 • 355pp • H/C (ISBN: 9781466646674) • US $185.00 (our price)

A Systemic Perspective to Managing Complexity with Enterprise Architecture
Pallab Saha (National University of Singapore, Singapore)
Business Science Reference • copyright 2014 • 327pp • H/C (ISBN: 9781466645189) • US $185.00 (our price)

Frameworks of IT Prosumption for Business Development
Małgorzata Pańkowska (University of Economics in Katowice, Poland)
Business Science Reference • copyright 2014 • 347pp • H/C (ISBN: 9781466643130) • US $185.00 (our price)

Handbook of Research on Enterprise 2.0 Technological, Social, and Organizational Dimensions
Maria Manuela Cruz-Cunha (Polytechnic Insitute of Cavado and Ave, Portugal) Fernando Moreira (Portucalense University, Portugal) and João Varajão (Universidade de Trás-os-Montes e Alto Douro, Braga, Portugal)
Information Science Reference • copyright 2014 • 603pp • H/C (ISBN: 9781466643734) • US $325.00 (our price)

Managing Enterprise Information Technology Acquisitions Assessing Organizational Preparedness
Harekrishna Misra (Institute of Rural Management Anand, India) and Hakikur Rahman (University of Minho, Portugal)
Business Science Reference • copyright 2013 • 344pp • H/C (ISBN: 9781466642010) • US $185.00 (our price)

Information Systems and Technology for Organizations in a Networked Society
Tomayess Issa (Curtin University, Australia) Pedro Isaías (Universidade Aberta, Portugal) and Piet Kommers (University of Twente, The Netherlands)
Business Science Reference • copyright 2013 • 432pp • H/C (ISBN: 9781466640627) • US $185.00 (our price)

Cases on Enterprise Information Systems and Implementation Stages Learning from the Gulf Region
Fayez Albadri (ADMO-OPCO, UAE)
Information Science Reference • copyright 2013 • 370pp • H/C (ISBN: 9781466622203) • US $185.00 (our price)

Business Intelligence and Agile Methodologies for Knowledge-Based Organizations Cross-Disciplinary Applications
Asim Abdel Rahman El Sheikh (The Arab Academy for Banking and Financial Sciences, Jordan) and Mouhib Alnoukari (Arab International University, Syria)
Business Science Reference • copyright 2012 • 370pp • H/C (ISBN: 9781613500507) • US $185.00 (our price)

Editorial Advisory Board

List of Reviewers

Ana Isabel Machado Silva, *Porto Business School, Portugal*
Marisa Carla Barros Fonseca Silva, *Escola Superior de Tecnologia e Gestão de Lamego, Portugal*
Dora Simões, *University of Aveiro, Portugal*
Fawzy Soliman, *University of Technology Sydney, Australia*
Ana Filipa Martins de Sousa, *University of Aveiro, Portugal*
Simona Sternad, *University of Maribor, Slovenia*
António Joaquim da Silva Teixeira, *University of Aveiro, Portugal*
Leonor da Conceição Teixeira, *University of Aveiro, Portugal*
Ana Isabel Perdigão Lopes Pereira Torres, *University of Porto, Portugal*
Iakovos S. Venieris, *National Technical University of Athens, Greece*
Miguel Angel Sánchez Vidales, *Universidad Pontificia de Salamanca, Spain*
Jelena Zascerinska, *Centre for Education and Innovation Research, Latvia*
Bruno Završnik, *University of Maribor, Slovenia*

List of Contributors

Table of Contents

Detailed Table of Contents

Volume I

Section 1
The Technological Dimension

Small and Medium-Sized Enterprises (SMEs) are socially and economically important, since they represent 98% of all enterprises, providing around 90 million jobs in the European Union, and contribute to entrepreneurship and innovation. However, SMEs face particular difficulties in order to be competitive in a global world. In recent time, technology applications in different fields, especially Business Intelligence (BI) have been developed rapidly and considered to be one of the most significant uses of information technology. BI is a broad category of applications and technologies for gathering, storing, analyzing, and providing access to data to help enterprise users make better business decisions. This represents a tremendous competitive advantage that allows achieving and exploring the collective intelligence of the organization, enabling contextual, agile, and simplified information exchange and collaboration among distributed workforce and networks of partners and customers, which can be defined as Enterprise 2.0. Despite these advantages, the companies applying such systems may also encounter problems in decision-making processes because of the highly diversified interactions within the systems. Hence, the choice of a suitable BI platform for SMEs is important to take the great advantage of using information technology in all organizational fields. The authors analyze seven open source Business Intelligence tools, free of charge, given that one of the main objectives is to reduce costs and enhance Enterprise 2.0 using new open source technologies.

A wealth of research is associated with virtual teams and collaboration technologies; however, no integrated model is available to guide decision-makers at large organisations in the strategic implementation and management of "virtuality." Whilst collaboration through technology has become commonplace in modern teams, it is not yet clear if Enterprise 2.0 organisations have made changes to accommodate and support this new mode of work. In other words, managing "virtuality" requires supporting tools and research in order to maximise the benefits and diminish the challenges inherent in it. This chapter presents findings of research relating to managing "virtualtiy" that culminates in the development and evaluation of a management model that guides large organisations in implementing and managing virtual teams. The findings demonstrate that there are benefits associated with virtual teamwork; however, a structured approach is essential to realise and maximise such benefits. The authors unçover several critical success factors in managing virtual teams, and they also learned that the implementation of enabling technologies must be carefully planned to ensure successful adoption by the intended audience. This chapter provides practitioners with a structured approach to implementing and managing virtual teams in an Enterprise 2.0 environment. Essential conditions for success are identified, specific organisational level tasks are presented, a process to ensure the introduction of new technologies is documented, and the critical success factors to create and manage virtual teams are synthesised and presented.

Until recently, a company's communications with the public were unidirectional and mostly limited to advertisements in mass media. This gave companies almost complete control over their brand and image. Nowadays, a new set of media, in which the public has similar capabilities for creating content as companies has emerged: social media. The growth of this medium has been exponential, endowing it with a reach that can dwarf traditional mass media. Having or not having a presence in such media is not just a choice of the company. The company's customers and the general public can generate content related to a company without the company's consent. There is no way for the company to avoid it. All they can do is listen to the conversations, engage in them, and try to dampen negative feelings while steering the overall conversation in positive directions. Given the size of social networks and the large number of conversations that they support on a daily basis, manual monitoring is impossible. In this chapter, the authors review and evaluate various tools to support the tasks of monitoring and managing the content of social media that is relevant for a company, a brand, or a product.

To some authors and scientists the concepts effectiveness and efficiency are significantly different. To others, they mean the same; while to a third group the truth about them lies somewhere between these two extremes. This chapter provides an overview of efficiency theories. It finds that the term efficiency covers both doing the right thing and doing the thing right. Efficiency is not limited to internal factors of success, nor should effectiveness only be seen as a term pertaining to the outer factors of success of a human origin, organization source, or inherent in national, local, or international regions.

Before the development of the Internet, there were only a few major media outlets that organizations could use to reach their target audiences. Subsequently, public relations practitioners were able to carefully control all forms of communication. The arrival of new media in the past few years has posed an array of new opportunities but also threats. The public has developed a need to access news and information practically before it exists, and so there is a growing desire to find out what's new via social network sites. With the introduction of social networks, business organizations should identify those social networks representing their target audiences; they should control and participate in them. This chapter describes basic characteristics of social networks and their role for public relations.

Values of individuals, culture of groups, ethics of communities, and the resulting influential norms (i.e. VCEN) are interdependent. VCEN tend to crucially influence development and application of knowledge, skills, talents, and other resources. In the current very competitive and increasingly global economy, organizations and countries become more successful if their economic culture is innovation friendly. Economic culture reflects itself in the economic part of VCEN of nations as well, because organizations, such as enterprises, play a crucial role in a nation's life. National resources are no longer enough, neither is investment, if it is not innovation enhancing. Thus, a new concept of economic VCEN is going to become necessary for people to find a new positive direction beyond the worrisome blind alley of the current economic crisis. The innovation of VCEN is, again, becoming more important than the technological innovation for development of countries and, indeed, for humankind. The contribution discusses two theses: (1) VCEN in organizations is importantly interdependent with the economic culture, and (2) the change of the economic culture in an organization is connected with the changes of the organizing methods and their management.

The past few years have seen a revolutionary transition in the field of project management that enlightened the strength of agile methodologies as a strategic attack towards the progressively faster development rhythms and growing innovation requirements. In this chapter, the authors present a study developed under this context that aims to discuss the suitability of agile project management to multimedia production through a case study focused on an academic context depleted in management formalities, the Laboratory SAPO/UA. The most prominent project of this setting is the SAPO Campus, and its team is analyzed and subjected to an agile project management model. Consequently, the authors anticipate an enhancement to the studied project and the gathering of arguments that empower a clear perspective on the fitness of agile project management to the context of multimedia development.

Web 2.0 technologies have fundamentally reshaped everyday users' perceptions regarding online services by strengthening the importance of individual participation. This profound change is expanding to substantially affect modern enterprise operations and especially corporate information management practices. Well-established business models are upgraded to capture value from the establishment of dynamic coalitions and virtual organizations among remote stakeholders. However, these collaboration formulations dictate the concentration, use, and circulation of corporate information and sensitive personal data, and thus ignite severe security and privacy concerns. Enterprises against this background are more than willing to invest in terms cost and time in order to enforce the necessary countermeasures and thus build and maintain the trustworthiness of involved operations. This chapter studies how legislation and inherent characteristics of this new collaboration paradigm affect the qualities of trust and highlights prominent features of security and privacy protection measures that can deal with emerging trust issues.

Knowledge management systems are a way to help tracking and keeping organizational knowledge. Typically, organizations value is greater than their tangible assets value. Human, structural, and relational capital is essential knowledge but difficult to evaluate because it tends to be tacit and spread in different organizational elements. The relational capital, as tacit knowledge, is not possible to capture its value as from accounting systems. There is a lack of models to evaluate the relational capital of organizations in a network perspective and this research question is: What is the value of this social network? SNARE (Social Network Analysis and Reengineering Environment) is a framework with engineering artifacts that can answer this question. With the aim of evaluating the relational capital of organizations, the authors develop three SNARE components: (1) SNARE-Language – a descriptive UML-based method that provides a representation of an abstract social network structure able to be extended and applied to organizations; (2) SNARE-RCO – a model to determine the relational capital of organizations; and (3) SNARE-Explorer – based on SNARE-Language, is a tool for social networks visualization able to simulate or use real social network scenarios. It also uses SNARE-RCO model to compute the value of the organizational relational capital. The chapter presents an approach for the measurement of the value of organizations' networks.

While evangelists and enthusiasts of Enterprise 2.0 praise the benefits of the use of social software in the workplace, the sceptics are not that convinced and some draw attention to the failures of the Knowledge Management concept and tools that were trendy some years ago. In parallel, board members and top management question the true business benefits of Enterprise 2.0 and demand proof of the potential business value prior to giving a green light to this type of investment. If it is true that some of the benefits of Enterprise 2.0 are intangible and therefore harder to measure, the impact on business performance should be observable and consequently measurable. This chapter reflects on the importance of addressing the topic of business performance when it comes to social software in the enterprise. It also discusses the importance of integrating social software into the flow of work in order to drive adoption and sustained use.

According to the literature, social relationships have a positive influence on work-related attitudes and behaviours. Taking into account that Online Social Networks (OSNs), brought about by Web 2.0, have become an international phenomena and have a considerable impact on the way people communicate and interact with each other, the chapter's purpose is to evaluate the effect that the use of OSNs has on the worker's attitudes and behaviours. In this way, the authors use a questionnaire to evaluate the attitudes of 157 faculty members in Higher Education Institutions (HEI). To assess the use of OSNs by faculty members, they use a binary variable. After analysing and discussing the results, the authors conclude that the use of OSNs influences the workers' performance traits. The relations they propose in what concerns the workers' attitudes are all empirically proven. At last, the authors describe the study limitations and suggest some perspectives for future research.

This chapter describes innovation and diversification policies (i + d) and analyzes the main drivers of innovation in financial institutions. In addition, recent examples of financial innovations and their effect on banking policies are discussed. Specifically, the Internet has been the key to enabling financial institutions to extend and optimize their business by improving the information and services they can offer to their customers and prospects. Due to innovations and changes, the banking sector now takes a new approach in the design of their offices ("bank branch 2.0") and Websites as a way to innovate and diversify business. This chapter explains the innovative strategies of the Urban@ program at the Caja Rural of Granada (Granada, Spain). The history and consolidation of the program, the internal institutional response, and the competition within the banking sector are described and analyzed. In general, the main strategies and achievements of this initiative are: (1) active customer listening, resulting in increased confidence and commitment from the staff; (2) use of up-sale strategies (cross-selling, reduced dropout rates, increased membership advantages), which increase both customer loyalty and customer satisfaction; and 3) a modern, more positive perception of the entity among the general public.

This chapter examines how the concept of social networks can be effectively transferred to a business context and why some of the promises associated with network use might be misleading. Special emphasis is given to the issue of co-determination within social networks in the light of networks' proposed benefits for modern companies. The chapter draws relevant insights from literature research and provides a comparison of social networks, user innovation communities, and company requirements. Findings are illustrated by three respective cases from the context of different networks, communities, as well as from network use in business contexts.

Volume II

Web 2.0 represents the second generation of the Web applications, based on online services collaboration and sharing that promote different ways of interaction between people. These applications provide several collaboration and communication opportunities, like social interaction, feedback, conversation, and networking, thus being a perfect environment for the teaching and learning context. The main goal of this chapter is to present the most used Web 2.0 tools, their major advantages and disadvantages, and their specificity when used in the teaching and learning process. It is believed that their use can greatly improve the teaching and learning process and, consequently, the need to adjust the traditional practice to the new technological paradigm emerges.

As each year sees an increase in the number of Internet users, so too the percentage of purchases made online increases. It is for this reason that firms are showing a growing interest in designing effective communication strategies that help to achieve their online business objectives. Online sales promotion is one of the most widely used communication tools on the Internet. However, there is little research into its effect on purchase intention and how this effect may vary depending on the type of incentive offered and the consumer's level of experience in using the Internet. This chapter seeks to analyze which types of online sales promotions (utilitarian vs. hedonic) are most effective at triggering online purchasing and whether the user's past experience of the Internet is capable of moderating the effect of the type of incentive on online purchasing.

The Information and Communication Technologies (ICT) contain properties that easily convert into solutions for people with special needs, contributing to their inclusion in everyday life. The possibility to intervene and participate in acts of communication in interpersonal settings and distance learning, or simply the possibility of using a device that simulates the vocalization of requests, greetings, and caresses gain a redoubled sense in the efforts to include citizens with special needs, as it does to the senior citizens, in societies attempting to promote equal opportunities among its members. This chapter focuses on the interaction between the elderly and the information and communication technologies and the impact that that interaction has on their participation in society.

Contemporary marketing recognizes the scope and complexities of marketing activities. It is a multi-dimensional and a dynamic concept, known as holistic marketing, that asks and allows for the support systems in order to permanently connect to the parties, to create value and long-term relationships among all. In this context, this chapter presents a wide review about conceptualization of relationship marketing and its evolution and integration within the broader concept of contemporary marketing. It highlights that the development of a program for implementing and managing a successful Customer Relationship Management (CRM) system is an essential part of a strategic contemporary marketing plan. Additionally, it is imperative to assess it to better demonstrate its success or failure. The metrics to do this are also revisited in this chapter. Still, the emerging capabilities of CRM systems using Internet technologies are putting tremendous challenges on organizations and their human resources. Reference is made to some social media tools that can be a cheap and useful support in marketing strategies.

Enterprise Resource Planning (ERP) systems have been implemented in numerous organizations over the last decade. However, research indicates that successful implementation of ERP solutions does not

Current enterprise architecture frameworks are inherently committed to the process paradigm by separating the data and application architectures. The N-tier architectural style is a good match to those methods, since it is based on the same separation principle. However, the process paradigm does not satisfy the information hiding and low semantic gap principles heralded by the object-oriented paradigm. This chapter presents an enterprise architecture framework that emphasizes the motivations (stemming from the business), the ends (expectations, what the business needs to achieve), and the means (what is needed to accomplish the ends), as the basis for a method to develop architectures better prepared for changes, either due to maintenance, adaptation, or enterprise integration and interoperability. The main tenets are to refine the ends into goals and objectives, increasing the level of concreteness as much as possible before delving into the design, and to adopt the service paradigm, for which a tierless architectural style is a more suitable match.

Engineering education is facing a challenge to bring e-business closer to student engineers. Enterprise 2.0 application in engineering education advances engineering students' enterprise for the development of innovative products, processes, and services. The aim of the research is to analyze student engineers' Enterprise 2.0 application underpinning elaboration of pedagogical guidelines on student engineers' Enterprise 2.0 application in engineering curriculum. The meaning of key concepts of Enterprise 2.0 and engineering curriculum is studied. Moreover, the study indicates how the steps of the process are related following a logical chain: Enterprise 2.0 → engineering curriculum design → modelling Enterprise 2.0 application in engineering curriculum → empirical study within a multicultural environment. The present empirical research was conducted during the Baltic Summer School "Technical Informatics and Information Technology" in 2009, 2010, and 2011. The findings of the research allow drawing the conclusions that student engineers' Enterprise 2.0 application in engineering curriculum is efficient.

This chapter summarizes several previous studies on the analysis of social networks and presents some challenges in monitoring and evaluating large-scale training programs that make use of social networks. The main objective is to understand the dynamics and identify how information is shared among the participating agents of the training program. In this regard, the authors present various algorithms that apply metrics to social network analysis to assess the evolution of networks throughout the training process, and specifically, to discuss the application of these metrics in the evaluation of large-scale training programs for digital inclusion.

Enterprise 2.0 aims to help employees, customers, and suppliers collaborate, share, and organize information. As governments are relevant partners for enterprises (legislation, contracts, etc.) e-government platforms need to be ready for Enterprise 2.0 to what concerns e-government interactions. The public sector holds huge quantities of information and just a small proportion is relevant to each enterprise. Enterprises should only be confronted with relevant information and not flooded with lots of data. This implies data organization with semantic description and services using open standards. The goal is to build a durable information infrastructure for government that can be readily accessed by enterprises. The authors propose a conceptual model for government information provisioning. The rationale for this proposal is to motivate the creation of durable, standard, and open government information infrastructures. The model acquires information from natural language documents and represents it using ontology. A proof-of-concept prototype and its preliminary results are presented.

Preface

This handbook of research represents a collection of the most recent developments on the technological, organizational, and social dimensions of Enterprise 2.0 that dictate a paradigm shift in organizations, society, and people. It covers the following dimensions:

- The technological dimension, addressing: emerging technologies, emerging architectures, Web 2.0 tools, standards and reference models, apps and platforms technology, and security.
- The impact on organizations, society, and individuals, covering: new business models, collaborative work, culture and internal communication, mobile enterprise people, social networks, studies on adoption, studies of impact, critical success factors, and level of preparedness of SME.
- Applications and solutions: application to different sectors, from business to government services, from education to eHealth, relevant developments, and technical considerations.

ORGANIZATION OF THE HANDBOOK

This handbook is a compilation of 33 contributions to the discussion of the main issues, challenges, opportunities, and developments related with Enterprise 2.0. They are arranged in a very comprehensive way in order to disseminate current achievements and practical solutions and applications. These 33 chapters are written by a group of 76 authors that include many internationally renowned and experienced researchers and specialists in the e-Business field and a set of younger authors, showing a promising potential for research and development. Contributions come from all over the world and from academia, research institutions, and industry, representing a good and comprehensive representation of the state-of-the-art approaches and developments that address the many dimensions of this quickly evolving theme.

The *Handbook of Research on Enterprise 2.0: Technological, Social, and Organizational Dimensions* is organized in three sections:

- **Section 1:** The Technological Dimension
- **Section 2:** Impact on Organizations, Society, and Individuals
- **Section 3:** Applications and Solutions

The first section, "The Technological Dimension," addressing technologies supporting Enterprise 2.0 applications, comprises five chapters that address relevant research and development contributions to the field of Enterprise 2.0, summarized below. Contributions include: "Emerging Business Intelligence Technologies for SMEs," "Managing 'Virtuality': An Integrated Model for the Implementation and Management of Virtual Teams," "A Review of Tools for Overcoming the Challenge of Monitoring of Social Media," "E-Health Sites Development Using Open Source Software and OMT Methodology as Support for the Family Doctors Activities: A Romanian Case Study," and "CommunicaME: A New Proposal for Facilitating Communication using NFC."

"Emerging Business Intelligence Technologies for SMEs"

Small and Medium-Sized Enterprises (SMEs) are socially and economically important, since they represent 98% of all enterprises, providing around 90 million jobs in the European Union, and contribute to entrepreneurship and innovation. However, SMEs face particular difficulties in order to be competitive in a global world. In recent time, technology applications in different fields, especially Business Intelligence (BI) have been developed rapidly and considered to be one of the most significant uses of information technology. BI is a broad category of applications and technologies for gathering, storing, analyzing, and providing access to data to help enterprise users make better business decisions. This represents a tremendous competitive advantage that allows achieving and exploring the collective intelligence of the organization, enabling contextual, agile, and simplified information exchange and collaboration among distributed workforce and networks of partners and customers, which can be defined as Enterprise 2.0. Despite these advantages, the companies applying such systems may also encounter problems in decision-making processes because of the highly diversified interactions within the systems. Hence, the choice of a suitable BI platform for SMEs is important to take the great advantage of using information technology in all organizational fields. The authors analyze seven open source Business Intelligence tools, free of charge, given that one of the main objectives is to reduce costs and enhance Enterprise 2.0 using new open source technologies.

"Managing 'Virtuality': An Integrated Model for the Implementation and Management of Virtual Teams"

A wealth of research is associated with virtual teams and collaboration technologies; however, no integrated model is available to guide decision-makers at large organisations in the strategic implementation and management of "virtuality." Whilst collaboration through technology has become commonplace in modern teams, it is not yet clear if Enterprise 2.0 organisations have made changes to accommodate and support this new mode of work. In other words, managing "virtuality" requires supporting tools and research in order to maximise the benefits and diminish the challenges inherent in it. This chapter presents findings of research relating to managing "virtualtiy" that culminates in the development and evaluation of a management model that guides large organisations in implementing and managing virtual teams. The findings demonstrate that there are benefits associated with virtual teamwork; however, a structured approach is essential to realise and maximise such benefits. The authors uncover several critical success factors in managing virtual teams, and they also learned that the implementation of enabling technologies must be carefully planned to ensure successful adoption by the intended audience. This chapter provides practitioners with a structured approach to implementing and managing virtual teams in an Enterprise 2.0 environment. Essential conditions for success are identified, specific organisational level tasks are presented, a process to ensure the introduction of new technologies is documented, and the critical success factors to create and manage virtual teams are synthesised and presented.

"A Review of Tools for Overcoming the Challenge of Monitoring of Social Media"

Until recently, a company's communications with the public were unidirectional and mostly limited to advertisements in mass media. This gave companies almost complete control over their brand and image. Nowadays a new set of media in which the public has similar capabilities for creating content as companies has emerged: social media. The growth of this medium has been exponential, endowing it with a reach that can dwarf traditional mass media. Having or not having a presence in such media is not just a choice of the company. The company's customers and the general public can generate content related to a company without the company's consent. There is no way for the company to avoid it. All they can do is listen to the conversations, engage in them, and try to dampen negative feelings while steering the overall conversation in positive directions. Given the size of social networks and the large number of conversations that they support on a daily basis, manual monitoring is impossible. In this chapter, the authors review and evaluate various tools to support the tasks of monitoring and managing the content of social media that is relevant for a company, a brand, or a product.

"E-Health Sites Development Using Open Source Software and OMT Methodology as Support for the Family Doctors' Activities: A Romanian Case Study"

E-health is the generic term used for the set of tools based on information and communication technology used to help prevent, diagnose, treat, and monitor the health and lifestyles and to improve these processes. These considerations are the starting point of this chapter, which presents a Website development solution for family doctors' consulting-rooms to meet the needs of potential patients, based on Object Modeling Technique (OMT) and Open Source Software (OSS) in a metropolitan area network infrastructure. Development of ICT leaves much more freedom to the consultants to accommodate organizations to other influences, both internal and external.

"CommunicaME: A New Proposal for Facilitating Communication Using NFC"

In a society that is clearly influenced by new technology, new advances in mobile technology have yielded important changes in the way users interact with information systems and contextual information. There is a need to provide technological solutions that help users communicate more easily. In this chapter, a novel solution that makes it easier for the elderly to use mobile phones is proposed. The senior population is rapidly growing; they represent 16-17% of the total population in developed countries. The use of a mobile device presents two large obstacles for this group: problems from disabilities due to age and problems associated with the lack of familiarity with mobile technology. The combined use of contactless technologies such as NFC and MiFARE eliminates the barriers encountered by older individuals. These technologies make it possible to use basic services of a mobile telephone, such as placing a call or sending a message, in a way that is easy, user friendly, and intuitive. The CommunicaME system makes it possible to place a call or send a SMS on a mobile by simply moving it closer to a contactless tag. The use of contactless technologies helps the user to carry out their daily tasks, and it also provides a new method of mobile communication that is both quick and secure. The results obtained with the defined and implemented prototype are presented in this chapter.

The seventeen chapters of section 2, "Impact on Organizations, Society, and Individuals," introduce the efficiency and impact of Enterprise 2.0 theories and practices. Section 2 consists of: "The Impact of Enterprise 2.0 Principles on Business Processes: Emphasizing Human Decisions," "Efficiency Theories: The State of the Art," "Use of Social Network for Business in Public Relations," "Impact of Economic Culture on the Development of Enterprises," "Agile Management for Multimedia: A Case Study," "Trust in an Enterprise World: A Survey," "How to Value and Monitor the Relational Capital of Knowledge-Intensive Organizations," "Critical Success Factors in Enterprise 2.0: The Importance of Business Performance," "The Influence of (Online) Social Networks on Workers' Attitudes and Behaviours in Higher Education Institutions," "Innovation and Diversification Policies in the Banking Sector: The Case of the Urban@ Program," "Internal Social Networks: The Danger of Misleading Promises," "The Impact of Web 2.0 in the Teaching and Learning Process," "Experts vs. Novices: Influence of Promotional Benefit Type on their Online Purchase Intention," "The Importance of ICT in the Social Support Networks and in the Citizenship of the Portuguese Elderly," "Impact of 2.0 on Contemporary Marketing," "Comparative Analysis of Acceptance Factors for SAP and Microsoft Dynamics NAV ERP Solutions in their Maturity Use Phase: Enterprise 2.0 Issues," and "Attributes of Innovation Leaders."

"The Impact of Enterprise 2.0 Principles on Business Processes: Emphasizing Human Decisions"

The impact of Enterprise 2.0 principles on business processes is a hot research topic and involves several aspects. In particular, this chapter addresses knowledge-intensive processes in which participants are not considered as mere resources needed to carry out tasks that are not automatable, but their involvement is required at a higher level where they can take decisions that affect the control flow of the process. Participants must be given as much information as possible on the decisions they have to take and on the business entities to be acted on and produced by the tasks they have to perform. For this reason, this chapter proposes a business process notation that integrates the data flow and the control flow and focuses on three kinds of decisions, referred to as data selection, task selection, and performer selection. It also illustrates the structure of to-do lists, which are the major interface between the participants and their tasks.

"Efficiency Theories: The State-of-the-Art"

To some authors and scientists the concepts effectiveness and efficiency are significantly different. To others, they mean the same; while to a third group the truth about them lies somewhere between these two extremes. This chapter provides an overview of efficiency theories. It finds that the term efficiency covers both doing the right thing and doing the thing right. Efficiency is not limited to internal factors of success, nor should effectiveness only be seen as a term pertaining to the outer factors of success of a human origin, organization source, or inherent in national, local, or international regions.

"Use of Social Network for Business in Public Relations"

Before the development of the Internet, there were only a few major media outlets that organizations could use to reach their target audiences. Subsequently, public relations practitioners were able to carefully control all forms of communication. The arrival of new media in the past few years has posed an array of new opportunities but also threats. The public has developed a need to access news and information practically before it exists, and so there is a growing desire to find out what's new via social network sites. With the introduction of social networks, business organizations should identify those social networks representing their target audiences; they should control and participate in them. This chapter describes basic characteristics of social networks and their role for public relations.

"Impact of Economic Culture on the Development of Enterprises"

Values of individuals, culture of groups, ethics of communities, and the resulting influential norms (i.e. VCEN) are interdependent. VCEN tend to crucially influence development and application of knowledge, skills, talents, and other resources. In the current very competitive and increasingly global economy, organizations and countries become more successful if their economic culture is innovation friendly. Economic culture reflects itself in the economic part of VCEN of nations as well, because organizations, such as enterprises, play a crucial role in a nation's life. National resources are no longer enough, neither is investment, if it is not innovation enhancing. Thus, a new concept of economic VCEN is going to become necessary for people to find a new positive direction beyond the worrisome blind alley of the current economic crisis. The innovation of VCEN is, again, becoming more important than the technological innovation for development of countries and, indeed, for humankind. The contribution discusses two theses: (1) VCEN in organizations is importantly interdependent with the economic culture, and (2) the change of the economic culture in an organization is connected with the changes of the organizing methods and their management.

"Agile Management for Multimedia: A Case Study"

The past few years have seen a revolutionary transition in the field of project management that enlightened the strength of agile methodologies as a strategic attack towards the progressively faster development rhythms and growing innovation requirements. In this chapter, the authors present a study developed under this context that aims to discuss the suitability of agile project management to multimedia production through a case study focused on an academic context depleted in management formalities, the Laboratory SAPO/UA. The most prominent project of this setting is the SAPO Campus, and its team is analyzed and subjected to an agile project management model. Consequently, the authors anticipate an enhancement to the studied project and the gathering of arguments that empower a clear perspective on the fitness of agile project management to the context of multimedia development.

"Trust in an Enterprise World: A Survey"

Web 2.0 technologies have fundamentally reshaped everyday users' perceptions regarding online services by strengthening the importance of individual participation. This profound change is expanding to substantially affect modern enterprise operations and especially corporate information management practices. Well-established business models are upgraded to capture value from the establishment of dynamic coalitions and virtual organizations among remote stakeholders. However, these collaboration formulations dictate the concentration, use, and circulation of corporate information and sensitive personal data, and thus ignite severe security and privacy concerns. Enterprises against this background are more than willing to invest in terms cost and time in order to enforce the necessary countermeasures and thus build and maintain the trustworthiness of involved operations. This chapter studies how legislation and inherent characteristics of this new collaboration paradigm affect the qualities of trust and highlights prominent features of security and privacy protection measures that can deal with emerging trust issues.

"How to Value and Monitor the Relational Capital of Knowledge-Intensive Organizations"

Knowledge management systems are a way to help tracking and keeping organizational knowledge. Typically, organizations value is greater than their tangible assets value. Human, structural, and relational capital is essential knowledge but difficult to evaluate because it tends to be tacit and spread in different organizational elements. The relational capital, as tacit knowledge, is not possible to capture its value as from accounting systems. There is a lack of models to evaluate the relational capital of organizations in a network perspective and this research question is: *What is the value of this social network?* SNARE (Social Network Analysis and Reengineering Environment) is a framework with engineering artifacts that can answer this question. With the aim of evaluating the relational capital of organizations, the authors develop three SNARE components: (1) SNARE-Language – a descriptive *UML-based* method that provides a representation of an abstract social network structure able to be extended and applied to organizations; (2) SNARE-RCO – a model to determine the relational capital of organizations; and (3) SNARE-Explorer – based on SNARE-Language, is a tool for social networks visualization able to simulate or use real social network scenarios. It also uses SNARE-RCO model to compute the value of the organizational relational capital. The chapter presents an approach for the measurement of the value of organizations' networks.

"Critical Success Factors in Enterprise 2.0: The Importance of Business Performance"

While evangelists and enthusiasts of Enterprise 2.0 praise the benefits of the use of social software in the workplace, the sceptics are not that convinced and some draw attention to the failures of the Knowledge Management concept and tools that were trendy some years ago. In parallel, board members and top management question the true business benefits of Enterprise 2.0 and demand proof of the potential business value prior to giving a green light to this type of investment. If it is true that some of the benefits of Enterprise 2.0 are intangible and therefore harder to measure, the impact on business performance should be observable and consequently measurable. This chapter reflects on the importance of addressing the topic of business performance when it comes to social software in the enterprise. It also discusses the importance of integrating social software into the flow of work in order to drive adoption and sustained use.

"The Influence of (Online) Social Networks on Workers' Attitudes and Behaviours in Higher Education Institutions"

According to the literature, social relationships have a positive influence on work-related attitudes and behaviours. Taking into account that Online Social Networks (OSNs), brought about by Web 2.0, have become an international phenomena and have a considerable impact on the way people communicate and interact with each other, the chapter's purpose is to evaluate the effect that the use of OSNs has on the worker's attitudes and behaviours. In this way, the authors use a questionnaire to evaluate the attitudes of 157 faculty members in Higher Education Institutions (HEI). To assess the use of OSNs by faculty members, they use a binary variable. After analysing and discussing the results, the authors conclude that the use of OSNs influences the workers' performance traits. The relations they propose in what concerns the workers' attitudes are all empirically proven. At last, the authors describe the study limitations and suggest some perspectives for future research.

"Innovation and Diversification Policies in the Banking Sector: The Case of the Urban@ Program"

This chapter describes innovation and diversification policies (i + d) and analyzes the main drivers of innovation in financial institutions. In addition, recent examples of financial innovations and their effect on banking policies are discussed. Specifically, the Internet has been the key to enabling financial institutions to extend and optimize their business by improving the information and services they can offer to their customers and prospects. Due to innovations and changes, the banking sector now takes a new approach in the design of their offices ("bank branch 2.0") and Websites as a way to innovate and diversify business. This chapter explains the innovative strategies of the Urban@ program at the Caja Rural of Granada (Granada, Spain). The history and consolidation of the program, the internal institutional response, and the competition within the banking sector are described and analyzed. In general, the main strategies and achievements of this initiative are: (1) active customer listening, resulting in increased confidence and commitment from the staff; (2) use of up-sale strategies (cross-selling, reduced dropout rates, increased membership advantages), which increase both customer loyalty and customer satisfaction; and 3) a modern, more positive perception of the entity among the general public.

"Internal Social Networks: The Danger of Misleading Promises"

This chapter examines how the concept of social networks can be effectively transferred to a business context and why some of the promises associated with network use might be misleading. Special emphasis is given to the issue of co-determination within social networks in the light of networks' proposed benefits for modern companies. The chapter draws relevant insights from literature research and provides a comparison of social networks, user innovation communities, and company requirements. Findings are illustrated by three respective cases from the context of different networks, communities, as well as from network use in business contexts.

"The Impact of Web 2.0 in the Teaching and Learning Process"

Web 2.0 represents the second generation of the Web applications, based on online services collaboration and sharing that promote different ways of interaction between people. These applications provide several collaboration and communication opportunities, like social interaction, feedback, conversation, and networking, thus being a perfect environment for the teaching and learning context. The main goal of this chapter is to present the most used Web 2.0 tools, their major advantages and disadvantages, and their specificity when used in the teaching and learning process. It is believed that their use can greatly improve the teaching and learning process and, consequently, the need to adjust the traditional practice to the new technological paradigm emerges.

"Experts vs. Novices: Influence of Promotional Benefit Type on their Online Purchase Intention"

As each year sees an increase in the number of Internet users, so too the percentage of purchases made online increases. It is for this reason that firms are showing a growing interest in designing effective communication strategies that help to achieve their online business objectives. Online sales promotion is one of the most widely used communication tools on the Internet. However, there is little research into its effect on purchase intention and how this effect may vary depending on the type of incentive offered and the consumer's level of experience in using the Internet. This chapter seeks to analyze which types of online sales promotions (utilitarian vs. hedonic) are most effective at triggering online purchasing and whether the user's past experience of the Internet is capable of moderating the effect of the type of incentive on online purchasing.

"The Importance of ICT in the Social Support Networks and in the Citizenship of the Portuguese Elderly"

The Information and Communication Technologies (ICT) contain properties that easily convert into solutions for people with special needs, contributing to their inclusion in everyday life. The possibility to intervene and participate in acts of communication in interpersonal settings and distance learning, or simply the possibility of using a device that simulates the vocalization of requests, greetings, and caresses gain a redoubled sense in the efforts to include citizens with special needs, as it does to the senior citizens, in societies attempting to promote equal opportunities among its members. This chapter focuses on the interaction between the elderly and the information and communication technologies and the impact that that interaction has on their participation in society.

"Impact of 2.0 on Contemporary Marketing"

Contemporary marketing recognizes the scope and complexities of marketing activities. It is a multidimensional and a dynamic concept, known as holistic marketing, that asks and allows for the support systems in order to permanently connect to the parties, to create value and long-term relationships among all. In this context, this chapter presents a wide review about conceptualization of relationship marketing and its evolution and integration within the broader concept of contemporary marketing. It highlights that the development of a program for implementing and managing a successful Customer Relationship

Management (CRM) system is an essential part of a strategic contemporary marketing plan. Additionally, it is imperative to assess it to better demonstrate its success or failure. The metrics to do this are also revisited in this chapter. Still, the emerging capabilities of CRM systems using Internet technologies are putting tremendous challenges on organizations and their human resources. Reference is made to some social media tools that can be a cheap and useful support in marketing strategies.

"Comparative Analysis of Acceptance Factors for SAP and Microsoft Dynamics NAV ERP Solutions in their Maturity Use Phase: Enterprise 2.0 Issues"

Enterprise Resource Planning (ERP) systems have been implemented in numerous organizations over the last decade. However, research indicates that successful implementation of ERP solutions does not necessarily lead to successful ERP usage. ERP systems benefit organizations only to the extent that users accept and utilize them frequently and extensively. To improve the efficiency and effectiveness of ERP systems in the operation phase, organizations need to research the factors that impact user satisfaction. In this area, the Technological Acceptance Model (TAM) proposed by Davis (1989) has been widely used as it can enhance understanding of the influences that increase the efficiency and effectiveness of ERP system use. Regardless of ERP complexity and ERP implementation failure, very few studies have been conducted to examine technology acceptance, especially when dealing with autonomous ERP users and including more external factors, which can influence users' acceptance of ERP system. Because ERP solutions are implemented by different methodologies and some are more present at large organizations than at small and mid-sized organizations, the authors research and compare the importance of external factors of two global solutions—namely, SAP and Microsoft Dynamics NAV—regarding user acceptance. The chapter contributes to the body of knowledge in this specific area.

"Attributes of Innovation Leaders"

Many innovative companies pass through a number of transformation stages. The transformation is considered a chain of activities that begins with information that leads to knowledge, then into learning before it can finally be used for innovation. The chapter shows that transformational leadership is a key factor for moving the organisation from being information-based into knowledge-based and then into a learning organisation and an innovative company. The six important characteristics of the transformational leaders for the transformation are shown to be courage to switch off or terminate projects, rewarding performing staff, ability to appropriately time release of products to the market, ability to release products to the market within budget, and ability to inspire and be a role model for other staff. The chapter also shows that there are fourteen transformational leadership attributes that may be considered less critical than the above-mentioned six characteristics. Those non-critical characteristics include: degree of passion for the job, attracting talent, ability to build teams, coaching subordinates, communicating at all levels, driving projects successfully, enabling project-supporting environments, advising others managers, advocating for improvement, encouraging self-goal setting, ability of self rehearsal, ability of self reinforcement, ability of self-observation, and ability of self-expectation.

Finally, Section 3, "Applications and Solutions," consists of a comprehensive collection of eleven chapters presenting relevant applications to different sectors of activity and target uses, such as "The Portuguese School of Macao, China: A Traditional/Web 2.0 Assessment Facing Different Learning Styles," "Visibility of the Airport Sector: Web 2.0 and Social Communication Networks," "Online Social Networks: Recommendation Diffusion and Co-Consumption Influence," "The Evolving Value of eTourism for Suppliers and Visitors," "Organizational Learning and Web 2.0 Technologies: Improving the Planning and Organization of a Software Development Process," "Valuing Learning Objects Shared in an Online Community," "A Framework Proposal to Assess the LARG Index of a Supply Chain in a Fuzzy Context," "Objective-Oriented Modeling of Enterprises under the Service Paradigm," "Enterprise 2.0 in Engineering Curriculum," "Brazilian Government's Training Network for Digital Inclusion: Analysis of Strategies for Improving Interactivity," and "Towards E-Government Information Platforms for Enterprise 2.0."

"The Portuguese School of Macao, China: A Traditional/ Web 2.0 Assessment Facing Different Learning Styles"

Technology is fundamental to the youth culture of today and high schools need to integrate it into live classes. This research hopes to provide a better understanding of the present learner styles and the technology impact towards enhancing and enriching the conventional learning process. Hence, the central focus of this writing is based on the four Index Learner Styles (Active VS Reflective, Sensing VS Intuitive, Visual VS Verbal, Sequential VS Global) of Felder and Soloman (1993, 2011) and on the teaching strategies impact that integrates technology (online lessons, blending learning topics, and collaboration software use) as a vehicle in the differentiation of the traditional learning curriculum. The field of experiment is the Portuguese language subject of the 8th grade students at the Portuguese School of Macau, China. One online survey and four tests (two for each class) are carried out to check whether the e-Learning perspective will benefit student learning in this new surrounded generation of mobile devices. Still, the main purpose relies on the learning style identification of high school scholars and to raise awareness of those personal characteristics to facilitate future development on personal learning strategies. Some other related topics are also highlighted such as Web 1.0 to Web 4.0 evolution and learning distance topics.

"Visibility of the Airport Sector: Web 2.0 and Social Communication Networks"

The aim of this chapter is to analyse the use of social communication media and Web 2.0 tools at airports to determine whether these technologies are being used as a means of raising the airports' visibility, enhancing their level of e-participation and improving corporate dialogue. In addition, the authors seek to determine which variables influence the use and development of these tools. The results obtained reveal a moderate use of Web 2.0 tools by airports, with the most noteworthy finding being their presence in social networks and the use of the latter as channels through which to increase e-participation.

"Online Social Networks: Recommendation Diffusion and Co-Consumption Influence"

The chapter is conceptual, based on analysis and synthesis of social network theory and e-consumer literature. Despite a broad spectrum of disciplines that investigate social networks and the interest of marketing practitioners in the consequences of social networks, there are still areas open for research into networked-consumer behavior in marketing. Based on previous theoretical and empirical research, this study examines and discusses the influence of social network structure and ties in matched dyads, recommendation diffusion, social contagion and co-consumption influence, and individual motivations to spread market information. The chapter proposes a theory of matched dyadic ties in close networks of connections as a proxy for information about the potential market that is difficult and expensive for businesses to measure or access directly.

"The Evolving Value of eTourism for Suppliers and Visitors"

The tourism industry is known to have an extensive use of the Internet, both on the supply and on the demand side. The steady and fast emergence of the Internet has dramatically changed the business processes within the sector, forcing suppliers and intermediaries to adapt to a scenario in which visitors have multiple and more flexible choices regarding the search, planning, booking, and purchase of tourism services and products. This chapter explores the main impacts and trends that the dynamic use of the Internet within the tourism sector—the so-called *eTourism*—has originated in each of the sector's main stakeholders, including suppliers, intermediaries, destination management organizations, and tourists.

"Organizational Learning and Web 2.0 Technologies: Improving the Planning and Organization of a Software Development Process"

The knowledge era redefines companies' scenarios and workers' profiles, requiring models and tools for Knowledge Management (KM) and Organizational Learning (OL) to respond to external demands. The growth of the Internet and the emergence of Web 2.0 created the conditions for Enterprise 2.0. This chapter analyzes Web 2.0 usefulness in the workplace and presents a software application for KM and OL that aims to support the software development process in software houses. The conclusion discusses controversial issues related to collaboration and competitive markets and presents some reasons for the apparent negative reaction of companies to adopt systems based on social networks.

"Valuing Learning Objects Shared in an Online Community"

In this chapter, the authors analyze and discuss how the activity inside a social network impacts on the value of a Learning Object (LO) used in a collaborative e-learning platform. Recent works propose metrics for measuring LO reusability based on a variety of approaches. In this work, they combine and extend these approaches in order to design a valuation strategy which helps to identify the usage of LOs inside a social network. Their proposal is to identify the factors that are relevant for the valuation of a LO and determine which of them can be computed automatically from its context of usage, the level of success of its authors and its metadata. The authors' analysis was performed on a particular social network called LOP (LO Poll) system, which strongly motivates the creation and collaborative valuation of LOs. They present preliminary conclusions obtained from an experiment performed in order to analyze the feasibility of the proposal.

"A Framework Proposal to Assess the LARG Index of a Supply Chain in a Fuzzy Context"

Bearing in mind the new Supply Chain Management (SCM) paradigms, it is important that supply chains be aware of the implementation level of the main practices associated to each SCM paradigm (Lean, Agile, Resilient, and Green, hereafter referred as LARG). The main objective of this chapter is to propose a framework, based on Enterprise 2.0 approach, for global supply chains to assess their LARG index in order to evaluate the leanness, agility, resilience, and greenness of their practices. Enterprise 2.0 technologies and Fuzzy Logic techniques are used as enablers to the proposed LARG evaluation model in the following assessment tasks: 1) determination of an adequate set of Lean, Agile, Resilient, and Green practices; 2) consensual definition of the relative weights of the considered practices; 3) adjustment of the evaluation policy to the particular supply chain; and 4) effective follow-up of the assessment results.

"Objective-Oriented Modeling of Enterprises under the Service Paradigm"

Current enterprise architecture frameworks are inherently committed to the process paradigm by separating the data and application architectures. The N-tier architectural style is a good match to those methods, since it is based on the same separation principle. However, the process paradigm does not satisfy the information hiding and low semantic gap principles heralded by the object-oriented paradigm. This chapter presents an enterprise architecture framework that emphasizes the motivations (stemming from the business), the ends (expectations, what the business needs to achieve), and the means (what is needed to accomplish the ends), as the basis for a method to develop architectures better prepared for changes, either due to maintenance, adaptation, or enterprise integration and interoperability. The main tenets are to refine the ends into goals and objectives, increasing the level of concreteness as much as possible before delving into the design, and to adopt the service paradigm, for which a tierless architectural style is a more suitable match.

"Enterprise 2.0 in Engineering Curriculum"

Engineering education is facing a challenge to bring e-business closer to student engineers. Enterprise 2.0 application in engineering education advances engineering students' enterprise for the development of innovative products, processes, and services. The aim of the research is to analyze student engineers' Enterprise 2.0 application underpinning elaboration of pedagogical guidelines on student engineers' Enterprise 2.0 application in engineering curriculum. The meaning of key concepts of *Enterprise 2.0* and *engineering curriculum* is studied. Moreover, the study indicates how the steps of the process are related following a logical chain: Enterprise 2.0 → engineering curriculum design → modelling Enterprise 2.0 application in engineering curriculum → empirical study within a multicultural environment. The present empirical research was conducted during the Baltic Summer School "Technical Informatics and Information Technology" in 2009, 2010, and 2011. The findings of the research allow drawing the conclusions that student engineers' Enterprise 2.0 application in engineering curriculum is efficient.

"Brazilian Government's Training Network for Digital Inclusion: Analysis of Strategies for Improving Interactivity"

This chapter summarizes several previous studies on the analysis of social networks and presents some challenges in monitoring and evaluating large-scale training programs that make use of social networks. The main objective is to understand the dynamics and identify how information is shared among the participating agents of the training program. In this regard, the authors present various algorithms that apply metrics to social network analysis to assess the evolution of networks throughout the training process, and specifically, to discuss the application of these metrics in the evaluation of large-scale training programs for digital inclusion.

"Towards E-Government Information Platforms for Enterprise 2.0"

Enterprise 2.0 aims to help employees, customers, and suppliers collaborate, share, and organize information. As governments are relevant partners for enterprises (legislation, contracts, etc.) e-government platforms need to be ready for Enterprise 2.0 to what concerns e-government interactions. The public sector holds huge quantities of information and just a small proportion is relevant to each enterprise. Enterprises should only be confronted with relevant information and not flooded with lots of data. This implies data organization with semantic description and services using open standards. The goal is to build a durable information infrastructure for government that can be readily accessed by enterprises. The authors propose a conceptual model for government information provisioning. The rationale for this proposal is to motivate the creation of durable, standard, and open government information infrastructures. The model acquires information from natural language documents and represents it using ontology. A proof-of-concept prototype and its preliminary results are presented.

EXPECTATIONS

Within these 33 chapters the reader is faced with the discussions and confirmation of the relevance and impact of this hot topic, providing professionals, researchers, and scholars with some of the most advanced research developments, solutions, state-of-the-art enabling technologies, discussions, and case studies on mobility and computing.

The handbook is expected to support a professional audience of top managers, IT professionals, technology solution providers, and an academic audience (teachers, researchers, and students, mainly of post-graduate studies). As an academic tool, it can be a support to disciplines of post-graduate studies on IT/IS.

We hope you find it useful. Enjoy your reading and study!

Maria Manuela Cruz-Cunha
Polytechnic Insitute of Cavado and Ave, Portugal

Fernando Moreira
Portucalense University, Portugal

João Varajão
Universidade de Trás-os-Montes e Alto Douro, Portugal

Acknowledgment

Editing a book is a hard but compensating and enriching task, as it involves a set of different activities, like contact with authors and reviewers, discussion and exchange of ideas and experiences, process management, organization and integration of contents, and many more, with the permanent objective of creating a book that meets the public's expectations. This task cannot be accomplished without the help and support of many sources. As editors, we would like to acknowledge the help, support, and belief of all who made this creation possible.

First of all, this book would not have been possible without the ongoing professional support of the team of professionals at IGI-Global. We are grateful to Dr. Mehdi Khosrow-Pour, Jan Travers, Kristin Klinger, and Erika Carter for the opportunity and belief in this project. A very special mention of gratitude is due to Joel Gamon, Development Editor, for his professional support and friendly words of advice, encouragement, and prompt guidance. We also address our recognition and appreciation to all the staff at IGI Global, whose contributions throughout the process of production and making this book available all over the world was invaluable.

We are grateful to all the authors for their insights and excellent contributions to this book. We are also grateful to the authors who simultaneously served as referees for chapters written by other authors, as well as to the external referees and to the members of the editorial advisory board for their insights, valuable contributions, prompt collaboration, and constructive comments. Thank you all, authors and reviewers, you made this book! The communication and exchange of views within this truly global group of recognized individuals from the scientific domain and from industry was an enriching and exciting experience!

Thank you.

Maria Manuela Cruz-Cunha
Polytechnic Insitute of Cavado and Ave, Portugal

Fernando Moreira
Portucalense University, Portugal

João Varajão
Universidade de Trás-os-Montes e Alto Douro, Portugal

Section 1
The Technological Dimension

Chapter 1
Emerging Business Intelligence Technologies for SMEs

Jorge Bernardino
Institute Polytechnic of Coimbra – ISEC, Portugal

ABSTRACT

Small and Medium-Sized Enterprises (SMEs) are socially and economically important, since they represent 98% of all enterprises, providing around 90 million jobs in the European Union, and contribute to entrepreneurship and innovation. However, SMEs face particular difficulties in order to be competitive in a global world. In recent time, technology applications in different fields, especially Business Intelligence (BI) have been developed rapidly and considered to be one of the most significant uses of information technology. BI is a broad category of applications and technologies for gathering, storing, analyzing, and providing access to data to help enterprise users make better business decisions. This represents a tremendous competitive advantage that allows achieving and exploring the collective intelligence of the organization, enabling contextual, agile, and simplified information exchange and collaboration among distributed workforce and networks of partners and customers, which can be defined as Enterprise 2.0. Despite these advantages, the companies applying such systems may also encounter problems in decision-making processes because of the highly diversified interactions within the systems. Hence, the choice of a suitable BI platform for SMEs is important to take the great advantage of using information technology in all organizational fields. The authors analyze seven open source Business Intelligence tools, free of charge, given that one of the main objectives is to reduce costs and enhance Enterprise 2.0 using new open source technologies.

1. INTRODUCTION

Data Warehouses (DWs) have become an essential component of modern decision support systems in most companies of the world. In order to be competitive, even Small and Medium Enterprises (SMEs) now collect large volumes of information and are interested in Business Intelligence (BI) systems (Lawton, 2009). BI is now widely used, especially in the world of practice, to describe analytic applications allowing companies analyze large amounts of information collected while do-

DOI: 10.4018/978-1-4666-4373-4.ch001

ing business to capture trends, gain insights, and draw conclusions about the organization.

SMEs are regarded as significantly important on a local, national, or even global basis and they play an important part in the any national economy (Mullins, et al., 2007). Only in European Union they represent 98% of all enterprises, providing around 90 million jobs. Micro, Small, and Medium-Sized Enterprises (SMEs) are the engine of the European economy. They are an essential source of jobs, create entrepreneurial spirit and innovation and are thus crucial for fostering competitiveness and employment. The category of micro, Small and Medium-Sized Enterprises (SMEs) is made up of enterprises which employ fewer than 250 persons and which have an annual turnover not exceeding 50 million euro, and/or an annual balance sheet total not exceeding 43 million euro (European Union, 2003).

However, they are often confronted with market imperfections. SMEs frequently have difficulties in obtaining capital or credit, particularly in the early start-up phase. Their restricted resources may also reduce access to new technologies or innovation. Therefore, support for SMEs is one of the European Commission's priorities for economic growth, job creation and economic and social cohesion (European Union, 2003). BI and Decision Support Systems (DSS) can help SMEs to be competitive in a global world. In spite of multiples advantages, existing DSSs frequently remain inaccessible or insufficient for SMEs because of the following factors (Grabova, et al., 2010):

- High price.
- High requirements for a hardware infrastructure.
- Complexity for most users.
- Irrelevant functionality.
- Low flexibility to deal with a fast changing dynamic business environment. (Xie et al., 2007)
- Low attention to difference in data access necessity in SMEs and large-scaled enterprises.

Today organizations compete in a hyper competitive business environment characterized by a massive influx of data. Information has gained significance as a key resource in organizations and it is undisputed that effective information use is a source of major competitive advantage (Bucher et al., 2009). In this dynamic environment, Business Intelligence (BI) is seen as a critical solution that will help organizations leverage information to make informed, intelligent business decisions to survive in the business world (Jordan & Ellen, 2009). BI describes the concepts and methods used to improve decision making using fact based systems (Watson & Wixom, 2007).

Using BI initiatives, businesses are gaining insights from growing volumes of data generated by applications such as customer relationship management, supply-chain management, and Web analytics. BI enables access to diverse data, manipulation and transformation of these data, and provide business managers and analysts the ability to conduct appropriate analyses and perform actions (Turban et al., 2008). As such, organizations are eager to adopt these technologies to take advantage of the power of BI. BI is seen as a critical solution that is a necessity to survive in the business world (Bucher et al., 2009). A survey of over 4000 Chief Information Officers (CIO) conducted by Gartner Group, revealed that business intelligence is rated as the number one technology priority in organizations (Strange, 2009). A similar survey of CIO's by IBM revealed that BI is the top visionary plan for enhancing enterprise competitiveness (IBM, 2009).

As a result, the BI field has experienced steady growth despite the recent economic downturn that has affected the growth of other IT applications. In its worldwide forecast for BI for 2007-2012, Gartner forecasts the BI market to grow at a compound annual growth rate of 8.1% through 2012, reaching $7.7 billion in 2012 despite the economic downturn (Knight, 2011).

Although BI and data warehousing is now considered a mature market, historically, failure rates have been high (Kelly, 1997). A recent assessment of data warehouse failure in 2007 suggests data warehouse failure rates can be as high as 50 percent (Embarcadero, 2008). Overtime, researchers have described many reasons for struggling and unsuccessful BI efforts (Watson et al., 1999; Watson, 2009); BI implementations come with a very high price tag (Mimno, 2002). Although BI initiatives have been undertaken for major industries, such as airlines (Anderson-Lehman et al., 2004) and telecommunications (Turban et al., 2008), there is still much to be learnt as to why organizations cannot successfully implement and grow their BI efforts to meet the needs of the organization.

In this manner, SMEs require lightweight, cheap, flexible, simple and efficient solutions. To aim at these features, we can take advantage of light clients with Web interfaces. For instance, Web technologies are utilized for data warehousing by large corporations, but there is an even greater demand of such kind of systems among small and medium enterprises. Usage of Web technologies provides cheap software, because it eliminates the necessity for numerous dispersed applications, the necessity of deployment and maintenance of corporate network, and reduces training time. It is simple for end-users to utilize Web-based solutions. In addition, a Web-based architecture requires only lightweight software clients (i.e., Web browsers).

The benefit from business intelligence platforms for organizations is extremely important. Traditionally, only technical specialists run BI tools and only for the benefit of organization management. Not allowing non-management employees to use the generated intelligence has limited BI's usefulness, resulting in a reduced rate of return on companies' large investments in technology. BI can also helps employees, customers and suppliers collaborate, share, and organize information, the main objective of Enterprise 2.0.

Currently, there are several known cases of success, from implementing business intelligence tools in various business segments. The resource to business intelligence platforms is extremely important in order to monitor market trends, technological innovation and make the most work activity of the company. The processes of business intelligence help make business more profitable and dynamic. When is time to choose one business intelligence platform is important that companies have some knowledge about existing platforms on the market. There are several tools in the business intelligence market with different types of licenses, which we can break up in two main groups: proprietary and open source platforms. Before making a decision for the business intelligence platform to acquire, business managers must take into account the features of the tool to satisfy the needs of the organization and check whether the minimum requirements of the platform are supported by the company computer system.

The implementation of business intelligence platforms in an organization requires some additional efforts. Some of the problems regarding the adoption of business intelligence for organizations is directly related to: acquisition of skilled human resources in the area of databases, changes in organizational structure forcing the inclusion of new employees, implementation of new standards of regulation and planning of new work methods.

As organizations today can no longer spend money on excessive infrastructure and technology that does not provide a quick impact on the business' bottom-line, Business Intelligence (BI) is becoming indispensable to an organization's success in the emerging global economy.

Historically Small and Medium Enterprises (SMEs) have been excluded of BI arena by excessive product costs and lack of accessibility. With the traditional BI architecture requiring a database, Extract, Transform, and Load (ETL) tools, reporting and OLAP software, the initial licensing fees from sustaining vendors can easily extend into six figures for a basic environment. For many businesses, this is simply an unviable proposition. Instead, they have been relegated to the limited BI capabilities of office productivity software or the inflexible reporting modules of their core transactional applications. Nowadays, though, these organizations can quickly download freely available Open Source Business Intelligence packages that include report development, ETL and OLAP tools. Now, there are some mature open source business applications and platforms, in the sales, finance and operational areas (Damiani, 2009).

Some of the open source BI platforms follow a model called "Commercial Open Source," where the advanced features are coded under a closed source license. This model usually gives origin to two or more editions of the same product: the "Community" edition, which includes only the open sourced functionalities and the "Enterprise" or "Full" edition, including all the features, and sold, like any other proprietary product. Other open source BI platforms follow the so-called "Free and Open Source" model, FLOSS (Free/Libre/Open Source Software), in which all the functionalities are available under an open source license, like GNU Public License (GPL) or a BSD-style license. These platforms usually only have one free edition.

In this chapter, we concentrate our work on the evaluation of FLOSS model solutions and the Community Edition of open source BI tools. Open-source BI has matured to the point where organizations can evaluate it to see whether it meets basic requirements, particularly when providing a low-cost solution is a priority.

This study analyzed open source tools, free of charge, given that one of the main objectives is to reduce costs and enhance enterprise 2.0 using new open source technologies. We evaluated and compared seven major Open Source Business Intelligence tools (Actuate/BIRT, 2011; Jaspersoft, 2011; Jedox/Palo, 2011; OpenI, 2011; Pentaho, 2011; SpagoBI, 2011; Vanilla, 2011).

2. OPEN-SOURCE SOFTWARE

Open Source Software (OSS) is primarily defined as software, which is freely redistributable and includes the source code (Varner, 1999). This is vastly different from the mainstream proprietary software industry where source code is highly guarded and programs are only distributed in their binary, non-modifiable format. The development process of OSS also differs as it involves large number of software developers at many different locations and organizations sharing code to develop and refine software programs.

While the attention of businesses to the phenomenon of OSS has been recent, the basic behaviors are much older in their origins. According to (Lerner & Tirole, 2002), the tradition of sharing and cooperation in software development began in early 1960s mainly with cooperative development efforts of the UNIX operating system where programmers in different organizations shared source code. The General Public License (GPL) was a noticeable innovation introduced by the Free Software Foundation (FSF) in response to intellectual property right enforcements by commercial companies in 80s. Users had to agree to make the source code freely available and not to impose licensing restrictions on others, in exchange for being able to use and modify GPL software. The widespread diffusion of Internet access in the early 1990s led to a dramatic acceleration of open source activity. As we will mention below, interactions between commercial companies and the open source community also became common place in the 1990s. These interactions created demand to bundle the cooperatively developed software with proprietary code and led to adoption of more flexible licenses. The licenses under which OSS is released today vary greatly, but two points that we mentioned in the beginning (freely redistributable and available source code) remain consistent. Some of these licenses and their characteristics are shown in Table 1.

In the past years, growing interest has brought large market diffusion and capital investment to

Table 1. Comparing open source software license types (Corbett & Ward, 2006)

License Type	Code protected by copyright?	Can code be used in Closed Source Project?	Can project that uses code, be sold?	Must Source Code be released?	Provides for patents?
Public Domain	No	Yes	Yes	No	No
BSD/MIT	Yes	Yes	Yes	No	No
GNU GPL	Yes	No	No	Yes	No
GNU Lesser GPL	Yes	Yes	Yes	Yes	No
Mozilla Public License MPL/ CDDL	Yes	Yes	Yes	Yes	Yes
Common/Eclipse Public License (CPL/EPL)	Yes	Yes	Yes	Yes	Yes

open source software. A number of open source products, such as the Apache Web server, dominate in their product category, while major corporations, including Hewlett Packard, IBM, Sun and Microsoft have launched own open source projects (Lerner & Tirole, 2002).

Today, major enterprises are running mission-critical functions on open source, big vendors have lined up to support it, and reliable applications have emerged. In a survey of 375 information executives, 54 percent said that within five years open source would be their dominant server platform; 59 percent of respondents said a lower Total-Cost-of-Ownership (TCO) is open source's primary strength and those who have implemented it confirm huge TCO reductions (Koch, 2003).

However, OSS has its own disadvantages. The same survey of IT executives shows that 52 percent mentioned a lack of vendor support as open source's primary weakness. To fill this gap, major vendors such as Dell, HP, IBM, Oracle and Sun recently have announced in various ways that they would begin supporting open source products (Koch, 2003).

3. OPEN SOURCE IN SMEs

The increasing focus on open-source software has reached the mainstream business intelligence market. As some organizations are looking to reduce costs in their large Business Intelligence (BI) deployments, they are hoping that open source gives them greater leverage for their money. Application developers that are looking for a way to embed BI functionality into their applications initiate other open-source BI deployments. Similarly, organizations often cannot afford to roll out BI technology to hundreds or maybe thousands of users, even from their preferred vendor, because of steep licensing costs and are therefore considering an open-source solution to complement the current infrastructure.

3.1. Information Systems Success Factors in SMEs

SMEs are defined by usage of qualitative and quantitative measures. We took the European Union (EU) definition as our basis. The EU describes an SME as a company that has fewer than 250 employees and has either an annual turnover not exceeding €50 million or an annual balance sheet total not exceeding €43 million (European Union, 2003).

Information Systems (IS) in SMEs have been addressed by a number of past works. They are mostly based on special IS problems such as Internet adoption (Mehrtens et al., 2001; Dholakia & Kshetri, 2004), system integration (Themistocleous & Chen, 2004), or IS management (Bhagwat & Sharma, 2006). In a more general approach, (Lefebvre, Harvey, & Lefebvre, 1991) identified four general success factors that influence the adoption of a new technology by SMEs: (1) the characteristics of the organization; (2) the competitiveness and management strategies of the organization; (3) the influences of internal and external parties on the adoption decision process; and (4) the characteristics of new technologies adopted. An important factor in at least three of these four points is the strong influence of the owners (Levy et al., 2002; Lybaert, 1998). While larger organizations have specialists for IS (IT department), in SMEs, investment decisions are often made among the owners who might not have deep IS knowledge and experience.

3.2. Advantages of Open Source

Evaluating open source BI is not cost-free, even though the software is freely available for download, and the labor costs should be dramatically lower. This is because the evaluation of open source BI is more likely to be "bottom up" rather than "top down". This means that the technical evaluation and even a pilot implementation may occur at minimal cost and effort before executives are involved.

One of the biggest problems with proprietary solutions is that all the costs are born upfront by the customer before there is any reward. This dynamic is one of the key reasons for the growth and popularity of the open source movement. While open source is evangelized on many fronts, including security, flexibility, and competitive advantage, organizations adopt open source primarily because of the price/performance ratio. With open source BI, organizations can adjust spending as they go, depending on the perceived returns. Almost all of the investment is spent configuring or customizing the solution to meet the organization's needs, not on a generic system that needs to be customized just to work.

Open Source Software/Free Software (OSS/FS) (also abbreviated as FLOSS – Free and Libre Open Source Software) has risen to immense notoriety. Briefly, FLOSS programs are those whose license allows the user to run and modify the program at will, including the right to redistribute copies of both the original and the modified versions. This kind of license usually requires that copyright notices are maintained but doesn't require royalty payments (Cossentino, 2007).

There are a multitude of FLOSS licenses, with varying degrees of openness or freedom, but all those licenses give open source software the possibility of being freely downloaded and used for any purpose that the user wishes, even if the developers never intended or predicted such uses. Redistribution, modification and unrestricted access to source code are also some possibilities present in every FLOSS license.

Nowadays, if an organization has the needed skills to implement, use and maintain the desired application, there are almost certainly one or two options of enterprise-class open source software. Some common benefits associated with open source software include (Bernardino & Ribeiro, 2011):

- **Short Product Cycle:** Software evolves most quickly when there are no restrictions to what programmers are allowed to do with the source code for a piece of software. If programmers can read, modify, and redistribute software at will, and more users are allowed to try that software, improvements, bug corrections, and general feature adoption tend to happen faster. The short product cycle and the fact that this software does not have license costs allows users to test and try new versions, and give feedback to developers more quickly than with traditional commercial software.
- **Reliable and Secure:** By giving access to source code to anyone, the chances that a security flaw is exposed increase, and that flaws can't be easily covered up and made "secret." Fixes are also more easily

obtained because we do not need to wait for an "official" release or such mechanism common in proprietary software. Anybody with the proper knowledge can devise a fix and patch the software.

- **Freedom from Vendor Lock-In:** Free and open source licenses, by their very nature, turns vendor lock-in in a non-issue. Allowing everyone to review the source code, assures the user that if some vendor vanishes other people can follow the work.
- **No Sales or License Costs:** There are no costs, regarding software licensing, allowing users to evaluate the software nearly for free. If organizations have internal knowledge, they can achieve a nearly cost-free implementation of the desired software. If an organization needs to contract external services, their budget is not impacted by software acquisition costs, typical of commercial applications. Thus, the money saved can be invested in other services, like training, hardware or other business requests.

While Linux, Apache, MySQL, and other open source software are routinely deployed in organizations, open source BI solutions are just at the point where they are sufficient mature to satisfy user requirements (OpenSourceInitiative, 2011). The major attraction of open source is to save time and money, but there is an extra dimension to open source BI – open source BI allows interaction and evolution in a way that proprietary BI does not. These are all good reasons to use open source BI in small and medium enterprises (SMEs).

3.3. Business Intelligence in SMEs

There are already a number of studies on BI success factors. (Hwang et al., 2004) identify factors in the dimensions of organization, environment, and project planning. They find especially strong support for organizational factors. In addition, earlier works discovered the importance of technical issues (Wixom & Watson, 2001; Joshi & Curtis, 1999; Rudra & Yeo, 1999) as well as personnel, educational, and business issues (Rist, 1997). However, some results might not be adoptable for the special case of SMEs. For example, Hwang et al. (2004) found the most significant factor to be the support provided by the top management. However, as discussed previously, in SMEs it is often the top management who also decide on IT issues. Therefore, top management support in SMEs is not a question of "success" but of general interest in BI systems.

Existing research suggests that SMEs, while using other types of IS, are modest in the adoption of BI (also known as management information or decision support) systems (Levy & Powell, 1998). However, a possible explanation might be that BI projects often require lots of capital which bigger organizations are more likely to have (Hwang et al., 2004). Bergeron (2000) reports similar findings and suggests that conventional BI systems, which are focused on large organizations, would not meet the needs of SMEs.

In the context of the above mentioned research, a couple of statements according to IT adoption in SME, BI adoption and BI success factors in a specific dimension already exist. What was missing is a link between BI adoption in SMEs with a focus on general BI success factors and general BI challenges as well as enterprise properties. In addition, it might be useful to focus on general possible benefits and problems prior to detailed facts as defined in previous studies, to give executives a first decision support on BI adoption. The results of our research can build a connection between intending BI adoption and the usage of in-depth planning using specific requirements and factor dimensions.

4. BUSINESS INTELLIGENCE OVERVIEW

The early focus of relational databases was on Online Transactional Processing (OLTP), designed to support the daily business operation requirements (Chen et al., 2000). Using Codd's normalization rules, operational systems are typically optimized for fast inserting and updating of data. As companies expanded the applications they supported and consequently, the data stored, attention turned to providing user access for reporting and decision support. However, a different architecture was needed where transactional data from operational systems could be extracted, transformed, integrated, and stored to support the reporting requirements (Devlin & Murphy, 1988).

The Data Warehouse (DW) utility was defined by four necessary components: Subject-oriented, Integrated, Non-volatile, and Time-variant (Inmon, 2002; Kimball & Ross, 2002). The DW is designed to collect disparate data from operational systems and uniquely store that data to allow end-users ready access for subsequent analysis. A DW is intended to provide integrated data from operational systems organized for reporting, whereas BI is intended to provide actionable information. BI can be defined as "...a set of concepts and methodologies to improve decision-making in business through use of facts and fact-based systems" (Snowden & Boone, 2007). Simply stated, BI provides the ability to transform data into usable and actionable information for business and organization purposes (Gonzales & Wells, 2006). BI is an encompassing term that combines data architectures, technical architectures, analytic tools, and methodologies (Turban et al., 2007).

There is significant synergy and overlap between DW and BI. While a DW is the core repository (Turban et al., 2007), BI requires an information infrastructure to provide actionable insight to decision-makers (Beyer, 2009b). The synergy between BI and DW has caused them to be viewed as one entity. An industry report (Beyer, 2009a) notes that "BI/DW is a strategic initiative that has the potential to deliver significant insights unavailable through other means".

4.1. History

In the early 1970s, decision-support systems were the first applications designed to support decision making. They were a contrast to transaction-processing or operational applications, such as order entry, inventory control, and payroll systems. Over the years, a variety of applications—executive information systems, online analytical processing, and dashboards—have been added to the family of decision support applications. In 1989, analyst Howard Dresner with market research firm Gartner Inc. coined the term "business intelligence," as an umbrella term to describe these analytical applications. Dressner defined BI "a set of concepts and appropriate methods to support decision making, using the data provided by support systems to business process" (Power, 2007). The concept subsequently took flight as companies began collecting and analyzing vast amounts of data stored in data warehouses, as well as in Enterprise Resource Planning (ERP) and other business systems.

However, the first probable reference to BI is said to be made in Sun Tzu's *Art of War*, where he claimed that to succeed in war, full knowledge on one's strengths and weaknesses as well as the strengths and weaknesses of the enemy must be known. Applying this to the modern business world, BI becomes the art of wading and sieving through tons of data, and presenting the overloaded data as information that provides significant business value in improving the effectiveness of managerial decision making (Turban et al., 2004). As such, BI is carried out not just for gaining sustainable competitive advantages, but it also has a valuable core competence in most instances. A variety of businesses have used BI for activities such as customer support and service, customer profiling, market research and segmentation, product profitability, inventory and distribution analysis, etc.

Originally, BI provided fairly simple operational information. However, the technology has changed dramatically during the past years. This is due to both technology improvements and business demands for better BI. Many companies want more information and more analysis, they want results faster, and they want them available to the employees who work directly with the business activity that relates to the data.

In BI's early days, developing queries was complex and required specialized programming knowledge, so obtaining answers could require days or even weeks. Now, systems can return results in real time. In addition, the cost of BI implementations has dropped significantly because processing and storage prices have fallen in recent years.

4.2. Business Intelligence Technologies

In a BI system, BI tools, data warehouse management tools, ETL (Extract, Transform, and Load) and data integration tools are some of the essential elements. BI tools are widely accepted as a new middleware between transactional applications and decision support applications, thereby decoupling systems tailored to an efficient handling of business transactions from systems tailored to an efficient support of business decisions. For a good review of BI technologies see (Chaudhuri et al., 2011). The main BI activities include query, reporting, On-line Analytical Processing (OLAP), statistical analysis, forecasting, data mining and decision support (see Figure 1). Ensuing subsections will describe OLAP, data mining, real time BI and data warehousing.

- **OLAP (On-line Analytical Processing):** It refers to the way in which business users can slice and dice their way through data using sophisticated tools that allow for the navigation of dimensions such as time or hierarchies. Online Analytical Processing or OLAP provides multidimensional, summarized views of business data and is used for reporting, analysis, modeling and planning for optimizing the business. OLAP

Figure 1. Business intelligence framework

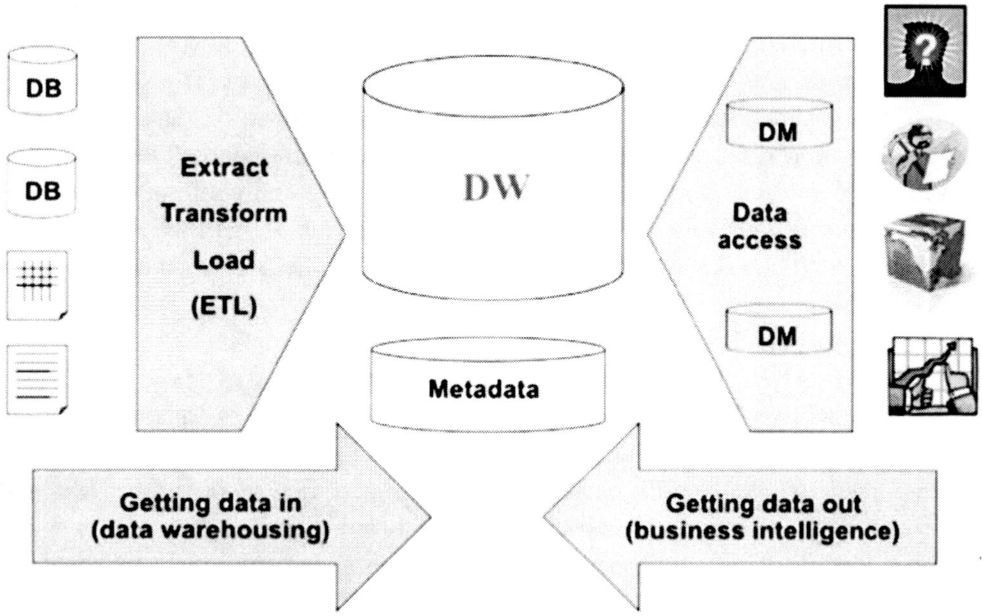

techniques and tools can be used to work with data warehouses or data marts designed for sophisticated enterprise intelligence systems. These systems process queries required to discover trends and analyze critical factors. Reporting software generates aggregated views of data to keep the management informed about the state of their business.

- **Advanced Analytics:** it is referred to as Data Mining, forecasting or predictive analytics, this takes advantage of statistical analysis techniques to predict or provide certainty measures on facts. Corporate Performance Management (Portals, Scorecards, Dashboards), usually provides a container for several pieces to plug into so that the aggregate tells a story. For example, a balanced scorecard that displays portlets for financial metrics combined with say organizational learning and growth metrics.
- **Real Time BI:** Business transactions are fed as they occur to a real-time business intelligence system that maintains the current state of the enterprise. The Real Time BI system not only supports the classical strategic functions of data warehousing for deriving information and knowledge from past enterprise activity, but it also provides real-time tactical support to drive enterprise actions that react to immediate events. As such, it replaces both the classical data warehouse and the enterprise application integration (EAI) functions. Real-time business intelligence is also known as event-driven business intelligence. In order to react in real-time, a business intelligence system must react to events as they occur – not minutes or hours later. With real-time business intelligence, an enterprise establishes long-term strategies to optimize its operations while at the same time reacting with intelligence to events as they occur.
- **Data Warehouse and Data Mart:** The data warehouse is the significant component of business intelligence. The data warehouse supports the physical propagation of data by handling the numerous enterprise records for integration, cleansing, aggregation and query tasks. It can contain the operational data, which can be defined as an updateable set of integrated data used for enterprise wide tactical decision-making of a particular subject area. A Data Mart (DM) as described by (Inmon, 2002) is a collection of subject areas organized for decision support based on the needs of a given department. Finance has their data mart, marketing has theirs, and sales have theirs and so on. And the data mart for marketing only faintly resembles anyone else's data mart. Perhaps most importantly, the individual departments own the hardware, software, data, and programs that constitute the data mart (Inmon, 2002). Each department has its own interpretation of what a data mart should look like and each department's data mart is peculiar to and specific to its own needs. Similar to data warehouses, data marts contain operational data that helps business experts to strategize based on analyses of past trends and experiences. The key difference is that the creation of a data mart is predicated on a specific, predefined need for a certain grouping and configuration of select data. There can be multiple data marts inside an enterprise. A data mart can support a particular business function, business process or business unit.
- **Data Sources:** Data sources can be operational databases, historical data, external data for example, from market research companies or from the Internet, or information from the already existing data warehouse environment. The data sources can be relational databases or any other

data structure that supports the line of business applications. They also can reside on many different platforms and can contain structured information, such as tables or spreadsheets, or unstructured information, such as plain text files or pictures and other multimedia information.

In Figure 1 we illustrate the BI framework. As figure shows, BI is a process that includes two primary activities: getting data in and getting data out.

5. OPEN SOURCE BUSINESS INTELLIGENCE TOOLS

Open Source solutions have become serious alternatives to traditional proprietary licensed software with many open source projects providing a wide variety of tools for data warehousing and full BI suites. The value of BI for business is predominantly expressed in the fact that such systems cast some light on information that may serve as the basis for carrying out fundamental changes in a particular organization, i.e. establishing new co-operation, acquiring new customers, creating new markets, and offering products to customers (Olszak & Ziemba, 2006).

Implementing BI technologies and applying its process can help make business more effective and more efficient, increasing revenue, decreasing costs, and improving relationships with customers and suppliers. BI platforms include *ad hoc* query, report writing, decision support systems, executive information systems (for example KPI - Key Performance Indicators), and techniques such as statistical analysis and Online Analytical Processing (OLAP) (Chaudhary, 2004).

Our work stems from the need to reduce costs in SMEs offering a survey of BI solutions on the market with minimal costs, increased ability to compete with other organizations and ability to structure and improve support decision making. We evaluated and compared seven Open Source Business Intelligence tools: Actuate/BIRT, Jaspersoft, Jedox/Palo, OpenI, Pentaho, SpagoBI, and Vanilla.

5.1. Actuate/BIRT

Actuate Corporation was founded in 1993 and is headquartered in San Mateo, California, with offices worldwide. In 2004 Actuate Corporation founded the Eclipse BIRT Project with the cooperation of the Eclipse Foundation, and continues to co-lead what has become the most successful open-source Business Intelligence (BI) toolset in existence today (Actuate/BIRT, 2011). Developers using BIRT (Business Intelligence Reporting Tools) number more than 750,000, proving that BIRT is easily adopted and is, for many, the development environment of choice, according to (Actuate/BIRT, 2011). BIRT has become the backbone of many enterprise-level BI deployments, and is an integral component of infrastructures everywhere. As open source has continued to gain momentum and acceptance, BIRT has pulled ahead of the pack due to its ease of use and flexibility.

BIRT, which runs on the Eclipse IDE, provides a set of reporting and data visualization tools and technologies used by developers to build rich information applications. It includes the basic tools required for reporting: the ability to design reports and to display report data. The technology underpinning these elements is complete, equipping developers with everything they need to access data sources, transform data, apply business logic to data, and, once the data has been filtered and formatted, present the results to users. Open Source BIRT includes the following functions and features: Multiple Development and Design Tools; Extensible Data Access; Data Customization; Programmability; Flexible Data Presentation; Component Reuse/Libraries; Easy Integration and Internationalization (Eclipse/BIRT, 2011).

Actuate continues to transition its product and marketing emphasis to its open-source commercial products based on Business Intelligence and Reporting Tools (BIRT). In September 2010, it announced ActuateOne, a unified suite for developing and deploying BI applications that include reports, dashboards, in-memory analytics, and mobile and cloud-based deployments that leverage BIRT. The output of existing e.Reports can be used as input to new applications. Actuate products add interactivity, dashboards, analytics, and deployment options for Web and mobile applications. Figure 2 shows different chart types available in BIRT.

The company's acquisition of Xenos, an e-presentment provider, was completed in early 2010 and has augmented its capability in leveraging untapped print stream data and in document transformation, specifically useful for the financial services sector and for meeting accessibility.

The Forrester Wave report, "The Forrester Wave™: Open Source Business Intelligence (BI), Q3 2010", rated Actuate as a Leader based on the company's pure play BI application and highly scalable, function-rich reporting. According to the report "Actuate BIRT reports can be used for mass (millions) report distribution and for highly complex (with scalability and load balancing challenges) BI applications like interactive online customer statements" (Evelson and Hammond, 2010).

In the most recent addition, Actuate also added BIRT data objects, which can be used for disk- or memory-based OLAP style analysis. Actuate is also investing heavily into mobile BI with BIRT iPhone application and BIRT Mobile virtual appliance, which can deliver BIRT content to most popular mobile devices (see Figure 3). Additionally, as BIRT is part of the Eclipse project, Actuate BIRT is also highly attractive to developers using Eclipse integrated development environment (IDE).

5.2. Jaspersoft

Jaspersoft was founded in 2001, headquartered in San Francisco, California and have an EMEA headquarters in Dublin, Ireland with global offices in Bangkok, Paris, Frankfurt, UK, Italy, Romania, Ukraine, Australia and India. This is an open BI

Figure 2. BIRT chart types (source www.eclipse.org/birt)

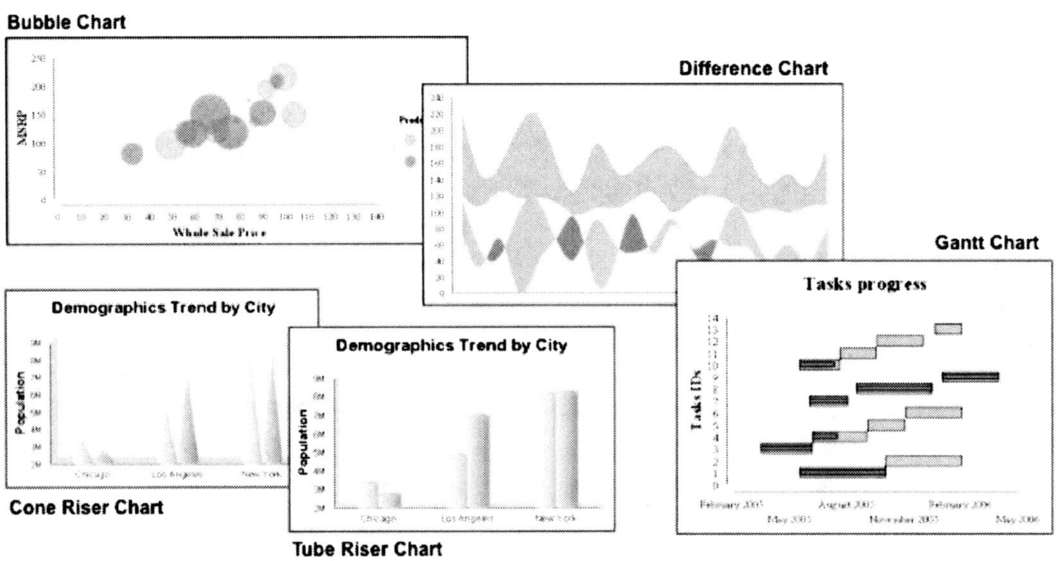

Figure 3. BIRT mobile (source www.birt-exchange.com)

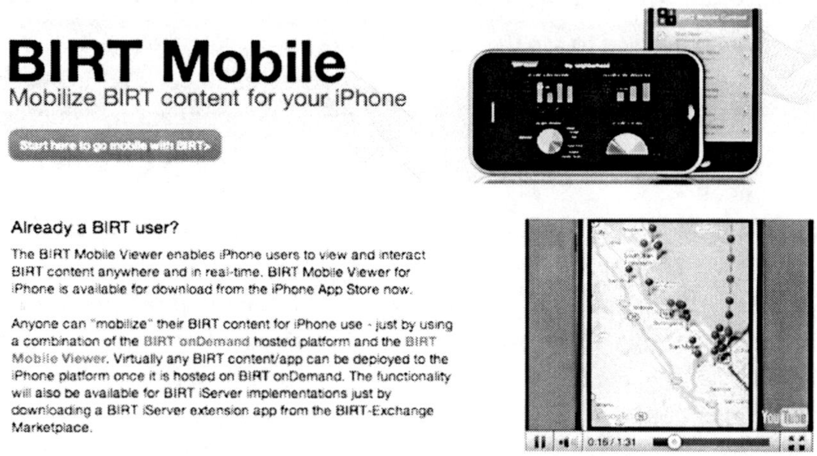

tool developed in Perl and Java, with a license GNU GPL (Jaspersoft, 2011).

Jaspersoft provides a complete BI platform for reporting and analysis, with shared services including a metadata and content repository, report management, security integration, interactivity, and scheduling. The BI platform has been designed for integration with other applications through Web Services, Java, and APIs, as well as being completely ready for stand-alone enterprise BI deployments. It also offers multi-tenancy for SaaS applications out of the box. The Jaspersoft BI stack is comprised of the following products: JasperReports Library, Jaspersoft iReport Designer, JasperReports Server, Jaspersoft OLAP, and Jaspersoft ETL. Figure 4 shows the Jaspersoft architecture.

Figure 4. Jaspersoft architecture (source www.jaspersoft.com)

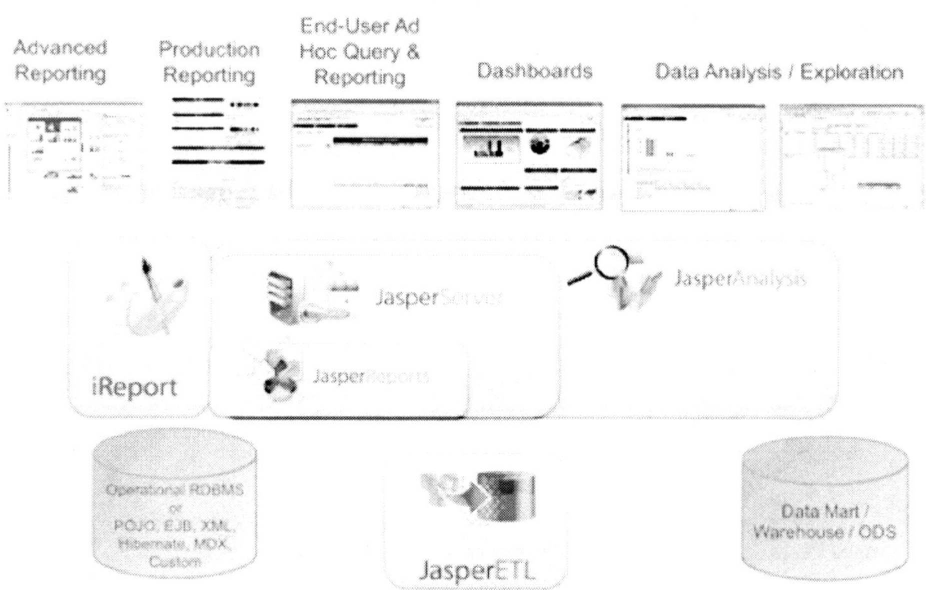

Jaspersoft is widely used to generate and distribute Web and printable invoices, forms, and all varieties of complex reports from production systems. Reports can also be used to tap the rich data stored in operational systems and business applications. Jaspersoft is qualified for embedding reports within a Web application or decoupled as a stand-alone BI application.

End users can design, configure, and deploy their own interactive BI dashboards. It's as simple as dragging and dropping reports and charts onto the Web-based dashboard designer. We can even "mash up" URL-addressable content, such as maps, videos, and content from other business application.

Jaspersoft claims to be the mostly-widely deployed BI vendor with 11 million product downloads, 13,000 commercial customers, and a community of 150,000 registered developers (Jaspersoft, 2011). They argue that its BI software is continually improved, tested, and successfully deployed across the widest range of applications.

With Jaspersoft mobile business users have the ability to view, explore, and create information on-the-go using an iPad or iPhone device (see Figure 5). JasperReports Server is accessible via a touch enabled iPad browser or through a native iOS application, which powers the mobile platform. Organizations now have the choice to build a native BI application with an open source mobile SDK or rapidly deploy through a browser interface.

Jaspersoft products are available as Professional and Enterprise editions with access to modifiable source code, and as open source Community projects. The Jaspersoft Community projects provide BI functionality for open source developers and technology enthusiasts who want to add reporting and analytics to their applications and operational processes. Community software is distributed by Jaspersoft "as-is" and can be modified and redistributed under the terms of GNU GPL open source license (Jasperforge, 2011).

Figure 5. Jaspersoft mobile (source www.jaspersoft.com)

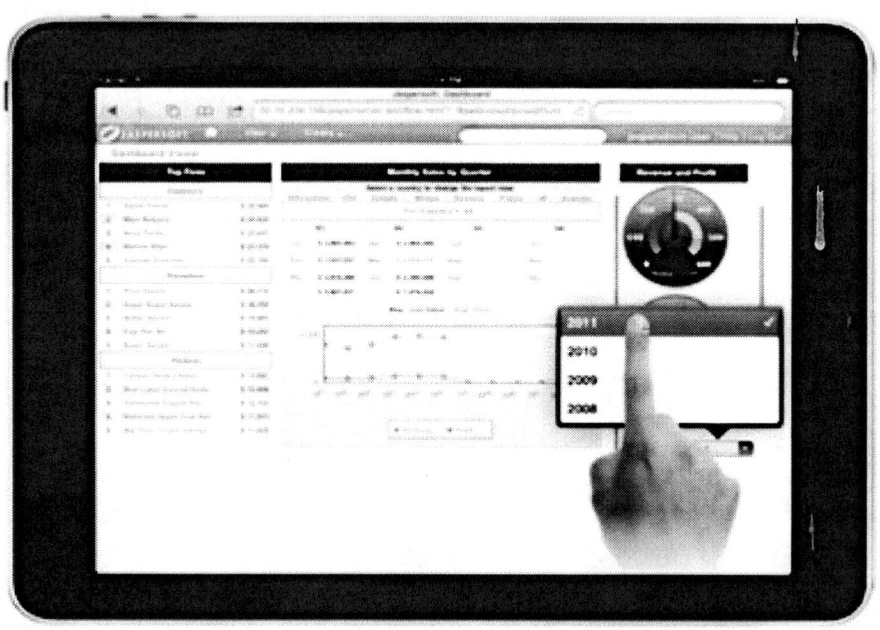

The Professional and Enterprise Edition products build on the Community Projects provide valuable benefits including: Professional technical support up to 24x7; Advanced product features such as Web based Ad Hoc reporting, Integrated In-Memory Analysis, Flash powered visualizations, Multi-tenancy, and enhanced manageability with Audit Logging but under a Commercial license that includes legal indemnification and product warranties.

Jaspersoft's strengths lie in its business model. By nature, open source solutions are built based on a strong interaction with the end user community. This means that solutions can be deployed more quickly because any issues regarding the solution or snags in implementation can be dealt with quickly. Overall, Jaspersoft had high services and support ratings and quick implementation times. Due to its subscription based licensing model, the ability to choose diverse licensing options does not exist. However, organizations pay a flat fee for use, meaning that overall costs can be lower for larger deployments.

5.3. Jedox/Palo

Palo is the MOLAP engine, implemented by Jedox Company, which is founded in 2002 (Jedox/Palo, 2011). The whole BI proposal of Jedox revolves around MOLAP engine, which is its distinguishing feature. If we implement a traditional data warehouse where the data are static and unchanging, Palo is not the correct solution. On the other hand, if we want to implement a BI environment where to be able to perform simulations, draw various scenarios, and work with manipulating data to see the different possible outcomes, then PALO is the solution.

The most important feature that contributes Palo being MOLAP is that enables us to edit the values and propagate changes based on business rules, create formulas for simulations, create scenarios, etc. Initially Palo MOLAP engine was programmed in C++ and a MS Excel plugging that allowed us to use the data from there. This nucleus initially grew with Palo Jpalo and Web client. It is a Java API to attack the engine from Java and a Web application that allows exploring dashboards from the browser.

Recently this has been integrated into the Palo Suite: a complete solution that provides the ETL, the engine and a Web interface to exploit it (Jedox/Palo, 2011). Palo Suite combines all three of Jedox's core applications — OLAP Server, Palo Web, Palo ETL Server and Palo for Excel — into one comprehensive and customizable Business Intelligence platform. The platform is completely based on Open Source products representing a high-end Business Intelligence solution, which is available entirely free of any license fees. Palo Suite is available as a community and a premium edition, with the premium version offering extended software assurance and support functionalities. An example of a Palo report is illustrated in Figure 6.

5.4. OpenI

OpenI (pronounced "Open Eye") start in 2005 as an open source project (OpenI, 2011). OpenI is a Web-based OLAP reporting application based on Java EE. OpenI's differentiator is that it strives to be BI application that a user can use right "out of the box" as opposed to an "SDK" on top of which a BI developer will build their BI application. This means a lot of work has gone towards making the installation increasingly easier, and we are able to just point to an OLAP data source and start publishing anlayses/dashboards without having to write code, supporting Microsoft Analysis services, etc. However, all this requires a BI platform underneath, and to date, OpenI has built its own platform using the same usual components (JPivot, Mondrian, etc.) that most other open source BI projects use.

The application provides end-to-end BI solutions: to complex ETL jobs, dimensional modeling, OLAP cube design, predictive models, interactive reporting and dashboards. All OpenI

Figure 6. Jedox/Palo report manager (source www.jedox.com)

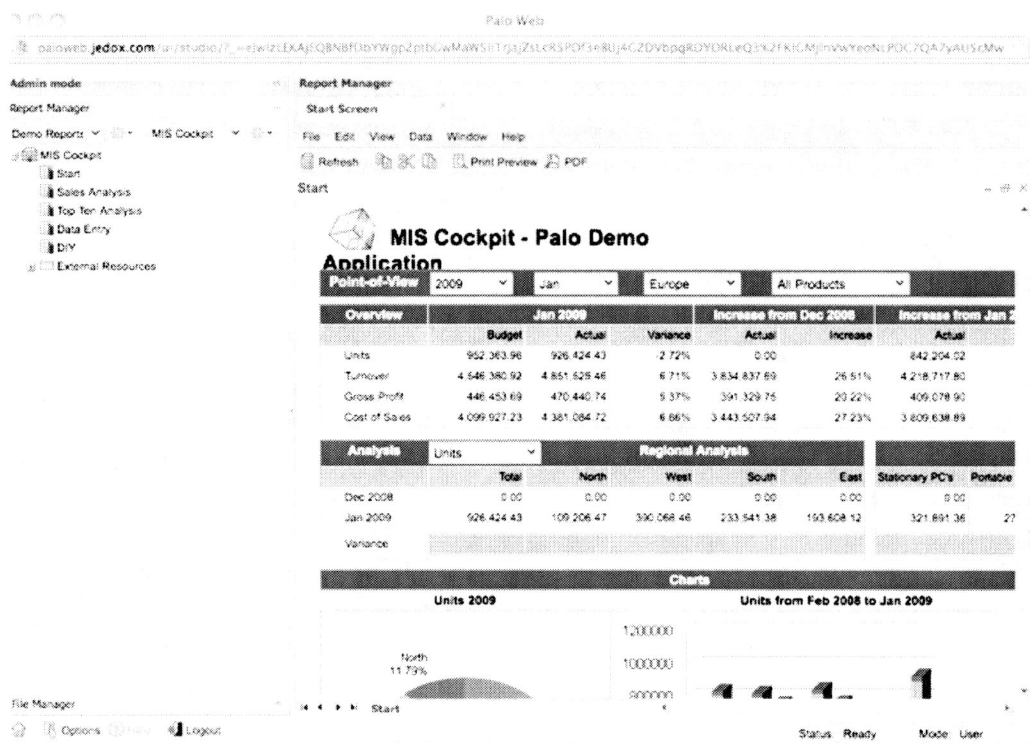

Figure 7. OpenI plug-in (source openi.org)

open source software is made available under GNU Public License Version 2 (GPL version 2). OpenI also provides commercial licenses for its software that includes support.

Recently OpenI announces some profoundly changes (OpenI, 2011). First - OpenI as a "BI platform" on its own will be discontinued. Instead, they will use Pentaho and Jasper as base platforms as needed. The approach is to release "OpenI plug-ins" for Jasper and Pentaho—so that they behave/appear in a manner very similar to OpenI. The first step in this direction is the "Plug-In" for Jasper that replaces its Jaspersoft OLAP (aka JasperAnalysis) user interface, which is basically JPivot as-is, with OpenI's user interface. They believe this is a greatly improved user interface for JasperServer users who need better interface for OLAP reporting and exploratory analysis (see a screenshot in Figure 7).

5.5. Pentaho

Pentaho BI provides a full spectrum of data integration and Business Intelligence (BI) capabilities including data Extraction, Transformation, and Loading (ETL), interactive reporting, *ad hoc* analysis, rich visualizations, data mining, and predictive analysis. Pentaho BI platform is one of the world's most popular open source BI, also providing broad enterprise data integration services for Big Data analytics and reporting (Pentaho, 2011).

Pentaho BI suite has the following modules: Pentaho Data Integration – cleanse and integrate data wherever it exists; Pentaho Reporting – point, click, and immediately gain access to information; Pentaho Analysis – discover, explore, and analyze information interactively; Pentaho Dashboards – discover, explore, and analyze information interactively; and Pentaho Data Mining – discover hidden patterns and indicators of future performance.

The Pentaho BI Platform, the core architecture and foundation of the Pentaho Open BI Suite, is process centric because the central controller is a workflow engine. The workflow engine uses process definitions to define the business intelligence processes that execute within the BI Platform. The processes can be easily customized and new processes can be added. The BI platform includes components and reports for analyzing the performance of these processes (see in Figure 8 an example of a report). The BI platform is solution-oriented because the operations of the platform are specified in process definitions and action documents that specify every activity. These processes and operations collectively define the solution to a business intelligence problem. This BI solution can be easily integrated into business processes that are external to the platform. The definition of a solution can contain any number of processes and operations.

The Pentaho BI platform provides the architecture and infrastructure required to build solutions to business intelligence problems. This framework provides core services including authentication, logging, auditing, Web services, and rules engines. Pentaho's commercial open source business model eliminates software license fees, providing support, services, and product enhancements via an annual subscription. The Community Edition is self supported open source software (Pentaho Community, 2011). The Enterprise Edition (EE) of the Pentaho BI platform is available as part of the Pentaho BI Suite EE which includes technical support, managed upgrades and enterprise features.

5.6. SpagoBI

The history of SpagoBI began in 2001, along with the necessity of the Architectures and Consulting Unit of Engineering Group (at that time called EngiWeb.com) to realize a Java Enterprise framework in order to develop some projects for its customers (SpagoBI, 2011). At the end of 2004, this framework was re-engineered and released in open source, as Spago, at first on SourceForge. In 2005 SpagoBI project was released and the solu-

Figure 8. Pentaho report (source www.pentaho.com)

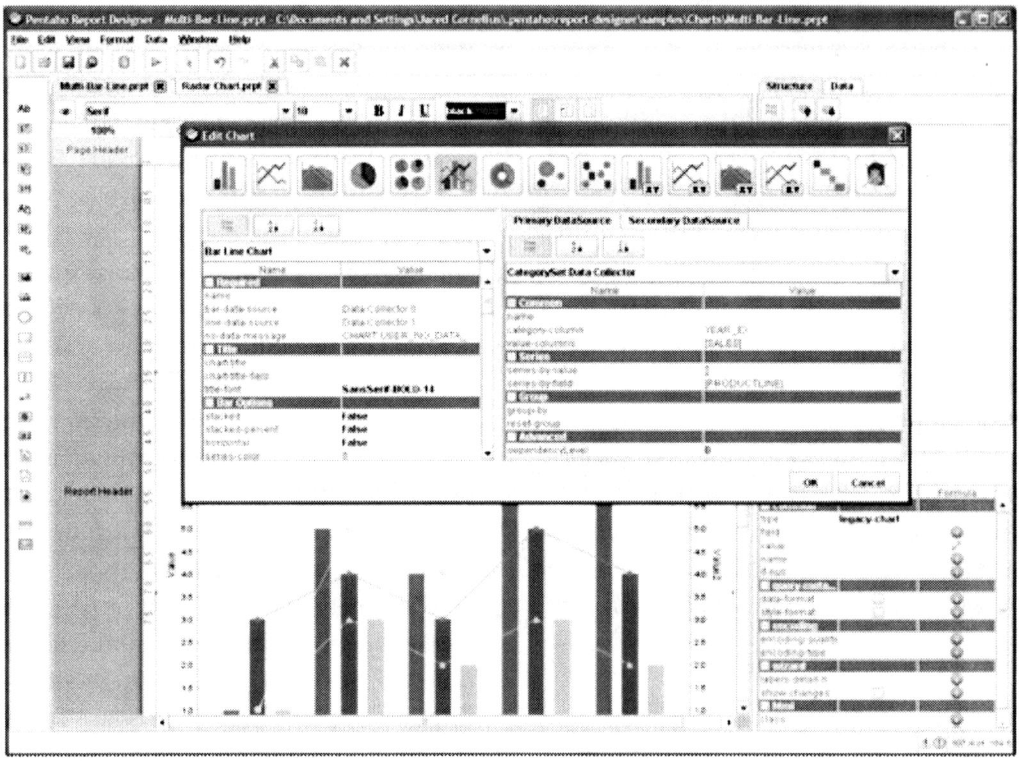

tions were transferred onto the forge of ObjectWeb Consortium. In 2006 SpagoWorld Initiative was launched and the merge of the ObjectWeb Consortium into the new OW2 Consortium began. In 2007 two more projects, Spagic and Spago4Q, were released. In 2010, after that Engineering Group joined the Eclipse Foundation, the eBAM, eBPM, and GeoBI, the first initiative launched by SpagoWorld, were announced. SpagoWorld is a Free (Libre) Open Source Initiative, founded and managed by Engineering.

All SpagoWorld solutions are 100% open source forever, they adopt the "pure open source" model and are released as only one stable version. They are an alternative to the "dual-licensing" or "open core" model, which also includes a parallel software release as a proprietary enterprise or professional version. In order to guarantee the open source transparency, openness, sustainability and availability over time, all the solutions are downloadable from the forge of open source, no-profit and independent communities, such as the OW2 Consortium and Eclipse Foundation.

More than usual reporting and charting tools, SpagoBI adds solutions such as: Geographical analysis, to thematize maps according to business data coming from several sources, relating them to different types of analysis (chart, dashboard, report). It allows to merge business data coming from a data warehouse and geographical data coming from a geographical system; QbE and Smart Filter, which allow advanced users to directly query data sources; Dossier, to generate new information, such as documents or presentations, through a collaborative approach based on annotations of existing analysis and on dedicated workflows; KPIs, to monitor the main business performance indicators; Interactive dashboards, to analyse one's business in an intuitive and interactive way; Ad-hoc reporting, allowing end-users to

Figure 9. SpagoBI suite - KPI (source www.spagoworld.org)

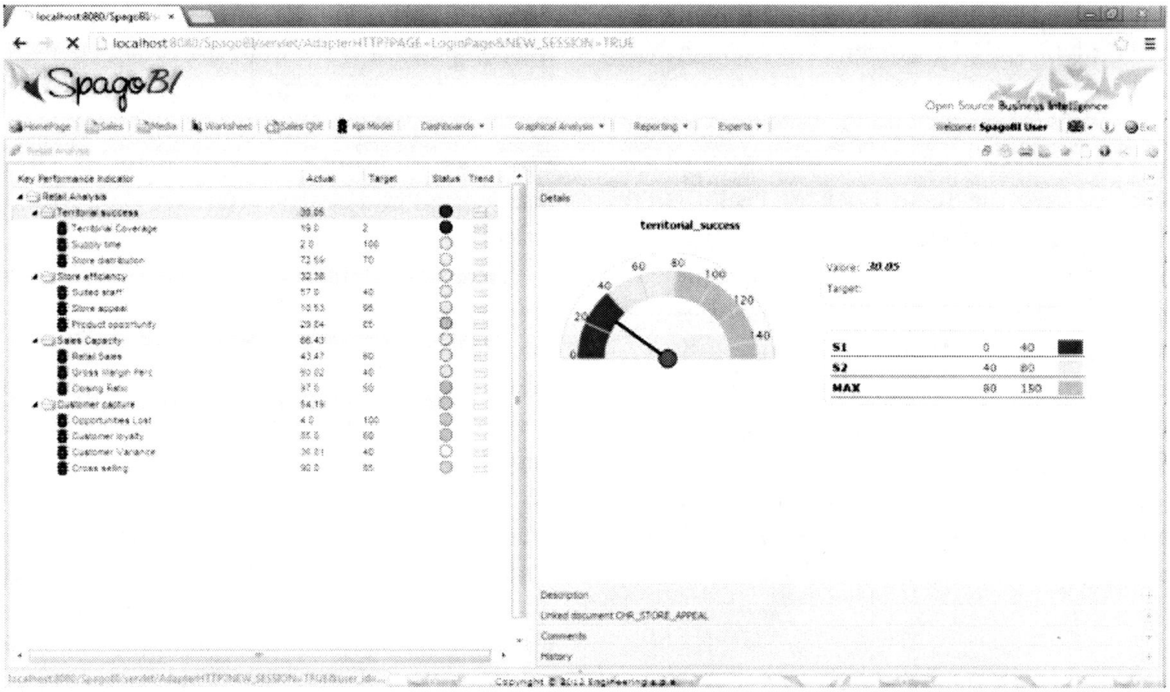

create their own multi-sheet reports, by defining simple tables, cross-tables and different chart types in their document layout; and Real-time events: they allow to detect events as soon as they occur, analyse them and react towards OLTP systems.

SpagoBI also offers a specific engine for the realization of complex cockpits, which allow to aggregate several documents into a single view, connecting them with one another, fostering their interactive and intuitive usage. Figure 9 shows an example of Key Performance Indicators using SpagoBI suite.

5.7. Vanilla

Vanilla is a true Open Source BI Platform sponsored by BPM-Conseil (Vanilla, 2011). BPM-Conseil has been a growing member of the Open Source Software Community since 2005. The Vanilla BI Platform is an Open Source BI Platform providing a complete state of the art Business Intelligence environment for a fraction of the running costs of a commercial platform.

With the new version, Vanilla provides new features such as multithread/cluster for servers, document management, tight integration between each component and also numerous new features in existing packages (ETL, Dashboard, OLAP, Metadata, KPI, Reporting, …). Vanilla also has the Enterprise Services that is the backbone of the Vanilla suit, allowing administrators to manage every security aspect of Vanilla components. Each user can be modified, each security group can be parameterized. It's the only administration tool to manage users, to define security rules, to manage contents, to manage server's configuration in all the BI open source suits. EnterpriseServices also provides some key features like exporting, importing a whole repository full of BI resources without any databases manipulations just by few clicks.

Vanilla provides a complete set of development modules: BI Metadata Designer, OLAP Schema Designer, BI Dashboard Designer, BI Workflow Designer, KPI Metrics Designer, KPI Maps Designer and Report Designer Plugins for iReport and BIRT. Using Vanilla a developer or administrator will safe time by managing a unique database of reference, and having all the component available when designing a BI document. For example, BI Workflow and BI Gateway leverage all the others Vanilla documents: reports, dashboard, cubes and KPI database. And all Vanilla Development packages have the same Look & Feel (BIRT alike), and are using the same set of components (for example: Oda drivers). For visual document integration, they provide Free Dashboard with a new set of features that allow BI developer to easily and visually integrate Report, Reports on Cube, standard reports, KPI and Maps, all documents being manage by FreeDashBoard filters. Figure 10 illustrates Vanilla Performance Dashboards, an innovative Excel-like way to present dashboards, complete with forms and tab folders.

6. EVALUATION OF OPEN SOURCE BUSINESS INTELLIGENCE TOOLS

We tested the public available demos, which can be downloaded or accessed through each platform Website in (Actuate/BIRT, 2011; Jaspersoft, 2011; Jedox/Palo, 2011; OpenI, 2011; Pentaho, 2011; SpagoBI, 2011; Vanilla, 2011). Table 2 presents the comparison of the most important characteristics of the open source business intelligence tools concerning information delivery (Reports, Dashboards, Ad-hoc Query, Microsoft Office Integration) and analysis (OLAP, Data Mining, Data Export and Scorecards).

Table 3 shows the platforms and programming languages supported by open source business intelligence tools. Since all the tools have a GNU GPL license, the last column shows which tools don't have a commercial version, implying that only have a free version of the software.

The first conclusion drawn from this study is that the SpagoBI tool is one of BI packages more complete and where the Community version, which is the only one, contains more features than most of the Enterprise versions of the remaining packages BI solutions analyzed. The OpenI tool has some weak points, such as the lack of proper methods of ETL and the inability to export data. It is therefore a most rudimentary tool when compared to the others. Pentaho is a fairly comprehensive and consistent tool together with

Figure 10. Vanilla performance dashboards (source www.bpm-conseil.com)

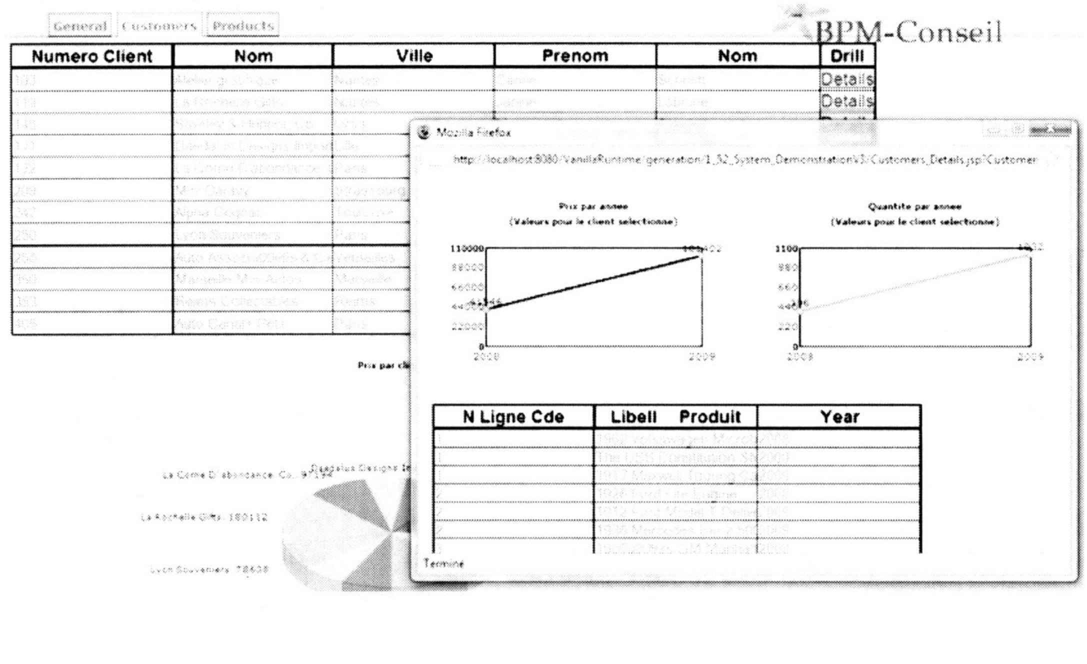

Table 2. Open source business intelligence tools information and analysis evaluation

	Reports	Dash-boards	Ad-hoc Query	MS Office Integration	OLAP	Data Mining	Data Export	Scorecards
Actuate/BIRT	✓	✓	✓	✓	✓	✓	✓	✓
Jaspersoft	✓	✓	✓	✓	✓	N	✓	N
Jedox/Palo	✓	✓	✓	✓	✓	N	✓	N
OpenI	✓	✓	N	✓	✓	N	N	N
Pentaho	✓	✓	✓	✓	✓	✓	✓	✓
SpagoBI	✓	✓	✓	✓	✓	✓	✓	✓
Vanilla	✓	✓	✓	✓	✓	N	✓	N

SpagoBI. Jaspersoft is a powerful BI tool, lacks only the process of Data Mining and Scorecards; when compared with SpagoBI and Pentaho is still more balanced analysis tools because it allows *ad-hoc* queries and managing location GEO/GIS. The Jedox/Palo tool does not support data mining processes, Scorecards and tracking features GEO/GIS. Jedox/Palo enables *ad-hoc* queries, which are a plus for this tool. Jedox/Palo has a relevant factor in the fact that you can add to Microsoft Excel and Open Office Calc. All BI tools provide integration with Microsoft Office, including support for document formats, formulas, data "refreshes" and pivot tables. Some ones support advanced integration including cell locking and write-back capabilities. An important point to note is that most of BI tools have a version for mobile devices, a factor that opens up important perspectives for future functionalities in open source BI. Jaspersoft is the only open source BI platform developed in Java and Perl. Vanilla is developed in PHP language and the remainders are implemented in Java.

7. FUTURE TRENDS IN BUSINESS INTELLIGENCE

One of the future trends to BI systems could be the use of the Software as a Service (SaaS) new paradigm (Cusumano, 2010). SaaS is a model for software delivery where a software company publishes one copy of their software on the Internet. It allows individuals and companies (multi-tenant architecture) to "rent" it through a subscription model (pay as you go model). The software com-

Table 3. Open source business intelligence platform and programming languages support

	Mobile	Windows	Linux	Unix	Java	Perl	PHP	Only Free version
Actuate/BIRT	✓	✓	✓	✓	✓	N	✓	N
Jaspersoft	✓	✓	✓	N	✓	✓	N	N
Jedox/Palo	✓	✓	✓	N	✓	N	N	N
OpenI	N	✓	✓	N	✓	N	N	N
Pentaho	✓	✓	✓	✓	✓	N	N	N
SpagoBI	✓	✓	✓	✓	✓	N	N	✓
Vanilla	✓	✓	✓	✓	N	N	✓	✓

pany centrally operates, maintains and supports all its customers using this centralized service. On-Demand and pay as you go models mean that in a SaaS model, costs are directly aligned with usage. The cost may increase as the usage of the application increases. Multi-tenant architecture model means that the physical backend hardware infrastructure is shared among many different customers but logically is unique for each customer (Cai, et al., 2011). Lower Total Cost of Ownership (TCO) and better Return On Investment (ROI) constitute the major benefits of SaaS (Spruit, & Abdat, 2012). Indeed, several factors contribute to making it considerably less expensive to implement a SaaS application than a traditional on-premises application. These factors include: (1) lower IT costs; since when you subscribe to a SaaS application, you avoid the overhead associated with implementing conventional software (installing and maintaining servers, etc.). (2) Economies of scale; subscription costs for SaaS applications reflect the economies of scale achieved by multi-tenancy; as example on database is used to store all customers data, so, this makes the overall system scalable at a far lower cost. (3) Pay as you go; companies who subscribe to a SaaS application pay a monthly or annual subscription fee, sometimes depending also on the number of users or transactions. Others key variables such as simplicity, flexibility and accessibility constitute the advantages of SaaS deployment model.

In recent years, SaaS is gaining momentum with more and more successful adoptions. Several companies including some well known names have embraced this new model for software distribution. As SaaS providers, we cite Salesforce.com for on-demand Customer Relationship Management (CRM) services; PeopleSoft On-Demand from Oracle provides SaaS infrastructure for enterprise applications; ShareMinds that offers an on-demand Enterprise Content Management (ECM). Google maps and apps (mail, docs, sites, etc.); and Microsoft, which announces Office Web Apps. Several business intelligence software solutions are exposed in a SaaS model. SAP BusinessObjects, the business intelligence software company launched a hosted on-demand platform (available at http://www.ondemand.com) to deliver analytic and reporting functionality. PivotLink is one of the major actors of the on-demand business intelligence (http://www.pivotlink.com). PivotLink offers a SaaS business intelligence solution covering data analysis, reporting and dashboards. LogiXML (http://www.logixml.com) provides Web-based *ad-hoc* reporting, analysis, dashboard and data integration (ETL) applications. LogiXML solution is one of the few solutions that offer a fully Web-based data integration environment. Talend (http://www.talend.com) one of the most known open-source data integration solutions, starts recently the Talend on-demand project. Talend on-demand is a centralized and shared repository hosted by Talend in order to consolidate Talend Open Studio metadata and project information in online and to facilitate collaboration, object and code reuse. However, it consists of a partial SaaS solution since the design of ETL package is made with Talend Open Studio, the on-demand service covers only uploading, sharing and collaboration functions. Finally, Open-Reports (http://oreports.com) is an open-source solution for Web-based business intelligence deployments that allows build and publish reports, analyses, and dashboards.

These solutions present many advantages derived in general from the advantages of the SaaS concept. But, not much information on the architecture of these on-demand solutions is provided. In addition, few solutions offer integrated platforms that cover all functional and technical aspects of the data warehousing architecture. Indeed, these tools focus only on the problem of the business intelligence services deployment and they provide a partial on-demand solution to the problem of data warehousing design. Furthermore, none of these solutions offer an integrated model driven DW development approach and a Web-based tool that support this approach.

Other future trends can be focusing on aspects such as performance issues concerning data throughput, processing and scalability, as well as the prediction algorithm's efficiency, joined with data privacy and security requirements.

The business intelligence sector has undergone major changes, impacting enterprise appetites for operational data and strategic insight, while enhancing the technology available to deliver these insights. Not every IT and software development organization can act on all of these trends. However, as BI strategies evolve and BI project decisions are made, understanding these trends can help enterprises reap maximum benefit from their BI investments.

The future of business intelligence is bright. BI is changing how companies are managed, decisions are made, and people perform their jobs. Top major vendors are increasing their commitment and investment in BI. And there are other developments on the horizon—the integration of structured and unstructured data, rules engines, guided analytics, and enhanced data visualization—that promise to keep BI fresh and exciting.

8. CONCLUSION

Many organizations today use a collection of Business Intelligence (BI) tools and applications to allow experts to gather information from a variety of sources, analyze it, and share it with managers and staff. However, ever-increasing business dynamics and increased competition means businesses now require a much higher level of value from their BI investments. BI must now help drive profitable growth, change, and many other operational and financial performance goals. Not only does BI need to deliver significant Return on Investment (ROI), but it also needs to be deployed in a manner that minimizes Total Cost of Ownership (TCO).

After several years in existence, Open Source Business Intelligence platforms are mature from the functional and business model point of view to become a solid option to meet and exceed the business intelligence needs of an organization. A mature set of open source solutions already exists as we have shown, that includes most areas of business intelligence functionality, with a common list of characteristics:

- The product is offered in an open source format (open source licensing and source code is available).
- A credible community exists that exerts extensive effort to be involved in the development of the product (some areas include bug detection, forums, documentation, source code and common licensing).
- Open source technology has evolved to now provide the same level of trust and comfort as traditional software does for enterprise adopters (in the areas of software maintenance, training, consulting, etc.) with the establishment and growth of successful vendor companies to support the software.

Organizations are increasingly considering what they believe to be low license price alternatives solutions such as Software-as-a-Service (SaaS) and open-source vendors to augment or replace highly priced and often incumbent platforms. Open source BI tools are just at the point where they are sufficient mature to satisfy SMEs requirements. The major attraction of open source is to save time and money, but open source BI also allows interaction and evolution in a way that proprietary BI does not.

From our analysis, we conclude that the Open Source Business Intelligence platforms are growing both in features, quality and visual appeal. Of the seven tools reviewed, OpenI is arguably the least developed and Birt, Jaspersoft, Pentaho and SpagoBI tools are those with the greatest potential to be exploit by SMEs.

REFERENCES

Actuate/BIRT. (2011). *BIRT open source*. Retrieved from http://www.actuate.com/

Anderson-Lehman, R., Watson, H. J., Wixom, B. H., & Hoffer, J. A. (2004). Continental airlines flies high with real-time business intelligence. *MIS Quarterly Executive*, *3*(4), 163–176.

Bergeron, B. (2000). Regional business intelligence: The view from Canada. *Journal of Information Science*, *26*(3), 153–160. doi:10.1177/016555150002600305.

Bernardino, J., & Ribeiro, P. (2011). Open source business intelligence: An alternative to proprietary tools. *International Journal of Electronic Business*, *9*(3), 219–237. doi:10.1504/IJEB.2011.042543.

Beyer, M. (2009a, February). Tutorial: Key roles for successful BI/DW delivery: Business intelligence solution architect. *Gartner*.

Beyer, M. (2009b, April). Fundamentals of data warehousing for the CIO. *Gartner*.

Bhagwat, R., & Sharma, M. K. (2006). Management of information system in Indian SMEs: An exploratory study. *International Journal of Enterprise Network Management*, *1*(1), 99–125. doi:10.1504/IJENM.2006.010068.

Bucher, T., Gericke, A., & Sigg, S. (2009). Process-centric business intelligence. *Business Process Management Journal*, *15*(3), 408. doi:10.1108/14637150910960648.

Cai, H., Reinwald, B., Wang, N., & Guo, C. (2011). SaaS multi-tenancy: Framework, technology, and case study. *International Journal of Cloud Applications and Computing*, *1*(1), 62–77. doi:10.4018/ijcac.2011010105.

Chaudhary, S. (2004). Management factors for strategic BI success. In *Business intelligence in digital economy: Opportunities, limitations and risks*. Hershey, PA: IDEA Group Publishing.

Chaudhary, S., Dayal, U., & Narasayya, V. (2011). An overview of business intelligence technology. *Communications of the ACM*, *54*(8), 88–98. doi:10.1145/1978542.1978562.

Chen, L., Soliman, K. S., Mao, E., & Frolick, M. N. (2000). Measuring user satisfaction with data warehouses: An exploratory study. *Information & Management*, 103–110. doi:10.1016/S0378-7206(99)00042-7.

Corbett, P., & Ward, D. (2006). *Open source reporting solutions for institutional reporting: The BIRT approach. Australasian Association for Institutional Research*. AAIR.

Cossentino, M. (2007). *Open source software*. Retrieved from http://www.pa.icar.cnr.it/cossentino/ICT/ppt/S11%20-%20Open%20Source%20Software.pdf

Cusumano, M. (2010). Cloud computing and SaaS as new computing platforms. *Communications of the ACM*, *53*(4), 27–28. doi:10.1145/1721654.1721667.

Damiani, E., Frati, F., & Monteverdi, C. (2009). *Open source BI adoption*. Retrieved from http://www.ow2.org/xwiki/bin/download/BusinessIntelligence/Documents/OSBIadoption-v10.pdf

Devlin, B. P., & Murphy, P. T. (1988). An architecture for a business and information system. *IBM Systems Journal*, *7*(1), 60–80. doi:10.1147/sj.271.0060.

Dholakia, R. R., & Kshetri, N. (2004). Factors impacting the adoption of the Internet among SMEs. *Small Business Economics*, *23*(4), 311–322. doi:10.1023/B:SBEJ.0000032036.90353.1f.

Eclipse/BIRT. (2011). *BIRT project*. Retrieved from http://www.eclipse.org/birt

Embarcadero Technologies. (2008). *Why data warehouse projects fail*. Retrieved from http://www.embarcadero.com/resources/technical_papers/Why-Data-Warehouse-Projects-Fail.pdf

European Union. (2003). The new SME definition: User guide and model declaration. *Official Journal of the European Union, 124*, 36.

Evelson, B., & Hammond, J. S. (2010). *The Forrester Wave™: Open source business intelligence (BI), Q3 2010*. Forrester Research.

Gonzales, M. L., & Wells, D. L. (2006). *BI strategy: How to create and document*. Austin, TX: HandsOn-BI, LLC.

Grabova, O., Darmont, J., Chauchat, J.-H., & Zolotaryova, I. (2010). Business intelligence for small and middle-sized entreprises. *SIGMOD Record, 39*(2), 39–50. doi:10.1145/1893173.1893180.

Hwang, H.-G., Ku, C.-Y., Yen, D. V., & Cheng, C.-C. (2004). Critical factors influencing the adoption of data warehouse technology: A study of the banking industry in Taiwan. *Decision Support Systems, 37*(1), 1–21. doi:10.1016/S0167-9236(02)00191-4.

IBM. (2009). *The new voice of the CIO*. Retrieved from http://www-935.ibm.com/services/us/cio/ciostudy/

Inmon, B. (2002). *Building the data warehouse* (3rd ed.). New York: Wiley and Sons.

Jasperforge. (2011). *Jasperforge*. Retrieved from http://jasperforge.org/

Jaspersoft. (2011). *Jaspersoft*. Retrieved from http://www.jaspersoft.com/ Jedox/Palo. (2011). *Open source business intelligence*. Retrieved from http://www.jedox.com/

Jordan, J., & Ellen, C. (2009). Business need, data and business intelligence. *Journal of Digital Asset Management, 5*(1). doi:10.1057/dam.2008.53.

Joshi, K., & Curtis, M. (1999). Issues in building a successful data warehouse. *Information Strategy: The Executive's Journal, 15*(2), 28–35.

Kelly, S. (1997). Data marts: The latest silver bullet. *Data Mart Review*, 12-16.

Kimball, R., & Ross, M. (2002). *The data warehouse toolkit: The complete guide to dimensional modeling* (2nd ed.). New York: John Wiley and Sons.

Knight, M. (2011). *BI growth to buck economic trends*. Retrieved July 14, 2011, from http://www.itpro.co.uk/183480/bi-growth-to-buckeconomic-trends

Koch, C. (2003). *Open source - Your open source plan*. Retrieved from http://www.cio.com/article/31768/Open_Source_Your_Opensource_Plan

Lawton, G. (2009). Users take a close look at visual analytics. *IEEE Computer, 42*(2), 19–22. doi:10.1109/MC.2009.61.

Lefebvre, L., Harvey, J., & Lefebvre, E. (1991). Technological experience and the technology adoption decisions in small manufacturing firms. *R & D Management, 21*(3), 241–249. doi:10.1111/j.1467-9310.1991.tb00761.x.

Lerner, J., & Tirole, J. (2002). Some simple economics of open source. *The Journal of Industrial Economics, 50*(2), 197–234. doi:10.1111/1467-6451.00174.

Levy, M., & Powell, P. (1998). SME flexibility and the role of information systems. *Small Business Economics, 11*(2), 183–196. doi:10.1023/A:1007912714741.

Levy, M., Powell, P., & Yetton, P. (2002). The dynamics of SME information systems. *Small Business Economics, 19*(4), 341–354. doi:10.1023/A:1019654030019.

Lybaert, N. (1998). The information use in a SME: Its importance and some elements of influence. *Small Business Economics, 10*(2), 171–191. doi:10.1023/A:1007967721235.

Mehrtens, J., Cragg, P. B., & Mills, A. M. (2001). A model of internet adoption by SMEs. *Information & Management, 39*(3), 165–176. doi:10.1016/S0378-7206(01)00086-6.

Mimno, P. (2002). *How to avoid data mart chaos using hybrid methodology*. TDWI Flash point column.

Mullins, R., Duan, Y., Hamblin, D., Burrell, P., Jin, H., Jerzy, G., ... Aleksander, B. (2007). A web based intelligent training system for SMEs. *The Electronic Journal of e-Learning, 5*, 39-48.

Olszak, C. M., & Ziemba, E. (2006). Business intelligence systems in the holistic infrastructure development supporting decision-making in organizations. *Interdisciplinary Journal of Information. Knowledge and Management, 1*, 47–58.

Open, I. (2011). *Open intelligence*. Retrieved from http://www.openi.org/

OpenSourceInitiative. (2011). Retrieved from http://www.opensource.org/

Pentaho. (2011). *Pentaho open source BI*. Retrieved from http://www.pentaho.com/

Pentaho Community. (2011). *Pentaho community home*. Retrieved from http://community.pentaho.com/

Power, D. J. (2007). A brief history of decision support systems, version 4.0. *DSSResources.com*. Retrieved from http://DSSResources.COM/history/dsshistory.html

Rist, R. (1997). Challenges faced by the data warehousing pioneers. *Journal of Data Warehousing, 2*(1).

Rudra, A., & Yeo, E. (1999). Key issues in achieving data quality and consistency in data warehousing among large organizations in Australia. In *Proceedings of the 32nd Hawaii International Conference on System Sciences*, (pp. 7012-7019). IEEE.

Snowden, D., & Boone, M. (2007). A leader's framework for decision making. *Harvard Business Review, 85*(11), 68–76. PMID:18159787.

Spago, B. I. (2011). *Spago business intelligence*. Retrieved from http://www.spagoworld.org/

Spruit, M., & Abdat, N. (2012). The pricing strategy guideline framework for SaaS vendors. *International Journal of Strategic Information Technology and Applications, 3*(1), 38–53. doi:10.4018/jsita.2012010103.

Strange, K. F. T. (2009). *Making BI and data warehousing strategic: The key issues, LE-19-4691*. Gartner Group.

Themistocleous, M., & Chen, H. (2004). Investigating the integration of SMEs' information systems: An exploratory case study. *International Journal of Information Technology and Management, 3*(2-4), 208–234. doi:10.1504/IJITM.2004.005033.

Turban, E. Aronson, Liang, & Sharda, R. (2007). Decision support and business intelligence systems (8th Ed.). Englewood Cliffs, NJ: Prentice Hall.

Turban, E., King, D., Lee, J. K., & Viehland, D. (2004). *Electronic commerce 2004: A managerial perspective* (3rd ed.). Englewood Cliffs, NJ: Prentice Hall.

Turban, E., Sharda, S., Aronson, J. E., & King, D. (2008). *Business intelligence: A managerial approach*. Upper Saddle River, NJ: Pearson Prentice Hall.

Vanilla. (2011). *True open source BI platform*. Retrieved from http://www.bpm-conseil.com/

Varner, P. E. (1999). *The economics of open source software*. Retrieved from http://www.cs.virginia.edu/~pev5b/writing/econ_oss/

Watson, H. J. (2009). Tutorial: Business intelligence–Past, present, and future. *Communications of the Association for Information Systems, 25*(39).

Watson, H. J., Gerard, J. G., Gonzalez, L. E., Haywood, M. E., & Fenton, D. (1999). Data warehousing failures: Case studies and findings. *Journal of Data Warehousing*, 44–55.

Watson, H. J., & Wixom, B. H. (2007). The current state of business intelligence. *IEEE Computer*, *40*(9), 96–99. doi:10.1109/MC.2007.331.

Wixom, B., & Watson, H. J. (2001). An empirical investigation of the factors affecting data warehousing success. *Management Information Systems Quarterly*, *25*(1), 17–41. doi:10.2307/3250957.

Xie, G., Yang, Y., Liu, S., Qiu, Z., Pan, Y., & Zhou, X. (2007). EIAW: Towards a business-friendly data warehouse using semantic web technologies. In K. Aberer, et al. (Eds.), *ISWC/ASWC '07: Proceedings of the 6th International Semantic Web Conference and 2nd Asian Semantic Web Conference* (LNCS), (vol. 4825, pp. 851-904). Berlin: Springer Verlag.

ADDITIONAL READING

Biere, M. (2010). *The new era of enterprise business intelligence: Using analytics to achieve a global competitive advantage*. IBM Press.

Castellanos, M., Dayal, U., & Markl, V. (Eds.). (2011). *Enabling real-time business intelligence - 4th international workshop, BIRTE 2010*. Berlin: Springer-Verlag.

Collier, K. (2011). *Agile analytics: A value-driven approach to business intelligence and data warehousing*. Reading, MA: Addison-Wesley Professional.

Davenport, T., & Harris, J. (2007). *Competing on analytics: The new science of winning*. Boston: Harvard Business School Press.

Howson, C. (2007). *Successful business intelligence: Secrets to making BI a killer app*. New York: McGraw Hill.

Kimball, R., Ross, M., Thornthwaite, W., & Mundy, J. (2010). *The Kimball group reader: Relentlessly practical tools for data warehousing and business intelligence*. Indianapolis, IN: Wiley Publishing, Inc..

Laursen, G. H. N., & Thorlund, J. (2010). Business analytics for managers: Taking business intelligence beyond reporting. New York: Wiley and SAS Business Series.

Loshin, D. (2003). *Business intelligence: The savvy manager's guide*. San Francisco, CA: Morgan Kaufmann Publishers.

Redman, T. (2008). *Data driven: Profiting from your most important business asset*. Boston: Harvard Business School Press.

Roebuck, K. (2011). *Business intelligence (BI) high-impact strategies - What you need to know: Definitions, adoptions, impact, benefits, maturity, vendors*. Tebbo Publisher.

Sabherwal, R., & Becerra-Fernandez, I. (2010). *Business intelligence: Practices, technologies, and management*. New York: Wiley.

Thomsen, C., & Pedersen, T. B. (2009). A survey of open source tools for business intelligence. *International Journal of Data Warehousing and Mining*, *5*(3), 56–75. doi:10.4018/jdwm.2009070103.

Turban, E., Sharda, R., & Delen, D. (2010). *Decision support and business intelligence systems* (9th ed.). Englewood Cliffs, NJ: Prentice Hall.

Turban, E., Sharda, R., Delen, D., & King, D. (2010). *Business intelligence* (2nd ed.). Englewood Cliffs, NJ: Prentice Hall.

Vercelli, C. (2009). *Business intelligence: Data mining and optimization for decision making*. New York: Wiley.

Vitt, E., Luckevich, M., & Misner, S. (2002). *Business intelligence: Making better decisions faster*. Redmond, WA: Microsoft Press.

Williams, S., & Williams, N. (2006). *The profit impact of business intelligence*. San Francisco, CA: Morgan Kaufmann.

KEY TERMS AND DEFINITIONS

Business Intelligence (BI): Mainly refers to computer-based techniques used in identifying, extracting, and analyzing business data. BI technologies provide historical, current and predictive views of business operations.

Data Mart (DM): Is a collection of subject areas organized for decision support based on the needs of a given department. A data mart can support a particular business function, business process or business unit.

Data Warehouse (DW): A data warehouse is a subject-oriented, integrated, time-variant and non-volatile collection of data in support of management's decision making process. A data warehouse is a copy of transaction data specifically structured for query and analysis.

Enterprise 2.0: Is the use of Web 2.0 technologies within an organization to enable or streamline business processes while enhancing collaboration - connecting people through the use of social-media tools. Enterprise 2.0 aims to help employees, customers and suppliers collaborate, share, and organize information.

OnLine Analytical Processing (OLAP): Is a decision support software that allows the user to quickly analyze information that has been summarized into multidimensional views and hierarchies. OLAP tools are used to perform trend analysis on sales and financial information. They enable users to drill down into masses of sales statistics in order to isolate products that are the most volatile.

Open Source: Open source does not just mean access to the source code. The distribution terms of open-source software must comply with the following criteria: 1) Free Redistribution; 2) Source Code; 3) Derived Works; 4) Integrity of The Author's Source Code; 5) No Discrimination Against Persons or Groups; 6) No Discrimination Against Fields of Endeavor; 7) Distribution of License; 8) License Must Not Be Specific to a Product; 9) License Must Not Restrict Other Software; 10) License Must Be Technology-Neutral. For the complete definition, see http://opensource.org/docs/osd.

Small and Medium-Sized Enterprise (SME): Is any enterprise which employ fewer than 250 persons and which have an annual turnover not exceeding 50 million euro, and/or an annual balance sheet total not exceeding 43 million euro.

Chapter 2
Managing "Virtuality": An Integrated Model for the Implementation and Management of Virtual Teams

Sandra Morley
National University of Ireland, Ireland

Kathryn Cormican
National University of Ireland, Ireland

Maébh Coleman
National University of Ireland, Ireland

ABSTRACT

A wealth of research is associated with virtual teams and collaboration technologies; however, no integrated model is available to guide decision-makers at large organisations in the strategic implementation and management of "virtuality." Whilst collaboration through technology has become commonplace in modern teams, it is not yet clear if Enterprise 2.0 organisations have made changes to accommodate and support this new mode of work. In other words, managing "virtuality" requires supporting tools and research in order to maximise the benefits and diminish the challenges inherent in it. This chapter presents findings of research relating to managing "virtualtiy" that culminates in the development and evaluation of a management model that guides large organisations in implementing and managing virtual teams. The findings demonstrate that there are benefits associated with virtual teamwork; however, a structured approach is essential to realise and maximise such benefits. The authors uncover several critical success factors in managing virtual teams, and they also learned that the implementation of enabling technologies must be carefully planned to ensure successful adoption by the intended audience. This chapter provides practitioners with a structured approach to implementing and managing virtual teams in an Enterprise 2.0 environment. Essential conditions for success are identified, specific organisational level tasks are presented, a process to ensure the introduction of new technologies is documented, and the critical success factors to create and manage virtual teams are synthesised and presented.

DOI: 10.4018/978-1-4666-4373-4.ch002

INTRODUCTION

Developments in communications technologies have changed the way we work. Organisations are no longer bound within physical confines, but have become more fluid, encompassing dynamic work groups and strategic alliances. These developments facilitate the co-ordination of knowledge work, making the ability to tap into knowledge workers wherever they are a competitive necessity (Bradley and Nolan, 1998). The need for collaboration beyond the physical margins of the traditional workplace has become critical for organisations. Virtual teaming has developed in response to the requirement for inter-organisational co-operation. In the past, organisations sought to maintain direct control of all processes from the acquisition of raw materials to the manufacture of finished goods, which often proved unmanageable. To counteract this, firms have begun to focus on their core, value-added processes, and divest peripheral businesses. Together, these factors have left organisations facing increased challenges to coordinate work activities across time zones, geographical locations and organisational boundaries. "Consequently, the virtual team has begun to emerge as a new form of structure, supported by enabling information and communication technologies, able to meet the challenges of this new work context" (Kayworth and Leidner, 2001).

"Virtual teams" can be defined as "groups of geographically and/or organizationally dispersed co-workers that are assembled using a combination of telecommunications and information technologies to accomplish an organizational task" (Townsend et al., 1998, p. 18), while "collaboration technologies' can be defined as information and communication technology applications that "support communication, co-ordination, co-operation, learning, and/or social encounters through facilities such as information exchange, shared repositories, discussion forums and messaging" (Andriessen, 2003, p. 10). Because of the ubiquity of some technologies, such as e-mail, most teams find that at least some of their work and a large number of their interactions with other team members are carried out electronically. This means that most teams can be considered 'virtual' to some degree. This increased use of the virtual team structure has developed gradually, as a result of the increased availability of technologies to facilitate collaboration.

Because of the natural evolution of this form of group work, most Enterprise 2.0 organisations have failed to implement the necessary structure to support teams working virtually. Studies have shown that investing in technologies while important is not sufficient. Benson-Armer and Hsieh (1997) report that many corporations have invested millions of dollars in technology, only to be disappointed when there is no commensurate improvement in performance. Consequently a number of management oriented problems have emerged, which centre around: the formalising of work processes and strategies (Lee-Kelley and Sankey, 2008; Lee, 2009; Gluesing and Riopelle, 2010); the composition and interaction of virtual team members (Rusman et al., 2010; Fan et al., 2011); virtual team building and reward structures (Rezgui, 2007; Shachaf, 2008; Bryant et al., 2009); virtual team leadership (Lee, 2009; Purvanova and Bono, 2009; Huang et al., 2010) and the role of technology in a virtual team environment (Harvey et al., 2004; Bryant et al., 2009). Clearly these problems must be addressed.

The goal of our research is to provide practitioners with a structured approach to the introduction and on-going management of virtual teams and associated technologies. It aims to provide managers with the necessary tools to help them manage cross-site virtual teams more efficiently and effectively. The objectives of this study are as follows:

- To examine the different types of technologies used by virtual teams to communicate and share information.

- To identify the characteristics of virtual teams and to determine the critical success factors associated with their successful implementation.
- To outline the recognised benefits and investigate the challenges faced by virtual teams, at individual, team and organisational levels and to identify the factors impacting the successful implementation and adoption of these technologies.
- To develop a model for the implementation and management of virtual teams using the information.

COLLABORATIVE TECHNOLOGIES

The growth of collaboration technologies can be traced back to the early 1970s, when the concept of using the processing and storage capabilities of computer networks to support communication processes within a group, as well as tailoring these processes to the needs of the application, and nature of the group itself was first developed (Hiltz and Turoff, 1993). Since that time, many researchers have studied this field in an attempt to understand the complex relationships that exist between the type of technology chosen, the context of its implementation and the factors impacting its acceptance and performance. In current literature, more generic terms such as Information and Communication Technology (ICT) and Collaboration Technology (CT) are more common. Andriessen (2003) defines ICT as "a mixture of hardware and software, of equipment and services" (p. 8). Table 1 illustrates the varied types and examples of collaborative technologies.

The advent of the personal computer was a great enabler of collaborative technologies. However, there is now a move away from desktop to mobile computing with the prevalence of laptops, Personal Digital Assistants (PDAs), wearables

Table 1. Types of collaboration technology

Category of Technology	Definition	Examples
Communication	Interpersonal communication through audio, text, video, etc. (Munkvold, 2003)	■ Telephone/Voice-mail ■ E-mail ■ Audio-conferencing ■ Video-conferencing ■ Chat systems ■ Instant Messaging
Information	Systems that 'represent, structure, and store information' (Mark et al., 1999)	■ Document sharing/management systems ■ Message boards/Electronic bulletin boards ■ Web-based team/project rooms ■ Data conferencing/application sharing
Coordination	Systems that manage interdependencies between participants and their activities (Munkvold, 2003)	■ Group calendars/scheduling systems ■ Workflow management systems ■ Notification systems ■ Command and control centre support systems
Co-operation/ Collaboration	Systems to improve teamwork by providing document-sharing and co-authoring capabilities and providing ability to co-ordinate work (Andriessen, 2003)	■ Shared CAD, whiteboard, word-processor, spreadsheet ■ Meeting support systems
Integrated Products	Products which 'combine features from several other categories' (Munkvold, 2003)	■ Collaboration product suites ■ Integrated team support technologies ■ e-Learning technologies
Social Encounter	Systems to 'make socialising possible at a distance' (Andriessen, 2003)	■ Media spaces ■ Virtual reality

(i.e., "a worn device which provides its user with access to computing and communications facilities wherever they are" (McAtamney and Parker, 2006), and even smartphones, which provide a wide range of platforms for individuals involved in group work (Olson and Olson, 2003). These systems allow people to work with information anywhere, at any time. More and more applications are being developed to operate across these diverse environments. With such an array of technologies available, choosing the most appropriate one can take considerable effort. However, choosing the right technology is not enough. The implementation strategy employed by the organisation's management is the key to ensuring its successful adoption. Kwon and Zmud (1987) introduced a six stage model for the implementation of information systems, covering all stages from project initiation and the acquisition of a new technology to the stage where the technology is fully 'internalised' in the daily work practices and the full benefits from the technology may be realised. This framework is summarised in Table 2.

Table 2. Six stage model of the IS implementation process (adapted from Cooper and Zmud, 1990)

Stages	Activities
Initiation	Scanning organisational problems/opportunities and IT solutions and choosing an appropriate technology.
Adoption	Negotiating to get organisational backing for IT implementation which includes assignment of appropriate resources.
Adaptation	Developing, installing and maintaining the IT application. Developing new organisational procedures. Training users. Deploying the technology.
Acceptance	Inducing the organisational members to use the technology.
Use	Enabling the IT application to be used as a normal activity.
Infusion	Encouraging and maintaining adoption rates. .

Although presented in a linear manner, the stages outlined in Table 2 should be considered to occur in parallel (Cooper and Zmud, 1990; Munkvold, 2003).

VIRTUAL TEAMS

Over ten years ago in 1998, definitions of the virtual team were emerging amongst researchers. Townsend et al. (1998, p. 18) defined virtual teams as "groups of geographically and/or organizationally dispersed co-workers that are assembled using a combination of telecommunications and information technologies to accomplish an organizational task". One year later in 1999, Jarvenpaa et al. (1999, p. 29) identified a virtual team as "a boundary-less network organization form where a temporary team is assembled on an as-needed basis for the duration of a task and staffed by members from different countries" where team processes are facilitated via shared communication systems. Huang et al. (2010) also posit that virtual teams are technology-enabled, and consist of members who can span different organizations, time zones, geographic locations, and cultures. Purvanova and Bono (2009) assert that virtual teams are characterized by; temporary lifespan and membership; spatial dispersion; and the use of predominantly computer-mediated communication infrastructures.

With time, increasingly virtual teams were being described in terms of their attributes, or the degree of virtuality as Table 3 shows. With increasing time 'virtuality' as a concept becomes more integral to function rather than form.

All agree that advances in collaborative technologies have made it possible for individuals separated by time, space and organisational barriers to work together with a common purpose, however what sets virtuality apart is that all employees act 'virtually' with regard to one or more elements of their work. Johnson et al. (2001) state that the term virtual team can just as easily be applied to groups of people who work no more than 50 feet apart. Kirkman and Mathieu (2005) agree that collocated, face-to-face teams can also exhibit high levels of virtuality.

Table 3. Definitions of "virtual teams"

Definition	Author(s)
"Virtual teams are groups of people who collaborate closely even though they may or may not be separated by space, time, and organizational barriers (Jennings, 1997) [....] A virtual team is usually going to be a cross-functional team that is pulled together for a specific purpose"	Johnson et al. (2001, p. 25)
"Virtual teams are groups of people who work interdependently with shared purpose across space, time, and organization boundaries using technology to communicate and collaborate"	Kirkman et al. (2002, p. 67)
"A group of people with complementary competencies executing simultaneous, collaborative work processes through electronic media without regard to geographic location"	Chinowsky and Rojas (2003, p. 99).
Virtual teams are "teams whose members use technology to varying degrees in working across locational, temporal, and relational boundaries to accomplish an interdependent task"	Martins et al. (2004, p. 808)
A virtual team must consist of two or more persons who: a) collaborate interactively to achieve common goals, while b) at least one of the team members works at a different location, organization, or at a different time so that c) communication and coordination is predominantly based on electronic communication media.	Hertel et al. (2005, p. 71)
'A virtual team typically has team members dispersed geographically, possibly with different times, organizational affiliations, and cultures. In general, the greater the dispersion or discontinuity, the more virtual the team.'	Munkvold and Zigurs (2007, p. 288)

There has also been much debate around the definition of 'virtual'. For example, Hertel et al. (2005) believe that the extent to which team members are dispersed and their reliance on electronic communication media should be considered dimensions, rather than "as dichotomized criteria that distinguish virtual teams from conventional 'face-to-face' teams" (p. 71). Thus, these authors believe that it would be better to consider the 'virtuality' of a team. In their review of virtual team literature, Martins et al. (2004) found that researchers appeared to be moving from defining virtual teams as a type of team that contrasts with a 'traditional' or 'conventional' face-to-face team (e.g. Guzzo and Dickson, 1996) to focusing on 'virtualness' as a potential characteristic of all teams (e.g. Griffith and Neale, 2001; Griffith et al., 2003; Munkvold and Zigurs, 2007). Several authors have characterised virtuality in terms of certain dimensions. See Table 4 for a summary.

Again, research is developing to recognise that the physicalities of purpose and form are becom-

Table 4. Dimensions of virtuality

Dimensions of Virtuality	Authors
Geographic dispersion Temporal dispersion Cultural dispersion Organizational dispersion	Zigurs (2003)
Spatial Temporal Cultural Organizational	Shin (2005)
Physical distance Time apart on tasks Level of technology support	Griffith et al. (2003)

Figure 1. A three-dimensional model of team virtuality (Kirkman & Mathieu, 2005, p. 705)

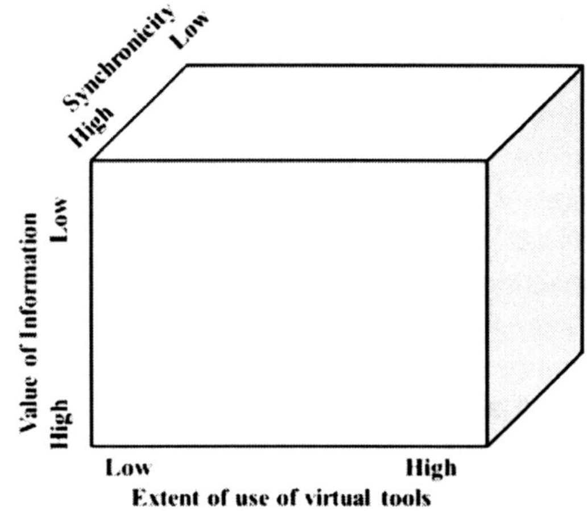

ing more blurred. In 2005 Kirkman and Mathieu characterise a three dimensional model of team virtuality which is based upon the use of virtual tools, the informational value of such tools and the synchronicity of interaction as shown in Figure 1.

Benefits of Virtual Teams

According to Zolin et al. (2004, p. 2). "cross-functional, geographically distributed workers provide great advantages by bringing to bear the diverse skills of scarce specialists on problems or projects that span traditional organizational boundaries". Many authors support the view that virtual teaming enables the successful management of knowledge within organisations (Bierly and Chakrabarti, 1996; Grant, 1996; Mowery et al., 1996), and according to Furst et al., (1999) "the effective use of virtual teams may become a prerequisite for organizations to compete successfully" (p. 253). The ability to create and disseminate knowledge in a timely fashion, especially in fast-changing business environments is essential where timely response and innovation is critical (Furst et al., 1999; Grant, 1996). Work methods of virtual teams can also become an important part of the organization's knowledge repository or 'organizational memory (Walsh and Ungson, 1991; Lewis, 1998), especially as the majority of team interactions is documented (e.g. through e-mail) and can be archived. Johnson et al. (2001) highlight additional benefits to employees, the organisation and society at large. Whilst the employee benefits from more flexible working hours and locations, the organisation can disperse improved business processes more widely and increase cross-functional and cross-divisional interactions and synergies.

The creation of virtual teams provides the opportunity to build teams from many countries and cultural backgrounds who could not possibly work together under traditional circumstances, allowing team leaders to access a greater pool of employees with the required expertise to address a wider range of problems (Townsend et al., 1998; Zaccaro and Bader, 2003). As Kayworth and Leidner (2000) point out, virtual teaming allows organisations to pool talent without having to physically relocate individuals. Anderson et al. (2007) believe that virtual teaming allows managers to rapidly pull together these individuals, as there is no need to travel or to commit to face-to-face meetings. It also allows organisations to use "the varying perspectives of different cultures and business customs to avoid counterproductive ethno-centric biases" (Solomon, 2001; Solomon, 1995) and societal benefits of a diverse work environment can extend to increased inclusivity for the physically challenged who cannot work in traditional environments.

Zaccaro and Bader (2003) believe that virtual team leaders and members potentially have access to a wider range of social contacts than would typically be available in more traditional teams. The authors believe that this 'social capital' (the quality of relationships and networks that leaders and team members form in their operating environment) is a "vital lubricant in work transactions and operations" (p. 380). As virtual team members are more likely to be drawn from differing social networks (to compensate for knowledge not available locally), Griffith et al. (2003) conclude that, as a result, the team will have "access to a potentially greater base of knowledge through their individual team members than collocated teams" (p. 268).

Additionally, Potter and Balthazard (2002) argue that although likely to communicate less frequently, "team members may express opinions more strongly as a compensatory measure or as a response to reduced social presence" (p. 2). The authors believe that communication technology may actually be superior to face-to-face communication in allowing for objective and accurate evaluation of the input of other team members leading to an authenticity that is not available in traditional work environments. According to Martins et al. (2004) (p. 806) "overall [virtual teams] provide an effective structural mechanism for handling the increased travel, time, coordination, and costs associated with bringing together geographically, temporally, and functionally dispersed employees to work on a common task".

Limitations of Virtual Teams

Although there are many benefits to be gained from the introduction of virtual teams in an organisation, research has shown that there are also a number of challenges and barriers that need to be addressed to allow the advantages outlined above to be realised. Townsend et al. (1998) outline that developing the technology and employee skills necessary for effective virtual team implementation carries a cost in time and financial investment that must be offset by the competitive advantage virtual teams afford. Virtual teams also require organisational restructuring and the introduction of new work technologies, which may result in resistance to change amongst other implementation problems.

Hertel et al. (2005) highlights that organisational challenges can include difficulties in supervising team members' activities and preventing unproductive developments in time and additional costs associated with the introduction of new technologies. Data security and training can also prove problematic whilst isolation for the virtual worker can pose problems in terms of motivation. Cramton (1997, 2001 and 2002) identifies five problems that can result in failures to establish and maintain mutual knowledge among dispersed team members. These are:

- Failures in communicating and retaining contextual information about other team members.
- Misunderstanding due to unevenly distributed information and team-level collaboration.
- Misunderstandings regarding the importance and relevance of information.
- Differences in speed of access to information.
- Difficulties in interpreting the meaning of silence/lack of communication.

Corso et al., (2006, p. 584) suggests that "these failures can have serious consequences for the viability of dispersed collaboration".

Whilst research has shown that cultural diversity can be one of the greatest benefits of virtuality in the workplace, creating many synergies and knowledge assets, there are also drawbacks. Maznevski and Chudoba (2000) define culture as "a set of deep-level values associated with societal effectiveness, shared by an identifiable group of people". Zolin et al. (2004) found that cultural diversity was associated with lower perceived trustworthiness (which is found to act as a barrier to knowledge sharing (Rosen et al., 2007) although they concluded that this may be the result of cultural misunderstandings rather than prejudices. Furthermore different culture-related cognitive schemata can act as 'filters' for team members which can become a source of misunderstanding and conflict in a virtual team (Rusman et al., 2010). Shapiro et al. (2002) note that members of trans-national teams may have difficulties in establishing a team identity due to the members' "national/cultural value diversity, global dispersion, and general tendency to not see each other" (p. 464). Ahuja and Galvin (2003) highlight socialization as one of the key challenges in the management of a virtual team

Hertel et al. (2005) note that the use of computer-mediated communication can result in increased chances of misunderstandings and conflict escalation. Shin (2005) states that virtual groups are more likely to engage in uninhibited behaviours such as insults and name-calling than more traditional groups and that conflict tends to occur more frequently in virtual contexts. The author lists the following sources of potential conflicts:

- Task/role/responsibility ambiguity
- Lack of trust
- Cultural differences
- Weak identity
- Low group cohesiveness

Many of the challenges outlined above arise because of the reliance on computer-mediated communication technology and the lack of face-to-face interactions between virtual team members. Handy (1995) questions whether virtual teams can ever function effectively in the absence of frequent face-to-face interaction. Cramton (2001) has noted that information may flow less easily in geographically distributed teams and that distributed workers may not develop the same understanding of the information that is shared.

With the potential benefits and challenges in mind, discussion can now centre on developing a model for implementing and managing virtuality using collaborative technologies in a team environment.

A MODEL FOR MANAGING VIRTUALITY IN LARGE ORGANISATIONS

A model for managing virtual teams in large organisations must endeavour to maximise the benefits whilst ameliorating or mitigating the challenges. This research has developed critical success factors to support the strength and integrity of an integrated model that implements and manages virtual teams in large organisations. Our research identified a number of recommendations and best-practices for the development and management of virtual teams, and for the implementation of technologies designed to optimise information exchange and communication in these teams. The knowledge gained from this review is summarised below where the key critical success factors are mapped across four categories.

Organisational Level

Specific human resource policies are needed to recognize, support, and reward virtual team members and leaders. Dedicated training is also required for team members and management. An appropriate organisational culture should also be created. For example a technologically advanced, non-hierarchical organisation with a history and culture of knowledge sharing is more likely to be successful. There must also be an appropriate infrastructure to successfully introduce and adapt technologies. Finally the continuous support of senior management is critical.

Team Processes and Virtual Environment

Opportunities for interaction and information exchange must be provided. The organisation must also provide opportunities for members to get acquainted at a social level, e.g. creation of personal Web pages. Furthermore, there is a need to provide visibility on activities, availability and work progress, and facilitate equal access to information. Open communication channels and participation in decision-making are also important. Clear roles and responsibilities within teams must be defined, along with formalised work practices such as strong communication and collaboration protocols, clear rules and terminologies. Norms around the use of technologies should also be established. The team's reporting structure should be clearly defined. It is important to define the team's role within the context of the organisation's greater mission. The team manager should re-iterate and continuously re-focus the team members on their ultimate goal. There is a need to provide adequate tools and technologies; the 'right' communication technology is required, i.e. simple, user-friendly and available to all team members.

A psychologically safe culture in the team should be established. This can happen by assessing the trustworthiness of each member (Fan et al., 2011) and creating trust and cohesiveness among leaders and team members. Team manager should visit remote members on a regular basis. Team-based reward systems should be established. Team empowerment should be supported, as it allows teams members to show high levels of initiative and proactivity. The virtual environment needs to support all aspects of the team's work, i.e. communication and information sharing at all levels of the team. The environment should also act as an integrated service, as it supports many people and is composed of many different components – from facilities to computer hardware and networks.

Management of Virtual Teams

Personality characteristics and psychological profile should be considered when choosing team members. Team members with appropriate skills should also be chosen. Examples of the skills required include:

- Self-discipline.
- Individual accountability i.e. responsibility and liability.
- Excellent team participation skills, i.e. able to assimilate quickly into the team.
- Excellent communication skills.
- Trust, i.e. have confidence that other members will fulfil their tasks and behave in a consistent and predictable manner.
- Suitable personality traits include: patience, perseverance, persistence, tolerance, flexibility, and understanding.

The managers of virtual teams also have a significant role to play. They should:

- Emphasise continuous communication.
- Engage in team building activities at the team's formation.
- Instil all team members with a sense of cultural awareness.
- Lead by example, i.e. exhibit the characteristics desired in virtual team members, use tools provided, and express flexibility and empathy toward all team members.
- Assess political and economic barriers to international communications.
- Set clear team goals and provide continuous performance feedback.
- Ensure assigned team roles are not in conflict with team members' commitments to other work units.
- Establish procedures to ensure minor disagreements do not escalate.
- Ensure that the assigned task is suitable for virtual teaming.

We found that the specific skills required by the manager of a virtual team include:

- Ability to effectively manage communication and to develop relationships with team members and to develop the team into a cohesive unit, shaping team processes, and monitoring and managing ongoing team performance.
- Choosing the appropriate medium for communications, e.g. using face-to-face encounters when necessary.
- Conflict resolution.
- Ability to recognise and encourage emergent leadership and self-leadership within team.
- Ability to recognise and address issues of low motivation.
- Sensitivity to the schedules of team members.

- Appreciative of team member opinions and suggestions.
- Exhibits care and concern over team member problems and expresses a personal interest in team members.
- Need to develop the team members and to develop other employees who can effectively participate in the virtual environment.

Introduction of New Technologies

Thorough mapping is required to ensure that technology fits the existing infrastructure and meets requirements of task to be completed. Furthermore, the design and implementation of the new technology should involve representations from different levels of the organisation. Any new technology adopted should be aligned with existing processes, platforms, and applications. Incentives for the adoption of the new technology should be developed, along with the identification of local champions. It is recommended that adequate support should be provided after the initial go-live of the technology. Finally clear guidelines for the use of the relevant technologies are essential.

AN INTEGRATED MODEL: IMPLEMENTATION AND MANAGEMENT

Whilst contemporary work practices mean that employees have embraced working virtually, organisational management practices do not always support this through a defined strategy which is why the development of an integrated model for implementation and management was necessary.

The section above has outlined the critical success factors associated with virtual teams and collaboration technologies. These factors have been expanded to develop a model that can be used by organisations to successfully implement and support virtual teams. This model is represented in Table 5 overleaf. The model identifies four key areas that need to be addressed to facilitate suc-

Table 5. Model for the implementation of virtual teams and associated technologies

1.0 Essential Conditions for Success	2.0 Organisational Level Tasks	3.0 Introduction of New Technologies	4.0 Creation and Management of Virtual Teams
1.1 Support of senior management 1.2 Robust IT Infrastructure 1.3 technologically Advanced Corporate Culture	2.1 Establish ownership for virtual team support 2.2. Identify collaboration tools already in use 2.3 Identify virtual teams that currently operate successfully 3.4 Develop toolkit for virtual teams 2.5 Develop training materials on tools 2.6 Develop Guidelines for Identifying and Introducing new technologies 2.7 Develop HR policies that support virtual teaming 2.8 Develop structure for creating and managing virtual teams 2.9 Raise awareness of virtual teaming	3.1 Detailed mapping to ensure technology fits 3.2 Design of new technology should involve future users 3.3 Where possible new technologies should be aligned with existing ones 3.4 Local champions should be identified 3.5 Rewards/benefits of new technologies should be emphasised 3.6 Adequate support should be provided for new technologies 3.7 Clear guidelines and training to be provided	4.1 Team manager must be trained on specific skills required to manage VTs 4.2 Chose team members with appropriate skills 4.3 Provide training on working in virtual teams including technologies 4.4 Teams reporting structure to be clearly defined 4.5 Provide opportunities for interaction and trust development 4.6 Establish rules of engagement 4.7 Establish clear goals and responsibilities 4.8 Ensure team are aware of how their work supports the overall goals of the organisation 4.9 Manager to visit remote team members as often as possible

cessful technology-enabled collaboration between work teams. These areas are:

- Essential conditions for success.
- Organisational level tasks.
- Introduction of new technologies.
- Creation and management of virtual teams.

Essential Conditions for Success

An organisation must have several fundamental characteristics in order to successfully support the implementation of virtual teaming and associated technologies. These form the basis for success; without them, there is little chance that the use of collaboration through technology will become an integral part of the organisation. The key 'conditions for success' are:

- **Support of Senior Management:** Like any organisation-wide initiative, the support of senior management is essential; not only to advocate the use of virtual teaming, but to drive the necessary corporate-wide changes to systems and policies that are required, and to ensure that the resources needed are made available.
- **Robust IT Infrastructure:** An up-to-date and well-maintained IT infrastructure is vital to ensure that new technologies can be accommodated and that increased network traffic can be facilitated. In multi-site, multinational organisations, a common IT infrastructure is a key requirement to ensure that all geographically-dispersed team members have equal access to information and the ability to fully utilise the relevant opportunities presented by the use of collaboration technologies.
- **Technologically Advanced Corporate Culture:** Successful virtual teaming can only really occur in organisations where the use of technology is already commonplace. Studies have shown that the process of implementing new collaboration technologies is considerably easier in non-hierarchical organisations that are already familiar and comfortable with the use of technologies and systems, with a history and culture of knowledge sharing. The organisation must be open and receptive to technological change (see Table 5).

Organisational Level Tasks

If the pre-requisites for successful virtual teaming outlined above are met, then the organisation must turn its attention to establishing policies and processes at an organisational level to support the establishment and management of virtual teams. These organisational level tasks are as follows:

- **Establish Ownership for Virtual Team Support:** Although the use of the virtual team model is not limited to one particular function or department, it is important that a responsible group is identified at an organisational level to provide focus for maintenance activities, to manage feedback, and to support virtual teams at other sites within the organisation. In large organisations, it is important to have a centralised owner of such an initiative to ensure that a common approach is maintained throughout, and to ensure that a common language is used when working with virtual teams. Without this focus, it becomes very difficult to ensure that relevant information (such as best-practice examples and any new technologies identified) is disseminated appropriately throughout the organisation.
- **Identify Collaboration Tools that are Already inUse:** At the outset of a formal virtual teaming initiative, it is important that time is spent on identifying collaboration tools that are already used successfully within the organisation. Some teams/sites

may already have identified or developed software solutions that could be used by other teams.

- **Identify Virtual Teams that Currently Operate Successfully:** In addition to determining the tools already in use, it is also important to identify existing teams in the organisation that are already successfully using technology to collaborate and communicate. The tools and methodologies used by these teams may form the basis of a best-practice model for the organisation.
- **Develop a Tool-Kit for Virtual Teams:** The identification of the existing collaboration tools in use and the tools and methodologies used by existing teams should form the basis of a tool-kit that can be used by virtual teams throughout the organisation, and can provide a starting point for new teams. This tool-kit should also include the guidelines on technology implementation and team creation in Sections 3 and 4 of this model.
- **Develop Training Material on Tools:** It is vital that corporate-wide training material be developed to ensure that the tools identified are fully utilised in a common way. This will ensure that all team members, regardless of location or native language, can derive the same benefits from using the tools available.
- **Develop Guidelines for Identifying and Introducing New Technologies:** Guidelines should be established at a corporate level to ensure that the risks associated with the introduction of new technologies are assessed consistently, and that lessons learned at one site can be communicated appropriately. The requirements for the introduction of new technologies are outlined in greater detail in section 3.0 of the model.
- **Develop HR Policies that Support Virtual Teaming:** HR policies relating to the selection of suitable virtual team managers and members should be established. Training must also be provided to increase awareness of suitable behaviours for members of a team that may never meet face-to-face, placing emphasis on the appropriate use of technology to communicate. It is also important that criteria are established for identifying and rewarding successful teams. Cultural sensitivity and awareness are key concerns for teams that consist of geographically dispersed members and should be formally addressed.
- **Develop a Structure for Creating and Managing Virtual Teams:** To enforce the training and tools provided, a structured approach to the creation and management of virtual teams is required. The key aspects of this structure are described in Section 4.0.
- **Raise Awareness of Virtual Teaming:** Chapter 5 concluded that an increased use of virtual teams is the most appropriate strategy to pursue for the multinational corporation analysed in order to maximise the potential of the available resources and, as a result, to facilitate innovation. The use of virtual teams, with members drawn from different locations or companies, as required, should be encouraged throughout the organisation.

Introduction of New Technologies

As outlined above, it is critical that a process is established to ensure that the introduction of new technologies to facilitate the communication of information and/or data between team members is carried out in a consistent manner. In addition, where teams are comprised of members from different geographical locations or organisations, any differences in the IT infrastructure need to be addressed.

- **Detailed Mapping Required to Ensure Technology 'Fits':** When a requirement for a new technology has been identified, detailed mapping of the existing tools used within the organisation, the experience of intended users, along with the capability of the IT infrastructure, must be completed to ensure that the proposed technology 'fits' the requirements of the team and the organisation. Before this mapping can take place, it is vital that there is a clear understanding of the tasks to be performed by the technology.
- **Design of New Technology Should Involve Future Users:** When a new technology or system needs to be designed, or customised to meet the needs of the organisation, it is vital that input is sought from the future users of the new system (ideally, at different levels and locations within the organisation). This will ensure that the 'right' technology to meet the current and future requirements of the business is selected. It is also important that the support of key stakeholders, such as the organisation's leadership, is established early in the project.
- **New Technologies Should be Aligned with Existing Ones:** Any new technologies to be introduced should be aligned to work in conjunction with existing technologies, systems, and business processes to maximise their usefulness and effectiveness, and to leverage the existing experience and knowledge of intended users.
- **Local Champions Should be Identified:** System experts and champions should be established at different levels in the organisation to facilitate the acceptance of the new technology.
- **Rewards/Benefits of New Technology Should be Emphasised:** Emphasis should be placed on the potential rewards and benefits presented by the new technology to ensure that these are fully understood by future users and to facilitate acceptance.
- **Adequate Support Should be Provided for New Technologies:** Technical support should be made available for new technologies, not only during the initial implementation phase, but on an on-going basis. It is also important to establish criteria to evaluate the success of the new technology by monitoring performance before and after implementation.
- **Clear Guidelines and Training to be Provided:** Formal training material should be developed for all new technologies, in addition to manuals and procedures governing the use of the system. The timing of the implementation should also be carefully planned to meet the needs of the organisation.

Creation and Management of Virtual Teams

The above sections combine to establish the right environment for the successful use of virtual teaming in an organisation. However, without the development of a structured approach to the creation and management of individual virtual teams, consistent success can not be achieved. There are a number of important factors that combine to make a virtual team successful. These are outlined below:

- **Team Manager has the Appropriate Characteristics and Skills Required to Manage the Virtual Team:** The managers of virtual teams require different skills to those required by the managers of traditional, collocated teams. These include:
  - Ability to effectively manage communication and to develop relationships with team members, recognising their opinions and suggestions.

- Ability to identify and address issues of low motivation.
- Conflict resolution.
- Encouragement of self-leadership and recognition of emergent leaders.
- Awareness of and sensitivity to team members' opinions, concerns, and constraints (such as increased workload, time zone, etc.).
- Promotion and maintenance of team trust and cohesion.
- Monitoring and management of team performance.
- Development of team into one cohesive unit.
- Ability to choose the right tasks for virtual teamwork, i.e. some tasks, such as conflict negotiation, are not appropriate for virtual teaming.
- Ensure that appropriate tools are available for all aspects of the work to be performed by the virtual team, from basic e-mails to formal meetings and presentations.
- Managers should lead by example, following outlined team processes and using collaboration tools available.
- Ability to assess potential barriers to communication, both political and economic.

- **Choose Team Members with the Appropriate Skills:** It is also important that the team members selected have the appropriate skills for working on a virtual team. These include:
    - Self-management and self-discipline, with individual accountability or culpability.
    - Comfort with technology and technological change.
    - Excellent communications skills.
    - Excellent team participation skills with experience of working in teams, particularly in using technology to communicate.
    - Propensity to trust, i.e. to have confidence in other team members to fulfil their tasks and to behave in a consistent and predictable manner.
    - Suitable personality traits include: patience, perseverance, persistence, tolerance, flexibility, and understanding.
- **Provide Training on Working in Virtual Teams (Including Technologies):** It is critical that team participants should be trained on how to work effectively in a virtual team, and that team members, regardless of location, should receive the same level of training. This should include guidelines on using communications tools such as e-mail, voicemail and audio- and video-conferencing effectively, and cultural awareness for multinational teams. It is also important to develop the team themselves and, in particular, to develop employees who can effectively participate in this virtual environment.
- **Team's Reporting Structure to be Clearly Defined:** It is important that team members understand where they fit within the team itself, and also where the team lies within the overall organisation.
- **Provide Opportunities for Interaction and the Development of Trust:** It is recommended that virtual teams should meet face-to-face, at least at the outset of the team, to help in the creation of relationships and trust between members. The establishment of trust and cohesion between team members and with the team's manager is vital, to ensure that ideas and opinions will be freely exchanged. Teams should be given opportunities to interact outside of formal group meetings; more informal, social interaction has been shown to lead to more productive teams as it helps to establish trust and to create a shared group

identity. Team-building activities are also recommended, especially early in the life of the team.

- **Establish Rules of Engagement:** Clear rules of engagement should be established during the team's formation. These should include:
  - The establishment of equal access to information for all members
  - Visibility to progress on the tasks assigned to team members and on the members' availability
  - Promotion of continuous communication between team members
  - Continuous performance feedback from the team manager
  - Establishment of norms around the use of communication technologies, including terminologies to support knowledge transfer.
  - Team empowerment: It is important that team members feel free to make decisions, to contribute to goals, and to develop and improve processes.
  - Establish a code of conduct, along with standards for availability and acknowledgement. Guidelines for meetings and discussions should also be established. These procedures should ensure that minor disagreements do not escalate.
- **Establish Clear Goals and Responsibilities:** To work effectively, clear goals and responsibilities should be established. Adherence to these should be monitored by the team manager. Team member expectations should be set and criteria established for assessing the team's success. It is important that the team roles assigned do not conflict with team members' commitments to other work units.
- **Ensure Team is Aware of how their Work Contributes to the Overall Goals of the Organisation:** To overcome feelings of isolation or a lack of motivation, the importance of the work carried out by the team in relation to the overall organisation should be emphasised.
- **Manager to Visit Remote/Isolated Team Members as Often as Possible:** Where regular face-to-face meetings are impossible, it is important for the team manager to visit remote team members to counteract any feelings of isolation that may arise.
- **Ensure Success is Rewarded:** Criteria for determining the success of the team must be established at the outset and successful teams should be rewarded accordingly.

BENEFITS AND LIMITATIONS TO THE MODEL

This model was implemented and tested in a large multinational medical device organisation in Ireland to establish its potential effectiveness. From this analysis the following benefits and limitations of the virtual team model were identified.

The model incorporates the critical success factors identified relating to virtual teams and collaboration technologies. Thus, recommendations from different fields of research are combined to form one set of criteria for an organisation to follow. It also provides a holistic framework for implementing virtual teaming in an organisation; from the requirements at the overall organisational level, to the specific skills and abilities that are most appropriate for working in a dispersed team. Furthermore, the virtual teams' model emphasises the importance of the organisation's culture and attitude towards change and incorporating new systems and processes and the need for senior management support to ensure that tools and techniques are disseminated appropriately throughout the business.

Full implementation of the model would mean a considerable investment of time and money to ensure that the organisation could meet the requirements of the model. Examples of this include:

- The technology infrastructure would need to be updated to ensure that it performed consistently across the organisation, and could support the integration of up-to-date systems.
- A substantial investment in training and recruitment would be required to ensure that employees have the most suitable skills and abilities for virtual teamwork.
- The model emphasises the importance of providing opportunities for interaction between team members, with face-to-face meetings at the beginning of the team's life highlighted in particular. The cost of facilitating face-to-face interactions for all the virtual teams in an organisation would prove prohibitive for most businesses.

It may be difficult to garner adequate support at all levels of the organisation to ensure that the guidelines outlined in the model are disseminated and integrated. This will be a particular problem in large organisations with employees from many different countries and cultures. Significant time and effort would be required to ensure that the message of virtual teaming is rolled out appropriately and consistently.

For the model to work in a dispersed organisation, an owner for the support of virtual teaming would have to be identified. Because virtual teamwork is something that can be used by any function or work group, it may be difficult to assign ownership to one function. A central source is required to ensure that best-practice methods are identified and rolled-out throughout the corporation; establishing this central source, that is accessible to all employees, may pose a considerable challenge for many organisations. Finally, choosing team members with the skills outlined in the model may not be possible. In many cases, teams are already in place, and managers do not have the opportunity of choosing new members.

CONCLUSION

Research results show that the use of collaboration technologies is not limited to certain groups within an organisation. Basic technologies, such as e-mail and voicemail, are used by most employees. Thus, the collaborative work carried out by the majority of today's teams can be said to be 'virtual' to some degree. Other factors, along with the advancements and proliferation of technology, have facilitated the growth of virtual teams. These include changes in the business environment that have forced organisations to become flatter and leaner, and the resultant drive towards inter-organisational co-operation.

We found that the virtual team is a commonly used work structure in the organisation examined. However, analysis showed that virtual teaming and the technologies associated with communications and information exchange between dispersed team members have not been implemented or managed in a structured way. As a result, the level of employee satisfaction with this mode of group work was low. To provide structure to the implementation and management of virtual teams, a model has been created based on the critical success factors identified during the literature reviews. This model proposes that, in order to successfully employ virtual teams, management need to evaluate their organisation to ensure the right environment for such work structures exist. In addition, specific activities at the organisational and team levels were identified, along with the steps needed to successfully implement new technologies. The model can be used to diagnose existing barriers to achieving the full benefits outlined in this research or to carry out a fresh implementation of new technology.

REFERENCES

Anderson, A., McEwan, R., Bal, J., & Carletta, J. (2007). Virtual team meetings: An analysis of communication and context. *Computers in Human Behavior, 23*, 2558–2580. doi:10.1016/j.chb.2007.01.001.

Andriessen, J. H. E. (2003). *Working with groupware: Understanding and evaluating collaboration technology*. London: Springer-Verlag. doi:10.1007/978-1-4471-0067-6.

Benson-Armer, R., & Hsieh, T. (1997). Teamwork across time and space. *The McKinsey Quarterly, 4*, 18–27.

Bierly, P., & Chakrabarti, A. (1996). Generic knowledge strategies in the U.S. pharmaceuticals industry. *Strategic Management Journal of Special Issue on Knowledge and the Firm, 17*, 123–135.

Bradley, S. P., & Nolan, R. L. (1998). Capturing value in the network era. In Bradley, S. P., & Nolan, R. L. (Eds.), *Sense & Respond: Capturing Value in the Network Era*. Boston, MA: Harvard Business School Press.

Bryant, S. M., Albring, S. M., & Murthy, U. (2009). The effects of reward structure, media richness and gender on virtual teams. *International Journal of Accounting Information Systems, 10*, 190–213. doi:10.1016/j.accinf.2009.09.002.

Chinowsky, P. S., & Rojas, E. M. (2003). Virtual teams: Guide to successful implementation. *Journal of Management Engineering, 19*(3), 98–106. doi:10.1061/(ASCE)0742-597X(2003)19:3(98).

Cooper, R. B., & Zmud, R. W. (1990). Information technology implementation research: A technological diffusion approach. *Management Science, 36*(2), 123–139. doi:10.1287/mnsc.36.2.123.

Corso, M., Martini, A., Pellegrini, L., Massa, S., & Testa, S. (2006). Managing dispersed workers: The new challenge in knowledge management. *Technovation, 26*, 583–594. doi:10.1016/j.technovation.2005.02.003.

Cramton, C. D. (1997). Information problems in dispersed teams. Academy of Management Proceedings, 298-302.

Cramton, C. D. (2001). The mutual knowledge problem and its consequences for dispersed collaboration. *Organization Science, 12*, 346–371. doi:10.1287/orsc.12.3.346.10098.

Cramton, C. D. (2002). Finding common ground in dispersed collaboration. *Organizational Dynamics, 30*(4), 354–367. doi:10.1016/S0090-2616(02)00063-3.

Cramton, C. D., & Orvis, K. L. (2003). Overcoming barriers to information sharing in virtual teams. In Gibson, C. B., & Cohen, S. G. (Eds.), *Virtual Teams that Work: Creating Conditions for Virtual Team Effectiveness*. San Francisco, CA: Jossey-Bass.

Fan, Z. P., Suo, W. L., Feng, B., & Liu, Y. (2011). Trust estimation in a virtual team: A decision support method. *Expert Systems with Applications, 38*(8), 10240–10251. doi:10.1016/j.eswa.2011.02.060.

Furst, S. A., Blackburn, R. S., & Rosen, B. (1999). Virtual team effectiveness: A proposed research agenda. *Information Systems Journal, 9*, 249–269. doi:10.1046/j.1365-2575.1999.00064.x.

Furst, S. A., Reeves, M., Rosen, B., & Blackburn, R. S. (2004). Managing the life cycle of virtual teams. *The Academy of Management Executive, 18*(2), 6–20. doi:10.5465/AME.2004.13837468.

Gluesing, J. C., & Riopelle, K. R. (2010). Correlating survey data and network data to understand performance in global virtual teams. *Procedia Social and Behavioral Sciences, 2*, 6551–6560. doi:10.1016/j.sbspro.2010.04.065.

Grant, R. (1996). Toward a knowledge-based theory of the firm. *Strategic Management Journal, 17*, 109–122.

Griffith, T. L., & Neale, M. (2001). Information processing in traditional, hybrid, and virtual teams: From nascent knowledge to transactive memory. *Research in Organizational Behavior*, *23*, 379–421. doi:10.1016/S0191-3085(01)23009-3.

Griffith, T. L., Sawyer, J., & Neale, M. (2003). Virtualness and knowledge in teams: managing the love triangle of organizations, individuals, and information technology. *Management Information Systems Quarterly*, *27*(2), 265–287.

Guzzo, R. A., & Dickson, M. W. (1996). Teams in organizations: Recent research on performance and effectiveness. *Annual Review of Psychology*, *47*, 307–338. doi:10.1146/annurev.psych.47.1.307 PMID:15012484.

Handy, C. (1995). Trust and the virtual organization. *Harvard Business Review*, *73*(3), 40–50.

Harvey, M., Novicevic, M. M., & Garrison, G. (2004). Challenges to staffing global virtual teams. *Human Resource Management Review*, *14*, 275–294. doi:10.1016/j.hrmr.2004.06.005.

Hertel, G., Geister, S., & Konradt, U. (2005). Managing virtual teams: A review of current empirical research. *Human Resource Management Review*, *15*, 69–95. doi:10.1016/j.hrmr.2005.01.002.

Hertel, G., Konradt, U., & Orlikowski, B. (2004). Managing distance by interdependence: Goal setting, task interdependence, and team-based rewards in virtual teams. *European Journal of Work and Organizational Psychology*, *13*(1), 1–28. doi:10.1080/13594320344000228.

Hiltz, S. R., & Turoff, M. (1993). *The network nation* (Revised Ed.). Cambridge, MA: MIT Press.

Huang, R., Kahai, S., & Jestice, R. (2010). The contingent effects of leadership on team collaboration in virtual teams. *Computers in Human Behavior*, *26*, 1098–1110. doi:10.1016/j.chb.2010.03.014.

Jarvenpaa, S. L., & Leidner, D. E. (1999). Communication and trust in global virtual teams. *Organization Science*, *10*(6), 791–815. doi:10.1287/orsc.10.6.791.

Johnson, P., Heimann, V., & O'Neill, K. (2001). The wonderland of virtual teams. *Journal of Workplace Learning*, *13*(1), 24–29. doi:10.1108/13665620110364745.

Kayworth, T. R., & Leidner, D. E. (2000). The global virtual manager: A prescription for success. *European Management Journal*, *18*(2), 183–194. doi:10.1016/S0263-2373(99)00090-0.

Kayworth, T. R., & Leidner, D. E. (2001). Leadership effectiveness in global virtual teams. *Journal of Management Information Systems*, *18*(3), 7–40.

Kirkman, B. L., & Mathieu, J. E. (2005). The dimensions and antecedents of team virtuality. *Journal of Management*, *31*(5), 700–718. doi:10.1177/0149206305279113.

Kirkman, B. L., & Rosen, B. (2000). Powering up teams. *Organizational Dynamics*, *28*(3), 48–66. doi:10.1016/S0090-2616(00)88449-1.

Kirkman, B. L., Rosen, B., Gibson, C. B., Tesluk, P. E., & McPherson, S. O. (2002). Five challenges to virtual success: Lessons from Sabre, Inc. *The Academy of Management Executive*, *16*(3), 67–79. doi:10.5465/AME.2002.8540322.

Kirkman, B. L., Rosen, B., Tesluk, P. E., & Gibson, C. B. (2004). The impact of team empowerment on virtual team performance: The moderating role of face-to-face interaction. *Academy of Management Journal*, *47*(2), 175–192. doi:10.2307/20159571.

Kwon, T. H., & Zmud, R. W. (1987). Unifying the fragmented models of information systems implementation. In Boland, R. J., & Hirschheim, R. A. (Eds.), *Critical Issues in Information Systems Research*. New York: John Wiley & Sons.

Lee, M. R. (2009). E-ethical leadership for virtual project teams. *International Journal of Project Management*, *27*, 456–463. doi:10.1016/j.ijproman.2008.05.012.

Lee-Kelley, L., & Sankey, T. (2008). Global virtual teams for value creation and project success: A case study. *International Journal of Project Management*, *26*(1), 51–62. doi:10.1016/j.ijproman.2007.08.010.

Lewis, R. (1998). Membership and management of a 'virtual' team: The perspectives of a research manager. *R & D Management*, *28*, 5–13. doi:10.1111/1467-9310.00076.

Mark, G., Grudin, J., & Poltrock, S. (1999). Meeting at the desktop: An empirical study of virtually collocated teams. In *Proceedings of ECSCW'99, the 6th European Conference on Computer Supported Cooperative Work*, (pp. 159-178). ECSCW.

Martins, L., Gilson, L., & Maynard, M. (2004). Virtual teams: What do we know and where do we go from here? *Journal of Management*, *30*(6), 805–835. doi:10.1016/j.jm.2004.05.002.

Maznevski, M. L., & Chudoba, K. M. (2000). Bridging space over time: Global virtual team dynamics and effectiveness. *Organization Science*, *11*(5), 473–492. doi:10.1287/orsc.11.5.473.15200.

Maznevski, M. L., Gomez, C. B., Noorderhaven, N. G., & Wu, P. (1997). *The cultural orientations framework and international management research*. Paper presented at the Academy of International Business Annual Meeting. Monterrey, Mexico.

McAtamney, G., & Parker, C. (2006). An examination of the effects of a wearable display on informal face-to-face communication. In *Proceedings of the SIGCHI Conference on Human Factors in Computing Systems*. Montréal, Canada: ACM.

Mowery, D., Oxley, J., & Silverman, B. (1996). Strategic alliances and interfirm knowledge transfer. *Strategic Management Journal*, *17*, 77–91.

Munkvold, B. (2003). *Implementing collaboration technologies in industry: Case examples and lessons learned*. London: Springer-Verlag. doi:10.1007/978-1-4471-0073-7.

Munkvold, B., & Zigurs, I. (2007). Process and technology challenges in swift-starting virtual teams. *Information & Management*, *44*, 287–299. doi:10.1016/j.im.2007.01.002.

Olson, G. M., & Olson, J. S. (2003). Groupware and computer-supported cooperative work. In Jacko, J. A., & Sears, A. (Eds.), *The Human-Computer Interaction Handbook*. London: Lawrence Erlbaum Associates.

Pape, W. (1997). The book of virtuals. *INC Technology*, *4*(19), 7–26.

Potter, R. E., & Balthazard, P. A. (2002). Understanding human interaction and performance in the virtual team. *Journal of Information Technology Theory and Application*, *4*, 1–23.

Purvanova, R. K., & Bono, J. E. (2009). Transformational leadership in context: Face-to-face and virtual teams. *The Leadership Quarterly*, *20*, 343–357. doi:10.1016/j.leaqua.2009.03.004.

Rezgui, Y. (2007). Exploring virtual team-working effectiveness in the construction sector. *Interacting with Computers*, *19*(1), 96–112. doi:10.1016/j.intcom.2006.07.002.

Rusman, E., van Bruggen, J., Sloep, P., & Koper, R. (2010). Fostering trust in virtual project teams: Towards a design framework grounded in a trustworthiness antecedents (TWAN) schema. *International Journal of Human-Computer Studies*, *68*(11), 834–850. doi:10.1016/j.ijhcs.2010.07.003.

Shachaf, P. (2008). Cultural diversity and information and communication technology impacts on global virtual teams: An exploratory study. *Information & Management*, *45*(1), 131–142. doi:10.1016/j.im.2007.12.003.

Shapiro, D. L., Furst, S. A., Spreitzer, G. M., & Von Glinow, M. A. (2002). Transnational teams in the electronic age: Are team identity and high performance at risk? *Journal of Organizational Behavior*, *23*, 455–467. doi:10.1002/job.149.

Shin, Y. (2005). Conflict resolution in virtual teams. *Organizational Dynamics*, *34*(4), 331–345. doi:10.1016/j.orgdyn.2005.08.002.

Solomon, C. M. (1995). Global teams: The ultimate collaboration. *The Personnel Journal*, *74*(9), 49–53.

Solomon, C. M. (2001). Managing virtual teams. *Workforce*, *80*(6), 60–64.

Townsend, A., DeMarie, S., & Hendrickson, A. (1998). Virtual teams: Technology and the workplace of the future. *The Academy of Management Executive*, *12*(3), 17–29.

Walsh, J. P., & Ungson, G. R. (1991). Organizational memory. *Academy of Management Review*, *16*, 57–91.

Zaccaro, S., & Bader, P. (2003). E-leadership and the challenges of leading e-teams: Minimizing the bad and maximizing the good. *Organizational Dynamics*, *31*(4), 377–387. doi:10.1016/S0090-2616(02)00129-8.

Zigurs, I. (2003). Leadership in virtual teams: Oxymoron or opportunity? *Organizational Dynamics*, *31*(4), 339–351. doi:10.1016/S0090-2616(02)00132-8.

Zolin, R., Hinds, P., Fruchter, R., & Levitt, R. (2004). Interpersonal trust in cross-functional, geographically distributed work: A longitudinal study. *Information and Organization*, *14*(1), 1–26. doi:10.1016/j.infoandorg.2003.09.002.

KEY TERMS AND DEFINITIONS

Collaborative Technologies: Hardware and software equipment used to facilitate information sharing, communication and coordination.

Critical Success Factors: Best practice traits or attributes.

Dispersed Teams: Teams that are not co-located.

Implementation: This refers to the roll out or deployment of something such as a model, technology or new practice.

Limitations: Challenges that are known to impact an issue.

Model: Conceptual framework or diagram that identifies and groups key issues.

Virtual Teams: Virtual teams can be defined as a group of people working towards similar goals who use information communication technology to interact and collaborate.

Virtuality: The level of distance between team members in terms of time, space, culture and organization.

Chapter 3
A Review of Tools for Overcoming the Challenge of Monitoring of Social Media

Carlos Figueroa
University of Turabo, Puerto Rico

Abraham Otero
University San Pablo, Spain

ABSTRACT

Until recently, a company's communications with the public were unidirectional and mostly limited to advertisements in mass media. This gave companies almost complete control over their brand and image. Nowadays, a new set of media, in which the public has similar capabilities for creating content as companies has emerged: social media. The growth of this medium has been exponential, endowing it with a reach that can dwarf traditional mass media. Having or not having a presence in such media is not just a choice of the company. The company's customers and the general public can generate content related to a company without the company's consent. There is no way for the company to avoid it. All they can do is listen to the conversations, engage in them, and try to dampen negative feelings while steering the overall conversation in positive directions. Given the size of social networks and the large number of conversations that they support on a daily basis, manual monitoring is impossible. In this chapter, the authors review and evaluate various tools to support the tasks of monitoring and managing the content of social media that is relevant for a company, a brand, or a product.

INTRODUCTION

Part of Web 2.0 is comprised of social networks, blogs, wikis, and other collaborative applications where end users are no longer mere spectators, but participants that generate content continuously and guide the direction of the conversation. In the past, business communications with the public were unidirectional and mostly limited to advertisements in mass media. Therefore, companies had strong control over their brand and image. Now the public has new ways to spread messages about

DOI: 10.4018/978-1-4666-4373-4.ch003

companies through social media. These messages sometimes have a reach equal to or even superior to the reach of mass media messages. Heinlein and Kaplan (2010) found that at least in one medium (Internet) companies have lost complete control of the messages related to their own brand and products, since the public can guide the conversation and respond to the company on equal terms. The lack of full control over this new media forces companies to monitor and react to what happens in these new avenues of communication. (O'Reilly, 2007; Gallaugher, 2010; Constantinides, et al., 2008; Dösinger, et al., 2007)

To monitor social media, large amounts of heterogeneous information such as text, images, audio, videos and other unstructured data need to be analyzed. Sometimes these contents are negative, requiring prompt intervention to reduce or prevent damage to the reputation, products and/or services of the business or organization (Heinlein, Kaplan, 2010; Constantinides, et al., 2008; Bhattacharya, Du, & Sen, 2010). When no adequate and prompt action is taken, the image of the company may be affected negatively (Constantinides, et al., 2008; Social Media Report, 2010; Sterne, 2010; Leganza, 2010; Hutley, 2009).

All social networks provide user interfaces, usually via the Web browser or mobile applications, for creating and accessing user-created content. But these interfaces are intended for personal use, and for accessing only the content created by users who have some relationship between them such as friends, followers, etc. They are not intended for use by several people working within the same account (a very common scenario in a company). They do not provide effective mechanisms for discovering or monitoring discussions on a certain topic throughout the entire network. In addition, they only allow the user to manage content within the social network itself, while a company must maintain a presence in multiple social networks simultaneously.

Currently, there are various monitoring tools that provide assistance in the overwhelming task of social media content monitoring. These tools can monitor the generation of new content relevant to a certain area (a company, a brand, a product...), analyze the scope of the conversation, provide a sentiment analysis classifying the discussions in categories such as "Positive," "Neutral," and "Negative" trigger alerts or actions whenever a conversation on a certain topic is started, etc. (Constantinides, et al., 2008; Sterne 2010; Leganza, 2010; FreshMinds Research, 2010; Koch & Richter, 2008). There are over a hundred monitoring solutions of this nature (A Wiki of Social media Monitoring Solutions, 2011), making it difficult to select the most appropriate tool/tools for the particular context and needs of each company (FreshMinds Research, 2010).

Well exploited, social media monitoring can not only be used to respond to negative content related to a company, but it can also be integrated into business processes in the areas of marketing, market research, customer service, public relations, and sales among others. With the adequate support of monitoring tools, these functions can be carried out in a more effective manner and at a lower cost than with traditional solutions (Gleanster, 2010). However, before such tools can be used effectively in a company, both the staff who is going to participate in the social media monitoring task and the management must understand the potential of social media and how it can make a difference in their company (Harvard Business Review Analytic Services, 2010).

In this chapter we will analyze the capabilities of the most popular tools currently available for monitoring and reacting to social media content. We will examine their ability to track, analyze, obtain metrics, manage, and respond to what is said about a given topic (in our case, a company, its products and its business) in social media. In the next section, we briefly present several case studies that demonstrate how the social media can provide considerable value if the business knows how to properly take advantage of it. However, when it is ignored or misused the social media can cause considerable damage to the brand and reputation of a business. The following section reviews the main tools that can provide support in the management of the social media presence of a company. Finally, we discuss the results of our review and provide some conclusions.

BACKGROUND

Well exploited, social media channels can be used for market research, and public relations. Starbucks is a poster child on how to use social media for this purpose. On their Website, MyStarbucksIdea (My Starbucks Idea, 2011) the company allows customers to suggest ideas to improve services, products, stores and the brand itself. These ideas can be voted and discussed by users. The ideas that receive the most votes not only tend to be good ideas from the point of view of increasing the quality of services or products, but the voting process itself is a prospective market study showing the support these ideas receive from the customers. And the company not only gets these ideas for free, but it increases the perception that it values and considers customers' opinions.

Starbucks also stands out for the speed and effectiveness with which they issue corrective replies to negative comments about the brand. For example, there is an urban legend that the firm does not send coffee to the U.S. military because of a corporate position against "the war" (whatever "the war" is at that moment). Users of the popular microblogging network Twitter often echo this legend in their messages, which are usually followed by a fast response from Starbucks stating that it is not true, and providing a link to a Web page that sets the record straight (Starbucks Newsroom, 2011). The company also maintains a presence in all the major social networks: Facebook (Starbucks-In Facebook, 2011), Youtube (Starbucks Producer, 2011), LinkedIn (Starbucks-In LinkedIn, 2011) and Twitter (Starbucks Coffee, 2011) among others. The pages of the company are updated regularly, show a high level of activity, and have fans numbering in the millions.

The computer maker Dell is a good example of using social media for promotional purposes. The company was an early adopter in the social media space and has mastered how to leverage blogs and community outreach. For example, it maintains multiple Twitter accounts tailored for content that may be of interest to different customer profiles. Through one of these accounts, Dell Outlet, which is being followed by more than a million and a half users, Dell offers promotions and discount coupons. According to the company, this account alone produces tens of millions of dollars in sales a year. The company also maintains Twitter accounts designed to provide technical support to customers, and accounts for keeping customers up to date with the latest news about Dell. In the latter case, the company has two different accounts, one for consumers and another for corporate clients, to target content to each of these two profiles.

These two case studies could lead the reader to think about social media as just another marketing channel. As is the case of any marketing channel, each company should evaluate whether it should maintain a presence in it or not, but there is no requirement for participation in the channel. This assumption is wrong. Social media is different from any other channel. Having or not having a presence in the channel is not a decision that depends entirely on the company, but it also depends on the customers. Customers can choose to talk about the company in the channel, both in positive or negative terms. There is nothing that the company can do to prevent this. The only thing it can do is engage in conversation. Failure to do this in time can have significant negative consequences.

Dell itself learnt this lesson the hard way. In June 2005, before Dell had a social media communication strategy, it began to receive major complaints concerning their customer support services; especially from the popular blogger Jeff Jarvis (Williams 2009). Recently he had bought a Dell laptop, as well as a four year in home warranty service plan. Just after he received the machine, it malfunctioned. Jarvis contacted Dell's customer support and learnt that he would need to send the machine back to the company because the technician wouldn't be able to get the parts needed to fix the laptop to his home. On June 21, 2005 he posted his first blog related to this matter in BuzzMachine.com (Jarvis 2005). This blog post, entitled "Dell lies. Dell sucks", was commented by 253 bloggers, who also had been receiving a poor customer service from Dell. In June 23, 2005 he wrote another blog post entitled, "Dell hell, continued" where he stated, "But that's what bothers me most: I bought that warranty, the top-of-the-line, most expensive warranty that warrant (Dell 2012) to send someone to my home to repair my machine. Except that's a big fat Dell lie. The person they would send to my home would not have the parts (or, according to some of my commenters, the expertise, training, and intelligence) to repair that machine". He kept on blogging for almost a month about Dell's poor customer service and also sending emails to Dell representatives at the same time; but he never received a reply from them. Jarvis blog Website caught the attention from many other bloggers that have had negative experiences with the Dell's technical support, triggering criticism and bad publicity through the net, and it finally was reported by Business Week Online. It is possible that the 5 points dropped on the score of the American Customer Satisfaction Index on August 2005 was related to the bad campaign generate by the blogosphere. If Dell had pay attention to claims and negative comments adequately, rather than remain in silent; the damage caused to the reputation of the company would have been minimal.

The songwriter and singer Dave Carroll (Rotman, 2010) after having a bad experience with his baggage, specifically with an expensive guitar that was damaged by United Airlines employees during a flight, uploaded a video entitled "United Breaks Guitars" to YouTube on July 6, 2009. This video was viewed by 150,000 people by the end of the first day, and had been seen by over five million people by August 15, 2009. It is possible that the 2009 reduction in passengers of 12.67% compared to 2008, and the decline in profits of 19.19% compared to the previous year bore some relationship to the negative promotion created by this video (Kaplan, 2010; Rotman, 2010; Soule, 2010). Currently, the video continues to accumulate views on YouTube and Dave Carroll has registered the domain http://www.UnitedBreaksGuitars.com to continue to focus attention on his case. The original video has been watched by more than 11 million people, and Dave Caroll has uploaded two more videos in which he criticizes different departments of the company for failing to satisfactorily address the problem. The damage to the image of the airline has been and is still considerable. An appropriate and prompt response by United would have completely avoided this situation.

Sometimes, these types of problems do not originate outside the firm. In 2009, employees of a Domino's Pizza outlet created what they thought would be a funny gross-out video for their friends and they posted on YouTube. The video showed the firm's brand alongside gross mishandling of the brand's food products. The video was seen by over 1 million viewers before it was removed from YouTube. The two employees who made the video were arrested and fired. The Domino's store where the incident occurred was closed, and the firm's president had to make a painful apology.

Companies cannot avoid conversations about their brands, their products or their services on the social media. All they can do is listen to the conversations and engage in them. Given the size of the social networks and the large number of conversations that occur in them every day, monitoring these conversations can only be done in an efficient manner with monitoring tools that help identify and manage the relevant content.

TOOLS TO MONITOR SOCIAL MEDIA AND GENERATE ENGAGEMENT

Materials and Methods

The authors of this paper have been early adopters of social networks, with six years of experience participating both at a personal level and in the role of "social media manager" of communities (mainly the javaHispano.org community [JavaHispano, 2011]). In the latter case, the social presence of the organization in Twitter, Facebook, Youtube, Google+, Vimeo, and the organization's own Website is not managed by a single person, but by a team geographically distributed among Spain, Mexico, Chile, Colombia and Peru. From the early days of social media, this led us to search for tools that enable collaboration among several persons to manage an organization's online presence, assigning tasks among the team members and monitoring activity relevant to the organization.

To this experience in the field of social media, we add a personal interest and curiosity about the whole ecosystem. This has led us to always keep track of the latest developments in the social media ecosystem, beyond the search for tools to support our own use of social networks. Therefore, even before starting the more formal and methodical study presented in this chapter we already had good knowledge of the social media field, the tools that can be used to maintain a presence more sophisticated than personal use requires, and the main players which develop tools to support building an online presence.

Building on this experience, we developed a draft list of tools to include in this study. We completed the list by querying Google for terms like "tool for monitoring social media," "support tools for social media managers", "online reputation" and so on. Based on our previous experience and the initial information we found regarding the different tools, more than 100 existing solutions were reduced to a total of 11 tools which were finally included in this study. The main criteria used in selecting the tools were the size of the tool's user base, the functionality it provides, and its suitability for use in a business environment. Inevitably, some readers will feel that some other tool should also have been included in this study. Unfortunately, time and space constraints forced us to limit the scope of the study to a manageable number of tools.

Again, relying on our previous experience, we defined a list of features that would be checked when evaluating all the tools. When evaluating a tool for functionality relevant to a business context, we sometimes found some feature that was not included in our initial feature list. In this case, we extended the list with the new functionality. The tools that had already been studied without evaluating this functionality were reviewed again to recheck whether or not they had a similar feature.

The list of features analyzed in each tool is:

- **The Social Networks Supported by the Tool:** Facebook and/or Twitter support is considered essential for inclusion in the study, given the prevalence and magnitude of these social networks (over 800 million in the case of Facebook [2011] and over 200 million in the case of Twitter, Shiels, [2011]). Support for other networks such as LinkedIn, Youtube, Vimeo, Google + or blogging sites was considered a plus. We also evaluated the tool for its capability of maintaining multiple identities in each of these social networks. As we have seen in the background section with the firm Dell, it is sometimes recommended that a company maintains more than one identity/user account on a given social network.
- **Support for Searching for Key Terms in Social Networks:** We also evaluated whether these searches were in real time ("live searches" that update themselves automatically), and the functionality that the tool provided to store search results.

- **Alarm Triggering:** We assessed the functionality that the tools had to generate warnings (sending e-mail, SMS or similar) to warn of certain events (such as a user with considerable influence in a social network that is talking negatively about a company's product).
- **Support for Sentiment Analysis of the Content:** It is often the case that a prompt reaction to negative content limits the damage it can cause to an organization, and stop its spread through a social network. Often the positive content does not require a response from the organization. Hence there is an interest in being able to identify content associated with an organization and classify it as positive, negative or neutral, and to be able to effectively prioritize content management.
- **Analysis of Influence of Social Network Users:** The content, either positive or negative, will have more impact and diffusion the more influence the user who created it has. Negative content from influential users must be addressed immediately. Positive comments by influential users may be encouraged with some kind of reward, for example, by sending him/her free evaluation units of their products. Sometimes, companies also contact these users for advertising purposes. In any case, knowing who the influential users are that speak of a company's products, services or brand is useful information.
- **Support for Teamwork:** The social presence of a medium or large company will often not be managed by a single person. The availability of tools to assign tasks to different team members, prioritize tasks, provide real-time collaboration between various team members, and support for multiple user profiles in the tool are useful features when more than one person will be responsible for managing the social presence.
- **Internationalization** of the user interface, and geo-targeting of the users who engage in conversations with our organization.
- **Possibility of integration** of the tool with internal information systems of the company, such as ERP, CMR, a marketing data base, etc.
- **Reporting Functionality:** Ideally, the tools should generate reports that summarize the organization's online activity, the activity of influential users who talk about the products, reports about discussions regarding a topic of interest for the company and other relevant information. They should also provide metrics such as number of clicks on links, or number of responses/comments generated by the content we create.
- **Price of the Tools:** Price is important, and can determine if, for example, a small business cannot afford to use a certain tool.
- **Clients Available for the Tool:** In almost all cases there are Web clients who can be accessed from any Web browser. The availability of mobile clients for smart phones or tablet devices is desirable.

To evaluate each of the tools, we started by reading the user guide of the tool. In most cases, videos showing diverse functionality of the tools were available. Whenever possible, we requested a demo of the product from a company representative who developed the tool. In this way we could see the tool being used by an expert user. We also used the tool ourselves. When necessary, we requested trial accounts for the testing. The tools were tested using social media profiles created specifically for the purpose of evaluating the tools. This permitted certain tests (such as the creation of negative content) to be carried out freely. The tools also were tested with real users' profiles that had a long time presence in social networks and a considerable number of followers (several thousands).

Results

There are some similarities and differences that should be pointed out in order to categorize the different tools according to their capabilities and functionalities. On one hand, we have those tools that are mainly used to monitor the social media, and on the other hand, those that also can generate content, promote engagement, and launch advertising or public relations campaigns. Trackur, Klout, Viralheat, StepRep, and Brandwatch are tools that are essentially used to perform monitoring activities. Radian6, SocialFlow, SproutSocial, Sysomos, Hootsuite, and TweetDeck are mainly used to monitor and generate engagement.

All the tools use some kind of dashboard from which monitoring, searching, engagement and other activities are launched. From the dashboard the operator or social media manager may perform different actions such as view user generated content from blogs, forums, YouTube, news and other traditional and non-traditional social media networks. Figure 1 shows how two different dashboards may present almost the same information, but in a different manner. The functionality and capabilities of each dashboard may differ in terms of user interface, arrangement, components, icons, links, tabs and other features that may comprise it. There are three common functionalities across all dashboards: to monitor or listen to what is said; search or query key terms, topics and other kind of information such as competitors; and generate engagement in a real time basis with fans (Facebook), followers (Twitter), or users from other social media content sites.

Most of the tools may monitor or listen to what has been said about a brand, product, or company. This ongoing process generates facts to which analytic techniques are applied to obtain statistics of mentions, reputation, reach, sentiment, posts' tone, influence, competitors, demographics, and even the number of clicks that users make to specific URL's links. StepRep, Brandwatch, Trackur, and ViralHeat have common grounds when it comes to monitoring the reputation of a brand, product or company; they all search different social media content for mentions and keywords to determine if what has been published affects the enterprises' reputation in a positive or negative manner; giving more emphasis to the negative content. This does not mean that other tools do not pay attention to the reputation dimension as part of their whole monitoring tasks. Sometimes, it is seen as a derived functionality of the monitoring process itself and it might be incorporated within the sentiment analysis functionality or even by means of other functions.

The ability to search social media for keywords, persons, competitors or topics in order to get a better picture of what is happening around a spe-

Figure 1. SproutSocial dashboard (top) and Sysomos Twitter dashboard (bottom)

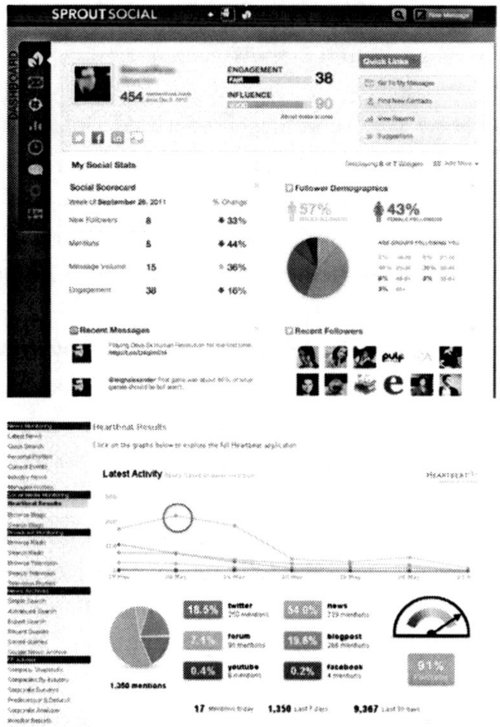

cific brand, product, or company is an invaluable feature. All the tools have searching capabilities, but they may differ in terms of how, what, where, and when a search is done.

- How the search is performed determines to some extent the results that will be obtained; some tools may search using some kind of query structure, but others may only search individual keywords, brands, or users.
- What can be searched refers to: keywords, topics, brands, user accounts or user identifier, businesses, places, videos, competitors, people, mentions, and Facebook wall content.
- Where the search is performed is about specific social media where user generated content is available: Twitter, Facebook, Linkedin, Google Buzz, YouTube, Blogs, Word press, Flickr, Foursquare, Go Walla, Yelp, Trip advisor, Tumblr, Instagram, last.fm, Yelp, Citysearch, Urbaspoon, Metacafe, bliptv, MySpace, Typepad, LiveJournal, Ping.fm, mixi, news sites, and forums. Some tools can be configured so the scope of the search can be limited to a specific region(s), country, city, or area in order to obtain results that are meaningful to an enterprise whose activities are limited to that region.
- When the search is going to be executed or in what interval of time will new results be obtained for a specific search. Some tools may provide options to save searches for future reference and execution. Most of the tools execute searches in a real time basis, which is an ideal situation for businesses that want to be aware of conversations in real time, especially of those that require a rapid response to mitigate negative publicity.

Searches are usually based on queries that are defined using a simple user interface that in many cases is part of the main dashboard. Constraints on the search can sometimes be imposed by means of combo boxes to constrain the media in which the search is performed (videos, images, news, Twitter, Facebook, etcetera) to city, country or any other predetermined constraints or filters. In some cases, the user may select or even write some logical or binary operators to combine several search terms and build the search query. Searches may be performed manually or automatically in time intervals (minutes, hours, days or even on a virtually continuously basis). Searches generate results that can be analyzed, graphed and displayed to obtain a better picture of who, what, when, where, and how (format used: text, image or video) something was said. Almost all tools have the capability of saving a searchable query for future references, modifications or for future use.

The counterpart of monitoring and searching is being able to generate engagement using real time conversations, posts or results from the executed searches. The solution used to reply to posts or conversations does not differ much between the tools, and it is influenced by the mechanism that each social network provides to perform this task. Almost all tools provide means to reply to posts or conversations by sending a direct message or writing into the user's Facebook wall; by adding a comment to a post or conversation, or by sending an email to the social media user account. Replying to posts or conversations is only part of the picture. The real power of the engagement functionality relies in the capability to launch or schedule advertising or public relations campaigns, as well as to publish messages in different social media networks at the same time. In many cases these messages may be composed of text, attachments, images, videos and even location information. Furthermore, some tools have mechanisms to track and assign posts or comments to other team members of the enterprise (for example, the sales force, customer service or any other member of the organization). Engaging with customers benefits business because each customer might influence a potential customer who, in turn, is connected to other users who influence others, consequently generating a domino effect.

Predominantly all dashboards are Web based client applications that are executed on the server side and the interface is provided by a Web server. The user only needs a Web browser to access the application. The only exception is the TweetDeck dashboard, whose interface runs as a standalone desktop application. Twitter and Facebook are the main social networks supported by the tools. Although Twitter is the main social network used by Trackur, SocialFlow and TweetDeck, most of these tools can collect information of what has been published from different social media networks, like: Linkedin, Google Buzz, YouTube, Blogs, Wordpress, Flickr, Foursquare, GoWalla, Yelp, Trip advisor, news sites, forums, and many other media that are not necessarily composed of text, links, and images.

The capability that some tools have to trigger alarms when some potentially damaging content is created by a user is a very useful feature. Many businesses are already well aware of the damage that a bad comment or post can do to their reputation. Almost all the tools have some kind of alarm function, but only a few can produce real alerts when a truly bad post, comment, image, video or news is published. An alarm should be triggered immediately by the monitoring tool as soon a harmful publication is identified, especially if the content has been originated by a user with well-known reputation that is highly influential. This alert can take the form of an email, an audible sound, a visible object on the screen, RSS feed or a combination of these.

Many of the tools generate some type of warning every time a comment or post is made regarding our company, or a new fan or follower signs in, or there is an update to the content of some social media and for many other reasons that do not require any prompt action (sometimes no action at all). In this study we have not considered these types of warnings as "alarms".

We shall now describe each of the tools included in this study, emphasizing the points which differentiate each tool from the others. Table 1 summarizes the results of our study.

Radian6

Radian6 is a high budget, real-time, multi-language monitoring tool which also has capabilities for engagement and workflow management. It allows a business to view, analyze and display in real time any relevant conversations by searching through more than 150 million public sites, including the open Facebook, API and the Twitter Firehose. Radian6 has a powerful dashboard that can be quickly setup using the Quick Start topic profile set-up tool. The dashboard can be customized with the Widget Gallery to only show items that are meaningful for a certain social media team. The workflow management tool is used to assign posts or comments to team members, add internal notes, flag priority, categorize, and classify conversations that are taking place.

The integration of CRM and Web analytics with the "river of news" created by Radian 6 generates a database that can be used by the sales force to create leads and by customer support. The engagement console can be used on the Web or as an iPhone application that filters conversations and enables engagement in real-time with collaboration throughout the entire enterprise improving effectiveness and efficiency without duplicating effort. The social profile of a person can be seen in detail in each social media network where it was created along with the entire history of conversations that the business has had with him/her including the replies. Reporting and measuring tied to analytics and social metrics are seamless capabilities that can be integrated with

Table 1. Summary of the features of each tool

	Radian6	Trackur	Klout	Socialflow	SproutSocial	Sysomos (Heartbeat)	ViralHeat	StepRep	Brandwatch	HootSuite	TweetDeck
Monitoring*	Strong	Average	Not supported	Average	Strong	Strong	Average	Average	Strong	Strong	Average
Engagement*	Strong	Weak	Not supported	Strong	Strong	Strong	Average	Average	Weak	Strong	Strong
Reputation*	Strong	Average	Not Supported	Weak	Average	Average	Strong	Strong	Strong	Average	Weak
Influence*	Strong	Average	Strong	Not Supported	Strong	Strong	Strong	Weak	Weak	Average	Weak
Preferred Network	Facebook & Twitter	Twitter	Facebook & Twitter	Twitter	Facebook & Twitter	Facebook & Twitter	Facebook & Twitter	Facebook & Twitter	Facebook & Twitter	Facebook & Twitter	Twitter
Social Network Support	Strong	Strong	Strong	Weak	Average	Strong	Strong	Strong	Strong	Average	Average
Multiple Profiles Support	Strong	Weak	Strong	Weak	Strong	Strong	Strong	Not Supported	Not Supported	Average	Strong
Search	Strong	Average	Not Supported	Average	Strong	Strong	Strong	Strong	Strong	Strong	Strong
Store searches	Strong	Strong	Not Supported	Not Supported	Strong	Strong	Strong	Average	Strong	Average	Strong
Alerts/Alarms	Strong	Average	Weak	Strong	Average	Strong	Average	Average	Average	Average	Average
Sentiment analysis	Strong	Weak	Not Supported	Not Supported	Average	Strong	Strong	Strong	Strong	Average	Not Supported
Influence Analysis	Strong	Average	Average	Not Supported	Strong	Strong	Strong	Weak	Strong	Average	Weak
Internationalization	Strong	Average	Weak	Weak	Weak	Strong	Weak	Weak	Average	Strong	Average
Geotargeting	Strong	Average	Weak	Weak	Strong	Strong	Strong	Weak	Average	Strong	Weak
Team collaboration	Strong	Average	Weak	Weak	Strong	Strong	Average	Weak	Strong	Strong	Weak
CRM Integration	Strong	Weak	Weak	Weak	Weak	Strong	Average	Weak	Average	Average	Weak
Min and Max Price (monthly payment)	\$600 -\$2,000	\$8 - \$377	Free	Starts at \$2,000	\$9 - \$899	\$500	\$9.99 - \$89.99	\$199	\$640 - \$2,325	\$5.99 - \$210	Free
Available Clients	Web & iPhone	Web	Web	Web	Web & iPhone	Web & iPhone	Web	Web & iPhone	Web	Web, iOs Android & Blackberry	Desktop, iPhone, Android

*Based on the top plan that each company can offer

business functions like marketing, public relations, sales, customer support and other administrative activities.

We may contract four plans with Radian6. All of them are paid monthly and the rate is based on the number of results returned by each topic. The basic plan, called: "Getting Started" has a price tag of $600 for 1 topic and up to 10,000 mentions. The "Advance" plan costs $4,000 and provides up to 6 topics and up to 200,000 mentions; it also includes Web analytics integration, using: Omniture, Webtrends, and Google Analytics. The "Enterprise" solution has a custom price and is intended for businesses that have more than 6 topics and a large number of members on the social media team. A plan called: "Agency" is designed for agencies that build and execute social media strategies for others and its price is $600 for 1 topic and up to 10,000 mentions. They offer a 50% discount for registered and qualified charitable organizations, but the organization must be validated by an account representative. This software runs as a Web client in any Web browser. There is also a smartphone application called, Radian6 Mobile for iPhone, which has most of the functionality of the Web client version.

Trackur

This is an online reputation tool used to search and keep track of mentions of keywords or topics in the Web; it is somehow similar to Google Alerts. Its searches can be saved and executed every 30 minutes generating graphs with the new mentions, velocity of the creation of mentions, and sources in the past 24 hours. Trackur has four different monthly plans that can be purchased; each plan has a specific number of searches that can be saved; from 5 searches in the Basic plan up to unlimited searches in the Ultimate plan. Trackur scours the Web using a tagging system to determine the mentions of a specific keyword, phrase or topic. It mostly searches in social media like Technorati, Flickr, Youtube, Reddit, Digg, Delicious, Twitter, and Facebook. It may be configured to update RSS feeds or send emails each time new mentions are detected for a specific search.

Trackur has four plans which differ in the permitted quantity of saved searches. All plans have RSS/Email alerts, manual sentiment tagging, CSV export, Twitter, Facebook & Google+ and other social media monitoring and influence metrics. Other features are only available on certain plans. These features are: Trackur Insights, Upload RSS Feeds, branding of the company in Trackur dashboard, and unlimited client logins. The only plan that includes all features is the Ultimate plan, which has a price of $377 per month and unlimited saved searches. The Premium plan costs $197 and provides 250 saved searches. The Plus plan costs $88 and provides 50 saved searches with one extra feature (Trackur Insights) than the Basic plan. The Basic plan costs $8 and provides 5 saved searches. Trackur offers a free plan limited to 1 save search and no Facebook, Google+ or Forums, slower updates, and no analytics. This tool can only be used as a Web application.

Klout

This is a free tool that uses a scoring system on a scale of 1 to 100 points, which is calculated using over 35 different variables to determine the social media reach of a business or person. The scores are grouped into three metrics: True Reach, Amplification Probability and Network Influence. Klout focuses on how influence and messages are spread within the social networks, mainly from Twitter and Facebook. Upon registration a business has to subscribe their Twitter and Facebook accounts through Klout, so it may have access to comments and messages generated by users within these networks. Klout classifies a person or business using a matrix of what they call "style", which describes how different people interact with one another in an online social media. Plot line charts display metrics for the three different scores and for an overall score that's related to clicks, comments, or retweets, depending on the social media site. True Reach uses engagement in terms of followers and friends that are listening and reacting to the posts. Amplification Probability measures how tweets are received, replied or retweeted in Twitter and how many comments or likes are received in Facebook. Network Influence or Impact is used to determine how much influence the business network has with the audience. Klout has neither sentiment analysis metrics nor other features like demographics, multi-language support, team tasks assignment, or other similar capabilities. The company aspires to be the online gold standard for measuring reputation.

SocialFlow

This is an engagement tool that uses Twitter accounts to determine the precise moment to post messages of certain topics or to start conversations that are more relevant for the best accessible audience at certain time frame. It may be used for optimizing outbound communications and to launch marketing and public relations campaigns. It uses bit.ly (bitly, 2011) to shrink domain names of the companies or brands and analyzes the number of clicks given to a certain link. Using the "Twitter Firehose", it can follow up to 400 keywords, 5,000 user identifiers, links that contain http, and https, "retweets", and other parameters enabling queries to get statistics of an IP's location and other filtered data. It may publish content in Twitter, Facebook and Google Buzz. The goal of the tool is to say the right thing at the right moment when conversations are shifting in any specific direction. It provides reports in real time about what is being said, and what the brand followers like and dislike. This tool is not actually used for monitoring purposes, but it may be used as an analytical tool.

SocialFlow prices are not public. According to an interview given by Frank Speiser, the founder of the company, prices start at $2000 per month, with the average price being about $ 5,000 per month (This WeekIn Startups-Producer, 2011) A free version of the product may be solicited, but it is limited to Reddit, Digg, delicious, Twitter and news sites and it has several other limitations. SocialFlow does not have a mobile application client; it only runs as a Web application.

SproutSocial

This is an all-in-one tool that monitors social media. It enables engagement and has reporting and analytics capabilities. Its dashboard can be customized to show several different widgets, which may provide a summary for engagement and influence scores, number of clicks, follower's demographics by age and gender, new followers, mentions, volume or tone of the messages, Twitter statistics, recent followers and messages. It has a "Social Inbox" where all the messages that come from different media are received, as if it were a personal email account. Within the Social Inbox a user can be followed back, his profile may be seen, messages can be replied to or flagged to get back to them later, and mentions can be looked for so a specific action can be taken.

Alerts may occur every time that a mention or a direct message is received in the Social Inbox. The user can see summary reports either daily or weekly of these mentions or the messages received. Messages from a particular contact can be stored if he has been added to the contacts list. Discovery is an option that enables searching for keywords that people write in their profiles such as "President" or "CEO". Using this option we can also search for competitors to compare ourselves to them in terms of engagement, influence, followers and demographics. All searches may be restricted to a geographical area. It has a variety of reports that include: a report of followers or friends, new followers or friends, clicks, messages sent, messages received and "retweets", summary of messages or mentions, demographic reports and others. Reports and analytics are executed automatically, or they can be restricted to specific dates.

SproutSocial offers four monthly plans: "Pro" for $9, "Small Biz" for $39, "Deluxe" for $59, and "Premium" for $899. All plans have access to Twitter, Facebook, LinkedIn and Google Reader. They all allow publishing to multiple accounts, scheduling messages, and posting from any Website. All plans share the same features for engagement: "Smart Inbox," contact management with conversation history, identification of influential users, RSS reader, and task creation from messages. But they differ in the analytics and reporting features, branding, monitoring, team support, and local business tools. The Pro plan only adds to the base features support for team work. The "Deluxe" and "Premium" plans have Foursquare, Gowalla, and Google Analytics support, flexible account grouping, report exporting, local search and targeting, check-in monitoring and reporting, and team collaboration features such as tasks and assignments. The "Premium" plan adds branded reports, and branded portal. SproutSocial can be used as a Web application or as an iPhone application.

Sysomos: Heartbeat

Heartbeat is a real-time monitoring tool, which is also used for engagement and to compare your business with competitors. It has a customizable user-friendly dashboard to display a snapshot of social media activity. The dashboard can display the most active keywords and graph the mentions of a brand or product in comparison with other competitor's mentions. A panel called; "Your Heartbeat", permits the managing of unlimited social media profiles and the monitoring of conversations that happen in real-time, enabling engagement with "fans" or followers.

Heartbeat uses a powerful search function based on queries filtered by one or more keywords, social media network, tags, sentiment, demography, country and many other options. A query may combine more than one filter using boolean operators. Although the user does not need to know anything about the syntax, the queries can be built as SQL-like statements. The results of queries can be tagged. These tags function as user-defined rules which are related to a product, brand, service, competitor, or any other topic that can be used to validate, classify or store query results for later analysis and graphic presentation. Searches can be stored and scheduled on a regular basis; monthly, weekly, daily. A list of keywords can be created and used to automatically delete messages or posts that contain one or more of these keywords. Alarms can be configured using a list of keywords defined by the user or from a list of terms predefined by Sysomos for a specific industry or business. The alerts generated by these alarms may be configured in a variety of forms.

This tool has the ability to classify the sentiment as negative, neutral or positive. To perform this classification previous conversations and top influencers are considered. Terms can be defined to support the classification of the conversations into one of the three categories, although a set of rules created by Sysomos are used. The other users' influence is measure and plotted automatically. The Social media Manager can drill-down into the chart, make comments and translate it into 20 different languages.

The workflow feature can assign one or more comments or tweets to be managed by a person or team within the organization, such as the "sales force team". Sysomos provides multiple metrics and graphs related to the demographics of the population (sex, age, language…), reports about the different geographical world regions where content is created or where emerging conversations have more influence, and reports comparing the business with competitors by different demographics and/or geographic world regions, by number of mentions, and by several other dimensions.

This tool has a monthly price of $500. Sysomos also offers an academic version for $250 with the same capabilities and functions, and which may also be used at the same time on multiple computers for educational purposes. This application runs as a Web client and doesn't have a mobile client yet.

ViralHeat

ViralHeat is designed for listening or monitoring social media; it does not have many engagement functionalities, except that it may identify the top influencers. The tool uses "profiles" to monitor content and perform advanced analysis on it. Each profile can be created with a user-friendly wizard or an advanced configuration interface. In both cases the profile will have its own name and it will be composed of one or more of the following: keywords or phrases to track for mentions; keywords or phrases that are going to be used to remove any mention when they are detected; location (e.g., Madrid, Spain) that will limit mentions to a specific city or within a specified radius; and an email reporting method to be used when a mention for the profile keyword(s) or phrase(s) is detected. ViralHeat enables producers of content to monitor the profiles in multiple social media networks in order to identify key trends and understand the participation of the community. This information is used to generate competitive analysis.

To monitor the social media in real-time, it uses over 200 video sharing sites, including YouTube, blogs, Twitter, Facebook, and other social networks. It can monitor tweets to realize a competitive analysis, discover new tracks and optimize marketing campaigns. It can discover new Fan Pages in Facebook which mention the brand, topic or product. It has built-in intelligence to analyze the ROI on Facebook campaigns.

Alerts can be defined as emails that can be sent (to more than one person) on a daily basis or each time a mention is detected for a specific profile. If the option called: "Daily Digest" is enabled, a summary of all profiles will be sent daily. ViralHeat adds comment stats for the sentiment of each post in Facebook, showing percentages for positive, neutral and negative sentiment.

ViralHeat has three monthly plans with prices of $9.99 (Basic), $29.99 (Professional), and $89.99 (Business). The Basic Plan permits 5 profiles, 7 days of previous data to analyze, and Twitter, Real-time Web, Facebook Fan Pages, and Viral Video analytics. The Professional Plan permits 20 profiles and adds viral content and sentiment analysis. It also has influencer analytics. The Business Plan permits 40 profiles, 30 days of previous data to analyze and 6 months of data archiving. It also adds Facebook link analytics (Real-time Web), the entire social graph of influencers (Twitter), Klout analytics (Twitter), and Twitalyzer analytics (Twitter). The Business plan also provides custom branding.

The cost of this plan is $199.99 per month which includes search for three of the following: competitors, key people, and terms that will create searches on Twitter. This tool runs as a Web application, but there is also a version of the Website optimized for mobile clients.

StepRep

StepRep started with a company called MyFrontSteps which was intended to connect service providers with their customers through social networks. This product was withdrawn from the market in 2009 and in 2010 StepRep took its place as a tool for corporate reputation management. The tool was created for small and medium-sized businesses. It uses a spider search engine to constantly search through comments, blogs, articles, links and any Website that might refer to a product, brand or company. It uses searches in the major search engines and some minor ones, plus searches that are executed within social media networks, such as Twitter, Flickr, YouTube, and Facebook. All searches are performed on an ongoing basis and the results may be seen in the dashboard as soon as they arise, or may be received via email anytime something new is found. Each search result might be composed of text, images, videos, articles or any other format. These results are displayed on a single page where they can be sorted, inspected and assigned a sentiment (negative, neutral or positive). If any of the results are classified as "Positive", they can be added to the StepRep widget and posted in the company blog, social media page or any other online Website where the company has presence. Duplicated results will be deleted and not shown more than once. Using a component called: "Visibility" a comprehensive search to determine if the company is listed in any search engines, line of business or social networking directories can be can performed.

The tool doesn't use social media accounts because it focuses on mentions rather than Twitter or Facebook pages. Mentions are places where a business appears; these might include a detailed article or a comment in Twitter. The tool graphs mentions by different sentiment type. The sentiment report shows those positive or negative mentions that obtained the highest relevance scores. Sentiment analysis uses various methods to analyze the sentiment, which are constantly evolving. These methods are: weighted scores based on normative emotional skills of commonly used English words; processing of natural language which includes techniques for determining sentiment based on context of the post, and a Bayesian statistical analysis of the sentiments assigned over time by the users.

Brandwatch

This is a social media monitoring tool used to constantly track reputation based on queries and workspaces. A query is composed of a set of parameters and criteria that are used to monitor or search the Web for mentions that meet such query. Each time a new query is created the tool generates a new workspace using a basic template which in turn is composed of several pages. Each query may be composed of one or more main terms, context terms, terms to be excluded, and Boolean operators: AND, OR and NOT. In addition one or more languages may be selected from where the mentions may arise. An industry filter may be chosen for the query from a list of predetermined industries; for example: learning, jewelry, loyalty, media, and retail among others. Once a query is created it might be tested to determine if the resulting mentions are related to the topic or if the theme is specified in the criteria. If the query brings spam results it can be modified until the desired results are obtained. Once the setup of a query has been finished, it will take between 25 to 30 minutes to check the 24 databases that the tool uses for this task; but in the meantime intermediate outcomes may be seen in the workspace. Once the process is completed an email will be sent by the tool indicating that the query results are available.

Each query can generate various graphs in real-time that may be drilled-down by the user clicking in any part of the plot lines and opening the comments. The common summary reports are: number of mentions, positive, negative and neutral sentiment, graphs indicating the origin of the mentions (news, blogs, etc.), history of entries by date, in addition to a summary by site (e.g. www, facebook.com, twitter.com, answers.yahoo.com, etc.). The "Share of Voice" functionality shows how a business is doing against the competition. The tool also has individual tabs for volume reports, graphics, feelings, site and recurring phrases, and honorable mentions. More details on each of these aspects can be obtained from the corresponding tab. Individual posts can be assigned to specific business areas, such as: customer service, support, or other areas. Posts are classified as open, answered or closed, and a priority (high or low) is assigned to them.

Brandwatch offers two monthly plans: "Pro" for $640 and "Enterprise" for $2,325. Both plans include unlimited users, sentiment analysis in 16 languages, free initial training, full API access, and multilingual coverage. The Pro plan is limited to 10 thousand mentions, which may seem at first glance as a good deal, but a single query may generate more than 10 thousand mentions.

Brandwatch provides two upgrades for the Pro plan that includes 20 thousand mentions for $1,125 or 50 thousand mentions for $1,525 per month. The Enterprise plan includes unlimited mentions and only 15 queries; if more queries are needed they are offered for an additional cost of $110 each. This tool can only be used as a Web application.

HootSuite

This is an affordable social media managing tool used to launch marketing campaigns, track conversations, make the audience grow, and distribute or schedule messages through multiple channels at the same time. Using the social media dashboard, teams can collaborate and schedule posts to Twitter, Facebook, LinkedIn, Word Press and other social media over the Web. The dashboard is composed of tabs and within each tab there are columns that can be associated with one or more accounts of Twitter, Facebook, LinkedIn, Ping.fm, WordPress, MySpace, Foursquare and Mixi. Each column is associated with a type of feedback, such as: home feed, mentions, direct messages, favorites, or others. Every time a stream or column is defined within a tab, key terms used to search can be defined. It is possible to search for multiple terms using multiple columns within the same tab associated with a social environment. Each tab is stored as part of the dashboard when it is configured initially. A user or group of users may be defined for a specific tab or column.

The number of simultaneous profiles in a single session depends on the plan we have bought; the Pro and Enterprise version have no limits of social profiles, the free version allows up to 5 social identities that may be used within any tab. Sentiment analysis is done automatically using an analyzer called Lymbix (Lymbix, 2011) which analyzes the text using four areas: emotional context (language learning), measurement of subjectivity (human emotions), construction of lexicons (data analysis) and delivery in real-time (sentiment black boxes). This tool measures the sentiment in several aspects, such as: condition, joy, excitement, happiness, sadness, anger, fear and humiliation. In general terms, any text may be analyzed, but the tool tends to analyze all tweets to determine the sentiment. The tool may be used in several languages: English, French, Italian, Spanish, Japanese, Arabic, Chinese, Czech, German, Greek, Indonesian, Korean, Norwegian, Persian, Polish, Portuguese, Romanian, Russian, Turkish, Dutch and Wales.

The graphics may reflect demographics of users that generate content relevant for a business by gender, age and others. Results from a query can be filtered by a specific geographical area. The tool permits the assignment of tasks to others within the work team with ease, but they may only become editors of one or more social media accounts already defined. At any time messages or comments can be assigned to someone on the team, but only the enterprise plan allows an unlimited number of contributors. If a particular stream wants to be included in a Blog or CRM site, the embedded code can be generated from the stream column top right hand menu; this feature is not available on the free plan. This tool has an impressive amount of customizable reports and graphs which can be saved and reused. Figure 2 shows one of the readymade analytic reports that may be used to display various results over a period of time; usually HootSuite uses the last 7 days from the current date.

HootSuite offers two monthly plans: "Pro" for $5.99 and "Enterprise" for $210. The Pro plan provides social analytics, unlimited Facebook or Twitter profiles, one team collaborator, and one report. It also includes integration with Google Analytics and several Facebook analytics. The Enterprise plan includes unlimited social network profiles, up to 10 reports, unlimited team members, unlimited RSS/Atom, enhanced analytics, priority technical support, VIP setup, free advertisement and 10 seats for the HootSuite certification program. There is a free plan called; "Basic", which includes: social analytics, 5 free profiles on either

Figure 2. Click analytics in HootSuite

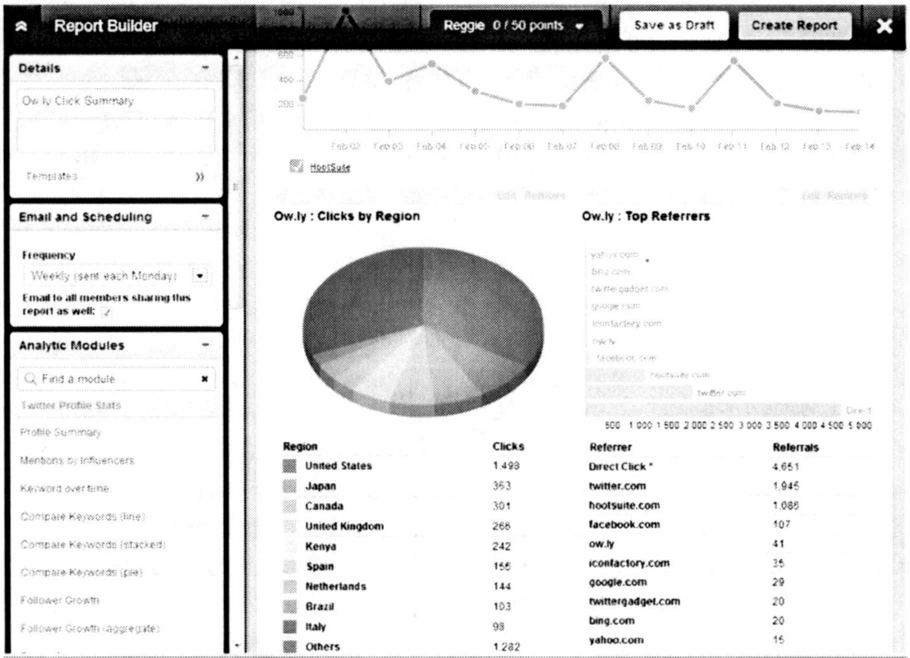

Facebook or Twitter and 2 RSS/Atom for blogs or news. The dashboard runs as Web based client, but there also are clients for iPhone, iPad, Android and BlackBerry.

TweetDeck

This is a free desktop application based on Adobe Air for a single-user. Its main purpose is to keep in touch with conversations and messages in various social media like, Twitter, Facebook, LinkedIn, Google Buzz and Foursquare, in addition to replying to (generate engagement) conversations or messages. It permits the use of multiple Twitter accounts at the same time; however it only allows one account from Facebook, LinkedIn, Google Buzz, MySpace and Foursquare. The dashboard is composed of columns to present information from the social media accounts, such as messages or comments. By clicking on a given user, we obtain a new column with the "posts" of that user. If the mouse pointer is dragged over the top of a user image, several small buttons will pop out. Depending on the account type, these buttons enable different tasks. If it is a Facebook account, the user may make comments on posts published by that user, click "Like", write into the users' wall, send a message to the user, send an e-mail, translate the message, or comment in the language selected in the configuration panel and perform the translation of the text automatically. If the column is associated with a Twitter account, the options are: send a tweet, replicate a tweet, follow the user, unfollow the user, see the profile, find the user in all tweets, retweets, mentions or posts generated, block a user or block the user and report him/her as spammer.

The search option for key terms is not available, but a keyword may be used to filter the content of a column. Real-time searches are limited to users' ids or lists of Twitter users. Once the user or list is found a column will be added where you can see the "posts" from that user or list. Audible alerts are generated when an incoming message is received, or a comment or image is added. Although it lacks the ability to identify the top influencers, each time a new message or comment is received from the user a red circle with a number in it indicates the total number of messages sent by the user. With this information we may determine whether or not the user is an influencer. TweetDeck has clients for iPhone and Android mobile devices.

DISCUSSION AND CONCLUSION

Social media is still a relatively recent phenomenon. Many companies still do not understand and do not know how to take advantage of it. Gradually, more managers are starting to grasp the potential of social media and how it can make a difference in their organization. The companies that embraced social media earlier on were often Information Technology (IT) related, especially large companies. Having an IT-related business increases the likelihood that the customers of the company are technology savvy. Consequently, they are often early adopters of social media. Because of the large size of the company, they are likely to generate a large volume of conversations. Therefore, these companies have seen the need for having full-time staff dedicated to monitoring and engaging in social media within their marketing departments. This is one of the main reasons why many of the tools reviewed in this article are oriented to the high end portion of the market, having prohibitively expensive prices for small businesses. Four of the 11 companies in our study have a minimum monthly fee over $ 500. The highest plan for eight of the 11 companies has a monthly cost over $ 200, with three of them being over $ 2000 per month.

For large businesses, having a strategy to manage their presence in social networks is of paramount importance. Given the volume of conversations they have to monitor and manage, the use of tools to support this task is mandatory. In these cases, where possibly more than one person will be managing the company's online presence, Radian6, Socialflow and Heartbeat are integral solutions to be considered. Brandwatch and Trackur also are interesting solutions which focus more on monitoring and comparison with the competition.

As the use of social media spreads further, more small business will understand its utility and the need to have a presence in social networks. As a consequence, we expect to see more tools tailored to their needs in the future. Nowadays having a presence in social networks is very desirable for a small business if it is related to technology. Otherwise having a good social media strategy can still be a competitive advantage and an excellent marketing tool. Of the tools studied here, we consider that HootSuite and ViralHeat offer a reasonable feature set for small and medium businesses at an affordable price. TweetDeck is also a good option if only a casual use of social media is intended.

One trend that will undoubtedly help to increase the use of social media by small businesses is "local". All the main social networks have local strategies that aim to connect users with other users living in the same city or neighborhood and that frequent the same locations. They also want to connect users with local businesses. This permits, for example, displaying advertising on the social network Website only to users who live in the same neighborhood where the small mom and pop store is located. The wide availability of smart phones, which often have GPS capabilities, also enable social networks to know exactly where the user is at every moment. This permits, for example, sending an SMS with a discount coupon or an offer just as the user enters the mall where the store is.

The goal of the local trend is to serve the long tail (Anderson, 2008) of small businesses that are only interested in reaching a geographically targeted and relatively small audience. These businesses can only make small investments to reach potential new customers. These investments will only pay off if the advertising is very well targeted. There are tens of millions of such businesses in the world; i.e., they can be a significant revenue source. The local features of social networks will make the presence of the small business in social media more appealing. Thus, they will increasingly need to use tools to manage their online presence. In the near future, we expect more development of tools to serve this purpose. In this scenario there will be no staff dedicated full time to manage the business presence in social networks. Features such as internationalization, team collaboration, and integration with the company information systems are irrelevant. Geolocation is crucial, but should be automatic and transparent to the user. On the contrary, having a highly intuitive user interface that has a very low learning curve will be very important given that it is not realistic to require from these users a long training process. Providing mechanisms for scheduling content creation will also be an important feature to maintain the online presence of the business when the person responsible for maintaining it is not on duty.

Many of the small and medium businesses will likely enter the social media world supported by a social media manager (Wollan, Smith, & Zhou, 2011). The role of these people will be crucial in defining the social media strategy of mom and pop stores, which are often run by non-tech savvy people. Social media managers will need tools designed specifically for them, which can manage the online presence of multiple businesses from a single integrated dashboard. Right now only Radian6 has plans specifically designed for social media managers, but we expect that in the future there will be more tools for this purpose.

Finally, we expect that eventually there will be some consolidation in the market of tools to support the management of the social media presence of a business. As usual in the IT field, when a new business opportunity appears many players jump into the new market. Ultimately, there is a consolidation in which some of them disappear and others are absorbed by the strongest leaving only a small number of players. It happened to the PC market, with the operating systems market and with Internet search engines, among others. Currently, there are over a hundred tools with a purpose similar to the 11 tools studied in this chapter. The 11 tools addressed in this chapter are among the strongest in the market (we believe they are the strongest), and thus have a good chance of survival, either independently or integrated into a larger company that acquires them. Whatever the case may be, we expect significant market consolidation in the near future.

REFERENCES

A Wiki of Social Media Monitoring Solutions. (2011). *Monitoring solutions master list*. Retrieved from http://wiki.kenburbary.com

Anderson, E. (2008). *The long tail: Why the future of business is selling less of more*. New York: Hyperion.

Bhattacharya, C. B., Du, S., & Sen, S. (2010). Maximizing business returns to corporate social responsibility (CSR): The role of CSR communication. *International Journal of Management Reviews, 12*(1), 6–19.

Bitly. (2011). *Bitly: Shorten, share and track your links*. Retrieved November 15, 2011, from https://bitly.com/

Coffee, S. (2011, November). *Freshly brewed tweets from Brad and Lee at Starbucks in Seattle, WA*. Retrieved from http://twitter.com/#!/starbucks

Constantinides, E., Gómez, M., & Lorenzo, C. (2008). Social media: A new frontier for retailers? *Europea Retail Research, 22*, 1–28.

Dell. (2012). *Peace of mind! We've got covered!* Retrieved from http://www.dell.com/content/learnmore/learnmore.aspx?c=us&l=en&s=dhs&~id=serv_inspn&~line=notebooks&~lt=popup&~series=inspn&ref=CFG#tn2

Dösinger, G., Stocker, A., Us, A., & Wagner, C. (2007). The three pillars of 'corporate web 2.0': A model for definition. In *Proceedings of I-MEDIA '07 and I-SEMANTICS '07*. Graz, Austria: IEEE.

Facebook. (2011). *Statistics*. Retrieved November 15, 2011, from http://www.facebook.com/press/info.php?statistics

FreshMinds Research. (2010). *Turning conversations into insights: A comparison of social media monitoring tools*. Retrieved from http://shared.freshminds.co.uk/smm10/whitepaper.pdf

Gallaugher, J. (2010). Get S.M.A.R.T. – Social media awareness & response team. In *Information Systems: A Manager's Guide to Harnessing Technology* (pp. 125–134). Flat World Knowledge.

Gleanster. (2010). *Gleansight: Social media monitoring*. Gleanster, LLC

Haenlein, M., & Kaplan, A. (2010). Users of the world, unite! The challenges and opportunities of social media. *Business Horizons*, *53*(1), 59–68. doi:10.1016/j.bushor.2009.09.003.

Harvard Business Review Analytic Services. (2010). *The new conversation: Taking social media from talk to action*. Boston: Harvard Business School Publishing.

Hutley, R. (2009). *Social networking as a business tool*. Cisco Internet Business Solutions Group.

Jarvis, J. (2012). *BuzzMachine*. Retrieved from http://buzzmachine.com/archives/cat_dell.html

JavaHispano. (2011, November 15). *Tu lenguaje, tu comunidad*. Retrieved from http://javaHispano.org

Koch, M., & Richter, A. (2008). Functions of social networking services. In *Proceedings of COOP '08: the 8th International Conference on the Design of Cooperative Systems*. COOP.

Leganza, G. (2010). *The top 15 technology trends EA should watch: 2011 To 2013*. Forrester Research, Inc.

Lymbix. (2011). *Add sentiment intelligence to your applications*. Retrieved from http://www.lymbix.com/

My Starbucks Idea. (2011, November). *Share. Vote. Discuss. See. Share your ideas, tell us what you think of other people's ideas and join discussion*. Retrieved from http://mystarbucksidea.force.com/

Newsroom, S. (2011, January). *Starbucks support of the troops/military*. Retrieved from http://news.starbucks.com/about+starbucks/myths+facts/militarydonations.htm

O'Reilly, T. (2007). What is web 2.0: Design patterns and business models for the next generation of software. *International Journal of Digital Economics*, *65*, 17–37.

Report, S. M. (2010). *Lightspeed research and the internet advertising bureau UK*. Retrieved from http://www.iabuk.net/en/1/socialmedialanding.html

Rotman, J. (2010). *Unite breaks guitars – Case study*. Toronto, Canada: School of Management, University of Toronto.

Shiels, M. (2011). Twitter co-founder Jack Dorsey rejoins company. *BBC News*. Retrieved from http://www.bbc.co.uk/news/business-12889048

Soule, A. (2010). *Fighting the social media wildfire: How crisis communication must adapt to prevent from fanning the flames*. (Thesis). University of North Carolina at Chapel Hill, Chapel Hill, NC.

Starbucks. (2011a). *LinkedIn*. Retrieved November 15, 2011, from http://www.linkedin.com/company/starbucks

Starbucks. (2011b). *Facebook*. Retrieved November 15, 2011, from http://www.facebook.com/Starbucks

Starbucks (Producer). (2011, October 28). *The create jobs for USA fund* [informative video]. Retrieved November 15, 2011, from http://www.youtube.com/user/Starbucks

Sterne, J. (2010). *Social media metrics: How to measure and optimize your marketing investment*. New York: John Wiley & Sons, Inc..

This WeekIn Startups (Producer). (2011, January 4). *This week in startups - Frank Speiser, founder of SocialFlow.com* [informative video]. Retrieved November 15, 2011, from http://thisweekin.com/thisweekin-startups/this-week-in-startups-105-frank-speiser-founder-of-socialflow-com/

Williams, K. T. (2009). Case study: Dell hell: The impact of social media on corporate communication. Hoboken, NJ: CorpCommCollab.

Wollan, R., Smith, N., & Zhou, C. (2011). *The social media management handbook: Everything you need to know to get social media working in your business*. New York: John Wiley & Sons, Inc..

ADDITIONAL READING

Asur, S., & Huberman, B. (2010). *Predicting the future with social media*. Retrieved from http://www.hpl.hp.com/research/scl/papers/socialmedia/socialmedia.pdf

Balasubramanyan, R. O'Connor, Routledge, B., & Smith, N. (2010). From tweets to polls: Linking text sentiment to public opinion time series. In *Proceedings of the International AAAI Conference on Weblogs and Social Media*. Washington, DC: AAAI. Retrieved from http://www.cs.cmu.edu/~nasmith/papers/oconnor+balasubramanyan+routledge+smith.icwsm10.pdf

Bale, K., & Lasica, J. (2011). *Top 20 social media monitoring vendors for business*. Retrieved from http://www.socialmedia.biz/2011/01/12/top-20-social-media-monitoring-vendors-for-business/

Balegno, S. (2010). *Social marketing ROAD map handbook: A method for mapping an effective social strategy*. Retrieved from http://www.marketingsherpa.com/heap/SocialMediaHandbookExcerpt.pdf

Bhattacharjee, B., Druschel, P., Gummadi, K., Marcon, M., & Mislove, A. (2007). Measurement and analysis of online social networks. In *Proceedings of the IMC'07*, (pp. 29-42). San Diego, CA: IMC.

Blackshaw, P., & Nazzaro, M. (2006). *Consumer-generated media (CGM) 101 word-of-mouth in the age of the web-fortified consumer*. Retrieved from http://www.nielsen-online.com/downloads/us/buzz/nbzm_wp_CGM101.pdf

Boyd, M., & Ellison, N. (2008). Social network sites: Definition, history, and scholarship. *Journal of Computer-Mediated Communication, 13*, 210–230. doi:10.1111/j.1083-6101.2007.00393.x.

Brandwatch Social media Monitoring. (2011). *Guest post: The fox news twitter hack*. Retrieved from http://www.brandwatch.com/2011/07/guest-post-the-fox-news-twitter-hack/

Bright, L., Daugherty, T., & Eastin, M. (2008). Exploring consumer motivations for creating user-generated content. *Journal of Interactive Advertising*, *8*(2), 16–25.

Chou, D., Fink, C., Llorens, A., & Kopecky, J. (2011). Coarse- and fine-grained sentiment analysis of social media text. *Johns Hopkins APL Technical Digest*, *30*(1). Retrieved from http://www.jhuapl.edu/techdigest/TD/td3001/Fink.pdf.

Corporate Executive Board. (2008). *Leveraging social networking sites in marketing communications*. Retrieved from http://www.ittoolbox.com/advertising/pdf/Leveraging-Social-Media-Networking-Sites-in-Marketing-Communications.pdf

Godbole, N., Skiena, S., & Srinivasaiah, M. (2008). *Large-scale sentiment analysis for news and blogs*. Retrieved from http://icwsm.org/papers/3--Godbole-Srinivasaiah-Skiena.pdf

Hackford, C., Morris, H., & Palomba, M. (2010). *Social media marketing – Protecting your brand online*. Retrieved from http://www.advertisingcompliancelaw.com/uploads/file/Social%20Media%20Marketing%20-%20Protecting%20your%20brand%20online.pdf

Han, J., Liu, L., Tang, J., & Yang, S. (2010). Mining topic-level influence in heterogeneous networks. In *Proceedings of the 19th ACM International Conference on Information and Knowledge Management (CIKM '10)*, (pp. 199-208). New York, NY: ACM Press. Retrieved from http://keg.cs.tsinghua.edu.cn/jietang/publications/KDD09-Tang-et-al-Social-Influence-Analysis.pdf

Hernández, S., & Sallis, P. (2011). *Sentiment-preserving reduction for social media analysis*. Paper presented at the XVI Iberoamerican Congress on Pattern Recognition CIARP. Pucon, Chile.

Huhtamaki, J., Poschko, J., Rubens, N., Rusell, M., Still, K., & Yu, J. (2011). *Social media: Reputation and branding of innovation hubs: A periscope using content analysis of twitter*. Retrieved from http://www.leydesdorff.net/th9/Social%20media,%20reputation%20and%20branding%20of%20innovation%20hubs.pdf

Lee, E. (2008). Warming up to user-generated content. *University of Illinois Law Review*, *5*, Retrieved from http://ssrn.com/abstract=1116671.

Lee, L., & Pang, B. (2008). Opinion mining and sentiment analysis. *Foundations and Trends in Information Retrieval, 2*(1-2), 1-135. Retrieved from http://www.cs.cornell.edu/home/llee/omsa/omsa.pdf

Michael, M. (2010). *The real questions about social media monitoring/web listening*. Retrieved from http://www.digital-mr.com/UserFiles/File/Social-Media-Monitoring-wp.pdf

Orcutt, M. (2011). *How occupy wall street occupied twitter, too: Software reveals how the occupy wall street idea spread across to the social web as protesters took to the streets*. Retrieved from http://www.technologyreview.com/blog/editors/27324/

Seiple, P. (2008). *How to leverage social media for public relations success: Using social media to generate media coverage and improve brand sentiment*. Retrieved from http://www.hubspot.com/Portals/53/docs/hubspot_social_media_pr_ebook.pdf

Steinert-Threlkeld, T. (2011). *How to deal with the brave new world of social network policies*. Retrieved from http://www.socialware.com/about/news-events/how-to-deal-with-the-brave-new-world-of-social-network-policies/

Sun, J., Tang, J., Wang, C., & Yang, Z. (2009). *Social influence analysis in large-scale networks*. Retrieved from http://keg.cs.tsinghua.edu.cn/jietang/publications/KDD09-Tang-et-al-Social-Influence-Analysis.pdf

Sysomos a Marketwire Company. (2011). *The 24/7 customer experience: Automating and improving customer service through the social web*. Retrieved from http://info.marketwire.com/rs/marketwire/images/Sysomos-Automate-Customer-Service.pdf

Tromp, E. (2011). *Multilingual sentiment analysis on social media*. (Master's Thesis). Eindhoven University of Technology, Eindhoven, The Netherlands. Retrieved from http://www.win.tue.nl/~mpechen/projects/pdfs/Tromp2011.pdf

KEY TERMS AND DEFINITIONS

Alert/Alarm: Action that is taken automatically in response to a mention, post, comment, image, video or news has been published. It might take form of an email, an audible sound, a visible object on the screen, an RSS feed or a combination of them.

Engagement: Interest and participation that the followers or fans demonstrate to the brand, product or company through concrete actions such as commenting content, sharing content, clicking a like button, retweeting, etc.

Influence Analysis: Metric to quantify the influence that certain social network users (influencers) have over other social network users because of their knowledge and reputation on a certain topic.

Monitoring: Action of identifying the creation of new content that can take the form of text, audio, video, images or any other kind of user generated content that can be posted or upload in any social media. The ultimate goal of this task is to identify what is being said about a company, competitor, product or brand.

Online Community: Group of people with common interests who use Internet-based applications to interact with each other and share information.

Reputation Analysis: Capability to automatically determine how different keywords, terms, topics or user generated content within the mentions may harm a brand name, product or company.

Search or Query: Consult looking for mentions of brands, companies, products, topics, keywords or key terms, persons, Twitter or Facebook account users, businesses, URL's, places, and other types of information on social media sites, news streams, and other Websites.

Sentiment Analysis: Capability to automatically classify user sentiment when performing a certain engagement action as, for example, negative, neutral or positive.

Social Media: Group of Internet-based applications where users can engage with other users and share ideas, messages, information, videos, images, and other content.

Social Profile: Account registered in some social media site that can be used to participate in the social media site, or to listen for user generated content or to launch marketing or public relations campaigns for a brand name, product, or company.

User Generated Content (UGC): Includes videos, images, audio files, messages in Facebook, posts in Twitter and other forms of media that can be created by social media users in any online community, and that is visible to others users in that online community, or to any Web user.

Chapter 4
E-Health Sites Development Using Open Source Software and OMT Methodology as Support for Family Doctors' Activities:
A Romanian Case Study

Sebastian Marius Rosu
Special Telecommunications Service, Romania

George Dragoi
University "Politehnica" of Bucharest, Romania

ABSTRACT

E-health is the generic term used for the set of tools based on information and communication technology used to help prevent, diagnose, treat, and monitor the health and lifestyles and to improve these processes. These considerations are the starting point of this chapter, which presents a Website development solution for family doctors' consulting-rooms to meet the needs of potential patients, based on Object Modeling Technique (OMT) and Open Source Software (OSS) in a metropolitan area network infrastructure. Development of ICT leaves much more freedom to the consultants to accommodate organizations to other influences, both internal and external.

DOI: 10.4018/978-1-4666-4373-4.ch004

INTRODUCTION

E-health is an emerging field in the intersection of medical informatics, public health and business, referring to health services and information delivered or enhanced through the Internet and related technologies - in a broader sense, the term characterizes not only a technical development, but also a state-of-mind, a way of thinking, an attitude, and a commitment for networked, global thinking, to improve health care locally, regionally, and worldwide by using information and communication technology (Eysenbach, 2001).

E-health includes the relationship between patients and healthcare providers, sharing information between the institutions of communication between patients and health professionals. It also includes relevant information networks, electronic medical record and personal portable communication systems used to monitor and assist patients. Because of e-Health tools, some information vital to saving a life may be available in place at the right time - which is critical, given the intensification of cross-border movement of citizens and patients.

E-health is rapidly emerging as an international priority in nations at all levels of development, yet the benefits and priorities have not clearly been defined (Bates & Wright, 2009). Although some authors have suggested that electronic records may be out of reach for developing nations, an increasing body of work shows that use of electronic tools can result in large health improvements, even in resource-poor environments (Siika, et al., 2005; Allen, et al., 2007; Were, Sutherland, Bwana, Ssali, Emenyonu, & Tierney, 2008; Blaya, Gomez, Rodriguez, & Fraser, 2008). Vast amounts of personal data are collected routinely by health and social care systems in order to support clinical management and patient care (Ford, et al., 2009).

Health professionals, patient organizations, and the pharmaceutical industry are using the Internet as a medium for communicating health information (Sittig, King & Hazlehurst, 2001; Bovi, 2003; Baker, Rideout, Gertler, & Raube, 2005; Brooks & Menachemi, 2006) while the most obvious use for patients is as a source of health information (Kummervold, et al., 2008).

E-Health can bring considerable benefits for the community by improving access to health care and improving them. It contributes to the establishment of citizen-oriented health systems and the efficiency, effectiveness and sustainability of the health sector. The European Union is moving towards a "European e-Health Area," coordinating actions and related policies and promoting synergies between stakeholders to develop better solutions, to prevent fragmentation and to disseminate best practices. The specific objectives are: the creation electronic medical records, supporting information sharing and standardization, the establishment of networks of health information between various care centers to coordinate the response to threat to health, providing medical services on line such as information on healthy lifestyles and disease prevention, and development of remote consultations (prescribing services, reference and electronic reimbursement). Ensure the success of this project is necessary to take into account the requirements of citizens, patients and healthcare professionals and their involvement in implementing strategies and projects.

It is clear that while research in this area is burgeoning, it remains a fact that there is little reliable evidence to demonstrate the measurable impact, risks, or cost-effectiveness of e-health innovations, except in a modest number of application areas (Johnston, Pan, Walker, Bates & Middleton, 2003; Chaudhry, et al., 2006; Pagliari, 2007). Designing effective e-health systems and services requires the application of expertise from diverse fields and will benefit from interdisciplinary collaboration - this may be eased by increasing familiarity with each others' terminologies, theoretical bases, and research methods, with the ultimate objective of achieving trans-disciplinary working (Pagliari, 2007).

E-HEALTH IN ROMANIA

Romania is a semi-presidential democratic republic where executive functions are shared between the president and the prime minister. Romania is divided into 41 counties – the municipality of Bucharest is considered also a county. The Ministry of Public Health (MPH) is responsible for the health policy, regulations, health programs and investments in public health establishments. The main regulatory law in the Romanian healthcare environment is currently the Law 95/2006 (with subsequent amendments) which establishes the organization of healthcare, institutions, financing, organization of health insurance, personnel (doctors, dentists, pharmacists etc.), their responsibilities and official organizations etc.

The public healthcare is financed from the state budget, local budgets, social health insurance and other sources (there is also an optional, voluntary health insurance network, for complementary and supplementary services) – the state and local budgets are mainly sustaining health programs and investments in buildings, appliances, endowment etc., while the health insurance covers mainly the healthcare services, the drugs reimbursement and the "per capita" wages of the general practitioners. As a result of the Romanian health reform, after 1999, most of the healthcare units, except the hospitals, were privatized (however, some new private hospitals were set up). Also, in the nineties, most of the pharmacies were privatized. Recently the number of hospital has been reduced and the Diagnostic Related Groups (DRG) system was adopted for budgeting over 180 hospitals – the health insurance system is operational but needs still to be improved (Moisil & Jitaru, 2006). Concerning Romania acquiring the technology or training the actors is not a problem but a very important problem is infrastructure.

In Romania, family doctors (General Practitioner – GP) are those who provide and coordinate personal health care, primary and continue individual and family (e.g. family goes to a family doctor the first time when have a health problem). One of the most important tasks of a family doctor is prescribing drugs in the list of cleared and recommendation based diagnostic investigations. The family doctor is referring his patients so they can make their free blood tests, x-rays or an electrocardiogram. Insured persons, identified with health problems that cannot be treated by a doctor, are directed at specialist clinics. GP issued registration certificates for the different exams and courses. The family doctor and certificates issued prenuptial death certificates and certificates for the firearm permit. He vaccinates, consults, and interprets test results and issue prescriptions free or fee. The GP program is on average five hours a day at practice and two hours on the ground. The family doctor is paid by National Health Insurance House. Payment of family doctors is a system which takes into account both the number of patients entered on the list – the doctor is paid whether or not the patient requested services and on the effective settlement services.

According to the latest survey results under SNMF (National Society of Family Medicine of Romania), 2 of 3 family physicians in Romania said they want to improve professionally through courses delivered online. Among the advantages of this mode of learning, are, according to respondents, and the ability to access desired information regardless of county or area they live in the country, whether living in a big city or rural area.

Real need of medical e-learning tools is evidenced by the fact that, according to the study, about one in two family doctors in Romania are already using the Internet routinely to document. Moreover, 60% of doctors were eager to show they have a portal where they can go through specially designed courses to meet their professional concerns. Besides the fact that most family doctors have a busy schedule in both the field and in medical offices (see Figure 1), have the duty to keep records and to process the whole data on the activities daily. The abundance of data and need proper management of their need to ensure

Figure 1. Two offices for family doctors (with medical analysis laboratory) in the same location in the Buzau city (Buzau county)

a competent medical act, to keep it in the medical arts, the need to harmonize with European trends, these are arguments for introducing widespread office software for proper development of activity in family medicine.

In general, using software by family doctors has the following advantages:

- Increasing revenue
    - Accurate reporting to National Health Insurance House standards SIUI local or other forms.
    - Proper records management insured.
    - Easy identification of patients who have lost their insured.
- More time available
    - Possibility of copying recipes chronically ill from month to month.
    - Easy printing on the forms of National Health Insurance House data entered into the computer: recipes, holidays, links, registry advice, patient chart.
    - Elimination of repetitive work to complete the general information available on all documents.
- Safety in daily activities
    - Eliminating risk of error in prescribing medicines recipe, thanks always updated list of medications to date.
    - Security of data about patients and diseases, the key systems of protection and privacy of personal information.
- More control in practice
    - Complete reports about the movement of patients and the services provided.
    - Ability to import list of patients from the Health Insurance House.
    - Check the light status of the insured patients.
    - Clear evidence of patients, consultants and prescribed recipes.
- Better personal image
    - Simple and quick release of medical records.
    - Ability to schedule more patients.
    - Automated and updated in terms of: the list of medicines, etc.

Current medical system in Romania is in constant development and transformation. Due to ever-increasing complexity increasingly required the introduction of modern computing techniques in this system.

This need is given by the dynamic character of development and system operation, particularly due to the impact that it has with the environment in which it belongs.

E-health refers today to the use of modern Information and Communication Technologies (ICT) to meet the needs of citizens, patients, healthcare professionals, healthcare providers, as well as policy makers.

At Romania level, the introduction of e-Health services is facilitating access to healthcare, whatever the geographical location, thanks to innovative telemedicine and personal health systems. In this view, e-Health is also breaking down barriers, enabling health service providers (public authorities, hospitals etc) from different regions to work more closely together.

Many other new e-Health projects have been proposed in the last time to the Ministry of Communications and Information Technologies in Romania, targeting strategies, critical healthcare, statistical reporting, family medicine, telemedicine, e-Prescription, health programs, imaging, laboratory, e-Health portal, GIS, broadband, resource management, ID, confidentiality, security, Procurement etc. Each of these projects is intended to ensure as far as possible compliance with the EU interoperability requirements. The implementation of these projects in Romania is likely to depend on support from European structural funds.

An important factor is created on 2 July 2008, where the European Commission published a proposal for a Directive on the cross- border provision of healthcare services in Europe, as part of its Renewed Social Agenda.

The aim or the principal target of this directive is called to codify and clarify the rules that have already been set down by the European Court of Justice on patients' rights to receive healthcare in another European Member State. Also, this directive on the application of patients' rights in cross-border healthcare will have a major impact on the way regions organize, manage and finance their healthcare services.

Under this Directive, the patients will be able to travel freely to another country and receive treatment there, in most cases, very important, without first getting the authorization of their domestic health system.

E-HEALTH NETWORK INFRASTUCTURE

Metropolitan Area Network corresponds to the interconnection of several locations in the same city. The aim is to interconnect LANs (local area networks) and management at a village level. A MAN network contains only a cable or two, do not contain switching elements that drive packages on one of several possible lines of output. An important aspect of this type of network is the presence of a broadcast environment where all computers are attached. These networks operate in general at the city level.

Some technologies used for implementation of metropolitan networks are ATM (Asynchronous Transfer Mode), FDDI (Fiber Distributed Data Interface) and SMDS (Switched Multi-megabit Data Service). But these old technologies are in the replacement process by Ethernet MAN (Metro-Ethernet). Many networks have been built wireless MAN due to the use of microwaves, radio waves or infrared laser waves. Many companies are rented or leased circuits with public transport (due to the high cost of pulling a cable through the city).

Metropolitan networks play a critical role in the overall expansion of network services because they not only provide for services within individual metropolitan areas, but they also serve as the gateways for wide-area national- and international-scale networks (Skoog, Von Lehmen, Clapp, Gannett, Kobrinski & Poudyal, 2004).

Over metropolitan networks can build virtual private network through which patients can connect to the site family doctor to access various information (e.g. in order to schedule a consultation). The Virtual Private Network (VPN) is a network emulated (the virtual) built on public infrastructure (shared), dedicated to a client (the private) to connect users in locations and to ensure similar conditions of integrity, confidentiality and quality similar with those of a private network. VPNs allows the provisioning of private network services for an organization or organizations over a public or shared infrastructure such as the Internet or service provider backbone network (Rosu & Dragoi, 2011).

In an e-health metropolitan area network, a large number of nodes are interconnected together through a computer network as follow (Youssef, Sait & Khan, 2002):

- **End-User Nodes:** Represented by access points such as workstations, personal computers, printers, mainframe computers, etc.
- **Network Active Elements:** Consist of devices such as multiplexers, hubs, switches, routers, and gateways; the active elements and links provide the needed physical communication paths between every pair of end-user nodes.

Possible solutions to implement a VPN structures (see Figure 2) can be (Rosu & Dragoi, 2011):

- Local VPN based on VLAN (Virtual Local Area Network).
- Local VPN based on IPSec (Internet Protocol Security).

A virtual local network is a logical grouping of local network components without regard to their physical grouping. IPsec is a framework of open standards for ensuring private communications over public networks. It has become the most common network layer security control, typically used to create a Virtual Private Network (VPN). IPSec Tunnel mode is used to secure gateway-to-gateway traffic. IPSec Tunnel mode is used when the final destination of the data packet is different from the security termination point. IPsec Tunnel mode protects the entire contents of the tunneled packets. The IPSec Tunnel mode data packets sent from the source device are accepted by the security gateway (a router or a server) and forwarded to the other end of the tunnel, where the original packets are extracted and then forwarded to their final destination device.

Because the new communication system enables many more interactions between many more participants, it has security requirements beyond the conventional confidentiality, integrity and availability properties provided by conventional security systems (Hauser, Bakken, Dionysiou, Gjermundrod, Irava, Helkey & Bose, 2008). Development of information technology and communication has led to widespread deployment of technical solutions for (Dragoi, Draghici, Rosu, & Cotet, 2010):

- Accessing and processing data and information.
- The transmission of data and information in a network environment with distributed destinations.

Figure 2. Local VPN based on VLAN and IPSec examples (more details in Rosu & Dragoi, 2011)

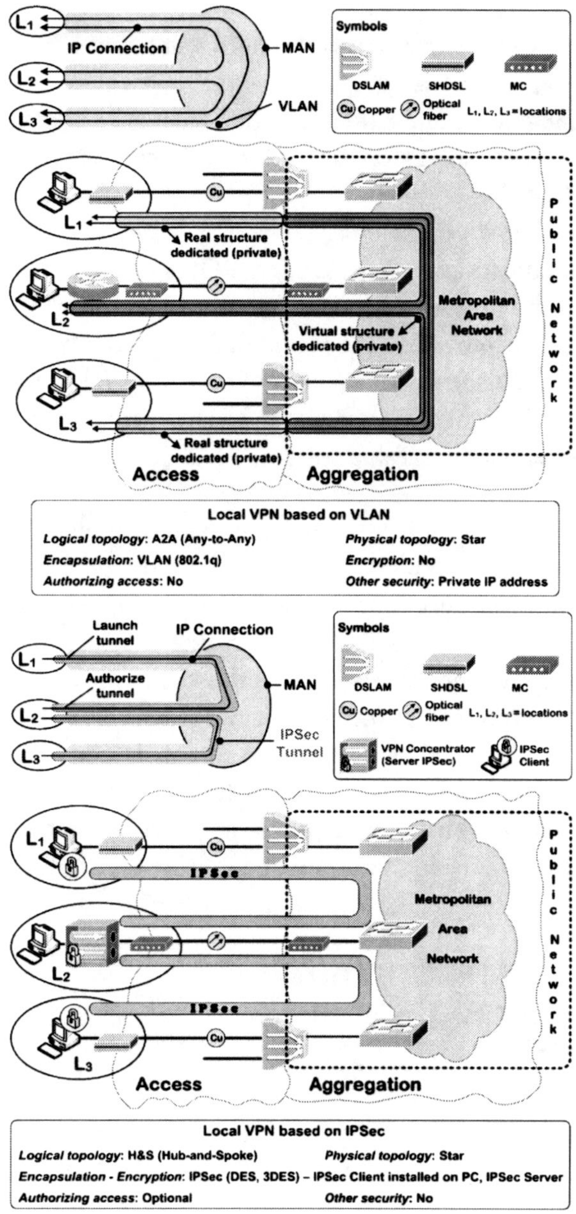

- Connect different users regardless of their geographical distance and position.

Development of ICT leaves much more freedom to the designers and consultants to accommodate organizations to other influences, both internal and external (Cudanov, Jasko, & Jevtic, 2009)

Most recent advancement in wireless communication systems namely 3G and 4G mobile communication networks and WiMAX broadband access now have the potential to importantly enhance telemedicine services by creating a flexible and heterogeneous network within and end to end telemedicine framework.

Radio waves emitted by WiMAX systems are today the subject to the same standards that are applied to radio waves from other radio products such as mobile phones and their base stations. In fact, the World Health Organization (WHO) recommends at this moment the standards, which governments and health agencies around the world have adopted. The standards establish today exposure limits to which products must comply and include substantial margins of safety to protect consumers and the general public.

AN E-HEALTH SITE GENERAL ARCHITECTURE USING OMT AND OSS

E-health sites can be developed using OMT (Object Modeling Technique) - methodology of analysis and object-oriented design. An object must have the following features (Rosu, Dragoi, Rosu & Guran, 2010):

- **Identity:** The object is a discrete entity, which is distinguished from other entities (e.g. a window on a workstation, an isosceles triangle, a list of people).
- **Classification:** Objects with the same attributes and operations are grouped into classes; each object with the same attributes and operations can be considered as an instance of a class (e.g. window, triangle, and list).
- **Polymorphism:** The same operation (with the same name) may have different behavior in different classes (e.g. move a window, move a triangle); operation *move* means different things depending on the subject on which it applies - concrete implementation of an operation in a class is called *method*.
- **Inheritance:** The attributes and operations are transmitted of all downward classes in a hierarchical relationship.

In building the model objects, the most important stage is the evidence that objects with their attributes and operations, and relations between them. Concepts used in this model are classes and objects, diagrams, attributes, operations and methods. Object model is the most important stage of the OMT methodology because it shows the static structure of real system.

Model objects are represented using graphs of objects that are graphs whose nodes are objects and whose arcs represent relationships between objects. Steps in obtaining the objects model are: identifying candidate classes, classes keeping accurate, the preparation of a dictionary, the identification of associations, associations keeping accurate, identifying attributes, attributes keeping accurate, refine the model and grouping classes into modules. The concepts used in implementing the model objects are: the class concept, the object concept, the attribute concept, the diagram concept, the operation concept, method, links and associations.

An object is an abstract concept and it is built for problem understanding before solution implementation. Generally, an object is an entity that can be distinguished among other entities and have significance in modeling application context. Each object has one specific identity even if it is similar to other objects. An object class describes a multitude of objects with similar properties, similar behaviors and similar relations regard others objects. In the modeling of objects held the following:

- Web page has been modeled as object (by means the item page will have the general characteristics of all elements contained in the hierarchy – these features will be: background, fonts, artistic effects, buttons navigation, etc.).
- Collection of Web pages with the same attributes will shape the class of objects.

For a site to a medical doctor, to meet the requirements of potential patients can highlight some key issues about how the application should look as follows:

- The program will have a graphic that will not be requiring special hardware or memory resources very much, also providing sufficient operational stability.
- The program will need to access a database containing information about patients.
- You have created a link between Web pages and database.
- The program must be easily improved by adding other requirements for the database is in constant change.

Application modules can be:

- User interface module medical records.
- Interface management module.
- Association module of the elements of Web pages with entries in the database.

For application system can distinguish the following subsystems: user interface to the main medical records, the main management interface, selecting and processing data and database.

User interface module, type the Web page actually includes a combination of several pages. Some items are shown on all pages of this site: the page title, logo, typeface, Website sections menu, footer. Access will be via a login form, based on authentication. Management interface module in all pages in this area will be password protected, contains the login form and forms to add, delete, or alter data on patients, medical records, and consultation by appointment on-line agenda.

Association module of the elements of Web pages with records in the database actually contains the user interaction. This module should be to answer certain types of queries such as: information about the patient, online schedule, patient medical record, etc.

Although currently there are a lot of software on the market for family doctors, many doctors in Romania considers that the costs of program management of patient's acquisition are high. Therefore we present a method (a didactical method) to build a site for managing patient information.

Regarding software, our option was to use Open Source Software (OSS) with free sources, these products having a remarkable quality because these projects often get together distinguished programmers and because everything is public, open and anybody can come. Sources access and modified possibility is a great advantage even if very rarely somebody makes these modifications.

Open Source Initiative (OSI), a non-profit corporation dedicated to managing and promoting the Open Source Definition give the definition for this software (www.opensource.org): Open source doesn't just mean access to the source code.

The distribution terms of open-source software must comply with the following criteria:

- **Free Redistribution:** The license shall not restrict any party from selling or giving away the software as a component of an aggregate software distribution containing programs from several different sources.

- **Source Code:** The program must include source code, and must allow distribution in source code as well as compiled form.
- **Derived Works:** The license must allow modifications and derived works, and must allow them to be distributed under the same terms as the license of the original software.
- **Integrity of the Author's Source Code:** The license may restrict source-code from being distributed in modified form only if the license allows the distribution of "patch files" with the source code for the purpose of modifying the program at build time. The license must explicitly permit distribution of software built from modified source code. The license may require derived works to carry a different name or version number from the original software.
- **No Discrimination Against Persons or Groups:** The license must not discriminate against any person or group of persons.
- **No Discrimination Against Fields of Endeavour:** The license must not restrict anyone from making use of the program in a specific field of endeavor. For example, it may not restrict the program from being used in a business, or from being used for genetic research.
- **Distribution of License:** The rights attached to the program must apply to all to whom the program is redistributed without the need for execution of an additional license by those parties.
- **License Must Not Be Specific to a Product:** The rights attached to the program must not depend on the program's being part of a particular software distribution. If the program is extracted from that distribution and used or distributed within the terms of the program's license, all parties to whom the program is redistributed should have the same rights as those that are granted in conjunction with the original software distribution.
- **License Must Not Restrict Other Software:** The license must not place restrictions on other software that is distributed along with the licensed software.
- **License Must Be Technology-Neutral:** No provision of the license may be predicated on any individual technology or style of interface.

For added, accessed, and processed database information is necessary to have a database administration system and for this site was used MySQL, a relational database management system that runs as a server providing multi-user access to a number of databases. A Relational Database Management System (RDBMS) is a complex software program, which purpose is to store, manage and retrieve data as quickly and reliable as possible. MySQL is a management relational database system, produced by Swedish company MySQL AB and distributed under the GNU General Public License. GNU GPL license does not allow embedding MySQL in commercial software. Those wishing to do so may purchase fee, a license to commercial production company, MySQL AB. The MySQL database has become the world's most popular open source database because of its high performance, high reliability and ease of use, and because MySQL runs on more than 20 platforms including Linux, Windows, Mac OS, Solaris, HP-UX, IBM AIX, giving you the kind of flexibility that puts you in control (www.mysql.com).

There were created user (with fields: id, user, password, name, age, etc.), calendar (with fields: id, event, user_id, received, etc.), data (with fields: id, address, phone, sex, citizenship, birth_date, birth_place, cnp - personal identification number, no_insurance, marital_status, employment, education, insurer), medical (fields: id, id_disease, document, diagnosis_date, name, etc.), and diseases (fields: diseases_id, name, category) tables in the database. The database development using this model requests an application server and a database server. Application servers are responsible for communications between users.

A language that can translate the browser request, process these request, interact with software on server to satisfy the requests and to indicate to the server exactly which need to send back to user's browser is request. These languages, which work with the server and can execute these, are middleware. Such as middleware languages class was used PHP, a server-side, Web scripting software. PHP is a scripting language specialized for the applications developing through code integration in the HTML document. PHP syntax derived from C, Java and Perl (www.php.net). The difference between PHP and other similar products, such as JavaScript is, that PHP is executing on the server when JavaScript is execute on the user computer. These languages, which work with the server and can execute these, are middleware. PHP (Hypertext Preprocessor) program is open source. You can use, modify and redistribute free this product.

For this site model were identified and created the following classes: index, config, pacient, data_patient, program_patient, login, mail, home, etc.

Usual steps in users working process with databases are the following (Rosu, Guran & Mateescu, 2007):

- The user makes a request for certain dates (e.g. a special form, a rapport or a situation).
- The application server receives the request, locates the files and gives request to PHP for processing.
- The PHP starts processing, makes the connection with database and sends the request.
- The Database server receives the request, processing and sent to PHP the result.
- PHP returns the result to application server.

Figure 3. Manage patient files web page

- Server applications send the result to the user.

The interfaces with users are indicating to be simply used, friendly, and attractive, without many graphical pictures or animations because they can make loading operation slower (see Figures 3 and 4). For the forms there can be used different language as HTML (Hypertext Markup Language), CSS (Cascading Style Sheets) or JavaScript. Easy to used is HTML because this language can be edited in any text editor software and integrated the PHP script. The most used HTML editors are Notepad for Windows and Pico for Linux.

HTML is one of fundamental first WWW (World Wide Web) fundamental elements and describe primary format in which documents are distributed and visualized on the Web. Between his advantages specify the platform independence, hypertext links and documents conformation. HTML documents are ASCII Format documents and can be created with anything texts editor. Hypertext is to say that any word, phrase, picture or any document element seen by user can make reference to another document. This property facilitates navigation between multiple documents or internal same documents. The strict documents structure admits their conversion from a format in another as well as databases formed by these query.

A HTTP (Hypertext Transport Protocol) server is requested for application rolling. A good choice is Apache because of its flexibility, portability, safety, and extensibility (www.apache.org). Apache has Apache Software License. This license is similar with BSD License (Berkeley Software Distribution - it is necessary just to keep the copyright and license information in the source code; it is imperative to mention "This product includes software developed by the University of California, Berkeley and its contributors") but is forbidden to put the name Apache in derived products without Apache Software Foundation accord. To apply the Apache License to your work, it's necessary

Figure 4. On-line programming consultations web page

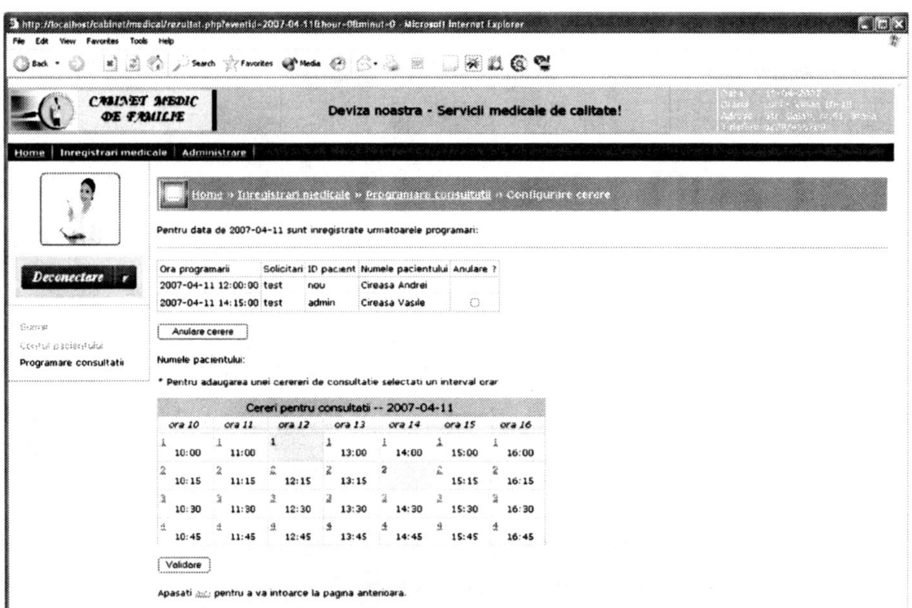

to attach the following boilerplate notice, with the fields enclosed by brackets "[]" replaced with your own identifying information. The text should be enclosed in the appropriate comment syntax for the file format. It's also recommended that a file or class name and description of purpose be included on the same "printed page" as the copyright notice for easier identification within third-party archives.

Here, we used a 3 level Client-Server architecture:

- Database server represents the first level and executes database requests management.
- Second level is applications level and represents logical level where functional components rolling.
- The last level is user's level and from here they access application.

This architecture use optimum the hardware and software resources because the functionalities are distributed between the two servers type: application server and database server. To implement this system we used Apache 2.2.17 and PHP 5.3.5 and the database server MySQL 5.1.54 (5.3.5.0 EasyPHP package).

FUTURE RESEARCH DIRECTIONS

Initiatives to promote and support technology transfer in the area of e-health structures and mechanisms for e-health related technology transfer were not observed in Romania. For example, according to a recent European Commission report in terms of broadband fixed point, Romania is one of the least developed markets in the EU penetration of 13% with a slow upward trend, being the second lower penetration in the EU (in Europe, 92% of hospitals have access to broadband Internet, while 80% have implemented electronic patient chart). Broadband coverage is still limited, especially in rural areas, resulting in low utilization of broadband Internet by households and enterprise. Terms such as telemedicine, e-patient, centralized electronic cards of the past patients are still new for patients and many clinicians in Romania.

Some successful e-health solutions are in progress to be rolled out, but they are isolated initiatives. We can say that the Romanian e-health is a growing business and the interest of IT companies is increasing.

We will continue in future to find other solutions to develop e-health applications.

Clinical productivity depends today on rapid access to information, seamless data flow, and reliable clinical networks and family doctors. Reducing complexity results in higher efficiency. That's why our e-Health Solutions provide you with a global ICT infrastructure for integrated healthcare based on both clinical, family doctors and IT security expertise. We focus in the future on Integrated Care Solutions that improve processes along the healthcare continuum and clinical pathways, e.g. by featuring an electronic health record. The target is to enable secure access and efficient administration. This adds up to effective cooperation for healthcare providers and a better quality of patient care at reduced costs, giving relevant answers to the demands of integrated healthcare.

In the view of the proposal of EU Commission on 2 July 2008, for a Directive on the cross- border provision of healthcare services in Europe, as part of its Renewed Social Agenda where the aim or target is to codify and clarify the rules that have already been set down by the European Court of Justice on patients' rights to receive healthcare in another European Member State, a number of questions for the regions is purposed today: Also, in this context, what will be the impact of patient mobility on the planning, management and delivery of healthcare services or without a prior authorization or warning system, how can regional authorities accurately estimate the number of patients they will treat and make the necessary logistic provisions?

Each Member State of EU is asked today to set up their own national plans in which they define their own targets in each of these areas. Further actions on EU level are designed to support this strategy.

CONCLUSION

The existing medical system is in continuous development and transformation. Due to the ever-increasing complexity requires more than the introduction of modern computing techniques in this system. This need is given by the dynamic nature of development and functioning, particularly due to the impact this has on the environment to which it belongs.

Here, it was presented few OSS products and an implementation model for a family doctor e-health site using OMT methodology and a metropolitan network infrastructure. The scope of this work (realized in the PREMINV Research Center) was to see if these products can represent alternative solutions to commercial software for Web sites development at the family doctor consulting room level.

Must be known than open source products aren't in all cases better then commercial software. There is software Open Source who excels any commercial alternative as performance, but there is inferior software to comparative commercial software. Open source software with free sources is a good option these products having a remarkable quality because of fact then often these projects get together distinguished programmers and everything is public, open and anybody can come.

ACKNOWLEDGMENT

This work was developed at PREMINV Research Center, University "Politehnica" of Bucharest.

REFERENCES

Allen, C., Jazayeri, D., Miranda, J., Biondich, P. G., Mamlin, B. W., & Wolfe, B. A. et al. (2007). Experience in implementing the OpenMRS medical record system to support HIV treatment in Rwanda. *Studies in Health Technology and Informatics*, *129*, 382–386. PMID:17911744.

Apache. (n.d.). Retrieved from www.apache.org

Baker, L., Rideout, J., Gertler, P., & Raube, K. (2005). Effect of an Internet-based system for doctor-patient communication on health care spending. *Journal of the American Medical Informatics Association*, *12*(5). doi:10.1197/jamia.M1778 PMID:15905484.

Bates, D. W., & Wright, A. (2009). Evaluating eHealth: Undertaking robust international cross-cultural ehealth research. *PLoS Medicine*, *6*(9), e10000105. doi:10.1371/journal.pmed.1000105 PMID:19753106.

Blaya, J. A., Gomez, W., Rodriguez, P., & Fraser, H. (2008). Cost and implementation analysis of a personal digital assistant system for laboratory data collection. *The International Journal of Tuberculosis and Lung Disease*, *12*(8), 921–927. PMID:18647452.

Bovi, A. M. (2003). Ethical guidelines for use of electronic mail between patients and physicians. *The American Journal of Bioethics*, *3*(3), 43–47. doi:10.1162/152651603322874771 PMID:12859845.

Brooks, R. G., & Menachemi, N. (2006). Physicians' use of email with patients: Factors influencing electronic communication and adherence to best practices. *Journal of Medical Internet Research*, *8*(1),

Chaudhry, B., Wang, J., Wu, S., Maglione, M., Mojica, W., Roth, E., et al. (2006). Systematic review: Impact of health information technology on quality, efficiency, and costs of medical care. *Annals of Internal Medicine*, *144*(10), 742–752. PMID:16702590.

Cordis. (n.d.). retrieved from cordis.europa.eu

Cudanov, M., Jasko, O., & Jevtic, M. (2008). Influence of information and communication technologies on decentralization of organizational structure. *Computer Science and Information System*, *6*(1), 93–109. doi:10.2298/CSIS0901093C.

Dragoi, G., Draghici, A., Rosu, S. M., & Cotet, C. E. (2010). Virtual product development in university-enterprise partnership. *Information Resources Management Journal*, *23*(3), 43–59. doi:10.4018/irmj.2010070104.

Europa. (n.d.). Retrieved from europa.eu

Eysenbach, G. (2001). What is e-health? *Journal of Medical Internet Research*, *3*(2), e20. doi:10.2196/jmir.3.2.e20 PMID:11720962.

Ford, D. V., Jones, K. H., Verplancke, J. P., Lyons, R. A., John, G., & Brown, G. et al. (2009). The SAIL databank: Building a national architecture for e-health research and evaluation. *BMC Health Services Research*, *9*, 157. doi:10.1186/1472-6963-9-157 PMID:19732426.

Hauser, C. H., Bakken, D. E., Dionysiou, I., Gjermundrod, H. K., Irava, V. S., Helkey, J., & Bose, A. (2008). Security, trust and QoS in next-generation control and communication for large power system. *International Journal of Critical Infrastructures*, *4*(1/2), 3–16. doi:10.1504/IJCIS.2008.016088.

Johnston, D., Pan, E., Walker, J., Bates, D. W., & Middleton, B. (2003). *The value of computerized provider order entry in ambulatory settings*. Wellesley, MA: Center for Information Technology Leadership.

Kummervold, P. E., Chronaki, C. E., Lausen, B., Prokosch, H. U., Rasmussen, J., & Santana, S. et al. (2008). eHealth trends in Europe 2005-2007: A population-based survey. *Journal of Medical Internet Research*, *10*(4), e42. doi:10.2196/jmir.1023 PMID:19017584.

Moisil, I., & Jitaru, E. (2006). E-health progresses in Romania. *International Journal of Medical Informatics*, *75*, 315–321. doi:10.1016/j.ijmedinf.2005.08.013 PMID:16275159.

MySQL. (n.d.). Retrieved from www.mysql.com

Open Source. (n.d.). Retrieved from www.opensource.org

Pagliari, C. (2007). Design and evaluation in eHealth: Challenges and implications for an interdisciplinary field. *Journal of Medical Internet Research*, *9*(2), e15. doi:10.2196/jmir.9.2.e15 PMID:17537718.

PHP. (n.d.). Retrieved from www.php.net

Rosu, S. M., & Dragoi, G. (2011). VPN solutions and network monitoring to support virtual teams work in virtual enterprises. *Computer Science and Information System*, *8*(1), 1–26. doi:10.2298/CSIS100127033R.

Rosu, S. M., Dragoi, G., Rosu, L., & Guran, M. (2010). Virtual enterprise network solutions to support e-learning sites development. In Katalinic, B. (Ed.), *DAAAM International Scientific Book 2010* (pp. 725–742). Vienna, Austria: DAAAM International. doi:10.2507/daaam.scibook.2010.63.

Rosu, S. M., Guran, M., & Mateescu, L. M. (2007). E-learning sites development using open source software support in the enterprise. In *Proceedings of the 4th Balkan Region Conference on Engineering Education & MSE* (pp. 98-103). Sibiu, Romania: MSE.

Siika, A. M., Rotich, J. K., Simiyu, C. J., Kigotho, E. M., Smith, F. E., & Sidle, J. E. et al. (2005). An electronic medical record system for ambulatory care of HIV-infected patients in Kenya. *International Journal of Medical Informatics*, *74*(5), 345–355. doi:10.1016/j.ijmedinf.2005.03.002 PMID:15893257.

Sittig, D. F., King, S., & Hazlehurst, B. L. (2001). A survey of patient-provider e-mail communication: What do patients think? *International Journal of Medical Informatics*, *61*(1), 71–80. doi:10.1016/S1386-5056(00)00134-9 PMID:11248604.

Skoog, R., Von Lehmen, A., Clapp, G., Gannett, J. W., Kobrinski, H., & Poudyal, V. (2004). Metro network design methodologies that build a next-generation network infrastructure based on this generation's services and demands. *Journal of Lightwave Technology*, *22*(11), 2680–2692. doi:10.1109/JLT.2004.836748.

Were, M. C., Sutherland, J. M., Bwana, M., Ssali, J., Emenyonu, N., & Tierney, W. M. (2008). Patterns of care in two HIV continuity clinics in Uganda, Africa: A time-motion study. *AIDS Care*, *20*(6), 677–682. doi:10.1080/09540120701687067 PMID:18576169.

Youssef, H., Sait, S. M., & Khan, S. A. (2002). Topology design of switched enterprise networks using a fuzzy simulated evolution algorithm. *Engineering Applications of Artificial Intelligence*, *15*, 327–340. doi:10.1016/S0952-1976(02)00066-0.

ADDITIONAL READING

Andersen, S. T., & Jansen, A. (2011). Innovation in ICT-based health care provision. *International Journal of Healthcare Information Systems and Informatics*, *6*(2), 14–27. doi:10.4018/jhisi.2011040102.

Burkhard, R. (2010). Patient-centered e-health. *International Journal of E-Health and Medical Communications*, *1*(1), 64–66. doi:10.4018/jehmc.2010010106.

Cruz-Cunha, M. M., Oliveira, E., Tavares, A., & Fereira, L. (2009). *Handbook of research on social dimensions of semantic technologies and web services*. Hershey, PA: IGI-Global. doi:10.4018/978-1-60566-650-1.

Cruz-Cunha, M. M., & Varajao, J. (2010). *Enterprise information systems design, implementation and management: Organizational applications*. Hershey, PA: IGI Global. doi:10.4018/978-1-61692-020-3.

Cugelman, B., Thelwall, M., & Dawes, P. (2011). Online interventions for social marketing health behavior change campaigns: A meta-analysis of psychological architectures and adherence factors. *Journal of Medical Internet Research*, *13*(1), e17. doi:10.2196/jmir.1367 PMID:21320854.

Fernandez-Luque, L., Karlsen, R., & Bonander, J. (2011). Review of extracting information from the social web for health personalization. *Journal of Medical Internet Research*, *13*(1), e15. doi:10.2196/jmir.1432 PMID:21278049.

Green, B. B., Anderson, M. L., Ralston, J. D., Catz, S., Fishman, P. A., & Cook, A. J. (2011). Patient ability and willingness to participate in a web-based intervention to improve hypertension control. *Journal of Medical Internet Research*, *13*(1), e1. doi:10.2196/jmir.1625 PMID:21371993.

Hood, C. C., & Bougourd, S. (2011). Research essay: The ethics of e-health. *International Journal of E-Health and Medical Communications*, *2*(2), 82–85. doi:10.4018/IJEHMC.2011040120110401006.

Miller, K., & Sankaranarayanan, S. (2011). Applications of policy based agents in wireless body sensor mesh networks for patient health monitoring. *International Journal of E-Health and Medical Communications*, *2*(2), 24–45. doi:10.4018/jehmc.2011040103.

Munoz-Cornejo, G., Seaman, C. B., & Koru, A. G. (2008). An empirical investigation into the adoption of open source software in hospitals. *International Journal of Healthcare Information Systems and Informatics*, *3*(3), 16–37. doi:10.4018/jhisi.2008070102.

Olla, P., & Tan, J. (2009). *Mobile health solutions for biomedical applications*. Hershey, PA: Information Science Reference. doi:10.4018/978-1-60566-332-6.

Parry, D., Parry, E., Dorji, P., & Stone, P. (2008). Open source software: A key component of e-health in developing nations. *International Journal of Healthcare Information Systems and Informatics*, *3*(3), 1–15. doi:10.4018/jhisi.2008070101.

Raychaudhuri, K., & Ray, P. (2010). Privacy challenges in the use of e-health systems for public health management. *International Journal of E-Health and Medical Communications*, *1*(2), 12–23. doi:10.4018/jehmc.2010040102.

Rocha, A. (2011). Evolution of information system and technologies maturity in healthcare. *International Journal of Healthcare Information Systems and Informatics*, *6*(2), 28–36. doi:10.4018/jhisi.2011040103.

Rosu, S. M., Dragoi, G., Cotet, C. E., & Guran, M. (2009). A didactical method for knowledge bases development at the SMEs level to professional risk assessment. In *Proceedings of the 5th Balkan Region Conference on Engineering Education & 2nd International Conference on Engineering and Business Education* (pp. 266-269). Sibiu, Romania: IEEE.

Rosu, S. M., Dragoi, G., Cotet, C. E., & Rosu, L. (2010). Professional risk assessment using knowledge bases in small and medium enterprises. *Environmental Engineering and Management Journal*, *9*(4), 489–493.

Rosu, S. M., Dragoi, G., Guran, M., & Dragomirescu, C. (2010). The SMEs knowledge management: Professional risk assessment using a KBS. In Katalinic, B. (Ed.), *DAAAM International Scientific Book 2010* (pp. 709–724). Vienna, Austria: DAAAM International. doi:10.2507/daaam.scibook.2010.62.

Saito, M., Wickramasinghe, M., Fuji, M., & Geisler, E. (2009). *Redesigning innovative healthcare operation and the role of knowledge management*. Hershey, PA: Information Science Reference. doi:10.4018/978-1-60566-284-8.

Sobol, M., & Prater, E. (2011). Adoption, usage and efficiency: Benchmarking healthcare IT in private practice. *International Journal of Healthcare Information Systems and Informatics*, *6*(1), 36–50. doi:10.4018/jhisi.2011010103.

Thompson, L. A., Black, E., Duff, W. P., Paradise-Black, N., Saliba, H., & Dawson, K. (2011). Protected health information on social networking sites: Ethical and legal considerations. *Journal of Medical Internet Research*, *13*(1), e8. doi:10.2196/jmir.1590 PMID:21247862.

Yu, J., Guo, C., & Kim, M. (2008). Developing a user centered model for ubiquitous healthcare system implementation: An empirical study. *International Journal of Healthcare Information Systems and Informatics*, *3*(3), 58–76. doi:10.4018/jhisi.2008070104.

KEY TERMS AND DEFINITIONS

E-Health: Is the generic term used for the set of tools based on information and communication technology used to help prevent, diagnose, treat and monitor the health and lifestyles and to improve these processes; is an emerging field in the intersection of medical informatics, public health and business, referring to health services and information delivered or enhanced through the Internet and related technologies.

Family Doctors (In Romania): Are those who provide and coordinate personal health care, primary and continue individual and family.

Internet Protocol Security (IPSec): Is a framework of open standards for ensuring private communications over public networks.

Metropolitan Area Network (MAN): Meet the interconnection of several departments or enterprises located in the same city, the objective is to interconnect and management LANs at a locality.

Middleware: Is a language that can translate the browser request, process these request, interact with software on server to satisfy the requests and to indicate to the server exactly which need to send back to user's browser is request.

Object Modeling Technique (OMT): Methodology of analysis and object-oriented design.

Open Source Software (OSS): Any computer software that: is distributed freely copy or use for anyone, is always distributed (and) the source code and whose study, change, improve and distribution are allowed to anyone.

Relational Database Management System (RDMS): Is a complex software program, which purpose is to store, manage and retrieve data as quickly and reliable as possible.

Virtual Private Network (VPN): Is a network emulated (the virtual) built on public infrastructure (shared), dedicated to a client (the private) to connect users in locations and to ensure similar conditions of integrity, confidentiality and quality similar with those of a private network.

Chapter 5
CommunicaME:
A New Proposal for Facilitating Communication Using NFC

Montserrat Mateos Sánchez
Universidad Pontificia de Salamanca, Spain

Roberto Berjón Gallinas
Universidad Pontificia de Salamanca, Spain

Juan Agustín Fraile Nieto
Universidad Pontificia de Salamanca, Spain

Miguel Ángel Sánchez Vidales
Universidad Pontificia de Salamanca, Spain

ABSTRACT

In a society that is clearly influenced by new technology, new advances in mobile technology have yielded important changes in the way users interact with information systems and contextual information. There is a need to provide technological solutions that help users communicate more easily. In this chapter, a novel solution that makes it easier for the elderly to use mobile phones is proposed. The senior population is rapidly growing; they represent 16-17% of the total population in developed countries. The use of a mobile device presents two large obstacles for this group: problems from disabilities due to age and problems associated with the lack of familiarity with mobile technology. The combined use of contactless technologies such as NFC and MiFARE eliminates the barriers encountered by older individuals. These technologies make it possible to use basic services of a mobile telephone, such as placing a call or sending a message, in a way that is easy, user friendly, and intuitive. The CommunicaME system makes it possible to place a call or send a SMS on a mobile by simply moving it closer to a contactless tag. The use of contactless technologies helps the user to carry out their daily tasks, and it also provides a new method of mobile communication that is both quick and secure. The results obtained with the defined and implemented prototype are presented in this chapter.

DOI: 10.4018/978-1-4666-4373-4.ch005

INTRODUCTION

Recent years the use of mobile telephony and mobile terminals has been widely integrated into modern society; they have seen an exponential growth that has surpassed 100 lines for every 100 inhabitants. Only in Spain had 109 lines for every 100 inhabitants (Comisión de Mercado de las Telecomunicaciones, 2010). Subgroups of the population, such as the elderly, are often excluded from accessing technological advances, primarily because of the barriers encountered in their use (del Arco Carabias & San Segundo Encinar, 2010; Al Mahmud, Mubin, Shaid, & Martens, 2008; Kurniawan, 2007).

One of the main problems for this subgroup are associated with the lack of familiarity with the mobile technology itself (Pavon & Casanova, 2006), although the difficulties experienced by these individuals are primarily derived by the actual characteristics of the terminals (small screens, shortcuts, touch screens, etc.).

If we consider that the subgroup of seniors is very high in all developed countries, this exclusion supposes a serious problem. Now in Spain the group of seniors citizens is already nearing 20% of the total population; also in a few years the number of people older than 65 in the United States will reach nearly 16% of the population; and in Asia, and specifically Singapore, it will reach nearly 18% within just over a decade (Keating, Nagai, Hadder, & Kowalsky, 2007; del Arco Carabias & San Segundo Encinar, 2010; Hix, 2011; Been-Lirn Duh, Yi-Luen Do, Billinghurst, Quek, & Chen Hsueh-Hua, 2010). So a high number of individuals could not use the most basic mobile services offered by the mobile devices, such as making a call or sending a message. Our society is concerned about the problems caused by the lack of adaptation to technological advances among seniors and programs are proposed to solve. For example, in Europe exits the AGE[1] platform whose ambit of operation includes a component specific to TICs. Also Spain has the Advancement Plan[2] that contains a proposal that would encourage the use of TICs (Information and Communication Technologies) among citizens aged 55 years and older.

This chapter presents a new proposal for facilitating the mobile communication for elderly. It is CommunicaME and it is a system that makes the communication more accessible through the use of a mobile telephone for senior citizens. For this subgroup of population, the simply task of writing a short message or searching the contact list for a telephone number is very complicate (Pavon & Casanova, 2006). The objective of this system is to provide a simple solution to this problem, and ensure that sub-groups of the population with difficulty adapting to mobile technology can place a call or send messages in a simple and intuitive way. This can be achieved by using contactless technologies such as NFC (Near Field Communication) (Roebuck, 2011; Finkenzeller, 2010), RFID and MiFare[3]. The combination of these technologies allows for the identification of objects and actions associated with these objects. A mobile device with NFC can identify an action that needs to be performed, such as sending a message or placing a call, by moving the mobile closer to an object containing an associated RFID or MiFare tag that represents these actions. Once the action has been identified, the same mobile device uses another MiFare tag to identify the person with whom one wishes to communicate.

In this chapter, in the next section, it is reviewed every area related with the project, such as, the problems that elderly have in accessing TIC; after that, it is described the contactless technologies used in this work as well as techniques for voice synthesis and recognition used to improve the accessibility of the system. Followed this, it is described the proposed solution and also it is explained a detailed presentation of the experiments that were carried out with the CommunicaME system with an emphasis on the results obtained. Finally, the conclusions are presented together on the innovative approach of this proposal.

BACKGROUND

Accessibility and Dependent Environments for the Elderly

When speaking of technology, it is generally more common to think of young people; rarely does one associate technology with senior citizens. Nevertheless, this is a group of individuals that, given the proper training and, in some cases, specific adaptations to lessen their limitations can benefit from the numerous advantages that technology offers to improve their quality of life (Been-Lirn Duh, Yi-Luen Do, Billinghurst, Quek, & Chen Hsueh-Hua, 2010). To do so, however, it is necessary to overcome certain obstacles (Huber, Walsh, & Varman, 2005) and find a way to point out how technology can improve their daily lives. This could increase their interest in working with different technological resources. The resources most used by seniors are the personal computer, landline telephone, mobile telephone and television. They use these resources to a lesser degree than the remainder of the general population, but according to statistics from the INE (National Institute of Statistics) (INE. Encuesta de Tecnologías de la Información en los hogares 2010, 2010), the number of older people using advanced technological resources is ever increasing. Among seniors, the mobile phone is the most prized resource, along with the television, as they consider these items to be necessary in their daily lives.

The dependent environment should provide services according different parameters and constraints. User preference and capacities deal with user profile aspect. Modeling the profile is the hardest task in this domain especially when dealing with dependent people who has motor inefficiency that reduces their capacities (Ghorbel & Mokhtari, 2005). Also, user location is very important and should be estimated as accurate as possible in order to perform service provision. There are different technologies (GPS, Radio Frequency tags,) to determine user location which differs in computing means and error margin. On the other hand, context awareness is an important aspect that matters in environment perception to make it smart and autonomous. This can be crucial to define the context of a dependent person living alone (Yang, Lim, King, & Helal, 2006). Also, personalization and adaptation assistive services are discovered based on previous parameters and also they have to be adapted for the user end-terminal and his input device. That deals mainly with User Interface adaptation (Ghorbel & Mokhtari, 2005).

We focus our investigation in the modeling aspects dealing with both actors: User and Mobile Service. The goal we want to achieve through user modeling is to design a user profile which describes specific characteristics of our targeted users. On the other hand, the personalization and adaptation of provided mobile services according to the user profile have to be considered since the service development phase. That is why a significant effort is required during the service modeling.

However, there are also a number of barriers that complicate and in some cases impede the use of TIC among the elderly. The aging process involves a progressive deterioration of both physical and cognitive capabilities, which assumes some limitations in accessing TIC (Hix, 2011). Neither personal computers nor mobile telephones in particular are designed to ensure easy access for those with limitations. In some cases, the size of the device or the amount of information displayed, the lack of a standard design or function, the volume, placement of the keys, etc., may create an obstacle impossible for many of these individuals to overcome (Abascal & Civit, 2000). The limitations that most commonly affect the elderly and prevent them from accessing or using TICs include: poor vision, loss of hearing, or reduced motor skills due to problems with articulation or coordination.

The majority of works or projects related to accessibility of mobile telephones focus on improving the services and content of mobile devices. One example is the WebA Mobile, an assistance tool for the design and evaluation of Websites for mobile devices (Mena Tobar, Latorre Andrés, & Lafuente Lapena, 2009). This line includes the W3C[4] mobileOK Checker validation tool (MobileOk Checker) or the Mobile Web Best Practices 1.0 practical recommendations (Mobile Web Best Practices Working Group). These tools and recommendations serve as a guideline for future developments aimed at improving the accessibility of the elderly to specific technological elements.

There are also numerous studies, such as that of Yelmo-Garcia et al. (Yelmo-García, San Miguel González, & Martín García, 2007), that focus on the accessibility of mobile services from mobile devices, particularly those related to Public Administration, Public institutions have tried to lead the way in ensuring that their services are accessible. Other authors, such as Lindholm et al. (Lindholm & Keinonen, 2003) have studied the general usability of mobile devices. The usability of mobile devices is directly related to their ability to provide accessible services.

Among projects with a broader scope, there are studies that deal with the interoperability of mobile devices, such as the INREDIS[5] project (Interfaces for Relations between People with Disabilities). The lines of investigation for this project include their objective of facilitating interaction between users and their environments by using mobile devices.

Other works, such as Abascal and Civit (Abascal & Civit, 2000), analyze the novelties that have become part of the daily lives of senior citizens with mobile technology, and point out the goals that stem from using the technology and usage guidelines for this group of individuals. The objective of other studies has been to understand the best use of technology for the elderly, with particular emphasis on mobile games (Been-Lirn Duh, Yi-Luen Do, Billinghurst, Quek, & Chen Hsueh-Hua, 2010). Keating et al. (Keating, Nagai, Hadder, & Kowalsky, 2007) studied the needs of the elderly and those with visual or audio impairment, and how these needs can be included in the design and development of future products.

Additionally, Thomson and Cupples (Thompson & Cupples, 2008) have analyzed the use of SMS, highlighting that its use, in addition to being a means of communication between people, is also a relationship or association between a mobile and a person. This relationship places great importance on the ease of use of the mobile device.

Notable among all the described research is the absence of specific systems aimed at simplifying the basic services offered by mobile telephones.

To ensure the full independence of elderly people, we should guarantee the continuity of assistance and accessibility overall their environment. This point is crucial and it should be involved during the establishment of the mobile service provision and the development of mobile services. The dependents environments have to be pervasive and should ensure proposed technical assistance. The mobiles devices must also let user interact with environments. Such environments have different characteristics due to geographical or functional difference. Those characteristics should be taken into account while designing mobile services. The CommunicaME system is a specific solution that aims to facilitate the interaction between the user and the mobile device through the use of NFC technology. Additionally, this project is innovative for its use of wireless NFC technology, which is integrated in the most innovative mobile devices.

CONTACTLESS TECHNOLOGY

There are different contactless or wireless technologies, such as Bluetooth, RFID, ZigBee or NFC, every one of them, incorporates interesting characteristics to offer or facilitate support services to the user. For example, Bluetooth is incorporated in the majority of mobile devices and is used to share information or files within a short range. ZigBee is oriented to the use of domotics.

Table 1. Comparison wireless/contactless standard

	International Standard	Operating Frequency	Maximum Data Rate	Maximum Distance	Power Consumption Rate
Bluetooth 3.0	IEEE 802.15.1	2.4 GHz	22 Mb/s	100 m	hours/days
Bluetooth 2.1	IEEE 802.15.1	2.4 GHz	3 Mb/s	100 m	days
NFC	ISO 14443	13.56 MHz	0.42 Mb/s	10 cm	∞
Wi-Fi B	IEEE 802.11b	2.4 GHz	11 Mb/s	100 m	hours
Wi-Fi G	IEEE 802.11g	2.4 GHz	54 Mb/s	100 m	hours
Wi-Fi N	IEEE 802.11n	5 / 2.4 GHz	144 Mb/s	100 m	hours
ZigBee	IEEE 802.15.4	2.4 GHz	0.25 Mb/s	100-1200 m	months/years

As it could be observed in Table 1, NFC technology is suitable to transfer small amounts data over short distances; the other contactless/wireless communication protocols, such as Wi-Fi or Bluetooth, are suited to transferring large amounts of data over long distances.

NFC has some advantages over other wireless technologies that make this technology very interesting for several projects. Some of these characteristics and advantages are: high usability (you only need a touch to use), user interaction with screen, keyboard, sounds or vibration, relatively safe, anti-collision mechanism available.

CommunicaME incorporates NFC because of its characteristics and relationship with mobile devices.

Near Field Communication (NFC) Technology

NFC[7] (Ahson & Ilyas, 2011) is based on short range wireless communication, which permits bidirectional communication between devices. It normally combines the interface of an intelligent contactless card with a reader within the same device. It was developed and approved by the ISO/IEC 18092 standard in 2003. It is also compatible with other pre-existing technologies that comply with the ISO-14443 standard.

Communication takes place by induction of a magnetic field and operates at a frequency of 13.56 MHz, a band that does not require an administrative license for its use. Its maximum range is approximately 20 centimeters, and its recommended usage is between 4 and 10 centimeters, which limits its use to operations performed at a short distance. Communication between devices takes place when the initiating device sends a signal and the receiving device sends a response. Thus, by the simple act of moving a mobile device close to an object, the mobile will receive information associated with that object.

There are different modes of communication: passive mode and active mode:

- With passive mode the initiator device provides a carrier fields and the target device answers by modulating the existing field. In this mode, the target device may draw its operating power from the initiator-provided electromagnetic field, thus making the target device a transponder.
- With active mode both, initiator and target device, communicate by alternately generating their own fields. A device deactivates its radio frequency field while it is waiting for data. In this mode, both devices typically have power supplies.

Also there are different NFC modes of operation: read/write, peer-to-peer communication, and card emulation:

- Read/write mode; with this mode the NFC phone reads and writes data to any of the supported tag types in a standard NFC data format.
- Peer-to-peer mode allows to two NFC-enabled devices exchange data or transfers data objects, such as business cards, digital photos, set up parameters to initiate a Bluetooth communication or to configure a Wi-Fi link.
- Card emulation mode turns, a NFC-enabled phone into a tag or into a contactless card or a into smartcard, it could just emulate a credit card to support paying or a transportations system access card. Each of these modes enables this innovative technology to be applied to different fields.

The CommunicaME system uses the read/write operating mode, whereby the mobile becomes a contactless reader/writer capable of reading/writing different types of contactless cards.

A NFC-enabled phone has 3 main components:

- **NFC Antenna:** NFC radio communications requires an antenna that allows communication and generates an electronic field used to transmit data.
- **Chip NFC or Controller NFC:** This component consists of an NFC hardware controller interface and an NFC modem. This component is the interface for all of these elements: the processor of applications, the phone, the antenna and the secure element.
- **Secure Element:** This is a component which is also used in smart cards. It consists of hardware and a smart card operating system. It is capable of storing and running multiple small applications known as applets; in this element also is possible store data and applications with high requirements security. Not all phones have available a secure element.

NDEF (NFC Data Exchange Format) messages are used to exchange information between NFC devices or between a NFC device and a tag. These NDEF messages define the way to encapsulate the information to be transmitted. It is possible to encapsulate one or more payloads of various sizes and types in a single NDEF message; this is achieved by means of NDEF records.

NFC PHONES AND TECHNOLOGIES OF DEVELOPMENT

There are several NFC-enabled handsets, and they are of different manufactures and they have different operating systems, such as Android, Bada, Symbian and others. Operating systems and technologies that support NFC-enabled devices are exposed above.

CommunicaME has been developed with Android and tested with Google Nexus S phones.

Java Me Technology

Java Platform Micro Edition (J2ME), or Java ME, is a Java platform designed for embedded systems, such as mobile devices. Some "features phones" support JavaMe or J2Me. In order to work and to develop application under JavaMe and interact with NFC technology is used the Contactless Communication API. The specification of this API is led by Nokia and defined under the Java Community Process as JSR-257. JSR-257 defines a set of APIs for proximity, contactless-based communication.

This API allows you to discover and exchange data with contactless targets such as NDEF tags, RFID tags, and external smartcards and provides support for visual tags.

Android Technology

Android is a Linux-based operating system that was originally intended for mobile terminals, although at present its use has expanded to include notebooks, tablets, PCs, etc. Its initial launch was towards the end of 2008. Despite its relatively short life, it is one of the most advanced systems used, and probably with the greatest future. In the United States, it is the leading operating systems in smartphone, with a market share of almost 50%[8]. In Spain, 39.2% of mobile terminals are Smartphone, of which 9% are Android[9].

Since the launch of Android 2.3 (Gingerbread) in February 2011, Android has supported NFC technology. The only operating modes currently available for Android are NFC read/write and peer-to-peer; the card emulation mode is not available. The Android devices that support NFC are Google Nexus S, Samsung galaxy SII and Sky Vega racer (available only in Korea).

Symbian Technology

Symbian is a mobile operating system and computing platform designed by Nokia Smartphone. Symbian OS is the predecessor to Symbian Platform and Nokia Series 60; the latest version, Symbian^3, was officially released towards the end of 2010, first used in the Nokia N8. In May 2011 an update, Symbian Anna, was officially announced, followed by Nokia Belle (previously Symbian Belle) in August 2011.

There are 3 options to develop applications based on NFC under Symbian devices: using APIs provided in Qt Mobility Connectivity, JavaMe or native Symbian C++. Between these options, using Qt is the recommended approach because it's the core development framework for Symbian; also the development of applications is easy and flexible. This API provides operations for interacting with tags and devices, including target detection and target loss, registering NDEF message handlers, reading and writing NDEF messages, etc. The JavaMe option is recommended for application development for S40 devices. And finally with the Symbian native C++, the developer has a low level control, so the developer is required to have an exhaustive platform knowledge.

Some Nokia terminals that support NFC are C7, 700, 701, or 603.

Bada Technology

Bada is a Smartphone platform which is created for wide range of device, unveiled in 2010. It was developed by Samsung Electronics. Samsung Bada is an user-interactive and service-oriented Smartphone that allows you to create feature-rich applications for bada devices using C++, flash and Web programming.

Samsung has launched a SDK for Bada 2.0. This is the new version of its mobile phone operating system which now includes support for NFC tag reading and writing and also it supports different events like tag discovery, message discovery, etc.

Some devices with Bada OS with NFC are Samsung Wave 578 and Samsung Wave 725.

BlackBerry Technology

BlackBerry OS is a proprietary mobile operating system developed by RIM (Research in Motion) for Smartphone and handheld devices. The operating system provides multitasking and supports specialized input devices that have been adopted by RIM for use in its handhelds.

Some BlackBerry NFC-enabled devices are BlackBerry Bold 9900 and 9930 and BlackBerry Curve 9350, 9360 and 9370. These Smartphones support reading/writting tags and card emulation mode, but they don't support peer-to-peer communication.

iPhone: Apple Technology

Iphone does not support NFC but there are two NFC/RFID reader and payment adaptors for iphone. iCarte 110 and iCarte 420. iCarte 420 is suitable for iPhone 4 and iCarte 110 is suitable for iPhone 3G, 3GS.

iCarte is an Iphone accessory attaching to the botton connector of the iPhone; this accessory turns the iPhone an NFC phone and an RFID Reader/Writer. The iCarte also contains an embedded secure element which can be configured as a debit, credit, pre-paid or loyalty card, turning the iPhone into an electronic wallet. The secure element has a NXP MiFare classic 1k tag and it is compliant with JCOPS OS.

Tag Types as Defined in the NFC Forum

The NFC Forum is a non-profit industry association that promotes the use of NFC. This association proposes and publishes the protocol specifications, among which are the specifications for the tag types supported by NFC terminals.

A NFC mobile telephone can normally read and/or rewrite 4 tag types defined by the NFC Forum; each card contains characteristics that determine how appropriate it will be with regards to the different types of services needed.

Tags are integrated circuits that store data that can be read by NFC-enabled devices to support these applications. By standardizing the tag types and formats with the specifications announced today, the NFC Forum is promoting interoperability across the NFC market, enabling low-cost volume production, and clearing a path to a global, cost-effective mass market. More than one billion NFC-ready tags are already deployed worldwide for use in areas such as accessing public transportation, hotel rooms, and offices.

By publishing these four tag types, the NFC Forum is taking great strides towards putting the power of NFC in the hands of consumers around the world. Building on existing technology, the Forum's tags are based on the International Organization for Standardization (ISO) 14443 Type A and B standards and Sony's FeliCa. The four tag types are all based on existing contactless products and are available commercially.

The NFC Forum has mandated that the four tag types be operable with NFC devices. This mandate is the backbone of interoperability between NFC tag providers and NFC device manufacturers to ensure a uniform user experience.

The tag specifications are the most recent in a series of specifications being developed by the NFC Forum. The operation specifications for the NFC Forum tag types, as shown in Table 2, providing the technical information required to implement the reader/writer and associated control functionality of the NFC device, enabling interaction with the tags. The four tag type specifications are:

- **NFC Forum Type 1 Tag Operation Specification:** Type 1 tag is based on ISO14443A. Tags are read and re-write capable; users can configure the tag to become read-only. Memory availability is 96 bytes and expandable to 2 kbyte; communication speed is 106 kbit/s.
- **NFC Forum Type 2 Tag Operation Specification:** Type 2 tag is based on ISO14443A. Tags are read and re-write capable; users can configure the tag to become read-only. Memory availability is 48 bytes and expandable to 2 kbyte; communication speed is 106 kbit/s.
- **NFC Forum Type 3 Tag Operation Specification:** Type 3 tag is based on the Japanese Industrial Standard (JIS) X 6319-4, also known as FeliCa. Tags are pre-configured at manufacture to be either read and re-writable, or read-only. Memory availability is variable, theoretical memory limit is 1MByte per service; communication speed is 212 kbit/s or 424 kbit/s.
- **NFC Forum Type 4 Tag Operation Specification:** Type 4 tag is fully compatible with ISO14443A and B standards. Tags are pre-configured at manufacture to be either read and re-writable, or read-only. Memory

availability is variable, up to 32 KBytes per service; communication speed is up to 424 kbit/s.

As it is shown in Table 2, memory availability for each tag type ranges between 48 bytes and 1Mbyte. They also have different transmission speeds and operate at different radiofrequencies. However, the user cannot read and rewrite with all types; applications that need to write information can only use tag types 1 and 2, which are the only ones that the user can reconfigure.

As the CommunicaME system needs to personalize tags for each contact and each type of action, tag types 1 and 2 were used.

RIFD Technology

RFID or Radio Frequency Identification (Finkenzeller, 2010) is a technology that uses radio waves as a mode of communication to exchange data between the reader and the RFID tag. During the World War II it is used as an espionage tool, it underwent development to become an Identification tool. After significant improvements in micro technology, miniature RFID tags are used widely today in consumer markets to identify items. RFIDs have found widespread use in today's world, they are expected to be used in many domains including transportation, logistics, mobile transactions, and medicine and emergency services.

Table 2. NFC tag types

	Type 1	Type 2	Type 3	Type 4
Read/ Rewrite capability	Yes	Yes	Preconfigured at manufacture	Preconfigured at manufacture
Speed	106 kbits/s	106 kbits/s	212 Kbits/s	106-424 Kbtis/s
Memory	96 Bytes – 2Kbytes	48 Bytes- 2 KBytes	< =1MB	32KBytes
Radiofrequency	ISO-14443 type A	ISO-14443 tipo A	Felica ISO 18092	ISO-14443 type A y B

RFID tags also have the advantage of being read from quite a distance, unlike bar codes, which needs to be shown to the reader. Multiple RFID tags can also be read simultaneously thus allowing parallel processing. These characteristics can be used to prevent theft or shoplifting using an alarm that goes off once a specific RFID (Radio Frecuency Identification) embedded product moves out of range. RFID typically have two parts: an integrated circuit for processing and storing information and an antenna for sending and receiving signals. Another source of resistance to the adoption of RFID by many organizations stems from, ongoing privacy concerns. One concern is that RFID tags can be scanned even after they exit the supply chain, and without anyone's knowledge. Anyone with an RFID scanner can conceivably access data encoded on an RFID tag.

In an increasingly fragmented, regulated, and uncertain world, RFID technology gives businesses, governments, and consumers a safe, private, and unobtrusive way to keep track of it all. Consumer's benefit from shorter lines at checkout counters, in hospitals, libraries, and gas stations because RFID fast tracks them to the front of the queue. The can also benefit from lower prices because of the efficiencies RFID brings to the supply chain. Business and institutions are turning to RFID technology as they comply with government product-tracking regulations, seeking to limit theft, reduce out-of-stock losses, strengthen brand loyalty, and make interaction with customers a more positive experience.

MiFare Technology

MiFare is owned by NXP Semiconductors and is the most widely used contactless intelligent card. It is compatible with the ISO 14443 Type A standard and operates at 13.56 MgHz, which makes it compatible with NFC. The distance for reading/writing is approximately 10 centimeters. It contains basic and simple control mechanisms, is very reliable and low cost. There are different types: classic, mini, ultralight, etc.

Given these characteristics, these both tags types, MiFare and RFID, are well suited for the CommunicaME system.

SPEECH SYNTHESIS AND RECOGNITION IN ACCESSIBLE SYSTEMS

Power and resources of computer technology have increased highly, so building natural-sounding synthetic voices has progressed from a knowledge-based approach to a data-based one. Rather than manually crafting each phonetic unit and its applicable contexts, high-quality synthetic voices may be built from sufficiently diverse single-speaker databases of natural speech. However, although certainly successful, there is always the issue of spurious errors. When a required sentence happens to need phonetic and prosodic contexts that are under-represented in a database, the quality of the synthesizer can be severely degraded. Even though this may be a rare event, a single bad join in an utterance can ruin the listeners' flow. It is not possible to guarantee that bad joins and/or inappropriate units will not occur, simply because of the vast number of possible combinations that could occur. However, it is often possible to almost always avoid these for particular applications. A speech synthesizer can be organized in two parts: front-end, which is in charge of receiving text and producing a phonetic linguistic representation; and back-end, which takes that representation and produces a synthesized wave that, is converted into sound. The low level speech synthesis in Android is achieved with TextToSpeech (TTS) API[10]. The TTS engine that ships with the Android platform supports a number of languages: English, French, German, Italian and Spanish. Also, depending on which side of the Atlantic you are on, American and British accents for English are both supported. The TTS engine needs to know which language to speak. The same word is pronounced differently in German and Italian. So the voice and dictionary are language-specific resources that need to be loaded before the engine can start to speak. Although all Android-powered devices that support the TTS functionality ship with the engine, some devices have limited storage and may lack the language-specific resource files. If a user wants to install those resources, the TTS API enables an application to query the platform for the availability of language files and can initiate their download and installation.

Voice recognition is a part of artificial intelligence; its objective is to achieve spoken communication between people and electronic devices. This type of system processes a voice signal and uses different techniques from different fields (physiology, acoustics, signal processing, and computation) to recognize the information contained in the voice signal and either transform it into text or identify orders or commands that the system must perform. Android supports voice recognition with the speech recognizer API[11].

Speech synthesis and voice recognition allow the systems in general and the mobile terminals in particular to be more accessible to persons with difficulties in accessing the screen text (Yang, Lim, King, & Helal, 2006). Even the blind or visually impaired use these techniques systematically, not only to read information, but to know where they are on the screen and to navigate through the computer.

The CommunicaME system uses both techniques to ensure that the system is more accessible by allowing the user to interact by voice to gather information as well as to send command information.

Figure 1. Flowchart

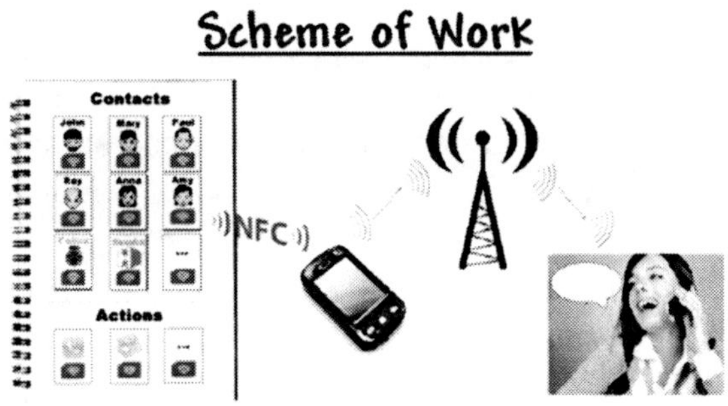

The CommunicaME System

CommunicaME is a system that facilitates and makes communication accessible to elderly in dependent environment. Using a NFC mobile telephone and tags that identify both people and actions, the user need only move the mobile close to the tag that represents the person or corresponding action.

The flowchart is represented in Figure 1. It includes a panel that displays a graphical representation of the list of contacts in a mobile telephone and the actions that can be performed. The contacts are displayed as photos and the actions as an image with which the user can very easily identify an action to be performed. Each of the objects (photo and image) are then associated with a NFC or MiFare or RFIF tag containing the contact information or the action to be performed. The user must have a mobile telephone with NFC technology in order to read the tags.

This system is composed of two applications: CommunicaME and CommunicaME Writer. With CommunicaME Writer, the panel is configured with the contacts and the actions by writing the information onto the contactless tags. This module is used by persons who do not have any problems using and handling mobile telephones.

In order to write the action (Figure 2), the user need only select the action and move the mobile close to the tag they want to record. To write a contact, the user can either select the list of contacts or input the telephone number of the contact. Once this is done, the user simply moves the mobile close to the tag that represents that contact.

CommunicaME is the application used by seniors to communicate in a way that is simply, easy and intuitive.

To place a call (Figure 3), the user performs the following steps:

1. The user selects the person to call by moving the mobile to the photo of that person.

Figure 2. Process to write a tag

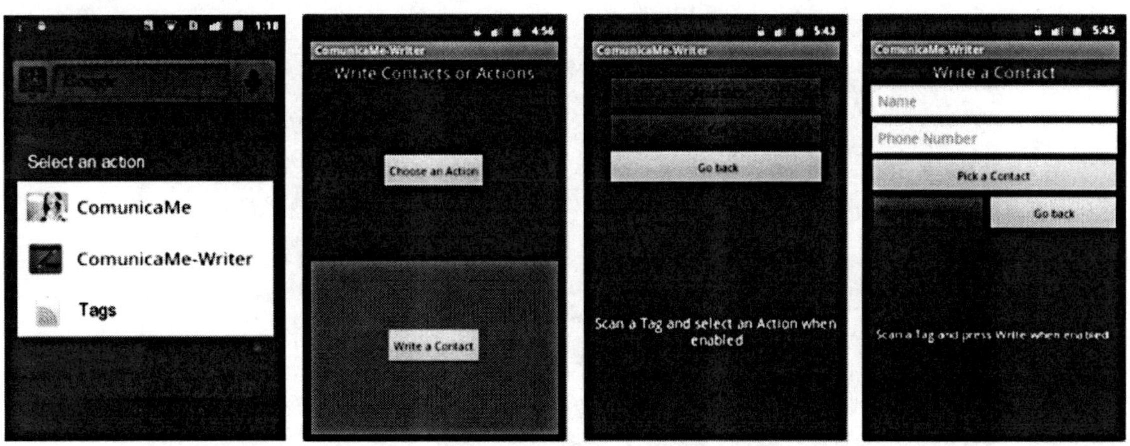

Figure 3. Making a call

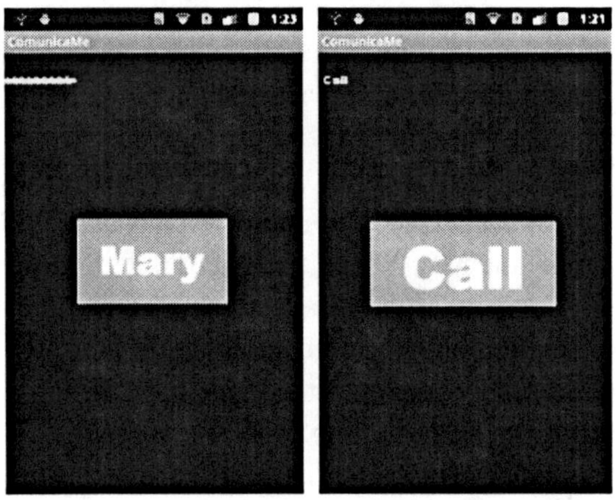

2. The mobile telephone uses NFC to read the NFC tag and obtain the telephone number of contact information for the person to be called.
3. The user selects the *call* action by moving the mobile close to the image that represents the action of calling.
4. The telephone uses the information to establish communication with the telephone number retrieved in step 2.

The user can send a short message (Figure 4) by following these steps:

1. The user selects the person to receive the message by moving the mobile phone near the photograph of that person.
2. The mobile telephone uses NFC to read the NFC tag and obtain the telephone number of the contact information for the person to receive the message.
3. The user selects the "send message" action by moving the mobile near the image that represents the action of sending a short message.
4. The telephone uses the speech recognizer to request the message to be sent.
5. The user speaks to transmit the message to be sent.
6. The telephone uses the speech recognizer to transcribe the voice message to text.
7. The telephone uses the mobile telephone line to send the text message to the number retrieved in step 2.

The primary innovation of the CommunicaME systems is in the combination of NFC mobile technology, MiFare/RFID technology and the connection between mobile devices and mobile communication networks. The combination of these technologies and means of communication ensure that mobile communication is simple and

Figure 4. Sending a SMS

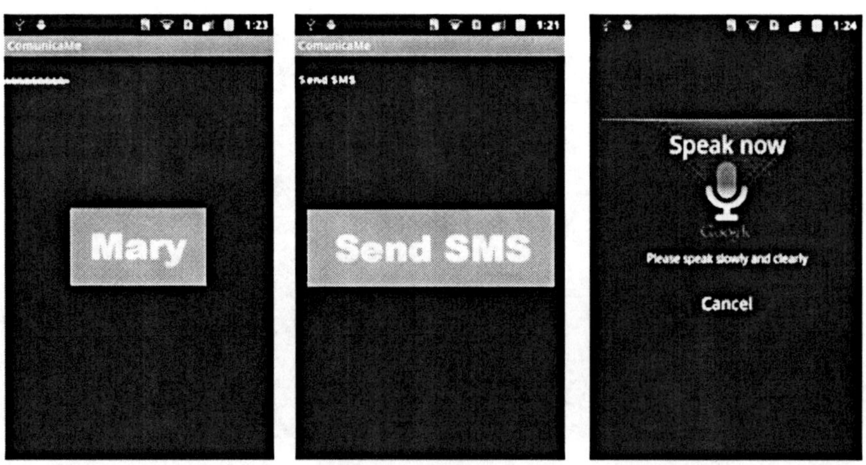

easy for seniors. Additionally, it does not require a complex technical infrastructure, and the development is simple. Because NFC technology is free, easy and secure, routine tasks can be carried out very easily by individuals of certain sectors of the population such as the elderly, who are normally quite reluctant to use new technologies.

Evaluation

In order to demonstrate the usability of the CommunicaME system, we developed a study involving 50 seniors of various ages. They were each provided with a panel as shown in Figure 1, which includes the tags that were correctly written with the photos of each person's contacts and the images for each action.

The following user variables were evaluated prior to the user having any knowledge or use of the application:

1. Previous experience of the user with mobile terminals. Rated on a scale of 0-10 with 0 being no experience and 10 much experience.
2. Frequency with which the user uses a mobile telephone. Rated according to the number of times per week.
3. Age of the user.
4. Does the user live alone? The answers have a value of either yes or no.
5. Does the user utilize other tele-assistance mechanisms? Which? The answers have a value of either yes or no. In the case of an affirmative answer, the mechanisms are identified.

The user first indicates previous experience with the CommunicaME system and then uses the system with the correctly configured panel of contacts. To evaluate the efficiency of the system, the following application variables were evaluated:

1. The user's rating of the system.
2. Rating the use of the call.
3. Rating the use of SMS messages sent by speech recognition.
4. Have you used the CommunicaME system?
5. Do you think the CommunicaME system has helped you in performing daily tasks with your mobile telephone?

The responses were ranked on a scale of 0-10, with 0 being the lowest score and 10 the highest.

Taking into account the previous experience of the user with mobile terminals variable; the users without or with little experience rate the system higher; little or no experience of the elderly with mobile terminals usually is caused mobile phones aren't designed to easy access for this group. These persons think that with this new system they can overcome the barriers that complicate and impede the use of mobile phone. Also they say that with CommunicaME system they use this technology further because it is easy and intuitive. Also they find the panel with frequent numbers very interesting because they usually communicate with the same people. The elderly with more experience rate the system much higher than those without or little experience; they find the system very useful because they think it is very agile and easier that search for contacts in the phonebook or type numbers and/or text messages.

The elderly without experience appreciates the call service, being the SMS service rate worst for them; this group think that the SMS is not useful. However, the experienced elderly using mobile phone make a rate positively of mobile services, call, and SMS. The SMS by speech recognition it is very useful because for them type a message with a touch-screen or a qwerty is a difficult and tedious task. About the questions if "they would use the system "or "the system would help them in performing daily task", there are no differences from those experienced and no experienced; all elderly think that the CommunicaME system is a great idea, and they use it every day.

About the frequency with which the user uses a mobile telephone variable, it is important to note that this variable is closely related to previous experience of the user with mobile terminals variable. It was observed during the system evaluation involves the disparity among the data gathered: on the one hand, there are persons with experience in using mobile devices who use them frequently, on the other hand are those with little experience who use the mobile devices sporadically. As observed in Figure 5, the application is ranked higher by those with more experience using a mobile phone, while those with less experience using mobile technology, although they believe that it is a good idea, and rate it lower. All users, however, are convinced that the CommunicaME system facilitates the daily tasks with the use of a mobile phone. A significant finding is that the SMS is not highly valued by users with little experience with mobile technologies.

After evaluating the system, we could appreciate the distinction between older (older than 75 years) and younger (between 65 and 74 years) seniors. Figure 6 shows that the younger seniors rate the application higher and use the system more than their older counterparts. We can also see that the automatic call service is ranked higher than the SMS service by the users.

In addition to these evaluations and about the user live alone variable, it is important note that only the 32% of respondents live alone. We were also able to note during the study that 95% of individuals living alone use the CommunicaME system and they highly appreciate it, being the call more appreciated; they claim that the panel should include as contact the emergency number or 112. By other hand, they claim that with CommunicaME system they are safer because make a call to a close relative or emergency number is very quickly and easy. The rest of elderly who live accompanied say that is a good idea but they do not believe it is as necessary as those that live alone.

Figure 5. Results based on experience/use

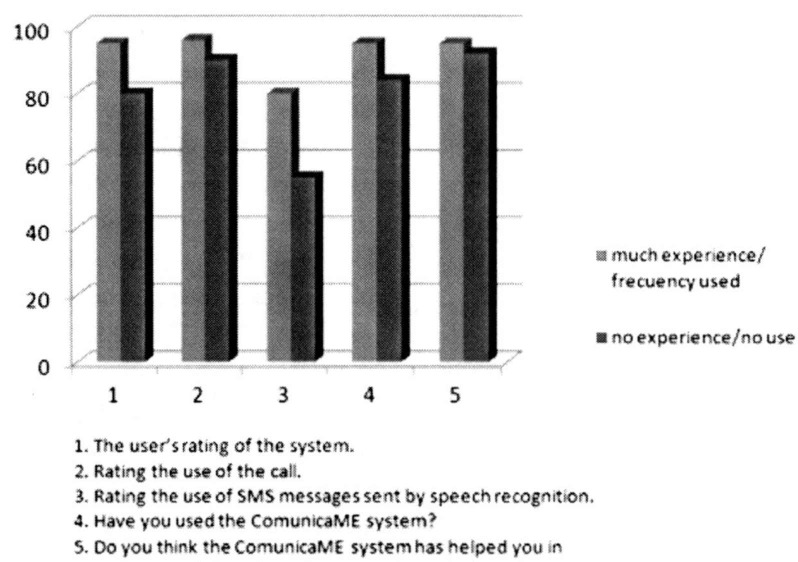

Figure 6. Results based on/considering age

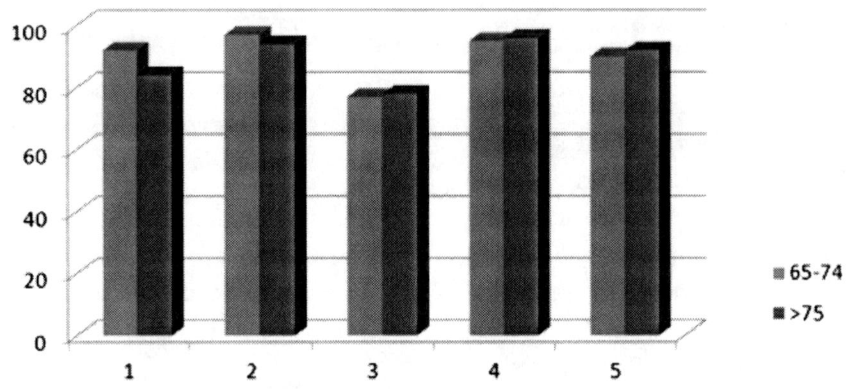

1. The user's rating of the system.
2. Rating the use of the call.
3. Rating the use of SMS messages sent by speech recognition.
4. Have you used the ComunicaME system?
5. Do you think the ComunicaME system has helped you in performing daily tasks with your mobile telephone?

For all seniors, only two of them utilize other tele-assistance mechanisms. One of this people has a phone that when he picks up it, the phone makes a call to specific person. The other person has a device that he can operate at any time and just in this moment the device makes a call to emergency service. These two elderly think that CommunicaME is also easy to use and with only one system can make calls to different numbers such as relatives or emergency or doctor.

After the study was concluded, we noted that, in general terms, in 90% of the cases, the users believe that the CommunicaME system is a good idea and that its use helps them to perform daily tasks.

The results of this study demonstrate the feasibility of the integration of the mobile services into CommunicaME. These results show that the performance of mobile services can simplify the daily tasks. This way, the integration of new mobile services enhances the ComunicaME system. The ComunicaME system has the possibility of working with Wireless communication Networks to perform an improved context-aware environment. Furthermore, the context of the environment and users can interact with other existing software in a transparent way.

CONCLUSION AND FUTURE WORK

Mobile technology is particularly promising as support tools for that improve quality of life. Tags and communication devices facilitate the process of sending and receiving information in a ubiquitous and non-intrusive manner. The ComunicaME system presented in this paper proposes an innovative technological solution consisting of an environment based on the use of NFC mobile devices and NFC tags. This system facilitates the use of mobile telephones and mobile communication networks, creating a more user-friendly experience. This project is oriented primarily to the elderly in dependent environments, but it may be used by any type of user.

The results obtained in the experiments are promising, but need to be improved using a more extensive dataset and evaluating the approach in real scenarios.

However, the system presents some disadvantages on distributing the majority of the systems' functionalities into remote and local services and applications. Our future work focuses on testing the system in different environments and looking for feedback to adjust and improve the proposed solution. Moreover, we will focus on distributing services and applications able to be invoked by the system acting as controllers and coordinators. That is our next challenge.

REFERENCES

Abascal, J., & Civit, A. (2000). Mobile communication for older people: New oportunities for autonomous life. In *Proceedings of the Worshop on Universal Accessibility of Ubiquitous Computind: Providing for the Elderly* (pp. 255-268). Firenze, Italy: European Research Consortium for Informatics and Matematics.

Ahson, S. A., & Ilyas, M. (2011). *Near field communications handbook*. Boca Raton, FL: CRC Press. doi:10.1201/b11226.

Al Mahmud, A., Mubin, O., Shaid, S., & Martens, J.-B. (2008). Desigining and evaluating the tabletop game experience for seniors citizens. In *Proceedings of the 5th Nordic Conference on Human-Computer Interaction: Building Bridges*. ACM.

Been-Lirn Duh, H., Yi-Luen Do, E., Billinghurst, M., Quek, F., & Chen Hsueh-Hua, V. (2010). Senior-friendly technologies: Interaction design for seniors users. In *Proceedings of CHI*. Atlanta, GA: ACM.

Comisión de Mercado de las Telecomunicaciones. (2010). Retrieved from http://informeanual.cmt.es/informe-sector/comunicaciones-moviles

del Arco Carabias, J., & San Segundo Encinar, J. M. (2010). *Los mayores ante las TIC: Accesibilidad y accesiquibilidad*. Fundacion Vodafone España.

Finkenzeller, K. (2010). *RFID handbook: Fundamentals and applications in contactless smart cards, radio frecuency identificacion and NFC*. New York: Wiley. doi:10.1002/9780470665121.

García Ponce, F. J. (2007). *Accesibilidad, TIC y educación. CNICE*. Centro Nacional de Información y Comunicación Educativa. Ministerio de Educación y Ciencia.

Ghorbel, M., & Mokhtari, M. (2005). Toward an assistive indoor/outdoor living environment for people with disabilities. [Boca Raton, FL: IOS Press.]. *Proceedings of ICOST*, *05*, 237–244.

Hix, B. (2011). Seniors, mobile communication, and health care. Boca Raton, FL: 3CInteractive, LLC.

Huber, J. T., Walsh, T. J., & Varman, B. (2005). Camp for all connection: A community health information outreach project. *Journal of the Medical Library Association*, *93*(3), 348–352. PMID:16059424.

INE. (2010). *Encuesta de Tecnologías de la Información en los hogares 2010*. Retrieved from www.ine.es

Keating, E., Nagai, E., Hadder, N., & Kowalsky, J. (2007). *The role of the mobile phone in the welfare of aged and disabled people*. Austin, TX: University of Texas / NTT DoCoMo, Inc..

Kurniawan, S. (2007). mobile phone design for older persons. *Design for Seniors: Innovations for Graying Tmes*, *14*(4), 24–25.

Lindholm, C., & Keinonen, T. (2003). *Mobile usability: How Nokia changed the FACE of the mobile phone*. New York: McGraw Hill.

Mena Tobar, L., Latorre Andrés, P., & Lafuente Lapena, E. (2009). WebA mobile (web analysis mobile), assistance tool for the design and evaluation of website for mobile devices. In *New Trends on Human-Computer Interaction. Research, Development, New Tools and Methods*. London: Springer. doi:10.1007/978-1-84882-352-5_13.

Mobile Web Best Practices Working Group. (n.d.). Retrieved from http://www.w3.org/2005/MWI/BPWG/

MobileOk Checker. (n.d.). Retrieved from http://www.w3.org/2005/MWI/BPWG/Group/TaskForces/Checker/

Pavon, F., & Casanova, J. (2006). Telefonía móvil y personas mayores: La accesibilidad como derecho. *Latinoamericana de Tecnología Educativa*, *5*(2), 385–395.

Roebuck, K. (2011). *Near field communication (NFC), hight-impact strategies - What you need to know: Definition, adoptions, impact, benefits, maturity, vendors*. Emereo Pty Limited.

Thompson, L., & Cupples, J. (2008). Seen and not heard? Text messagind and digital sociality. *Social & Cultural Geography*, *9*(1), 95–108. doi:10.1080/14649360701789634.

Yang, H., Lim, S., King, J., & Helal, A. (2006). Open issues in nomadic pervasive computing. In *Proceedings of UbiSys'06 (LNCS)*. Berlin: Springer.

Yelmo García, J. C., San Miguel González, B., & Martín García, Y. S. (2007). *Análisis del potencial de las comunicaciones móviles para la mejora de los servicios proporcionados por la administración pública a las personas con discapacidad*. Retrieved from http://www.tecnimap.es

KEY TERMS AND DEFINITIONS

Accessibility: Applied to the use of objects and technologies, and especially in relation to certain groups of people with functional difficulties, it means the benefits of interaction with the environment or other people. Accessibility enables people to participate in social activities for which designed the built environment.

Contactless Technology: Contactless technologies or short-range technologies, reach up to 10 cm, and are bidirectional transmission. A clear example of what these technologies are the contactless smartcards, or cards intelligent and Near Field Communication (NFC).

Dependent Environment: A dependent is one who can not fend for themselves and need assistance. These people need to interact with a dependent environment adapted to their needs.

MiFARE: MIFARE is a technology contactless smart card. Typical reading distance is 10 cm. The reading distance depends on the reader module power, and there are readers of higher and lower range. MIFARE is the property of NXP Semiconductors.

Mobile Communication: We understand by mobile communication as the use of technology that allows us to communicate with others in different locations without the use of cables. Mobile communication makes our life easier, saves time and effort.

Mobile Services: They are the services associated with mobile technology. Mobile services allow you to have more features and greater interactivity between people.

NFC (Near Field Communication): Is a protocol based on a wireless interface. Communication takes place between two entities. The protocol establishes a wireless connection between network applications and electronic devices. It works in the band of 13.56 MHz, this causes no restriction does not apply and does not require any license for use. In this protocol there is always one that initiates the conversation and it is this that will monitor the same, this role is interchangeable between the two parties involved.

RFID: The technology of Radio Frequency IDentification (RFID) refers to the use of radio frequency through a reader to detect and read information from a device commonly known as RF Tag or also known as "tag." Unlike bar codes, RFID does not require a direct field of view between the RF tag and reader.

ENDNOTES

1 http://www.age-platform.org/

2 http://www.planavanza.es/Paginas/Inicio.aspx

3 http://www.mifare.net/products/mifare-smartcard-ic-s/

4 www.w3c.es

5 http://www.inredis.es

6 http://java.sun.com/developer/technica-lArticles/javame/nfc_bluetooth/

7 http://www.nfc-forum.org/home/

8 http://www.comscore.com/Press_Events/Press_Releases/2011/8/comScore_Reports_July_2011_U.S._Mobile_Subscriber_Market_Share

9 http://blog.nielsen.com/nielsenwire/global/nearly-40-of-mobile-spaniards-now-sport-smartphones/

10 http://developer.android.com/resources/articles/tts.html

11 http://developer.android.com/reference/android/speech/package-summary.htm

Section 2
Impact on Organizations, Society, and Individuals

Chapter 6
The Impact of Enterprise 2.0 Principles on Business Processes:
Emphasizing Human Decisions

Giorgio Bruno
Politecnico di Torino, Italy

ABSTRACT

The impact of Enterprise 2.0 principles on business processes is a hot research topic and involves several aspects. In particular, this chapter addresses knowledge-intensive processes in which participants are not considered as mere resources needed to carry out tasks that are not automatable, but their involvement is required at a higher level where they can take decisions that affect the control flow of the process. Participants must be given as much information as possible on the decisions they have to take and on the business entities to be acted on and produced by the tasks they have to perform. For this reason, this chapter proposes a business process notation that integrates the data flow and the control flow and focuses on three kinds of decisions, referred to as data selection, task selection, and performer selection. It also illustrates the structure of to-do lists, which are the major interface between the participants and their tasks.

INTRODUCTION

During the past few years, organizations have taken important steps to make their business practices explicit and shared through the adoption of the business process technology (Davenport & Short, 1990). However, most of the attention was devoted to processes aimed at repetitive, standardized work and the point of view adopted is that of a central coordinator who orchestrates the work among the various participants involved, which may be persons (referred to as participants) playing

DOI: 10.4018/978-1-4666-4373-4.ch006

specific roles or automated services. Participants receive work assignments through to-do lists; by clicking on the entries of their to-do lists, they can perform the corresponding tasks, usually by means of graphical user interfaces. When a task has been completed, a notification is sent to the process engine, which goes on with the next step in the process description. Process descriptions contain sufficient information for the engine to be able to decide which task to activate next. Although participants may exert influence on such decisions, they do so within the tasks assigned to them; they are not able to autonomously decide what has to be done next.

The impact of Enterprise 2.0 principles (Carbone, Contreras & Hernández, 2010) on business processes is a hot research topic and involves several aspects. In particular, this chapter addresses knowledge-intensive processes (Marjanovic & Freeze, 2011), in which participants are not considered as mere resources needed to carry out tasks that are not automatable; instead, their involvement is required at a higher level where they can take decisions that affect the control flow of the process.

In the domain of Process-Aware Information Systems (Dumas, van der Aalst & ter Hofstede, 2005), participants, by taking decisions and performing tasks, are meant to act on the business entities residing in the underlying information system. The data flow is then essential to give the readers of process models clear indications on which entities the tasks are performed and the decisions are taken. Participants' decisions affect the control flow of the process, but, in their turn, they are affected by the entities to be acted on. A stronger integration between the control flow and the data flow is then needed, and, to this end, a clear distinction must be made between intrinsic decisions and extrinsic ones.

Intrinsic decisions are limited in scope as they affect the entities involved in the execution of tasks; an example is the evaluation of a conference paper. In this case, the decision may simply amount to selecting a score in a given range, but nevertheless, it may be a difficult one. Extrinsic decisions are broader in scope; they are needed when: a) there are several tasks that can be performed with the same data and a choice has to be made, b) when it is up to the performer to select the input data from among those available before working with them, or c) when the performers of subsequent tasks are decided by the performers of previous tasks. These three kinds of extrinsic decisions are referred to as task selection, (input) data selection, and performer selection, respectively.

To show how such decisions can be represented in process models, this paper introduces a notation, called Chant, in which the control flow and the data flow are integrated. As to its graphical representation, Chant draws on Petri nets (Murata, 1989) and hence it is made up of places and transitions connected by oriented arcs. Transitions represent tasks and places represent run-time entities called events: events point to business entities.

This chapter is organized as follows. Section 2 presents background information on flexible business processes, on the complementarity of activity-centric models and information-centric ones, and on the role of to-do lists. Section 3 describes the Chant notation with the help of an example. Section 4 illustrates the basic data-flow rules that establish the input and output requirements for the tasks. Section 5 addresses decisions and the grouping of tasks implied by decisions. Section 6 deal with the organization of to-do lists, which are the major interface between the participants and their tasks. Section 7 presents the final considerations.

BACKGROUND

Processes aimed at repetitive, standardized work received great attention in past research and efficient solutions based on the notion of orchestration have been proposed (Weske, 2007). Orchestration is the distribution of work among the various participants involved, which may be persons playing specific roles or automated services; in this chapter, term participant will be used to indicate a person having a part in the process. The work distribution is carried out by a process engine which interprets detailed process descriptions. Participants receive work assignments through to-do lists; by clicking on the entries of their to-do lists, they can perform the corresponding tasks, usually by means of graphical user interfaces. When a task has been completed, a notification is sent to the process engine, which goes on with the next step in the process description. Process descriptions contain sufficient information for the engine to be able to decide which task to activate next. Although participants may exert influence on such decisions, they do so within the tasks assigned to them; they are not able to autonomously decide what has to be done next. This approach does not imply that their work is not a knowledge-intensive one; the task of reviewing a conference paper requires specific skills and experience, but these abilities operate at a local level.

In current research, growing attention is dedicated to situations calling for creativity and adaptation to specific circumstances (Alvesson, 2004). Participants are not considered as mere resources needed to carry out tasks that are not automatable, but their involvement is required at a higher level where they can take decisions that affect the control flow. Enhancing flexibility in the control flow is a hot issue and several approaches have been proposed (Nurcan, 2008). A first step in this direction is the notion of ad hoc sub-process, which, in Business Process Model and Notation, or BPMN, (OMG-BPMN, 2011), is a group of tasks to be carried out in any number and order as decided by their performers. This solution may be too flexible, and therefore it needs to be balanced by the introduction of constraints. Late modeling is adopted in the Business Process Constraint Network, or BPCN, approach (Lu, Sadiq & Governatori, 2009): when the process engine assigns an ad hoc sub-process to a certain performer, they have first to produce an actual sequence of steps conforming to the constraints, and then the process engine will proceed. In the Declare approach (van der Aalst, Pesic & Schonenberg, 2009), there is no need to define a complete variant in advance, but any task of the ad hoc sub-process can be performed as long as the mandatory constraints are not violated.

Growing attention is being dedicated to leveraging the complementary aspects of business processes and information systems (consisting of interrelated business entities).

In the case-handling approach (van der Aalst, Weske & Grünbauer, 2005) a process is meant to take care of a specific entity (for example, an insurance claim), called the process case: the process evolution depends on the state of the case and not only on the tasks performed (Künzle & Reichert, 2009).

Recent work addresses the relationships between activity-centric models and information-centric ones. The latter (also called artifact-centric models) focus on the life cycle of the entities involved and on the synchronizations caused by the common tasks (Hull, 2008). The two kinds of models are substantially equivalent: an algorithm generating an information-centric model from an activity-centric one was presented by Kumaran, Liu and Wu (2008), while the opposite transformation was addressed by Küster, Ryndina, and Gall (2007). Since artifacts may be handled by participants playing different roles, it is important to take into account the different perspectives they may have on the same entities (Yongchareon & Liu, 2010).

To-do lists are widely used to organize personal work (Riss, Rickayzen, Maus & van der Aalst, 2005): they are fed by tasks generated by their owners (Bellotti et al., 2004) and may also include tasks automatically produced from emails (Grebner & Riss, 2008). Through task delegation, the members of a team can assign tasks of their to-do lists to each other, and this allows informal collaborative processes to take place (Stoitsev, Scheidl & Spahn, 2007).

OVERVIEW OF CHANT

Chant takes its place in the domain of Process-Aware Information Systems (Dumas, van der Aalst & ter Hofstede, 2005): participants, by taking decisions and performing tasks, are meant to operate on the business entities residing in the underlying information system. By means of suitable graphical user interfaces, they can generate new business entities, retrieve, modify, and delete existing ones, as well as establish or remove associations between entities.

Chant purpose is to give participants as much information as possible on the tasks they have to perform and on the decisions they have to take.

Three kinds of decisions are addressed: they are referred to as task selection, data selection and performer selection. Task selection occurs when a participant can operate on the same input data with a number of tasks and they have to make a choice: for example, after receiving a request for quote, an account manager may directly provide a quote or start a reselling initiative that first implies contacting a number of potential suppliers. Data selection takes place when a task can operate on a number of input entities and it is up to its performer to select which to act on from among those available: for example, a distributor may assemble several customer orders into a bulk order for a supplier, and they have to decide which customer orders match up. Task selection and data selection may occur jointly: for example, a broker may match purchase requisitions to offers (data selection), but they may also discard items pending for too long (matching and discarding are mutually exclusive tasks). Performer selection is about the distribution of work: the performers of subsequent tasks may be decided by the performers of previous tasks. For example, a conference chairman can decide which reviewers will be asked to review an incoming paper.

As to its graphical representation, Chant draws on Petri nets (Murata, 1989) and hence it is made up of places and transitions connected by oriented arcs. Transitions represent tasks and

Figure 1. Fragment of Chant model (a); part of the corresponding information model (b)

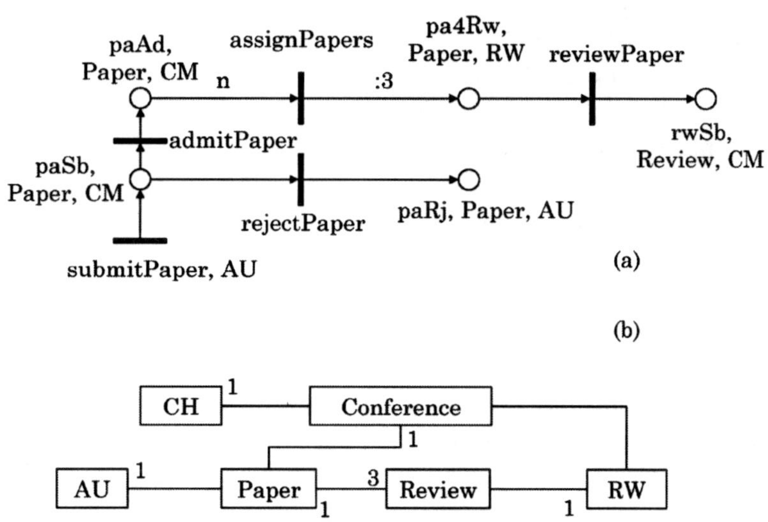

Legend
paSb: paper submitted | paAd: paper admitted | paRj: paper rejected
pa4Rw: paper for review | rwSb: review submitted
AU: author | CM: chairman | RW: reviewer

places provide information on the local data flow. The data flow and the control flow are integrated as both are based on tokens, which, in Chant, are called events.

The example in Figure 1a shows a fragment of a process handling paper submissions: it will be used to illustrate the role of places and the meaning of the inscriptions on the arcs.

The requirements of the process are as follows. Basically, authors submit papers to conferences, conference chairmen assign the papers to three reviewers, and reviewers provide their reviews. In particular, authors are allowed to submit one paper at a time; chairmen reject the papers not complying with the conference requirements and admit those compliant. Chairmen assign papers to reviewers in blocks so as to balance the reviewers' load while matching the topics of papers to the preferences of reviewers.

The information model in Figure 1b shows the entities and relationships involved. The notation used is that of UML (Unified Modeling Language) class models (OMG-UML, 2011).

In Chant, places represent run-time entities called events. From a structural point of view, events are entities that have a name and are connected to two other entities, one is an information entity referred to as the payload of the event, and the other denotes the intended recipient. The meta-model of Chant is illustrated in section "To-do lists."

The three labels of places provide the name of the events, the type of their payloads and the role of their recipients, respectively. The process fragment in Figure 1a shows four kinds of events concerning papers: paSb (paper submitted), paAd (paper admitted), paRj (paper rejected) and pa4Rw (paper for review). From an operational point of view, an event represents a request for work addressed to the participant represented by the recipient of the event, and the payload provides the entity to be acted on. Entity types AU, CH and RW represent the participants on the basis of the roles they play.

Tasks are responsible for the local data flows and the readers of Chant models can easily understand what the local data flows imply, by taking into account the types of the event payloads and the labels of the arcs (called weights). There are a number of data flow rules which are illustrated in the next section. In this section, an informal description is given with reference to the process fragment in Figure 1a.

The number of the input events to be consumed is given by the input weight, which is a label associated with an input arc (of a task). The weight may be an integer number > 0 or a symbol like m or n, which stands for a number not known a priori. In the second case, the exact number is decided by the performer when carrying out the task; such a decision involves selecting the appropriate events from those available. If the weight is equal to 1, it may be omitted.

Output arcs (of tasks) have two weights, separated by a colon: the first is the number of payloads produced by the task and the second is the number of recipients associated with each payload. The two weights are called output payload weight and recipient weight, respectively. The total number of events produced is given by the product of the two weights. If the output payload weight is equal to the input weight, it may be omitted.

When a chairman carries out an instance of assignPapers, they may consume a number of paAd events and, for each of their payloads, they produce three pa4Rw events. This occurs because the input weight and the output payload weight are identical and the recipient weight is 3. In addition, since the payload types of the places are identical, the payloads are transferred from the input events to the output ones. Therefore, for each paper taken, three requests for reviews are generated, all related to the same paper but each directed to a different reviewer.

The recipients of the output events may be decided by the performer of the task, as it takes place for task assignPapers, or they may be determined automatically, on the basis of rules either implicit or explicit. The first case occurs when it is part of the job of the performer to do so; the second case takes place when the recipients are designated by means of associations already established in the underlying information system or they are determined on the basis of business rules. From a notational point of view, when recipients are not selected by the performer of the task, the recipient weight is shown within parentheses. The recipient weight may be omitted if it is equal to one and the recipient is automatically determined.

Usually tasks consume input events and produce output ones, but there may be tasks, like submitPaper, that produce output events without consuming any input event. The former are called event-driven tasks and the latter free tasks.

Task submitPaper is meant to enable authors to submit one paper for each execution and the recipient is automatically selected: as a matter of fact, the chairman of the conference to which the paper is submitted is the participant to be involved.

The papers rejected are directed to the corresponding authors through events paRj: since place paRj is a sink place, the corresponding events represent notifications and do not solicit direct reactions from their recipients.

Task reviewPaper enables reviewers to provide a review for each paper assigned to them. The payloads of the input event and that of the output one are different, i.e., Paper for the former and Review for the latter. As a matter of fact, this task generates a new review for each input paper; it follows the generation pattern illustrated in the next section. The recipient of the review is the conference chairman and is automatically determined since the recipient weight is omitted.

For each paper submitted, chairmen can choose between admitting and rejecting it: place paSb involves a simple choice as explained in section "Decisions".

DATA-FLOW RULES

The purpose of data-flow rules is to give the readers of Chant models indications on: a) the events consumed and produced by the tasks, b) the correspondences between the payloads of the input events and the payloads of the output ones, c) the number of the recipients of the output events.

These rules depend on the types of the places and on the weights of the arcs. They are first presented in relation to linear tasks and then to nodal tasks.

A task is called linear if both its fan-in and fan-out are equal to 1. The fan-in of a process item (place or task) is the number of its input arcs; the fan-out is the number of its output arcs. Nodal tasks are those tasks having two or more input places. Data-flow rules concerning process variables were defined by Russell, ter Hofstede, Edmond, and van der Aalst (2005); here, they address systems consisting of interrelated business entities.

Transfer Rule

If the types of the input and output payloads are identical, then the payloads released by the task are the input ones (possibly updated by the task). Therefore, the number of the input payloads and that of the output ones are identical and only the first needs to be indicated. Tasks admitPaper, rejectPaper, and assignPapers in Figure 1a follow this rule.

Indirect Transfer Rule

The purpose of this rule is to release entities that are different from the input ones but related to them.

An example is shown in Figure 2a. Task ask4Evaluations takes one customer order (which is made up of a number of order lines) and releases some of its lines for separate evaluations. The fragment of the information model (Figure 2b) shows that classes CO and COL are linked by

Figure 2. Example of transfer rule (a); part of the corresponding information model (b)

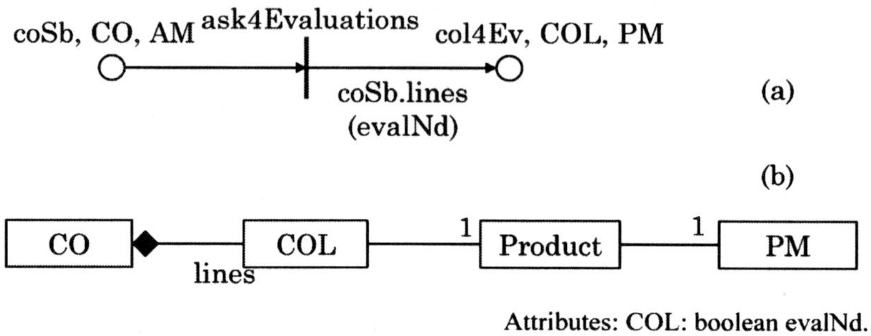

Legend
CO = customer order (co)
coSb: co submitted
evalNd: evaluation needed
AM: account manager
COL = customer order line (col)
col4Ev: col for evaluation
PM: product manager

means of a composition relationship: associative attribute lines returns the collection of lines associated with a customer order.

The output weight is a logical weight in that it does not consist in a number but in a navigational expression denoting the output payloads. The purpose of this task is to enable an account manager to get support for critical lines from product managers. The account manager is supposed to select the lines to be evaluated by setting line attribute evalNd (evaluation needed) to true.

The logical weight, i.e., "coSb.lines(evalNd)", indicates that the lines of the input order for which boolean attribute evalNd is true are released as the output payloads. The input order is referred to by means of the event name (coSb). There is one recipient for each line, automatically selected: as a matter of fact, an order line points to one product and a product is handled by one product manager. Chant navigational expressions draw on OCL (Object Constraint Language) (OMG-OCL, 2010).

Figure 3. Examples of generation patterns: n,1 (a), 1,n (b), m,n (c)

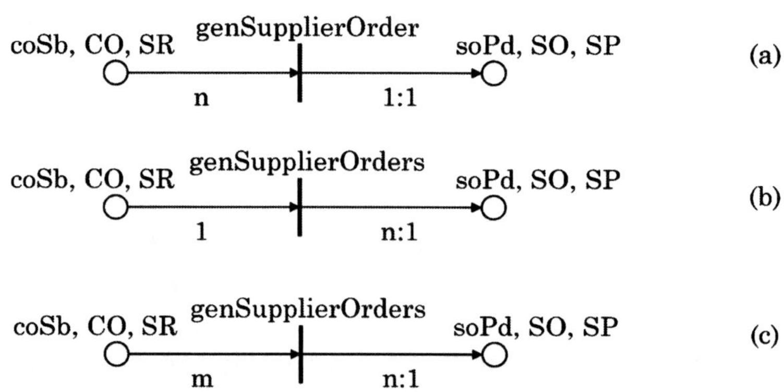

Legend
CO = customer order (co)
coSb: co submitted
SR: sales representative
SO = supplier order (so)
soPd: so produced
SP: supplier

Generation Rule

If the types of the input and output payloads are different and there is no logical weight, then the output entities are generated by the task, which usually links them with the input entities either directly or indirectly. The output weight specifies the number of the newly generated entities; if it is 1, it may be omitted.

Task reviewPaper in Figure 1a follows this rule; the output review is connected to the input paper as shown in the information model. Task reviewPaper is a case of 1-from-1 generation pattern; other typical combinations of input and output weights are shown in Figure 3.

The information models are omitted, but they can be deduced from the descriptions of the examples.

The example in Figure 3a shows a one-from-many generation pattern. Task genSupplierOrder enables a sales representative to build a supplier order from a number of customer orders; the recipient, i.e. a supplier, is selected by the performer. Task genSupplierOrders in Figure 3b is about producing several supplier orders from one customer order: the performer can split the lines of the customer order into several groups for which they produce distinct supplier orders. The last example presents a many-from-many generation pattern: a sales representative can build several supplier orders from a number of customer orders by distributing the lines of the customer orders to different supplier orders.

Long-Lasting Events

Normally, the execution of a task implies the deletion of the input events and the release of new output events. In some situations, this simple mechanism might be too rigid. For example, one execution of task genSupplierOrders in Figure 3c is assumed to distribute all the lines of the input orders to the newly generated output orders. While this is certainly possible, it might be too demanding: a more flexible solution is to allow the performer to build provisional supplier orders with which they may associate the lines of customer orders a few at a time. This solution implies that the execution of a task may not delete the input events; in addition, if there are provisional output events, they have to be explicitly confirmed during the execution of the task in order for them to become available to the subsequent tasks. The input events that may be acted on in several executions of a task are called long-lasting events: they have to be explicitly deleted by the performer.

In order to graphically show these features of events, dashed arcs are used as shown in Figure 4.

In the first case, there are long-lasting input events but not provisional output events; in the

Figure 4. Examples of flexible patterns

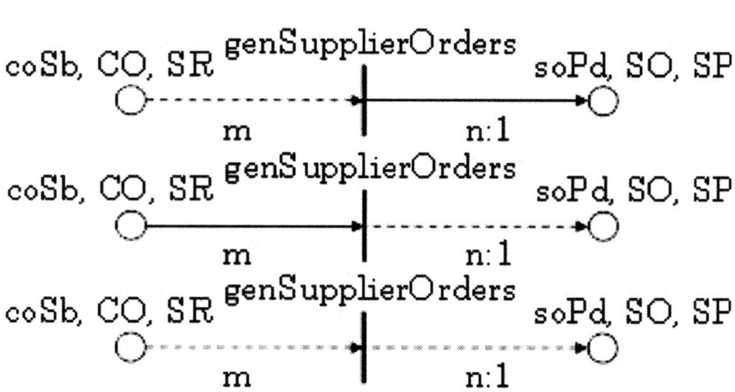

second case, the situation is reversed; and in the third case, there are both long-lasting input events and provisional output events.

Nodal Tasks

Nodal tasks enable their performers to combine input entities of different types: this feature is called combined data selection and is illustrated in the examples of Figure 5.

Task genTransaction produces one transaction out of one request and one offer; a transaction is a newly generated entity related to the request and the offer and hence path "(rqSb,ofSb)-trPd" follows a generation pattern. Transactions are sent to a treasurer automatically selected. The performer is a broker and their job is to find an offer that matches a request or vice versa. The weight of the input arcs is 1, but could be greater: for example, the broker could match a group of requests to a single offer or vice versa or even a group of requests to a group of offers.

Task genTr2 is a variant of the previous task: it joins the two input flows and produces three output flows. In addition to producing a transaction, it sends acceptance events to the buyer (who sent the offer) and the seller (who sent the request). Besides the generation rule, there are two transfer rules, i.e., "rqSb-rqAc" and "ofSb-ofAc."

DECISIONS

While data selection has been illustrated in the previous section, this section deals with task selection in two typical situations, referred to as simple choices and complex ones. Choices bring about groupings of tasks; the resulting groups, which are called primary tasks, are the major entries of to-do lists, as will be discussed in the next section.

Simple Choices

When a place is the only input place of two or more tasks, a simple choice is involved; in Petri net literature (Murata, 1989), it is called free choice. In this chapter, such tasks are called rival tasks as they are in competition with each other.

Figure 5. Examples of combined data selection

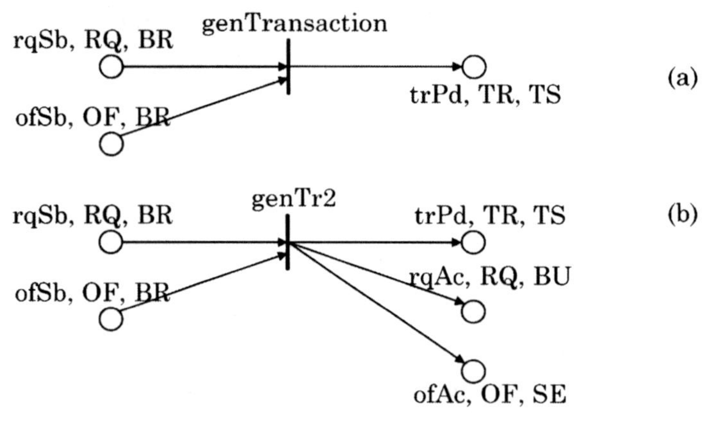

Legend

RQ = request	OF = offer	TR = transaction
ofSb = offer submitted	rqSb = request submitted	trPd = transaction produced
ofAc = offer accepted	rqAc = request accepted	
BR = broker	TS = treasurer	
BU = buyer	SE = seller	

If the input weights of the rival tasks are all equal to 1, the input events are handled individually; otherwise they are handled in groups and data selection takes place at the same time as task selection. Events paSb in Figure 1a bring about simple individual decisions.

Extended simple choices (also called extended free choices) take place when there are two or more places that are the only input places of a number of tasks. This situation involves combined data selections as the rival tasks have two or more input places.

Complex Choices

Complex choices are situations in which there is no direct competition among all the rival tasks, but there may be a task, say, t1, in competition with another task, say, t2, that is in competition with a third task, say, t3. An example is shown in Figure 6: a request may be combined with an offer, but requests and offers may be discarded if they are waiting for too long.

Task genTransaction is in conflict with both task discardRq and task discardOf, but these two tasks are not in conflict with each other. Brokers first have to look at the available requests and offers and then they decide what to do; they cannot select a task a priori, without considering the input events. Complex choices imply combined data selections as there is at least one task with two or more input places.

Primary Tasks

Selecting one task among a number of rival tasks implies a careful evaluation of the input entities; in complex cases, the help of a decision-support system may be required. For this reason, the rival tasks may be thought of as being encompassed by a container task that enables the performer to carry out all the analyses and comparisons needed before selecting one of them along with the input entities to be acted on. The container task in which the rival tasks are subsumed is called primary task. Primary tasks do not need any graphical representation, as they mainly address operational issues; however, they have a great impact on the structure of to-do lists as will be discussed in the next section.

In order not to introduce new names, the name of a primary task is obtained from the name of one

Figure 6. Example of complex choice and of primary task

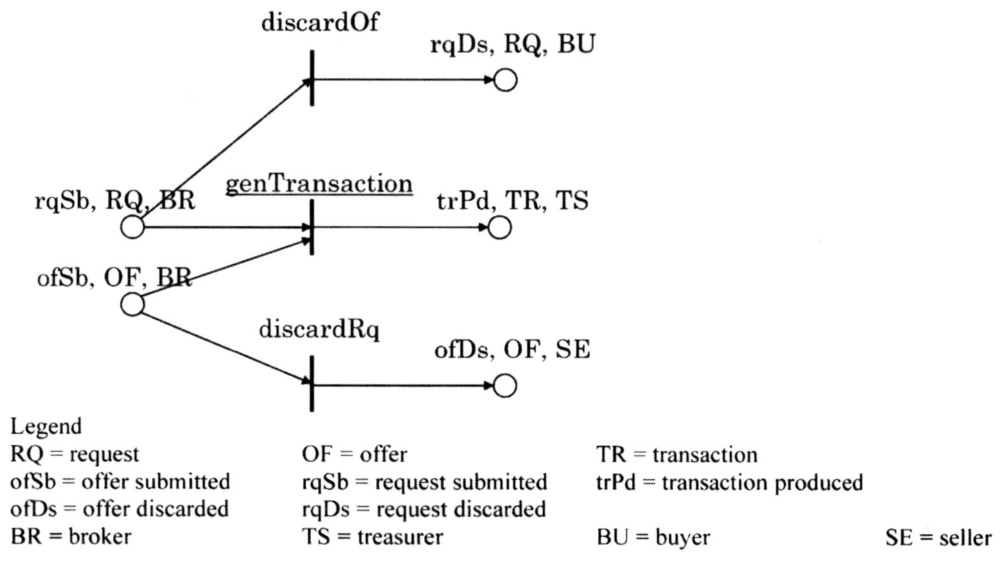

of the corresponding rival tasks and is followed by a "?". The rival tasks that give their names to the primary tasks are underlined in the models, as shown in Figure 6; they are called the representatives of their groups. From a computational point of view, primary tasks are obtained from the transitive closure of the tasks that have some input places in common. The three tasks in Figure 6 form one primary task called "genTransaction?"

By extension, primary tasks are also those tasks that have no rivals, i.e. tasks having no input places in common with other tasks. They are called simple primary tasks. Tasks assignPapers and reviewPaper are two examples that, however, differ in the data selection aspect; task reviewPaper acts on individual papers, while task assignPapers acts on groups of papers. The nodal tasks in Figure 5 are other examples: having more than one input place, they perform combined data selection.

TO-DO LISTS

In the domain of business processes, to-do lists are the major interface between the participants and the tasks orchestrated by the process engine. The to-do lists resulting from Chant models show the primary tasks assigned to participants; they are obtained from queries on the underlying information system.

A short description of the Chant meta-model is needed before such queries are explained. A simplified version of the Chant meta-model, i.e. the information model concerning the design entities and the run-time ones of Chant, is presented in Figure 7.

The right part addresses the structure of processes and is a typical meta-model for Petri nets; the left part focuses on the events. As mentioned in section "Overview of Chant," an event is related to a business entity (its payload) and to a recipient. The Entity abstract class is the bridge between the business information model and the Chant meta-model: any entity belonging to a class that inherits from Entity can be referred to by a Chant event. Class Actor represents the participants. Events are grouped in process instances (ProcessI). A process instance may take care of a particular business entity (its case) according to the case-handling approach (van der Aalst, Weske & Grünbauer, 2005). Events point to the corresponding places and these links allow the design entities (places and transitions) to be reached from the run-time ones, i.e. the events.

A preliminary analysis of a Chant process determines the primary tasks: since primary tasks induce the partition of the places into distinct sets, each place has a fourth attribute (in addition to the name, the payload type and the recipient role introduced in section 2) which receives the name

Figure 7. Simplified version of the Chant meta-model

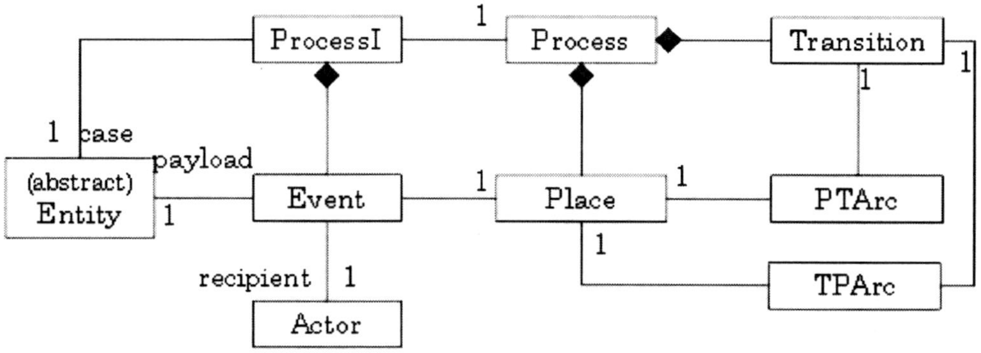

of the corresponding primary task. By extension, the events get the primary task name from the places they are connected to.

Chant to-do lists are organized in two levels at most: the first-level entries (called primary entries) correspond to the events grouped by process instance and primary task name. In particular, primary entries show the primary task names and the number of pending events. When a primary entry is clicked, the result depends on a number of factors, as follows.

If the primary task is a simple one and corresponds to a linear task, e.g., reviewPaper and assignPapers in Figure 1a, the result depends on whether the task handles input events individually or in groups. In the first case, the events are shown as secondary entries in the to-do list: when the performer clicks one of them, the task application is activated. In the second case, the task application is directly activated by a click on the primary entity, since the selection of the input entities is part of its job; a primary task corresponding to a nodal task is handled likewise.

Secondary entries also appear if the primary task corresponds to a simple choice in which the events are handled individually, e.g., "admitPaper?" in Figure 1a (assuming that admitPaper is the representative of the group of tasks consisting of admitPaper and rejectPaper). An example of to-do list for a chairman is shown in Figure 8. Three secondary entries are shown for primary task

Figure 8. Example of to-do list for a conference chairman

```
+ admitPaper?        3
          title of paper x
          title of paper y
          title of paper z
assignPapers         10
```

"admitPaper?"; each entry presents some information taken from the payload of the corresponding event, e.g., the title of the paper submitted.

When one such entry is clicked, a primary-task application is activated: it enables the chairman to examine the paper and then to decide whether to admit or reject it.

In the remaining cases, primary-task applications allow the performers to carry out data selection and, if needed, task selection as well.

CONCLUSION

The notation, Chant, proposed in this chapter integrates the control flow and the data flow owing to its Petri-net structure. Such integration is based on the notion of event. An event basically denotes a business entity in a particular point of its life cycle where it is to be handled by a specific participant who will perform an appropriate task, possibly after carrying out a data selection and/or a task selection. Events and states are similar notion, but they are not equivalent. A Chant event is a kind of request for work directed to a particular participant; states can be obtained from the events grouped by payload (i.e. by ignoring the recipients).

What characterizes Chant is the emphasis put on three kinds of decisions, i.e. data selection, task selection and performer selection. By looking at the places (and their output transitions) associated with their roles, participants get informed of the decisions to take and the tasks to perform; the weights on the arcs of the tasks give them information on the data flow involved.

The infrastructure for the implementation of Chant processes is light as the burden of decisions falls to the participants. The to-do lists are populated by queries on the events directed to the primary tasks and, for this reason, they are rather straightforward. The implementation of the primary tasks, i.e. the task applications, varies depending on the complexity and mix of data selection and task selection; however, the notion of primary task and the data flow rules provide the general requirements for the architecture of such applications.

Current work is dedicated to the customization of to-do lists, so as to provide more detailed information to their owners. For example, primary tasks fed by events coming from a number of places, only show the number of pending events regardless of their source places, while it may be useful for the performers to know their distribution.

Chant models draw on two major components representing complementary viewpoints: the process model addressing tasks and events, and the information model defining the structure of the business entities. Events are explicitly represented in process models as the precedence relationships between tasks may be mediated by the payloads of events. A third component to be added is a rule model, which is meant to specify conditions of activation of the tasks and the intended effects of their execution (zur Muehlen & Indulska, 2010). Such rules will be expressed in Chant with the OCL (Object Constraint Language) notation (OMG-OCL, 2010) in order to take advantage of the underlying information model. In alternative, textual representations based on Semantics of Business Vocabulary and Business Rules, or SBVR, will be examined so as to make the rules easier to read by non-technical users. Transformations from OCL to SBVR and vice versa have been proposed: an example of the first is given by Cabot, Pau & Raventós (2010), while Bajwa, Bordbar & Lee (2010) provide an example of the second.

REFERENCES

Alvesson, M. (2004). *Knowledge work and knowledge-intensive firms*. Oxford, UK: Oxford University Press.

Bajwa, I. S., Bordbar, B., & Lee, M. G. (2010). OCL constraints generation from natural language specification. In *Proceedings of the 14th IEEE International Enterprise Distributed Object Computing Conference* (pp. 204-213). New York: IEEE Press.

Bellotti, V., Dalal, B., Good, N., Flynn, P., Bobrow, D. G., & Ducheneaut, N. (2004). What a to-do: Studies of task management towards the design of a personal task list manager. In *Proceedings of the SIGCHI Conference on Human Factors in Computing Systems* (pp. 735-742). New York: ACM.

Cabot, J., Pau, R., & Raventós, R. (2010). From UML/OCL to SBVR specifications: A challenging transformation. *Information Systems*, *35*, 417–440. doi:10.1016/j.is.2008.12.002.

Carbone, F., Contreras, J., & Hernández, J. Z. (2010). Enterprise 2.0 and semantic technologies for open innovation support. *Lecture Notes in Computer Science*, *6097*, 18–27. doi:10.1007/978-3-642-13025-0_3.

Davenport, T. H., & Short, J. E. (1990, Summer). The new industrial engineering: Information technology and business process redesign. *Sloan Management Review*, 11–27.

Dumas, M., van der Aalst, W. M. P., & ter Hofstede, A. H. M. (2005). *Process-aware information systems: Bridging people and software through process technology*. New York: Wiley. doi:10.1002/0471741442.

Grebner, O., & Riss, U. (2008). Implicit metadata generation on the semantic desktop using task management as example. In *Proceedings of the Conference on Formal Ontologies Meet Industry* (pp. 33-44). Amsterdam: IOS Press.

Hull, R. (2008). Lecture Notes in Computer Science: *Vol. 5332. Artifact-centric business process models: Brief survey of research results and challenges* (pp. 1152–1163). Heidelberg: Springer. doi:10.1007/978-3-540-88873-4_17.

Kumaran, S., Liu, R., & Wu, F. Y. (2008). On the duality of information-centric and activity-centric models of business processes. *Lecture Notes in Computer Science*, *5074*, 32–47. doi:10.1007/978-3-540-69534-9_3.

Künzle, V., & Reichert, M. (2009). Towards object-aware process management systems: Issues, challenges, benefits. *Lecture Notes in Business Information Processing*, *29*, 197–210. doi:10.1007/978-3-642-01862-6_17.

Küster, J. M., Ryndina, K., & Gall, H. (2007). Generation of business process models for object life cycle compliance. *Lecture Notes in Computer Science*, *4714*, 165–181. doi:10.1007/978-3-540-75183-0_13.

Lu, R., Sadiq, S., & Governatori, G. (2009). On managing business processes variants. *Data & Knowledge Engineering*, *68*(7), 642–664. doi:10.1016/j.datak.2009.02.009.

Marjanovic, O., & Freeze, R. D. (2011). Knowledge intensive business processes: Theoretical foundations and research challenges. In *Proceedings of the IEEE 44th Hawaii International Conference on System Sciences*. New York: IEEE Press.

Murata, T. (1989). Petri nets: Properties, analysis and applications. *Proceedings of the IEEE*, *77*(4), 541–580. doi:10.1109/5.24143.

Nurcan, S. (2008). A survey on the flexibility requirements related to business processes and modeling artifacts. In *Proceedings of the IEEE 41st Hawaii International Conference on System Sciences*. New York: IEEE Press.

OMG-BPMN. (2011). *Business process model and notation*. Retrieved October 14, 2011, from http://www.omg.org/spec/BPMN/

OMG-OCL. (2010). *Object constraint language*. Retrieved October 14, 2011, from http://www.omg.org/spec/OCL/

OMG-SBVR. (2008). *Semantics of business vocabulary and business rules*. Retrieved October 14, 2011, from http://www.omg.org/spec/SBVR/

OMG-UML. (2011). *Unified modeling language: Superstructure*. Retrieved October 14, 2011, from http://www.omg.org/spec/UML/

Riss, U. V., Rickayzen, A., Maus, H., & van der Aalst, W. M. P. (2005). Challenges for business process and task management. *Journal of Universal Knowledge Management*, *2*, 77–100.

Russell, N., ter Hofstede, A. H. M., Edmond, D., & van der Aalst, W. M. P. (2005). Workflow data patterns: Identification, representation and tool support. *Lecture Notes in Computer Science*, *3716*, 353–368. doi:10.1007/11568322_23.

Stoitsev, T., Scheidl, S., & Spahn, M. (2007). A framework for light-weight composition and management of ad-hoc business processes. *Lecture Notes in Business Information Processing*, *4849*, 213–226.

van der Aalst, W. M. P., Pesic, M., & Schonenberg, H. (2009). Declarative workflows: Balancing between flexibility and support. *Computer Science -. Research for Development*, *23*(2), 99–113.

van der Aalst, W. M. P., Weske, M., & Grünbauer, D. (2005). Case handling: A new paradigm for business process support. *Data & Knowledge Engineering*, *53*(2), 129–162. doi:10.1016/j.datak.2004.07.003.

Weske, M. (2007). *Business process management - Concepts, languages, architectures*. Berlin: Springer.

Yongchareon, S., & Liu, C. (2010). Lecture Notes in Computer Science: *Vol. 6426. A process view framework for artifact-centric business processes* (pp. 26–43). Heidelberg: Springer. doi:10.1007/978-3-642-16934-2_6.

zur Muehlen, M., & Indulska, M. (2010). Modeling languages for business processes and business rules: A representational analysis. *Information Systems*, *35*, 379–390. doi:10.1016/j.is.2009.02.006.

ADDITIONAL READING

Alter, S. (2008). Defining information systems as work systems: Implications for the IS field. *European Journal of Information Systems*, *17*, 448–469. doi:10.1057/ejis.2008.37.

Austin, J. L. (1976). *How to do things with words*. Oxford, UK: Oxford University Press.

Davenport, T. H. (1993). *Process innovation*. Boston: Harvard Business School Press.

Davenport, T. H. (2005). *Thinking for a living*. Boston: Harvard Business School Press.

Dietz, J. L. G. (2006). The deep structure of business processes. *Communications of the ACM*, *49*(5), 59–64. doi:10.1145/1125944.1125976.

Goldkuhl, G., & Lind, M. (2004). The generics of business interaction - emphasizing dynamic features through the BAT model. In M. Aakhus & M. Lind (Eds.), *9th Conference on the Language-Action Perspective on Communication Modelling*. New Brunswick, NJ: IEEE.

Hofreiter, B., Huemer, C., & Winiwarter, W. (2005). Business collaboration models and their business context-dependent Web choreography in BPSS. *International Journal of Web Information Systems*, *1*(1), 33–42. doi:10.1108/17440080580000081.

Holt, A. W. (1985). Coordination technology and Petri nets. *Lecture Notes in Computer Science*, *222*, 278–296. doi:10.1007/BFb0016217.

Ould, M. (2005). *Business process management: A rigorous approach*. London: The British Computer Society.

Russell, N., ter Hofstede, A. H. M., Edmond, D., & van der Aalst, W. M. P. (2005). Workflow data patterns: Identification, representation and tool support. *Lecture Notes in Computer Science*, *3716*, 353–368. doi:10.1007/11568322_23.

Russell, N., van der Aalst, W. M. P., ter Hofstede, A. H. M., & Edmond, D. (2005). Workflow resource patterns: Identification, representation and tool support. *Lecture Notes in Computer Science*, *3520*, 216–232. doi:10.1007/11431855_16.

Schmidt, K., & Simone, C. (1996). Coordination mechanisms: Towards conceptual foundation of CSCW systems design. *Computer Supported Cooperative Work*, *5*, 155–200. doi:10.1007/BF00133655.

Suchman, L. A. (1987). *Plans and situated actions: The problem of human-machine communication*. Cambridge, UK: Cambridge University Press.

van der Aalst, W. M. P., ter Hofstede, A. H. M., Kiepuszewski, B., & Barros, A. P. (2003). Workflow patterns. *Distributed and Parallel Databases*, *14*, 5–51. doi:10.1023/A:1022883727209.

Zaha, J. M., Dumas, M., ter Hofstede, A. H. M., Barros, A., & Decker, G. (2008). Bridging global and local models of service-oriented systems. *IEEE Transactions on Systems, Man and Cybernetics. Part C, Applications and Reviews*, *38*(3), 302–318. doi:10.1109/TSMCC.2008.919193.

KEY TERMS AND DEFINITIONS

Business Process: A standard way of organizing work in a business context. It consists of a number of process actions to be performed by a process engine.

Data Flow: The information items used and produced by the tasks.

Data Selection: A situation in which a performer has to select the input data before performing the task.

Performer: For a given task, the user in charge of performing it.

Task: A unit of work in the system.

Task Selection: A situation in which a performer may operate on the same input data with a number of alternative tasks.

To-Do List: A list of pending tasks for a certain performer. By clicking an entry, he/she can perform the specific work related to the task.

Chapter 7
Efficiency Theories:
The State-of-the-Art

Vojko Potocan
University of Maribor, Slovenia

Matjaz Mulej
University of Maribor, Slovenia

ABSTRACT

To some authors and scientists the concepts effectiveness and efficiency are significantly different. To others, they mean the same; while to a third group the truth about them lies somewhere between these two extremes. This chapter provides an overview of efficiency theories. It finds that the term efficiency covers both doing the right thing and doing the thing right. Efficiency is not limited to internal factors of success, nor should effectiveness only be seen as a term pertaining to the outer factors of success of a human origin, organization source, or inherent in national, local, or international regions.

INTRODUCTION

The Selected Framework for Consideration of the Efficiency Concept

When dealing with various human associations/organizations, one recurrently faces the question: "What is new concerning (the understanding and consideration of) efficiency of their working (and behavior)?" But this question is much easier to pose than to respond to with an answer that leaves no room for doubt.

The concept of efficiency is so wide-reaching that it is in reality not possible to define in a unified and holistic way. It is a concept/word/term used in most sciences, be they natural, technological, or social. At the same time, this concept - especially in the social sciences - is used for the consideration on different levels of human activity (e.g. from the individual to the world-wide scope). In addition, there are several different, and even

DOI: 10.4018/978-1-4666-4373-4.ch007

non-comparable, divisions of these levels. For example, in economy, efficiency is used for dealing with activities on the macro (national economy), mezzo (sectors of economy), and micro (businesses) levels. On the other hand, the concept of efficiency is used in several disciplines, such as organization and management for dealing with the whole organization (as in the macro level), parts of an organization (as in the mezzo level), and groups within those parts (as in the micro level). Other social science disciplines, such as geography, sociology, psychology, logistics, human resource management, and so on, are also facing similar definitional differences.

From the entire range of all sciences, we will therefore limit ourselves to dealing with those social sciences that predominantly consider organizations and how they work, which means: the macro level covers the organization, the mezzo level its parts, and the micro level the constituent groups (that is: those inside it).

The Selected Problem and Related Theses

Existence and development of (most) organizations depend on their attainment of suitable outcomes of their productive working and behavior (Quinn, 1992; Porter, 1998; Magretta, 1999; Steffen, 2006). In order to attain aimed-for results, the organization under review must fulfill at last two preconditions in its point of departure – that is, it must appropriately use its available (given or potential) resources for attainment of its results suitably, and it must attain results meeting demands and needs of its (internal and external) social, business, and natural environments (Drucker, 1946; Magretta, 1999; Potocan and Rebernik, 2002; Potocan, 2003; Potocan, 2006; Steffen, 2006).

Attainment of such results is far from simple in an organization, which is a complex and complicated feature in objective reality. It faces many problems concerning selection and application of approaches, methods, methodologies, and techniques of understanding and consideration of the particular organization being considered (Daft, 2000; Mulej, 2000; Potocan, 2003; Potocan, 2004; Wren, 2004; Daft, 2006; Potocan, 2006).

The existence of an organization crucially depends on the attainment of appropriate outcomes of its working and behavior. When dealing with the outcomes, we face problems of diverse and different understanding of the content of working and behavior of the organization being studied, as well as a variety of potential ways of achieving its aimed-for outcomes (Porter, 1998; Potocan, 2003; Pettinger, 2007).

Hence, we would like to present from our education, research, and experience (in business, organization, systems, and innovation theories) the following contributions concerning efficiency. Our theses result from relevant literature and read as follows:

1. Efficiency has been and is an important point of departure and objective factor and outcome of working in and behavior of (diverse) organizations.
2. In terms of conceptualization, there are at least two basic approaches to the understanding and consideration of efficiency in any organization under the spotlight/use or book reference.
    a. The first approach is based on the original (and unchanged) findings of theoreticians, who have defined efficiency and its attributes a century ago.
    b. The second approach attempts to deal with the concept of efficiency more holistically in line with needs and requirements of the working of organizations in the contemporary environment.
3. In terms of content, the concept of efficiency is not understood, defined, and considered in a unified way. Differences may (partially, at least) make sense in consideration of efficiency in/ between different sciences, but they certainly make less sense within the same science.

4. In terms of methodology, efficiency has never been dealt with in a unified way. There exists a partially unified methodological consideration of single, synthetic, or analytical elements of efficiency, but even this exists inside single disciplines only. However, there is no unified methodology of meeting the need to consider efficiency in a synthesis of its single parts, their mutual relations, or of efficiency as a whole. Thus, this thesis does not only apply across a spectrum of various / different sciences but it also applies inside the framework of single sciences.
5. There are both in theory and practice various, diverse efficiency constructs that are partially in opposition to, and excluding, each other; though, the various well-known efficiency constructs tend to be more or less either correct or wrong in terms of methodology and contents. Their authors are namely entitled to, and do, take into account a defined and, of course, selected understanding of, and approach to, their own selected viewpoints, areas, and levels of consideration of efficiency. They may be correct in their own framework, but wrong or less correct from a different selected starting point.

On this basis, our actual theses read as follows:

1. A suitable understanding of efficiency must be requisitely holistic, and hence result from a consideration of the interdependence between.
   a. Efficiency as a starting point (and resulting objective/goal) under consideration.
   b. Efficiency as a factor of working (and behavior).
   c. Efficiency as an outcome of working activity.
2. A suitable understanding of efficiency must be requisitely holistic and hence be based on interdependence of consideration of its (1) concepts, (2) contents, and (3) methods and methodologies. Detection of their synergetic unity in diversity can enable formation of a suitable environment and framework for humans to understand and consider efficiency more, or even requisitely, holistically.
3. A suitable understanding of efficiency must be requisitely holistic and hence based on interdependence of consideration (and application) of various and different ways of one's approach to consideration, and understanding of its (1) concepts, (2) contents, and (3) methods and methodologies. Detection of their synergetic unity in diversity can enable formation of a suitable environment and framework for humans to understand and consider efficiency more, or even requisitely, holistically.
4. Complexity of the problematique under consideration (this includes complexity of the concept of efficiency, and complexity of application of the concept of efficiency in various sciences) does not allow humans to form a unified and requisitely holistic model, in terms of content and methodology and secondly in terms of their synergies, of efficiency of working and behavior of organizations—either in theory or in practice.

But a shared methodological framework can be created and such a framework should help humans achieve more unity and comparability of different considerations of efficiency along with taking specifics of single considerations into account.

For further consideration, we will choose from the entire problematique ... the research, the starting points, attributes, and impact of efficiency of working (and behavior) of organizations inside the viewpoints of the social sciences, especially those pertaining to organization and management of organizations as business systems (Potocan et al., 2005).

CONSIDERATION OF THE EFFICIENCY CONCEPT

Our Understanding of Efficiency (Within Our Selected Frame of Research)

In our research of organizations, we use efficiency to more holistically identify, define, and analyze organizations, and to influence them. Various known considerations of efficiency differ crucially in authors' understandings and according to (their) definitions of business. They, thus, define goals of their consideration of efficiency of organization as, for example, economic, business, organization, management, sociological, psychological, human, technological, production, and so on, as the context/s of organizational working and behavior.

Therefore, the question arises as to what efficiency (from the viewpoint of organization) is and how to define it for our research. Up to now, the term has been used in various contexts and for different purposes and has had different meanings. Today, efficiency is one of the most wide-spread (and frequently used) terms of the modern world. Yet, the meaning of efficiency is not essentially unified.

In modern literature, many diverse definitions of the term efficiency may be found. For example, the Webster Dictionary (Gove, 2002) gives 14 different definitions for efficiency (and more than 50 synonyms for efficiency). Some of them are related to different viewpoints of treatment of organizations. The definitions include the following:

- The ratio of the output to the input of any system (WD, 1913; Funk, 1992; Gove, 2002).
- Skillfulness in avoiding wasted time and effort (WD, 1913; EAHD, 2000; Gove, 2002).
- The quality or property of being efficient (Gove, 2002).
- The quality or degree to which someone or something possesses adequate skill or knowledge for the performance of a duty (Funk, 1992; EAHD, 2000; Gove, 2002).
- The ratio, expressed as a percentage, of the output to the input of power (energy or work per unit time) (McGraw-Hill, 1989).
- Cost of inputs for each unit of output produced (Siegel and Shim, 2000).
- The power or capacity to produce a desired result (Gove, 2002).
- The measure of the effectiveness with which a system performs. It is stated as the ratio of a system's work output to its work input (Encyclopaedia Britannica, 2007).
- "Efficiency is doing better what is already being done." (Drucker, 1946).
- In human movements, the relationship between the amount of work done and the energy expended during the work (See Encyclopedia of Sports and Science Medicine, http://sportsci.org/encyc/index.html).
- Economic efficiency is a general term for the value assigned to a situation by some measure designed to capture the amount of waste or "friction" or other undesirable economic features present (see also Pareto efficiency, Kaldor-Hicks efficiency, X-efficiency, allocative efficiency, distributive efficiency, productive efficiency, optimization of a social welfare function) (EAHD, 2000; Gove, 2002; http://www.wikipedia.org).
- Mechanical efficiency (in natural and technical sciences – for example in physics), that is, the ratio of the work done to the effort used (the quality of energy will always decrease) (see thermal efficiency, electrical efficiency, etc.) (McGraw-Hill, 1989; http://www.wikipedia.org).

For the purpose of our research of efficiency, the different definitions of efficiency may be classified into a small number of basic groups:

- Efficiency as a base or starting point (e.g., as purpose and/or goal) of working (and behavior) of an organization, and/or efficiency as an interest, supporting the activity.
- Efficiency as an element of operating and/or behavior of an organization.
- Efficiency as a result of working and/or behavior of an organization.

Efficiency as a factor of working (and behavior) is what we are studying. In doing so, we use efficiency as a starting point, and we see the resulting objective/goal as a basis and tool having impact over working and behavior of the organization being considered. On the other hand, efficiency as a result provides information about the actual productive working and about the necessary measures for calibration of the planned and actual situation(s).

Therefore, efficiency may be understood (and requisitely holistically) defined on the basis of an adequate (synergetic) understanding and use of all content definitions mentioned above. A more detailed definition of the term efficiency depends on the selection and use of the methodology for its consideration (e.g., the selected viewpoints, methods, and methodologies).

Why? Efficiency is an elaborate (complex and complicated), dynamic and comprehensive phenomenon, which can, in our opinion, be adequately conceived and defined only in a requisite holistic, systemic treatment. It makes sense to analyze it within this framework as a network of all selected significant viewpoints, levels and areas of activity and the analysis must include all their synergies.

In the case of efficiency of business organizations, we attempt to consider the activity of a (specific) group of (profit-oriented) organizations (and/or people) from a dialectical system of viewpoints (e.g. organizational, management, economic, and business, in synergy); this approach should enable the requisite holism for consideration according to the business organization's purpose and goals of its activity.

Based on the above-mentioned findings of various authors and (the presented) starting points, efficiency of business organizations can be best defined in the broadest terms as follows:

Efficiency (as we define it) (see Potocan, 2004, 2005; Potocan et al., 2005) can be described in the most general terms as a requisitely holistic measure of working of the reviewed business system, that has been created because humans deemed that there is a possibility to attain the desired outcomes of organizational performance from the vantage point of various constituencies directly and indirectly affected by the organization. It is stated as the general (requisitely holistic) and (as a rule) synthetic criterion that is basically aimed at the evaluation of productive working (and behavior) of the transformation system of the organization. It is due to the selected viewpoint (or, hopefully, the dialectical system of viewpoints) defining the approach, field, and level of consideration and the chosen methodology (methods and techniques) of consideration. (For more about the transformational system of an organization, see: Honeycutt and Richards, 1989; Quinn, 1992; Parolini, 1999; Galbrait, 2002; Magretta, 2002; for more about the dialectical system, see Mulej, 2000, and earlier, since 1974; and Mulej et al., forthcoming in 2012).

A discussion about the definition of efficiency triggers the issue of the relationship between the concepts of efficiency and effectiveness. They are differently understood and defined in different sciences and even inside the same sciences (Potocan, 2004, 2005). The well-known solutions differ very much and include a large variety of definitions. For example:

- In economics and business economics, as well as in most of the natural and technological sciences, they (the practitioners) use the concept of efficiency solely to deal with suitability of the entire working of the organization, including the internal and external parts of the business process and environments.
- In organizational theory they (the theoreticians) make a distinction between efficiency and effectiveness and they use both terms. So, for instance, some authors define the suitability of the entire working of the organization being reviewed with the term efficiency, while others describe this as effectiveness.
- In management science, they (the scientists) rather strictly delimit efficiency and effectiveness.

Differences and similarities of both concepts can be (partially) objectively explained with differences in authors' understanding of the topics in the given outer, i.e. objective, reality, such as concerning organizations, and of their relations with their environments. In the earlier phases of coping with the theoretical consideration of the organization, authors understood it as a closed system with clearly defined boundaries separating it from its environment. Under such conditions, it made sense to separately and independently consider:

- Efficiency as a goal, factor, and measure of the internal processes (e.g., doing things right).
- Effectiveness as a goal, factor, and measure of the external processes (e.g., doing the right things).

On the other hand, the contemporary conditions cause differences between efficiency and effectiveness to grow smaller because of their invisible interdependence in organizations as open systems. Due to the contemporary division of work and related specialization,

- Boundaries between organizations and their environments are becoming less and less clear.
- One must consider very many internal and external environments, e.g. by in-sourcing and out-sourcing, long-term co-operation, etc., and view them as being interdependent.
- One must attain the requisite holism of consideration of the working and behavior of organizations, and do so in a manner beyond the formally and/or institutionally defined boundaries of the organization at issue in order to cover the entire transformation process, the value chain, etc.

This is why efficiency and effectiveness are used as interchangeable terms in those fields. But various sciences have diverse and different practices, which force us to take into account some facts in order to make the problematique easier to understand. The following are some of the practices:

- On one hand, we consider efficiency with two criteria:
    - Efficiency in the narrower sense covers authors from the earlier period of research, who have understood the organization as a closed and clearly delimited subject, leaving its environment aside as another topic.
    - Efficiency in the broader sense covers more recent authors who view the organization as an open system and hence work on the suitability of its working activity and behavior inside and outside the organization and detect its suitability in an appropriate

way, e.g. by comparing the attained and the planned outcomes, or the expected and real ones, etc.

- On the other hand we still use the term effectiveness, putting it equal to efficiency in the broader sense, in order to pay tribute to the scientific correctness related to findings and references of various sciences. This applies especially to sciences of organization and management, in which many authors pay much attention to the efficiency concept.

The presented definition is formed to meet the needs of consideration of efficiency of working and behavior of the transformation process of organizations and individuals as the so-called business organizations emphasizing the so-called business viewpoints rather than the natural and / or technical / technological, social, psychological, etc, viewpoints of consideration of features, events and processes of real life.

Of course, this brings us back to questions that the authors have raised in their famous book 'New Perspectives on Organizational Effectiveness' (see Goodman and Pennings, 1977) and to Pfeffer and Salancik with their 1978 work (Pfeffer and Salancik, 1978): Who wants what and how important is it that the demand be satisfied? And what are the implications of the satisfaction of one demand for the satisfaction of other demands?

But: a definition of efficiency on its own provides a response to the important open issues of understanding and consideration of efficiency, such as:

- How can a definition of efficiency be requisitely holistic and hence suitably applied to the working and behavior of an organization in terms of concept, content, and methodology?
- How can a definition of efficiency be requisitely holistic and hence suitably understood in the context of its purpose and goals?
- How can a definition of efficiency be requisitely holistic and hence suitably understood in the context of outcomes of working and behavior of an organization?

Conceptual Issues of Understanding and the Consideration of Efficiency

Various well-known ways of understanding and of considering the concept of efficiency can, for the purpose of this contribution, generally be included in two basic groups—in terms of their approach and scope of understanding of the problematique of efficiency.

The first group can include those approaches that are based on findings of the earlier researches of organizational effectiveness, e.g. by Taylor, Gilbert M., Gilbert L., Weber, Follett, Bernard (See also Mogensen (1932), Barnard (1938), and Thorndike (1949); see in Price (1980), Hall and Clark (1980), Chandler (1996), Kanigel (1999), and Wren (2004). In the framework of our contribution they can be called approaches in the narrower sense of the efficiency concept. The priority of these earlier authors was consideration of efficiency as an internal attribute of the working of the organization.

The more important attributes of first group include: 1) the macro approach (focusing their attention exclusively on such organization-wide variables as profit, productivity, and so on); 2) (as a rule) a lack of systems approach; 3) a (more or less) one-sided understanding and consideration; 4) a quantitative consideration; 5) an aim to consider single (and/or specific) attributes; 6) orientation to an analytical consideration (favoring parts over the whole) of single elements of efficiency (or parts of the holistic efficiency); 7) a predominantly normative approach to understanding and consideration; 8) use of single-variable models; 9) a static consideration of efficiency; and 10) focusing on the shorter term effects of time.

In the second group approaches can be assembled that attempt to more holistically understand and consider the complex problematique of efficiency in terms of needs and requirements of the working of organizations in the contemporary environment. These include most of the more complex considerations of efficiency over the recent 30 years (See, e.g., Goodman and Pennings, 1977; Steers, 1977; Cameron and Whetten, 1982; Quinn and Rohrbaugh, 1983; Zammuto, 1984; Russ-Eft and Preskill, 2001). In the framework of our contribution they can be called approaches that fit the broader sense of the efficiency concept. Their aim is to consider the entire range of efficiency, including both the internal and the external working.

The more important attributes of the second, more contemporary, group include: 1) combining the macro and micro approaches; 2) a more holistic (systemic) approach; 3) effort aimed at a (more or less) holistic understanding and consideration; 4) combining the synthetic and analytical considerations, including elements, their synergies, and the whole, by considering their individual, group-specific, and general parts of attributes together; 5) combining the qualitative and quantitative consideration; 6) orientation to a requisitely holistic consideration of all levels of efficiency (of the whole, its parts, and their components and relations); 7) combining the normative and descriptive approaches; 8) use of multi-variant models (attempting to measure effectiveness/efficiency in terms of the sum, a set, or even synergy of relevant criteria); 9) dynamic consideration of the values and time of the effectiveness construct; and 10) focusing on the longer term effects of time.

Single well-known approaches, as a rule, do not have all attributes of these two groups, and can hence be classified by their prevailing attributes (Potocan, 2004, 2005). However, the basic problem of approaches is less in their classification and more in their practical application. The latter compels us to face the dilemma of definition of their mutual relations:

- Many authors maintain that only one specific approach may and can be used, since there can only be one correct approach. These one-sided and self-sufficient viewpoints (also) cause the unfortunate situation concerning the Efficiency Theories: definitions and considerations of efficiency are not unified either inside groups of various sciences, or within single sciences, or even inside single (sub)-disciplines of a single science.
- On the other hand, there are well-known solutions attempting to deal with efficiency by considering both above approaches. Their basis is the cognition, that: 1) both approaches support comprehension of the problematique in the real world; 2) both of them can be correct or wrong, which depends on the selected viewpoint, area, and level of consideration; and 3) both of them are interlinked and even interdependent.

In order to use the various approaches correctly, one should define an interval between: 1) a totally one-sided approach to anything, as the first extreme, and 2) a totally holistic approach to it, as a second extreme (given that the holistic approach can, of course, only be attained in theory). Single given approaches find their position somewhere between the two extremes, depending of their prevailing attributes.

This interval-approach also allows us to classify the various (more outstanding) well-known approaches to consideration and understanding of efficiency in literature such as:

- Goal based approaches (See Perrow, 1961; Lawrence and Lorsch, 1967; House, 1971; Porter, 1998).

- Systems approaches (See: Yuchtman and Seashore, 1967; Evan, 1976; Russ-Eft and Preskill, 2001).
- Constituency approaches (See: Goodman and Pennings, 1977; Connolly et al., 1980; Zammuto, 1984).
- Contingency approaches (See Fiedler (1967), in Wren, 2004).

The cited approaches present, of course, only the basic trends in development; these trends have in turn provided bases for several (various) specific approaches to surface (see Strasses et al., 1981; Cameron and Whetten, 1986; Etzioni, 1997; Fare et al., 2004; Wren, 2004; Coelli et al., 2005).

What must be mentioned, too, is the issue of the either normative (e.g. Connolly et al., 1980), and/or descriptive (e.g. Salancik and Pfeffer, 1974; Goodman and Pennings, 1977; Tsui, 1990) approaches to the consideration of efficiency. A possible option of a choice between these two approaches, which might come closest to the requisite holism, could be the combination of both of them. This solution is proved by comparative studies (about approaches, methodologies, and models) in the area of efficiency. For example, Steers (1975) compares 17 different models of efficiency, 13 of which were normative, and the other 4 were descriptive. Zammuto (1984) quotes 19 different models of organizational efficiency that belong to five approaches and include, mostly, normative approaches with some elements of the descriptive ones. Our study of 14 contemporary models of organizational efficiency (Potocan, 2005) provides a growing number of models, most of which are normative, but descriptive approaches are included as well, e.g. multiple constituency models (Tsui, 1990).

This finding can help us overcome two problems of consideration of efficiency, at least, which covers consideration of its components, relations, and synergies:

- An organizational factor can be defined at the same time as a normative, descriptive and/or normative/descriptive one, depending of the selected approach and viewpoint of consideration.
- Delimitation of types of understanding and consideration of efficiency into the humanistic and the mechanical ones inside the framework of various sciences, especially the natural and technological ones. In consideration of the organizational efficiency, namely, every component of it presents an interdependent entity of subjective and objective characteristics.

Understanding of various conceptual approaches cannot and may not be dealt with independently from the issue of understanding, cognition, and definition of the content of efficiency, of course.

Issues Concerning Content in Understanding and Consideration of Efficiency

Efficiency (and/or Effectiveness) Theories provide for at least two terms, which various authors use to define efficiency in terms of its content (Goodman and Pennings, 1977; Zammuto, 1984; Etzioni, 1997; Potocan, 2004, 2005). The first term is perspectives, which some authors propose to cover e.g. the realistic, power and social justice approaches and evolutionary perspectives. Perspective responds largely to what we have called the selected viewpoint so far on the basis of the Dialectical Systems Theory (see Mulej, 2000). The second term is the generalization about effectiveness with the value-based and time-specific nature of an effectiveness construct.

Concepts in both terms depend, more or less, on the concept of understanding of efficiency, and can (and must) therefore be considered in relation with findings concerning the conceptual definition, e.g. inside single approaches.

The term perspectives of efficiency is a construct that is frequently equated in the literature to the term approach, which causes an additional muddle and confusion in the research of efficiency (Potocan, 2004, 2005). If one wishes to formulate a unified consideration of efficiency, such equating of these terms is senseless and unnecessary. The theory acknowledges, first of all, the relativism, power, social justice, and evolutionary perspectives. Perspectives, which include various ethical, interests, and sustained perspectives, are newer (Lawler et al., 2006). Given the same underlying empirical framework, each perspective renders a different interpretation of organizational performance. We will try to very briefly present their vital attributes.

- **Relativism:** The relativistic perspective of research can be defined as an empirical technique for the collection of information about organizational performance from organizational constituencies. One knows of several models of relativism, and the most accepted is the "concept minimalistic" model (Connolly et al., 1980). Within this context, effectiveness is not treated as a single statement about organizational performance, but as "a set of several (or perhaps many) statements, each reflecting the evaluative criteria to a greater or lesser degree with the organization". Overall judgment of organizational effectiveness is viewed as being neither possible nor desirable because this perspective does not make any assumptions concerning the relative primacy of one-component judgments over those of any other component-dimension judgment. Instead, the relativistic evaluator takes the position that overall judgments should be made by someone else, preferably the consumer of the evaluative information.
- **Power Perspective:** The power perspective on organizational effectiveness is based on a resource dependence model (Emerson, 1962; Hickson et al., 1971; Salancik and Pfeffer, 1974) and is most closely associated with the work of Goodman and Pennings (1977), and Pfeffer and Salancik (1978). In terms of distributive issues, the power perspective suggests that the effective organization is the one that satisfies the demand of the most powerful members of the dominant coalition so as to ensure their continued support and the survival of the organization. The power is clearly evident in their treatment of the implications of these constituent judgments for organizational action.
- **Social Justice Perspective:** The social justice perspective is based on Rawls' (1971) theory of justice. One knows several applications of this theory in consideration of efficiency, such as, e.g., in the work by House (1980). Rawls' concept of justice allows neither inequalities unless they benefit the least advantaged, nor trade-offs to be made between basic liberties and social or economic advantages. The effective organization seeks to minimize constituents' regret over the actual consequences of their participations within the organization. Comparatively, the most effective organization would be the one that minimizes the regret of its most regretful constituency.
- **Other Ethical Perspectives:** In organizational and management sciences, especially, one knows also of ethical perspectives, which are used (also) for consideration of efficiency. They include, e.g., the utilitarian perspectives (Mill, 2002), individualism perspectives (Trevino and Nelson, 2006), moral-rights perspectives (Kekes, 1989; Schultz, 2001), and other justice perspectives (e.g. distributive justice, procedural justice, compensatory justice) (Singer, 1999; Lebacqz, 1986; Lawler et al., 2006). They are applied in consideration of effi-

ciency on the same basis as in the social justice perspectives, but they use different criteria for evaluation.

- **Evolutionary Perspective:** Zammuto (1982) proposes an evolutionary perspective that views evolution of organizational effectiveness as a selection process in societal evolution. Within the evolutionary framework, constituent preferences are treated as being insufficient for assessing the effectiveness of organizational performance, because they do not reflect the potential limits of performance. Consideration of the constraints defining an organization's niche is seen as essential because such constrains form the outermost boundaries of possible performance at any given time. The emphasis of the model is on the continual process of becoming effective rather than on being effective, because the substantive definition of effective organizational performance continually changes.
- **Interest Perspective:** In the organizational and management sciences the interest perspective has shown up, too. It stems partially from the areas of organizational development and political economy (e.g., Costantino, 1996). It is aimed at understanding (and studying) efficiency inside the entire political and professional interest in efficiency. At first sight, this view looks quite similar to the power perspective, but there are essential differences. Its basis is namely the understanding of the organization as an interest-based association of its (internal and external) participants. The interest perspective on organizational effectiveness is based on an interest-dependence model.

The second criterion above is the generalization about effectiveness with the value-based and time-specific background of the effectiveness construct (Cameron and Whetten, 1982; Zammuto, 1984; Wagner and Schneider, 1987; Tsui, 1990; Etzioni, 1997; etc.). The value-based nature of the effectiveness construct is generally ignored in (most) of earliest researches of organizational effectiveness. Values form the core assumptions (Lakatos and Musgrave, 1970; Etzioni, 1997) that direct each model's path of inquiry. All evaluations of organizational effectiveness consist of two components: elements of facts and elements of values (Simon, 1976, Etzioni, 1997). Only when elements of facts and values are coupled can evaluative judgments be made (Etzioni, 1997). The element of values provides the basis for the evaluative interpretation of facts in every assessment of effectiveness (Zammuto, 1984; Tsui, 1990; Etzioni, 1997).

The differences among the core values assumptions of the different perspectives become clear when examining the guidance, which they provide in:

- The selection of constituencies for inclusion in an evaluation.
- The basis of the judgment of the effectiveness of organizational performance.
- The background of the managerial implications that would be derived subsequently.

The differences in the values assumption embodied in the different perspectives have fueled the debate concerning the appropriateness of each of the perspectives for judging the effectiveness of organizational performance. The above-mentioned cognitions lead to the conclusion that theoretically there are a potentially infinite number of value perspectives about the desired state of social arrangement on which these judgments could be based. As a result, there are a potentially infinite number of effectiveness concepts (and/or models).

The second area in which variations among the later perspectives (and their models) provide insight, concerns the effects of time (see Hay and Gray, 1974; Zammuto, 1984; Tsui, 1990; Etzioni,

1997). The temporal effects summarized briefly below are not inherent in any of the perspectives, with the exception of the evolutionary perspectives. Generally, the relativistic, power, and social justice perspectives have focused on the shorter-term effects of time. The evolutionary, interest, ethics, and sustainable perspectives have considered the longer-term effects. Four effects of time, ranging from short term to long term, can be discerned from the different perspectives: 1) on the organization's ability to sequence its attention to constituent demands for performance; 2) on the composition of the pool of organizational constituencies; 3) on the preferences that constituencies have for the outcomes of organizational performance; and 4) on the societal context within which constituent preferences are formed.

Insight into generalization about effectiveness with the value-based and time-specific nature of the effectiveness construct helps us to understand more easily the development of the efficiency construct and various models of efficiency up till now. The evaluation of organizational effectiveness has not been random, but it has paralleled change in the perspective of (the most advanced) management in the course of the 20th and 21st centuries.

These changes largely reflect modification in society's definition of acceptable organizational behavior. In turn, acceptable behavior is reflected in the outcomes of an organization's performance and this behavior is required, if the organization is to thrive within its social setting. Various authors (see Hay and Gray, 1974; Kotler and Lee, 2004; Werther and Chandler, 2005) have suggested that since the turn of the century there had been two shifts in managerial perspectives, which reflect the changing public expectations that are naturally based on prevailing values, cultures, ethics, and norms. At the beginning of the 20th century, in keeping with the tenets of classical economics and free enterprise capitalism, the perspectives of an organization's owners was of the central concern to managers. This perspective was reflected in early goal-based researches of organizational effectiveness in their emphasis on the financial performance criteria such as profit and return on equity.

Public dissatisfaction with the performance of businesses increased during the first third of the 20th century following business excesses of the late 1800s and early 1900s. In the wake of the 1930s depression (especially in USA) governments enacted legislation to protect the interests of a variety of direct organizational participants. Hay and Gray (1974) and Werther and Chandler (2005) noted that this dissatisfaction then led to the emergence of managerial perspectives that considered the preferences of these participants in management decision making.

This perspective was fairly well entrenched in American management by the 1950s and in European management during 1960s. Various constructs of the organizational effectiveness formulated during the 1960s reflected a shift in public expectations and managerial orientation. This was accomplished through the addition of criteria that reflected aspects of organizational functioning beyond those represented by financial criteria. Effectiveness was operationally defined in many different ways, including job satisfaction (Bowers and Seashore, 1966; Box and Cosgrove, 1968), managerial task skills (Goodman, 1970; Seashore and Yuchtman, 1967), managerial interpersonal skills (Bowers and Seashore, 1966), turnover (Bowers, 1964; Grusky, 1963), product quality (Beek, 1964; Student, 1968), group cohesion (Lodahl and Porter, 1961), etc. This new understanding of reality was consistent with the systemic understanding of efficiency being introduced in the organizational sciences during the 1960s (Cunningham, 1977; Zamuto, 1982; Ostroff and Schmitt, 1993).

Public dissatisfaction with the performance of public institutions increased during the 1960s and 1970s as the civil rights, environmental, and other social movements grew. Legislative regulations of the activities of organizations were enacted during this period, presenting the public definition of acceptable organizational behavior, and these concepts continued to evolve. The public began to require that organizations take into account the preference of indirect constituencies—those affected by the externalities of organizational performance—as well as the preferences of the direct constituencies of the organizations. The emergence of multiple constituency models during the 1970s paralleled this change by incorporating the preferences of both direct and indirect constituencies into the evaluation process. And much of the confusion that surrounds the definition and criteria of effective /efficient organizational performance in current discussion is related to the slow and uneven acceptance of changing social expectation(s).

Discussion about General and Content-Related Consideration of Efficiency Theories

On the basis of the selected viewpoint or viewpoints, or a requisitely holistic dialectical system of viewpoints (or perspective/s), the author selects (his or her or their) approach. He, she, or they may consider generalization of effectiveness/efficiency with their value-based and time-specific background of their chosen effectiveness/efficiency construct. After that phase, researchers choose their way/methodology and content of consideration of the efficiency construct that suits their purpose and goal of research. Of course, this selection depends on the interdependence inside the entity of (selected) important viewpoints (Potocan, 2004, 2005).

As we have demonstrated in the Dialectical Systems Theory (Mulej, 2000, and earlier, since 1974; Mulej et al., 2012), no process of work starts well, unless it starts with the definition of the (desired) goals or objectives. Desires do not tend to be requisitely holistically grounded and hence realistic. Desires are, in fact, an irrational, emotional component of values, which are interdependent with knowledge, like the right and left brain hemispheres. And there are also outer circumstances. We call the former 'the subjective starting points' and the outer 'the objective starting points', which we divide into needs and possibilities that exist out there. On the basis of our human subjective starting points all of us consciously or subconsciously select our viewpoint or, hopefully, our dialectical system of viewpoints. A single selected viewpoint makes us one-sided in our perception, thinking, reflection, decision-making, communication, and action; oversights result from one-sidedness and cause failures, all the way to world-wars and their causes. On the other hand, a dialectical system of viewpoints enables the requisite holism averting crucial oversights and resulting failures. On the basis of the selected viewpoint/s one perceives the objective starting points, and formulates the perceived needs and perceived possibilities. Usually, as economics teach us according to experience, the perceived needs require more than the perceived possibilities are able to offer. Sociology and psychology add needs beyond the biological and economic ones to ones' perceived needs, often moving needs and possibilities even further apart. Hence, in the next step, we must select the preferential needs and the corresponding possibilities. Only in the next step of the process of human working, we have a chance to define well grounded, and therefore realistic, goals. Afterwards, the definition of tasks and of the ways of performing the tasks follows, and only then comes the operational work, leading to attainment of the goals. Often, the entire process must be repeated to achieve a good outcome, because some oversights occurred in the first round or new circumstances have shown up since.

Efficiency depends on all these steps of the process, but most of all on the first ones and on the interdependence and synergetic interaction of their components. Thus, efficiency theories should cover all components and process steps, and interactions among them to meet the law of requisite holism, to consider the law of hierarchy of the process and interdependence, and thus to fight the law of entropy as the permanent natural tendency of everything to regress towards destruction often by eroding towards some other lesser form.

From the research on the content-related understanding and consideration of efficiency viewpoint we can draw the following conclusions:

- Very many different content-related definitions of efficiency are known in both theory and practice.
- These definitions are impossible to compare requisitely holistically, because they are based on different objective and subjective starting points and pursue, as a rule, different goals that are, as a rule, not very well, i.e. requisitely holistically, grounded.
- But one can, partially at least, unify attributes of similar models inside the framework of single approaches, and compare them afterwards, on a framework basis.
- Most of the contemporary considerations of efficiency take into account the value-based and time-specific nature of the effectiveness construct.
- Most of the contemporary considerations use the transformation model as their basis of understanding the efficiency of working and behavior of organizations.

Thus, these models may be judged as approaching a kind of the requisite holism, although no final phase of this trend is visible as yet. One measure that needs to be undertaken by authors and users to come closer to a requisitely holistic definition of the concept of efficiency is learning to know the methodological bases for making and using the effectiveness construct.

ISSUES CONCERNING METHODOLOGY IN UNDERSTANDING AND CONSIDERATION OF EFFICIENCY

The need for requisite holism of consideration of efficiency requires the methodological bases of the efficiency construct to be requisitely holistic as well. This fact opens issues of concept and content of methodology of consideration of efficiency (Potocan, 2004, 2005). Two aspects (or viewpoints or perspectives) require our priority attention in this respect:

- A (minor) part of the methodology for dealing with an efficiency construct depends on the framework given by the selection of the approach for dealing with the efficiency construct.
- A (larger) part of the methodology depends on the chosen methodology of dealing with the organization, and choice which measure of efficiency is a side-effect of the work.

Dealing with the efficiency construct is easier and simpler, if both methodologies are in accord. But, in organizational practice, this accord is rather an exception than the rule. Organizations, or even their single parts, may, and frequently do, practice diverse and different combinations of methodological starting points of consideration of efficiency. Methodology is a part of knowledge, thus a part of the subjective starting points rather than of the objective ones.

Some options for combining different methodological starting points are (also) considered in some other contributions (see e.g. Parra-Luna, 2000, 2003; etc.).

But some open methodological issues should be exposed anyway, because they have an important and, first of all, limiting, impact on the attempt to requisitely holistically research organizations as wholes/entities and to research the efficiency construct specifically (Potocan, 2005, 2006; Potocan and Kuralt, 2007). Dealing with the efficiency construct depends essentially on how these issues are understood, be the topic at stake a single criterion (where e.g. it may follow a single value presenting a single aspect of efficiency) on the one extreme, or the most complex and complicated composition or system of all criteria (that e.g. a situation that attempts to reach beyond the requisite holism of consideration of all criteria toward a total holism) on the other extreme of the span of options.

Some open issues tackle the problems of dealing with several factors and entire entities, e.g. factors (or components) of the organization and/or efficiency, factors inside these frameworks (or inside partial criteria or sub-criteria and/or single synthetic criteria of efficiency), or with the whole entity (the whole organization and the total system of criteria of efficiency).

The more important open issues of consideration of factors (or components) and/or criteria of efficiency (such as single-criterion indicators) include:

- A requisitely holistic definition of criteria (e.g. what has a primary or a secondary importance: e.g. is technology an internal or an external factor of efficiency; what is the structure of the factor at stake: the consumed work hours as an entity made up of many kinds, types and forms of work expressed in time units; etc.).
- Monitoring and assessment (e.g. ways to—as objectively as possible—perceive, measure and evaluate the objective and the subjective factors; how to define the quality level of products and processes quality; how to define the level of innovativeness of a work unit; how to objectively measure employee satisfaction, if only an indirect tool of their opinion about their satisfaction is available; etc.).
- The need to understand (and use) an evaluated factor and/or criterion inside a context of contents (e.g. how to understand and/or compare the same level of productivity of two organizations with different levels of technological equipment; how to understand different levels of absenteeism in two different units of the same organization; etc.).
- Learning to know and to define—both direct and indirect—impacts on a factor and/or criterion and of the impact of this factor and/or criterion on its environments, both internal and external.

On the level of composed factors and/or criteria all cited and similar issues keep making sense, since the field of study is open, but new unsolved issues are added all the time.

The critical conceptual issues include synergies and related (requisitely) holistic consideration of their working. Relatively many organizations try to learn to know and understand important synergies of their working, but relatively few organizations include synergy on a requisitely holistic basis in their actual dealing with their own working and behavior.

Yet another issue considers a requisitely holistic dealing with the working of an organization (as a rule reaching beyond its formal and institutional boundaries) and it does so, e.g., in terms of its entire transformation process, the entire business process (including all suppliers and all buyers and customers), value chains, interest chains, etc.

Concerning composed factors and/or composed criteria (e.g. multi-criteria indicators) the open issues include:

- The selection of critical components to be considered (i.e. which are the unavoidable criteria for an objective assessment of a topic – e.g. Steers (1975) finds that the available models of efficiency include 3 to

14 criteria, of those mostly 5 are critical criteria).

- Relations between single factors and/or partial or sub-criteria (how are they related to each other, to environments, to the entire whole, etc.).
- What is the way and strength of impact of single factors and/or partial or sub-criteria (what and how it impacts them; what are their impacts over each other like; what is their impact over the whole like; what are their impacts over their environment like; etc.).
- Detecting the synergies inside consideration of factors and/or partial or sub-criteria (what are synergies like between them, inside the whole, with their environments, etc.).

If there are several levels, further issues show up such as the following:

- Links between different efficiency approaches and different kinds, types, and forms of efficiency.
- Links between single efficiency construct and different kinds, types, and forms of efficiency.
- Links between an efficiency construct (with the given approaches, kinds, types, and forms of efficiency) and its possible (and/or real) influence (on working and behavior of organization and/or organizational environment/s).
- Links between an efficiency construct (with the given approaches, kinds, types, and forms of efficiency) and its possible (and/or real) influences (on results of organization and organizational environment/s).

A more/requisitely holistic investigation of this topics will require further research with further contents- and methodology-related issues, including, e.g.:

- Potential consideration of different efficiency construct(s) and different kinds, types, and forms of efficiency in a given organization.
- Potential impact of different kinds, types, and forms of efficiency over business of organizations.
- Bases for a requisitely holistic approach to consideration of efficiency constructs, different kinds, types, and forms of efficiency, and their impact over business and other working and behavior of different organizations.

Solutions and Recommendations

Efficiency is a much more complex concept, if one takes a thorough look at it, than is apparent in the daily superficial use of the word. It shows up in many rather different sciences and their (sub)-disciplines. Their authors use many diverse perspectives/viewpoints, which they are fully entitled to select as they deem appropriate in their research. Thus, no unified definition is possible. The huge variety of approaches causes a similarly huge variety of definitions. An overview in terms of contents is provided here as is an overview of dilemmas in terms of methodology of consideration. No final or unique answer is offered, because this would make no sense. What is required, though, is for every author to attempt to do two things:

- To explicitly state the framework and viewpoint applied.
- To explicitly and rigorously define what is included in the dialectical system of the applied viewpoints, so that some kind of a requisite holism might be attained in research and/or management, both of theory and practice.

The modern business conditions require humans, enterprises and other organizations to take a less narrowly specialized methodological approach and apply new methods in order to manage requisitely holistically rather than apply their one-sided approach to holism, entanglement and dynamics, which the old, less complex, conditions used to require.

In our contribution, we discuss different approaches to research of efficiency. Most of the newer approaches deal with complex rather than complicated efficiency constructs; thus, most of them have tried to stress relations between parts of reality, which have usually up to now been considered in separation and hence one-sidedly rather than (requisitely) holistically, in other, mostly older, approaches.

Different authors define efficiency differently, because they use different understanding and definitions (e.g. different conceptual bases, different content bases, and different methodological bases) according to their selected viewpoints. Generally, one takes either one of the traditional approaches or the systems/systemic approach.

From our viewpoint the systems approach is the most interesting and promising. If one adds, in order to be less abstract and closer to reality, the consideration of the influential role of the selected viewpoint/s and of humans defining them, one comes closer to an array of the different less traditional Systems Theories. This does not yet provide a unified definition of the systems approach. Much depends on the authors too—often not only in details, but also in the basic definition of the approach. In some cases of the systems approach, interdependence between the following relations can be seen: inside the entity / system under consideration / impact / viewpoints. It is less often extended to the relations between the object under consideration and the humans dealing with it, and still less often extended to the relations between viewpoints of consideration, e.g. of efficiency. (See: François, 2004).

Our understanding of possible ways for the creation of different efficiency constructs is presented in Figure 1.

Figure 1. Our understanding of possible ways for the creation of different efficiency constructs

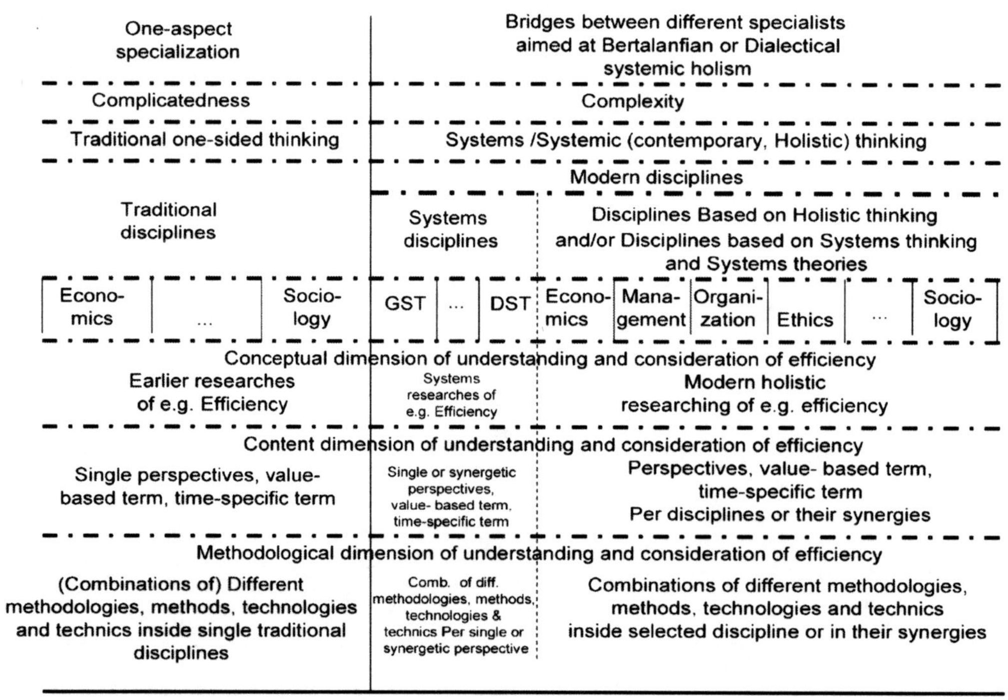

FUTURE RESEARCH DIRECTIONS

Cognitions that a more holistic understanding and research of efficiency is possible might enable more of the necessary requisite holism in consideration of organizations. This need requires consideration of interdependence and synergetic working of the business reality, systems thinking (i.e. the methodological approach enabling the requisite holism of understanding of e.g. the business practice), and the Efficiency construct (i.e. methodology of impacting the business reality).

In general this makes room for the requisitely holistic understanding and research of efficiency.

At the same time, there is a need for a requisitely holistic consideration of the organization as an entity/system made up of the network/system of: (1) general, (2) group-specific, and (3) individual attributes. Based on these terms, one can formulate efficiency as one possible specification of the general and the group-specific attributes of working and behavior of organizations. Its definition is a generalization of many individual attributes on the basis of their common attributes.

In terms of contents, efficiency can be defined as a measure for and of success and as a general term for requisitely holistic understanding of outcomes and preconditions. A specialized research and action on the basis of its (1) specific area, and (2) specific methods of dealing with this area is required. This requires application to an organization and investigating the organization-related specifics in order to requisitely holistically deal with business issues of organizations/humans from the crucial viewpoints in the selected dialectical systems. In terms of methodology, efficiency applies selected content to organization, based on selected (dialectical systems of) viewpoints, purposes, goals, methods, methodologies, circumstances of use, and characteristics of its users.

When we define the role and significance of efficiency, we are facing new dilemmas, such as:

- How are we to create and implement the general methodology for requisitely holistic cognition, implementation, and management of (efficient) working to typical organizations?
- What are the required and adequate conditions for the division of the entire business into the general and specialized possible specific content, such as efficiency?
- What are the criteria for the definition of an individual specialized definition of efficiency?
- What is the relationship between different narrow specialized areas of efficiency within social, technical or natural sciences?

These are some of the issues for further research.

REFERENCES

Beek, H. (1964). The influence of assembly line organization on output, quality, and morale. *Occupational Psychology*, *38*(3/4), 161–172.

Bowers, D. (1964). Organizational control in insurance company. *Sociometry*, *27*(2), 230–244. doi:10.2307/2785719.

Bowers, D., & Seashore, S. (1966). Predicting organizational effectiveness with a four-factory theory of leadership. *Administrative Science Quarterly*, *11*(2), 238–263. doi:10.2307/2391247.

Box, S., & Cosgrove, S. (1968). The productivity of scientists in industrial research laboratories. *Sociology*, *11*(2), 163–172. doi:10.1177/003803856800200202.

Cameron, K., & Whetten, D. (Eds.). (1982). *Organizational effectiveness: A comparison of multiple models*. New York: Academic Press.

Cameron, S., & Whetten, D. (1986). Effectiveness as paradox: Consensus and conflict in conceptions of organizational effectiveness. *Management Science, 32*(5), 539–553. doi:10.1287/mnsc.32.5.539.

Chandler, A. (1996). *Strategy and structure: Chapters in the history of the American industrial enterprise*. Cambridge, MA: MIT Press.

Coelli, T., Prasada Rao, S., O'Donnell, C., & Battese, G. (2005). *An introduction to efficiency and productivity analysis*. New York: Springer.

Connolly, T., Conlon, E., & Deutsch, S. (1980). Organizational effectiveness: A multiple-constituency approach. *Academy of Management Review, 5*(2), 211–217.

Costantino, C. (1996). Using interest-based techniques to design conflict management systems. *Negotiation Journal, 12*(3), 207–214. doi:10.1111/j.1571-9979.1996.tb00095.x.

Cunningham, B. (1977). Approaches to the evaluation of organizational effectiveness. *Academy of Management Review, 2*(3), 463–474.

Daft, R. (2000). *Management*. Fort Worth, TX: The Dryden Press.

Daft, R. (2006). *Organization theory and design*. Cincinnati, OH: South Western College Publishing.

Drucker, P. (1946). *Concept of corporation*. New York: Harper and Row.

Editors of the American Heritage Dictionaries (EAHD). (2000). *The American heritage dictionary of the English language*. Boston: Houghton Mifflin.

Emerson, R. (1962). Power-dependence relations. *American Sociological Review, 27*(1), 31–41. doi:10.2307/2089716.

Encyclopaedia Britannica. (2007). *Britannica concise encyclopedia*. London: Encyclopedia Britannica.

Etzioni, A. (1997). *Modern organizations*. London: Profile Books.

Evan, W. (1976). Organizational theory and organizational effectiveness. *Organizational and Administrative Science, 7*, 15–28.

Fare, R., Grosskopf, S., & Fukuyama, H. (2004). *New directions: Efficiency and productivity*. Boston: Springer.

Funk, W. (1992). *Word origins: An exploration and history of words and language*. Gravesend, NJ: Bell Publishing Company.

Galbrait, J. (1995). *Designing organizations: An executive briefing on strategy, structure, and process*. San Francisco, CA: Jossey-Bass.

Goodman, P., & Penningss, J. (Eds.). (1977). *New perspectives on organizational effectiveness*. San Francisco, CA: Jossey-Bass.

Goodman, R. (1970). Organizational preference in research and development. *Human Relations, 23*(4), 279–298. doi:10.1177/001872677002300403.

Gove, P. (Ed.). (2002). *Third new international dictionary of the English language*. Chicago: Merriam-Webster.

Grusky, O. (1963). Managerial succession and organizational effectiveness. *American Journal of Sociology, 69*(1), 21–31. doi:10.1086/223507.

Hall, R., & Clark, J. (1980). An ineffective effectiveness study and some suggestions for future research. *The Sociological Quarterly, 21*, 119–134. doi:10.1111/j.1533-8525.1980.tb02203.x.

Hay, R., & Gray, E. (1974). Social responsibilities of business managers. *Academy of Management Journal, 17*(1), 135–143. doi:10.2307/254777.

Hickson, D., Hinings, C., Lee, C., Schneck, R., & Pennings, J. (1971). A strategic contingencies' theory of inter-organizational power. *Administrative Science Quarterly, 16*(3), 216–229. doi:10.2307/2391831.

Honeycutt, A., & Richards, B. (1989). An organizational transformation model: The road to renewal. *Educational Technology*, *29*(10), 42–45.

House, R. (1971). A path goal theory of leader effectiveness. *Administrative Science Quarterly*, *16*(3), 321–339. doi:10.2307/2391905.

House, R. (1980). *Evaluating with validity*. Beverly Hills, CA: Sage Publications.

Kanigel, R. (1999). *The one best way: Frederick Winslow Taylor and the enigma of efficiency*. New York: Viking.

Kekes, J. (1989). *Moral tradition and individuality*. Princeton, NJ: Princeton University Press.

Kotler, P., & Lee, N. (2004). *Corporate social responsibility: Doing the most good for your company and your cause*. Hoboken, NJ: Wiley.

Lakatos, I., & Musgrave, A. (Eds.). (1970). *Criticism and the growth of knowledge*. Cambridge, UK: Cambridge University Press.

Lawler, E., Worley, C., & Porras, J. (2006). *Built to change: How to achieve sustained organizational effectiveness*. San Francisco, CA: Jossey-Bass.

Lawrence, P., & Lorsch, J. (1967). Differentiation and integration in complex organizations. *Administrative Science Quarterly*, *12*(1), 1–30. doi:10.2307/2391211.

Lebacqz, K. (1986). *Six theories of justice: Perspectives from philosophical and theological ethics*. Augsburg, Germany: Augsburg Books.

Lodahl, T., & Porter, L. (1961). Psychometric score patterns, social characteristics, and productivity of small industrial work groups. *The Journal of Applied Psychology*, *45*(2), 73–79. doi:10.1037/h0043379.

Magretta, J. (1999). *Managing in the new economy*. Boston: Harvard Business School.

Magretta, J. (2002, May). Why business models matter. *Harvard Business Review*, 86–92. PMID:12024761.

McGraw-Hill Company. (1989). *McGraw-Hill encyclopedia of science and technology*. New York: McGraw-Hill Company.

Mill, S. (2002). *Utilitarianism*. Indianapolis, IN: Hackett Pub..

Mulej, M. (1974). Dialectical systems theory. *Our Economy*, *21*(3-4), 207–212.

Mulej, M., et al. (2000a). *Dialectical and other soft systems theories*. Maribor, Portugal: FEB.

Mulej, M. et al. (2012b). *Dialectical systems thinking and the law of requisite holism*. Phoenix, AZ: ISCE Publishing.

Ostroff, C., & Schmitt, N. (1993). Configurations of organizational effectiveness and efficiency. *Academy of Management Journal*, *36*(6), 1345–1361. doi:10.2307/256814.

Parolini, C. (1999). *The value net: A tool for competitive advantages*. Chichester, UK: Wiley.

Parra-Luna, F. (2000). *The performance of social systems*. New York: Kluwer Academic / Plenum Publishers. doi:10.1007/978-1-4615-4251-3.

Parra-Luna, F. (2003). *Elementos para un teoria formal del sistema socia: Una orientacion critica*. Madrid, Spain: Universidad Complutense.

Pennings, J. (1975). The relevance of the structural-contingency model for organizational effectiveness. *Administrative Science Quarterly*, *20*(3), 393–410. doi:10.2307/2391999.

Perrow, C. (1961). The analysis of goals in complex organizations. *American Sociological Review*, *26*(6), 854–866. doi:10.2307/2090570.

Pettinger, R. (2007). *Introduction to management*. Chicago: Palgrave MacMillan.

Pfeffer, J., & Salancik, G. (1978). *The external control of organizations*. New York: Harper & Row.

Porter, M. (1998). *Competitive advantage of nations*. New York: Free Press.

Potocan, V. (2003). Transition from ethics of independence to ethics of interdependence as a factor of sustainable development. In *Proceedings of the 10th Interdisciplinary Information Management Talks,* (pp. 123-130). Linz, Austria: Universitätsverlag Trauner.

Potocan, V. (2004). *Operations management.* Maribor, Portugal: FEB.

Potocan, V. (2005). Efficiency or effectiveness? *Organization*, *38*(10), 570–576.

Potocan, V. (2006). Business operations between efficiency and effectiveness. *Journal of Information and Organizational Sciences*, *30*(2), 251–262.

Potocan, V., & Kuralt, B. (2007). Synergy in business: Some new suggestions. *The Journal of American Academy of Business*, *12*(1), 199–204.

Potocan, V., Mulej, K., & Kajzer, S. (2005). Business cybernetics: A provocative suggestion. *Kybernetes*, *34*(9/10), 1496–1516. doi:10.1108/03684920510614786.

Potocan, V., & Rebernik, M. (2002). Achieving synergy of business system via anticipatory system. In *Proceedings of the AIP Conference,* (pp. 441-447). AIP.

Price, J. (1972). The study of organizational effectiveness. *The Sociological Quarterly*, *13*(4), 3–15. doi:10.1111/j.1533-8525.1972.tb02100.x.

Quinn, R. (1992). *The intelligent enterprise: A knowledge and service based paradigm for industry*. New York: Free Press.

Quinn, R., & Rohrbaugh, J. (1983). A spatial model of effectiveness criteria: Toward a competing values approach to organizational analysis. *Management Science*, *29*(3), 363–377. doi:10.1287/mnsc.29.3.363.

Rawls, J. (1971). *A theory of justice*. Cambridge, MA: Harvard University Press.

Russ-Eft, D., & Preskill, H. (2001). *Evaluation in organizations: A systemic approach to enhancing learning, performance, and change*. Cambridge, MA: MIT Press.

Salancik, G., & Pfeffer, J. (1974). The bases and uses of power in organizational decision making: The case of a university. *Administrative Science Quarterly*, *19*(4), 453–473. doi:10.2307/2391803.

Schultz, W. (2001). *The moral conditions of economic efficiency*. Cambridge, UK: Cambridge University Press. doi:10.1017/CBO9780511549649.

Seashore, S., & Yuchtman, E. (1967). Factorial analysis of organizational performance. *Administrative Science Quarterly*, *12*(3), 377–395. doi:10.2307/2391311.

Siegel, J., & Shim, J. (2000). *Accounting handbook*. New York: Barron.

Simon, H. (1976). *Administrative behavior: A study of decision-making processes in administrative organizations*. New York: Free Press.

Singer, P. (1999). *Practical ethics*. Oxford, UK: Oxford University Press.

Steers, R. (1975). Problems in the measurement of organizational effectiveness. *Administrative Science Quarterly*, *20*(4), 546–558. doi:10.2307/2392022.

Steers, R. (1977). *Organizational effectiveness: A behavioral view*. Santa Monica, CA: Goodyear.

Steffen, A. (2006). *Worldchanging: A user's guide for the 21st century*. New York: Harry N. Abrams.

Strasses, S., Eveland, J., Cummins, G., Deniston, L., & Romani, J. (1981). Conceptualizing the goal and systems models of organizational effectiveness – Implications for comparative evaluation research. *Journal of Management Studies*, *18*(3), 321–340. doi:10.1111/j.1467-6486.1981.tb00105.x.

Student, K. (1968). Supervisory influence and work group performance. *The Journal of Applied Psychology*, *52*(3), 188–194. doi:10.1037/h0025886 PMID:5659502.

Trevino, L., & Nelson, K. (2006). *Managing business ethics: Straight talk about how to do it right*. New York: Wiley.

Tsui, A. (1990). A multiple-constituency model of effectiveness: An empirical examination at the human resource subunit level. *Administrative Science Quarterly*, *35*(3), 458–483. doi:10.2307/2393313.

Wagner, J., & Schneider, B. (1987). Legal regulation and the constraint of constituency satisfaction. *Journal of Management Studies*, *24*(2), 189–200. doi:10.1111/j.1467-6486.1987.tb00943.x.

Webster Dictionary (WD). (1928). *An American dictionary of the English language*. Retrieved September 16, 2011 from http://www.cbtministries.org/resources/Webster1828.htm

Werther, W., & Chandler, D. (2005). *Strategic corporate social responsibility: Stakeholders in a global environment*. London: SAGE.

Wren, D. (2004). *The history of management thought*. Upper Saddle River, NJ: Pearson Prentice Hall.

Yuchtman, E., & Seashore, S. (1967). A system resource approach to organizational effectiveness. *American Sociological Review*, *32*(6), 891–903. doi:10.2307/2092843.

Zammuto, R. (1982). *Assessing organizational effectiveness: Systems change, adaptation and strategy*. Albany, NY: SUNY Press.

Zammuto, R. (1984). A comparison of multiple constituency models of organizational effectiveness. *Academy of Management Review*, *9*(4), 606–618.

Zenko, Z., Mulej, M., & Marn, J. (2004). Innovation before entry into the EU: The case of Slovenia. *Post Communist Economies*, *16*(2), 169–189. doi:10.1080/1463137042000223877.

KEY TERMS AND DEFINITIONS

Approaches to Consideration of Efficiency: In literature authors mentioned some various well-known approaches to consideration and understanding of efficiency such as: Goal based approaches, Systems approaches, Constituency approaches, and Contingency approaches.

Concept of Efficiency: In economics and business economics, as well as in most of the natural and technological sciences, the practitioners use the concept of efficiency solely to deal with suitability of the entire working of the organization, including the internal and external parts of the business process and environments. In organizational theory the theoreticians make a distinction between efficiency and effectiveness and they use both terms. In management science, the scientists rather strictly delimit efficiency and effectiveness.

Content of Efficiency: Efficiency Theories provide for at least two terms which various authors use to define efficiency in terms of its content. The first term is perspectives, which some authors propose to cover e.g. the realistic, power and social justice approaches and evolutionary perspectives. The second term is the generalization about effectiveness with the values-based and time-specific nature of an effectiveness construct.

Efficiency: Efficiency can be described in the most general terms as a requisitely holistic measure of working of the reviewed business system; it has been created because humans deemed that tone can attain the desired outcomes of organizational performance from the vantage point of various constituencies directly and indirectly affected by the organization.

Methodology of Efficiency: The need for requisite holism of consideration of efficiency requires the methodological bases of the efficiency construct to be requisitely holistic as well. In that framework, two aspects require priority attention. i.e.: A (minor) part of the methodology for dealing with an efficiency construct depends on the framework given by the selection of the approach for dealing with the efficiency construct, and; A (larger) part of the methodology depends on the chosen methodology of dealing with the organization, and which measure of efficiency is a side-effect of the work.

Chapter 8
Use of Social Network for Business in Public Relations

Damjana Jerman
International Business School Ljubljana, Slovenia

Bruno Završnik
University of Maribor, Slovenia

ABSTRACT

Before the development of the Internet, there were only a few major media outlets that organizations could use to reach their target audiences. Subsequently, public relations practitioners were able to carefully control all forms of communication. The arrival of new media in the past few years has posed an array of new opportunities but also threats. The public has developed a need to access news and information practically before it exists, and so there is a growing desire to find out what's new via social network sites. With the introduction of social networks, business organizations should identify those social networks representing their target audiences; they should control and participate in them. This chapter describes basic characteristics of social networks and their role for public relations.

INTRODUCTION

People often associate social networks with socialization and interconnection of a group of people with similar interests. Social networking is becoming inevitable part of life and work on the field of communication. It represents communication channels for active communication with users with the help the companies to follow new trends. Social networks are especially appropriate for the increase brand awareness, recognition of a company and its offer, for the improvement of customer relationship and for creation of new groups of users. To achieve those goals it is necessary to analyze current conditions and create corporate communication strategy. The organization must carefully combine and coordinate different strategies, tactics, messages, and communication channels for the creation of the message to be clear and impressive to users. And most importantly,

DOI: 10.4018/978-1-4666-4373-4.ch008

this message must be shared and recommended to friends and acquaintances by users.

Communication is at the heart of the management of relationships with stakeholders. The organization develops and forms its relationships with different publics through communication. Organizations inform customers of new products and prices, remind them of their existing offerings, and attempt to favourably influence their perceptions by using various communication tools. Likewise, organizations communicate with various other stakeholders, such as employees, government, suppliers, intermediaries and investors, in their attempts to manage relationships for mutual benefit. Until recently the nature of this communication has tended mostly to be unidirectional and simple. The Internet is changing the nature of an organization's communication with its stakeholders in ways that are unprecedented. Stakeholder communication will no longer be unidirectional, and as stakeholders increasingly communicate with each other (either about or not about the organization, as the case may be) this communication becomes infinitely more complex. Public relations becomes more than the management of effective communication with stakeholders – it evolves to become the management of communication between stakeholders as well (Van der Merwe *et al.,* 2005).

The definition of a news release has also expanded. The press release is no longer exclusively a media relations tool; now, with the Internet's search capabilities, consider it a direct to-consumer online page of Web content. This sea change for news releases means that consumers now access releases simultaneously with journalists. This has important implications for news release content, style and format (Croft, 2008).

The initial period of Internet was characterized by the Internet user who had in relation to the Website completely passive role - the visitor. The user read and accepted only what firms or individuals offered on their Web sites. With the development of new services, arising of programming language, Internet connections, the growth of these users are becoming more curious, difficult, important and active. The dialogue and the relationship began to emerge between the site and its visitors. In addition to the establishing two-way communication, social networking allows users to add comments, participate in forums, add pictures and videos on the Web site, assessing the author's contributions and content, integrating with other site visitors, sharing opinions and building a network of contacts (Skrt, 2007).

Social networking is a way of communicating and making friends online. There are various popular networking sites and if they are used effectively it can produce a positive image for the business. Social networks mean that there are Web sites where people can find and connect with each other and can have an impact on a specific target public. The advantages of building social networks as a tool of public relations for the organization are the following. Social networks can increase the production of content by user organizations. Also, social networks can help to set up the systems feedback, create members of online social networks and can allow sharing interests and may begin to build relationships. Organizations can build a company brand or its product brand with Facebook and Linkedin profiles or a Twitter account. Through these entities organizations could benefit consistent and efficient corporate communications (Hozjan, 2010).

In the literature social networks is often mentioned as the essential factor for business success and has been given considerable attention. This article challenges this view by pointing out positive effects of social networks on reaching success in the filed of public relations in general.

The methodology used in this paper refers to a review of basic literature in the field of public relations, review of the literature in the field of the Internet as a social space and social networks. We will use secondary data sources.

Our contribution consists of three sections. In the first section we introduce the concept of communications and different definitions of public relations. The following section refers to computer-supplied information and the definition of the Internet as a medium. The differences between Internet and traditional media are presented; we also tried to set the Internet in a social context. The communication is the essence of the Internet and through communication; the relations between people are established. So, the Internet is creating virtual communities. So in the followed section we define the concept of virtual communities and present their characteristics. People are increasingly connecting through social media on the Internet, so we present their growing importance for public relations. In the third section we discuss the use of social media in public relations. Internet is changing the practice of public relations, so we introduced these changes.

Overall, in this paper is to present a study, the objectives of which are:

- To explore the concept of communications and different definitions of public relations.
- To outline basic characteristics of social networks and its role for public relations.
- To explore different instruments of public relations and the importance of development of social responsibilities of businesses for communication and corporate objectives achievement.
- To improve the understanding of using social networking to create a positive company image.

THE ROLE OF COMMUNICATION IN SOCIAL NETWORK

The role of communications is the focus of research or discussion of many authors. However, the role of communication within organisations is far from clear, and the large array of academic terms in usage has made it difficult to establish "common definition." Parallel to this, it is difficult to define also the term "communications professionals" – a term often hears being used in academia and business, too (Kalla, 2005).

There are various interpretations of the term communication(s). At its simplest, the definition for communication is social interaction through messages (Kalla, 2005). On the other hand, Oliver (1997, p. 64) provides a more comprehensive definition of communication as "an interchange of ideas, facts and emotions, by two or more persons, with the use of words, letters and symbols based on the technical problem of how accurately the symbols can be transmitted, the semantic problem of how, precisely, the symbols convey the desired meaning, and the effectiveness of how the received meaning affects conduct in the desired way". In order to understand better the nature of communication(s) and some of the definitions for communications will now be explored.

The impact on the communication profession over the next few years will mean a renewed focus on crisis management and the role communication plays to ensure companies, employees, clients and customers have the tools and mechanisms in place for business continuity, minimal confusion and chaos, and zero human casualties. Crisis communication planning and the ability to lead come hell or high water may become a required skill set for professional communicators (Kalla, 2005).

Some authors distinguish between communication and effective communication (Bove´e & Thill, 2000); whereas others take communication to always refer to effective communication (Oliver, 1997). For example, Bove´e and Thill (2000, p. 4) believe that effective communication only takes place when participants "achieve a shared understanding, stimulate others to take actions, and encourage people to think in new ways." On the other hand, Oliver (1997) argues that communication is always a persuasive two-way process.

Some authors also distinguish the concept of integrated internal communications. This concept is seen as being composed of all the academic disciplines at the cross-section between communication and organisational life, i.e. business, organisational, management, and corporate communication. Similarly, Grunig and others (2002) define organizational communication as a specialized subject to discipline, which examined how employees interact in the organization and the nature of the effectiveness of communication within the organization. Furthermore, integrated internal communications are not limited to the formal tasks performed by the corporate communication function; instead all formal and informal communication taking place inside an organisation is included (Kalla, 2005).

The Definition of Communities and Social Network

Many important aspects of social life are organized as networks. Social networking at its beginning means chatting of secondary school pupils and students groups on the Website MySpace. Today, many Websites are available for creating social networks. Users are increasingly recognizing the usefulness of portals for business purposes. Using these portals to work is becoming more common and many of professional networks have already been created. Date back to 1995, when it was founded Web site Classmates.com, which is one of the sites that have started to build a community network. Over the years, the Website was followed by the online sites like Epinions.com, Friendster.com, MySpace.com, YouTube.com and others.

Tönnies began a systematic study of communities in "Gemeinschaft und Gesellschaft". He developed a dichotomy between community and society. Both dimensions are pure theoretical concept. "Gemeinschaft" or community is characterized by the traditional, inarticulate, based on personal relationships, unity, traditions and religions. It is characterized by organic will, which provides for thinking and produced naturally. This theoretical concept is operationalized as a private, natural form, such as understanding, traditions, beliefs, which are private decisions. From these resulting collective forms like style, customs and religion; these are common emotions. On the other hand, "Gesellschaft" or society means urban, industrial, rational organization. Relations in it are impersonal; there are special interests, conventions, laws, law. It is based on the reflective forms which encompasses free will. It has a natural shape: the agreement, low, the doctrine of generating complex forms: conventions, legislation and public opinion. It can achieve a high degree of consensus (Splichal, 1997).

A common definition of social network don' exists. Muniz and O'Guinn (2001) therefore summarize the main features of social network, which are common to most definitions. The common consciousness is an internal connection that community members feel to one another. It is also important feeling of being different from those who are not members of this community. It is therefore a collective sense of belonging to certain common network (Muniz & O'Guinn, 2001). We can also define social network as common rituals and traditions, deriving from a common history, culture, and consciousness. They can reinforce the norms, values and community solidarity. Social network can also be conceptualized as a sense of moral responsibility, which is reflected as an obligation to all communities and individual members (Muniz & O'Guinn, 2001).

Indicators of network are the social relations that arise between individuals, groups and institutions. It is important to the saturation of networks, power connections, and relationships, rate heterogeneity among the units in the network, the impact of situations on the individual and collective action. All this can also be found in social networks (Jankowski, 2009).

Instead of analyzing individual behaviours, attitudes or beliefs, social network put its attention on social entities or actors in interaction with one another and how these interactions constitute a framework that can be studied (Wasserman & Galaskiewicz, 1994).

The Definition of Public Relations

Public relations tell an organization's story to publics to foster goodwill and understanding. Public relations practitioners help shape the company's practices by counselling top management on public opinion and issues, and on the positive and negative implications of certain behaviours. Public relations often moves at a dynamic pace and is driven by a changing competitive landscape and unpredictable shifts in publics opinions. Public relations are a component of the management who are responsible for the effectiveness and efficiency of the relationship between the organization and its public. The process of public relations management processes consist of making sense, directing, planning, organizing, implementing, monitoring and evaluation of projects.

However, there are different definitions of public relations. Among these are differences which arise because the authors of these definitions are not uniform in view of public relations and communication. Some practitioners define communication broader than public relations. Communication is seen as the management of communication functions within an organization.

Public relations on the other site is seen as one of the sub-functions, mostly as publicity, media relations or marketing support. For example Kotler and others (1999) defined public relations as one of the most important marketing tools. The public is any group that has an actual or potential interest or impact on the company's ability to achieve its goal.

Other authors have different view on public relations and they see it as a broader concept.

Cutlip and other authors defined public relations as a management function that establishes and maintains mutually beneficial relationships between the organization and the public, which determine the performance of the organization. Regardless of definition public relations is viewed as a management function that conducts research to identify public attitudes, then plans and executes communications programmes designed to earn public understanding and acceptance (Cutlip *et al.,* 2000).

Similarly, Gruban and others (1997) argued that public relations are systematically planned process to influence the creation of public positive impact through mutual communication. With the help of long-term internal and external communications company can maintain or improve the company's reputation. Indirectly by the company pursues its stated business goals (Gruban *et al.*, 1997). Grunig and Grunig (2002) have developed a theory that says that public relations impact on the effectiveness of organizations by providing strategic public in the environment and the consequent development of communications programs to build a long term and stable relations with them. This definition presupposes that public relations serves the public interest, develops mutual understanding between organizations and their publics, contributes to informed debate about issues in society, and facilitates a dialogue between organizations and their publics. These are some characteristics of the basic definitions of public relations.

Kitchen (1997) in its survey of definitions of public relations found the following repeating patterns:

- Public relations are essentially a communication function, with emphasis on two-way communication.
- Public relations are concerned with establishing and maintaining mutual understanding between the organization and its public.
- Public relations serve as the intelligence function, which analyzes and interprets trends and topics in an environment that could have implications for the organization and its stakeholders.
- Public relations help organizations to design and achieve socially acceptable goals.

The opportunities for professional development in the public relations and communication are many. The vast array of available resources provides practitioners many intellectual feasts.

SOCIAL NETWORKS AND PUBLIC RELATIONS

The Internet is changing communication between stakeholders. In the past, communications between the stakeholder of an organization and the organization itself were relatively simple. They either used the telephone or wrote a letter to the organization. Electronic communications changed that. Faxes, voice mail systems and now e-mail and the Internet creates more channels of communication, it promotes open communication and, frankly, complicates matters to a large extent (Sherman, 1998). There are great advantages inherent to these new technologies, but organizations have to realize that their communication channels are being transformed, and they need to be aware of the different ways the Internet can be utilized to facilitate communication. This section describes some examples of where this has already occurred.

All indications are that the business, social, political, economic and human environment will change dramatically in the next 10 years and. As a result, so this will change the way we communicate with customers, employees and one another in general. Internet technology is transforming corporate communications, because it is changing channels, publicity, communication tools, form and content of communications, strategic planning and the ability to send feedback. Information technology is changing the structure and the relationship between companies and their publics. In parallel with this it also a shift from traditional vertical and horizontal communication paradigms. An important feature is that the stakeholders get to the Internet a mass medium, where you can access the information by them and thus produce a greater power (Ihator, 2001).

The Internet has experienced a new wave of development in recent years. Some have called this new wave Web 2.0, in contrast to the Web 1.0 of the previous Internet era (O'Reilly, 2005). These two phases differ in the way information is shared. In the Web 1.0 era, information was usually disseminated over the Internet by service providers. For example, Yahoo! provided news, stock quotes, etc. These providers controlled both the content and the distribution channels; there was little opportunity for users to participate. These changes are illustrated by the rapid growth of Weblogs (blogs), which evolved from personal Web pages. People use blogs to express their opinions and thoughts, as well as to share these with people they may, or may not, know. Concurrent with the burgeoning use of blogs, "sharing" gradually became a trend on the Internet. Many Internet companies realized that user participation is important to their success and have started using Web 2.0 to build their social networks and their reputation. The willingness of people to share online has been crucial for the development of Web 2.0 and the success of virtual communities. As sharing takes time and effort, the reason that people are willing to share is a topic of interest to researchers (Shu & Chuang, 2011).

The Internet has increased the quantity, quality and speed of information flow. As a result, transformational change in the world of media and in the practice of corporate communication is occurring at an accelerating rate of speed. Goldstein (2006) states some examples:

- The press is in decline. The standards of accuracy and rules of journalism are being eroded by the pressures to compete with Internet blogs and Web advocacy groups and the growing influence of the entertainment side of the media business. The media reporting of blog information increases their acceptance as legitimate news sources, becomes a basis for news reporting.

- Companies face an enormous challenge in trying to communicate their messages clearly and effectively. The chatter and noise factor will grow. The Internet has levelled the playing field and disgruntled stakeholders and advocacy groups will gain increasing influence.
- Communication strategists will increasingly look to adopt market research methods like focus groups to pre-assess and post-assess messaging strategies. Brand and messaging strategies will become more targeted and values-driven. And to compete, companies will create their own direct channels to reach stakeholders with Internet broadcasting, e-mail and other direct marketing techniques. Companies will establish their own databases of stakeholders and customers willing to defend the firm.
- Political campaigns have already become the laboratories for testing new communication theory and as a training ground for communication professionals who think strategically. In time, experience in politics will be as important as journalism as a criteria for corporate communicators.
- The art of writing will once again be the most valued skill a communicator can offer. In a crowded marketplace of ideas and opinions, the crafting of words that are impactful will be critical in distinguishing and differentiating companies and their messages.

There has been an increased attention given by public relations practitioners to the Internet in recent years with the focus on how best to adapt traditional practices to the new technologies (Ryan, 2003). Public relations concern itself with the management of relationships with the organization's stakeholders. The public relations function will in most cases be the department dealing with these unplanned messages. As stakeholder strength increases, public relations practitioners will have to develop strategies that deal with the rising power of different stakeholders on the Web (Van der Merwe *et al.,* 2005).

There are some differences between traditional and new media. Many of the journalists manning various "new" media can hardly claim the same experience, objectivity and credibility as a traditional print or electronic journalist. Their result often tends to lack objectivity credibility. Instead of waiting patiently for the scheduled evening/morning newscast or print run, the public has developed a crushing need to access news and information practically before it exists, and so there is a growing dash to find out what's new or breathtaking as quickly as possible via blogs, podcasts, social network sites and other "new" media that mushroom exponentially on a daily basis (Croft, 2008).

In addition, it has become disturbingly clear that the growing popularity of new media and its ability to address specific target audiences has the potential to impact negatively on public relations agencies' ability to continue to earn a good living. Especially if an agency is still running largely in tandem with traditional media to meet client business and communications needs and has not developed awareness of or the skills necessary (Croft, 2008).

Internet provides better information to the public and they consequently require organizations to be more informed. That is, organizations must adapt and become available to users also on the Internet. For the effective and successful communications, company has to accurately identify their target audiences. In the past it was much easier to target certain target groups and organizations to choose the appropriate medium for reaching them. Internet has due to its geographical features of breaking national, cultural and political boundaries and, therefore, determines target audiences and communicates with them more difficult. At the same time we are witnessing the traditional media moving online, which means to attract both old and new audiences, and this imposes difficulties when trying to accurately determine its public (Ihator, 2001). We must choose a different approach and identify those social communities where our target audiences gather; we must monitor them and participate in them. This allows controlling the situation, while providing opportunities for two-way communication. It is also easier to determine who are the opinion leaders and give more attention to them.

One of the major differences between traditional media and the Internet are therefore modified characteristics of the public. Burnett and Marshall (2003, p. 201) state that "Internet enable its public to make the transition from passive, hierarchy, centralization and isolation to a more active involvement in the production of meanings, interactivity, nonlinearity, coherence and decentralized. Internet as a medium also differs from than traditional media in its hypertexts, multimedia, reciprocity, and timeliness. It represents a complex communication platform that produces complex Web of interconnected activities and communications arenas." So, the interactivity creates Internet. The information is changed; the newly applied and sent to other receives. It is a cultural production, it is that access and opportunity to create content and indirectly increase the effectiveness of the Internet as a cultural phenomenon (Burnett & Marshall, 2003).

Before the introduction of the Internet, organizations were able to carefully monitor all forms of communication. With the introduction of Internet organization should identify those social networks representing their target audiences. Social capital can be seen in the context of the term social networks i.e. personal connections between participants (Hanson, 2001). The advantages of building social networks as a tool of public relations for the organization is that public relations on the Internet also cost-effective, because there is no intermediary, and we also implement virtual events, conferences and research.

Social networks are a type of virtual communities which can be affected by the online environment and can be defined as a social network of individuals who communicate through a specific and well-defined medium. Each social network that is connected to the organization represents a potential target organization. Each should therefore be assessed in terms of potential impact on the organization. We also have to set the level of cooperation of the organizations in it and build a relationship with it. When users for some time participate in such social network, gain some confidence of other members. Organizations can set up their fields of knowledge and other users can turn on them when they need advice. Those who are most trusted and most know, have also a higher status than other participants. There exist internal norms and rules of behaviour, conflicts fight for control in times of crisis as well as integration to achieve common interests. When such a community is growing, is also growing their impact (Holtz, 2002).

It is not necessarily to restrict organizations to already established social networks, they can build themselves. The structures are established when members recognized common communication features of their professional, social characteristics, or common values that they want to maintain or expand. Parallel to the establishment of such structures, additional sources of information, communication, according to hierarchical levels, common tasks is created. Additional resources are forcing people to communicate and further specifying the topics of communication.

Using Social Networks in the Field of Public Relations

As demonstrated by the popularity of social networking sites such as Facebook and Twitter, Internet-based social networks have become an important part of daily life, and many businesses are now involved in such networks either as service providers or as participants. Furthermore, inter-organizational networks are becoming an increasingly common feature of many industries, not only on the Internet. However, despite the growing importance of networks for businesses, there is little theoretical study on the social responsibilities of businesses in such networks, and how these responsibilities are affected by different types of networks (Chen & Bouvain, 2009). We describe social responsibilities of businesses in social networks, which have been developed from studies of social networks of individuals and can be used to shed light on corporate responsibilities in social networks.

Corporate social responsibility of each organization results from the impact of its activities on society in terms of improving the welfare of society. At the same time organizations want to obtain a personal benefit. Special role in the revised context of social responsibility also have public relations. We encountered the creation of the international campaigns of social networks also in the field of public relations, particularly with regard to charitable events. Donors usually identify the key public relations tool, which helps your target audience. One of the most important tools of public relations is also social networks. Through social networks, organizations can raise funds for the preparation of charity events, or organize a virtual charity conference. Create a charitable event communication is just one of the instruments of public relations. Through online social networks, organizations can achieve the objectives in the field of public relations, including through the implementation of virtual events and conferences for charitable purposes. For example, organizations wants to make its vast resources of information more accessible and readily available and launch a multi-language online advertising campaign as the human rights charity ups its digital activity. The international campaigning group can appointed search agency to manage its natural and paid search, as well as to look at how it can utilise social networks and online public relations. The charity has to identify key target social and demographic groups towards which organization can focus its online efforts (Copper, 2008). In this way it can concentrate on different target groups.

With the introduction of social networks, public relations have the opportunity to use new digital media and thus become more important in their communication strategy. Social networks are a type of virtual communities, which have an impact on a particular group of consumers. We are talking about the personal impact when communication is carried directly. The emphasis is on members of the network in their personal relationships and how to understand each other. Users social networks indicate some common features such as searching for information, and also participant in these networks want to encourage interaction and dialogue.

The function of public relations is not only to inform the public of crisis situations, but most important, and according to some authors like Sears (2009), the equivalent part of marketing communication mix. Through public relations firm builds its image, identity, and reputation. Public relations help to impact on consumer attitudes, which are consequently reflected in the shopping (and other) decisions to the public, which company is involved. Advantages of public relations compared to other marketing communication tools are mainly the following: lower costs, greater confidence, capacity to reach specific groups, but require careful strategic planning and choosing the right activities at the right time.

Social networks are also used in other areas of marketing communications, for example in the field of sales promotions. Some companies support the use of social networks for business purposes, because they believe that the positive effect and encourage the testing of certain products or services (Sears, 2009). Organizations that use of social networks should be aware that through social networks they can not directly sell their products, but they can build certain relationships through forums, blogs and other forms of social media.

Another area of marketing communications is the development of an interactive Internet home page. With the increased popularity of the Internet, companies are spending a great deal of money on establishing Web sites processes and protocols that encompass sophisticated tools for handling purchase transactions, providing customer information, gathering competitive market intelligence data, and monitoring site performance. However, organizations would like to know just how effective the Web is or can be as a marketing tool before they adopt it as part of their marketing strategy (Lynn, 2002).

Twitter has become the latest medium in the field of public relations, where you can find the most new information, themes, and responses to them. Many public introduce their products or services to the public via Twitter, which has a strong influence on some other forms of public relations (Žbogar, 2010). Yaxley (2008) noted some examples how should public relations practitioners engage with social networking:

- Social networking is about engaging in conversations, so organization has to be prepared to leave comments.
- Organizations should also monitor what is being said about the organization or the brand using Google Alerts (http://www.google.com/alerts).
- There is also important to pro-actively manage organisation's online footprint, because it is important to be aware of what is being said, and ensure there is accurate, reliable information available.
- It is important to connect with others online – the point of networking is to make connections with colleagues, contacts, and information resources.
- With sharing information, organizations add value to its presence – what information can organization share or offer that will be of use to others and help build organizations online reputation?
- Blogging and participation in social networking can optimise the organization presence online and make what organization has to say more prominent.
- Social networking is a great sucker of time so be purposeful in your use of online tools rather than aimlessly engaging with trivia, and look for smart opportunities to engage with the media, such as via mobile technologies.
- Professional communicators use video and audio as well as the written word, so organization has to look out for useful podcasts and vcasts which you can download to an iPod or mobile phone to keep up with the latest online happenings.

As the Internet evolved as a marketing tool, consumers have faced the challenge of marrying an anonymous Web visit with offline data to facilitate targeting. Banner-ad targeting rheas on online behavioural indicators like the keywords visitors search on or the pages they viewed in the past which are recorded by cookies (Goodwin, 2007).

In the case that organizations reach a specific goal, it is necessary to possess a certain level of impact on social networks. The degree of influence is a term that is closely linked with power. The impact of social networks can often be described as capacity or as something that allows it to do things or to do other than we want. Like Gruning and others (2002) argued, those organizations that have an excellent level of communication and those organizations with their managers positioned in a higher position, have the greater power to influence the entire organization's reputation and values.

Although importance will be placed on understanding the proliferation of channels driven by technology, the range of options available, and the strengths and weaknesses of each, a fascination with channels shouldn't distract communicators from addressing the bigger issue of having poor content to communicate in the first place.

FUTURE RESEARCH DIRECTIONS

We are facing the change in the communication professions, but this is not enough to challenge the controlled messaging and traditional media utilization that have served communicators well for decades, but which have now been rapidly altered by new realities of globalization, technology and new patterns of audience behaviour.

The future research should also highlight the issues like international communication and the role of social media. We have to be aware of trends like globalization and internationalization of the business, so more attention should be given to research of international communications strategy. The media is also becoming more globalized and that in turn is leading to some globalization of social and cultural factors in the business environment. For example, interest in environmental issues is growing in many countries and the media has played a major role in this. Likewise, the globalization of the media has also helped create some globalized social phenomena such as the international teenage culture whose are familiar with the usage of social network.

The implications of this would be that organizations could target groups of consumers who have similar wants and needs on a global or maybe European basis, without the need to refer to national differences. This would open up new opportunities for the usage of public relations techniques and social media. There should also be very beneficial the research of cross-cultural communications and its impact in on public relations practice and social media, too.

Following the last information trends, it will be helpful to more deeply explore the concept "next frontier" of technologies beyond multimedia and discusses streaming video, broadcasting, virtual worlds, and mobile communications. All these issues should be discussed by to public relations professionals looking to optimize their communications in today's competitive business environment.

CONCLUSION

Globalization and the Internet have transformed the function of public relations, outlining best practices and providing strategic advice for communicating. Organizations can use a variety of techniques like popular social networking tools like Twitter and Facebook and reach new online audiences and create new marketplaces. The role of public relations is no longer in doubt. It is a function that plans and manages relationships with key target audiences and company stakeholders. Public relations allows organization to alter opinions, views, attitudes, goals, products, countries, companies, institutions and individuals, no matter in what capacity the individual act and what are the mutual expectations of the environment. The function of public relations is to be the equivalent part of marketing communication mix. Through public relations firm builds its image, identity, and reputation. Public relations help to impact on consumer attitudes, which are consequently reflected in the shopping (and other) decisions to the public, which company is involved.

By the introduction of the Internet environment is changing the practice of public relations. The Internet is both a medium and a social space where social networks are formed. These are based on the interaction between participants, through which they establish a relationship, common awareness, a sense of belonging and moral responsibility to the community. Social networks have changed the role of public relations, and we need to include them as the individuals and as a company.

Virtual communities are manifested through social media, which also include a social network. For organizations, it is important that these proactive media work, joining the conversation virtual communities perform other activities such as gathering feedback, conflict resolution, and support for consumers, which can be seen in virtual communities and businesses. We can conclude that social media can be an effective tool for public relations.

First, this article has presented a way of looking at communications through the changing word of communication, enabling us to see it as all different aspects of information technology changing the way of communication, which is taking place within communication. Second, viewing social network as a medium used in public relations field may help us to understand how communication contributes to the organisation's competitive advantage. This warrants further research to be conducted.

REFERENCES

Bove'e, C. L., & Thill, J. V. (2000). *Business communication today* (6th ed.). Upper Saddle River, NJ: Prentice-Hall.

Burnett, R., & Marshall, D. I. (2003). *Web theory: An introduction*. London: Routhledge.

Chen, S., & Bouvain, P. (2009). Is corporate responsibility converging? A comparison of corporate responsibility reporting in the USA, UK, Australia, and Germany. *Journal of Business Ethics, 90*(4), 523–536. doi:10.1007/s10551-010-0604-0.

Copper, W. (2008). *Amnesty looks to utilise social media in latest global campaign*. Retrieved October 25, 2011 from http://www.mad.co.uk/Main/Search/MadSearchResults/Articles/2bd0e47f9b3247719c112e0bf3968aaf/Amnesty-looks-to-utilise-social-media-in-latest-global-campaign.html

Croft, A. C. (2008). Emergence of new media moves PR agencies in new directions: Competitive pressure threatens agencies' livelihood. *Public Relations Quarterly, 52*(1), 16–20.

Cutlip, S. M., Center, A. H., & Broom, G. M. (2000). *Effective public relations*. Englewood Cliffs, NJ: Prentice Hall.

Goldstein, S. Z. (2006). Fast forward: Future trends in corporate communication: A checklist of top priorities for professionals in 2006. *Strategic Communication Management, 10*(1), 14–17.

Goodwin, C. (2007). *Getting through*. Retrieved October 25, 2011 from www.directmag.com

Gruban, B., Verčič, D., & Zavrl, F. (1997). *Pristop k odnosom z javnostmi*. Ljubljana, Slovenia: Pristop.

Grunig, A. L., Grunig, E. J., & Dozier, M. D. (2002). *Inside the organization: Culture, structure, systems of internal communication, gender and diversity V: Excellent public relations and effective organizations*. Hoboken, NJ: Lawrence Erlbaum Associates, Inc..

Grunig, E. J., & Grunig, A. L. (2002). Implications of the IABC excellence study for PR education. *Journal of Communication Management, 7*(1), 34–42. doi:10.1108/13632540310807232.

Hanson, K. O. (2011). The long history of conscious capitalism: A response to James O'Toole and David Vogel's "Two and a half cheers for conscious capitalism". *California Management Review, 53*(3), 77–83. doi:10.1525/cmr.2011.53.3.77.

Holtz, S. (2002). *Public relations on the internet*. New York: Amazon.

Hozjan, T. (2010). *Spletne skupnosti kot orodja odnosov z javnostmi*. Ljubljana, Slovenia: Fakulteta za družbene vede.

Ihator, S. A. (2001). Communication style in the information age. *School of Journalism and Broadcasting, 6*(4), 199–204.

Jankowski, N. W. (2009). Creating community with media: History, theories and scientific investigations. In Lievrouw, L. A., & Livingstone, S. M. (Eds.), *Handbook of new media: Social shaping and social consequences of ICT's* (pp. 55–74). Los Angeles, CA: Sage.

Kalla, K. H. (2005). Integrated internal communications: a multidisciplinary perspective. *Corporate Communications: An International Journal, 10*(4), 302–314. doi:10.1108/13563280510630106.

Kitchen, P. (1997). *Public relations: Principles and practice*. London: International Thomson Business Press.

Kotler, P., Armstrong, G., Saunders, J., & Wong, V. (1999). *Principles of marketing*. London: Prentice Hall.

Lynn, G. S., Lipp, S., Akgün, A. E., & Cortez, A. Jr. (2002). Factors impacting the adoption and effectiveness of the world wide web in marketing. *Industrial Marketing Management, 31*, 35–49. doi:10.1016/S0019-8501(00)00104-8.

Muniz, A. M., & O'Guinn, T. (2001). Brand community. *The Journal of Consumer Research, 27*, 412–432. doi:10.1086/319618.

O'Reilly, T. (2005). *What is web 2.0: Design patterns and business models for the next generation of software*. Retrieved August, 16, 2008 from http://www.oreillynet.com/pub/a/oreilly/tim/news/2005/09/30/what-is-Web-20

Oliver, S. (1997). *Corporate communication: Principles, techniques and strategies*. London: Kogan Page.

Ryan, M. (2003). Public relations and the web: Organizational problems, gender and institutional type. *Public Relations Review, 29*(3), 335–349. doi:10.1016/S0363-8111(03)00040-7.

Sears, N. (2009). Measures should be taken to provide granular control over each social networking site. *Engineering & Technology, 6*, 6.

Sherman, K. (1998, November 1). Let the seller beware. *CIO Magazine, 1*.

Shu, W., & Chuang, Y.-H. (2011). Why people share knowledge in virtual communities? *Social and Personality, 39*(5), 671–690. doi:10.2224/sbp.2011.39.5.671.

Skrt, R. (2007). *Spletne socialne mreže*. Retrieved October 25, 2011, from http://www.mojmikro.si/preziveti/kar_tako/spletne_socialne_mrezenavidezna_indija_koromandija

Splichal, S. (1997). *Javno mnenje: Teoretski razvoj in spori v XX*. Ljubljana, Slovenia: Fakulteta za družbene vede.

Van der Merwe, L. F., Pitt, L.P., & Abratt, R. (2005, Spring). Stakeholder strength: PR survival strategies in the internet age. *Public Relations Quarterly*, 39-48.

Wasserman, S., & Galaskiewicz, J. (1994). *Advances in social network analysis: Research in the social and behavioural sciences*. Thousand Oaks, CA: Sage Publications.

Yaxley, H. (2008). *How PR practitioners should engage with social networking*. Retrieved October, 25, 2011 from http://greenbanana.wordpress.com/2008/02/28/how-pr-practitioners-should-engage-with-social-networking/

Žbogar, D. (2010). *Vpliv družbenih medijev na prakso odnosov z javnostmi*. Ljubljana, Slovenia: Fakulteta za družbene vede.

ADDITIONAL READING

Andresen, E., Bergman, A., & Hallen, L. (2003). *Electronic commnication in strategic networks*. Paper presented at the 19th IMP conference. Lugano, Switzerland. Retrieved June, 23, 2005 from http://www.impgroup.org/paper_view.php?viewPaper=4285

Ballantine, P. W., & Brell, M. (2005). Forming parasocial relationships in online communities. *Advances in Consumer Research. Association for Consumer Research (U. S.), 32*, 197–202.

Berthon, P., Nikala, L., Leyland, P., & Watson, R. T. (1998). The world wide web as an industrial marketing communication tool: Models for the identification and assessment of opportunities. *Journal of Marketing Management*, *14*, 691–704. doi:10.1362/026725798784867635.

Cross, S. (2009). Social networking: The business case. *Engineering & Technology*. Retrieved October 25, 2011, from www.theiet.org/magazine

Daugherty, T., & Reece, B. B. (2002). The adoption of persuasive internet communication in advertising and public relations curricula. *Journal of Interactive Advertising*, *3*(1), 1–21.

Egbert, H. (2009). Business success through social networks? A comment on social networks and business success. *American Journal of Economics and Sociology*, *68*(3), 665–677. doi:10.1111/j.1536-7150.2009.00643.x.

Fiske, J. (1990). *Introduction to communication studies* (2nd ed.). London: Routledge.

Goczol, J., & Scoubeau, C. (2003). Corporate communication and strategy in the field of projects. *Corporate Communications: An International Journal*, *8*(1), 60–66. doi:10.1108/13563280310458920.

Grunig, J. E., & Grunig, L. A. (1998). The relationship between public relations and marketing in excellent organizations: Evidence from the IABC study. *Journal of Marketing Communications*, *4*, 141–162. doi:10.1080/135272698345816.

Kitchen, P. J., & Schultz, D. E. (2003). Integrated corporate and product brand communication. *Advances in Competitiveness Research*, *11*(1), 66–86.

Krippendorff, K. (2009). Mathematical theory of communication. In Littlejohn, S. W., & Foss, K. A. (Eds.), *Encyclopedia of Communication Theory*. Los Angeles, CA: Sage Publication. doi:10.4135/9781412959384.n229.

Lichtenthal, D. J., & Eliaz, S. (2003). Internet integration in business marketing tactics. *Industrial Marketing Management*, *32*, 3–13. doi:10.1016/S0019-8501(01)00198-5.

McAlexander, J. H., Schouten, J., & Koenig, H. (2002). Building brand community. *Journal of Marketing*, *66*, 38–54. doi:10.1509/jmkg.66.1.38.18451.

Miller, K. (2003). *Organizational communication: Approaches and processes* (3rd ed.). Belmont, CA: Wadsworth.

O'Reilly, C. A. III. (1982). Variations in decision maker's use of information sources: the impact of quality and accessibility of information. *Academy of Management Journal*, *25*(4), 756–771. doi:10.2307/256097.

Olkkonen, R., Tikkanen, H., & Alajoutsijarvi, K. (2000). The role of communication in business relationships and networks. *Management Decision*, *38*(6), 403–409. doi:10.1108/EUM0000000005365.

Pavlou, P. A., & Stewart, D. W. (2000). Measuring the effects and effectiveness of interactive advertising: A research agenda. *Journal of Interactive Advertising*, *1*(1), 1–28.

Peltier, J. W., Kleimenhagen, A. K., & Naidu, G. M. (1996). Integrating multiple publics into the strategic plan. *Journal of Health Care Marketing*, *16*(1), 35–37. PMID:10157976.

Peltier, J. W., Schibrowsky, J. A., & Schultz, D. E. (2003). Interactive integrated marketing communication: Combining the power of IMC, the new media and database marketing. *International Journal of Advertising*, *22*(1), 93–115.

Proctor, T., & Kitchen, P. (2003). Communication in the postmodern integrated marketing. *Corporate Communications: An International Journal*, *7*(3), 144–154. doi:10.1108/13563280210436754.

Rowley, J. (1998). Promotion and marketing communications in the information marketplace. *Library Review*, *47*(8), 8, 383–387. doi:10.1108/00242539810239543.

Sinickas, A. (2005, January-February). Forecasting and evaluating the impact of marketing communication. *Communication World*, 14.

Smith, P. R., Berry, C., & Pulford, A. (2002). *Strategic marketing communications: New ways to build and integrate communications*. London: The Kogan Page.

Theaker, A. (2001). *The public relations handbook*. London: Routlledge, Taylor, & Francis Group.

Tian, R. G. (2011). International communications strategy: Development in cross-cultural communications, PR and social media. *Journal of Consumer Marketing*, *28*(3), 242–244.

Tourish, D., & Hargie, O. (2004). The communication consequences of downsizing trust, loyalty, and commitment. In Tourish, D., & Hargie, O. (Eds.), *Key Issues in Organizational Communication* (pp. 17–36). London: Routledge.

Van Doren, D. C., Fechner, D. L., & Green-Adelsberger, K. (2000). Promotional strategies on the world wide web. *Journal of Marketing Communications*, *6*, 21–35. doi:10.1080/135272600345534.

Weinstein, S. (1999). Integrate communication technologies. *Advertising Age's Business Marketing*, *84*(11), 48.

KEY TERMS AND DEFINITIONS

Public: Different stakeholders like local community, employees, customers, and others.

Public Relations (PR): Actions of an organization, an individual, a government, and others, in promoting goodwill between itself and the public.

Social Media: The use of Web-based and mobile technologies to turn communication into an interactive dialogue.

Social Network: A social structure made up of individuals (or organizations) which are tied (connected) by one or more specific types of relationship.

Social Responsibility: A theory that an organization has the obligation or fell the responsibility to benefit to society. The organization performs action which can benefit the system where it performs activities.

Stakeholder: An organization, a person, a community who affects or can be affected by an organization's actions.

Virtual Community: A social network of individuals who interact through interactive media in order to pursue mutual interests or goals.

Chapter 9
Impact of Economic Culture on the Development of Enterprises

Vojko Potocan
University of Maribor, Slovenia

Zlatko Nedelko
University of Maribor, Slovenia

ABSTRACT

Values of individuals, culture of groups, ethics of communities, and the resulting influential norms (i.e. VCEN) are interdependent. VCEN tend to crucially influence development and application of knowledge, skills, talents, and other resources. In the current very competitive and increasingly global economy, organizations and countries become more successful if their economic culture is innovation friendly. Economic culture reflects itself in the economic part of VCEN of nations as well, because organizations, such as enterprises, play a crucial role in a nation's life. National resources are no longer enough, neither is investment, if it is not innovation enhancing. Thus, a new concept of economic VCEN is going to become necessary for people to find a new positive direction beyond the worrisome blind alley of the current economic crisis. The innovation of VCEN is, again, becoming more important than the technological innovation for development of countries and, indeed, for humankind. The contribution discusses two theses: (1) VCEN in organizations is importantly interdependent with the economic culture, and (2) the change of the economic culture in an organization is connected with the changes of the organizing methods and their management.

INTRODUCTION

Although they are called by many different names business systems have become very influential institutions of the modern age (Schumpeter, 1934; Kuratko, 2008; Baumol, 2010). Since the great majority of business systems are Small and Medium Enterprises (SMEs), it is almost impossible to reach any goal in the society without also engaging the SMEs (Hebert & Link, 1989; Fink & Kraus, 2009; Greene, 2009; Lerner, 2009). In recent decades the attempts by SMEs to become

DOI: 10.4018/978-1-4666-4373-4.ch009

more efficient, have ranged from synergetically adding quality, range, uniqueness, and sustainability (Collins, 2001; Potocan & Mulej, 2007, 2010; Buchanan & Huczynski, 2010; Mullins, 2010). This requires on-going innovations, both of the technological and even more of the non-technological aspects, especially the economic culture.

Innovation is defined as every novelty found beneficial in the experience of its users (Afuah, 1998; Rogers, 2003; EU, 2006; Martin, 2009). Or, in other words: Innovation = invention + (its) commercialization (Afuah, 1998).

Modern SMEs face at least two important challenges: 1) How to satisfy demanding customers' requirements, and 2) How to make their own business innovative to make customers happier with it. For that reason, SMEs must structure and implement a process of thinking of/about everything crucial on the same level or even on a level higher than that performed by the bigger enterprises. Meeting these requirements depends on influential humans, and does not only depend on the institutional order alone. Thus, most SMEs can innovate their style of working and behavior, including the application of ethics of interdependence within the organization, in the market, and in society at large. Therefore, it makes sense to consider the preconditions for humans to be innovative about SMEs as business systems.

We discuss here the issue of improving the level of innovativeness on the basis of knowing: the innovative working of SMEs, possibilities to assure the human bases for innovativeness, and the link between change in economic culture and the innovativeness of SMEs.

BACKGROUND

Literature on innovation abounds. Today there are many more authors and contributions about different aspects of the innovativeness of SMEs than ever before (Lester & Piore, 2004; Leydesdorff, 2006; Sheshimski et al., 2007; Fink & Kraus, 2009; Chesbrough, 2009; etc.). Pyka and Scharnhorst (2009) offer an interesting new approach to change and learning. Leydesdorff (2006) offers an interesting new concept of modeling, measuring and simulating the knowledge-based economy. Schwartz (2006) is trying to help people be more entrepreneurial. Lester and Piore (2004) warn – when discussing the need for building interpretation capacity – that the contemporary American education lacks schooling that fosters the capacity for creative interdisciplinary co-operation, which is a precondition for success in active innovation.

Nussbaum et al. (2005) raises awareness that despite spending huge sums on R&D, most corporations have dismally low levels of effective and productive innovation—up to 96 percent of all new projects fail—and offers suggestions how to get better at this. McGregor (2006) points to attributes of the most innovative companies of today. Huston and Sakkab (2006) are given space in Harvard Business Review to describe their new model for innovation. Business Week decided to focus on innovation for its 75th anniversary issue under the label "The Innovation Economy" in its special report. In June 2006, Business Week published its inaugural issue of IN: Inside Innovation with these words from its editor: "We dedicate ourselves to the proposition that making innovation work is the single most important business challenge of our era. Our goal is to make a meaningful difference in the difficult journey toward building innovative business cultures" (Nussbaum et al., 2005; Potocan & Mulej, 2007; Kelley, 2009).

There is no way that we can include all references to innovation in economic, sociological, psychological, and similar literature; it is no longer a technological topic only. IBM (2006) reports on a worldwide survey finding that innovation of business is even more crucial than the technological innovation (Potocan, 2008; Shane, 2008; Conway & Steward, 2009; Korten, 2009; etc.).

In other words: SMEs are becoming more innovative mainly on the base of innovative working and behavior of their members. The important action of improving the level of innovativeness of SMEs members also establishes the importance of Values/Culture/Ethics/Norms (VCEN) for all SMEs members, and state (i.e. level of current) of especially their economic culture connected with innovativeness.

IMPACT OF ECONOMIC CULTURE ON THE DEVELOPMENT OF SMEs

SMEs are Transformed into Entrepreneurial Business Systems by Influential Humans

The basic problem looked at in this contribution is linked to the fact that a modern organization of any type "per se" is an empty legal shell (and/or organizational structure). That is also true of Small and Medium Enterprises (SMEs). It is the owners that define the SMEs' goals and operations that make their SME efficient, effective and successful, and it obviously comes about with the help of all other stakeholders in the SME (Hebert & Link, 1989; Afuah, 1998; Baumol, 2001; Fink & Kraus, 2009; Baumol, 2010; Berkun, 2010).

The SME is a product of the owners'/managers' endeavor to exploit a business opportunity and to capitalize on it. But the management of SMEs is a complex process, and the entrepreneur who runs it has to play many different roles (Lawrence & Weber, 2007; Korten, 2009; Martin, 2009). On the other hand, there is no guarantee that the entrepreneurial efforts will be applied in a way that matches the innovative and constructive image we usually have of economic entrepreneurship. Not every entrepreneurship results in development; it can even turn out to be unproductive or destructive (Baumol, 2001; Kaplan & Warren, 2009; Baumol, 2010).

In working on the development of SMEs, entrepreneurs encounter a number of problems. Firstly, they must define (and refine) their basis for understanding of modern economic conditions (crisis, etc.). In the next step, entrepreneurs need to define the starting points and characteristics of their work within the frame of globalization. And finally, they must define their own place in working on their SME's development. Their success depends both on their knowledge and their VCEN (Morgan, 1986; Rhinesmith, 1999; Mullins, 2006; Daft, 2007; Buchanan & Huczynski, 2010; Potocan & Mulej, 2010).

How can SMEs successfully participate in the market game under modern conditions?

Globalization Calls for Management Innovations within SMEs to Make the SMEs More Entrepreneurial

Neither the globalization nor the financial crisis allows long-term stability to be attained by routinism, like it used to be (Porter, 1990; Boisot, 1998; Florida, 2002; Potocan, 2005; EU, 2006; Lawrence & Weber, 2007; Potocan, 2009).

Therefore, the new bases of modern SMEs may include serious novelties aimed at becoming management innovations such as: 1) SME owners must be highly entrepreneurial and innovate their operations to improve the competitiveness of their SMEs, 2) Entrepreneurial SMEs must create their operations globally, and act locally, 3) Transition from the commanding hierarchy to the "process-based" specialization and interdisciplinary creative cooperation is of special importance, and 4) There is a growing need for entrepreneurial SMEs to extend their ability to seek and apply interdisciplinary knowledge.

For these reasons, SMEs that wish to be entrepreneurial must innovate their work processes to meet the newly emerging market conditions. They need to create a set of new goals and new innovative behavior for their own work (Ireland & Hitt, 1997; Rhinesmith, 1999; Potocan, 2002; Rogers, 2003; Cole, 2004; Jennings, 2005; Potocan & Mulej, 2007). Some of the basic tasks for achieving that include the following (see Rogers,

2003; Potocan, 2005; Potocan & Mulej, 2007; Potocan, 2008; Potocan & Mulej, 2010):

- A timely and therefore anticipatory and sufficiently complete formulation/reformulation of the concept of the SME and its competitiveness. Such an SME will have to be created on the basis of co-operation between all partners in its value chain, and cooperation with institutions in its environment.
- Anticipation of changes in the industrial dynamics, and the resulting adoption and adaptation by SMEs of available and potential resources to help them accommodate these changes.
- Creation of flexible operations, which will enable, on an anticipatory basis, a (re)configuration of resources to suit the SME's new possibilities of operations - market, and other challenges.
- Development of the SMEs' capability for global operations. Depending on their industry and vision, many SMEs must extend their operations globally and position them locally at the same time and accordingly establish their relations with buyers, suppliers and other partners.

Entrepreneurial SMEs must redefine their goals and tasks, rethink areas of their own work, and innovate the characteristics of their own operation. Thus, they can make the process of redefining their own operations a fundamental source of the SME's potentially higher competitiveness and consequently of profit.

In which way can entrepreneurial SMEs improve their innovativeness? Theoretical cognitions and our work experience indicate that innovation of human working is the least considered but most promising area for action/ because of its impact on the economic culture of an SME.

Approach to Innovation of Human Working in SMEs

Entrepreneurial humans support innovation (Daft, 2003; Katz, 2003; Lester & Piore, 2004; Leydesdorff, 2006; Chesbrough, 2009; Tidd & Bessant, 2009; Govindarajan & Trimple, 2010; Lafley & Johnson, 2010). Though, entrepreneurship can be considered from different viewpoints - at the very least it should be regarded as producing synergy of the following aspects:

- A legal feature, i.e. ownership of enterprises (Florida, 2002; McGregor, 2006; Daft, 2007; Mulej et al., 2008).
- An economic feature, i.e. searching for, creating, and using of new business opportunities to produce innovations (Schumpeter, 1934; Mulej, 2000; Mullins, 2006; Kuratko, 2008; Lafley & Johnson, 2010).
- A psychological and sociological attribute of the entrepreneur as a person (Barabba, 2004; Daft, 2007; McAuley et al., 2007; Potocan, 2009; Quick & Nelson, 2009; Govindarajan & Trimple, 2010).

But in reality, both groups of change agents of SMEs—those concerned with SMEs as BSs, and those concerned with innovativeness as the only way of humankind's survival—have obviously not done enough to get all influential persons and organizations to recognize the importance of the emergence and act of innovation.

Normally specialists display one-sided behavior - i.e. perception, thinking, decision making, and action. Some owners, entrepreneurs, and managers of SMEs are often quite close to this danger of one-sided behavior for different reasons. A wide selection of authors (Katz, 2003; Barabba, 2004; Nussbaum et al., 2005; Potocan & Mulej, 2007; Potocan, 2008; Chesbrough, 2009; Fink & Kraus, 2009; Lafley & Johnson, 2010), list the following:

1. Those running SMEs often do not have many co-workers.
2. Some people who run an SME are very good in a technical profession, but less good or even completely uneducated in running a business such as an SME.
3. On the other hand a genuine entrepreneur who does not suffer from such one-side behavior produces an enterprise rather than a product.

In the current economic circumstances, actual SMEs must obviously be viewed as inventions that are supposed to become innovations, and that innovations are not to be limited to the SMEs' products. All influential stakeholders must be persuaded through a communication process for the transition from invention to innovation to happen. This also includes surpassing the customers' expectations in terms of price, quality, range, uniqueness, and environmental impact (de Geus, 1988; Mulej, 2000; Alvesson, 2002; Lafollette, 2005; IBM, 2006; Daghfous, 2007; Potocan & Mulej, 2007; Potocan, 2008; Certo & Certo, 2009).

The invention-innovation-diffusion process can, in terms of content, be defined as an entity made (up) of discovering and formulating of new ideas and of turning them in inventions, suggestions, potential innovations, and finally innovations and stretching to broadly diffused innovations. This invention-innovation-diffusion process must become a beneficial routine, over a period of time (Albert & Bradley, 1997; Afuah, 1998; Mulej & Kajzer, 1998; Mulej, 2000; Florida, 2002; Gallagher, 2002; Rogers, 2003; McGregor, 2006; Mulej et al., 2008). Over time, new innovation replaces the prior innovation.

All process participants make use of both their subjective starting points (knowledge, values, emotions, talents) and their objective starting points (needs in the market, possibilities in organization) in order to develop an innovative application of all requisite and available knowledge, entrepreneurial spirit, entrepreneurship, cooperation capacity, and ethics of interdependence (More about ethics of interdependence see: Mulej & Kajzer, 1998; Mulej, 2000; Potocan, 2005; Potocan & Mulej, 2007).

The process is finished once all opportunities have been dealt with, and the names on the list of opportunities are depleted through diffusion. Success in diffusion provides investors courage to repeat the entire process. They may imagine that success in this process is normal but this is not so: even official innovation projects succeed in less than five percent of cases (Katz, 2003; Nussbaum et al., 2005; Huston & Sakkab, 2006; Daghfous, 2007; Kaplan & Warren, 2009; Schermerhorn, 2009; Lefley & Johnson, 2010).

On the base of all these mentioned cognitions a new question arises, and that is: Who is in charge of making it all happen in the case of an SME? How are we to change the attitude of members of SMEs, if we want to improve their level of understanding innovativeness?

The Human Preconditions for a Successful Innovative Business

Around the world, 80% of humankind lives in the less innovative countries (Mulej, 2000; Potocan, 2005; Potocan & Mulej, 2007; Mulej et al., 2008; Skarzynski & Gibson, 2008; Korten, 2009; Berkun, 2010). Everywhere, making innovative business the prevailing practice requires new thinking and practice to change the inherited culture and practice.

Traditional economists tend to suppose that the institutions on their own can work well enough (White, 2005; Shashimski et al., 2007; Mullins, 2006; Lawrence & Weber, 2007; Kuratko, 2008; Kelley, 2009; Baumol, 2010). Influential persons in SMEs tend to read the institutional systems measures from their own viewpoints. Therefore, the business reality is not only based on economics, but also and of equal importance, on management and the organization of human relations within SMEs.

Inter-disciplinary co-operation plays a central role in the innovative business and therefore such co-operation is also central to interdependence of the professional invention-innovation-diffusion teams. The tendency of growing specialization put all professions in danger of being closed-in and of ignoring interdisciplinary co-operation (Barabba, 2004; Potocan & Mulej, 2007; Potocan, 2008; Buchanan & Huczynski, 2010; Mullins, 2010). This danger impacts SMEs, their owners, managers, employees, consultants, and other business partners.

The contemporary need for success requires professionals to accept their practical inter-dependence and enter into interdisciplinary co-operation concerning all invention-innovation-diffusion processes and all resulting novelties – suggestions, inventions, potential innovations, and, at the very end of this long and very selective process, innovations and their diffusion in markets. Even if co-operation of all stakeholders of SMEs is approaching the holistic ideal, everything cannot be foreseen, and in every phase mentioned above only a small portion of its intermediate outcomes proceeds to the next stage.

In the invention-innovation-diffusion process very different people show up, from different functional areas, from different professions, having different human personality attributes, values, etc. (Mulej, 2000; Potocan, 2005; Mulej et al., 2008; Potocan, 2008, 2009). SMEs must lead them and manage their different cultures (See Figure 1).

This requirement for all stakeholders of SMEs has been emphasized for eight decades since Mogensen's first publication in 1926 (for more about Mogensen work see Wren, 2004), but again and again new methods had to be invented e.g. they ranged all the way to Business Reengineering and Twenty Keys, etc. of today (see Jennings, 2005; Lawrence, Weber, 2007; McAuley et al., 2007; Quick, Nelson, 2009; Buchanan, Huczynski, 2010). The basic three interdependent groups of sources of cultural differences are:

1. Psychological sources of cultural differences.
2. Sociological sources of cultural differences.
3. Economic sources of cultural differences (Waterman & Peters, 1982; Schein, 1992; Deal & Kennedy, 2000; Hofstede & Pedersen, 2004; Schein, 2004; Cameron & Quinn, 2005; Lafollette, 2005; White, 2005; Potocan & Mulej, 2006; Mullins, 2010).

For these reasons, all stakeholders of SMEs need to start developing their personnel's capacities of creativity and co-operation. Thus, cultural differences need to be bridged. And people must learn to use their creativity in a co-operative way. (Schein, 1992; Hofstede & Pedersen, 2004; Mullins, 2006; Potocan & Mulej, 2007; Certo & Certo, 2009; Schermerhorn, 2009; Buchanan & Huczynski, 2010).

In which way does innovative and economic culture influence development of SMEs? Theo-

Figure 1. Circular interdependence of values, culture, ethics, and norms

Individual values (interdependent with knowledge)	↔	Culture = values shared by many, habits making them a rounded-off social group
⇕	X	⇕
Norms = prescribed values on right and wrong in a social group	↔	Ethics = prevailing values on right and wrong in a social group

retical cognitions and our experiences indicate that economic culture has an especially important influence on assets, technology, knowledge, and values of modern SMEs.

How We Understand the Relations between Economic Culture and Economic Development

We understand the definition of economic culture as a component of VCEN, which is the accepted emotional reflection of the economic processes in society and accepted by the prevailing and significant humans, such as opinion makers and their followers (See Figure 1).

The economic culture tells us right from wrong in economic life based on the criteria of the prevailing social group (Lafollette, 2005; White, 2005; Lawrence & Weber, 2007; Daft, 2009; Buchanan & Huczynski, 2010; Mullins, 2010). If culture is primarily based on values, this cannot mean that culture is independent of other emotions and from all types of knowledge and from external circumstances. If external aspects and forces change, culture changes, and if culture changes, they change, too. At least in a longer term and indirectly they are interdependent.

We may summarize as follows (For details see: Potocan & Mulej, 2007; Potocan, 2008; Potocan & Mulej, 2010):

- Culture is no isolated issue, but essentially interdependent with both the trends of the economic and social development and its current phase.
- Culture cannot be impacted only by motivation and ideological persuasion, although both these tend to form values and cultures, including economic ones, and ethics.
- Ethics cannot be impacted only by teaching of facts – i.e. creating knowledge by the means of education, public relations, political speeches, public media, etc.
- Culture of a person or group includes in its sources their own as well as other persons' experiences, and these go beyond the education received in school and elsewhere.
- Culture is a synergetic consequence of all those mentioned and other impacts. Some impacts are explicit, others are tacit, some have immediate impact, and for some the impact requires a long lead time.
- Hence, every culture is a more or less an easily visible reflection of the entire network and synergy of such impacts.

The "open innovation" concept might crucially replace the R&D, based on an SME's own human resources only, and even result in the shelving of the unused novelties (Katz, 2003; Lester & Piore, 2004; Shane, 2008; Chesbrough, 2009; Kaplan, 2009; Potocan, 2009; Govindarajan & Trimple, 2010). In terms of such conclusions from findings and experiences, the process of transition from one phase of the SME life cycle to another phase of its life cycle is also a process of transition of culture. It is only partly reflected in legal frameworks and other means of socio-economic institutional order, while it is partly reflected in the human's perception and their acceptance of this order and their resulting practical behavior.

Solutions and Recommendations: Impacts of Changing Economic Culture on the Organizations of Today

The development of the economic culture in modern organizations is connected to the changes in the organizing methods and their management, among other impacts (See: Alvesson, 2001; Schein, 2004; Cameron & Quinn, 2005; Potocan, 2005; Mullins, 2006; Mulej et al., 2008; Certo & Certo, 2009; Uick & Nelson, 2009; Buchanan & Huczynski, 2010; Mullins, 2010). Therefore, in organizations as business systems at least the following instances of interdependence are worthy of consideration (Potocan & Mulej, 2006; Mulej et al., 2008; Potocan, 2009).

Economic Culture and Assets

The understanding of the role and importance of assets in modern organizations is connected with two areas: the organization's assets, and the related organization structure. Various asset forms and various organization processes can have an impact on each other and be combined into various organizational forms (Galbraith, 2002; Cole, 2004; Hofstede & Pedersen, 2004; Daft, 2007; Certo & Certo, 2009; Schermerhorn, 2009; Mullins, 2010).

Every organization has both soft elements (the knowledge capital possessed by the organization and inherent in its people, embedded in equipment and records) and hard elements (the physical business factors, the equipment and technology it uses to maintain and develop its networks and people) (Galbraith, 2002; Certo & Certo, 2009; Mullins, 2010). The satisfaction of an organization's needs calls for getting the requisitely holistic mix of the soft and hard elements with the purpose and goals of organization.

Economic culture helps us understand the need to apply simultaneously different kinds of assets acting in synergy in an organization's working. The latter is a permanent/continuous process that unavoidably requires organizations to use all available resources, including all available kinds of assets. Due to the need for synergetic action one must, hence, form a set of various kinds of assets in order to be able to get results from the action embarked on under the given conditions.

On the basis of prevailing economic culture one can also understand an entity's need for various types of organizing forms and their synergetic use. In its action, a firm can use various types of organization in order to run their activities properly various conditions. Combining organizing forms helps to attain requisite holism.

Economic culture greatly helps us to understand an organization's need to simultaneously use various kinds of organization in synergy. Thus, the need to act synergetically presupposes a simultaneous use of various forms of organization.

Economic Culture and Technology

The development of the economic culture in modern organizations is connected with the changes of technology, especially information and communications technology (Ireland & Hitt, 1997; Cole, 2004; Leydesdorff, 2006; Lerner, 2009; Tidd & Bessant, 2009; Mullins, 2010). Today, information and communications technology consists of the Internet and broadband communication technology. This has several immediate consequences.

In economic terms, the new technology allowed companies to reduce internal transaction costs, both directly, through costs savings, and indirectly, by speeding up information transactions and saving time. In organizational terms, it increased the managerial span of control in terms of physical space, allowing managers to contact and stay in touch more easily with colleagues and subordinates in physically distant places.

This in turn has led to a reversal of a century-long trend towards concentration and building (vertical) hierarchies aimed at creating economies of scale. In the early twentieth century, firms sought to grow and create economies of scale in part in order to "internalize" functions which had formerly been undertaken out of house, so as to reduce transaction costs and increase competitiveness. But, paradoxically, reducing transaction costs also often meant reducing flexibility and efficiency as large organizations become rigid and bureaucratic. The new technology offers business the opportunity to improve this situation. Peripheral business activities could be sent out of house once more, allowing organizations to scale down and concentrate on their core business while at the same time keeping transaction costs low (or at least, lower than the corresponding added value the external sub-contracting organization is able to provide).

Thus, on the one level, technology has greatly increased our ability to do business virtually, and has created an apparent revolution in how and where we work. But at the same time, it has done so not by overturning all of the old certainties about management but by providing us with a powerful tool which we can use to manage more effectively. It is for this reason that Goldman et al. (1995) argue that while technology is important to modern organizations, but it is not essential (see also Govindarajan & Trimple, 2010).

It is the "soft" technology of human beings—their brains, and senses and hands—that continue to manage, direct, and staff business organizations, and it is human beings who continue to be the customers. As long as this remains the case, therefore, managers in modern organizations must strive to find a second balance: between the needs and/or utility of people and those of machine technology.

The decision about employing "soft" or "hard" technology encounters two dimensions: the organization's technology, and its organizing. For human beings, too, work in virtual space. Machines create virtual space by networks of communication. People also create virtual space, using their own memories and imaginations. All of us store, retrieve, and use virtual data, information, and knowledge in our working lives, and we do so not only as individuals, but also as groups.

Boisot (1995) has referred to what he calls "information space", a kind of realm of the imagination which exists in every organization and is a core part of its culture, determining what kinds of knowledge and information are transmitted, how and to whom. Not all modern spaces are happy places to be. Depending on how they are constructed and the purpose they are intended to serve, they can be free, creative and exciting places to work, or they can be what Morgan (1986) so eloquently describes as "psychic prisons", where imagination and flexibility are restricted and inhibited.

A critical challenge facing managers in modern organization is the management of the interface between "soft technology" that is people, and those other physical systems. People and technology function according to fundamentally different rules: computers and software can be replicated and will function in the same way, while people, as biological organisms, are unique. This applies to each one of us.

Economic Culture and Knowledge

The idea of the modern organization overlaps with several other recent organization concepts, notably knowledge organization and the learning organization (Deal & Kennedy, 2000; Wren, 2004; Cole, 2004; Jennings, 2005; Potocan, 2005; Daft, 2007; Mulej et al., 2008; Schermerhorn, 2009).

The idea of the learning organization goes at least as far back as management gurus, Waterman and Peters (1982), who used the phrase "learning organization" to denote companies that invested in research and development and viewed knowledge as an organizational asset. The phase "thinking organization", current in the 1920s, expressed some of the same ideas (see Wren, 2004).

The notion that knowledge could be considered an asset in its own right came to the fore with the work in the late 1980s of de Geus and Senge at Royal Dutch Shell and MIT, and it was de Geus (1988) who made the now famous statement "that in future a company's only sustainable competitive advantage may be its ability to learn faster than its competitors."

This in turn led to the idea of "knowledge capital," where knowledge as a factor input is regarded on the same basis as the traditional factors of production, labor and (money) capital. Warner and Witzel (2004), for example, suggested that one of the key tasks of the general manager was the acquisition, use, creation and diffusion of knowledge within the firm, and went on to develop a model of knowledge production and dissemination. On a broader scale, Albert and Bradley (1997) have commented on the rise of knowledge-based industries, showing how knowledge is being used to create and add value in a variety of economic settings.

The relationship of these developments to modern organizations is simple: the technology networks on which these organizations are founded exist to transmit knowledge. This knowledge can take a variety of forms, ranging from hard data, to receiving knowledge disseminated in a variety of forms. Knowledge is not only a factor input; its creation, transmission, and use are implicit in almost everything a modern organization does.

According to Japanese management authors Nonaka and Takeuchi (1995), a network can be used not just to circulate but to directly create knowledge. In either case, however, it is the function of networks to transmit knowledge. Clearly when there is no knowledge to transmit, then the network is idle and useless.

How does a knowledge-based organization differ from traditional organizations? The differences are not so much in the importance of knowledge itself, but rather in the kinds of knowledge that are pursued and the ways in which knowledge is used. And, just as technology networks are inert without knowledge to pass along them, so in modern organizations knowledge is beneficial, because the networks exist along which it can be transmitted.

The decision whether to implement *traditional* knowledge or *modern* knowledge has two dimensions according to the role of knowledge in the organization.

In the traditional organization the ruling paradigm is based on mechanical systems and targeting efficient performance. The second dimension is the modern paradigm of organization, which is based on natural, biological systems and where it targets to be a learning organization.

Technology and knowledge are two important ingredients in the modern organization recipe. Neither will become active without the addition of the third important element, people. It is no accident that new theories such as the learning organization, and knowledge as capital, and knowledge management put such a strong emphasis on the human element within the organization. The same must be true for the actual modern organization. For that reason, the modern organization is primarily a human-oriented concept in which the management of people is more important that the managing of technology; but neither one can be wholly separated from the other.

Even more important: knowledge is no longer used solely or mainly for routine and mastering well-defined problems, but increasingly for innovation.

Economic Culture and General VCEN in the Organization

Working and behavior of an organization critically depends (also) on the system of prevailing values (see Figure 1). Therefore, the decision to be a "traditional" or "modern" organization depends on the perception of the relation between two dimensions: the general organization's VCEN, and the organization itself (Porter, 1990; Gallagher, 2002; Daft, 2003; Jennings, 2005; Lafollete, 2005; White, 2005; Potocan & Mulej, 2006; McAuley et al., 2007; Daft, 2009; Potocan, 2009; Buchanan & Huczynski, 2010; Mullins, 2010).

What are organizational VCEN for, and how do they affect behavior? VCEN provide general criteria, standards, or guiding principles that people use to define which types of behavior, events, situations, and outcomes are desirable or undesirable. There are two kinds of VCEN: terminal and instrumental. Instrumental VCEN help the organization achieve its terminal goals.

Organizational VCEN develop from the interaction of four interdependent factors (Potocan & Mulej, 2006; Mulej et al., 2008; Potocan, 2008, 2009):

- The personal and professional values of people within the organization. People may be attracted to an organization whose values match their own values. Similarly and keeping things in balance, an organization selects people who share its values. Hence, values are a relation making a specific synergy.
- Organizational culture, organization ethics, organizations norms. Many values derive from the personality and beliefs of the founder and influential members of an organization and are in a sense beyond the control of the organization. Organizational cultural, ethics, norms and values (beliefs, and the rules) establish the appropriate way for organizational members to deal with one another and with all other members of the organization's environments (both internal and external).
- The property and other rights that the organization gives to employees. The values in an organization reflect the values of individuals in the organization, of professional groups, and of the surrounding society in which the organization exists. The values in an organization also stem from how the organization distributes property rights – the rights that an organization gives to its members, for instance granting them the right to use organizational resources.
- The structure of the organization.

The interaction of these factors produces different values in different organizations and causes changes in values over time.

The traditional organizational VCEN is focused on defining:

1. **Workplace:** By way of the perceived importance of physical assets, structured (localized) work, dependable employees.
2. **Forces of Organization:** There is a perceived importance of mechanical technology, perceived importance of the local market, homogenous workforce, stability and efficiency as goals of business; calm, predictable everyday events.
3. **Management Competencies:** Autocratic leadership, focus on profits, doing work by individuals, and having conflict and competition as basis of relationships.

One of primary characteristic of a modern organization is expressed in strong organization VCEN. In addition, the VCEN of a modern organization encourages dynamic change and adaptation. Some important VCEN of modern organization are: 1) The whole is more important than the parts and boundaries between parts are reduced or done away with, 2) Equality is a primary value, and 3) The modern organizational culture encourages risk taking, change, and ongoing improvement.

VCEN of a modern organization encourages openness, equality, continuous improvement, and risk taking. Even though the internal VCEN are strong, the VCEN encourages a healthy and ready adaptation to a changing external environment. This means organizations must adapt their VCEN to changing environmental circumstances.

Economic Culture and Management

Management is an important factor in the adaptation of the traditional to the modern organization (Gallagher, 2002; Daft, 2003; Cole, 2004; Jennings, 2005; Potocan, 2005; Daft, 2007; Certo & Certo, 2009; Mullins, 2010). Therefore, the decision "traditional" or "modern" requires us to understand relations between the following two dimensions: the organization's management, and the (actual) organization itself.

In terms of its contents, the process of management development can be seen as being composed of the following phases:

- The practice of management can be traced to the very distant past, but the formal study of management is relatively recent.
- The modern era of management began with the classical management perspective in the late nineteenth and early twentieth century. Two subfields of the classical perspective are the scientific and administrative principles.
- Following the classical theory, other academic approaches emerged to address issues, such as the social context and workers' needs. This more humanistic perspective contains three subfields: the human relations movement, the human resources approach, and the behavioral sciences approach.
- The management science perspective is characterized by its application of mathematics, statistics, and other quantitative techniques to management decision making and problem solving.
- After the World War II, the following two trends emerged from the humanistic perspective: applications of systems theory and contingency theory.
- Systems theories (e.g. the viable systems theory, dialectical system theory) describe organizations as open systems that are characterized by entropy, synergy, and subsystem interdependence.
- Contingency theory presents an extension of the humanistic perspectives in which the successful resolution of organizational problems is thought to depend on managers' identification of key variations in the situation at hand. This theory favors a new, more flexible approach to management and organizational design.

Over the past 30 year more than 150 different management theories and techniques have appeared (Daft, 2003; Jennings, 2005; Daft, 2007; Certo & Certo, 2009; Mullins, 2010). Of course, their development reflects and leads to changes in atributes of management. In our case one can view it as a development from a traditional to a modern organization. The traditional organization might include management attributes in its early development stage, especially the classical perspective of 1900s to 1940s. The modern organization might cover, first of all, the current directions in management thinking, such as system theory, contingency theory, being a learning organization, and having a technology-driven workplace.

Basic steps in the transition from traditional to modern management are: 1) structure – from vertical to horizontal structure, 2) tasks – from routine tasks to empowered roles, 3) organizational arrangements – from formal control systems to shared information, 4) strategy – from competitive to collaborative strategy, and 5) culture – from rigid to adaptive culture.

CONCLUSION

The challenge of managing in modern organization is to achieve and sustain the requisitely holistic mix between the people, technology and knowledge the organization possesses. To do this, managers must first ensure that they have set their goals requisitely holistically and on a well grounded basis. Managers also need to map out a workable strategy to achieve the goals. They must then develop requisitely holistically their organizational processes and structures with the best possible mix of attributes for meeting that goal.

Authors use different approaches to describe the running of the modern organizations. In accordance with their intentions authors also adhere to their unique viewpoints of an organization's activity – for example they could pursue the organizational, managerial, or ethical point of view.

Making an SME successful must be considered as an invention-innovation-diffusion process that tackles both the businesses mix (of the given size), and the SME itself as an entrepreneurial achievement. Thus, all preconditions concerning both the content and the process of innovation must be considered, which requires consideration of all crucial attributes and therefore systemic rather than limited one-sided thinking/behavior as is common among specialists. Hence, VCEN of all members of SMEs must also be innovated along with their knowledge. Then, interdisciplinary creative cooperation can result even when cultural and professional differences do occur.

Despite their differences, researchers share the opinion that transforming the traditional organization into a modern organization is not possible without an innovative change of economic culture of all important people in an organization. The development and innovation of the economic culture in SMEs in a modern environment tackles many important relations between assets, technology, knowledge, and values of the given SME, its business partners, competitors, and society at large.

We considered economic values as a part of synergetic entity of values of individuals, culture of groups, ethics of communities, and resulting influential norms (i.e. VCEN). VCEN tend to crucially influence development and application of knowledge, skills, talents, and other resources.

If we wish to have an efficient modern organization, we must find answers to two key questions: 1) what are important economic cultural characteristics of an organization, and 2) how to put the appropriate economic culture into operation during the process of transforming a traditional organization into a modern organization. All these cultural characteristics are also reflected in the economic part of VCEN of nations because organizations, such as enterprises, play a crucial role in a nation's life.

REFERENCES

Afuah, A. (1998). *Innovation management*. New York: Harvard Press.

Albert, S., & Bradley, K. (1997). *Managing knowledge: Experts, agencies and organizations*. Cambridge, UK: Cambridge University Press. doi:10.1017/CBO9780511582486.

Alvesson, M. (2002). *Understanding organizational culture*. London: SAGE.

Barabba, V. (2004). *Surviving transformation*. Oxford, UK: Oxford University Press.

Baumol, W. (2001). When is inter-firm co-ordination beneficial? *International Journal of Industrial Organization*, *19*(5), 727–737. doi:10.1016/S0167-7187(00)00091-6.

Baumol, W. (2010). *The micro-theory of innovative entrepreneurship*. Princeton, NJ: Princeton University Press.

Berkun, S. (2010). *The myths of innovation*. Cambridge, UK: O'Reilly Media.

Boisot, M. (1998). *Knowledge assets: Securing competitive advantage in the information economy*. New York: Oxford University Press.

Buchanan, F., & Huczynski, A. (2010). *Organizational behaviour*. Harlow, MA: Pearson.

Cameron, K., & Quinn, R. (2005). *Changing organization culture*. New York: Wiley.

Certo, S., & Certo, T. (2009). *Modern management*. New York: Pearson.

Chesbrough, H. (2009). *Open innovation: The new imperative for creating and profiting from technology*. Boston: Harvard Business Press.

Cole, A. (2004). *Management*. London: Thomson.

Collins, J. (2001). *Why some companies make the leap ... and others don't*. Sydney, Australia: Random Books.

Conway, S., & Steward, F. (2009). *Managing and shaping innovation*. Oxford, UK: Oxford University Press.

Daft, R. (2003). *Management*. Cincinnati, OH: South-Western College.

Daft, R. (2007). *Organization theory and design*. Cincinnati, OH: South-Western College.

Daft, R. (2009). *The new era of management*. Cincinnati, OH: South-Western College.

Daghfous, A. (2007). Absorptive capacity and innovative enterprise systems. *International Journal of Innovation and Learning*, *4*(1), 60–73. doi:10.1504/IJIL.2007.011475.

De Geus, A. (1988, March-April). Planning as learning. *Harvard Business Review*, 70–74.

Deal, T., & Kennedy, A. (2000). *Corporate cultures*. Jackson, MI: Perseus Books Group.

European Union (EU). (2006). *Implementing the partnership for growth and jobs*. Brussels, Belgium: EU.

Fink, M., & Kraus, S. (Eds.). (2009). *The management of small and medium enterprises*. New York: Routledge.

Florida, R. (2002). *The rise of the creative class*. New York: Basic Books.

Galbraith, J. (2002). *Designing organizations*. New York: Wiley and Sons.

Gallagher, R. (2002). *The soul of an organization*. New York: Kaplan Business.

Goldman, J. et al. (1995). *Competitors and virtual organizations*. London: Van Nostrand Reinhold.

Govindarajan, V., & Trimple, C. (2010). *The other side of innovation*. Boston: Harvard Business Press.

Greene, C. (2009). *Entrepreneurship: Ideas in action*. Mason, GA: South-Western.

Hebert, R., & Link, A. (1989). In search of the meaning of entrepreneurship. *Small Business Economics*, *1*(1), 39–49. doi:10.1007/BF00389915.

Hofstede, G., & Pedersen, P. (2004). *Cultures and organizations*. New York: McGraw-Hill.

Huston, L., & Sakkab, N. (2006, March). Connect and develop: Inside Procter & Gamble's new model for innovation. *Harvard Business Review*, 1–9.

IBM. (2006). *The global innovation outlook*. Armonk, NY: IBM.

Ireland, R., & Hitt, M. (1997). Performance strategies for high growth entrepreneurial firms. *Frontiers of Entrepreneurship Research*, *9*(1), 101–104.

Jennings, M. (2005). *Business: Its legal, ethical and global environment*. Brentford, UK: SW Pub..

Kaplan, J., & Warren, A. (2009). *Patterns of entrepreneurship management*. New York: Wiley.

Katz, R. (Ed.). (2003). *The human side of managing technological innovation*. Oxford, UK: Oxford University Press.

Kelley, D. (2009). Adaptation and organizational connectedness in corporate innovation programs. *Journal of Product Innovation Management*, *26*(5), 487–501. doi:10.1111/j.1540-5885.2009.00676.x.

Korten, D. (2009). *Agenda for a new economy*. San Francisco, CA: Berrett-Koehler.

Kuratko, D. (2008). *Entrepreneurship: Theory, process, and practice*. Cincinnati, OH: South-Western College.

Lafley, A., & Johnson, M. (2010). *Seizing the white space: Business model innovation for growth and renewal*. Boston: Harvard Business Press.

Lafollette, H. (Ed.). (2005). *The Oxford handbook of practical ethics*. Oxford, UK: Oxford University Press. doi:10.1093/oxfordhb/9780199284238.001.0001.

Lawrence, A., & Weber, J. (2007). *Business and society*. New York: McGraw-Hill.

Lerner, J. (2009). *Boulevard of broken dreams: Why public efforts to boost entrepreneurship and venture capital have failed and what to do about it*. Princeton, NJ: Princeton University Press.

Lester, K., & Piore, M. (2004). *Innovation - The missing dimension*. Cambridge, MA: Harvard Business Press.

Leydesdorff, L. (2006). *The knowledge-based economy*. Boca Raton, FL: Universal Publishers.

Martin, R. (2009). *Opposable mind: Winning through integrative thinking*. Boston: Harvard Business Press.

McAuley, J., Duberley, J., & Johnson, P. (2007). *Organization theory: Challenges and perspectives*. Harlow, MA: Pearson.

McGregor, J. (2006, April 24). The world's most innovative companies. *BusinessWeek*, 63-74.

Morgan, G. (1986). *Images of organization*. Beverly Hills, CA: SAGE.

Mulej, M. (2000). *The dialectical systems theory*. Maribor, Slovenia: FEB.

Mulej, M., et al. (2008). *Management of innovation processes*. Maribor, Slovenia: FEB.

Mulej, M., & Kajzer, S. (1998). Ethics of interdependence and the law of requisite holism. In M. Rebernik & M. Mulej (Eds.), *Proceedings of STIQE 1998* (pp. 24-34). Maribor, Slovenia: FEB.

Mullins, L. (2006). *Essentials of organizational behavior*. Harlow, MA: Prentice Hall.

Mullins, L. (2010). *Management and organizational behaviour*. New York: Prentice Hall.

Nonaka, I., & Takeuchi, H. (1995). *The knowledge creating company: How Japanese companies create the dynamics of innovation*. New York: Oxford University Press.

Nussbaum, B., Berner, R., & Brady, D. (2005, August 15). Special report. *Business Week*, 51-68.

Porter, M. (1990). *Competitive advantage of nations*. New York: Free Press.

Potocan, V. (2005). Efficiency or effectiveness? *Organization*, *38*(10), 570–576.

Potocan, V. (2008). Why we need trust in organization?. *Issues in GRBE*, 102-115.

Potocan, V. (2009). What culture do we need for economic development? *Business Review (Federal Reserve Bank of Philadelphia)*, *12*(1), 102–107.

Potocan, V., & Mulej, M. (2006). Ethics of a sustainable enterprise. *Systemic Practice and Action Research*, *19*(6), 35–47.

Potocan, V., & Mulej, M. (2007). *From an institutional transition to a real one*. Maribor, Slovenia: FEB.

Potocan, V., & Mulej, M. (2010). *From an institutional transition to a real one into an innovative enterprise*. Maribor, Slovenia: FEB.

Pyka, A., & Scharnhorst, A. (2009). *Innovation networks*. Berlin: Springer. doi:10.1007/978-3-540-92267-4.

Quick, D., & Nelson, J. (2009). *Principles of organization behavior: Realities and challenges*. Cincinnati, OH: South-Western College.

Rhinesmith, S. (1999). *A manager's guide to globalization*. Chicago: Erwin.

Rogers, E. (2003). *Diffusion of innovation*. New York: The Free Press.

Schein, E. (1992). *Organizational culture and leadership: A dynamic view*. San Francisco, CA: Jossey-Bass.

Schein, E. (2004). *Organization culture and leadership*. New York: Wiley.

Schermerhorn, J. (2009). *Management*. New York: Wiley-Blackwell.

Schumpeter, J. (1934). *The theory of economic development*. Cambridge, MA: Harvard University Press.

Schwartz, J. (2006). *The magic of thinking big*. London: Simon & Schuster.

Shane, S. (2008). *The handbook of technology and innovation management*. New York: Wiley-Blackwell.

Sheshimski, E., Strom, R., & Baumol, W. (2007). *Entrepreneurship, innovation, and the growth mechanism of the free-enterprise economies*. Princeton, NJ: Princeton University Press.

Skarzynski, P., & Gibson, R. (2008). *Innovation to the core*. Boston: Harvard Business Press.

Tidd, J., & Bessant, J. (2009). *Managing innovation: Integrating technological, market and organizational change*. Chichester, UK: Wiley.

Warner, M., & Witzel, M. (2004). *Managing in virtual organizations*. London: Thomson.

Waterman, R., & Peters, T. (1982). *In search of excellence*. New York: Harper Collins.

White, J. (2005). *Contemporary moral problems*. Surrey, UK: Wadsworth.

Wren, D. (2004). *The history of management thought*. New York: Wiley.

KEY TERMS AND DEFINITIONS

Development of Organization: Is a term that generally refers to the sustained, concerted effort of all (internal and external) stakeholders of organization to achieve desired results of organization and selected standard of working and behavior in organization.

Economic Culture: We understand the economic culture as a component of VCEN, which is the accepted emotional reflection of the economic, processes in society in the feelings of the prevailing humans, such as opinion makers and their followers.

Ethics: In a general sense, ethics is the code of moral principles and values that govern the behaviors of a person or group with respect to what is right or wrong.

Innovation: Is defined as every novelty found beneficial in the experience of its users.

Organization: We understand organization as a social entity that is goal directed and deliberately structured. Social entity means being made up of two or more people. Goal directed means designed to achieve some outcomes, such as make a profit, win pay increase for members, meet spiritual needs, or provide social satisfaction. Deliberately structured means that tasks are divided and responsibility for their performance is assigned to organization members. This definition applies to all organizations, including both profit and not-profit.

Organizational Change: Is the process by which organizations move from their present state to some desired future state to increase their efficiency and effectiveness.

Organizational Culture: Is defined as "A pattern of shared basic assumptions invented, discovered, or developed by a given group as it learns to cope with its problems of external adaptation and internal integration" that have worked well enough to be considered valid and therefore, to be taught to new members as the correct way to perceive, think and feel in relation to those problems" (Schein, 1992, p. 9).

Chapter 10
Agile Management for Multimedia:
A Case Study

Ana Filipa Sousa
University of Aveiro, Portugal

Ana Margarida Almeida
University of Aveiro, Portugal

ABSTRACT

The past few years have seen a revolutionary transition in the field of project management that enlightened the strength of agile methodologies as a strategic attack towards the progressively faster development rhythms and growing innovation requirements. In this chapter, the authors present a study developed under this context that aims to discuss the suitability of agile project management to multimedia production through a case study focused on an academic context depleted in management formalities, the Laboratory SAPO/UA. The most prominent project of this setting is the SAPO Campus, and its team is analyzed and subjected to an agile project management model. Consequently, the authors anticipate an enhancement to the studied project and the gathering of arguments that empower a clear perspective on the fitness of agile project management to the context of multimedia development.

INTRODUCTION

Since the beginning of the last decade, the growing needs for innovation and the constant turbulence of business markets have forced companies worldwide to change many of their established practices. New product development styles have shifted from "predictive" to "adaptive" and traditional approaches have found themselves continually opposed by the numerous benefits and the increasing use of agile approaches (Highsmith, 2004). And project management did not escape such revolution. The tight association between this area and the society it escorts has always determined its evolu-

DOI: 10.4018/978-1-4666-4373-4.ch010

tion as a journey of progressive adaptation, where its methods, instruments, and strategies are clearly influenced by the society's multiple dimensions. But what was once a mere set of handy processes, it is now a structured discipline crucial for the survival in the enterprise context and achieving project management excellence became a priority to the majority of businesses (Kerzner, 2010). The need to fight the business market volatility and the awareness towards how a rigorous project management accession is fundamental to that fight are strengthening agile project management as a possible solution. Thereupon, this period brings out the relevance of understanding how can agile methodologies be adapted to the management of a specific type of business where innovation is at its fastest pace: multimedia production. Driven from a greater purpose of discussing such fitness, this case study aimed to comprehend how to specify an agile management model for an academic context. To accomplish such proposition, three specific objectives were defined: to adequately diagnose the management status of an academic context, to respond to it by developing an appropriate agile management model and to validate such model after its implementation. The focus of the study was Lab SAPO/UA, an academic context of multimedia product development which enclosed a set of projects functioning in the absence of any kind of formal management processes or practices. This nonexistence became the starting point for the methodology specification.

Chapter Organization

In this chapter, the Background begins by providing a contextual framing to agile project management, with particular focus on agile values and its relevance to today's enterprise. Then, the Case Study section presents the involving scope of the studied object and describes the different study phases. To attempt a lighter and hence clearer reading, the latter section will combine each phase with the data we have collected during it. This chronological line will be preserved during the debating of analyzed data in the Discussion section and in Future Research Directions new possibilities of investigation are presented. Finally, the Global Conclusions synthesizes the most relevant aspects of the chapter.

BACKGROUND

The past 10 years have witnessed a non-stopping technological progress that not only transformed almost every little aspect of the common citizen's quotidian as contributed to the increasing volatility of the business industry. In this "rapidly developing digital media industry, only change has been permanent" (Pelkonen, 2008, p. 26) and the next step on the evolution of project management became finding an answer on how to be prepared for the uncertain. According to Cooper, as cited by Highsmith (2004), the ability to quickly and competently mount an attack is critical to win the battle of new product development on this present scenario. Due to a greater vulnerability to the influences of the society's technological progress, this description becomes particularly relevant to the sectors of information and communication technologies and even more so to the specific context of multimedia production. The consecutive modifications that the technological spiral of innovation determines on chains of value and business models are of primary influence on multimedia production due to its central need of producing creative contents and innovative applications (Bruck & Boumans, 2008). The combination of the particular needs for speed in the development and innovation of obtained results and the uncertainty of the economic scenario build a frame against which all the anticipatory methods, linear thinking and prescriptive, fixed processes (that characterized the product development in the past) become inadequate – and progressively adaptive development methods (as agile methodologies), that try to take advantage of the emergent changes to benefit the result, become the solution. England and Finney (2007) recognize this transition as essential to the production of interactive media and alert on how important it is for teams to identify the increasingly stronger gap between initial and final project goals and to act on it to avoid or balance its influence on time and cost variables. However, one must understand this new direction has to influence more than just the product development approaches. As Higsmith (2004) points out, project management also needs to change; it needs to be faster, more flexible and more assertive in its response to the client's needs. According to this author, agile project management is the appropriate solution to this transition because it combines principles and practices that allow for the project to accompany the realities of modern development.

Agile Methodologies

Since its formal debut through the Agile Manifesto, agile methodologies have grown and multiplied with a fastness that suits the designation and hence embodied a true revolution against obsolete and decayed management methods. Along such vastness, the accommodation of a clear apprehension demands us to evoke the values that guide all the ensuing methods.

For starters, agile methodologies focus on the individuals and encourage cooperation above processes and tools, since the latter are useless without the right, result-producing people (Highsmith, 2009). The priority given to collaboration is also patent when it comes to the relation with the client: this must be a true cooperation, where the team values the client's contribution and the client trusts technical decisions to the team (Sliger & Broderick, 2008), and never compromised with unwise contract stipulations. Agile approaches also concentrate on the iterative development of working product versions over comprehensive documentation, as they believe it allows the team to collect an advanced and frequent feedback that guides the project onwards to the most valuable components (Cohn, 2005) but also because building working software is the way to appropriately respond to the project status (Sliger & Broderick, 2008). The final value points to responding to change as more important the sticking to a plan, an idea clearly driven from the volatility of the economic scenario – agilists believe in planning, but refuse to rigorously follow outdated plan designed at the beginning of the project. The planning issue reflects one of the most referred agile concepts: adaptation. All agile philosophies seem to nourish from the idea that accepting and dealing with change is the way to face the economic instability. And to detain such capability of adjusting to the context, agile methodologies pursue a simplifying attitude towards management without ignoring the importance of structure – the solution is "to strike an effective balance of right-sized, just-enough, and just-in-time practices" (Rico, 2009, p. 69).

Agile Basis to Enterprise 2.0

During its first decades of formal existence, project management implementation focused on quantitative and behavioral tools, but the latest years have witnessed the focus switch to the implementation of companywide project management applications (Kerzner, 2010), which evinces the need for revising project management concepts on the light of a new, faster and more competitive product development environment. This impelling journey towards excellence was busted throughout the years by several advents, namely Web 2.0 and, little by little, enterprise 2.0. This "use of emergent social software platforms within companies, or between companies and their partners or customers" (McAfee, 2006, para. 2) became the vanguard of outlooks for project management. By combining an agile attitude and practices with Web 2.0 tools, enterprise 2.0 turns into a crucial concept of the new project management approach. Filev (n.d.) believes companies benefit from the bottom-up knowledge dispersed across them and from a permanent dialogue between all business participants (from managers and clients to team members or stakeholders); and enterprise 2.0 builds up the capability of people to create, modify and manage that kind of information easily. This blending of top-down and bottom-management approaches advised by the author is also his answer to the ongoing agility gap that results from the clash of the rapidly ascending of new technologies, markets and competitors with the growth of organizations and consequent difficulty of reacting to changes with the intended fastness (Filev, 2007).

CASE STUDY

This study aimed its attention towards a particular multimedia product development context. The Laboratory SAPO/UA is a physical workspace within the Communication and Art Department of the University of Aveiro (Portugal), established since May 2008, where the efforts of students, teachers and researchers are combined to develop innovative projects in the field of information technology. The particular focus was its SAPO Campus project, a Web 2.0 education platform. The choice of this set was motivated by the lack of a formal base of management processes and practices for its projects. Despite a previous effort in engaging with management practices, the team's only significant attempt with a specific methodology, SCRUM (Schwaber, 2004), came quickly to an end. Once the opportunity arose, the challenge of testing management practices on a multimedia context was accepted – through the diagnosis of the referred situation and the development, implementation and validation of an appropriate agile management model

Space and Participants

The Laboratory is an area of collective work divided into an open office workroom and an annexed conference room. Despite the existence of designated areas of labor for each member in the workroom, the receptiveness and informality of the Laboratory encourages the repeated attendance from individuals outside the projects' teams.

As to the SAPO Campus team, it is composed of a project manager and eight developers and these members compose the group of participants of the study. The manager is generally responsible for the coordination of the entire project (including managing the team, work priorities and schedules, and external issues); and as to the developers, four of them are full time workers and the other four are undergraduate or master's degree students who work as part-time employees.

Methodological Approach

The development of the premises upon which this investigation was set up took the form of an analysis model, a structure leveled in dimensions and indicators (see Table 1) suggested by Quivy and Campenhoudt (2008), built in order to define and delimit the field analysis.

Likewise, this case study approach embodied a role of participant observer, during the earlier mentioned four months (February to July, 2010), which translated in a frequent attendance at the laboratory and project meetings and in the access to two communication channels used by the team (the bug tracking platform and the team's mailing list).

STUDY PHASES AND DATA COLLECTION

Established the case study premises, we must now expose and depict its different phases. A comprehensive approach to this composition, from its chronology to the data collection techniques used at each stage, is displayed by Figure 1, and a more elaborate description of each phase will be approached on the following subsections.

Table 1. Analysis model

Concepts	Dimensions	Indicators
Team	Hierarchical organization	Functions and roles
		Decision making processes
	Interaction and communication	Frequency
		Type of interaction
		Communication channels
		Addressed subjects
Collaboration	Client collaboration	Involvement of the client in the decision making process
		Face-to-face interactions
		Communication with the team
	External collaborations	Involvement of the collaborators in the decision making process
		Face-to-face interactions
		Communication with the team
Development and Management	Project life cycle	Time phasing
		Common practices
		Deadlines
	Meetings	Frequency
		Addressed subjects
	Verification	Planning practices
		Control practices
		Review practices
		Retrospective practices

Preliminary Phase: Building the Instruments

The first stage of the study featured an exploratory approach that allowed the merging of initially determined guidelines, resultant of literature revision, with all the information that gradually emerged from the researcher's presence in the setting. This initial step ensured a proper time frame to build the necessary data collection instruments and to gain a progressive awareness towards particular cautions related to the exercise of the researcher's role.

Initial Phase: Diagnosing the Project

The second phase was defined along two main purposes: a first advance to the data collection and the subsequent design of the management model. The initial data collection consisted in the first formal performance of the selected techniques, namely, the interview, the participant observation and the documentary analysis. This process, specially the interviews, were conducted in a very laid-back mode, ensuring a complete comfort and openness that indulge a sincere sharing of opinions and the overture of the study to important aspects which may have dodged the boundaries of the research field.

Figure 1. Study phases and data collection procedures/techniques

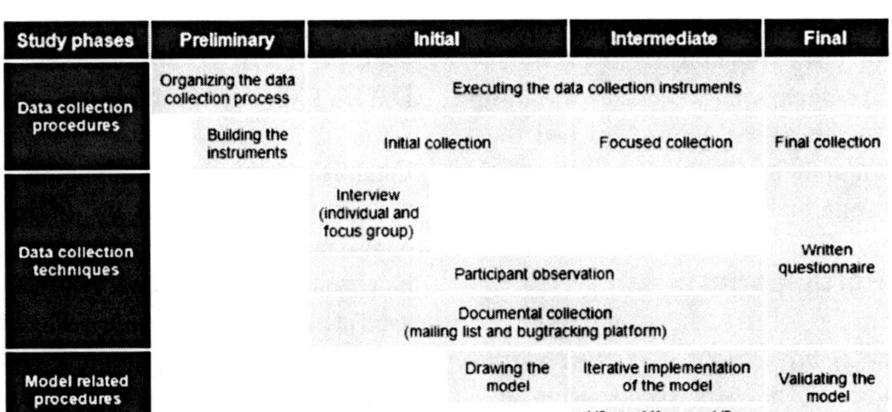

Initial Collection

The gathering of information along this initial phase was a process oriented by the indicators listed in the analysis model previously presented (see Table 1). To achieve a suitable translation between the abstract concepts of the structure and the latent objective data, each one of the indicators was associated with one or more objective categories and subcategories so the collected data could be processed with the support of qualitative analysis software (QSR NVivo8). The most important data resultant from this content analysis is summarized in Tables 2 to 4, arranged according to the methodological dimensions.

Table 2. Information related to the team concept

<table>
<tr><th colspan="4">Hierarchical organization</th></tr>
<tr><td rowspan="4">Functions and tasks</td><td colspan="3">Each SAPO Campus member has a different development role</td></tr>
<tr><td colspan="3">The development roles are directly related to their working skills</td></tr>
<tr><td colspan="3">Although stable, these functions can be changed if necessary</td></tr>
<tr><td colspan="3">The performed tasks are substantially diverse</td></tr>
<tr><td rowspan="3">Three hierarchical levels, obvious to the team</td><td colspan="3">Project manager</td></tr>
<tr><td colspan="3">Oldest developers (contractually commitment to SAPO, with more valuable qualifications and more meaningful responsibilities)</td></tr>
<tr><td colspan="3">Remaining members</td></tr>
<tr><td colspan="4">The hierarchy does not affect the comfort to share opinions and the respect for each opinion</td></tr>
<tr><td rowspan="3">Decision making trends</td><td colspan="3">General project issues discussed between all team members</td></tr>
<tr><td colspan="3">Individual work issues decided by the accountable member (despite the help of other members)</td></tr>
<tr><td colspan="3">Remaining decisions tend to involve the individuals whose opinion is considered to be pertinent to the discussed issue</td></tr>
<tr><th colspan="4">Interaction and communication</th></tr>
<tr><td colspan="4">Frequency of interaction</td></tr>
<tr><td colspan="4">Very frequent interactions between all team members</td></tr>
<tr><td colspan="2" rowspan="3">Influent factors to this frequency</td><td colspan="2">Presently developed work</td></tr>
<tr><td colspan="2">Proximity between physical work spots</td></tr>
<tr><td colspan="2">Outer common routines</td></tr>
<tr><td colspan="2">Interaction motives</td><td colspan="2">Communication channels</td></tr>
<tr><td>Express/Ask for opinion</td><td>29,1%</td><td>Oral</td><td>65,8%</td></tr>
<tr><td>Inform/Question</td><td>27,2%</td><td>Platform tickets</td><td>23,7%</td></tr>
<tr><td>Offer help/Ask for help</td><td>16,8%</td><td>E-mail</td><td>8,6%</td></tr>
<tr><td>Personal nature</td><td>11,8%</td><td></td><td></td></tr>
<tr><td colspan="3">Addressed subjects</td><td></td></tr>
<tr><td>Professional issues</td><td>88%</td><td>Personal issues</td><td>8,1%</td></tr>
<tr><th colspan="4">Nature of the interaction (initial nature and evolution)</th></tr>
<tr><td>Starts from one to one</td><td>50,3%</td><td>Relational dynamics maintained</td><td>73%</td></tr>
<tr><td>Starts from one to many</td><td>46,9%</td><td>New relational dynamics created</td><td>27%</td></tr>
<tr><td>Starts from many to many</td><td>2%</td><td>Same/Less participants</td><td>19%</td></tr>
<tr><td>Starts from many to one</td><td>1%</td><td>More participants</td><td>8%</td></tr>
</table>

Table 3. Information related to the collaborations concept

Client collaborations			
Project's clients	Academic community (final users of the platform)	University Rectory	SAPO company (funding entity)
Project manager as mediator	Guarantees the expression of every client's voice		
	Keeps everyone updated on how the interactions are running		
	Regulates the communication process		
	Represents the team in meetings		
No fixed regularity	Team and client communicate or gather their representatives whenever necessary		
External collaborations			
Examples of collaborators: college students, teachers, researchers and assorted entities			
Project manager as mediator	The responsibilities are mainly assumed by the manager but can shift to developers if necessary		
No fixed regularity	The interaction between team and partners occurs when necessary		

Drawing the Agile Management Model

As to the process of designing the management model, it developed from the gradual reading of collected data allied to a research of agile practices presented as effective and appropriate to the team. Since the participants of the study had already experimented SCRUM (as short as the experimentation might had been), and since the leeway given to the researcher to modify established habits was quite reduced, this methodology easily became a starting point for the model. Overall, this was essentially a process of understanding the benefits and risks of each regarded practice, of converting and adapting those practices to the context of the study and of conceiting new ideas which could suitably fill in the model. The result of this process is exposed in the subsection ahead.

Intermediate Phase: Implementing the Model

The middle phase of the study was characterized by a more empiric accession, in which the several management practices selected were experimented with the participants. Once the first version of the model was presented to the team, along with the explanation of each rule and its potential advantages, there was a discussion in order to identify positive/negatives aspects. According to this dialogue's assessments, the model was adjusted and officially adopted by the team. The implementation of the model was clearly experimental in the first week and formally settled in two ensuing periods (of five and four weeks, respectively). Also noteworthy, the iterative nature of the model demanded an extension of the data collection (through participant observation and documentary analysis) and a particular concern in its exercise and in the reading of the gathered data. This was a collection focused on the evidences related to the new implemented practices (what went right or wrong, what changed or remained the same). In light of this data, we repeated the design process, with new adjustments and further rules. A fresh cycle began with a new presentation and discussion of the modified version of the model, which ultimately resulted in a series of models.

Focused Collection

As mentioned, the data collection in this particular phase was mainly focused on the management rules. To enlighten such process, Figure 2 synthe-

Table 4. Information related to the development and management concepts

<table>
<tr><th colspan="4">Development</th></tr>
<tr><td colspan="2">Strategy of continually delivering new features</td><td colspan="2">In practice, periods of great pressure and fast development are combined with less frequent periods of tranquil reconstructions</td></tr>
<tr><td colspan="4">Project life cycle</td></tr>
<tr><td colspan="2">Absence of formal phases</td><td colspan="2">The project phases are merely distinguished by its typical practices</td></tr>
<tr><td colspan="2">Fast consecution and overlapping of phases</td><td colspan="2">Nevertheless, the dependency between goals can eventually assemble different members on a similar phase</td></tr>
<tr><td colspan="2">Conformity to the projects</td><td colspan="2">Though chaotic at times, the team appreciates the flexibility and doubt of the effectiveness of a more linear time management</td></tr>
<tr><td colspan="2" rowspan="5">Two types of deadlines (though not commonly established)</td><td rowspan="2">Project deadlines</td><td>Related to meaningful and ample targets</td></tr>
<tr><td>Usually connected to a client</td></tr>
<tr><td rowspan="3">Team deadlines</td><td>Related to specific tasks or features</td></tr>
<tr><td>Decided by the project manager</td></tr>
<tr><td>Assumed as ineffective by the team</td></tr>
<tr><th colspan="4">Meetings</th></tr>
<tr><td colspan="2" rowspan="4">Occasional assembling of the team</td><td colspan="2">One meeting every two weeks</td></tr>
<tr><td colspan="2">Conducted by the project manager</td></tr>
<tr><td colspan="2">Roughly organized and scheduled on short notice</td></tr>
<tr><td colspan="2">Motivated by specific needs, not by any given regularity</td></tr>
<tr><td colspan="2" rowspan="4">Addressed subjects</td><td colspan="2">General project issues</td></tr>
<tr><td colspan="2">Client/collaboration related issues</td></tr>
<tr><td colspan="2">Current development status and task assignment</td></tr>
<tr><td colspan="2">New ideas</td></tr>
<tr><td colspan="2">Frequent spontaneous gatherings</td><td colspan="2">For example, a member needs help from his colleagues to solve a more complex issue</td></tr>
<tr><th colspan="4">Management</th></tr>
<tr><td rowspan="4">Planning</td><td>Activities</td><td colspan="2">Simple task assignment, commonly during team meetings</td></tr>
<tr><td rowspan="2">Responsibilities</td><td colspan="2">The manager is responsible for assigning tasks to members, establishing development priorities and adjusting time restrictions to a task execution</td></tr>
<tr><td colspan="2">The developers are responsible for planning their subtasks</td></tr>
<tr><td>Support tool</td><td colspan="2">No formal use of a support tool (at most, a few notes are taken)</td></tr>
<tr><td rowspan="4">Control</td><td>Activities</td><td colspan="2">No formal activities</td></tr>
<tr><td rowspan="2">Responsibilities</td><td colspan="2">The manager is responsible for accompanying the progress of general team work but his lack of availability to regularly do so is roughly compensated by occasional efforts of casually questioning each developer.</td></tr>
<tr><td colspan="2">Each developer is responsible for controlling the current statues of his tasks</td></tr>
<tr><td>Support tool</td><td colspan="2">No formal use of a support tool (at most, a few notes are taken)</td></tr>
<tr><td rowspan="4">Review</td><td>Activities</td><td colspan="2">No formal activities; the gathering of the team to present concluded features and discuss everyone's opinion occurs only once in a while</td></tr>
<tr><td rowspan="2">Responsibilities</td><td colspan="2">The manager is responsible for accompanying the progress of general team work but his lack of availability to regularly do so is roughly compensated by occasional efforts of casual questionings to each developer.</td></tr>
<tr><td colspan="2">Each developer is responsible for controlling the current statues of his tasks</td></tr>
<tr><td>Support tool</td><td colspan="2">No formal use of a support tool (at most, a few notes are taken)</td></tr>
<tr><td rowspan="4">Retrospective</td><td>Activities</td><td colspan="2">No formal activities</td></tr>
<tr><td rowspan="2">Responsibilities</td><td colspan="2">The manager claims to privately address issues he thinks are in need of retrospective when the situation gets problematic</td></tr>
<tr><td colspan="2">Each developer has to figue out which practices went right/wrong and to adapt his practices along the way (sometimes with the help of other members)</td></tr>
<tr><td>Support tool</td><td colspan="2">No formal use of a support tool</td></tr>
</table>

sizes the most relevant information regarding the implementation of the agile management model.

Final Phase: Validating the Model

At the end of the implementation phase, began the validation of the designed model, a process that was carried out with the help of a written questionnaire, submitted to the team, which gathered all its participants' perspectives.

Written Questionnaire

By the end of the implementation period, all team members were submitted to a written questionnaire which helped us to understand not only the team members' opinions regarding the dimensions defined by the methodological premises of this investigation but also their perspectives on the agile model, its suitability to the team and eventual modifications. The most significant considerations are synthesized in Figure 3.

Figure 2. Agile management model and data related to its implementation

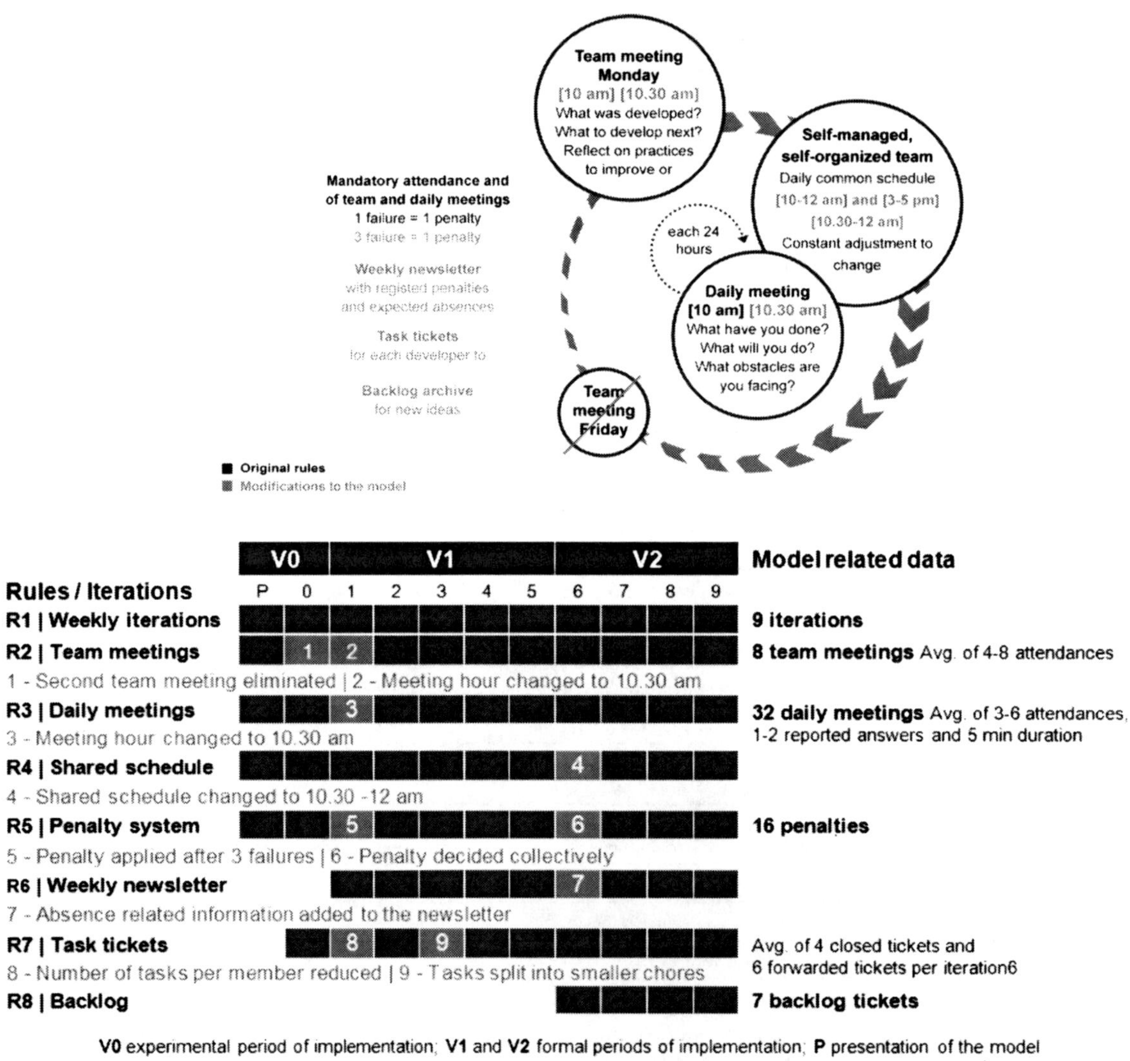

DISCUSSION

To preserve the sequential course of this reading, this section will separately discuss the data collected in the Initial, Intermediate and Final study phases.

Initial Phase: Initial Collection

Hierarchical Organization

The SAPO Campus team behaves as a heterogeneous entity where every member assumes unique development responsibilities - a multidisciplinary aspect that goes beyond the complexity of the executed work and results from taking advantage of each member's strongest abilities. Cohn (2005) mentions this option as the most appropriate way

Figure 3. Summary of collected opinions

Analyzed dimensions	Collected opinions
Hierarchical organization	General satisfaction towards assumed functions and tasks Certain discrepancy between the actual importance to each accounted priority in the decision making process and the importance members give them
Interaction and communication	General agreement on effectiveness of the communication process among the team, adequacy of its frequency, channels and subjects Scattering of opinions when the process involves clients / collaborators
Development	Dissonant opinions about the suitability of the existing project phases, their duration and practices – strong disagreement from a few members
Management	Individual work planning and control of developed work as most frequent management practices Retrospective of working methods as the less frequent practice Resort to a planning tool for collective work as least suitably performed practice
Agile model rules	Concurrence towards the majority of implemented rules General disagreement towards the day and time schedules for team meetings
General opinion of the management model	General agreement on the importance of management rules and on the particular need for an established management model With exception of one team member, all participants affirmed the developed agile model as an adequate solution for the team
Suggested adjustments	Different day an time for the team meetings Expansion and early beginning of the shared schedule Clarifying near everyone the importance of daily meetings and of respecting established schedules Daily meetings in the form of an e-mail report

of choosing the right people for the team, which brings out the SAPO Campus team as the agile methodologies prefer, as a group of people with the right skills for the function they're in charge. Also important, and despite a certain stability of assumed functions, these may be altered along the way (for example, when the direction of the product varies or when some features get restrained and lose priority), which means team members need to be prepared to assume new development accountabilities, whenever the surrounding scenario demands it, as it demanded in the past. Naturally, the agile concept of adaptation does not relate solely to the project but also to the team: to have processes and practices compliant with changes in the context is, first and foremost, to have a team of people able and willing to change.

Another important consideration relates to some attributes that assimilate all team members - the general easy-going attitude towards sharing opinions and a belief that every given opinion is valued – and to some others which demarcate them - the fact that only some of the developers tend to eagerly participate in a discussion and that there are some distinctions relating development responsibilities that indicate the oldest and more technically capable members as more prominent. By recalling the agile value technical excellence, this distinction of members with higher technical skills, allied to a sense of antiqueness (which allows them to be more accustomed to the project and to its context) can only be interpreted as a legitimate result of the project's characteristics. But despite this, the effort needed to assure a comfortable environment for sharing and discussing ideas cannot be forgotten and has to be extended to every member. To accomplish such conditions, it is imperative that newer or less capable members of the team do not feel inhibited to take part on any given discussion. Good results depend on trying over and over and again; the project manager needs to guarantee that no fear of failing limits the experimentation attitude of the team.

Regarding the decision making process, general issues are commonly discussed with all team members. This attitude is an effort towards real collaboration, which you can only accomplish when all the members feel their opinions as fundamental to the project's decisions, as Highsmith (2004) points out. At the same time, it is also a step towards a collective harmony: by assembling everyone to discuss project issues, the manager is congregating every existing perspective in a single space and time and confronting them with relevant questions. On a set like this, every member has the opportunity to cross an opinion not with a discussed matter but with other opinions; the dynamic here created and its repetition can create favorable conditions for each member to adequately articulate and recreate the product and project visions (and therefore improve and update them).

The idea of SAPO Campus team as truly agile is also sustained by the remaining trends of the decision making process. Firstly, the fact that individual tasks are a result of unilateral options made by the developer accountable for them embodies the concept that this team is self-organized and self-managed - a team that delegates in each member the responsibility of taking care of their own work. Secondly, the fact that only a few members of the team take part on decisions regarding more specific issues indicates there's no need to extend each and decision to all team members. If agile teams need to be prompt, need to be efficient on a daily basis, there cannot be constant interruptions to the working rhythm. This means, agile teams must find some sort of balance in the decision making process – and SAPO Campus team has found its own.

Interaction and Communication

There is no regular frequency in the interactions between the SAPO Campus team members; it depends on several factors, from the number of people occupying the Laboratory, to the type of work each member is developing at the moment. But it's easy to affirm the existing interaction as strong, and essentially amplified by the openness and informality of the work space, as it's easy to understand that the team takes advantage of what authors Sliger and Broderick (2008) point out as the richest form of communication, the one that creates the greater potential for effective understanding – face-to-face communication. Still, it is also of relevance to assert that the quotidian at the Laboratory is also characterized by moments of practically absent interaction, simply justified by the silence and quietness one needs to adequately focus on programming activities. For that, one may say the open environment and frequent interaction do not interfere with the ability of each member to set apart and accurately assume their tasks.

Other aspects we've analyzed were the nature and evolution of the interaction and although most of the registered interactions maintain its initial nature, one third of the total has spread into new relational dynamics. When crossing the information of these two parameters, we have noted that the interactions beginning with two members are those, which are most likely to maintain its dynamic; on the other hand, those beginning as "one-to-many" are more likely to evolve to new relational dynamics. This proliferation of interactions is, once more, an indicator of the strong collaboration between team members.

Regarding motives and subjects, the purposes of "asking for / giving opinion" were the most frequent, followed by those of "ask for / offer help" and the most predominant subjects were those of professional magnitude. For all this, one can attest that the work developed at the SAPO Campus project derives from a frequently collaborative effort and that, in spite of the preponderance of individual goals, team members count on each other to accomplish every target throughout and attainable and often spontaneous approach.

Client Collaboration

Agile defenders exalt how the relation between team and client needs to be fully cooperative and how it cannot be restricted by any previously stipulated rules – the SAPO Campus team does not believe in establishing, in advance, a specific set of features to develop in the future, manifesting a very lucid awareness of how unreasonable this kind of approach is. And for that, the interaction between team and client is not limited to a single phase of the project, but instead, a continuous flow of information between two parts – the team is always available to gather feedback from the client and use it to adjust different aspects of the development process. This symbiosis between team and client that progressively evolves throughout the project is what Sliger and Broderick (2008) recommend when discussing the agile collaboration with a client. Still, the project requires some level of rules and commitments, mainly proceeding from organizational demands and especially complex due to the existence of multiple clients and multiple requests. But it seems that, although the perception of the project's expansion regarding the client dimension exists, the only registered measure to prevent future risks of such growth is the delegation of some responsibilities related to the team-client relation to some members of the team – sharing the responsibility to avoid overload.

External Collaborations

By simultaneously providing resources and constraints, the external collaborators of the SAPO Campus project can be considered as stakeholders. The recommended agile collaboration with these participants is achieved by involving them in the project and making sure they get exactly what they need from the team (Highsmith, 2004). At the SAPO Campus project, each involvement is a straight repercussion of the specific needs of the collaborator and the guarantee of obtaining what he needs depends on how influent he is to the project.

This condition may seem to lack agility, but is essentially substantiated by the number of collaborators working with the team and by the reduced availability of the manager to assume specifically management tasks. Considering there's no time and no conditions to give the proper attention to everyone, those who influence the most gain priority, and having that, these collaborations are prompt and efficient.

Despite all said the risks that emerge from the complexity of the context must be avoided by a certain set of regulating processes and practices, even if no more than a few. Similarly to the status of the team-client collaboration, and as much as the approach towards these external partners seems sharp and resourceful, the need for some structure cannot be ignored.

Development

The data analysis indicated the absence of rigorously delimited phases of the project life cycle; as the development cycles are scattered over all members, each service or feature advances at a specific pace, something managed by the developer in charge. But this self-management still requires a more general coordination of all rhythms and all overlaying phases and although agile methodologies discard the necessity for considerable formalities in this management, the arrangement of the project development practices is insufficient. If the team is determined to continually deliver something new, that intention need to be reflected in a set of organized and timely regulated practices. Establishing iterations may seem more of an improvement when all team members are focused on the same target, when the development phases are more linear. But, since the plurality of working paces is quite common among multimedia production projects and since imposing a unique development rhythm can't certainly be the right thing to do, an adequate and careful maintenance of the different flows must be considered. Only this observant attitude can prepare the team to take advantage of upcoming opportunities and to measure the speed of each development by progressively comparing it against a rhythmical axis embodied by the project as a whole.

In the SAPO Campus project, the establishment of deadlines can be divided into those more of greater formality: typically of greater time amplitude and associated with clients and more significant risks, or those of lesser formality, commonly related to the team and easily considered too unrealistic by the developers. The latter situation is substantiated by a tendency of the manager to firstly ask for a prediction of how much time the developer assumes to need for executing a specific task and then reduce that period to half, an attitude determined to stimulate the working flow. But since the developers repeatedly face this advancement as extreme, they consequently tend to disregard many of these deadlines; this potentially harmful situation demands a careful revision.

Management

Planning

Planning the team work at this project consists of mere task priority and distribution decisions, usually during team meetings. This easiness and lack of structure are not compatible with the agile planning definitions, which aim to a considerable level of commitment and discipline. There is no organized effort to display the information relating the desired features for the product in the form of an accessible artifact that can guide a collective outlook – even if short and long-term conceptions of the product features may be part of the team's product vision, there is no condensation of such vision in any minimally formal plan. This situation is certainly influenced by the belief, shared by some of the developers, that organized planning activities are equivalent to wasting time, but as Highsmith (2004) underlines, it is essential for the team to acknowledge the importance of agile planning, of the advantages it brings and of the risks the project incurs in when lacking it. Individual planning may be granted with a very reasonable leeway, but the need for a consonant planning of the collective work remains.

Control

In this project, the practices of controlling the developed work are as casual and laidback as the previously discussed planning tasks, which lead to the reinforcement of equivalent arguments: despite the clear conception of the status of each tasks (by the developers) or the supposedly attentive general idea of the whole picture (by the project manager); the absence of a minimal, regular and managed action of control will elicit obstacles, problems and risks. To some point, we can rely on the team's strong sense of responsibility to avoid the expansion of these problematic situations into disasters, but the uncertainty of the context should not be challenged. No exaggerated monitoring is necessary, as it would only stifle the development. A simple and balanced effort to assure the satisfactory attention to each change that comes into view will empower the team to aware of any potential problems and to solve them (or at least react on them) as quickly and adequately as possible.

Review

The SAPO Campus team does not take on an agile review process as Sliger and Broderick (2008) recommend. Reviewing the project is not a practice repeated after a determined time frame or after a feature completion – the gathering of the team or of its representative(s) with the client side happens solely when such reunion is considered needed or relevant, a scenario sustained by several factors that add complexity to the project's context. Still, the process of cyclically examining the product in development and of consequently adjusting it according to the observed modifications is of major importance, essentially for two reasons: for ensuring that the team is continuously working on what truly matters and for establishing the team as integrant part of the (present and future) product vision. No matter how complex the context may be and how many limitations it imposes, it is fundamental for the team to come up with a solution that combines the right amount of flexibility with discipline in order to guarantee an effective reviewing process. Only then will the team be allowed to master a well-founded perception of the current project's status that can lead the product development to greater results today and tomorrow.

Retrospective

There is no general concern for reviewing or evaluating working methods used by the SAPO Campus team members; they take on an individual approach to the retrospective process and perform it only when something goes wrong. Although we can, once again, to some point rely on the agility of the team when it comes to development processes to assure the most efficient working methods, without the occasional reflection, the risk of grasping working routines or courses beneath the desired efficiency will always be there. Agile projects do not settle down; they constantly evolve thanks to a frequent effort of regularly questioning if every option has been associated with the best solution. And this standpoint must spread to another aspect of the retrospective process, as defended by Derby and Lasser (2006) – the personal and relational concerns of the team. As the analysis made clear, there are a few troublesome issues regarding the sharing of opinions and, naturally, to avoid these type of disagreeable situations to grow into a generally spread discomfort among the team, the team needs to reconsider how they deal with these scenarios. In an agile frame, it would clearly be advised a definition of a brief period, continually performed over the project duration, for solving relational dynamics' issues between team members, for scheduling incompatibilities, for discussing how comfortable team members are towards their roles/functions of even towards the physical environment of the workspace. The motivation of the team is a prime aspect of the project success and cannot be disregarded.

Intermediate Phase: Focused collection

Rule 1: Establishment of Weekly Iterations

Highsmith (2004) defends the establishment of iterative cycles of development as a way of creating a tangible outcome that allows the team to react to the true state of the project; therefore, agile development is achieved with consecutive adjustments (based on attentive product and project visions) in its own course. Since the definition of this project's iterations was reduced to a development policy of permanently delivering something, the designed model previewed the fractioning of the time scope into periods of one week.

Rule 2: Team Meetings

In order to regulate the frequency of team meetings and to guarantee the achievement of management goals, the second rule established the scheduling of one of these moments every week, with a fixed week day and hour. The previous patterns of assembling the team were maintained and throughout the implementation period the only necessary adjustment was related to the starting hour (from 10.15 to 10.30 am), due to the manifested difficulty of some members to adapt to a new and earlier routine. But these previous patterns overlapped the researcher's intervention, interfering with the performance of the management processes week after week, and even some intercessions made to underline arising problems or existing dependencies were not sufficient to fight it.

Rule 3: Daily Meetings

As previously stated, the model here presented was clearly influenced by the SCRUM methodology (Schwaber, 2004) and the daily meetings are a specific example of that influence. These meetings essentially consisted of inquiring three questions which every member should answer quickly ("What have you done since the last meeting?"; "What will you do until the next meeting?" and "Which impediments is your work facing right now?"). These moments were also required to be as brief as possible (and by that reason performed with everyone standing) and any impediment towards its attendance would have to be reported along with the answers for each question until the staring hour; this way the information could be shared with the rest of the team. And due to the lack of availability of the project manager, the meetings were conducted by the researcher and, similarly to what happened to team meetings, the only adjustment of the rule was the starting hour (from 10.15 to 10.30 am).

As other aspects of the inspirational model, these meetings make for a quite practical example of the agile principles, as they concentrate all team in a very effective, quick and basic process of control. Since many team members did not portrait an optimist vision of organized management processes this model, it was very important for these moments not to be interpreted as time misuses, and for that the original duration (15 minutes) was hastened. But soon it was clear that many members did not understand the potential benefits of this practice and such situation became ambiguous – on one hand, it was required a more intruding figure to adequately "sell" the agile advantages in this specific context; on the other, laying down explicit and enforced comments about agile approaches" benefits on the team was a measure avoided to assure all the gathered opinions would be as genuine as possible (and these needed to be a reaction to the model and not a reaction to the mode's advertising).

Rule 4: Shared Schedule

The shared schedule rule defined a daily time period during which the attendance was binding to all team members, firstly within two intervals (10-12.30 am and 3-5 pm) and later adjusted to a single one (10.30-12 am). The need for this adjustment was determined by the considerable number of registered failures, definitely encouraged by such aspects as the different work schemes, the academic obligations of some of the members and the flexible schedules the team was used to.

The establishment of a common daily margin was an attempt to guarantee two fundamental aspects for a smooth running of the project: the collective interaction of the team, essential for sharing and debating ideas that can drive innovation (no matter how much motivational flexible scheduling may seem, there's always the need for a time period that allows the team members to cooperate and good ideas to emerge, and by that avoiding the dispersion of time routines); and the management of dependency issues, crucial to speed up the project rhythm without having to waste time on work liabilities (since respecting this margin can facilitate this kind of issues by ensuring there's a daily space for them to be solved).

Rule 5: Penalty System

The penalty system consisted of fining all unjustified failures related to the attendance of team and daily meetings (and respective binding answers), initially according to a proportion of one fine per failure and down the line altered to one fine for every three failures – an adjustment to ease the adaptation of the team to the system. This idea, originally retrieved from SCRUM, was implemented to insist on the team's responsibility and despite not being an ideal approach, due to its rigidness, it was a necessary measure, due to the lack of time and of intervention authority. It was very important to discern if team members would not adapt to the rules of if they wouldn't even try to. The alternative, to only respect the rules to escape being fined, can reasonably be discarded when considering the frail intervention and authority of the researcher and the significant number of registered fines.

Regarding the execution of such penalties, and due to the systematic rejection by some members of all the proposed suggestions, for not finding them suitable for every team member or for disagreeing with monetary fines, the decision was eventually transferred to team meetings purposes. This way, everyone could take part on the discussion and consider each penalized individual before deciding how to execute the penalty. And as to the team behavior, half of the team members acted according to all rules most of the time – which allows the optimist prediction that, in a long-term adaptation of the team to the rules, the penalty system would not be necessary. On the other hand, insisting on the penalty system could help to ensure the fulfillment of management tasks, especially when you consider how complicated it is to the future characteristics of the project, of the development process and of the team. But in case of this continuity, the team would have to seriously reflect on how to implement the penalties, a process that needs to balance cost and comfort.

Rule 6: Weekly Newsletter

Though not directly driven from an agile premise, the composition of a weekly newsletter, that included all the registered penalties of the week, to be sent to every member of the team resulted from the adaptive attitude the model tried to engage. Once again as a way of insisting on the team's sense of responsibility, particularly on the sense of the more defaulting members, this rule aimed the exposure of every performance. The risk of offending these members was considered and assumed (namely for realizing how evident were the easiness of the environment and of the process of implementing the rules) and although the accomplishment of the mentioned goal turned out unsatisfactory, it is also certain that this rule did not harm the entire process.

In a later period, information about expected absences to the current week, previously collected at team meetings, was added to the newsletter. This addition aimed to take advantage of weekly meetings to understand which absences could interfere with the development process and to guarantee every member could have an anticipated impression of which members would or wouldn't be available during the subsequent iteration.

Rule 7: Task Tickets

In order to establish a planning record composed of tasks that every member could define and update according to its progress, the model recommended the use the platform tickets. Despite the far from ideal suitableness of the platform, these task tickets were originally created by the researcher and to be continually updated by the respective developers. By the end of the iteration, if a task ticket was not completed, it would move forward to the next iteration.

Due to the significant number of tasks left unconcluded along the rule implementation period, two modifications were applied. Initially, we insisted near the team members to avoid the aggregation of more than two tasks for iteration on a single member. After that, we requested the fraction of attributed tasks into subtasks whenever necessary, therefore allowing them to fit more suitably into the weekly period of the iteration. But this was not an easy adjustment – the developers did not reveal a sharp perspective of the time consumed by each task and reinforcing this procedure would require, even if temporarily, the support of the project manager's technical profile.

Rule 8: Backlog

The rule that previewed the existence of an archive on which records of hypothetical implementations could be stored only came to being in a more advanced stage of the implementation period and depended on the bugtracking platform once more, where a milestone was created for new development ideas. Although the reduced number of registered ideas and eminence of this backlog, the value of this procedure is still justified, since it has effectively allowed for a physical space where emergent ideas, once defined, could not simply be forgotten.

Final Phase: Final Collection

Adequacy of the Agile Management Model to the SAPO Campus Team

All team members have great consideration for the implementation of management rules and believe that the SAPO Campus project demands a valid management model. But, when regarding the elaborated set of rules to the team, one member has assumed his opposition, adding that "the team, more than the project, lacks of more clearly defined management rules." In the light of the collected information, this discordant opinion must be refuted – without overlooking the need of each individual to search, in his own course, a progressively better performance, this study has identified a more significant number of problematic situations resulting from the lack of minimal collective structure than those of individual failure. Nonetheless, the opinion resists (possibly derived from other not verbalized considerations) and the insistence in the individual responsibility is of great significance.

Suggestions to the Model

The analysis enlightened some suggestions we now briefly approach:

- Preferring a different day and time for team meetings, namely to held them by the end of the last day of the iteration, indicates us this team will probably be more prepared for the meeting's purposes after engaging with the project for a few days; we risk to say this team will, whenever possible, avoid to lose any time in meetings; if after a weekend pause the exercise of returning to their work role seems to take a little while, then an alternative to an early morning meeting must be considered;
- Suggesting the expansion and early beginning of the shared schedule (daily common margin) assists, once more, to the sense of responsibility amongst the team SAPO Campus – they may not have respected it at all times, but they do understand the basic need of a common schedule;
- Mentioning the need to break down the importance of daily meetings and of respecting the designated schedules reveals the incapability of the researcher's effort in doing so; it also raises the idea that values are the real motivational factors, not practices;
- Probably related to the previous statement, the suggestion of reporting the daily meeting's answers by e-mail should be considered for two different aspects: the first one is that by suggesting it, the team member in regard overlooked the daily meeting's potential as a moment during which information is actively shared and gathered; the second is that following the given suggestion would lead to an almost certain waste of time, since it's much likely that none of the team members would care to read all the answers every single day – reporting the answers is a mere compensation for not attending, a guarantee that basic and relevant information will be shared;
- As to other suggestions, the team has referred to a firmer establishment of deadlines, an individual controlling mechanism of labor hours and a greater delimitation of team member's roles – all of these aspects add to the team's consciousness of how important it is to define some project management processes and how team members need to feel oriented and organized.

FUTURE RESEARCH DIRECTIONS

In a future scenario, it would be interesting to expand the study here presented in different directions. One of these directions would be to elongate the model implementation period in order to experiment new management rules (these could be related to the already addressed aspects as well as to new ones). A second possibility would be to carry on an analysis regarding an appropriate support tool for the different management practices (both individual and collective ones). Finally, another research direction could be to conduct a study similar to this one but ensuring a data collection and analysis settled on more strictly defined and suited metrics. For example, the critical factors Boehm and Turner (2003) list as fundamental to determine the fitness of an agile methodology to a specific project (size, criticality, dynamism, personnel and culture) could work as an adequate metric set and define a control point that could clearly differentiate the pre-model period from the post-model one.

GLOBAL CONCLUSIONS OF THE STUDY

The exploratory attitude of every multimedia project matches the adaptive attitude of agile methodologies and of the enterprise 2.0 organizational structures, from searching a permanently better product result to searching an ever growing professional performance. But in order to fully understand the suitability of the agile methodology of project management to multimedia production, we must underline the most and least compatible aspects of this symbiosis.

Adequacy of Agile Project Management to Multimedia Production

With regard to the product, it is widely recognized by multimedia professionals that the developed product's characteristics can only be tested through the closest possible versions of the final product, a consideration that determined prototyping as such a frequent technique in the sector. To provide effective feedback, client and user must face a tangible outcome and to do so a multimedia project requires the iterative development exalted by agile methodologies. However, the high costs of building functional multimedia artifacts and the difficulty of establishing a fluid monetary dynamics between team and client resist as disadvantages.

Concerning the professional's performance, the multimedia production is used to deal with the constant emergence of new programming languages, platforms and paradigms – and ensuring the progressively accommodation of the team to the new elements is, indeed, a vital function to agile approaches. Still, when considering the multimedia project manager's performance, one has to assume the complexity of the challenge, as achieving the desired technical excellence consists in frequently mastering too many knowledge areas.

Finally, respecting management issues, it is clear that the self-management embodied by agile teams allows for a multimedia team, multidisciplinary by nature, to provide an adequate leeway to all the combined abilities and developed work, instead of constraining them to a single unifying methodology. But, since this premise can undermine the team's sense of unity and encourage team members to disperse (particularly within a context filled with different backgrounds and competences), it is critical for the management of a multimedia project to be based on a true sense of union, engaged in an allied vision of the product, a collaborative decision-making process and, above all, a strong interaction and collaboration between all members. The two latter are also crucial to this sector, due to the growing competitiveness for innovation that determines the success of the product and demands for each team the necessary conditions for a frequent exchange of ideas that encourage creativity.

SAPO Campus Agile Management Model

In spite of some generalized opinions about possible alterations and of one discordant opinion about the adequacy of the model to the team, the agile model designed in the context of this study was approved by the majority of the team and this is an encouraging result. In fact, SAPO Campus team has proved to be agile in attitude when facing practically every facet of the project's scope – except management. The almost complete absence of formal management processes and practices does not echo the dedication and discipline recommended by agile methodologies nor the attitude embodied by the team, for example, when facing development issues. In order to set the project on route towards agile management, it is imperative for the team to be conscious of the advantages some structure can add to the project's course and of the risks they are taking in the absence of a more rigorous preoccupation towards management issues. After establishing that awareness, begins a repetitive process of finding the right dosage of structure in every management dimension – and finding the best solution will require successive experimentations, as the team already does during the development process of the SAPO Campus platform.

Limitations of the Study

As it is not possible to summarize every limitation faced by this study, we shall point out those of greater strength:

- **Performance of the researcher's role while immersed in the context of the study case:** the lack of experience of the researcher became a limitation to the interpreted role and to the conduction of the study as it determined an easy absorption into the environment; ideally, the researcher would have remained distant from the studied object at all times and focused on researching goals;
- **Extension of the analyzed data:** this was a process of repeated blockages, retreats and reformulations that impeded an adequate work rhythm;
- **Nature of the attempted implementation:** since the rules of the model aimed to change behaviors already settled, there were time and authority limitations, which hindered a smooth transition of everyone's habits and a proper clarification of the importance of individual and collective responsibility in management processes.

But despite these limitations we believe this study contributes to a better understanding of the possibilities of fitting agile approaches to the multimedia production sector, as well as to a more comprehensive perspective on enterprise 2.0.

REFERENCES

Boehm, B., & Turner, R. (2003). *Balancing agility and discipline: A guide for the perplexed*. Boston: Pearson Education, Inc..

Cohn, M. (2005). *Agile estimating and planning*. Upper Saddle River, NJ: Pearson Education, Inc..

Derby, E., & Larsen, D. (2006). *Agile retrospectives: Making good teams great*. New York: The Pragmatic Bookshelf.

England, E., & Finney, A. (2007). *Managing interactive media: Project management for web and digital media*. Harlow, MA: Pearson Education, Inc..

Filev, A. (2007, September 29). *How do enterprise 2.0 technologies make companies more agile?* [Web log comment]. Retrieved from http://www.wrike.com/projectmanagement/09/29/2007/How-Do-Enterprise-2-0-Technologies-Make-Companies-More-Agile

Filev, A. (n.d.). *Project management 2.0: Blending bottom-up and top-down approaches*. Retrieved from http://www.wrike.com/apple_booklet_for_Web.pdf

Highsmith, J. (2004). *Agile project management: Creating innovative products*. Redwood City, CA: Addison Wesley Longman Publishing Co., Inc..

Kerzner, H. (2010). *Project management best practices: Achieving global excellence* (2nd ed.). Hoboken, NJ: John Wiley and Sons, Inc..

McAfee, A. (2006, May 27). *Enterprise 2.0, version 2.0*. [Web log comment]. Retrieved from http://andrewmcafee.org/2006/05/enterprise_20_version_20/

Pelkonen, T. (2008). Value creation patterns and current trends in digital media service creation: A case study of the Finnish digital media industry. In Bruck, P. A., & Boumans, J. M. (Eds.), *High Performance Multimedia: A Reader on the Technological, Cultural and Economic Dynamics of Multimedia* (pp. 23–65). Amsterdam: IOS Press.

Quivy, R., & Campenhoudt, L. (2008). *Manual de investigação em ciências sociais* (5th ed.). Lisboa, Portugal: Gradiva.

Rico, D. et al. (2009). *The business value of agile software methods: Maximizing ROI with just-in-time processes and documentation*. Fort Lauderdale, FL: J. Ross Publishing.

Schwaber, K. (2004). *Agile project management with scrum (Vol. 7)*. Redmond, WA: Microsoft Press.

Sliger, M., & Broderick, S. (2008). *The software project manager's bridge to agility*. Boston: Pearson Education, Inc..

Wysocki, R. (2011). *Effective project management: Traditional, agile, extreme* (5th ed.). Indianapolis, IN: Wiley Publishing, Inc..

ADDITIONAL READING

Cleland, D., & Ireland, L. (2006). *Project management: Strategic design and implementation* (5th ed.). New York: McGraw-Hill Professional.

Cobb, C. (2011). *Making sense of agile project management: Balancing control and agility*. Hoboken, NJ: John Wiley and Sons, Inc. doi:10.1002/9781118085950.

Frappaolo, C., & Keldsen, D. (2008, March 24). *Enterprise 2.0: Agile, emergent & integrated*. Retrieved from https://confluence.delhi.edu/download/attachments/2389/AIIM+Enterprise+2.pdf?version=1&modificationDate=1216403360000

Jyothi, V., & Rao, K. (2011). Effective implementation of agile practices: Ingenious and organized theoretical framework. *International Journal of Advanced Computer Science and Applications*, *2*(3). Retrieved from http://thesai.org/Downloads/Volume2No3/Paper%208-%20Effective%20Implementation%20of%20Agile%20Practices%20-%20Ingenious%20and%20Organized%20Theoretical%20Framework.pdf.

Oosterbaan, M., & Fischer, L. H. (2004). *Developing multimedia: A holistic approach*. Copenhagen: Nyt Teknisk Forlag.

PMI. P. M. I. (2008). A guide to the project management body of knowledge: PMBOK guide (4th ed.). Newton Square, NY: Project Management Institute.

Schwalbe, K. (2010). *Information technology project management* (6th ed.). Florence, Italy: Cengage Learning Custom Publishing.

KEY TERMS AND DEFINITIONS

Agile Management: A non-prescriptive management approach that confronts the volatility of the industry through a strategy of permanent attention and adjustment, focused on simplifying management processes, guaranteeing the tangibility of the product and ensuring a dynamic collaboration among all involved.

Agility: The ability to regularly and rapidly identify potential opportunities/problems and to attack/correct them.

Enterprise 2.0: A strategic use of Web 2.0 platforms and applications within a company's context to improve knowledge information sharing, collaboration between workers and customers and the company's ability to rapidly take advantage of each emergent opportunity.

Iterative Development: An approach to development based on a succession of time limited periods and oriented to the creation of a tangible outcome; the developed product is expanded during each period and evaluated by its end, in order to define the direction taken in the sequent period.

Multimedia Production: Development sector for products that combine different types of media (image, audio, video, animation ...), typically characterized for following the technology field's innovations, for the creative nature of its industry and for the multidisciplinary character of its teams.

Project: A time-limited activity based on the completion of established goals.

Project Management: A discipline oriented to the systematizing of time limited and goal defined efforts of development, from the project phases to the people, resources, time and costs involved.

Chapter 11
Trust in an Enterprise World: A Survey

Fotios I. Gogoulos
National Technical University of Athens, Greece

Georgios V. Lioudakis
National Technical University of Athens, Greece

Anna Antonakopoulou
National Technical University of Athens, Greece

Dimitra I. Kaklamani
National Technical University of Athens, Greece

Iakovos S. Venieris
National Technical University of Athens, Greece

ABSTRACT

Web 2.0 technologies have fundamentally reshaped everyday users' perceptions regarding online services by strengthening the importance of individual participation. This profound change is expanding to substantially affect modern enterprise operations and especially corporate information management practices. Well-established business models are upgraded to capture value from the establishment of dynamic coalitions and virtual organizations among remote stakeholders. However, these collaboration formulations dictate the concentration, use, and circulation of corporate information and sensitive personal data, and thus ignite severe security and privacy concerns. Enterprises against this background are more than willing to invest in terms cost and time in order to enforce the necessary countermeasures and thus build and maintain the trustworthiness of involved operations. This chapter studies how legislation and inherent characteristics of this new collaboration paradigm affect the qualities of trust and highlights prominent features of security and privacy protection measures that can deal with emerging trust issues.

INTRODUCTION

Recent advances in information technologies are fundamentally reshaping the modus operandi of online markets around the globe. Enterprises on intra and inter organizational level are moving from monolithic client-server architectures towards dynamic clouds of resources. Collaborative Web 2.0 technologies have become the leading edge of this rapid transformation and have set the foundation for the emergence of a new business operation and collaboration paradigm labeled as

DOI: 10.4018/978-1-4666-4373-4.ch011

Enterprise 2.0. The term Enterprise 2.0 coined by (McAfee, 2006a) as the adoption of Web 2.0 services to improve knowledge workers' productivity and augment the effectiveness and competence of organizations does not necessarily embrace explicit technological tools; it rather introduces a groundbreaking model for an enterprise's knowledge structure, information management and resources sharing.

Determinants in the process of Enterprise 2.0 adoption constitute the empowerment of users, the bottom-up formulation of new processing patterns, the emergence of free-flowing collaborative engagements, and the effective guidance of possible participants (De Hertogh, Viaene & Dedene, 2011). That is, Web 2.0 initiatives call for a profound shift of dynamics from a top-down to a bottom-up business logic; business value is built collectively by knowledge workers and is not simply imposed from a small number of key stakeholders. In this context, emerging electronic transactions have become highly dynamic in their nature, while involved work and data flows are suffused over totally decentralized collaboration parties employing distinct roles in the service provision chain.

However, inherent characteristics of the 2.0 epoch described above can ignite severe trust issues among participating entities. Whereas enterprises traditionally enforce strict centralized controls regarding information access and dissemination in the context of emerging transactions, openness and collective participation attributes of Web 2.0 tend to pose significant information security and individuals' privacy risks and thus call for immediate action. In a time where European citizens declare their concerns regarding their personal data and private life protection (Gallup Organization, 2008; European Opinion Research Group, 2011), it becomes evident that it is the level of user's trust and confidence regarding these emerging technologies that can either boost their applicability and effectiveness or comprise a heavy obstacle in the way of their diffusion.

On an international level, companies involved in e-business transactions have reached this realization; while exposing their resources through collaboration initiatives the respective potential information security and confidentiality attack surface is widened. Ultimately, the key to the successful and beneficial adoption of Enterprise 2.0 is acquiring the appropriate balance between vast user empowerment and strict privilege control. Against this background, information security and privacy as means to instill trust into potential collaborators has become a salient issue for enterprises and their key personnel in the 2.0 era (Milojicic, 2008). Evidently, along with trustworthiness privacy and security measures bring commercial value to organizations, a value greatly enhanced by the fact that privacy is increasingly becoming a legislated area. Awareness of the public regarding personal data protection, strengthened by legislation on an international level, affects collaborators' online behavior when involved in commercial activities (Acquisti, 2010) and thus motivates enterprises to adopt appropriate business models. In this climate, a number of keynote information security specifications and standards issued by leading institutions further intensify the organizations' perception of trust and sensitivity about risks stemming from privacy infringement and security breaches.

Ultimate objective of this chapter is to provide a concrete theoretical and technological roadmap for trust in the 2.0 era; from privacy and security related legislation and Web 2.0 operation patterns to explicit trust requirements and from the latter to compliance through respective technical trust management approaches and solutions. Major information security standards, privacy related legislation, along with the particularization of trust in Enterprise 2.0 environments and the specification of trust requirements comprise the content of the next section. The chapter then delves into the literature and provides an overview of the most important, characteristic and influential trust inducing models. Before concluding with a short overview of the future research directions, the chapter provides an overview of the studied trust models.

BACKGROUND

Overview of the Legal and Regulatory Background

The current trend among organizations in a worldwide level towards the adoption of concrete security and privacy policies is driven by the underlying legislation. In fact, legislation provides the means for the efficient orchestration of common security and privacy mechanisms and their composition into robust holistic trust solutions. In this context, legislation compliance and technical requirements of trust frameworks obtain a linear relation.

Since user participation comprises the cornerstone of Web 2.0 principles, privacy protection becomes crucial. Undoubtedly, Directive 95/46/EC (European Parliament and Council, 1995) and complementarily Directive 2002/58/EC (European Parliament and Council, 2002) comprise the most influential statutory laws regarding privacy in the E.U. region. Disciplines of the above Directives constitute formalizations of the fundamental principles, set forth by the Organization for Economic Co-operation and Development in its milestone guidelines (OECD, 1980). The legal and regulatory requirements (OECD, 1980; European Parliament and Council, 1995; European Parliament and Council, 2002; Lioudakis, et al., 2010) that should be taken into account for privacy protection in online market environments can be summarized as follows:

- Guarantee the lawfulness of the data processing.
- Identification of the purposes for which data are processed.
- Assurance of the necessity, adequacy, and proportionality of the data processed.
- Protection of the quality of the data processed.
- Retention of identifiable data only for the period required for the fulfillment of the processing purpose.
- Notification and other authorizations from competent Privacy Authority.
- Information to the data subjects.
- Consent and withdrawal of consent from data subjects.
- Exercising rights of the data subject.
- Enforcement of data security and confidentiality.
- Processing of special categories of data is performed in compliance with the specific data protection legislation.
- Data access limitation.
- Dissemination of data to third parties and transfer of data to third countries is performed in compliance with the underlying fair data practices, the contract with the data subject and the specific provisions ruling the transfer of data.
- Supervision and sanctions by competent Privacy Authority.
- Lawful interception by competent Privacy Authority.

It should be noted that, unlike the E.U., the U.S. have retained a less holistic and cross-disciplinary approach towards privacy legislation enacting different laws for each distinct business environment. For some insights in the frameworks of the U.S. and other countries, the reader is referred to Solove's excellent essay (Solove, 2006).

Information security is defined as the protection of information from unauthorized access, usage, disclosure, and modification in order to provide integrity, confidentiality and availability. Obviously, individual privacy protection is greatly dependent on information security practices. The E.U. has therefore accordingly legislated supplementary

Directives to meet requirements in individual domains such as the 1999/93/EC Directive (European Parliament and Council, 1999). More recently, Trust and Security was recognized as one of the Pillars of the Digital Agenda for Europe (European Commission, 2010a), an initiative emerged in the context of the Europe 2020 Strategy (European Commission, 2010b). This climate in favor of information security practices has turned the spotlights on popular information security standards and business best practices specifications. Driven by the original OECD privacy guidelines (1980) several information security management standards have been established in the last decade. Keynote specifications have been publicized by the National Institute of Standards and Technology (Swanson, M., & Guttman, B, 1996), the Information Systems Security Association (ISSA, 2004), the International Organization for Standardization (ISO/IEC 27002, 2005) and the Information Security Forum (ISF, 2007). Focusing on information security in different levels from a technological perspective the above disciplines converge into the following action points:

- Establishing information security policie.
- Enforcing identification and authentication.
- Enforcing access control.
- Assuring compliance with legal, regulatory, and contractual requirements of information security.

Establishing online trust constitutes the ultimate objective of all previous specifications. On the one hand, privacy principles derived from the OECD and E.U. legislative guidelines aim at protecting the user's privacy and instilling trust towards electronic transactions. On the other hand, security principles extracted from current security standards focus on protecting the most important asset of our times: information, and thus work towards motivating compliant enterprises to collaborate online. Formal pieces of documents such as the above constitute the best incentive for customers and enterprises for realizing the importance of online trust and becoming compliant with identified principles.

Trust in the Enterprise 2.0 Context

The alternation in the state of mind of enterprises regarding security and privacy enhancement measures is radical; protection technologies have turned from social added value services to be regarded as actual economic enablers. Enterprise and Web 2.0 particularities systematize this shift.

Studying the patterns of Enterprise 2.0 diffusion, Bughin (2008) recognizes that in order for companies to uphold a competitive advantage in the 2.0 era the following actions are required: loosening hierarchical structures, rewarding active and valuable participation, moving from central to "edge" competencies by means of exploiting knowledge workers outside of the corporation' s boundaries and gaining the trust of customers and suppliers. Bin Husin and Swatman (2008) suggested a four-category model denoting how organizations can benefit from Enterprise 2.0 technologies including the 4Cs: Communication, Cooperation, Collaboration and Connection. These approaches in grounding Enterprise 2.0 principles converge into the following contradiction: Enterprise 2.0 frameworks can through their embedded characteristics both instill as well retrieve confidence and trust beliefs to and from their users. On the one hand, the dynamics of Web 2.0 tools, the transparency of transactions (as the collaborating party becomes an integral part of processes), the feeling of collectiveness and the user-centric nature of operations empower the user and cultivate a mood of trust towards the underlying technology. On the other hand, the extension of the service provision chain with unknown participating parties, the obscurity of collaborators' roles and responsibilities throughout transactions and the lack of central information management leading to hard to monitor work and data flows build insecurity and lack of confidence towards active involvement in operations. Hints of distrust and lack of confidence towards the emerging alteration in information building and sharing culture are prominent in recent surveys. More specifically, results of research studies have indicated that in many cases despite the great popularity of Web 2.0 tools users are not aware of risks regarding their information security (Rudman & Steenkamp, 2010). Risks and distrust reside on the enterprise side as well. By extending the user participation base and by extending collaborations outside the company's boundaries organizations in the Enterprise 2.0 era are inherently broadening their potential attack zones and become vulnerable to opportunistic and malicious behaviors. Besides, according to a Eurostat Press Release (2010) during 2009 one out of twenty enterprises in the E.U. has reported incidents involving the destruction or corruption of data due to malicious software infection or unauthorized access.

Information security and privacy protection measures adapted to the 2.0 principles can work towards this direction; protecting end-points (customers and enterprises), enhancing the privacy of involved resources and most importantly of information and eventually instilling trust to all collaboration parties. In accordance with the underlying legal and regulatory framework and the inherent Enterprise 2.0 characteristics, for the purposes of this chapter we adopt a technological perspective of trust (Ratnasingam, 2005). Technology trust is defined as the organizations' confidence founded on the belief that the underlying technology infrastructure is capable of supporting transactions according to their expectations. Dimensions of technology trust formulate the following trust requirements:

- **Confidentiality:** Means for the protection of personal privacy and proprietary information should be provided. Compliance with the legal and regulatory background described above is crucial.
- **Integrity:** Safeguard measures against improper and unwanted information modification should be enforced.
- **Authentication:** Identification mechanisms for confirming the truth regarding users' identities should be applied.
- **Non-Repudiation:** Challenging the validity of one's performed actions should be unsuccessful through the exploitation of respective acknowledgement procedures.
- **Access Control:** Restrictions on access and disclosure of information should be applied according to the enforcement of required criteria.

The above principles constitute broad definitions that mandate specific characteristics for information security and privacy protection mechanisms in the process of protecting traditional online transactions and its actors. However, Enterprise 2.0 attributes further particularize those generally accepted trust requirements. Therefore protection measures and approaches that should be promoted for adoption are those which conform to its inherent characteristics:

- **Decentralized Networks:** Services, processes and relevant information are spanned across administratively and geographically dispersed peers.
- **Independent Trust Domains:** Collaborating peers are ruled by heterogeneous security policies adapted to their own needs and requirements.
- **Dynamic Communities Coalitions:** Collaboration and information sharing in the Enterprise 2.0 context are often performed on the basis of ad-hoc and dynamic formulations of user communities.
- **User Empowerment:** Web 2.0 attributes are summarized into this key principle; moving from top-down to bottom-up business logics and thus strengthening the centrality of the user's role.

Figure 1. Trust specification in the enterprise 2.0 context

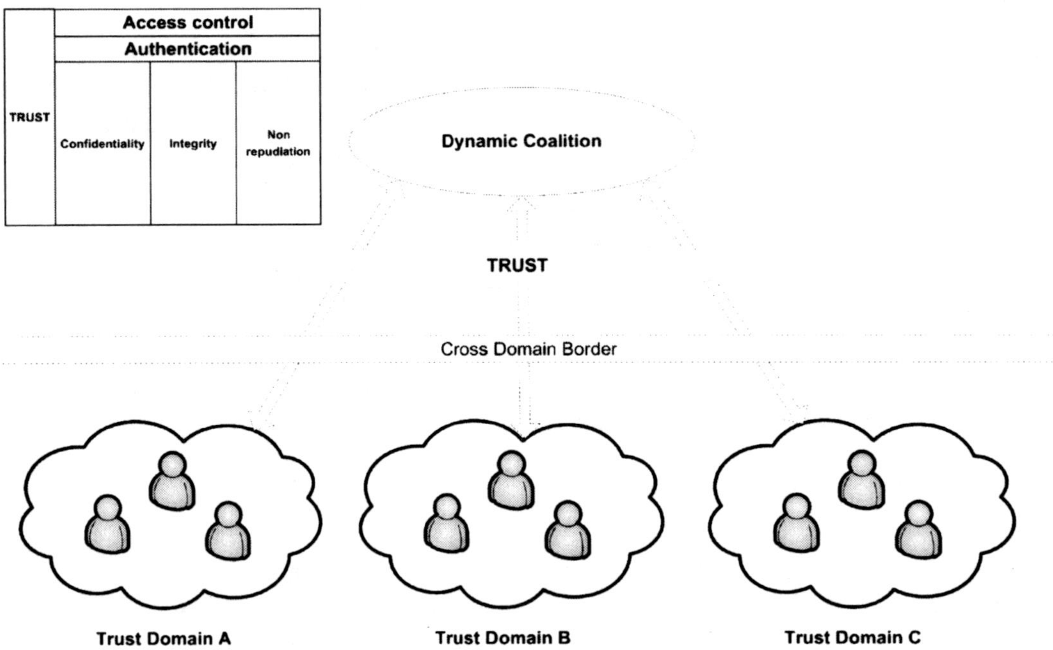

Figure 1 summarizes the adopted trust requirements applied in the context of Enterprise 2.0 operations.

MEETING THE REQUIREMENTS

Trust Issue and Countermeasures

Despite the reasonable diffusion rates of Web 2.0 among enterprises (Bughin & Manyika, 2007) a significant portion of organizations and respective employees remains quite skeptical towards Enterprise 2.0 adoption. This adoption reluctance, known as the *Empty Quarter* phenomenon (McAfee, 2006b) is grounded on a variety of reasons such as the possible low interest in and fear of innovative technologies and the existence of strongly established corporate cultures. However, it is evident that information security and privacy concerns further motivate users to position themselves in the Empty Quarter (McAfee, 2008; Lin, Lee, & Lin, 2010). Consequently, trust remains in the spotlight and as Kwan and Ramachandran (2009) state: "since the raison d' être of Web 2.0 is collaboration—often with strangers—trust is the linchpin of this new continuum of participation" (p. 2). In this context, enforcing strong trust measures for addressing trust requirements defined in the previous section becomes a key issue for organizations.

Generally, security frameworks in computer science can be categorized into hard and soft security systems (Rasmusson & Janson, 1996). This conceptual categorization can be adopted in the realm of trust: hard security is achieved by traditional security mechanisms making use of concrete evidence such as digital credentials and security tokens in order to make trust decisions according to specified security policies, while soft security systems employ social control mechanisms taking advantage of metrics regarding notions such as recommendations and reputation in order to evaluate trust. Indeed, the flexibility and openness of social control measures are well suited to the dynamic and user-centric nature of Enterprise 2.0. Therefore, whereas both approaches retain their own pros and cons, hybrid models employing hard security methods on the basis of "soft information" can be applicable and effective in many risk limited cases (Varadharajan, 2009). For instance, soft security mechanisms can be crucial for the establishment of *initial trust* (McKnight, Cummings, & Chervany, 1998) among potential collaborators. Despite the usefulness of soft techniques, hard security constitutes the main target of this review. This choice, apart from being compatible with the technological perspective of trust adopted here, is not unreasonable; social control mechanisms are characterized by great volumes of uncertainty in contrast to firmness derived from "harder" security mechanisms. Recommendations and reputation metrics provided by third parties although indicative of the trustworthiness of the target under consideration are prone to opportunistic behaviors, such as distorting information and misleading partners.

Whereas the vast majority of current research surveys focuses on investigating and analyzing partial views of the trust issue (i.e., trust definition, trust by means of secure authentication, trust by means of effective authorization, trust by means of reputation and recommendations) this chapter provides an overview of trust enhancing approaches which when appropriately adopted and combined can adequately address trust requirements in the 2.0 era. Hence, goal of our review is not to provide an exhaustive view of each trust mechanism, but rather a representative description of current approaches towards security and privacy issues within the Enterprise 2.0 world. In that respect, hard security and privacy measures comprise the content of the following analysis. Investigated technologies will be presented in the context of two broad categories: trust representation and exchange and trust establishment and enforcement. The above comprise two distinct stages of trust accomplishment; the first step to trust an entity is the acknowledgement of its identity and qualities, while the second includes the determination of its privileges and the enforcement of final trust decisions.

Trust Representation and Exchange

The term trust representation and exchange in the context of a digital partnership refers to the accumulation and circulation of tangible evidence regarding information related with potential cooperating parties. Prior to being able to negotiate and establish trust relationships, entities willing to engage in collaboration need to demonstrate valid proofs of their identity and attributes. In that sense, authentication is inherently related to trust representation and exchange. Online authentication has been studied thoroughly and from different disciplines from the early beginnings of e-commerce and e-business. Generally, two forms of authentication evidence prevail in current online transactions: biometrics and digital credentials. While digital credentials employ cryptography for depicting and verifying identities and attributes, biometric authentication technologies exploit physical features of humans for their identification, such as fingerprint scanning (Jain, Ross, & Pankanti, 2006), face recognition (Dabbah, Woo, & Dlay, 2007), iris scanning (Ganorkar & Ghatol, 2007) and signature verification (Bandopadhaya, et al., 2008). Several hybrid models integrating cryptographic techniques along with biometric matchers have also been proposed (Xinyi, et al., 2011).

However effective and liable biometrics may have turned out in the process of identities recognition, respective mechanisms suffer from a number of vulnerabilities. More specifically, unlike digital identification tokens, biological characteristics cannot be without difficulty altered and revoked. Furthermore, the disclosure of biometric traits is treated with skepticism and emotional-behavioral reservations by users due to its conceptual correlation with fingerprint matching in crime investigations. Last but not least, biometric authentication inherently ignites severe privacy issues. Respective technologies can be maliciously handled for inferring further information from biological measurements such as genetic information and for effectively attacking users' anonymity (Prabhakar, Pankanti, & Jain, 2003). Hence, biometric measures fail to conform to the confidentiality trust requirement and thus are not part of our analysis.

Public key cryptography and asymmetric key algorithms can efficiently enforce integrity, confidentiality and non-repudiation and offer the possibility to authenticate the identity of entities by validating the possession of a private key associated with a known public key. This association is depicted in the form of a digital certificate. Although alternative certificate specifications have emerged over the years, the most widely diffused is found in the International Telecommunications Union X.509 standard (International Telecommunication Union, 2005). Authentication in distributed environments by the exploitation of digital certificates has been fundamentally related with two key mechanisms that prevail in the online market: Public Key Infrastructures (PKI) and Federated Identity Management (FIdM) Systems.

Public Key Infrastructure

Public Key Infrastructure (PKI) and Privilege Management Infrastructure (PMI) constitute the most influential representatives of public key cryptography employment for the creation, distribution, validation and revocation of digital certificates (depicting identities in PKIs and attributes in PMIs). The above operations comprise typical responsibilities of Certification Authorities (CAs), entities whose role in an effective PKI installation is of crucial importance since they work as the user's trust point in the infrastructure. The placement of CAs within a PKI instance affects fundamental aspects of the mechanism such as validation of certificates and cross domain trust relationships establishment. Traditional PKI schemes, such as single CAs, hierarchically organized CAs and the employment of mesh of CAs are notoriously insufficient to support large and widely distributed interactions mainly due to scalability reasons (Polk, Hastings & Malpani, 2003) stemming from heavy computations required in tracking remote users' trust points and estimating the accuracy and validity of involved digital certificates.

In order to leverage the capabilities of PKIs the concept of Bridge Certification Authorities (BCAs) has been introduced. Designed to counter traditional vulnerabilities of conventional PKI architectures BCAs and their derivatives Bridge Validation Authorities (BVAs) connect disperse existing trust domains (PKIs), reduce certificate validation paths, equate different policies of existing corporate PKIs and thus become more adaptable to the demands of widely distributed systems. It should be noted that BCAs do not issue certificates to users and are not regarded as user trust points. That is, distinct trust domains retain their own internal PKI architecture based on traditional approaches, while a BCA facilitates their interconnection and efficient cooperation. Over the last years, several interesting solutions have been proposed for trust management based on BCA and BVA architectures. More indicative of the adherence, adaptation and acceptability qualities of BCAs in e-business are implementations put forth by acclaimed organizations on an international level:

- European Bridge-CA employs secure communication channels among businesses, banks, assurance, telecommunication companies and public authorities around Europe.
- Chinese Taipei BCA connects through certification services public and privates CAs.
- Federal Bridge Certification Authority (FBCA), which enforces secure interoperability among U.S. entities cross-certified with the FBCA.

Despite the demonstration of the above PKI success stories, many researchers argue that PKI has never met the initial high expectations of the research community for supporting the build-up of a unique global trust infrastructure. Operational and technical issues have critically obstructed the wide PKI diffusion in highly distributed and dynamic environments (Wilson, 2008). However, BCA architectures evidently constitute an important step forward. Statistics and pending attempts towards the support of large scale Bridge Certification Authorities and Bridge Validation Authorities constitute perfect examples of this PKI achievement. The fact remains, that the introduction of PKI substantially raised awareness of the public regarding the appliance of digital proofs of identities and attributes through digital certificates in online markets.

Federated Identity Management

Identity Management (IdM) systems emerged as a convenient approach towards the organized management of individual's identities and attributes. Enterprise 2.0 architectures and tools, based on users collaboration, federated work groups formulation and resources integration qualities, enlarge the need for organized online authentication mechanisms and most importantly for the management of diverse user identities. The involvement in Web 2.0 and social network communities offers a great example of users owning multiple identities, utilized in different environments and for dissimilar purposes. However, centralized and top-down logic based architectures, such as PKIs and IdMs although building the foundation for more advanced identity solutions, fail in standalone mode to conform to the dynamics of the emerging 2.0 landscape. Federated Identity Management (FIdM) systems (Shim, Bhalla & Pendyala 2005; Camenisch & Pfitzmann, 2007) supplement traditional approaches and work towards satisfying the need for an organized identification framework, by providing the means for tracking and accumulating entities' identities and attributes, stored across multiple and diverse identity management systems. A federated identity enables the user to roam seamlessly among multiple service providers, eliminates the need for numerous authentications and thus providing the comfort of Single-Sign-On, increases the portability of digital identities and leverages the flexibility of users in participating in dynamic coalitions.

A wide variety of FIdM solutions have been proposed, each handling the issue of federating identities across multiple remote trust domains from different viewpoint and discipline. In 2002, the Liberty Alliance group proposed the Identity Federation Framework – ID-FF, which later evolved to reach its current version of ID-FF 1.2 (The Liberty Alliance Project, 2005). The key contribution of the Liberty Alliance specifications is found at the interconnection and integration of all personal information related to distinct service providers residing in the federation group into one unique federated identity. Based on the Liberty Alliance specifications, the Organization for the Advancement of Structured Information Standards formed the Security Assertion Markup Language (SAML), an XML based standard for data exchange between identity and service providers. In its current version, SAML 2.0 (OASIS, 2005) constitutes the prevalent framework for identity management in federations. Other FIdM technologies include the user-centric Microsoft's InfoCard (Bertocci, Serack & Baker, 2007), the SAML based Shibboleth (MACE, 2001) and OpenID (Recordon & Reed, 2006). The OpenID approach limits the need for multiple identities by exploiting the utilization of unique Uniform Resource Locator based identifiers. OpenID is fast evolving into becoming the default solution for secure authentication in the Internet due to its simplicity and user-friendliness. Furthermore, its user-centric nature promotes OpenID based solutions for adoption in the Enterprise 2.0 context. Nevertheless, the employment of unique identifiers and the consequent possibility of different service providers correlating users' activities are aspects that hurdle the trustworthiness of OpenID despite its wide popularity (OpenID is supported by worldwide vendors such as AOL, Google, IBM and Microsoft).

The issue of privacy uncertainty is not unusual in federated identity solutions. In fact, FIdM can ignite severe privacy issues regarding users' attributes and identities secrecy. Sharing personal identifiable data and information among service providers endangers the confidentiality of users, attacks users' anonymity and enables malicious activities such as identity theft. An interesting approach for addressing these uneasiness with FIdM is reflected in research activities proposing the exploitation of cryptography for anonymizing identification proofs. In that respect, a rapid trend towards the integration of mechanisms for the usage of pseudonyms in federated identity certificates has been built in the respective literature. Idemix (Camenisch & Van Herreweghen, 2002) an anonymous credential provider system and SPARTA (Bianchi et al., 2008) constitute indicative examples of this tendency. Furthermore, projects PRIME (FP6 IST project PRIME) and PrimeLife (FP7 IST project PrimeLife) based on digital signature schemas and cryptographic zero-knowledge proofs extend FIdM operations for achieving stronger privacy protection and effective multiple credential usage. The latter projects provide a wide variety of functionalities in the identity management area while focusing on privacy and the centrality of the user's role.

Federated identity solutions have been evolving to meet the requirements of emerging trends on the Internet leading to the concept of Identity 2.0. The most intriguing feature of this evolution, is the relocation of the user into the centre of identity management. Users in Identity 2.0 are allowed to organize and distribute their personal identifying information according to their own security and privacy preferences. Approaches that combine the utilization of pseudonyms while being compliant with the key attribute of Web 2.0 which is decentralization, constitute the perfect candidates for adoption in the realm of Enterprise 2.0. PRIME and PrimeLife attributes highlight the required qualities and reflect perfect examples of Enterprise 2.0 trust compliant solutions.

Trust Establishment and Enforcement

The term trust establishment and enforcement reflects operations taking place subsequent to the trust representation and exchange phase, that is after parties under collaboration have identified and acknowledged each other. In this phase and based on the accumulated identifying information, participants in an online partnership are called to take trust decisions and accordingly adjust their behavior. In that sense, trust establishment and enforcement operations are inherently related to authorization. Indeed, resource sharing mandates the enforcement of authorization algorithms which finalize into explicit decisions regulating the access of information on the basis of who has access rights, what kind of access privileges are acknowledged and when those privileges should be activated. Traditionally, organizations have been employing access control models and trust management technologies for these purposes.

Access Control

Trust violations in the Enterprise 2.0 world include unlawful access to respective data; in that respect access control technologies constitute highly important mechanisms for personal data protection and confidentiality enhancement. However, traditional access control models such as Discretionary Access Control (DAC), Mandatory Access Control (MAC) and Role-Based Access Control (RBAC), fail to conform to the sum of special requirements which rule trust establishment and enforcement in dynamic and complicated environments, covering only partial views of the problem. In that respect, during the last years several mechanisms have emerged extending traditional models by introducing concepts such as obligation, purpose, context, separation of duties and conflicts resolution and integrating them into their semantics.

In Purpose Based Access Control model (Byun, Bertino & Li, 2005) privacy policies allow the disclosure of information only if the purpose of the access request is related to that information, highlighting the notion of purpose. Working towards the same direction, the Purpose-Aware Role-Based Access Control model (Masoumzadeh & Joshi, 2008) defines the concept of purpose as an intermediate entity between roles and permissions in order to perform purpose aware access control decisions. Location and temporal based approaches have also been proposed. In GEO-RBAC model (Bertino et al., 2005), a complete specification of spatial constraints is utilized by means of a geometric model for the representation of objects, user positions and roles. Furthermore, the Generalized Temporal Role Based Access Control (Joshi et al., 2005) model contains significant characteristics that are related to privacy aspects. The described model supports temporal authorizations in an efficient and completed way. It also includes the concepts of dynamic and static separation of duties as well as constraints related with spatial context. In Generalized Temporal History Based Access Control Model (Ravari et al., 2010) the authorization decision is taken after the evaluation of the relevant security rules along with the temporal constraints related with the history of accesses. Moreover, the Privacy-Aware Role Based Access Control model (Ni et al., 2010) deals with the most significant attributes of an emerging family of access control models, privacy aware access control. Concepts such as purposes, obligations and conditions comprise the foundation of the model. Finally, the Organization Based Access Control framework (Cuppens & Cuppens-Boulahia, 2008) provides the means for the specification of dynamic, flexible and privacy-aware access control policies. Organization Based Access Control is centered on the concept of the Organization, i.e., the entity responsible for managing a security policy. Respective policies are modeled at the organizational level on the basis of the roles that subjects, actions or objects play in the organization.

Clearly, the aforementioned access control models take one step forward towards addressing issues of complex authorizations in online transactions. However, key characteristics of Privacy-Aware Role Based Access Control and Organization Based Access Control are better suited in the context of performing trustful Enterprise 2.0 operations. Introduced notions such as obligations and conditions in the former and organizations in the latter seem to be compliant with the specification of trust in Enterprise 2.0 provided in the previous section.

The specification patterns of the above models have been based on a single organization's point of view and thus lack formulations that could capture potential conflicts between heterogeneous security policies of disperse collaborating entities. In dynamic collaborations reconciliation and mapping methods should be applied on the security policies of distributed parties in order for an orchestrated access control decision to be extracted. Research on security policies integration and reconciliation in distributed environments has produced some interesting results. In (Hao et al., 2004) a formal framework for the hierarchical representation of security policies is provided. Hierarchies are then exploited to identify policies structures and consequently to apply an efficient reconciliation algorithm. In (Yau & Chen, 2008), the proposed policy integration solution takes into account the dynamics of collaborations when participating nodes are joining and leaving the partnership in an arbitrary fashion. While being ontology based the proposed approach utilizes a similarity based security policy adaptation algorithm and a negotiation based model for generating concrete sets of security policies which can be acknowledged and accepted by all involved participants. Authors in (He & Yang, 2009) proposed a Policy Driven Authorization Control framework for access controls in cross domain collaboration environments. The framework introduces the notion of collaboration patterns and collaboration policies in order for possible policy inconsistencies to be identified. In a recent work Sun & Chen (2011) proposed a collaborative authorization framework based on XACML (OASIS, 2004) policies. Collaborative policies are generated by applying combining algorithms on sets of binary expressions referring to XACML encoded policies and the collaboration intents of participating parties.

In our perspective, the combination of policy reconciliation and mapping algorithms with high acclaimed access control models as those described above is the ultimate key for specifying a unified collaborative access control scheme. Such integrations constitute perfect candidates for adoption in the dynamic and decentralized environment of Enterprise 2.0.

Trust Management

One of the earliest attempts in highlighting the importance of trust in highly distributed environments was trust management. Introduced by Blaze, Feigenbaum, and Lacy (1996), trust management established a general viewpoint towards building online trust, while attempting to address the problem holistically through a unified mechanism for specifying and interpreting security policies, credentials, and relationships. Trust management frameworks deal with authorization in highly distributed systems by generalizing traditional access control models and by eliminating the closed world assumption according to which all collaborating parties are known (Weeks, 2001), a perspective partially adopted in access control models described above.

Following the introduction of the PolicyMaker trust management system (Blaze et al., 1996), a variety of solutions have been proposed. The Keynote system (Blaze et al., 1999) utilized authorization mechanisms that given a set of assertions return with compliance values denoting the degree to which the request under investigation complies with written policies. The SPKI/SDSI framework (Ellison et al., 1999) emerged after the integration of the Simple Public Key Infrastructure with the Simple Distributed Security Infrastructure. SPKI enriched the SDSI with more sophisticated and distributed systems oriented authorization policies. In SPKI/SDSI, identifiers are directly bound to capabilities through authorization certificates, which can be delegated at will by their owners. The RT family of trust management frameworks includes a number of different trust management systems, starting from the role based RT0 (Li, Winsborough & Mitchell, 2001). The basic RT0 language has provided the foundation for the build-up of several follow-ups, such as RT1 and RTT (Li, Mitchell & Winsborough, 2002) for the integration of parameterised roles and separation of duties attributes and RTC (Li & Mitchell, 2003) for inserting constraints on previously integrated parameterised roles. OASIS (Dim mock et al. 2004) is another trust management solution, where users can earn their membership into role categories by demonstrating compliance with security policies of certificate authorities. The ownership of a valid role membership, represented by a relative certificate, is equal to a positive authorization. Finally, the role based Cassandra (Becker & Sewell, 2004) utilizes parameterised roles, permissions as well as role activations and deactivations.

Although not directly related to Enterprise 2.0 concepts, well known and widely deployed grid authorization frameworks such as Privilege and Role Management Infrastructure Standard (Chadwick et al., 2008), Virtual Organization Membership Service (Alfieri, 2003) and Akenti (Akenti, 2009) own useful features that can be exploited in Enterprise 2.0 oriented trust management systems. Prominent qualities of the above models are the employment of PMI attribute certificates which decouple users' privileges from their local identities and their high level of scalability when operating in the context of large virtual organizations (Jie et al., 2011).

Overview

We argue that trust in online contexts has a qualitative rather than a quantitative value. Even though several trust metrics have been proposed in the literature based on reputation, recommendations and past behavior evaluation they fail to clearly capture the notion of trust. Of course the importance of soft security mechanisms cannot be neglected; they provide fruitful information that can undoubtedly affect online behavior and most importantly found a layer of initial trust towards online transactions. From our perspective, soft security features should be utilized in combination with concrete hard measures that fundamentally create trust. This reasoning is compliant with the respective legislation as well as with keynote security specifications published by well acclaimed international vendors. In this context, trust is inherently interconnected with mechanisms which effectively establish information security and protect individuals' privacy. Obviously, trust inducing mechanisms in the Enterprise 2.0 world should be analyzed through the prism of the Web 2.0 inherent attributes.

The analysis undertaken on the basis of two fundamental online transaction phases has as its primary goal to highlight the attributes that can promote a security and privacy protection approach to be regarded as trust 2.0 compliant. User centric, dynamic aware, heterogeneity responsive and decentralized solutions clearly stand out from this investigation. Furthermore the exploitation of cryptography for ensuring integrity non-repudiation as well as for advocating strong authentication and authorization techniques is mandated. In this context, several conclusions can be drawn.

- Trust management systems provide the more holistic approach for addressing the trust issue in decentralized dynamic environments. Especially, grid oriented solutions provide features for the formulation of virtual organizations, a notion directly related to Enterprise 2.0.
- The foundation of a strong trust management system is to be found within its implemented access control model. Access control models conceptualize trust requirements and provide the basis for enforcing explicit authorization decisions. Notions such as purpose, privacy and organization introduced in several access control models presented here are of crucial importance.
- Trust management systems and access control models capitalize on demonstrated proofs of identities and attributes in order to authorize requests. Organized circulation of digital proofs by FIdM systems, should be user centric and provide the necessary flexibility to users in order to manage their own identity profiles.
- PKIs and PMIs in their federated formation can be employed in large scale environments in order to trustfully connect independent trust domains. BCAs worldwide work towards this direction.

FUTURE RESEARCH DIRECTIONS

Undoubtedly, more than 30 years after the original OECD privacy guidelines, obtaining and maintaining trust remains vital to organizations. "Questions remain, however, as to the best combination of policies and tools to protect privacy and preserve (or restore) trust in this evolving landscape" (OECD, 2011, p. 25). Future research directions covering Enterprise 2.0 technologies involve solutions towards this direction: integration of tools. The requirement for more holistic security and privacy solutions is in the 2.0 epoch more prevalent than ever. Therefore in the future, greater interest should be shown in integrating existing innovative solutions in order to provide an holistic trust solution in the context of Enterprise 2.0 functionalities. Correlations studied among Identity Management and Automated Trust Negotiations (Bhargav-Spantzel, Squicciarini, & Bertino, 2007) and Federated Identity Management and Privilege Management Infrastructures (Bhatti, Bertino, & Ghafoor, 2007) pave the way for relative research activities.

Furthermore, one interesting trend in the trust literature refers to the association of trust metrics with risk management methodologies. While conceptually trust and risk qualities are strongly interrelated, several recent studies have built on this relationship in order to provide risk based access control features. Whereas risk management methodologies are largely active in the enterprise field, integrating risk aware security and privacy components into the Enterprise 2.0 world is of great interest.

Finally, although soft security measures such as privacy seals and reputation based security systems are not considered concrete trust frameworks and hence not a part of this chapter, when appropriately employed they can provide fruitful information as input to trust decisions. From our point of view, the combined utilization of soft and hard security mechanisms constitutes an extremely interesting approach. Some early work has already been done in this area, where hybrid models founded on the combination of vertical and horizontal trust are proposed (Lee & Yu, 2009). In the future, it is anticipated that the literature density regarding relative hybrid trust models will be greatly enhanced.

CONCLUSION

This chapter investigated the notion of trust in the Enterprise 2.0 context through a legal, regulatory, and technological perspective and has presented a variety of trust enhancing solutions found in the respective literature. Inherent characteristics of Enterprise and Web 2.0 tools along with the extracted trust requirements provided the guide for narrowing the range of investigated security and privacy enhancing solutions. The analysis undertaken while not exhaustive, provided a multidisciplinary overview of mechanisms employed in different stages of trust establishment in online collaborations and highlighted the key primitives that should characterize any adopted trust inducing technology. Results of this work can provide a useful input for extended research activities, such as analyzing selected threads of the trust issue or producing respective effective trust solutions.

REFERENCES

Acquisti, A. (2010). The economics of personal data and the economics of privacy. *WPISP-WPIE Roundtable*. Retrieved on November 3, 2011, from http://www.oecd.org/dataoecd/8/51/46968784.pdf

Akenti. (2009). *Amentia distributed access control*. Retrieved November 29, 2010, from http://dsd.lbl.gov/Akenti

Alfiery, R. (2003). Managing dynamic user communities in a grid of autonomous resources. In *Proceedings of the Conference for Computing in High Energy and Nuclear Physics*. IEEE.

Bandopadhaya, S. K., Bhattacharyya, D., Mukherjee, S., Ganguly, D., & Das, P. (2008). Statistical approach for offline handwritten signature verification. *Journal of Computer Science*, *4*(3), 181–185. doi:10.3844/jcssp.2008.181.185.

Becker, M. Y., & Sewell, P. (2004). Cassandra: Distributed access control policies with tunable expressiveness. In *Proceedings of the Fifth IEEE International Workshop on Policies for Distributed Systems and Networks* (p. 159). Washington, DC: IEEE Computer Society.

Bertino, E., Catania, B., Damiani, M. L., & Perlasca, P. (2005). GEO-RBAC: A spatially aware RBAC. In *Proceedings of the 11th ACM Symposium on Access Control Models and Technologies (SACMAT '06)* (pp. 29-37). New York: ACM.

Bertocci, V., Serack, G., & Baker, C. (2007). *Understanding Windows CardSpace: An introduction to the concepts and challenges of digital identities*. Reading, MA: Addison-Wesley.

Bhargav-Spantzel, A., Squicciarini, A. C., & Bertino, E. (2007). Trust negotiation in identity management. *IEEE Security & Privacy*, *5*(2), 55–63. doi:10.1109/MSP.2007.46.

Bhatti, R., Bertino, E., & Ghafoor, A. (2007). An integrated approach to federated identity and privilege management in open systems. *Communications of the ACM*, *50*(2), 81–87. doi:10.1145/1216016.1216025.

Bianchi, G., Bonola, M., Falletta, V., Proto, F. S., & Teofili, S. (2008). The SPARTA pseudonym and authorization system. *Electronic Notes in Theoretical Computer Science*, *197*(2), 57–71. doi:10.1016/j.entcs.2007.12.017.

Bin Husin, M. H., & Swatman, P. M. C. (2010). Removing the barriers to enterprise 2.0. In *Proceedings of the 2010 IEEE International Symposium on Technology and Society (ISTAS)* (pp. 275-283). IEEE.

Blaze, M., Feigenbaum, J., Ioannidis, J., & Keromytis, A. D. (1999). *RFC-2704: The keynote trust management system version 2*. Geneva, Switzerland: Internet Engineering Task Force.

Blaze, M., Feigenbaum, J., & Lacy, J. (1996). Decentralized trust management. In *Proceedings of the 1996 IEEE Symposium on Security and Privacy* (pp. 164-173). IEEE Computer Society Press.

Bughin, J. (2008). The rise of enterprise 2.0. *Direct. Data and Digital Marketing Practice*, *9*(3), 251–259. doi:10.1057/palgrave.dddmp.4350100.

Bughin, J., & Manyika, J. (2007). *How businesses are using web 2.0: A McKinsey global survey*. Retrieved November 3, 2011, from http://www.mckinseyquarterly.com/article_page.aspx?ar=1913

Byun, J.-W., Bertino, E., & Li, N. (2005). Purpose based access control of complex data for privacy protection. In *Proceedings of the 10th ACM Symposium on Access Control Models and Technologies (SACMAT 'O5)* (pp. 102-110). New York: ACM.

Camenisch, J., & Pfitzmann, B. (2007). Federated identity management. In Petkovic, M., & Jonker, W. (Eds.), *Security, Privacy, and Trust in Modern Data Management* (pp. 213–238). Berlin: Springer-Verlag. doi:10.1007/978-3-540-69861-6_15.

Camenisch, J., & Van Herreweghen, E. (2002). Design and implementation of the idemix anonymous credential system. In *Proceedings of the 9th ACM Conference on Computer and Communications Security (CCS '02)* (pp. 21-30). New York: ACM.

Chadwick, D., Zhao, G., Otenko, S., Laborde, R., Su, L., & Nguyen, T. A. (2008). PERMIS: A modular authorization infrastructure. *Concurrency and Computation*, *20*(11), 1341–1357. doi:10.1002/cpe.1313.

Cuppens, F., & Cuppens-Boulahia, N. (2008). Modeling contextual security policies. *International Journal of Information Security*, *7*(4), 285–305. doi:10.1007/s10207-007-0051-9.

Dabbah, M. A., Woo, W. L., & Dlay, S. S. (2007). Secure authentication for face recognition. In *Proceedings of the IEEE Symposium on Computational Intelligence in Image and Signal Processing* (pp. 121 – 126). IEEE.

De Hertogh, S., Viaene, S., & Dedene, G. (2011). Governing web 2.0. *Communications of the ACM*, *54*(3), 124–130. doi:10.1145/1897852.1897882.

Dim Mock, N., Belokosztolszki, A., Eyers, D., Bacon, J., & Moody, K. (2004). Using trust and risk in role based access control policies. In *Proceedings of the 9th ACM Symposium on Access Control Models and Technologies* (pp. 156-162). New York: ACM.

Ellison, C., Frantz, B., Lampson, B., Rivest, R., Thomas, B., & Ylonen, T. (1999). *RFC-2693: SPKI certificate theory*. Geneva, Switzerland: Internet Engineering Task Force.

European Commission. (2010a). *Communication from the commission to the European parliament, the council, the European economic and social committee and the committee of the regions: A Digital Agenda for Europe, L 245*. Brussels, Belgium: European Commission.

European Commission. (2010b). *Communication from the commission to the European 2020: A strategy for smart, sustainable and inclusive growth*. Brussels, Belgium: European Commission.

European Opinion Research Group. (2011). *Attitudes on data protection and electronic identity in the European Union. Technical Report Special Eurobarometer 359*. Bruxelles, Belgium: European Commission.

European Parliament and Council. (1995). Directive 95/46/EC of the European parliament and of the council on the protection of individuals with regard to the processing of personal data and on the free movement of such data. *Official Journal of the European Communities*, *281*, 31–50.

European Parliament and Council. (1999). Directive 99/93/EC of the European parliament and of the council on a community framework for electronic signatures. *Official Journal of the European Communities*, *13*, 12.

European Parliament and Council. (2002). Directive 2002/58/EC of the European parliament and of the council concerning the processing of personal data and the protection of privacy in the electronic communications sector (directive on privacy and electronic communications). *Official Journal of the European Communities*, *201*, 37–47.

FP6 IST Project PRIME (Privacy and Identity Management for Europe). (n.d.). Retrieved November 3, 2011, from https://www.prime-project.eu/

FP7 IST Project PrimeLife (Privacy and Identity Management in Europe for Life). (n.d.). Retrieved November 3, 2011, from http://www.primelife.eu/

Gallup Organization. (2008). *Data protection in the European Union: Citizens' perceptions – Analytical report (flash eurobarometer 225)*. Retrieved November 3, 2011, http://ec.europa.eu/public_opinion/flash/fl_225_en.pdf

Ganorkar, S. R., & Ghatol, A. A. (2007). Iris recognition: An emerging biometric technology. In *Proceedings of the 6th WSEAS International Conference on Signal Processing, Robotics and Automation* (pp. 91 – 96). WSEAS.

Hao, W., Jhat, S., Livny, M., & McDaniel, P. D. (2004). Security policy reconciliation in distributed computing environments. In *Proceedings of the 5th IEEE International Workshop on Policies for Distributed Systems and Networks (POLICY'04)* (pp. 137-146). IEEE.

He, D. D., & Yang, J. (2009). Authorization control in collaborative healthcare systems. *Journal of Theoretical and Applied Electronic Commerce Research*, *4*(2), 88–109.

Information Security Forum (ISF). (2007). *The standard of good practice for information security*. ISF.

Information Systems Security Association (ISSA). (2004). *Generally accepted information security principles*. GAISP.

International Telecommunication Union. (2005). *Information technology – Open systems interconnection – The directory: Public-key and attribute certificate frameworks*. ITU-T Recommendation X.509. Retrieved November 29, 2010, from http://www.itu.int/rec/T-REC-X.509-200508-I

ISO/IEC 27002. (2005). *Information technology - Security techniques - Code of practice for information security management*. ISO/IEC.

Jain, A. K., Ross, A., & Pankanti, S. (2006). Biometrics: A tool for information security. *IEEE Transactions on Information Forensics and Security*, *1*(2), 125–144. doi:10.1109/TIFS.2006.873653.

Jie, W., Arshad, J., Sinnott, R., Townend, P., & Lei, Z. (2011). A review of grid authentication and authorization technologies and support for federated access control. *ACM Computing Surveys*, *43*(2), 12:1-12:26.

Joshi, J. B. D., Bertino, E., Latif, U., & Ghafoo, A. (2005). A generalized temporal role-based access control model. *Journal of IEEE Transactions on Knowledge and Data Engineering*, *15*, 4–23. doi:10.1109/TKDE.2005.1.

Kwan, M., & Ramachandran, D. (2009). Trust and online reputation systems. In *Computing with Social Trust* (pp. 287–311). Berlin: Springer-Verlag. doi:10.1007/978-1-84800-356-9_11.

Lee, A. J., & Yu, T. (2009). Towards a dynamic and composable model of trust. In *Proceedings of the 14th ACM symposium on Access Control Models and Technologies (SACMAT '09)* (pp. 217-226). New York: ACM.

Li, N., & Mitchell, J. C. (2003). Datalog with constraints: A foundation for trust management languages. In *Proceedings of the 5th International Symposium on Practical Aspects of Declarative Languages* (pp. 58-73). IEEE.

Li, N., Mitchell, J. C., & Winsborough, W. H. (2002). Design of a role-based trust management framework. In *Proceedings of the 2002 IEEE Symposium on Security and Privacy* (pp. 114-130). IEEE.

Li, N., Winsborough, W. H., & Mitchell, J. C. (2001). Distributed credential chain discovery in trust management: Extended abstract. In *Proceedings of the 8th ACM Conference on Computer and Communications Security (CCS '01)* (pp. 156-165). New York: ACM.

Lin, T. C., Lee, C. K., & Lin, J. C. C. (2010). Determinants of enterprise 2.0 adoption: A value-based adoption model approach. In *Proceedings of the 2010 International Conference on Information Society (i-Society)* (pp. 12-18). i-Society.

Lioudakis, G. V., Gaudino, F., Boschi, E., Bianchi, G., Kaklamani, D. I., & Venieris, I. S. (2010). Legislation-aware privacy protection in passive network monitoring. In Portela, I. M., & Cruz-Cunha, M. M. (Eds.), *Information Communication Technology Law, Protection and Access Rights: Global Approaches and Issues*. Hershey, PA: IGI Global. doi:10.4018/978-1-61520-975-0.ch022.

Masoumzadeh, A., & Joshi, J. B. D. (2008). PuRBAC: Purpose-aware role-based access control. In *Proceedings of the On the Move to Meaningful Internet Systems: OTM 2008* (LNCS), (vol. 5332). Berlin, Germany: Springer Berlin / Heidelberg.

Mcafee, A. P. (2006a). Enterprise 2.0: The dawn of emergent collaboration. *IEEE Engineering Management Review*, *34*(3), 38. doi:10.1109/EMR.2006.261380.

McAfee, A. P. (2006b). Evangelizing in the empty quarter. In *The Business Impact of IT*. New York: Wordpress.

McAfee, A. P. (2008). Some questions you might get asked. In *The Business Impact of IT*. New York: Wordpress.

McKnight, D. H., Cummings, L. L., & Chervany, N. L. (1998). Initial trust formation in new organizational relationships. *Academy of Management Review*, *23*(3), 473–490.

Middleware Architecture Committee for Education (MACE). (2001). *Shibboleth system*. Retrieved November 3, 2011, from http://shibboleth.Internet2.edu/

Milojicic, D. (2008). Interview with Rich Friedrich, Dave Cohen, and Alex Dreiling. *IEEE Internet Computing*, *12*(1), 10–13. doi:10.1109/MIC.2008.15.

Ni, Q., Bertino, E., Lobo, J., Brodie, C., Karat, C. M., Karat, J., & Trombetta, A. (2010). Privacy-aware role-based access control. *Journal of ACM Transactions Information System Security*, *13*(3), 1–31. doi:10.1145/1805974.1805980.

Organization for Economic Co-Operation and Development (OECD). (1980). *Guidelines on the protection of privacy and transborder flows of personal data*. Retrieved November 3, 2011, from http://www.oecd.org/document/18/0,3343,en_2649_34255_1815186_1_1_1_1,00.html

Organization for Economic Co-Operation and Development (OECD). (2011). *The evolving privacy landscape: 30 years after the OECD privacy guidelines*. Retrieved November 3, 2011, from http://dx.doi.org/10.1787/5kgf09z90c31-en

Organization for the Advancement of Structured Information Standards (OASIS). (2004). *OASIS eXtensible access control markup language (XACML) TC*. Retrieved November 3, 2011, from http://www.oasis-open.org/committees/xacml/

Organization for the Advancement of Structured Information Standards (OASIS). (2005). *Security assertion markup language (SAML) v2.0*. Retrieved November 3, 2011, from http://docs.oasis-open.org/security/saml/v2.0/saml-2.0-os.zip

Polk, W. T., Hastings, N. E., & Malpani, A. (2003). Public key infrastructures that satisfy security goals. *IEEE Internet Computing*, *7*(4), 60–67. doi:10.1109/MIC.2003.1215661.

Prabhakar, S., Pankanti, S., & Jain, A. K. (2003). Biometric recognition: Security and privacy concerns. *IEEE Security & Privacy*, *1*(2), 33–42. doi:10.1109/MSECP.2003.1193209.

Rasmusson, L., & Janson, S. (1996). *Simulated social control for secure internet commerce*. New York: ACM Press. doi:10.1145/304851.304857.

Ratnasingam, P. (2005). Trust in inter-organizational exchanges: A case study in business to business electronic commerce. *Decision Support Systems*, *39*(3), 525–544. doi:10.1016/j.dss.2003.12.005.

Ravari, A. N., Jafarian, J. H., Amini, M., & Jalili, R. (2010). GTHBAC: A generalized temporal history based access control model. *Journal of Telecommunication Systems*, *45*(2), 111–125. doi:10.1007/s11235-009-9239-9.

Recordon, D., & Reed, D. (2006). OpenID 2.0: A platform for user-centric identity management. In *Proceedings of the 2nd ACM Workshop on Digital Identity Management (DIM'06)* (pp. 11-16). New York: ACM.

Rudman, R. J., & Steenkamp, L. P. (2009). Potential influence of web 2.0 usage and security practices of online users on information management. *South African Journal of Information Management*, *11*(2).

Shim, S. S. Y., Bhalla, G., & Pendyala, V. (2005). Federated identity management. *IEEE Computer*, *38*(12), 120–122. doi:10.1109/MC.2005.408.

Solove, D. J. (2006). A brief history of information privacy law. In Wolf, C. (Ed.), *Proskauer on Privacy: A Guide to Privacy and Data Security Law in the Information Age* (pp. 1–46). New York, NY: Practising Law Institute.

Sun, Y., & Chen, C. (2011). Towards coequal authorization for dynamic collaboration. [LNCS]. *Proceedings of Active Media Technology, 6890*, 229–240. doi:10.1007/978-3-642-23620-4_26.

Swanson, M., & Guttman, B. (1996). Generally accepted principles and practices for securing information technology systems. Washington, DC: National Institute of Standards and Technology (NIST).

The Liberty Alliance Project. (2005). *Liberty alliance identity federation 1.2 (ID-FF 1.2) specifications*. Retrieved November 3, 2011, from http://www.projectliberty.org/liberty/resource_center/specifications/liberty_alliance_id_ff_1_2_specifications/

Varadharajan, V. (2009). A note on trust-enhanced security. *IEEE Security & Privacy, 7*(3), 57–59. doi:10.1109/MSP.2009.59.

Weeks, S. (2001). Understanding trust management systems. In *Proceedings of the 2001 IEEE Symposium on Security and Privacy* (p. 94). Washington, DC: IEEE Computer Society.

Wilson, S. (2008). Public key superstructure it's PKI Jim, but not as we know it! In *Proceedings of the 7th Symposium on Identity and Trust on the Internet (IDtrust '08)* (pp. 72-88). New York: ACM.

Xinyi, H., Yang, X., Chonka, A., Jianying, Z., & Deng, R. H. (2011). A generic framework for three-factor authentication: Preserving security and privacy in distributed systems. *IEEE Transactions on Parallel and Distributed Systems, 22*(8), 1390–1397. doi:10.1109/TPDS.2010.206.

Yau, S., & Chen, Z. (2008). *Security policy integration and conflict reconciliation for collaborations among organizations in ubiquitous computing environments. Ubiquitous Intelligence and Computing (LNCS)* (*Vol. 5061*, pp. 3–19). Berlin: Springer.

ADDITIONAL READING

Antonakopoulou, A., Lioudakis, G. V., Gogoulos, F., Kaklamani, D. I., & Venieris, I. S. (2012). Leveraging access control for privacy protection: A survey. In Yee, G. (Ed.), *Privacy Protection Measures and Technologies in Business Organizations: Aspects and Standards* (pp. 65–94). Academic Press.

Basu, A., & Muylle, S. (2003). Authentication in e-commerce. *Communications of the ACM, 46*(12), 159–166. doi:10.1145/953460.953496.

Belanger, F., Hiller, J. S., & Smith, W. J. (2002). Trustworthiness in electronic commerce: The role of privacy, security, and site attributes. *The Journal of Strategic Information Systems, 11*(3), 245–270. doi:10.1016/S0963-8687(02)00018-5.

Bruno, A., Marra, P., & Mangia, L. (2011). The enterprise 2.0 adoption process: A participatory design approach. In *Proceedings of the 13th International Conference on Advanced Communication Technology (ICACT' 11)* (pp. 1457 - 1461). ICACT.

Camenisch, J., Leenes, R., Hansen, M., & Schalaböck, J. (2011). An introduction to privacy-enhancing identity management. In Camenisch, J., Sommer, D., & Leenes, R. (Eds.), *Digital privacy*. Berlin: Springer-Verlag. doi:10.1007/978-3-642-19050-6_1.

Cavoukian, A., & Tapscott, D. (2006). Privacy and the enterprise 2.0. In Learning, (pp. 1-26). New Paradigm Learning Cooperation.

Chadwick, D. W., Otenko, S., & Nguyen, T. A. (2009). Adding support to XACML for multi-domain user to user dynamic delegation of authority. *International Journal of Information Security*, *8*(2), 137–152. doi:10.1007/s10207-008-0073-y.

Chen, J., Wu, G., & Ji, Z. (2011). Secure interoperation of identity managements among different circles of trust. [Amsterdam: Elsevier Science Publishers B. V.]. *Computer Standards & Interfaces*, *33*(6), 533–540. doi:10.1016/j.csi.2011.02.008.

Christidis, K., Mentzas, G., & Apostolou, D. (2011). Supercharging enterprise 2.0. *IT Professional*, *13*, 29–35. doi:10.1109/MITP.2011.70.

Giorgini, P., Massacci, F., & Zannone, N. (2005). Security and trust requirements engineering. [LNCS]. *Proceedings of the Foundations of Security Analysis and Design III*, *3655*, 237–272. doi:10.1007/11554578_8.

Gutmann, P. (2007). PKI design for the real world. In *Proceedings of the 2006 Workshop on New Security Paradigms (NSPW '06)* (pp. 109-116). New York: ACM.

Hawkey, K. (2009). Examining the shifting nature of privacy, identities, and impression management with web 2.0. In *Proceedings of the 2009 International Conference on Computational Science and Engineering* (Vol. 4, pp. 990-995). Washington, DC: IEEE Computer Society.

iDABD – European eGovernment Services. (2010). *Completion of the framework for signature validation services*. Retrieved November 3, 2011, from http://ec.europa.eu/idabc/en/document/7764

Jøsang, A., Ismail, R., & Boyd, C. (2007). A survey of trust and reputation systems for online service provision. [Amsterdam: Elsevier Science Publishers B. V.]. *Decision Support Systems*, *43*(2), 618–644. doi:10.1016/j.dss.2005.05.019.

Kerr, R. C. (2007). *Toward secure trust and reputation systems for electronic marketplaces*. A (Thesis). University of Waterloo, Waterloo, Canada.

Kumari, A., Mishra, S., & Kushwaha, D. S. (2010). A new collaborative trust enhanced security model for distributed system. *International Journal of Computers and Applications*, *1*(26), 117–124.

Li, N., Mitchell, J. C., & Winsborough, W. H. (2005). Beyond proof-of-compliance: Security analysis in trust management. *Journal of the ACM*, *52*(3), 474–514. doi:10.1145/1066100.1066103.

Madsen, P., & Itoh, H. (2009). Challenges to supporting federated assurance. *Computer*, *42*(5), 42–49. doi:10.1109/MC.2009.149.

Murugesan, S. (2007). Understanding web 2.0. *IT Professional*, *9*(4), 34–41. doi:10.1109/MITP.2007.78.

Myhr, T. (2008). Legal and organizational challenges and solutions for achieving a pan-european electronic ID solution or i am 621216-1318, but I am also 161262-43774.1: Do you know who I am? *Information Security Technical Report*, *13*, 76–82. doi:10.1016/j.istr.2008.06.001.

Patton, M. A., & Jøsang, A. (2004). Technologies for trust in electronic commerce. *Electronic Commerce Research*, *4*(1-2), 9–21. doi:10.1023/B:ELEC.0000009279.89570.27.

Ruohomaa, S., & Kutvonen, L. (2005). Trust management survey. In *Proceedings of the ITRUST 2005* (LNCS), (vol. 3477, pp. 77-92). Berlin: Springer-Verlag.

Scherp, A., Schwagereit, F., Ireson, N., Lanfranchi, V., Papadopoulos, S., & Kritikos, A. … Smrz, P. (2009). Leveraging web 2.0 communities in professional organisations. In *Proceedings of the W3C Workshop on the Future of Social Networking*. Barcelona, Spain: W3C.

Shafiq, B., Bertino, E., & Ghafoor, A. (2005). Access control management in a distributed environment supporting dynamic collaboration. In *Proceedings of the 2005 Workshop on Digital Identity Management (DIM '05)* (pp. 104-112). New York: ACM.

Siponen, M. T., & Oinas-Kukkonen, H. (2007). A review of information security issues and respective research contributions. *SIGMIS Database*, *38*(1), 60–80. doi:10.1145/1216218.1216224.

Tapscott, D. (2006). Winning with the enterprise 2.0. In Learning, (pp. 1-59). New Paradigm Learning Cooperation.

Tredinnick, L. (2006). Web 2.0 and business - A pointer to the intranets of the future? *Business Information Review*, *23*(4), 228–234. doi:10.1177/0266382106072239.

KEY TERMS AND DEFINITIONS

Access Control: The mechanisms for allowing access to resources, systems or services to authorized persons or other valid subjects and denying unauthorized access.

Enterprise 2.0: The adoption of Web 2.0 services in business environments in order to improve knowledge workers' productivity and augment the effectiveness and competence of organizations.

Identity Management: The mechanisms for identifying individuals in a system and controlling the circulation of established identity profiles in order to deal with access to the resources in that system.

Information Security: The protection, in terms of integrity, confidentiality, authenticity and availability, of information from unauthorized access, usage, disclosure, modification, or destruction.

PKI: The sum of mechanisms for exploiting public key cryptography in order to create, distribute, validate, and revoke digital certificates.

Privacy: The claim of individuals, groups, or institutions to determine for themselves when, how and to what extent information about them is communicated to others.

Trust Management: A unified approach for specifying and interpreting security policies of a system, credentials of involved users and relationships among them.

Chapter 12
How to Value and Monitor the Relational Capital of Knowledge-Intensive Organizations

Alexandre Barão
Instituto Superior Técnico, Portugal

Alberto Rodrigues da Silva
Instituto Superior Técnico, Portugal

ABSTRACT

Knowledge management systems are a way to help tracking and keeping organizational knowledge. Typically, organizations value is greater than their tangible assets value. Human, structural, and relational capital is essential knowledge but difficult to evaluate because it tends to be tacit and spread in different organizational elements. The relational capital, as tacit knowledge, is not possible to capture its value as from accounting systems. There is a lack of models to evaluate the relational capital of organizations in a network perspective and this research question is: What is the value of this social network? SNARE (Social Network Analysis and Reengineering Environment) is a framework with engineering artifacts that can answer this question. With the aim of evaluating the relational capital of organizations, the authors develop three SNARE components: (1) SNARE-Language – a descriptive UML-based method that provides a representation of an abstract social network structure able to be extended and applied to organizations; (2) SNARE-RCO – a model to determine the relational capital of organizations; and (3) SNARE-Explorer – based on SNARE-Language, is a tool for social networks visualization able to simulate or use real social network scenarios. It also uses SNARE-RCO model to compute the value of the organizational relational capital. The chapter presents an approach for the measurement of the value of organizations' networks.

DOI: 10.4018/978-1-4666-4373-4.ch012

INTRODUCTION

Knowledge may be tacit or explicit. It can refer to an object, a cognitive state or a capability. Knowledge may reside in individuals, social groups, social systems, documents, processes, policies, physical settings, or computer repositories (Alavi & Leidner, 2001).

Knowledge Management (KM) refers to identifying and leveraging the collective knowledge in an organization to help the organization compete (Krogh, 1998). Knowledge Management Systems (KMS) relate to a class of information systems applied to managing organizational knowledge, and are developed to support and enhance the organizational processes of knowledge creation, storage/retrieval, transfer, and application (Alavi & Leidner, 2001).

Typically, the value of organizations tends to be greater than their tangible assets, and so KM and KMS are a way to help tracking and keeping tacit knowledge inside organizations. Human, relational and structural capitals are essential knowledge assets of organizations (Anklam, 2007). Human capital is the knowledge, skills and experience of individuals. Structural capital is the set of procedures, processes, and internal structures that contribute to the implementation of organization's objectives. Finally, the relational capital is the value of social relationships in a given organization, which contributes to achieve its objectives; i.e., it is the value of internal and external relationships of an organization.

The intangible value of the organization is mostly generated from informal, non-contractual activities that help build business relationships and contribute to operational effectiveness (ValueNetworks, 2010). Intangible assets can result from these non-contractual activities. Intangible assets can be seen as the knowledge and benefits extended or delivered by an individual or group, which are non-contractual, but still have value for the organization. The combination of all intangibles—i.e. human, structural, and relational capital—is called intangible or intellectual capital (Adams & Oleksak, 2010).

Although the value of intangibles can be difficult to identify through financial transactions, the use of nonfinancial indicators is a way to provide intellectual capital measurement (Adams & Oleksak, 2010). However, it is not always possible to capture the intellectual capital in accounting systems of organizations, because the intellectual capital is almost invisible in conventional forms of information systems (Adams & Oleksak, 2010). Also, there is a lack of standard approach to evaluate the relational capital of organizations (Zadjabbari, Wongthongtham, & Hussain, 2008).

We think of social networks as assets that are part of organizations. The value of a social network represents a contribution to satisfy a given demand. This demand is fulfilled by its social entities. In this sense, the value of a relation reflects the link between a thing (a good or service) and the social entities that are connected within a given context (Barão & Silva, 2011).

Social network systems identify relations between social entities and provide a set of automatic inferences on these relations, promoting better interactions and collaborations between these entities. Social Network Analysis (SNA) (Faust & Faust, 1994) is the foundation of several areas such as: Organizational Network Analysis (ONA) (Cross & Parker, 2004), Value Network Analysis (VNA) (Alee, 2008), and Dynamic Network Analysis (DNA) (Carley, Diesner, Reminga, & Tsvetovat, 2007). For example, they provide methodologies for studying communication in organizations with quantitative and descriptive techniques for creating statistical and graphical models of the individuals, tasks, groups, knowledge, and resources of organizational systems. In this sense, SNA methodologies are important to discover individual roles in organizations, identify social collaboration patterns, and evaluate the value of intellectual capital.

The question that we want to address and discuss in this research is: What is the value of this social network? Starting from this question, we argue that it is possible to define the relational capital of knowledge-intensive organizations.

The state of art analysis led us to conclude that any metric for assessing the relational capital of an organization should include aspects of human and structural capital. To evaluate the relational capital of an organization it is necessary to know various assessment approaches. There are several evaluation approaches for studying aspects such as economic impact or operational impact. However, there is a lack of methodologies for an organizational assessment that combines techniques derived from social network analysis and its relation to intellectual capital. The SNARE-Framework combines techniques from social network analysis and intellectual capital evaluation with the assessment of an organizations' relational capital.

In this chapter we firstly overview organizational evaluation issues and intellectual capital main concepts and measurement challenges. Also, an introductory description of SNA, ONA, VNA and DNA is given. Next, we present the SNARE-Framework components to evaluate organizations' relational capital. A methodology to evaluate the relational capital of organizations is suggested and three validation cases presented. Finally, we will briefly outline future research directions and present our research conclusion.

BACKGROUND

In this section we overview organizational evaluation issues, intellectual capital main concepts, intellectual capital measurement challenges, and current methods used for measuring it. Also, a description of four major areas to uncover network properties, evaluate and analyze social networks is given, namely: Social Network Analysis, Organizational Network Analysis, Value Network Analysis and Dynamic Network Analysis.

Organizational Evaluation

Organizational evaluation can be helpful in identifying (FAO, 2010): (1) whether or not the objectives and goals originally established are being achieved, as well as their expected effects and impact; (2) whether the organization is adapting to new environments, such as changing technology and alterations in other external variables so as to efficiently use the available resources; (3) areas which need to be improved, modified or strengthened; and (4) different ways to better fulfill the needs of the clients. Also, to evaluate an organization there are several steps and the evaluator must be aware of them (FAO, 2010): Objectives of the assessment exercise; Size and nature of the organization; Areas to be covered during the assessment exercise; Potential users of the assessment results and recommendations; Organizational model on which the assessment methodology is to be based on; Framework for conducting the assessment exercise; Data evaluation; Methods of collecting data; Methodology for conducting the assessment exercise; and Results, analysis and recommendations.

Information measures can be used to evaluate any kind of organization, since an organization is based on interrelations among parts.

Intellectual Capital Concepts

Current economy is supported by information and communication technologies. The processing of information and knowledge creation are the main sources of productivity. An organization has tangible and intangible capital. Tangible capital is what can be measured (e.g. the value of a product or service). Intangible capital is the result of the organization's informal and non-contractual activities, such as interpersonal relationships, which tend to be ignored by the organization's accounting systems. These intangibles can help and contribute to the operational effectiveness of an organization. So, in fact, they are not intangibles if they can be: detectable as an amount, thus observable and measured (Hubbard, 2010). The combination of all intangibles of an organization is intangible capital, also called Intellectual Capital (IC) (Adams & Oleksak, 2010).

From the book The Knowledge Evolution (Allee, 1997), Anklam summarizes (Anklam, 2007): Human Capital (HC) is the knowledge, skills, and experience of the individuals required to provide solutions to customers, its core competency; Structural Capital (SC) can be viewed as the internal procedures, processes, and organizational structures that have evolved to enable the organization to function as it does, for example, standard methods or heuristics passed on from person to person; and Relational Capital (RC) is the value of an organization's relationships with customers, suppliers, and others it engages with to accomplish its business; for example, its access to specific markets or resources.

We must refer that many intangibles (e.g. relations) are not owned by organizations and it is hard to separate them from the HC and SC. Also, their value can be difficult to identify through a financial transaction, and the use of nonfinancial indicators is a way to provide intangible capital measurement (Adams & Oleksak, 2010).

As previously stated, an organization has tangible and intangible capital. It is difficult to separate HC, SC, and RC factors, and KM is starting to become a core process as well as a fundamental competence of all knowledge workers, because they have to develop a better understanding of the information they need at the work. However, knowledge assets are not captured in accounting systems and are almost invisible in other conventional forms of management information (Adams & Oleksak, 2010). We consider intangible capital assets in organizations to be (Adams & Oleksak, 2010): Human Capital (e.g. Competencies, Experience, Longevity, Attitude, and Management); Structural Capital (e.g. Culture, Organizational Knowledge, Intellectual Property, and Processes); and Relational Capital (e.g. Customers, Partners, Brands, Reputation, Shared Knowledge).

Intellectual Capital Measurement Challenges

There are three basic challenges associated to intellectual capital (Buono, 2003) (Greene, 1999). In essence how can we: Value (measure) intangibles better; Create more value (i.e. invest and manage) from intangible capital; and Retain more (conversion) of this capital?

These questions are still a challenge. Mary Adams and Michel Oleksak argue that "In Europe and Asia, a number of tools have been created by governments as part of competitive initiatives to help training managers in Small and Medium-Sized Enterprises (SMEs) so that they can leverage their knowledge capital". However, to date, there is no dominant model for intellectual capital assessment (Adams & Oleksak, 2010). Also, Zadjabbari argues that "There is a lack of standard metric method to measure this kind of knowledge and assets" (Zadjabbari, Wongthongtham, & Hussain, 2008). So, when trying to solve this problem in order to create an IC assessment system, the main parameters are (Adams & Oleksak, 2010): Scope, after defining the scope (e.g. human, relationship or structural capital) it is possible to evaluate and measure intangibles; Rating System, this can be extremely valuable for turning data into actionable goals (e.g. using a rating scale from 1 to 10 or letter grades such as A, B, C, etc.); and Standard of Measurement in all kinds of assessments within the organization in order to achieve a cohesive picture.

Measurement can be seen as a result of observations that quantitatively reduce uncertainty. A reduction, not necessarily elimination of uncertainty, will suffice for a measurement because it is an improvement on prior knowledge (Hubbard, 2010). Toward a universal approach to measure intangibles in business, Douglas Hubbard recommends the following five steps framework (Hubbard, 2010): (1) Define a decision problem and the relevant uncertainties; (2) Determine what you know; (3) Compute the value of additional information; (4) Apply the relevant measurement instruments; and (5) Make a decision, act on it, return to step (1) and repeat. Even when some amount of error is unavoidable, it can be an improvement on prior knowledge of a system (Hubbard, 2010).

Methods for Measuring Intellectual Capital

Researches of measuring the intellectual capital of organizations have produced several methods and theories over the last years. A very good overview of intangible measuring theories can be found in (Sveiby, 2010) and also in (Bontis, 2001). According to Sveiby, the main problem with measurement systems is that it is not possible to measure social phenomena with anything close to scientific accuracy. All measurement systems have to rely on their proxies, such as dollars, euros, and other indicators (Sveiby, 2010). The common reason for measuring and reporting is to improve internal performance, i.e. management control. However, the problem is that people do not like to be measured (Sveiby, 2010). To sum up, there are four common approaches for measuring intangibles (Sveiby, 2010): Direct Intellectual Capital methods (DIC) estimate the $-value of intangible assets by identifying its various components. Once these components are identified, they can be directly evaluated, either individually or as an aggregated coefficient; Market Capitalization Methods (MCM) calculate the difference between a company's market capitalization and its stockholder's equity as the value of its intellectual capital or intangible assets; Return on Assets methods (ROA), standard pre-tax earnings of a company for a period of time, are divided by the average tangible assets of the company; and Scorecard Methods (SCM), the various components of intangible assets or intellectual capital, are identified and, afterwards, indicators and indices are generated and reported in scorecards or as graphs.

There is no standard IC measures/metrics because every company needs a unique understanding of which intangible assets are really valuable for the organization. Some of the indicators are financial but it is possible to use nonfinancial indicators to provide the most basic parameters for intangible capital. Nevertheless, there is no dominant model because every company has specific IC evaluation purposes. Also, there is a lack of standard metric tools used.

Social Network Analysis

Social Network Analysis (SNA) represents a method for achieving analytical results in about almost any group interaction in which social entities are present. In SNA scope, group dynamics are studied to identify relations and interactions among their members. Starting from these interactions, it is possible to identify social patterns (Haythornthwaite, 2005) and to detect or propose social or organizational changes that reveal how networks grow or should change. Also, it is likely to find potential causes and consequences of a network change, predicting and controlling networks' evolution (Churchill & Halverson, 2005). These features are dependent on metrics which allow group properties' identification or characterize individual influence on a specific group.

To perform SNA it is necessary to define measures that can be compared between actors or networks. Measures in SNA can be distinguished as those that evaluate the entire network and the ones that only assess a specific node (Faust & Faust, 1994). SNA can be used in an organization to better understand the social capital (Borgatti & Foster, 2003); support partnerships and alliances (Cross & Parker, 2004); measure the degree of embedment of the actors as well as their importance in the network; support knowledge management policies; identify who really knows what happens in the company (Helms & Buijsrogge, 2005); integrate networks across core processes; promote innovation; integrate new members or organizational changes; support the development of informal communities of practice; improve leadership effectiveness; replicate high performance throughout an organization and understand and improve the disconnections between groups in the organization or between groups and the outside world (Cross & Parker, 2004).

Organizational Network Analysis

Organizational Network Analysis (ONA) is a powerful mean of making invisible patterns of information flow and collaboration in strategically important groups visible (Cross & Parker, 2004). In organizations, ONA methodology can be helpful to uncover network value questions, namely: "Does the network have adequate resources to create value, both tangible and intangible?", "Does the network produce appropriate value for its stage in its development cycle?", "Are there performance metrics for tangible value produced?", "Is the network's value-producing model sustainable?", and "Are all stakeholders receiving the value that they are expecting?" (Anklam, 2007).

Value Network Analysis

Value Network Analysis (VNA) is focused on: Providing a perspective for understanding value, creating roles and relationships, both internal and external, upon which an organization depends on; Offering dynamic views of how both financial and non-financial assets can be converted into negotiable forms of value that have a positive impact on those relationships; Explaining how to more effectively attain value for each role and how to use tangible and intangible assets for value creation; and Providing a systematic analysis of how one type of value is converted into another (Alee, 2008).

Value networks are sets of roles, interactions and relationships generating economic, social or environmental value, and so any purposeful organization can be understood as a value network (Alee, 2003). VNA fills the analytical and managerial gap between other organizational tools, because it provides a network perspective into how processes and people create value. Also, it shows unique relationships and transactions as well as sequences of value flows (ValueNetworks, 2010). A transaction occurs when a deliverable originated by a role is conveyed to and received by another and two or more reciprocal transactions are an exchange (Alee, 2008). Value conversion is the act of converting or transforming financial to non-financial value; it can also imply changing an intangible input or asset into a financial value or asset (Alee, 2008).

Value interactions are of two types: (1) tangible deliverables, which are contractual or mandated interactions between participants; and (2) intangible deliverables, that are informal and more personal (e.g. knowledge exchange, favors, and benefits) (ValueNetworks, 2010). The roles and deliverables are made visible through a simple visual mapping technique and the diagrams link a variety of tools, such as cost/benefit analyses, to increase value outputs, leverage knowledge and intangibles for improving financial and organizational performance and find new value opportunities (ValueNetworks, 2010).

Dynamic Network Analysis

Dynamic Network Analysis (DNA) is a scientific field that combines social network analysis, link analysis and multi-agent systems within network science and network theory (Carley, Diesner, Reminga, & Tsvetovat, 2007). There are two aspects to be considered: (1) statistical analysis of data and (2) simulation to address issues of network dynamics. DNA networks vary from traditional social networks in that they are larger, dynamic, multi-mode (multiple types of nodes), multiplex networks (multiple types of links), and may contain varying levels of uncertainty (Carley, Diesner, Reminga, & Tsvetovat, 2007). The difference from DNA to SNA is that the first one takes the domain of time into account, i.e. DNA takes snapshots of the same network from different intervals and observes and analyzes its evolution.

Carley suggests an approach to DNA based upon the combined use of multi-agent modeling, machine learning and a metamatrix approach to network representation (Kathleen, 2003). This metamatrix is a multiplex representation of entities and connections that enriches the traditional one-dimensional representation. Carley combined knowledge management, operations research and social networks techniques to create the notion of metamatrix. The metamatrix approach provides a representational framework and a family of methods for the analysis of organizational data. Under this model, organizations are conceived of as being composed by a set of elements, each of which belongs to one of five classes (Personnel, Knowledge, Resources, Tasks, and Organization) (Carley, Diesner, Reminga, & Tsvetovat, 2007).

SNARE FRAMEWORK

SNARE is acronym for "Social Network Analysis and Reengineering Environment". This framework is able to represent social networks and it allows researchers to design and build real scenarios for social networks extraction and analysis (Barão & Silva, 2008). SNARE framework has engineering artifacts to: (1) Represent social network structures; (2) Define relations, social entities, properties and surveys; (3) Store, manage and visualize the information required for social network analysis; and (4) Monitor the relational capital of a social network in real-time.

SNARE framework provides mechanisms to extract data sets from other systems and it is designed to pull out data from a generic system by mapping data extraction components.

SNARE-Language

The SNARE-Language (Barão & Silva, 2010) provides a representation of a social network structure using UML (OMG, 2010) as a descriptive method. Through the application of SNARE-Language it is possible to graphically design social entities and the multiple relations among them. SNARE-Language main concepts are: Social Entity, Relation, Role, Action and Event. Figure 1 depicts the SNARE-Language Meta-Model.

Conceptualizing social structures of a network using SNARE-Language to model social networks is a process, which requires the instantiation of social entities, roles, relations, actions and events.

Figure 1. SNARE-language meta-model

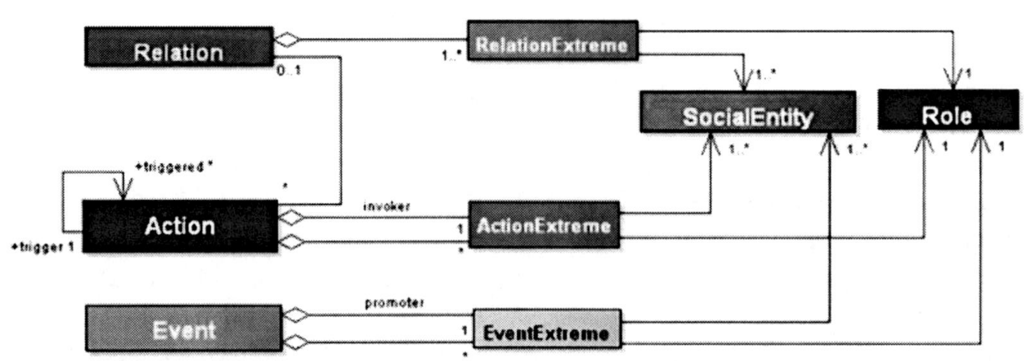

To do this, a set of stereotypes can be used. The richness of this language to model social networks comes from the flexibility to combine these stereotypes. Flexibility is expressed by all possible links that may exist on a network without adding redundant instantiations, e.g., a social entity can play several roles in the same relation, and this concept should be achieved through the instantiation of a factorized *Role* stereotype. Regarding the connection patterns we studied, SNARE-Language captures most of the possible social network relations. SNARE-Language is flexible to fit the needs of modeling social networks. When compared to other social networks representation techniques, SNARE-Language includes a new collection of diagrammatic model elements, which are more significant when capturing social network semantic concepts. Also, they are unambiguous and supported by UML tools.

SNARE-RCO

SNARE-RCO is a model to evaluate the relational capital of organizations; it combines techniques derived from social network analysis with aspects of organizational assessment, and considers dynamic properties from the social entities intellectual capital (Barão & Silva, 2011) .

To analyze the Relational Capital Value (RCV) of a given organization, SNARE-RCO model proposes three kinds of assessment inputs: organizational factors, network factors and social entity factors. These inputs are dynamic, i.e. defined by the analyst, because they depend on the target organization. SNARE-RCO model is used to compute the RCV of organizations. Figure 2 depicts the referred assessment inputs to compute RCV.

Figure 2. SNARE-RCO flows to compute RCV

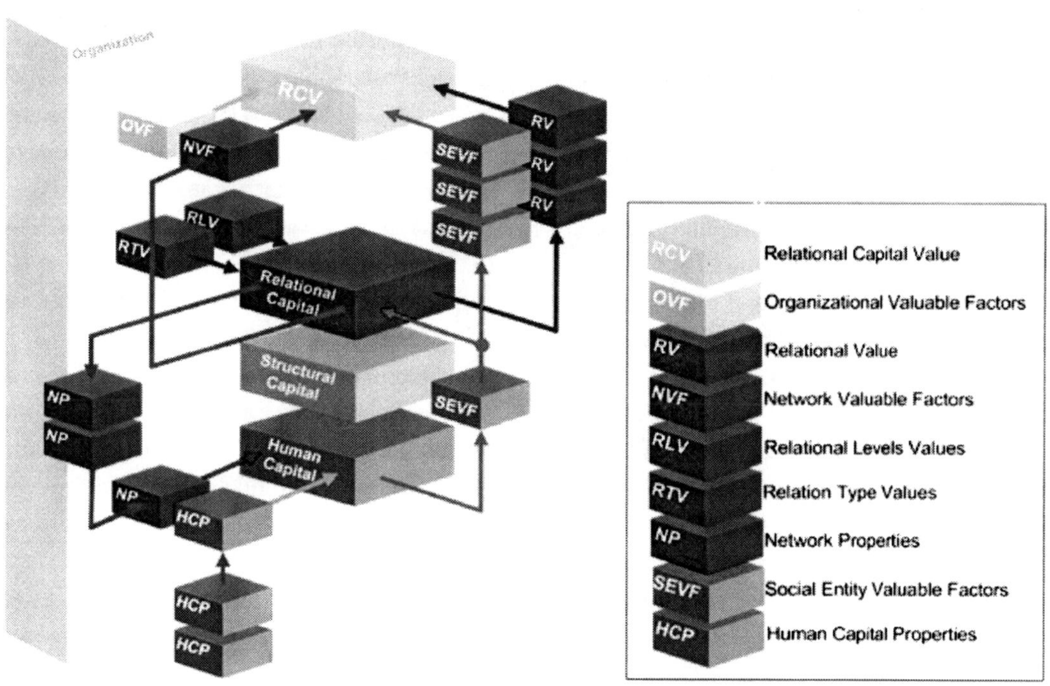

Organizational Valuable Factors (OVF) are attributes of the organization, for example: number of active customers; number of partners; and, number of brands.

Network Valuable Factors (NVF) are properties of the organization's social network. These properties can be derived from the analysis of social networks, for example size and density.

Social Entity Valuable Factors (SEVF) are properties assigned to each social entity. The analyst can use Network Properties (NP) from the analysis of social networks, such as centrality indegree or centrality outdegree. The analyst might also consider Human Capital Properties (HCP). These properties are role dependent and may result from previous human resources management analysis like questionnaires or other evaluation techniques. Examples of HCP properties are: Analytical Problem Solving; Creativity and Innovation; Problem Diagnosis and Solution; Technical Expertise; and Time Management.

Relations can be of numerous types (e.g. Collaboration/Information or Collaboration/Problem solving relation type) and for each several Relation Type Values (RTV) can be assigned. These values are weights to compute RCV. Also, in a given social network relation, different levels values could be assigned. These values are Relational Levels Values (RLV). Examples of relational values include: Very near; Near; Regular; Far; and Very far.

Relational Values (RV) are computed for each network and include a combination of RTV, RLV and SEVF factors in offer-demand logic.

To compute the RCV, the definition and classification of parameters, such as OVF, NVF, NP, RTV, RLV, and HCP, may change depending on the type of the analyzed network. This way SNARE-RCO is flexible because it allows adapting parameters definitions and classifications. Moreover, any of these parameters can be calibrated or even neutralized according the analyst's purposes. Besides computing the RCV, this model allows us to identify and compute the value of human capital in a given network.

In general terms, this model enables us to measure the relational capital of social networks from organizational units and organizations, content management systems, or social media platforms. Combining techniques derived from social network analysis with organizational aspects and its relation to intellectual capital, the SNARE-RCO model helps to answer the question "What is the value of this social network?" Three key-concepts to compute the organizational network RCV are: (1) the value of a social network is a contribution to satisfy a given demand; (2) this demand is conducted by its social entities; and (3) the value of relations in a given context reflects offers and demands from social entities (Barão & Silva, 2011).

SNARE-Explorer

SNARE-Explorer is a desktop-based interface for data analysis and rich visualization developed with Java technology (Barão & Silva, 2008). This system is able to store, manage, and visualize the information required to dynamically reconstruct real scenarios for social network analysis extraction and relational knowledge discovery. This tool is based on the SNARE-Language meta-model supporting different types and instances of social entities (e.g. people, organizational-units, and organizations), roles, or relations. Also, it supports different integration approaches and it is able to manage and automatically collect social networks data from legacy information systems, through transparent or intrusive approaches. Target systems are accessed by a sophisticated visualization tool, which includes specific heuristics to address the different types of data analysis required, and a set of spatial graphics and diagrams able to depict new data views.

As an engineering tool, SNARE-Explorer is able to simulate scenarios in real-time and uses

SNARE-RCO model to compute and visualize the value of the organizational relational capital. Figure 3 depicts the SNARE-Explorer Relational Capital Monitoring System interface.

RELATIONAL CAPITAL EVALUATION

For a relational capital evaluation using SNARE-Framework, first we describe a methodology to evaluate the relational capital of organizations and, after, present three distinct evaluation cases.

A Methodology to Evaluate the Relational Capital of Organizations

We present the SNARE-Methodology to be applied to evaluate the relational capital of organizations. This methodology has four main processes: Diagnosing, Designing, Executing, and Reporting. Methodology roles and artifacts are also described in this section.

In organizational context, stakeholders are participants that are normally associated with specific roles such as: sponsors, employees, customers, and suppliers (Anklam, 2007). In social

Figure 3. SNARE-explorer relational capital monitoring system

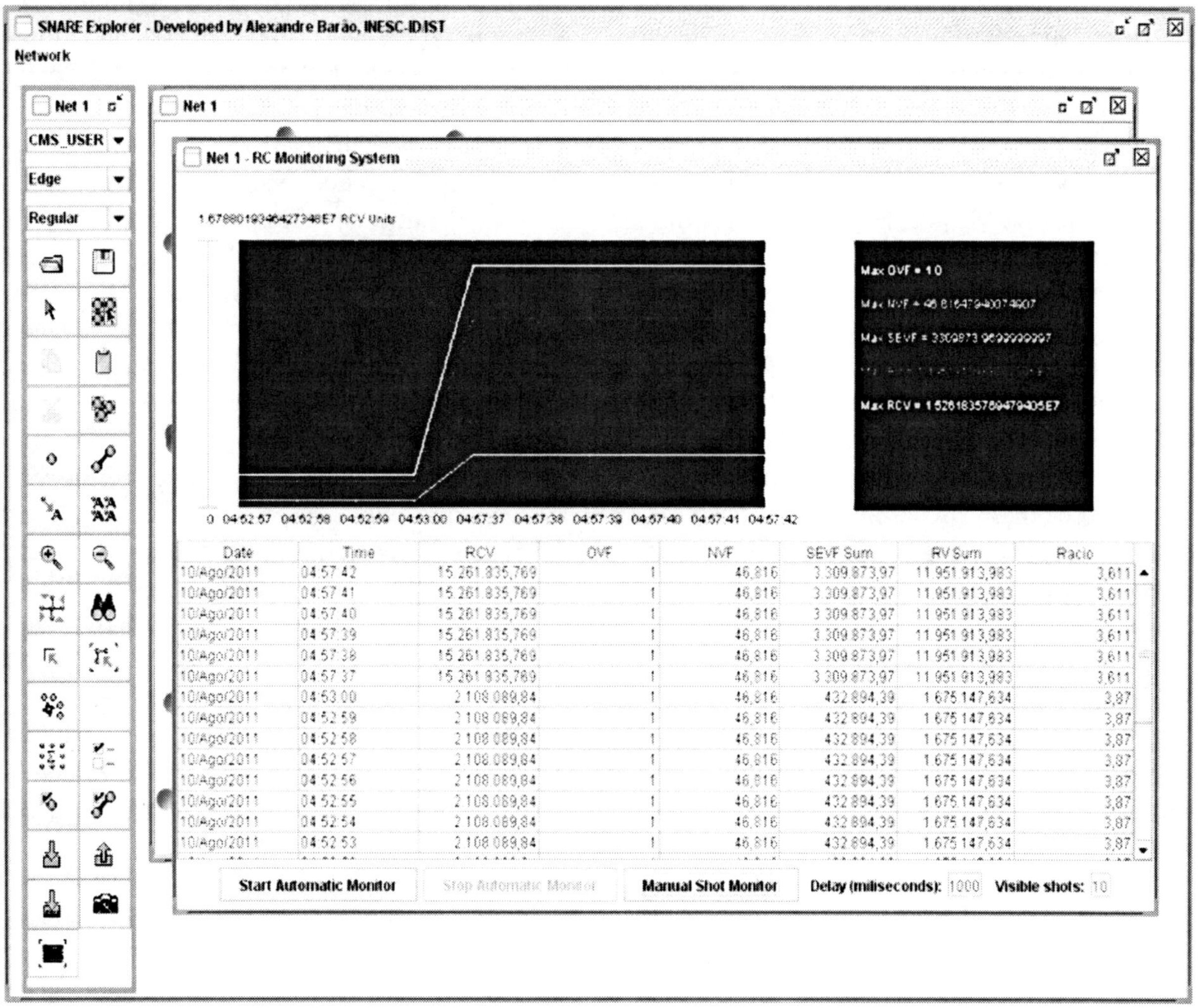

terms, sponsors are network investors or funders; employees are network core group members; customers are members of the network; and, suppliers are partners (Anklam, 2007). Employee roles are dependent on the target organization, which has a specific organizational structure that expresses allocation of responsibilities for different functions and processes to separate entities like departments, workgroups, and individuals.

Aiming at evaluating the relational capital of organizations, the SNARE-Methodology has four roles: Analyst, Sponsor, Manager, and Team. The Analyst is the SNARE framework expert, and s/he can lead to shifts in management thinking and improvements in the relational capital value of the organization. The Sponsor's primary objective is the preservation of organizational investments. In the organization, the Sponsor can be an individual or a group and assumes strategic responsibilities and decisions. The Manager serves as an agent to provide access to the organization's private information systems. The Team involves all the individuals, typically people who work part-time or full-time under a contract of employment.

SNARE-Methodology considers the use/development of several artifacts namely: Organizational Context, Organizational Structure, Project Charter, Analysis Pack, Evaluation Report and Evaluation Presentation. The Organizational Context is a document that results from the organization's elicitation and contains its introductory description. Based on SNARE-Language, the Organizational Structure is a document that identifies the social entities of the organization as well as the roles and social relations (relational actions) to be analyzed. The Project Charter contains four sections: (1) General Information; (2) Overview; (3) Project Approach; and (4) Project Approval. The Analysis Pack is a set of analysis documents, namely: Interviews and/or Questionnaires, Network Analysis, Social Entity Analysis, Relational Analysis, and Relational Capital Value Report. Interviews and/or Questionnaires contain Team answers which help the Analyst identify organizational relations. Network Analysis is a document which includes: Network Layouts (to depict network views with node type differentiation), Network Properties (to show social entity centrality degrees or other SNA applied measures), and Network Valuable Factors (to identify overall network properties such as density or number of social entities). Social Entity Analysis is a file that includes: Human Capital Properties Analysis (to compare human capital properties), Social Entity Valuable Factors Analysis (to analyze the RCV contribution of each social entity), Node Type Analysis (to study social entities' predominant network node types), and Organizational Valuable Factors (to spot attributes of the organization that may contribute to the evaluation system). Relational Analysis is a document that firstly includes definitions for Relation Type Values (to differentiate relational action values) and Relational Levels Values (to distinguish proximity relational values). Secondly, it comprises the Relational Value Analysis, which is a description to understand each relational action RCV contribution. Relational Capital Value Report is a document that describes the global RCV of the network and may include simulated scenarios to analyze RCV changes. Evaluation Report is a private file which may include insights and recommendations to improve the relational capital of the organization. Finally, Evaluation Presentation is a public domain document with evaluation results.

SNARE-Methodology makes use of a tool and two models. The tool is SNARE-Explorer (Barão & Silva, 2008) and the models are SNARE-Language (Barão & Silva, 2010) and SNARE-RCO (Barão & Silva, 2011). The SNARE-Language model is used to produce the Organizational Structure document. SNARE-RCO model is employed to classify relational input parameters and compute the relational capital of the organization. Finally, SNARE-Explorer is the desktop tool application that uses SNARE-Language and SNARE-RCO. The Analysis Pack is produced by SNARE-Explorer tool, but other tools can be used, particularly: ETL tools, spread sheets and word processors.

As stated before, SNARE-Methodology is based on four main processes, namely: Diagnosing, Designing, Executing, and Reporting. These processes tend to be sequentially performed. In the Diagnosing process (See Figure 4), the Analyst presents the SNARE-Methodology to the Sponsor and the Team. The SNARE-Methodology presentation includes an overview of the SNARE-Language, SNARE-RCO, and SNARE-Explorer tool. After the SNARE-Methodology presentation, the Analyst produces the Organizational Context document in collaboration with the Sponsor and the Team. Then, using SNARE-Language, the Analyst writes the Organizational Structure document and, finally, produces the Project Charter, which must be formally signed by him and the Sponsor.

In the Designing process (See Figure 5) using the identified Organizational Structure, the Analyst starts to request information access to the Manager. After that, the Analyst and the Manager can determine how organizational data will be gathered from the organization's knowledge base. For the next step, the Analyst defines analysis metrics, which are SNARE-RCO metrics. Finally, when appropriate, analysis instruments, such as interviews and/or questionnaires, are defined by the Analyst. These instruments must be approved by the Sponsor.

In the Executing process (See Figure 6), the Analyst starts having interviews and/or launching questionnaires to the Team. Interviews and questionnaires will be analyzed next by the Analyst. The Manager grants the Analyst access to necessary organizational information systems such as: the relational knowledge base, social networks, or Enterprise Resource Planning (ERP) systems. With this, the Analyst is able to start tasks like extract, transform and load data. These will populate SNARE-Databases and, using SNARE-Explorer, the Analyst can start to examine data, monitor, and evaluate relational capital. As a

Figure 4. Diagnosing process

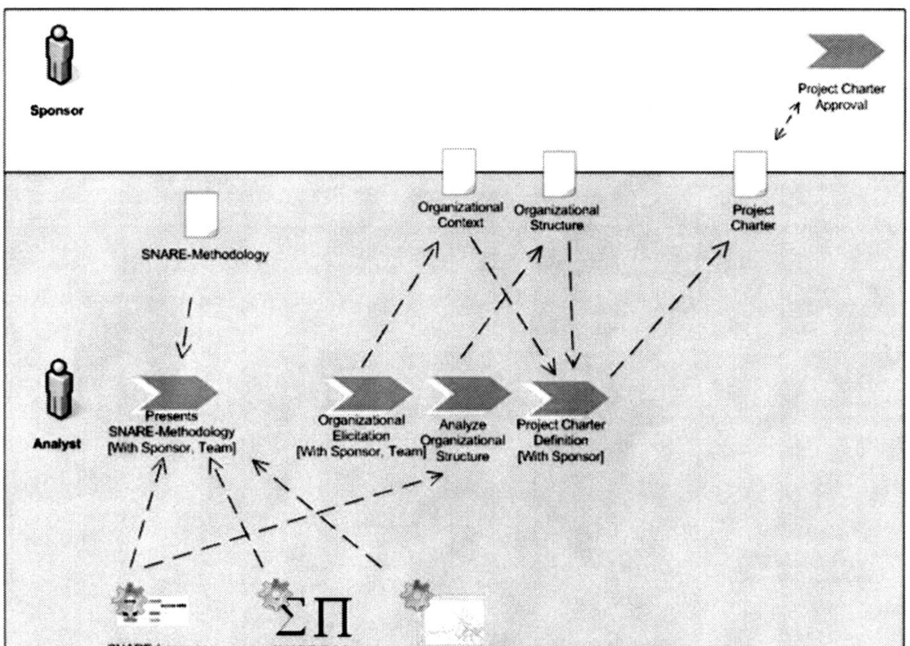

Figure 5. Designing process

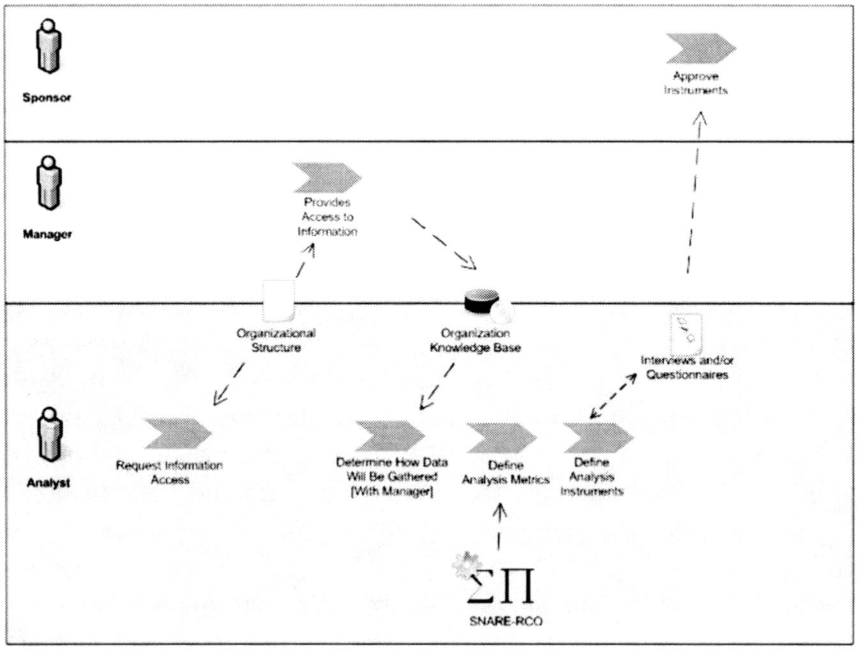

result, the Analysis Pack is produced. This pack includes processed Interviews and/or Questionnaires, Network, Social Entity and Relational Analysis, and also Relational Capital Value Report.

In the Reporting process (See Figure 7), the Analyst starts to review the Analysis Pack with the aim of producing the Evaluation Report. This report will be delivered to the Sponsor. The

Figure 6. Executing process

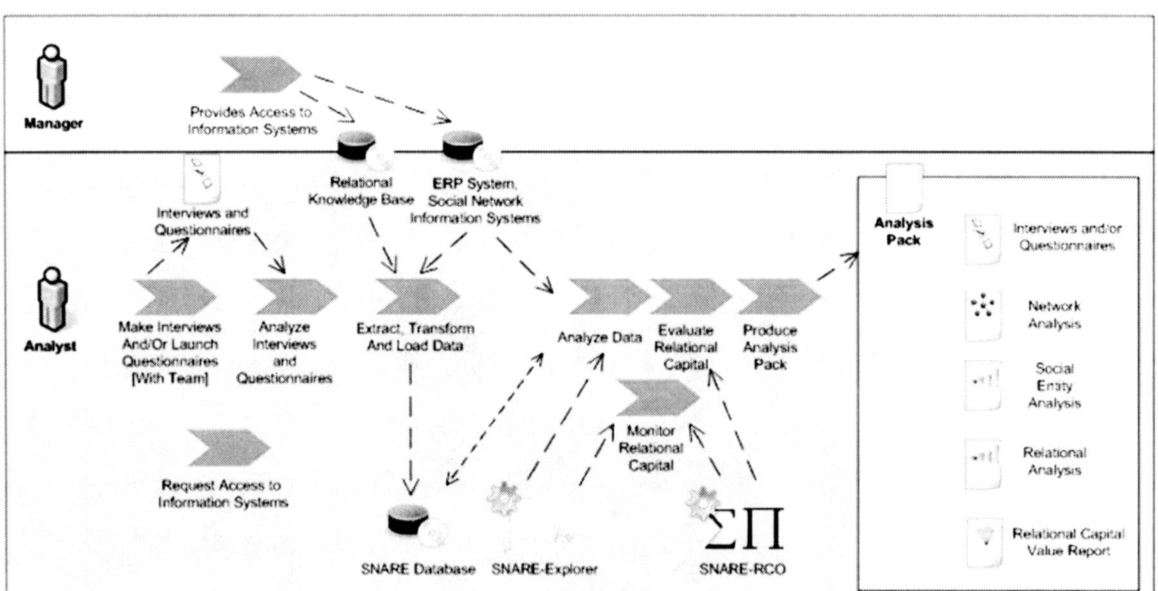

Figure 7. Reporting process

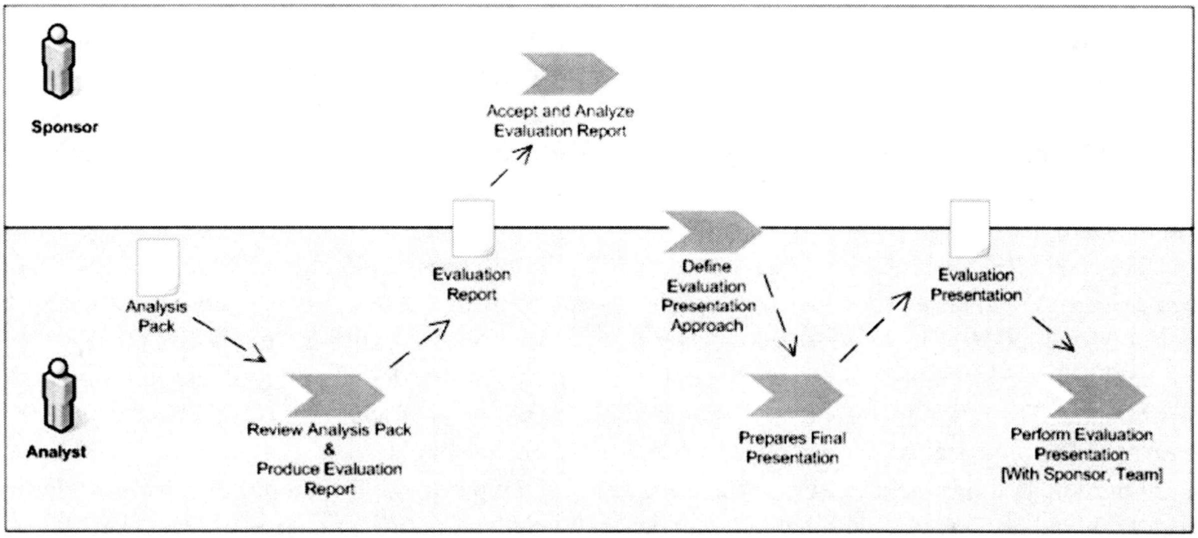

Evaluation Report contains data, some of which may be private, and it is necessary to define the Evaluation Presentation approach with the Sponsor, i.e. define what kind of results can be presented to the Team. Finally, the Analyst prepares the final presentation which will be performed to the Sponsor and the Team.

Using this methodology it is possible to define relational capital assumptions and help organizations to identify and solve problems. This methodology can promote ways for organizational characterization and/or change processes. Characterization or change begins with awareness and the Analyst and Sponsor work together for that purpose that is to evaluate the relational capital of the organization for a better characterization, and to find possible organizational changes to improve the organizational knowledge. Increasing the organizational understanding for both Sponsor and Analyst, regarding the relational capital, is to be aware of possible ways to change the organization. As described, with this methodology, the Analyst and the Sponsor participate in iterative and reflective processes.

With this methodology, the Analyst's presence can probably affect the situation on the experiment field because it allows direct intervention of analysts into events, e.g. the Analyst can be seen as a co-worker. However, intervention improvements can be reflected on an increase of relational capital which is an essential organizational knowledge.

Organizational Evaluation

Using SNARE framework and methodology, we have chosen to apply SNA and RC evaluation in the context of two organizations: (1) Case A – Services Support Group at Vodafone Portugal (GSS), a group responsible for the operation and support in networking services that is composed by more than half-a-hundred collaborators, most of them allocated to the different functional areas; and (2) Case B – A School in Lisbon, which employs over 200 people, namely teachers, technical assistants and operational assistants.

Case A was focused on the analysis of the Relational Capital of six teams from a Vodafone Portugal Unit: GSS. The study analyzed team resilience as a function of its dependency of specific members. Centering the analysis on GSS Unit, the main objectives were to: identify central elements on each team; obtain the RCV of each team; and analyze how RCV varies depending on the type of relational action. Also, in order to verify the GSS network importance, three additional goals were defined: to compute the global RCV of the network; to simulate the absence of central elements and measure the impact on the network RCV; and to replicate the removal of GSS Unit and measure the network RCV impact.

Using SNARE-Methodology, data was collected from Vodafone's workflow tool in the period from June 2011 to July 2011. Logs were gathered from the Vodafone workflow system for two months. This allowed insight into the tree main business processes in which the Unit under study participated on: Incident (Processes used to identify and respond to events that fall outside normal operations, including the recording, analysis and categorization of these events, along with measures taken to address the underlying causes and restore normal service operation as quickly as possible to minimize the adverse impact on business operations); Change (Processes used to manage any kind of change to existing technology, including definition of procedures; capturing, analysis and formal approval of change requests;, testing authorization, implementation and review of changes); and Problem (The process responsible for managing the lifecycle of all problems with the goal of preventing incidents from happening, and for minimizing the impact of incidents that cannot be prevented). The analysis repository was enriched with the log information from the Information Sharing used by the Unit under study. Both records belonging to Business Processes and Information Sharing were processed and analyzed with SNARE-Explorer Tool. These relational actions Change, Incident, Problem and Information Sharing were imported by CSV SNARE-Explorer mechanisms.

To perform Relational Analysis, Relation Type Values (RTV) and Relational Levels Values (RLV) were firstly determined. In this study, RTV was defined as 0.1 for all relations, and RLV as 1 (regular). Using these definitions, RV Sums for each relational action were computed. The following figure shows RV Sum values for each type of relational action. The predominant relational capital value refers to the Information Share relational action, and relational action Problem has the lowest RCV (See Figure 8).

Figure 8. Case A, RV sum per relational action

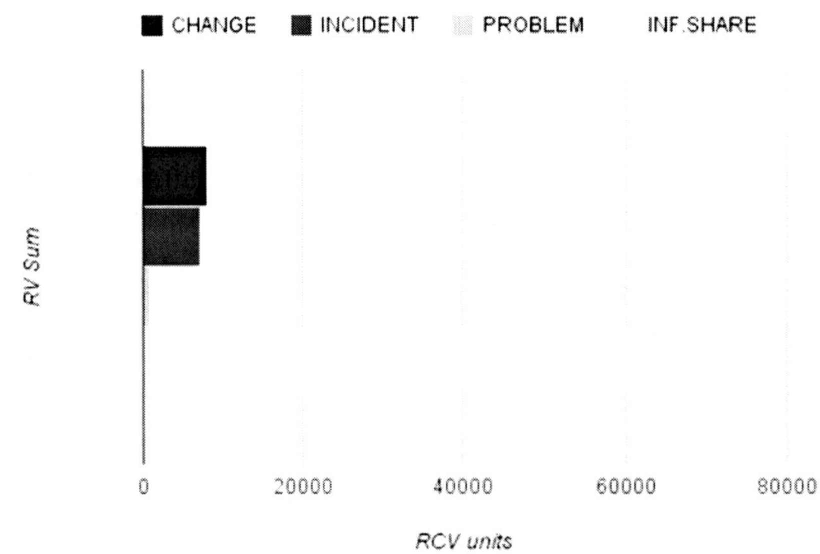

Using the SNARE framework, we successfully identified the central elements of GSS teams. Also, we determined the RCV of each one and analyzed how RCV varies depending on the type of relational actions. Finally, we computed the RCV of the overall network, replicated the absence of central elements and measured the impact on the RCV network. Using SNARE-Explorer tool, we also simulated the removal of GSS Unit and measured the network RCV impact. From this study, we further concluded that network properties and relational value can be a way to translate team resilience in this specific case. The study has validated *Sponsor* expectations, namely: homogeneous groups, in which all members execute similar functions and are expected to equally distribute effort among its members; in addition, if Network Properties (NP) are equally distributed, groups can be more resilient. Notwithstanding, members with NP higher than the average can be a risk of dependency while members with NP lower than the average can represent elements not entirely integrated into their teams.

Repeated over time, this study can help understand: what the impact of improvement measures is; what the consequences of an individual absence are; and how long it takes to fully replace one individual.

Case-B was focused on the analysis of mechanisms of communication and information to transmit knowledge in a given school in Lisbon. This school has over 200 employees and they are divided into three major categories: teachers, technical assistants and operational assistants.

The study's aim was to answer the question: "Is the organization optimized to produce and transmit knowledge?" If sharing knowledge is improved, then scientific articulations can be perfected and this is better for students. To reach an answer to the above question, several main goals were defined, namely to: identify central elements in the organization; spot central groups in the organization; obtain RCV for each relational action; and compute the RCV of the network. Also, two additional goals were outlined: to simulate the absence of central elements and measure the impact on network RCV; and to reproduce the removal of peripheral elements and measure the impact on network RCV.

Using SNARE framework, this study was conducted with the collaboration of the School Quality Observatory throughout April 2011.As a result, several recommendations to improve knowledge sharing emerged. With this study, a network analysis was first performed at the school. With the aim of analyzing organizational mechanisms of communication and information to transmit knowledge, we developed a questionnaire with several questions to the local community. Data about employees was collected from the school's Human Resources (HR) system. The target universe contained 229 employees. 207 questionnaires were delivered and collected (162 Teachers, 11 Technical Assistants and 34 Operational Assistants). The questionnaire contained several questions, and the closed-answer questions were defined as follows: "Who transmits important information to carry out your functions?"; "Who do you ask for help when you have to solve a new problem?"; "Who do you particularly appreciate for professionalism and/or scientific knowledge?"; and, "Who communicates with you using information technology?". These questions were inspired in Rob Cross' work Questions to Uncover Important Network Relationships (Cross & Parker, 2004). Using SNARE framework, these four questions were analyzed, and for each relational action, a name was correspondingly assigned: TransmitInformation; AskForHelp;WhoRecognizes; and CommunicateWithIT.

TransmitInformation captured a greater number of responses and CommunicateWithIT a lower one. In addition, when answering the questions listed above, people were also asked to rate their peers in terms of five descriptors: prestige, competence, experience, friendship, and proximity.

All questions were initially processed using an online spreadsheet and imported after by CSV SNARE-Explorer mechanisms.

To perform Relational Analysis, Relation Type Values (RTV) and Relational Levels Values (RLV) were defined first. In this study, RTV was set to 0.1 for all relations and RLV was defined as 1 (regular). The main responsible relational action for RCV increase is TransmitInformation. AskForHelp and CommunicateWithIT are the lowest RCV contributors. This is a remarkable fact because it proves that communication and transmission of organizational knowledge can be optimized (see Figure 9).

It was also observed that a relatively small number of people play a central position in the organization. Furthermore, a problem was detected: a significant amount of people are dependent on information provided by a restrict group. To increase this problem, communication with IT has captured low RCV values. This aspect reveals that to rationalize the information transmission using IT and redistributing workloads can release significant resources for other important tasks. Even when using IT, information senders are typically the network core members. Besides, after analyzing network layouts, we encountered another problem: people receive the same information from several sources.

The SNARE-RCO model evaluation provided very objective information to support decision making. Also, in the future, it can be used to compare several schools. This study has showed that the school is not optimized to produce and transmit knowledge, and a change of plan was recommended by the Observatory of Quality to the School's commission board. The plan was accepted and change actions started in September 2011. Some time from now, it would also be interesting to involve students in order to capture their perception about the school community.

Extending Evaluation to Content Management Systems and Social Media Platforms

We chose to apply SNA and RC evaluation to a Web-based collaborative and social platform (Case C). In particular, the Learning Objects Pool[1] (LOP) platform which has hundreds of users (Silva & Silva, 2009). This system is a repository of learning objects (Carlota, Silva,

Figure 9. Case B, RV sum per relational action

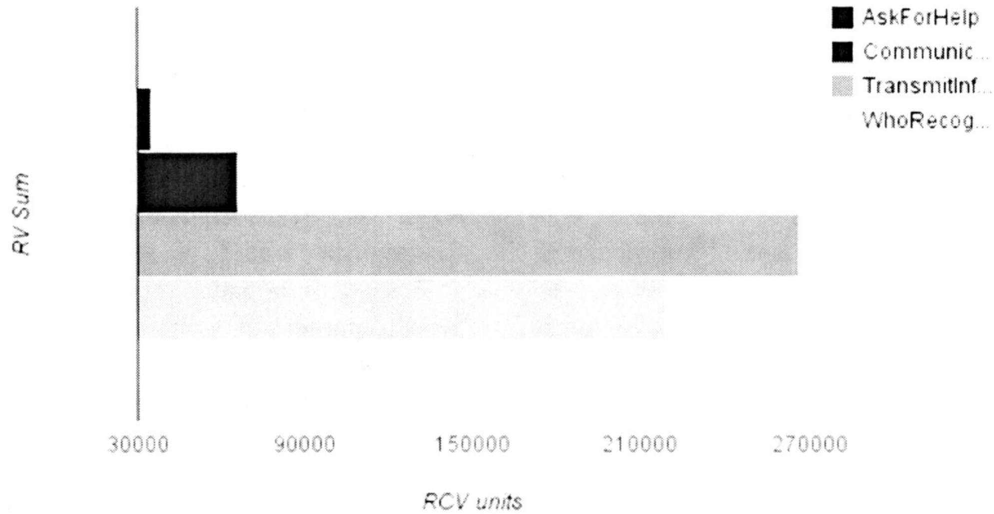

& Silva, 2009). A Learning Object (LO) is defined as any digital resource that can be reused to support learning (Wiley, 2000), and LOP is built around the "stock exchange" metaphor, pushing users motivation to produce good learning objects as well as to cooperate with other users, either by submitting suggestions, comments or by rating existing learning objects (Silva & Silva, 2007). To achieve this level of motivation and interest, some kind of competition is promoted, assigning credits to users and setting a value cost for each learning object. This credit-based system allows us to create users and learning objects rankings, rewarding those that collaborate with the system.

As stated before, LOP is built around the "stock exchange" metaphor, i.e. users are ranked through an offer-demand credit system, and the major aim was to compute its network RCV by analyzing two major LOP relational actions: downloads and comments. Data was collected from LOP database and 268 users were imported by SNARE-Explorer using CSV mechanisms, as well as associated relational actions: download and comment learning objects.

To perform Relational Analysis, Relation Type Values (RTV) and Relational Levels Values (RLV) were defined. In this case, RTV was set to 0,1 for relational action downloads, and to 0,2 for relational action comments. In this case, comments have a higher weight since they trigger interactivity between social entities. RLV was outlined as 1 (regular). Using these definitions, RV Sums for each relational action were computed. Figure 10 shows the RV Sum for each type of LOP analyzed relational action. The predominant relational action to produce RCV capital is Downloads.

On the one hand, in the LOP system network layout, a significant number of isolated nodes was observable. They are registered users but never make a single LO download or comment. This means that LOP gave them starting credits to use the system but they are not LOs authors. On the other hand, a small number of users with a high centrality degree were detected. These users are LO authors. In addition, we found an expressive correlation between NP computed properties and user credits imported from LOP system. This fact proves that SNARE-RCO model is able to evaluate registered users with similar computed LOP results. The study has also identified network

Figure 10. Case C, RV sum per relational action

central members, and proven that SNARE framework can be applied to monitor the relational capital of a CMS system. Relational actions were measured and the RCV was computed for the overall network.

From this study, we believe that it is possible to apply SNARE-RCO model to evaluate the relational capital of systems such as Moodle[2], LinkedIn[3], or Facebook[4]. Consider Table 1 in which the analyzed platform LOP is compared with possible applications to those systems. In the platforms Moodle, LinkedIn, and Facebook, demands are conducted by users, e.g. reading a document (Moodle), viewing a job description (LinkedIn), or viewing user photos (Facebook). These demands are relational actions and can be evaluated by the SNARE-RCO model, thus, using SNARE-RCO features, Table 1 shows several examples of possible scenarios to enforce the SNARE-Framework ability for evaluating the relational capital of these systems.

Table 1. SNARE framework platforms application

Platform	**LOP**	**Moodle**	**LinkedIn**	**Facebook**
Context	CMS	CMS	Social Media	Social Media
Network Analysis				
Network Layouts Depict network views with node type differentiation	Authors and readers	Teachers and students	Colleagues and friends	Friends and family
NP Detect social entity centrality degrees	Users	Teachers and students	Colleagues	Friends
NVF Compare overall network properties	Number of users	Number of teachers and students	Number of network members	Number of friends
Social Entity Analysis				
HCP Analysis Compare human capital properties	User credits	Students assessments	Professional skills	Activities and interests
SEVF Analysis Analyse the RCV contribution of each social entity	Recognized authors	Best students	Skilled workers	Friends interests
Node Type Analysis Analyse social entities network predominant roles	Users	Teachers and students	Colleagues	Friends
Relational Analysis				
RTV Differentiate relational actions value	Downloads comments	Forum replies submitted works	Status post recommendation	Like comment
RLV Differentiate relational levels value	Users co-authors	Users class mates	Friends colleagues	Friends family
RV Analysis Understand each relational action RCV contribution	Download comments	Forum replies submitted works	Status posts recommendations	Photo uploads comments
RCV Evaluate the relational capital of the network	LOP value	Classes value	Colleagues network value	Friends network value

FUTURE RESEARCH DIRECTIONS

The evaluation of relational capital of organizations is already a reality, and managers should encourage organizations to adopt it. Towards an evaluation system, the relational capital evaluation research can be useful to increase organizational awareness. In this sense, we believe that new relational capital research efforts will emerge in areas such as Enterprise Architecture, Business Processes Engineering, Organizational Learning, and Knowledge Management.

CONCLUSION

As stated initially, our research was driven by the following question: What is the value of this social network? To answer this question we developed a strategy. Our first challenge was to define a way to better design social network structures in order to graphically design social entities and multiple relations among them. To answer this issue we defined SNARE-Language to design social network structures in which organizations are present. The flexibility of this language is expressed by all possible links that may exist on a social network.

Second, to answer the question "How to measure the relational capital of social networks?" we defined a relational capital evaluation model: SNARE-RCO. Using this model, it is possible to define metrics for analyzing the relational capital of a given organization (or corresponding content management system, or social media platform).

Third, to answer to the question "How to visualize the relational capital value of an organization's social network?" we created a prototype system to show how to compute, visualize and monitor the relational capital. This prototype system is SNARE-Explorer, and it enables us to visualize organizational social networks, to evaluate them, and monitor the relational capital.

Fourth, we validated results through controlled case studies using the SNARE-Methodology. With a set of roles, artifacts, and using SNARE-Explorer tool and SNARE models, SNARE-Methodology has four main processes: Diagnosing, Designing, Executing, and Reporting. These processes promote iterative ways for organizational analysis. We chose three validation scenarios: (1) A telecommunications company; (2) a school; and (3) a CMS platform. From the validation conclusions we showed that SNARE Framework can be applied to evaluate organizations as well as their KMSs such as those based on content management systems or social media platforms.

Besides the use of SNARE framework in processes of organizational consulting, the following items pose further research that could be pursued in line with our work: (1) Comparing RCV from organizations of the same kind. An interesting study would be applying simultaneously SNARE models in the evaluation of several organizations such as schools. Using the same parameters of analysis, it would be possible to compare the RCV of various schools. Other issues to explore include increasing the analysis period and consider the relational capital of organizations in real-time; (2) Extending SNARE-Explorer with SNA tools integration features. Since there are already popular tools for social network analysis, we consider that the SNARE-Explorer may include new data integration features with those tools. E.g. importing and exporting compatible files with Pajek[5] and UCINET[6] tools. Thus, with these new features, in order to evaluate the relational capital of networks, the SNARE-Explorer may be used by the scientific community that already employs these tools; and finally, (3) Extending SNARE-Explorer with social platforms integration features. Using public application programming interfaces, we also would like to extend SNARE-Explorer data integration features to compute and visualize the relational capital value of platforms such as Moodle, LinkedIn and Facebook in real-time.

To compute the relational capital of an organization, the appraisal system should combine techniques derived from social network analysis, with aspects of organizational assessment. Furthermore, it must consider dynamic properties from the social entities intellectual capital.

REFERENCES

Adams, M., & Oleksak, M. (2010). *Intangible capital - Putting knowledge to work in the 21st-century organization*. Santa Barbara, CA: Praeger.

Alavi, M., & Leidner, D. (2001). Knowledge management and knowledge management systems: Conceptual foundations and research issues. *Management Information Systems Quarterly, 25*(1), 107–136. doi:10.2307/3250961.

Alee, V. (2003). *The future of knowledge: Increasing prosperity through value networks*. Burlington, MA: Elsevier Science.

Alee, V. (2008). Value network analysis and value conversion of tangible and intangible assets. *Journal of Intellectual Capital, 9*(1).

Allee, V. (1997). *The knowledge evolution: expanding organizational intelligence*. Burlington, MA: Butterworth-Heinemann.

Anklam, P. (2007). *Net work - A practical guide to creating and sustaining networks at work and in the world*. Oxford, UK: Elsevier.

Barão, A., & Silva, A. (2008). SNARE - Social network analysis and reengineering environment: Architecture overview. In *Proceedings of WEBIST - International Conference on Web Information Systems and Technologies*. Funchal, Portugal: WEBIST.

Barão, A., & Silva, A. R. (2010). The SNARE language overview. In *Proceedings of the 12th ICEIS - International Conference on Enterprise Systems, ICEIS'2010*. INSTICC.

Barão, A., & Silva, A. R. (2011). A model to evaluate the relational capital of organizations SNARE-RCO. In M. M. Crus-Cunha et al. (Eds.), *CENTERIS - Conference on Enterprise Information Systems*, (pp. 400-409). Berlin: Springer.

Bontis, N. (2001). Assessing knowledge assets: A review of the models used to measure intellectual capital. *International Journal of Management Reviews, 3*(1). doi:10.1111/1468-2370.00053.

Borgatti, S., & Foster, P. (2003). The network paradigm in organizational research: A review and typology. *Journal of Management, 29*(6).

Buono, A. F. (2003). *Enhancing inter-firm networks and interorganizational strategies*. Charlotte, NC: Information Age Publishing Inc..

Carley, K., Diesner, J., Reminga, J., & Tsvetovat, M. (2007). *Toward an interoperable dynamic network analysis toolkit*. Retrieved in January 2010, from https://community.bus.emory.edu/dept/ISOM/Shared%20Documents/Hightower%20Speaker%20Papers/KathleenCarley.pdf

Carlota, J., Silva, A. R., & Silva, P. (2009). The learning object pool and the BOA-GPI case study. In *Proceedings of the Iberoamerican Congress on Telematics (CITA-2009)*. CITA.

Churchill, E., & Halverson, C. (2005). Social networks and social networking. *IEEE Internet Computing, 9*(5). doi:10.1109/MIC.2005.103.

Cross, R., & Parker, A. (2004). *The hidden power of social networks: Understand how work really gets done in organizations*. Boston: Harvard Business School Press.

FAO. (2010). *Organizational evaluation*. Retrieved in January 2010, from http://www.fao.org/docrep/w7510e/w7510e05.htm

Faust, W., & Faust, K. (1994). *Social network analysis: Methods and applications: Structural analysis in the social sciences*. Cambridge, UK: Cambridge University Press.

Greene, D. (1999). *Measuring what matters: The paths of intangible value*. Paper presented at the Institute for International Research. San Diego, CA.

Haythornthwaite, C. (2005). *Social network methods and measures for examining e-learning*. Graduate School of Library and Information Science.

Helms, R., & Buijsrogge, K. (2005). *Knowledge network analysis: A technique to analyze knowledge management bottlenecks in organizations*. Paper presented at the Sixteenth International Workshop on Database and Expert Systems Applications. New York, NY.

Hubbard, D. W. (2010). *How to measure anything - Finding the value of intangibles in business* (2nd ed.). Hoboken, NJ: John Wiley & Sons, Inc..

Kathleen, C. (2003). *Dynamic social network modeling and analysis: Workshop summary and papers*. Washington, DC: National Academy Press.

Krogh, G. (1998). Care in knowledge creation. *California Management Review*, *40*(3), 133–153. doi:10.2307/41165947.

OMG. (2010). Retrieved in January 2010, from www.uml.org

Silva, P., & Silva, A. (2007). Design experiences with the learning objects board system. In *Proceedings of the Hawaii International Conference on System Sciences (HICSS-40)*. IEEE Computer Society.

Silva, P., & Silva, A. R. (2009). Application scenarios for the learning objects pool. *Journal of Universal Computer Science*, *15*(7).

Sveiby, K.-E. (2010). *Methods for measuring intangible assets*. Retrieved in July 2010, from www.sveiby.com/articles/IntangibleMethods.htm

ValueNetworks. (2010). *What is value network analysis (VNA)?* Retrieved in December 2010, from www.valuenetworks.com

Wiley, D. (2000). *Connecting learning objects to instructional design theory: A definition, a metaphor, and a taxonomy*. Retrieved from http://reusability.org/read/chapters/williams.doc

Zadjabbari, B., Wongthongtham, P., & Hussain, F. K. (2008). Towards an ontological intellectual capital based model in sustainable business performance. In *Proceedings of CIMCA*. IEEE.

ADDITIONAL READING

Alee, V. (2009). Value creating networks: Organizational issues and challenges. *The Learning Organization*, *6*(6).

Amaratunga, D., Baldry, D., Sarshar, M., & Newton, R. (2001). *Quantitative and qualitative research in the built environment: Application of mixed research approach*. Paper presented at the 1st International Postgraduate Conference - School of Construction and Property Management at the University of Salford. Salford, UK.

Atkinson, P., & Hammersley, M. (1994). Ethnography and participant observation. In *Handbook of Qualitative Research* (pp. 248–261). Thousand Oaks, CA: SAGE.

Baskerville, R. L. (1999). Investigating information systems. *Communications of the Association for Information Systems*, *2*(19).

Borgatti, S. (2003). *The state of organizational social network research today*. Boston: Department of Organization Studies, Boston University.

Brass, J., Greve, H., & Tsai, W. (2004). Taking stock of networks and organizations: A multilevel perspective. *Academy of Management Journal*, *47*(6). doi:10.2307/20159624.

Carrington, P., Scott, J., & Wasserman, S. (2005). *Models and methods in social network analysis: Structural analysis in the social sciences*. Cambridge, UK: Cambridge University Press. doi:10.1017/CBO9780511811395.

CASOS. (2007). *MetaMatrix: Tools for the analysis of organizational structure*. Retrieved from http://www.casos.cs.cmu.edu/projects/MetaMatrix/index.html

CASOS. (2011). *Computational models and social network tools*. Retrieved from http://www.casos.cs.cmu.edu/computational_tools/tools.html

Eynde Van, D., & Bledsoe, J. (1990). The changing practice of organization development. *Leadership and Organization Development Journal*, *11*(2), 25–30. doi:10.1108/01437739010135529.

Freitas, H. B., Barão, A., & Silva, A. (2009). Social networks in information systems: Tools and services. In *Handbook of Research on Social Dimensions of Semantic Technologies and Web Services*. Hershey, PA: IGI Global. doi:10.4018/978-1-60566-650-1.ch020.

Hannenman, R. A. (2010). *Introduction to social network methods*. Retrieved from www.analytech.com/networks.pdf.

Jamali, M., & Hassan. (2006). Different aspects of social network analysis. In *Proceedings of the 2006 IEEE/WIC/ACM International Conference on Web Intelligence*. IEEE.

Licamele, L., Getoor, L., & Roussopoulos, N. (2005). Capital and benefit in social networks. In *Proceedings of LinkKDD'05*. ACM. doi:10.1145/1134271.1134278.

Masolo, C., Bottazzi, E., Catenacci, C., Ferrario, R., Gangemi, A., & Guarino, N. (2004). Social roles and their descriptions. In *Proceedings of the Ninth International Conference on the Principles of Knowledge Representation and Reasoning*. IEEE.

McInerney, C. (2002). Knowledge management and the dynamic nature of knowledge. *Journal of the American Society for Information Science and Technology*, *53*(12). doi:10.1002/asi.10109.

Mika, P. (2005). Ontologies are us: A unified model of social networks and semantics. In *Proceedings of the 4th International Semantic Web Conference* (LNCS), (vol. 3729). Berlin: Springer-Verlag.

Provan, K. G., Fish, A., & Sydow, J. (2007). Interorganizational networks at the network level: A review of the empirical literature on whole networks. *Journal of Management*, 33.

Snijders, Steglich, & Schweinberger. (2007). Modeling the co-evolution of networks and behavior. In K. van Montfort, H. Oud, & A. Satorra (Eds.), *Longitudinal models in the behavioral and related sciences*. Mahwah, NJ: Lawrence Erlbaum.

Snijders, T. (2001). The statistical evaluation of social network dynamics. In Sobel, M. E., & Becker, M. P. (Eds.), *Sociological methodology*. Boston: Basil Blackwell. doi:10.1111/0081-1750.00099.

Sveiby, K.-E. (2001). *The intangible assets monitor*. Retrieved from www.sveiby.com/articles/CompanyMonitor.html

KEY TERMS AND DEFINITIONS

Human Capital: Human capital is the knowledge, skills and experience of individuals.

Intangible Capital: Intangible capital is the combination of all intangibles of an organization (i.e., human, structural, and relational capital).

Organizational Network Analysis: Organizational Network Analysis (ONA) involves the use of Social Network Analysis in organizational contexts in order to help managers to better understand relationships inside and outside the organization.

Relational Capital: Relational capital is the value of internal and external social relationships of a given organization.

SNARE Framework: SNARE is an acronym for "Social Network Analysis and Reengineering Environment." SNARE framework has engineering artifacts with the aim of evaluating the relational capital of organizations. SNARE main components are: SNARE-Language; SNARE-RCO; and SNARE-Explorer.

Social Network: A social network is generally defined as a set(s) of actors and the relation(s) defined for them. Actors, also defined as social entities, can be individual or collective social units that are connected by links. Links constituting a social network may be directed, undirected, or mixed. Social Networks can be analyzed using defined measures, and their results may be compared with those from similar networks. Each actor's position and connections could also be individually analyzed and compared with those of other actors in order to understand their relative importance in the network and highlight network bottlenecks and cutpoints as well as isolated and equivalent actors.

Social Network Analysis Measures: Measures in SNA are the metrics through which networks and social actors can be evaluated and compared. SNA measures can be distinguished into those which evaluate the entire network and those that only assess a specific node. At the individual level, the most frequently analyzed measure is centrality; this can be measured using nodal degree, betweeness, and closeness. At the network level, it is important to understand how the network is structured; it is, therefore, key to measure network cohesion, centralization, and clustering and to identify important nodes like cutpoints.

Social Network Tools: Social Network Tools are software tools that can be used to represent, visualize, and analyze social networks. These tools can usually read and write in common formats and use matrices to compute social networks as well as graphs, called sociograms, to represent them.

Structural Capital: Structural capital is the set of procedures, processes, and internal structures that contribute to the implementation of the objectives of an organization.

ENDNOTES

1 http://www.vemaprender.net

2 http://www.moodle.org

3 http://www.linkedin.com

4 http://www.facebook.com

5 http://pajek.imfm.si, Pajek is a Windows program for analysis and visualization of large networks. It is freely available for noncommercial use.

6 http://www.analytictech.com/ucinet/, UCINET is a social network analysis program developed by Borgatti, Everett and Freeman. UCINET works in tandem with freeware program NETDRAW for visualizing networks.

Chapter 13
Critical Success Factors in Enterprise 2.0:
The Importance of Business Performance

Ana Silva
Porto Business School, Portugal

ABSTRACT

While evangelists and enthusiasts of Enterprise 2.0 praise the benefits of the use of social software in the workplace, the sceptics are not that convinced and some draw attention to the failures of the Knowledge Management concept and tools that were trendy some years ago. In parallel, board members and top management question the true business benefits of Enterprise 2.0 and demand proof of the potential business value prior to giving a green light to this type of investment. If it is true that some of the benefits of Enterprise 2.0 are intangible and therefore harder to measure, the impact on business performance should be observable and consequently measurable. This chapter reflects on the importance of addressing the topic of business performance when it comes to social software in the enterprise. It also discusses the importance of integrating social software into the flow of work in order to drive adoption and sustained use.

INTRODUCTION

The enterprise of the 21st century will be a connected entity: one that leverages internal and external networks of people and knowledge to gain competitive advantage and face the increasing challenges of a highly mutable external environment.

The profound economy crisis, coupled with a deep social unease, has set the scenario for the rethinking, on a global scale, of the future of public and private institutions, of society as a whole and of work. Individuals and groups' opinions and actions are all being shared and amplified via a new generation of media—social media—that has given voice at a large scale to previously

DOI: 10.4018/978-1-4666-4373-4.ch013

anonymous people. As authors Hagel, Brown and Davison (2010) recently said in their recent book The Power of Pull "each of us, individually and together, are now, for the first time in history, in a position to collaborate in a complete reimagination of our biggest private- and public-sector institutions that will eventually remake society as a whole" (p. 159).

Authors such as Don Tapscott and Gary Hamel have well described some of the key concepts that will influence the future of organizations and work: openness, connectedness, mass collaboration, agility, and transparency. And social tools are playing an important part in enabling this internal and external connectivity and collaboration in companies big and small. For both leaders and employees the construction of the new enterprise presents new opportunities, but also new challenges and new work concepts to grasp, creating a mixture of excitement and fear.

A key concept in the modernization and adaptation of the enterprise to the challenges it will increasingly face is that of Enterprise 2.0: the deployment of Web 2.0-style tools (social software) and practices with the purpose of fostering collaboration and collective intelligence inside organizations.

But while evangelists and overall enthusiasts of Enterprise 2.0 praise the benefits of the use of social software in the workplace, the sceptics are not that convinced and some draw attention to the failures of the Knowledge Management concept and tools so trendy some years ago. In parallel, board members and top management question the true business benefits of Enterprise 2.0 and demand proof of the potential business value prior to giving green light to this type of investment.

If it is true that some of the benefits of Enterprise 2.0 are intangible and therefore harder to measure, especially those related to employee satisfaction and engagement, the impact on business performance should be observable and consequently measurable, demonstrating to companies' executives the concrete value of Enterprise 2.0.

In this chapter, we look at the importance of tying Enterprise 2.0 projects to the topic of business performance, as a way of measuring value to the organization, and also the need for integrating social software in the flow of work, as a critical success factor when it comes to driving adoption.

ENTERPRISE 2.0: CURRENT CHALLENGES

Andrew McAfee (2009) wrote in his Enterprise 2.0 book about one of the big shifts witnessed from Web 1.0 to Web 2.0 which was "the realization that software could be social – that in addition to making individuals more productive and automating away their roles in a process, software could and should be used to let people find one another and form communities" (p. 139).

Several years before, in the spring of 2006, the same McAfee published in the MIT Sloan Management Review magazine an article entitled Enterprise 2.0: The Dawn of Emergent Collaboration. The article, taking on the example of the investment bank Dresdner Kleinwort Wasserstein (DrKW) to reflect on the use of Web 2.0 tools inside organizations, is generally viewed as the text that coined the Enterprise 2.0 expression. And it opened up with a question: "Do we finally have the right technologies for knowledge work?" (McAfee, 2006, p. 21). That article is said to be one of the first case studies that shows how the use of software—in the particular form of social software—could help an organization work and share knowledge in a more efficient and human way.

Several years have passed now but the concept, its frontiers, advantages and challenges are still being discussed and researched, as more and more companies use the so-called social tools internally and report their experience and results.

And several years after that groundbreaking article the division persists: on one side the evangelists and overall enthusiasts of Enterprise 2.0

praise the benefits of the use of social software in the workplace, while on the other side the sceptics are less convinced and compare it to the promise, to many undelivered, of the Knowledge Management tools and practices some years ago.

Miller, Marks and DeCoulode (2011) from The Deloitte Center for the Edge state that Enterprise 2.0 is very different from traditional Knowledge Management methodologies and tools as the use of social software inside companies allows them to go one step further. With Enterprise 2.0 tools and methodologies, companies can actually create new knowledge whereas Knowledge Management was usually confined to the capture and sharing of existing knowledge.

But if it is true that Enterprise 2.0 draws on something that Knowledge Management seemed to miss – the importance of human-to-human interactions and conversations (thus the social component) in sharing tacit knowledge, the hardest form of knowledge to capture, and as well as in creating new knowledge – it is also true that some, if not most, of the social software experiences inside the enterprise are failing to deliver the expected adoption rates and return on investment (ROI).

Many Enterprise 2.0 projects are just pushed at executives, middle-managers and employees as Knowledge Management 2.0 projects or as a new way to communicate, with very little focus on performance improvement (Miller, Marks & DeCoulode, 2011).

In parallel, board members and top management usually question the true business benefits of Enterprise 2.0 and demand proof of the potential business value prior to supporting groundswell initiatives or to giving green light to investments in more customized and comprehensive (hence costly) platforms. As McKinsey stated in their late-2010 research on the use of social tools for business "management is trying to understand if they are a passing fad or an enduring trend that will underwrite a new era of better corporate performance" (Bughin & Chui, 2011, p. 2).

John Stepper, collaboration and social media evangelist at the Deutsch Bank, told the audience of the 2011 Enterprise 2.0 conference in Boston how his pitch for senior executives, asking for an investment sum for an enterprise platform and a small team, was received with the following reaction: "What problem are you trying to solve?" (Stepper, 2011, para. 11). This example helps to demonstrate the point of this chapter: the impact on business performance, including problem solving issues, should be considered from the outset when it comes to planning and implementing an Enterprise 2.0 project. And for that impact to be accomplished and noticeable, adoption of these social tools in the context of how work gets done is essential. For this matter, social software needs to be integrated into business processes and in the flow of work.

ENTERPRISE 2.0 AND BUSINESS PERFORMANCE

Current Challenges and Considerations in Enterprise 2.0 Implementation

As with any other concept or technology, implementation and adoption are two key issues when discussing Enterprise 2.0. The big questions of what (a single Enterprise 2.0 platform or several applications that can be integrated), how (bottom-up or top-down approach; led by managers or led by the IT department; starting with a small pilot project or going enterprise-wide) and when (advance now or wait until some applications and players mature) naturally emerge. But most importantly, organizations should start by defining why: what are the key goals of an Enterprise 2.0 project.

Before diving into the topic of the why, the key focus of this chapter, let us explore briefly the topic of the what—the technology side of the

Enterprise 2.0 project—leaving aside the how and when, less relevant for this particular discussion.

Understanding the different capabilities that social software enables, and in turn the impact of each technological functionality in enabling those capabilities, is very important when it comes to defining the technology focus of an Enterprise 2.0 project. Different authors look at these capabilities and tools from different perspectives, thus generating distinct frameworks.

Cook (2008) classified the different functionalities according to four Cs—communication, cooperation, collaboration, and connection—placing them on a matrix formed by two axes: the level of interaction enabled by a certain technology and the level of formality required by each technology. According to Cook, connection and collaboration require more formality than communication and cooperation mainly because they rely on people doing things in a more structured way. And collaboration and cooperation require higher levels of interaction because they have a higher focus on group than on individuals.

The two axes of interaction and formality, and the resulting four quadrants, thus serve as a guide for companies to prioritize the introduction of different forms of Enterprise 2.0 software (deciding where to focus their time and effort) into their organizations. For that, consider that interaction refers to the relations between different groups inside a company, and that formality looks at the organizational structure of that company. So, a company with predominantly formal organizational structures and a culture of group interaction will benefit most from software that enables collaboration. Similarly, an organization with an informal structure and a culture that rewards individual effort may prefer to invest in tools for communication purposes.

The framework by Miller et al. (2011) from The Deloitte Center for the Edge outlines five main capabilities: identifying expertise, facilitating cross-boundary communication & conversation, preserving institutional memory, harnessing distributed knowledge and discovering emerging opportunities. Each capability can then be more or less enabled depending on the technology functionalities employed. For example, social networking functionalities are very relevant for identifying internal expertise but not so much for preserving institutional memory. Wikis, on the other hand, are particularly relevant when it comes to preserving institutional memory but less adequate for facilitating cross-boundary communication & conversation.

So Miller et al. (2011) have also put together a matrix that combines the five main capabilities with the different categories of social technology (wikis, blogs, etc.), with an indication, using a relevance scale that goes from not applicable to high, of the fit between a certain capability and a certain tool. When compared to the framework proposed by Cook (2008), this matrix seems grounded on concepts that are more concrete, and therefore easier for executives to understand and use.

Nonetheless, whatever framework a company uses as a guide, it should first think about the objectives that an Enterprise 2.0 project will help enable and only then return to the chosen framework in order to understand the pieces of technology (blogs, wikis, etc.) that need to be deployed.

Coming back to the topic of the why, usually the main driver of an Enterprise 2.0 project, common to the vast majority of companies, will be to harness their internal collective intelligence, preparing the company for the connectedness demanded by the challenging environment of the 21st century, and trying to derive an important competitive advantage. Nevertheless, and in order to achieve this key long-term goal, an Enterprise 2.0 project will need to serve some smaller and short to medium-term objectives that help prepare for the future accomplishment of the greater strategy. No organization transforms itself overnight into a 21st century connected entity. Enterprise 2.0 is a road, not a destination. So companies usually set goals such as improving knowledge sharing and collaboration internally, breaking down departmental or geographical silos, and improving ideation and innovation processes. A new way of working, collaborating and sharing knowledge in the medium run is thus generally the overall aim.

But as Marks and Patel (2010) recently pointed out, using social software to help enable the values of transparency, openness, agility and collaboration, key factors of the future of work and businesses, whilst generating value to the business, together with managing the envisioned change in the way employees work and share knowledge, can be extremely challenging.

An Enterprise 2.0 project will have to solve specific business problems that are currently preventing an organization from reaping the benefits of their collective thinking: it will pave the road to guarantee a smooth ride. So companies should first start by identifying opportunities for improvement, or business problems that need to be addressed, and then evaluate how an Enterprise 2.0 project could help bridge the gaps. Only after defining the objectives can a company think about the how, what and when. But identifying the specific problems that these new social technologies will help solve, and defining the metrics and methods to measure the efficiency of these projects from a business perspective, are two key challenges often cited. So, where do companies start?

Current Research and the Importance of Business Performance

The topic of the use of social software inside companies and business performance has been address in one way or the other in recent research. At the beginning of 2011 Gartner's research of 200 successful social media implementations indicated that, when it came to the use of social tools inside organizations, "pursuing collective intelligence to achieve operational effectiveness is one of the most successful social media adoption trends" (Gartner, 2011, para. 6).

The consultancy company McKinsey has been doing some important, and pioneering, work in trying to sense and evaluate the impact of Web 2.0 in the enterprise, conducting an annual worldwide survey on the use of social tools for internal and external purposes (in this last case, connecting and collaborating with stakeholders such as customers or suppliers). In the 4th edition of their annual survey, McKinsey asked respondents to report measurable business benefits obtained from the use of these social tools for business. Amongst organizations using them for internal purposes, 40% reported a decrease in operational costs and 29% a reduced time to market for products and services (Bughin & Chui, 2010).

But why is it important to address the topic of business performance and operational efficiency when considering the use of social software inside the enterprise? Isn't business performance being accounted for by existing technologies? What could be the impact of these social tools in operational efficiency?

Marks and Patel (2010) pointed to something that helps frame the issue: when it comes to repeatable and clearly defined business processes, current technologies in place seem fairly capable of contributing to operational efficiency, aiding workers in their day-to-day tasks. But challenges arise when exceptions that disrupt the clearly defined processes emerge, calling for human intervention, brainstorming and collaboration, many times with the need to go beyond the boundaries of departments or business divisions to find the right solutions or internal expertise. This same view on the deficiencies of existing technologies to cope with the challenges of managing the 21st enterprise is shared in the research of Miller et al. (2011). And here is precisely where social software inside the enterprise can make a difference: it can help employees reach for valuable weak ties inside their organizations.

In the article "Managing the 21st Century Organization," Krebs (2007) demonstrated the value of using social network analysis inside companies to visualize the networked enterprise: the representation of how individuals and teams inside organizations are really connected and how knowledge is shared. In a nutshell, visualizing how work really gets done when we look beyond the hierarchical representation of a company. As Krebs (2007) noted, "an organization's knowledge sharing and learning are often informal processes dependent upon social ties for transmission" (p. 3), adding an important reminder that "better connections are those that provide you access to nodes that you currently do not have access to." (p. 4).

The importance of these so called weak ties has been stressed in the work of Granovetter (1973) that in his paper The Strength of Weak Ties concluded that "weak ties... are here seen as indispensable to individuals' opportunities and to their integration into communities." (p. 1378). The concept of strong and weak ties resurfaced in the context of social tools inside companies in McAfee's 2009 book Enterprise 2.0. There McAfee (2009) explained that "the ability to form, maintain, and exploit weak ties and the ability to convert potential ties into actual ones (either strong or weak) are both hugely valuable assets, both to individuals and to enterprises in which they work." (p. 88).

Social software is an important enabler of network connections inside an organization, especially amongst those colleagues that do not already form part of the same working groups or departments and thus rarely have the chance to connect (the weaker ties), this being particularly true in, but not exclusive of, large and geographically dispersed organizations. Truth is that many times the answer to an employee's business problem or the piece of information that she is looking for is already inside the organization, if only she knew who to contact. Reaching to a network of ties inside the company is especially valuable because an employee can speedily and in an agile way tap into those ties to get the answer she was looking for. And chances are that the answer is probably in a weak tie.

It is also true that we generally prefer to find and connect to another person when looking for help in addressing a certain problem or searching for a certain solution, more than just searching for and retrieving a document. The recommendation, help or knowledge of another colleague adds an important layer of context to a static piece of information. Semple (2007) emphasized the importance of context when in an article he wrote "having context in the question, context in the answer and the collective memory of your corporate meatspace, empowered by the mighty hyper-link, in between is hard to beat" (para. 5).

Coming back to the note made by Marks and Patel (2010) regarding how employees are dealing with exceptional situations that occur ever more frequently, meaning that they need to reach out to other colleagues in an agile and speedy way, and taking into consideration the importance of looking at the enterprise as a networked entity that needs tools to stimulate and enable that connectedness, we can see the important role that social tools can play inside companies. And, as we begin to understand, this important role of providing the connectivity tissue of an organization, giving context to information and strengthening social ties, can (and should) have an impact on business performance.

In 2011 the research from The Deloitte Center for the Edge explored the link between social software and business performance with greater detail, and the result can be summed up to this: "social software has the potential to address operational "pain points" and significantly enhance business performance in the short-term and transform it in the long-term" (Miller et al., 2011, p. 4). The *father* of the Enterprise 2.0 concept, Andrew McAfee, praised such a research for being "the first long-term, before-and-after data on Enterprise 2.0 that I'm aware of, and I'm grateful for the team's work" (McAfee, 2011a, para. 13).

The reason for focusing such a research on business performance is that The Deloitte Center for the Edge believes that if social software implementation does not impact business performance then it will fail to deliver concrete value to the organization. And if value cannot be achieved and measured, then the concept of Enterprise 2.0 will fall short of its promise. In other words, implementation of social software in the enterprise needs to go beyond the focus of what could be seen as vague goals (such as better collaboration and greater employee engagement), to more concrete objectives of improving business performance, especially in what concerns operational efficiency. And metrics need to go beyond adoption figures, like the number of users registered or the number of blog posts created, metrics that usually fail to capture frequency or sustained use, to metrics that show improved performance.

This is not to say that those adoption metrics, easier to track and share, are not valuable, nor that they should not be captured or shared. These adoption figures, together with small anecdotes derived from the first interaction of employees with the tools, form many times the first set of *success* stories told around the use of social software inside companies, acting as small *quick wins* to get other employees or departments to join the effort. They are many times the prime (and sometimes even the sole) material that internal evangelists can use to *spread the word*. But it should be noted that they shouldn't be the only set of metrics the company is tracking, or intends to track and measure, in order to understand the progress of the implementation of an Enterprise 2.0 project.

The focus on business performance is also important for another set of reasons. A research entitled Social Business Systems - success factors for Enterprise 2.0 applications, conducted in 2011 by the Association for Information and Image Management (AIIM), asked respondents what were the three biggest issues with Enterprise 2.0 applications in their respective organizations. Two of the three most cited issues were non-involvement of senior staff, referred by 36% of those surveyed, closely followed by too much social, not enough business, cited by almost 25% of respondents (AIIM, 2011). If senior staff fails to see the business value of these social tools in the enterprise, then they will surely not feel the appeal to participate. And they will also most certainly refrain from approving investments in this area, as the story shared by Stepper (2011) cited previously clearly showed.

But if the need to demonstrate business value is critical for getting the top management to approve investments in social tools, and also to guarantee their involvement and leadership by example when projects are implemented, employees too need to understand the value and impact that this new way of working will have in their daily work.

The top issue revealed from that same AIIM (2011) survey was the reluctance of staff to contribute. The reasoning here can be two-fold. First, the organization's culture—the beliefs, values, norms, and habits that embody the way things get done around here—may not be one that stimulates participation. Companies cannot expect to simply deploy the tools and have an army of employees eager to jump on board and share their knowledge (the build it and they will come belief has generally proven to be false).

Secondly, employees may not feel that contributing will help them in any way. In a time where they are expected to work under a more, better, faster motto, surrounded by an increasingly challenging competitive environment that demands them to be ever more agile and productive, the introduction of new tools that demand their attention, dedication and time without helping them improve their performance is doomed to fail. The new tools will become, sooner or later, just another component of an already complex landscape of enterprise applications, intranets and the like that seem to provide little real value when it comes to day-to-day tasks and problems. This topic will be addressed later in this chapter.

But if results from recent research point to the need of grounding Enterprise 2.0 projects to concrete business objectives, especially those related to business performance, how do companies determine exactly which objectives to tie in to the implementation of social tools? Again, the research of Miller et al. (2011) from The Deloitte Center for the Edge provides some important guidance. No one doubts that we currently face challenging times, with a fast pace of change that demands great adaptability and agility from organizations big or small. One of the consequences of this increasing pace of change, and the complexity it generates, is the growth in the number of exceptional situations that employees are faced with: situations that escape predefined and clearly mapped business procedures. Think of occurrences like a customer with a particular problem or requirement, demanding (or at least expecting) a speedy feedback and resolution.

These exception handling situations are increasingly frequent. Hagel and Brown co-authored an article for the Harvard Business Review Blog Network where they stated that "in our informal surveys, we have found that as much as two-thirds of headcount time in major enterprise functions like marketing, manufacturing and supply chain management is spent on exception handling" (Hagel & Brown, 2010, para. 12).

As had already been hinted in this chapter, this is one of the areas where social software brings great potential value to businesses by improving the access to people, data and knowledge not easily accessible in the context of clearly defined business processes. And it is, thus, a first and important lead of the linkage between social technologies inside the enterprise and business performance: improving agility and swiftness in problem solving when exceptions occur. In other words, improving speed and agility of response and therefore operational performance.

Miller et al. (2011) summed the importance of looking at this topic when they referred that "while social software can be applied against a variety of business challenges to yield performance improvement, exception handling offers one of the best opportunities to prove the concept and overcome skepticism" (p. 7). It is to say that the disruption and unbalance caused by the increase in exceptional situations impacting operational activities of organizations, consuming time and energy from employees that struggle to find the right resource or piece of information to deal with those exceptions, combined with the capabilities of social tools in solving those problems, set a powerful starting point when it comes to defining the purpose and key initial focus of an Enterprise 2.0 project.

So how would a framework for developing an Enterprise 2.0 project in light of the business performance focus look like? Companies should start by recognizing a situation (pain point) that could be addressed by social tools in the enterprise, identify the associated operating metric (and preferably also the related financial metrics), reflect on which social software capabilities are critical to help deal with that pain point, and only then think about the technology side of the equation. This is what Miller et al. (2011) call a focused implementation: one that starts by looking at a particular problem or difficulty, one that impacts business performance, and only then starts developing the basis for the Enterprise 2.0 project. "Clarity about goals brings clarity about means", wrote McAfee (2009) in his book on Enterprise 2.0 (p. 142).

The research by Miller et al. (2011) cites the example of OSIsoft, a US company developing enterprise software to manage real-time data and events, which used social software to improve an operating metric—average time to issue resolution—affected by the increasing difficulties of the customer support team in quickly providing accurate answers to customer questions. The company followed a focused implementation: identifying the capabilities that needed to be leveraged—identifying expertise, improving cross-boundary communication and conversation, preserving institutional memory, and harnessing distributed knowledge—and the corresponding social tools functionalities. The result? A 22% improvement in average issue resolution time and, according to that same research, "reductions in average time to issue resolution translated to cost savings and increased productivity" (Miller et al., 2011, p. 10), which means that the impact on an operational metric also derived benefits at the financial level.

Another starting point may be to begin looking for initiatives already underway in the company that can be substantially leveraged by the use of social software. Many companies, especially in manufacturing sectors, may already have internal communities of practice that get together to share and discuss best practices leading to overall operational improvements through cost savings or improved efficiency. These communities, especially in larger and geographically disperse organizations, can receive a significant boost in performance and agility with the use of social tools to facilitate contextual communication, discussion, and sharing. So an Enterprise 2.0 project should look internally for good examples of multi-disciplinary groups already working together towards performance improvement and collective problem solving and think: how can social software help gather momentum for these initiatives or make group discussions more nimble and rich?

Of course this approach needs to leave space for other important topics that are bound to be crucial in later stages of the project: scalability and emergence. There is the danger that an Enterprise 2.0 project that is too focused on the needs of certain areas of the company (in the case of a focused implementation as the one developed for OSIsoft those areas more closely related to customer service), will encounter difficulties when trying to scale to an enterprise-wide level.

Also, the 21st century enterprise, as an internal and externally connected entity, is one that evolves with the interaction of the different nodes and clusters in the network (Krebs, 2007). Think of life in perpetual beta but for organizations. This draws attention to the concept of emergence outlined by Hinchcliffe (2007) referring to a system that co-evolves with its users. In both cases the flexibility and adaptability of the chosen social tool is important and should also be considered from the outset of the project. Adapting a well-known mantra—start small, move fast, think big—we could think of Enterprise 2.0 as a start focused, move fast, think enterprise-wide project.

When it comes to measurement of results obtained, this is usually one of the most difficult items in many software projects, and an Enterprise 2.0 implementation, with the added complexity of being more than just a software project, is no exception. There is much discussion in the Enterprise 2.0 space around the topic of Return On Investment (ROI) and also around the lack of use cases that report more than just vague and cumulative adoption metrics such as the number of blog posts or entries to wikis. On this last issue some claim that if companies are deriving real competitive advantage from the internal use of social software then they may not be very open to publicly sharing their achievements, as author McAfee (2011a) emphasized.

Authors, such as Newman and Thomas (2009) sometimes distinguish between *soft* and *hard* benefits, the first set referring to metrics such as increased employees' productivity and satisfaction or better collaboration, usually captured via internal surveys or small anecdotes collected to help prove the validity and results obtained with the internal use of social tools. The second set usually includes benefits such as reduced email volume (communication moves from the inbox to the social tools), decrease in travel costs (as online collaboration improves) or increase in revenues from ideas generated using social software.

When it comes to measuring the impact on business performance, a focused implementation, starting with a clearly defined problem or pain point that has an associated operating indicator, gives a concrete indication on the key metric (or set of metrics) that should be tracked and evaluated. Of course one might question if concurring factors are easy to isolate. Was OSIsoft's performance improvement achieved only due to the use of social software? Could other factors be in fact contributing to this improvement? It is up to each company to try to isolate as much as possible the effects of the use of social tools from other also positive benefits.

A focused implementation seems to help address two key challenges discussed previously: the scepticism of executives regarding the benefits and impact of social software, and also the low level of participation by employees. As the research of Miller et al. (2011) indicated "showing how a social tool can improve an operational metric can prompt managers to use social software and to encourage their employees to use it as well" (p. 9).

But is employee adoption something that you dictate by mandate? If it is true that employees are likely to be more motivated to use a tool that directly addresses a problem (pain point) that they face in a certain business process, is this sufficient to encourage them to use it? This brings us to the topic of employee adoption.

Road to Adoption: Integrating Social Software into the Flow of Work

The nature of the Enterprise 2.0 concept has always been grounded on principles of openness, emergence, willingness to participate and voluntary action. Social tools in the enterprise are usually non-obligatory, following an opt-in concept that accommodates for both the voluntary nature of the concept (people participate because they want to connect with colleagues, share their knowledge and expertises, and participate in online internal communities) and also for legal questions regarding individual privacy, especially in the European Union (Frappaolo, 2010).

Previously in this chapter we have seen how an AIIM (2011) survey pointed to the reluctance of staff to contribute as a top issue in what concerns Enterprise 2.0 adoption. The question is that an Enterprise 2.0 project that fails to reach, inside the organization, the equivalent of the Internet concept of critical mass, will hardly produce the expected results because it will be lacking a base of committed users that give life to a networked and user-generated ecosystem.

This means that adoption clearly matters. If so, how to drive adoption of social software inside an organization? Opinions diverge but overall there's a consensus that the strategy to get employees on board may be very different from one organization to another and, therefore, that no unique solution exists. Some companies, striving to break down information silos, may try to enforce the use of social tools as a substitute for email communications in the management of projects, for example, while others may opt for strategies of raising awareness to the benefits of the social tools vis-à-vis existing ones, though not enforcing them onto their workforce. Some companies may also tie some of the employees' incentives and rewards to their collaborative effort, measured through their contributions to the wikis, comments, and so forth.

But an important aspect needs to be taken into account: the company's culture may be one that does not stimulate employees' participation and therefore just throwing some technology at the problem will certainly not solve it. Some companies, understanding this, seem prepared to embark into a change management journey to adapt to a new way of working.

But another reason may help explain why many companies deploying social software internally usually report difficulties in adoption: in the words of Buczek (2011), a practitioner in the area of Enterprise 2.0, "the big failure of social business is a lack of integration of social tools into the collaborative workflow" (para. 3). This empirical view from someone responsible for leading an internal social collaboration effort for a large global enterprise is corroborated by the results of some research and by the opinions of many thought leaders in the field of Enterprise 2.0, such as Dion Hinchcliffe, Andrew McAfee, Bertrand Duperrin or Emanuele Quintarelli.

The motive seems quite straightforward: if social tools are yet another addition to the already complex puzzle of technology that employees have at work, usually consisting of a variety of systems, intranets and extranets with little integration between them, they will ask themselves how the new tools will improve their productivity and help them do their job. If they cannot find real value in them, the initial enthusiasm caused by the novelty of those social tools will quickly fade away as the normal rhythm of day-to-day tasks and challenges imposes itself. Sooner or later the project team of the Enterprise 2.0 project, in many cases stimulated by the initial uptake in the number of employees visiting or contributing to the internal digital social environment, will struggle to boost adoption rates or to maintain sustained rates of usage.

This argument was supported by the research done by the McKinsey Group in 2009 with their 3rd edition of the annual survey on the use of social tools for business. When reflecting on the results from that research, and on the conclusions they could draw on which were the key success factors for making social software work inside the enterprise, Chui, Miller, and Roberts (2009) clearly stated that "participatory technologies have the highest chance of success when incorporated into a user's daily workflow" (p. 4). In fact, 75% of respondents to McKinsey's survey that claimed to be observing measurable benefits from those technologies said that one of the most important practices for success of social tools for business was integrating the use of Web 2.0 into employees' day-to-day work activities (Bughin, Chui & Miller, 2009).

This conclusion was reinforced in the findings of the 4th edition of that same survey in 2010 when McKinsey's researchers, reflecting on the findings, suggested as a specific step: "integrate the use of Web 2.0 into employees' day-to-day work activities. This practice is the key success factor in all of our analyses, as well as other research we have done" (Bughin & Chui, 2011, p. 8).

The research from The Deloitte Center for the Edge, already cited in this chapter, studied social software adoption at Alcoa Fastening Systems, a global business unit of Alcoa that designs and manufactures fastening systems for the aerospace and industrial industries, and discovered that as employees realized that the use of the social tools helped them perform better at work, they integrated their use into the workflow (Miller et al., 2011). We shouldn't forget, however, that the project at Alcoa is an example of a focused implementation, with a clear emphasis on improving productivity and reducing exception handling, which could in fact favour employees' perception on the positive impact that the use of social tools could have in their daily work.

The research of AIIM (2011) pointed to the need of firmly embedding social tools in business processes and applications, as a means to guaranteeing adoption. Hinchcliffe (2011), reflecting on the integration and connection of social tools to the workflow, articulated that "the isolation of social business platforms from the key operational activities of the organization is increasingly understood as a root cause of slower adoption and lower relevance" (para. 4). These two authors take the concept of integration into the flow of work one step further, as embedding of social tools may imply the tight integration of a social dimension into existing processes and systems as Customer Relation Management (CRM), for example, giving rise to concepts such as social CRM that we will not explore in this chapter. This calls for a tighter connection between systems of records (tools such as Enterprise Resource Planning – ERP – or CRM where structured work gets done) and systems of engagement (social tools that strengthen ties and communication between employees).

McAfee (2011b) also explored the topic of the connection of what he called formal (structured and pre-defined) and informal (unstructured and emergent) work by claiming that "the digital environments that support the formal and informal work should also be very close to each other, either within the same application or across tightly integrated ones" (para. 5).

With more or less integration, it all boils down to demonstrating the value of social software in employees' productivity and problem-solving capabilities, and thus making sure that those social tools serve in fact as regular work tools. A focused implementation, with a key emphasis on improving business performance and satisfying business needs as in the case of Alcoa Fastening Systems mentioned earlier, will certainly be conductive to workers realizing the benefits of social tools for their productivity.

Besides that, companies too often presume that their workforce will know how to use that technology in the context of work, when most of them are only used to resorting to similar tools in the social Web to connect with family and friends. This means that, besides resorting to focused implementations and integrating social software into the flow of work, companies also need to educate their employees on how those tools can help them improve their productivity. Leading by example is important and thus management sponsorship and role model behaviour are also important success factors to driving adoption in a business context.

FUTURE RESEARCH DIRECTIONS

Following some maturity of the Enterprise 2.0 concept and practices, especially in the United States, and the outcomes from the initiatives of the early adopting companies, there has been one main discussion topic generating much debate when it comes to the topic of social in a business context. Some call it Social Business, others focus on specific business processes and speak of Social CRM or others, thus with an implied concept of socializing the value chain. Carter (2011) reflects on the distinction between social media and Social Business as she states that the later "expands the usage and efficiencies beyond "media and marketing" to all of a company's processes, both internal... and external" (p. 5). Quintarelli (2011) focused on the topic of socializing the extended value chain, reflecting on the challenges that companies currently face, how different social technology vendors are approaching these challenges, and thinking about a four steps approach to that topic.

No matter how wide or narrow the focus is, truth is that these concepts are still in their infancy and therefore more research is needed to study the challenges and results of companies that *went social*, both internally and externally, and tightly integrated these two dimensions as one single social enterprise. Furthermore, greater consensus on the definitions and frontiers of each concept—Enterprise 2.0, Social Business, etc.—would be greatly valuable to advance the discussion beyond the basics or the buzzwords. The road to prepare businesses for the 21st century is still being paved.

CONCLUSION

Many Enterprise 2.0 implementations are failing to produce the expected results and adoption levels, and several executives are still sceptic about the benefits of social software for business. To this reality surely contributed an excessive emphasis on vaguer concepts such as better collaboration or an empowered workforce, and a lack of focus on business performance. The problem is that if projects cannot impact business processes and performance then they will hardly impact business value.

The concept of focused implementation helps address this issue, looking at operational problems (*pain points*) and applying social software capabilities to help solve them. The emphasis is thus on business needs and problem solving, striving for a concrete and measurable impact on business performance, especially at the operational level. This also helps address the always cumbersome task of tracking the right metrics when it comes to measuring Enterprise 2.0 success: by focusing on clearly identified business problems and needs at the operating level, the identification of the correct metrics is facilitated.

But adoption also needs to be stimulated to make sure that a threshold level of participation is attained in order to guarantee that network effects are facilitated. Too often the initial enthusiasm with social tools at the office soon fades away as the regular workload gets in the way. To overcome this, and really derive benefits from Enterprise 2.0 projects, social tools need to be integrated into the flow of work. Employees need to understand the benefits of social software to improve their productivity and problem solving skills, and should also be educated on the use of social tools in a work context.

The discussion on the use of social software for business is now heading for the bigger picture of the Social Business concept: the enterprise as an entity that embeds social into business processes, touching beyond its own borders to connect with external stakeholders. Further discussion is needed to reach consensus on the concept and future research needs to concentrate on the benefits and challenges that fully networked (both internally and externally) businesses are encountering.

REFERENCES

Buczek, L. (2011). *The big failure of enterprise 2.0 social business*. Retrieved October 1, 2011, from http://www.lauriebuczek.com

Bughin, J., & Chui, M. (2011). The rise of the networked enterprise: Web 2.0 finds its payday. [from http://www.mckinseyquarterly.com]. *The McKinsey Quarterly*, *22*, 2–9. Retrieved September 15, 2011

Bughin, J., Chui, M., & Miller, A. (2009). McKinsey global survey results: How companies are benefitting from web 2.0. *The McKinsey Quarterly*. Retrieved September 3, 2009, from http://www.mckinseyquarterly.com

Carter, S. (2011). *Get social: Using social media to create a new type of social business*. Hoboken, NJ: IBM Press.

Chui, M., Miller, A., & Roberts, R. P. (2009). Six ways to make web 2.0 work. [from http://www.mckinseyquarterly.com]. *The McKinsey Quarterly*, 1–7. Retrieved April 24, 2009

Cook, N. (2008). *Enterprise 2.0: How social software will change the future of work*. Hampshire, UK: Gower Publishing Limited.

Frappaolo, C. (2010). Implementing enterprise 2.0 within the European Union. *The 2.0 Adoption Council*. Retrieved September 1, 2011, from http://info.newsgator.com

Gartner. (2011). *Gartner says enterprises that harness the power of collective behaviors will be the ultimate winners with social media*. Retrieved February 28, 2011, from http://www.gartner.com

Granovetter, M. (1973). The strength of weak ties. *American Journal of Sociology*, *78*(6), 1360–1380. doi:10.1086/225469.

Hagel, J., & Brown, J. S. (2010). *The enterprise value of social software*. Retrieved September 1, 2011, from http://blogs.hbr.org

Hagel, J. III, Brown, J. S., & Davidson, L. (2010). *The power of pull: How small moves, smartly made, can set big things in motion*. New York: Basic Books.

Hinchcliffe, D. (2007). *The state of enterprise 2.0*. Retrieved September 1, 2011, from http://www.zdnet.com

Hinchcliffe, D. (2011). *Integration and connection to work are central to social business success*. Retrieved September 15, 2011, from http://www.ebizq.net

Krebs, V. (2007). Managing the 21st century organization. *IHRIM Journal*, *9*(4), 2–8.

Marks, O., & Patel, S. (2010). Enterprise 2.0 white paper: Accelerating business performance. *Sovos Group*. Retrieved September 1, 2011, from http://sovosgroup.com

McAfee, A. (2006). Enterprise 2.0: The dawn of emergent collaboration. *MIT Sloan Management Review*, *47*(3), 21–28.

McAfee, A. (2009). *Enterprise 2.0: New collaborative tools for your organization's toughest challenges*. Boston, MA: Harvard Business Press.

McAfee, A. (2011a). *Data from the edge*. Retrieved September 15, 2011, from http://andrewmcafee.org

McAfee, A. (2011b). *Putting enterprise 2.0 into context*. Retrieved September 15, 2011, from http://andrewmcafee.org

Miller, M., Marks, A., & DeCoulode, M. (2011). Social software for business performance. *The Deloitte Center for the Edge*. Retrieved February 23, 2011, from http://www.deloitte.com/

Newman, A. C., & Thomas, J. G. (2009). *Enterprise 2.0 implementation*. New York: McGraw Hill.

Quintarelli, E. (2011). *Socializing the extended value chain*. Retrieved September 30, 2011, from http://www.socialenterprise.it

Semple, E. (2007). *Survey proves 90% of managers are clueless*. Retrieved September 1, 2011, from http://www.fastforwardblog.com

Social Business Systems. (2011). *Success factors for enterprise 2.0 applications*. Retrieved October 30, 2011, from http://www.aiim.org

Stepper, J. (2011). *Don't retweet the revolution*. Retrieved October 1, 2011, from http://johnstepper.com

ADDITIONAL READING

Baird, C. H., & Parasnis, G. (2011). From social media to social CRM. *IBM Global Business Services*. Retrieved October 30, 2011, from http://www-935.ibm.com

Dawson, R. (2009). *Implementing enterprise 2.0: A practical guide to creating business value inside organizations with web technologies*. Advanced Human Technologies.

Duperrin, B. (2010). *A process approach to enterprise 2.0*. Retrieved October 1, 2011, from http://www.duperrin.com

Eccles, R. G., & Davenport, T. H. (2010). *Cognizant 2.0: Embedding community and knowledge into work processes embedding*. Boston: Harvard.

Hamel, G., & Labarre, P. (2011). *Inventing management 2.0*. Retrieved February 21, 2011, from http://blogs.wsj.com

Haque, U. (2010). *From social media to social strategy*. Retrieved September 15, 2011, from http://blogs.hbr.org

Hinchcliffe, D. (2010). *Communicating the value of social business*. Retrieved September 15, 2011, from http://www.dachisgroup.com

Lavoy, D. (2011). *Social business doesn't mean what you think it does, neither does enterprise 2.0*. Retrieved October 1, 2011, from http://www.cmswire.com

Li, C. (2010). How openness transforms organizations. In Li, C. (Ed.), *Open Leadership: How Social Technology Can Transform the Way You Lead* (pp. 243–269). San Francisco, CA: Jossey-Bass.

Moore, G. (2011). *Systems of engagement and the future of enterprise IT*. Retrieved October 30, 2011, from http://www.aiim.org

Patel, S. (2011). *BIG brands collaborate to accelerate performance*. Retrieved October 30, 2011, from http://www.pretzellogic.org

Rangaswami, J. P. (2011). *Curation in the enterprise: Actionable information*. Retrieved October 30, 2011, from http://confusedofcalcutta.com

Shah, R. (2011). *What do i do with this customer lead from my social network?* Retrieved November 4, 2011, from http://www.forbes.com

Tapscott, D. (2006). *Winning with the enterprise 2.0*. Retrieved October 30, 2011, from http://newparadigm.inorbital.com

Tapscott, D., & Williams, A. D. (2008). The wiki workplace. In Tapscott, D., & Williams, A. D. (Eds.), *The Wikinomics* (pp. 239–267). London: Atlantic Books.

Transforming collaboration with social tools. (2011). Retrieved October 30, 2011, from http://www.pwc.com

Weinberger, D. (2009). The hyperlinked organization. In Levine, R., Locke, C., Searls, D., & Weinberger, D. (Eds.), *The Cluetrain Manifesto: The End of Business as Usual* (pp. 187–231). New York: Basic Books.

KEY TERMS AND DEFINITIONS

Adoption: Use of social software, whether by simply registering/creating an account (less participatory) or by actively participating through comment, discussing, etc.

Business Performance: Balance of the outcomes of a company in key areas, usually associated with business processes, against the goals initially defined.

Business Processes: Set of activities and tasks associated with the completion of a certain output, be it a project or a product.

Collective Intelligence: Shared knowledge jointly constructed by a group of people through their collaboration and interactions.

Enterprise 2.0: Deployment of Web 2.0-style tools and practices inside organizations with the purpose of fostering collaboration and collective intelligence (employee-oriented).

Knowledge Management: The concept of capturing, retaining, and managing organizational knowledge, either tacit or explicit, with the purpose of guaranteeing that it can be kept and reused.

Social Business: A company that embeds social tools and practices both internally (employee-oriented) and externally (oriented to other stakeholders such as customers or other business partners) with an integrated approach.

Social CRM: The embedding of social tools and practices into the process of Customer Relationship Management with the purpose of better serving and understanding the market.

Social Software: Software inspired by the functionalities of Web 2.0 tools such as blogs, wikis, microblogging, social networks, and others.

Chapter 14
The Influence of (Online) Social Networks on Workers' Attitudes and Behaviours in Higher Education Institutions

Vera Silva Carlos
University of Beira Interior, Portugal

Ricardo Gouveia Rodrigues
University of Beira Interior, Portugal

ABSTRACT

According to the literature, social relationships have a positive influence on work-related attitudes and behaviours. Taking into account that Online Social Networks (OSNs), brought about by Web 2.0, have become an international phenomena and have a considerable impact on the way people communicate and interact with each other, the chapter's purpose is to evaluate the effect that the use of OSNs has on the worker's attitudes and behaviours. In this way, the authors use a questionnaire to evaluate the attitudes of 157 faculty members in Higher Education Institutions (HEI). To assess the use of OSNs by faculty members, they use a binary variable. After analysing and discussing the results, the authors conclude that the use of OSNs influences the workers' performance traits. The relations they propose in what concerns the workers' attitudes are all empirically proven. At last, the authors describe the study limitations and suggest some perspectives for future research.

DOI: 10.4018/978-1-4666-4373-4.ch014

INTRODUCTION

Nowadays, electronic social networks, the so-called Web 2.0, have taken on a high role and importance in the relationships between people and organizations. Castilla (2005) refers that social relationships are an important tool for the understanding of the workers' outcomes in the organizations and that it is necessary to understand the dynamics of these interactions. In this perspective, the main purpose of this study consists of evaluating the influence of Online Social Networks (OSNs) on the workers' attitudes and behaviours. Specifically, it is intended to evaluate to what extent the use of OSNs to maintain contact with co-workers influences job satisfaction, organizational commitment, organizational citizenship behaviours and individual performance. On the other hand, the intention is to verify whether there are positive relationships between the workers' attitudes and behaviours—some of them already proved in previous studies—specifically between satisfaction and commitment, satisfaction and organizational citizenship behaviours, satisfaction and performance, commitment and organizational citizenship behaviours, commitment and performance and organizational citizenship behaviours and performance. When the proposed relations are proved, it will be possible to broaden the understanding of each of the concepts being studied and increase their importance in the organizational context.

More than organizations in most sectors, Higher Education Institutions (HEI) know a great deal about facilitating environments in which people collaborate to create, share and advance knowledge. HEI should in this sense be very well prepared to reap value from the new online tools (Barnatt, 2008). In this scenario, it seems adequate to resort to the Higher Education (HE) context to investigate the proposed relations. HEI are characterized as community service providers, specifically of transference and economic value increase of the scientific and technological knowledge, which are autonomous and should define good management practice codes. The knowledge transference increase, as well as the fact that HE teachers have the duty to cooperate, justify the choice of context and the answering of a questionnaire given to the Professors as an instrument to gather data.

Firstly, the concepts that are being studied are briefly summarized. Then, two research models, based on 10 hypotheses, are proposed. After explaining and stating the hypotheses, the methodology is described and the results are presented and discussed. Finally, we describe the findings, the limitations of the study are explained and some guiding lines for future research are suggested. The methods used to analyse the results are the t-student test and the PLS method. It is possible to conclude that the use of OSNs to maintain contact with co-workers influences performance, specifically the individual's performance traits. We also verify that satisfaction positively influences commitment, organizational citizenship behaviours and performance, that commitment has a positive impact on organizational citizenship behaviours and on performance, and that organizational citizenship behaviours have a positive effect on performance.

THE WEB 2.0

Web 2.0 refers to the appearance of the Internet as an interpersonal resource and a service delivery platform (Barnatt, 2008). The term Web 2.0 is used to describe applications that distinguish themselves from preceding generations of software by a number of principles. Existing work shows that Web 2.0 applications can be successfully exploited for technology learning enhancement (Ullrich et al., 2008).

The second incarnation of the Web (Web 2.0) has been called the 'social Web', because, in contrast to Web 1.0, its content can be more easily generated and published by users, and because the collective intelligence of users encourages more democratic use. Originally, the World Wide Web (WWW) was intended to be used to share ideas and encourage discussion within a scientific community. Web 2.0 heralds a return to these original uses, and prompts important changes in the ways the World Wide Web is being used in education. In this context, there is a need to raise awareness of Web 2.0 tools and the possibilities they offer, and an imperative need to carry out quality research to inform better use of Web 2.0 applications (Boulos & Wheeler, 2007).

Web 2.0 sociable technologies and social software work as enablers for organizations. They include social networking services, collaborative filtering, social bookmarking, social search engines, file sharing and tagging, instant messaging, and online multi-player games. The more popular Web 2.0 applications in education, namely wikis, blogs and podcasts, are but the tip of the social software iceberg. Web 2.0 technologies represent a revolutionary way of managing and repurposing online information and knowledge repositories—including research information—in comparison with the traditional Web 1.0 model (Boulos & Wheeler, 2007)

Online Social Networks (OSNs)

According to Hoang and Antoncic (2003), there are three components that characterize a network: the content of relationships, its regulation and the structure or pattern that results from it. As to what the content is concerned, the relationships are seen as a means through which one of the parts has access to a variety of resources that the other part has. Regarding the regulation of relationships, the authors refer that there are several mechanisms that coordinate the exchanges in a relationship. The trust among the parts involved in the relationship, for example, constitutes a critical element, which improves the quality of the flow of resources in the relationship of exchange. The regulation of the networks can also be defined as the trust in implicit open contracts, which are based on social mechanisms, and not legally imposed. The structure of the network is defined as a pattern of relationships that are formed from the direct and indirect bonds among the organizational actors.

Bunt, Wittek, and Klepper (2005) state that there are two types of motives in the evolution of a network: expressive and instrumental. Many intra-organizational networks models postulate that relational dynamics are directed, primarily, by expressive motives. In this case, the reduction of cognitive dissonance in affective triads and the tendency that the individual has to bind with the ones he considers similar act as the main mechanisms for the formation of relationships. So, individual cognitions and attributes are the main factors that contribute to the evolution of networks. Other models have suggested that the work environment creates specific restrictions to the formation of social ties, which may limit or impede the mechanisms underlying the evolution of networks in 'natural' groups. There are two instrumental perspectives. One of them emphasizes the impact of the formal structures of the organizations, particularly the functional interdependences and the formal control strategies associated to the individuals' hierarchic position. At this rate, the interpersonal trust is modelled as a function of formally defined interdependence and power patterns. Individuals adapt to their formal work environment and manage critical dependences, incorporating them into social exchanges. Therefore, the dynamics of the informal networks is contingent to the formal organizational structure. The second instrumental perspective suggests that the interpersonal trust is a result of the individual's effort to optimize the benefits that his/her personal networks may generate, independently of his/her position in the formal structure. Based on these models, and after an empirical test, the authors conclude that both types of motives influence the evolution of networks, specifically organizational networks.

When it comes to organizational networks, it is relevant to refer that they function as communication channels and make the existence of resources exchange possible to several levels, including to the ideological level, as a form of spreading and sharing ideas. The formal transmission of knowledge among work groups, as well as the exchange of information that occurs in the organization, are fundamental aspects for the success of the network (Barbeira & Franco, 2009).

The use of OSNs has become an international phenomenon (Sledgianowski & Kulviwat, 2009; Benson, Filippaios, & Morgan, 2010), so they have a great impact on the way people communicate and interact with each other (Grabner-Kraeuter & Waiguny, 2011), providing an efficient and user-friendly way to maintain social relationships and share information. They have been shown to facilitate business relationships (Benson, Filippaios, & Morgan, 2010) and to build social capital (Benson, Filippaios, & Morgan, 2010; Young, 2011).

Modern technology has progressively transformed social interactions among people. With the emergence of Web 2.0 technologies, media such as blogs, instant messaging and social networking Websites are becoming ubiquitous, and they all provide a 'map' of communication paths among their users. Social networking sites such as MySpace and Facebook are particularly interesting examples, because they represent rich and popular communication interfaces for hundreds of millions of users. On these sites, users exhibit their demographics as well as their preferences by carefully editing their profiles. More important, they explicitly link to their friends and, in doing so, they reveal their likely communication patterns (Sledgianowski & Kulviwat, 2009).

OSNs function as tools to help individuals in the workforce organize their workload and life. When appropriately used and integrated into an organization's business plan and model they enable the organization and its workers to:

- Increase customer satisfaction \ timely responses to customer inquiries.
- Facilitate communication between customers and experts to share knowledge in areas of interest.
- Find experts within the organization as well as those outside with similar interests.
- Provide the whole product to fully meet a customer's needs, since customers can easily reveal their needs.
- Understand and visualize real communication paths within an organization and entire business process transaction.
- Extend the shelf life of conferences and organization meetings with an online network of attendees and databases (Asunda, 2010).

According to Young (2011), OSNs like Facebook strengthen existing friendships by supplementing traditional forms of communication (like face to face or telephone). Also, participation in the Facebook community enables efficient and convenient contact to be maintained with a larger and more varied group of acquaintances, thus, as mentioned before, extending potential social capital, that's a sociological concept related to the connections between social networks. An online social life does not detract from offline relationships. On the contrary, OSNs like Facebook provide an additional form of contact which is convenient when face-to-face or telephone is not possible or not desirable because the person is only a casual acquaintance.

Foster, Francescucci and West (2010) state that some participants of the OSNs have privacy concerns and may not have developed the confidence to contribute to new communities. Therefore, it is important that technology designers consider how to add in information about privacy settings into their site, as well as define better options to ensure that participants feel comfortable and that their privacy is protected. Having appropriate protection of privacy and personal information will develop and enhance trust within the community so that participants increase their confidence level to contribute in relevant and meaningful ways to the conversation. As it was mentioned before, trust is a critical element for the quality of the exchanges in a relationship.

WORK-RELATED ATTITUDES AND BEHAVIOURS

Job Satisfaction (JS)

There are few, if any, more central concepts for organizational psychology than for job satisfaction. (Judge et al., 2001, p. 25)

JS began to gather the interest of theorists, researchers and managers since the Taylorist model was compromised and the human factor in the company was given more importance (Vala et al., 1995). The concept has been originating some controversy (Staw, 1986), since it is characterized as a "complex emotional reaction to work" (Locke, 1968, p. 9) or as an attitude (Saari & Judge, 2004). Either way, satisfaction consists of a positive emotional state or a positive attitude towards work and the experiences that occur in the work environment (Vala et al., 1995).

In an effort to characterize and explain JS, several theories emerged. These theories are categorized in agreement with the two perspectives mentioned before: satisfaction as an emotional state, feelings and affective responses, and satisfaction as a generalized attitude towards work. There are also two distinct dimensions in what concerns JS: the global approach, based on the attitude towards work in general, not being a result of the sum of different aspects related to work, but depending on them, and the multidimensional approach, which is described as the satisfaction that reverses from a number of factors associated with work, and it is possible to measure satisfaction for each one of them (Alcobia, 2001).

JS theories may also be divided according to the following classification: (1) situational theories, which support that satisfaction is a result of the nature of work and environmental factors, (2) dispositional theories, according to which satisfaction results from personal and personality factors, (3) interactive theories, which suggest that JS derives from the interaction between personality factors and factors inherent to the situation. Dispositional theories are the most recent, but also the less developed ones. However, individual differences have been considered since investigation related to JS began (Judge et al., 2001).

The job characteristics model was suggested by Hackman and Oldham (1976) to measure three classes of variables: work objective characteristics, mediator psychological stages and individual needs of growth. According to this model, the central characteristics of each task – like the variety of competencies, the identity and the meaning of the tasks, the autonomy, the level of information provided to the worker about his/her performance, that is, the feedback – influence the individual's psychological stage. The function characteristics and satisfaction are also regulated by the worker's need for growth. The model can be used as a concept basis to identify the potential of job motivation, the workers' availability to respond positively to work improvement and to redesign specific characteristics of the jobs that need to be modified. Judge *et al.* (2001) state that, in this perspective, the jobs that have intrinsically motivating characteristics will lead to higher levels of motivation and even to a better performance. However, it is necessary to keep in mind that the individuals that want greater challenges and reveal a greater interest for work are, generally, more motivated and happier (Hackman & Oldham, 1976).

Organizational Commitment (OC)

Meyer and Herscovitch (2001) argue that the OC definitions, presented in the literature, have two common aspects: (1) commitment consists of a force of connection – a psychological or attitude stage, and (2) commitment determines a direction at the level of the individual's behaviour.

From the previous definitions of OC, Allen and Meyer (1990) created a commitment model, according to which the concept is composed of three dimensions: (1) affective, which consists of a connection, identification and involvement with the organization; (2) continuance, referring to the commitment based on the cost that the individual associates with leaving the organization; and (3) normative, related to the feelings of obligation to stay in the organization.

The perspective that will be adopted in this research is the one proposed by Cook and Wall (1980), who argue that the OC refers to the affective reactions to the characteristics of the employer organization. It is related to the worker's feelings of connection with the goals and values of the organization; to the role that he adopts in relation to them and to the connection with the organization with the aim of benefitting it, and not just for its instrumental value. Since this is a positive result of the experience of quality work, the concept can be considered a contributing factor to the well-being at work.

Organizational Citizenship Behaviours (OCB)

OCB are defined as 'extra-role' behaviours (Rego, 2002). The concept has different origins: (1) in Barnard's proposal (1938), according to which, the workers' will to cooperate is indispensable for the organization, (2) in the Katz and Khan (1970, 1974, 1987) distinctions in behavioural typologies facing the organizations, (3) in Organ's essay, which states that people can adopt a cooperative behaviour in order to respond reciprocally to the work experiences that provide satisfaction, as opposed to the behaviours inherent to the role, which depend on certain restrictions. Based on Organ's work (1977), Bateman and Organ (1983) measured this new kind of performance. From then on, several definitions and dimensions were proposed for the concept (Williams & Anderson, 1991; Graham, 1991; Van Dyne, Graham, & Dienesch, 1994; Organ & Moorman, 1993; Konovsky & Organ, 1996; Podsakoff, et al., 2000).

According to Rego (2002) and González and Garazo (2006), there are five dimensions of OCB that are more frequently used, which is in agreement with the literature:

1. **Altruism (Podsakoff, MacKenzie & Fetter, 1993; Organ & Lingl, 1995; Konovsky & Organ, 1996; Podsakoff & Mackenzie, 1997; Rego, Ribeiro & Cunha, 2009):** defined as 'helping behaviour' (Lo & Ramayah, 2009).
2. **Civic Virtue (Podsakoff, MacKenzie & Fetter, 1993; Organ & Lingl, 1995; Konovsky & Organ, 1996; Podsakoff & Mackenzie, 1997; Rego, Ribeiro & Cunha, 2010):** The responsibility of the subordinates to participate in the life of the organization (Podsakoff, et al., 2000).
3. **Sportsmanship (Podsakoff, MacKenzie & Fetter, 1993; Organ and Lingl, 1995; Konovsky & Organ, 1996; Podsakoff & Mackenzie, 1997; Rego, Ribeiro & Cunha, 2009):** Behaviour of warmly tolerating unavoidable irritations. Workers will assume new responsibilities and learn (Podsakoff & MacKenzie, 1997).
4. **Conscientiousness (Podsakoff, MacKenzie & Fetter, 1993; Rego, Ribeiro & Cunha, 2010):** Based on how organized, hardworking and responsible the worker is (Lo & Ramayah, 2009).
5. **Courtesy (Organ & Lingl, 1995; Konovsky & Organ, 1996; Rego, Ribeiro & Cunha, 2009):** Related to the prevention of problems at the work place (Lo & Ramayah, 2009).

Lo and Ramayah (2009) adopted Organ's conceptualization, according to which the OCB are 'extra-role' behaviours that arise as a way of acting beyond what is defined by work requirements, which means that the workers do non-mandatory tasks without expecting any rewards or recognition. The authors developed an instrument which contained the five dimensions more frequently found in literature, as it was mentioned before. The perspective of OCB adopted by these authors will be the one used in this study.

Individual Performance (IP)

Viswesvaran (2001) defines IP as behaviours that can be evaluated, but he points out that the difference between behaviours and results is not clear, since IP is composed of several behavioural manifestations, that are identifiable only through operational measures and that differ depending on the context in which they are applied.

In agreement with the theory of social capital, according to which the organizational theories focused on costs and on human capital are not adequate to respond to rapid changes on the nature of work, on the organizational structures and on the inter-organizational competitiveness (Dess & Shaw, 2001), a worker, fundamental for the organization, may be recognized for his/her capacity to have a high performance, as well as for his/her capacity to create value for the organization. In this way, the fundamental workers are those who have an influence on the other workers, who have knowledge and whose performance is characterized by the following aspects: (1) Skills to deal with organizational networks; (2) Skills to transmit organizational memory; (3) Flexible confidence; (4) Skills to energetically act in a team; (5) Influence in the performance chain/net; (6) Difficulty in being replaced; (7) Innovation traits (Xiaowei, 2006).

RESEARCH MODELS AND HYPOTHESIS

Literature points out the existence of positive relations among the social relationships established at work and:

1. Job Satisfaction (JS) (Castilla, 2005; Hurlbert, 2001)
2. Organizational Commitment (OC) (Donaldson, Ensher & Grant-Vallone, 2000)
3. Organizational Citizenship Behaviours (OCB) (Donaldson, Ensher & Grant-Vallone, 2000)
4. Individual Performance (IP) (Castilla, 2000)

Thus, we formulate the following research hypothesis:

- **H_1:** The use of OSNs to maintain contact with co-workers (OSN) influences JS.
- **H_2:** OSN influences OC.
- **H_3:** OSN influences OCB.
- **H_4:** OSN influences IP.

The hypotheses can be summarily represented by the research model in Figure 1.

According to some authors (Chang & Chang, 2007; Eker, Eker & Pala, 2008; Malik, Nawab & Naeem, 2010), satisfaction has a positive influence on commitment. In an attempt to assert these studies we propose H_5.

- **H_5:** JS has a positive impact on OC.

Literature also points out that satisfaction is positively related to OCB (Donavan, Brown, & Mowen, 2004; González & Garazo, 2006; Jones, 2006). Thus, we formulate the following hypothesis:

- **H_6:** JS has a positive impact on OCB.

Figure 1. Model 1

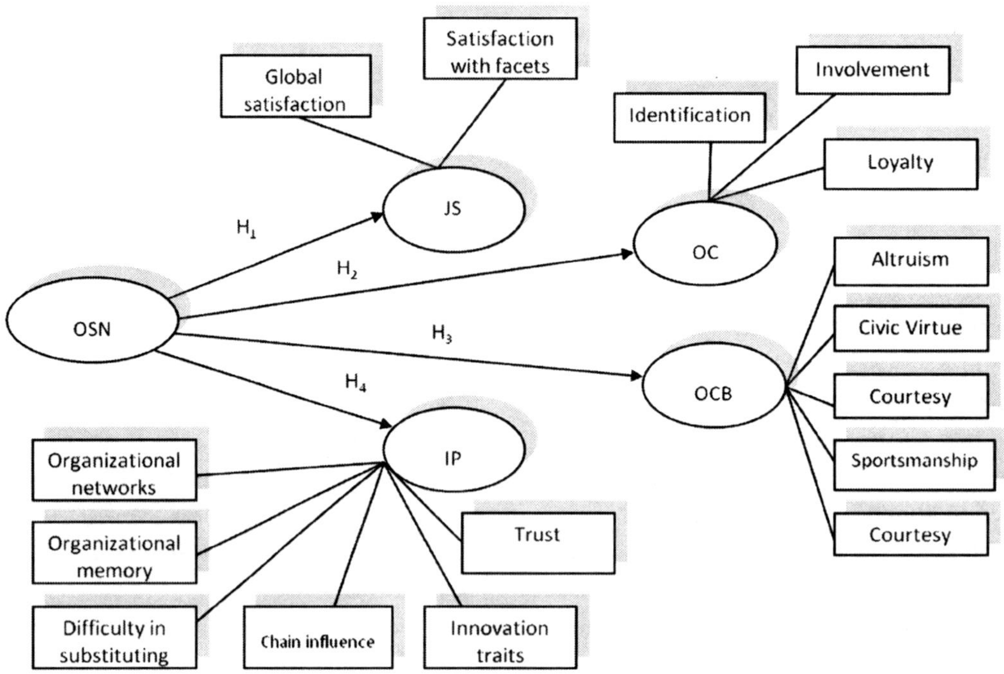

Samad (2005) and Jones (2006) refer that performance is positively influenced by satisfaction. These studies allow the formulation of the following hypothesis:

- **H_7:** JS has a positive impact on IP.

According to Donavan, Brown, and Mowen (2004), commitment has a positive impact on the OCB, specifically on the 'altruism' dimension. Lavelle *et al.* (2008) also investigated the relationship between OC and OCB and concluded that the affective commitment has an impact on OCB, characterized by the authors as the participation in meetings or events related to the organization. These studies allow the formulation of the following hypothesis:

- **H_8:** OC has a positive impact on OCB.

Samad (2005) found a positive impact of commitment on performance. The author adopts the perspective of Mowday *et al.* (1982), in which OC is defined as (1) the belief in the organization and the acceptance of its values and goals, (2) the will to make an effort to the well being of the organization and (3) the will/wish to stay in the organization. Locke, Latham and Erez (1988) argue that the strength of this relationship will depend on the amount of variance in the commitment. According to Meyer *et al.* (2002) commitment has an impact on performance, being this impact positive for to the affective and normative commitment, and negative for the continued commitment. In an attempt to assert these studies we propose H_9.

- **H_9:** OC has a positive impact on IP.

Following Podsakoff and MacKenzie (1997), there is a positive relation between OCB, in the perspective as helping behaviours, and the effectiveness of the organizations. Consequently, a relationship between the OCB and IP is supposed to exist and the following hypothesis is formulated:

Figure 2. Model 2

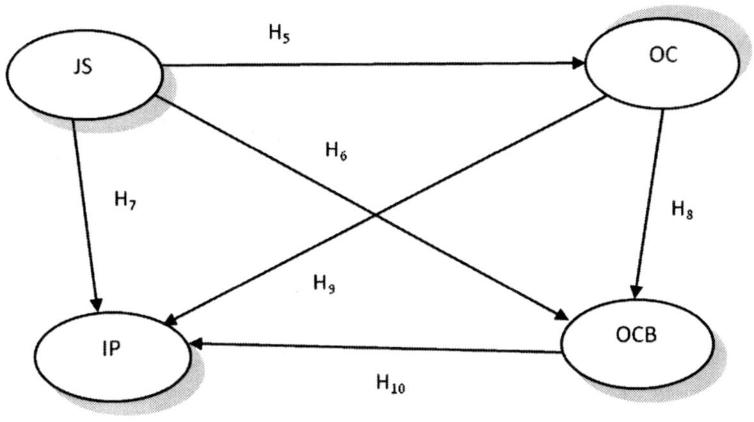

- **H_{10}:** OCB has a positive impact on IP.

The six hypotheses can be summarily represented by the research model in Figure 2.

METHODOLOGY

Sample and Data Collection

This research, descriptive in nature and quantitative, is carried out through the deductive method (Ciribelli, 2003) and is based on a model that tries to relate the following variables: the use of OSNs to maintain contact with co-workers (OSN), Job Satisfaction (JS), Organizational Commitment (OC), Organizational Citizenship Behaviours (OCB), and Individual Performance (IP).

The HE system in Portugal includes (1) the public higher education system, constituted by the institutions belonging to the State, (2) the private higher education system, composed of institutions belonging to private and cooperative entities. According to article 5, the HEI integrate (1) the university institutions incorporate the universities and the non-integrated university institutions, (2) the polytechnic institutes, incorporating the polytechnic institutes and the non-integrated polytechnic institutes.

Following the information of the National Institute of Statistics[1], updated on the 31st May, 2007, the number of Professors in higher education is 37,281, both in the in the public sector (26,098) and in the private sector (11,183). The sample in this study is composed by 157 Professors, of which 137 work in public HEI and 20 in privately-held ones; 101 teach in universities and 56 in polytechnic institutions.

We built a questionnaire in order to assess the use of OSNs. To evaluate the work-related attitudes and behaviours, four instruments were gathered on 7 points *Likert* type scale, where 1 means 'completely disagree' and 7 means 'completely agree'. This scale allows a wide appreciation of the worker's perception about the variables under study. It was necessary to validate the instruments for the Portuguese population by translating them into Portuguese and convert them back into English. The second translations were compared to the original instruments and some mistakes corrected. Because we were dealing with HEI, it was necessary to substitute the expressions 'firm' and 'organization' for the expression 'teaching institution', or just 'institution'. A pre-test was given to 6 individuals, which led to the need to make some changes. After these changes were made, the questionnaires were revised. Then, the final questionnaire, divided in five parts, was made available online and all the Portuguese HEI, public and private, were requested, via e-mail, to invite the Professors to participate in this study.

Development of Measures and Scales

Online Social Networks (OSN)

To evaluate the use of OSNs, we built a questionnaire that contained the following questions: (1) Do you use OSNs? (Yes/No), (2) If you answered 'yes', indicate which ones you use, (3) If you answered 'yes', indicate the how often you use OSNs, (4) If you answered 'yes', indicate with who you maintain contact with on OSNs (friends/family/co-workers/unknown people/other), (5) If you answered 'no', indicate why you don't use OSNs (lack of time/lack of interest/high personal exposure/other). OSN is assessed through a 0-1 variable. Since our purpose is to evaluate the influence of OSNs on work-related attitudes, we'll consider the use of OSNs to contact with the co-workers as the independent variable for model 1.

Job Satisfaction (JS)

Job Diagnostic Survey (JDS) was developed to measure three classes of variables: objective characteristics of work, critical psychological states and individual needs for growth. This measurement evaluates the global satisfaction and the satisfaction with job facets. Global satisfaction is measured through three dimensions, which include general satisfaction (5 items), internal work motivation (6 items) and satisfaction with growth (4 items). JDS also measures satisfaction with the following job facets: job security (2 items), pay (2 items), social (3 items) and supervision (3 items). The scores of items 3, 5 and 9 have to be reversed for statistical analysis (Hackman and Oldham, 1975).

Organizational Commitment (OC)

This measure, developed by Cook and Wall (1980), describes, in general, the worker's commitment towards the organization he/she works for. It has nine items, three of them measuring the identification with the organization, other three the involvement with the organization and, the remaining, loyalty. Three of the items are written in the negative form and their score was reversed later for statistical analysis purposes.

Organizational Citizenship Behaviours (OCB)

The scale used to evaluate the OCB was developed by Lo and Ramayah (2009). The instrument is composed of 20 items, which describe five dimensions of the OCB: (1) civic virtue, (2) conscientiousness, (3) altruism, (4) courtesy, and (5) sportsmanship. Four of the items were withdrawn from the scale by the authors, since they did not apply to the cultural context in which they used the instrument. However, those items were used in this study. One item is written in the negative form, so the score was reversed for statistical analysis purposes.

Individual Performance (IP)

In this study, the concept of 'individual performance' is measured using the performance traits that characterize the worker. Xiaowei (2006) developed a self-assessment measure of the performance traits, based on the revision of other authors' work. Seven dimensions were considered: the relationship among organizational networks (3 items), the transmission of organizational memory (2 items), trust (4 items), group synergy (2 items), chain influence on performance (2 items), difficulty in substituting (2 items) and innovation traits (3 items). On the whole the measure is made up of 18 items. Seven of the items are written in the negative form, so their score was reversed later for statistical analysis purposes.

Apart from the use of five scales to assess these variables, the respondents were requested to provide further information, such as age, gender, and nature of the HEI where they work (public/private and university/polytechnic).

Data Analysis Methods

To analyse the results we used the statistical package *SPSS,* version 18.0.

In this study, among other objectives, we intend to verify whether the means, for each variable, are statistically different depending on the use of OSNs to maintain contact with co-workers. In this case, the method used was the t-student test, for independent samples, which makes it possible to test whether the means of two populations are significantly different (Maroco, 2007).

To test model 2, we used the PLS method. This method has been increasingly used because of its ability to shape latent constructs under conditions of non-normality and small to medium samples. As a technique to create models based in components of structural equations, it's similar to the regression, but it models simultaneously the structural paths, i.e., the theoretical relationships among the latent variables, and it measures the paths, i.e., the relations among a latent variable and its indicators (Chin, Marcolin, & Newsted, 2003). This method was used to study the relationships when the independent variables were not solely 0-1 variables.

FINDINGS AND DISCUSSION

Sample Characterization

The sample is composed mostly by female individuals (62.4%). In what concerns age, the majority of the individuals is 30 to 49 years old (73.8%). A larger number of individuals belong to polytechnic institutions (64.3%) and to a public HEI (87.3%).

Utilization of OSNs

The majority of the sample uses OSNs (72.6%), but out of 157 individuals only 29.9% uses OSNs on a daily basis and only 10.8% uses three or more OSNs. Most of the individuals (57.2%) use OSNs to maintain contact with co-workers, although some of them also use it to contact friends, family, or unknown people.

The reason most often identified by faculty members not to use OSNs is 'high personal exposure', followed by 'lack of interest' (19), 'lack of time' (15), and, finally, 'unawareness' (1).

The concerns shown by faculty members that do not use OSNs suggest that there may be a lack of trust on OSNs, especially with respect to the reason 'high personal exposure'. According to Foster, Francescucci and West (2010), even some individuals that use OSNs have privacy concerns and don't have the confidence to contribute to new communities.

Group Comparisons (Model 1)

In order to evaluate the influence of the use of OSNs to contact with co-workers on work-related attitudes and behaviours, we used, as mentioned before, the t-student test for independent samples.

As shown on Table 1, for the Levene's test, 'Sig.' is higher than .05 in what concerns OCB. Consequently, at a level of significance of 5%, the hypothesis of homochedasticity cannot be rejected. Thus, the test statistic to be used is the one that assumes equal variances. It is possible to check, regarding the variable 'OCB', that *p-value* = .177 > .05, so we don't reject H_0, which means that there is no significant statistical difference between the means for the individuals that use OSNs to maintain contact with co-workers and the ones that don't, in what concerns OCB.

For the Levene's test, 'Sig.' is lower than .05 in what concerns JS, OC and IP. Thus, the test statistic to be used is the one that doesn't assume equal variances For the variables 'JS' and 'OC', p-value > .05, and so H_0 is not rejected, which

Table 1. T student test regarding the work-related attitudes and behaviours

		Levene's test					
		F	Sig.	T	df	Sig. (2-tailed)	Mean Difference
JS	Equal variances not assumed	.531	.467	-.677	152.748	.500	-.07007
OC	Equal variances not assumed	1.358	.246	-1.019	147.309	.310	-.16985
OCB	Equal variances assumed	.428	.514	-1.357	155	.177	-.12028
IP	Equal variances not assumed	.886	.348	-2.152	149.182	.033	-.17133

means there is no significant difference between the means for individuals that use OSNs to maintain contact with co-workers and the ones that don't. It is possible to check, regarding the variable 'IP', that p-value = .032 < .05, so we reject H_0, which means that there is a significant statistical difference between the means for the individuals that use OSNs to maintain contact with co-workers and the ones that do not.

The results described above allow the corroboration of H_4 and the rejection of H_1, H_2 and H_3. The use of OSNs to maintain contact with co-workers influences IP, but not JS, OC or OCB. In what concerns commitment, the results found may be due to the fact that the definition of OC is directed towards the employer organization and not to co-workers.

Considering that the results weren't significant for JS, OC, and OCB, we also evaluated the influence of OSN on the different dimensions that constitute these concepts (see Table 2).

As we can see, the variable 'OSN' has a significant positive influence on satisfaction with job facets (p-value=.048). This means that the individuals that use OSNs are more satisfied in what concerns job facets, such as job security, pay, social and supervision, in comparison to those who do not use OSNs.

The variable 'OSN' also has a significant positive influence on civic virtue (p-value=.006), one of the dimensions of OCB, which means that the individuals that use OSNs demonstrate more OCB related to the dimension 'civic virtue', that is behaviours that reveal the responsibility to participate in the life of the organization, in comparison to those who don't use OSNs.

These results partially corroborate H_1 and H_3.

PLS Method (Model 2)

We used the PLS method to test the relations among the worker's attitudes and behaviours.

The results show that there are positive correlations among all the variables, although the correlations among JS and OCB, JS and IP, OC and OCB, OCB and IP are low. The correlations among the other variables are moderate.

To test the significance of the relations, we utilized the bootstrapping method, which is used to create a high number of samples (in this case, 1000) from the original sample, through systematic eliminations of observations. When $\alpha > .05$ in what concerns a certain relation between variables, that is, when the relation is not supported by the data, we eliminate it from the model. In this study, there was no need to eliminate any of the relations, since they are all significant.

Table 2. T student test regarding the dimensions of JS, OC, and OCB

		Levene's test					
		F	Sig.	T	df	Sig. (2-tailed)	Mean Difference
Global satisfaction (JS)	Equal variances assumed	.431	.513	-.046	155	.964	-.00427
Satisfaction with job facets (JS)	Equal variances not assumed	2.989	.086	-1.998	147.324	.048	-.31842
Organizational identification (OC)	Equal variances assumed	.110	.741	-.783	155	.435	-.16623
Organizational involvement (OC)	Equal variances not assumed	3.120	.079	-1.141	140.209	.256	-.17019
Organizational loyalty (OC)	Equal variances not assumed	2.611	.108	-.744	145.768	.458	-.17312
Civic Virtue (OCB)	Equal variances not assumed	8.808	.003	-2.811	133.752	.006	-.38413
Conscientiousness (OCB)	Equal variances assumed	.436	.510	-.509	155	.612	-.05087
Altruism (OCB)	Equal variances assumed	.021	.885	-1.242	155	.216	-.14579
Courtesy (OCB)	Equal variances assumed	.403	.526	.546	155	.586	.05717

In what concerns the Cross loadings, there were some problems with the correlations among certain indicators, but we did not consider they were important enough to alter the model, also because that could imply the loss of validity of the scale contents (see Figure 3).

Figure 3. Final model and direct effects

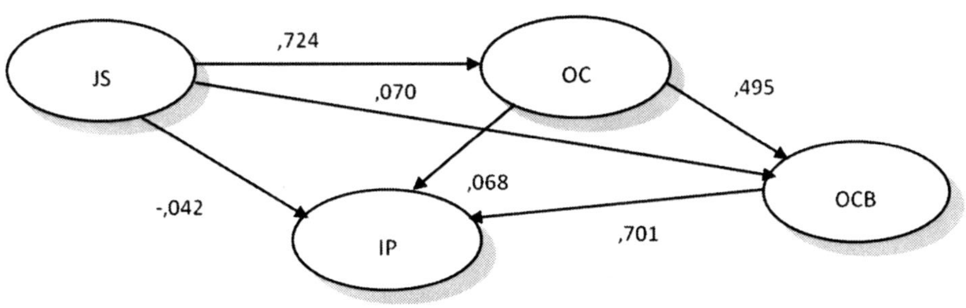

In what concerns the direct effects of the model, JS has a direct positive impact of .724 on OC (H_5), an impact of .070 on OCB (H_6) and it has a negative impact of -.042 on IP. When considering the direct effects between the variables, OC explains 49.5% of OCB (H_8), but only 6.8%

Table 3. Indirect effects for model 2

	JS	OC	OCB	IP
JS			.35838	.2512
OC				.3469
OCB				
IP				

Note: Not significant if α>.05

of IP (H_9). Finally, OCB explains 71.7% of IP (H_{10}) (see Table 3).

There are also indirect positive effects between JS and OCB, mediated by OC, between JS and IP, mediated by OC and OCB, and between OC and IP, mediated by OCB.

According to the results shown on Table 4, JS has a positive impact of .724 on OC (H_5), a positive impact of .429 on OCB (H_6) and it explains 30.9% of IP (H_7). OC explains 49.5% of OCB (H_8) and 41.6% of IP (H_9). Finally, OCB explains 70.1% of IP (H_{10}). Using another explanation, when, for example, OCB raises one unit, IP raises .701. These results are in agreement with the studies we identified in the literature review, so all the hypothesis included in model 2 are supported.

Explanatory Capacity of the Model and Internal Consistency of the Measures

In order to complete the analysis of the model, it is necessary to verify its explanatory capacity. The R^2 allows verifying what proportion of the variation of Y is explained by the variable X (Manso, 1996). The variable 'OC' explains 52.5% of the model, OCB explains 30.1% and IP explains 52.1% of the variation in the model. The variable 'JS' doesn't explain any variation in the model because it appears as the predictive variable.

A high composite reliability is a necessary condition to obtain a high validity and it's an important pre-requisite in the application of measures used to evaluate behaviours (Raykov

Table 4. Total effects for model 2

	JS	OC	OCB	IP
JS		.724	.429	.309
OC			.495	.416
OCB				.701
IP				

Note: Not significant if α>.05

Figure 4. Combination of model 1 and model 2

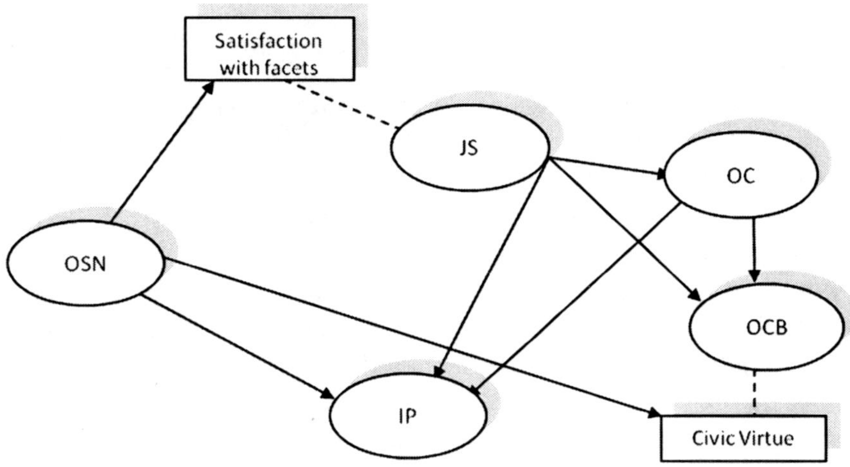

& Grayson, 2003). The value for IP is moderate, while the values for the other variables are high.

Cronbach's alpha allows us to analyse the internal consistency of a measure and provides a sub-estimate of the real credibility of the analysed instrument (Maroco & Garcia-Marques, 2006). The alpha values of Cronbach for the scale that measures JS, OC and OCB are relatively high (respectively .8841, .8525, and .8806). However, the value for the scale of IP is somewhat low (.6071), which means that further improvement of the scale may be needed.

As we can see on Figure 4, the use of OSNs to maintain contact with co-workers only has an effect on IP, if we do not consider the dimensions of the concepts. When considering the dimensions of JS, OC and OCB, we find that OSN influences the dimension 'satisfaction with facets' (JS) and the dimension 'civic virtue' (OCB). The results show that the use of OSNs to maintain contact with co-workers does not influence, at all, commitment.

In what concerns satisfaction with facets (job security, pay, social and supervision) the results make sense, since the variable OSN is related to the use of OSNs to maintain contact with co-workers, and so this may have a positive effect on social relationships at work, including with supervisors.

We explain the influence of 'OSN' on 'civic virtue' by the fact that OCB are also related to the worker's performance, and specifically this dimension of OCB could easily be confused with in-role behaviours. On the other hand, the contact that the worker maintains on OSNs with the co-workers could enhance the worker's will to participate actively in the organization's life due to a possible exchange of information regarding the organization on OSNs.

In what concerns the relations among work-related attitudes and behaviours, we verify that IP is also influenced by JS, OC, and OCB. OC is positively influenced by JS and OCB is positively influenced by JS and OC.

CONCLUSION

The results allow us to conclude that the individuals who maintain contact with co-workers on OSNs show more performance traits that lead to a higher performance, when compared to those that do not use OSNs. Curiously, some of the dimensions that compose the performance measure are directly connected to concepts related to networks, such as 'relationship among organizational networks,' 'transmission of organizational memory/knowledge,' 'trust,' and 'chain influence on performance.'

Although we found that the use of OSNs does not influence commitment, in what concerns JS and OCB, we found that the individuals that maintain contact with co-workers on OSNs show more satisfaction with job facets—job security, pay, social, and supervision—which may be explained by the fact that the variable OSN is related to the use of OSNs to maintain contact with co-workers, and so this may have a positive effect on the worker's social relationships at work, including with supervisors.

The fact that no significant relation between the use of OSNs to contact co-workers and commitment was found may be due to the fact that commitment is related to the affective reactions to the characteristics of the employer organization, and not to the interpersonal relationships established in the work environment. However, the use of OSNs to maintain contact with co-workers has a positive influence on the participation in the life of the organization (OCB), which may seem contradictory. Nevertheless, OCB refer to extra-role performance but, as mentioned before, 'civic virtue' behaviours could easily be confused with in-role performance. On the other hand, there might be an exchange of information regarding the organization on OSNs that may raise the worker's will to actively participate on the organization's life.

It seems important to mention that the motive 'high personal exposure' identified more often by the workers as the reason they do not use OSNs, reveals a lack of trust on OSNs, a fact that is in agreement with one study we found, that refers that even the individuals who use OSNs do not contribute as much as they could to online communities due to privacy concerns.

With respect to the worker's attitudes and behaviours, we have empirically supported all the proposed relations, which had already been found in previous studies. This way, we assure their value for HEI and we reaffirm their importance in the organizational context, which is particularly relevant nowadays, if we consider the current worldwide crisis.

Besides OSNs, one other concept that is central in this study is, possibly, performance. The concepts of satisfaction and OCB, as a whole, and the concept of commitment were not found to be significantly influenced by the use of OSNs to maintain contact with co-workers. However, performance was. On the other hand, we found that performance is also positively influenced by satisfaction, commitment and OCB.

The results found in this study allow us to conclude that, to keep workers that show a high performance in the HEI, the use of OSNs to maintain contact with co-workers should be encouraged. Our conclusion is in agreement with the study carried out by Boulos and Wheeler (2007). The authors mention the need to raise awareness of Web 2.0 tools and the possibilities they offer in the educational context. Moreover, HEI know a great deal about facilitating environments in which people join forces to create, share and advance knowledge, so they should be prepared to reap value from the new online tools (Barnatt, 2008). Furthermore, HEI should assure that their workers are satisfied, thus enhancing commitment and, consequently, OCB and performance.

FUTURE RESEARCH DIRECTIONS

The use of OSNs to maintain contact with co-workers could have been more deeply evaluated. We slate the replication of the study considering the types of exchanges made with co-workers on OSNs.

The relation between the use of OSNs to maintain contact with co-workers and OCB should be studied in more depth, using a different instrument and/or resorting to a different context. We suggest asking respondents what type of information they exchange with co-workers, in order to allow to draw more deep conclusions in what concerns the influence of 'OSN' on the dimension 'civic virtue'.

We also propose the evaluation of the quality of interpersonal relationships at work. This way, it will be possible to understand the effect that the use of OSNs to maintain contact with co-workers has on the relationships that workers maintain in the work environment.

In the future, this investigation should be enlarged, to include other organizational variables, such as motivation or work-related stress, so the understanding of the concepts used in this study can be enhanced.

We also propose the use of other measures to evaluate performance, as well as the replication of the study in other contexts, such as service or sales companies, with the aim of making comparisons and extending the empirical evidence of the proposed relations.

ACKNOWLEDGMENT

Research supported by: Programa de Financiamento Plurianual das Unidades de I&D da FCT – Fundação para a Ciência e Tecnologia, Ministério da Ciência, Tecnologia e Ensino Superior.

REFERENCES

Alcobia, P. (2001). Atitudes e satisfação no trabalho. In Ferreira, J. M., Neves, J., & Caetano, A. (Eds.), *Manual de psicossociologia das organizações*. Lisboa, Portugal: McGraw-Hill.

Allen, N., & Meyer, P. (1990). Organizational socialization tactics: A longitudinal analysis of links to newcomers' commitment and role orientation. *Academy of Management Journal*, *33*(4), 1–18. doi:10.2307/256294.

Asunda, P. (2010). Productivity, social networks and net communities in the workplace. *Techniques: Connecting Education and Careers*, *85*(5), 38–41.

Barbeira, M. R., & Franco, M. J. (2009). Um sistema de gestão do conhecimento como fomentador de redes estratégicas interorganizacionais. *Revista Ibero-Americana de Estratégia*, *8*(2), 5–29.

Barnard, C. (1938). *The functions of the executive* (2nd ed.). Boston: Harvard University Press.

Barnatt, C. (2008). Higher education 2.0. *International Journal of Management Education*, *7*(3), 47–56. doi:10.3794/ijme.73.250.

Bateman, T., & Organ, D. (1983). Job satisfaction and the good soldier: The relationship between affect and employee 'citizenship'. *Academy of Management Journal*, *26*(4), 587–595. doi:10.2307/255908.

Benson, V., Filippaios, F., & Morgan, S. (2010). Online social networks: changing the face of business education and career planning. *International Journal of e-Business Management, 4*(1), 20-33.

Boulos, M. N., & Wheeler, S. (2007). The emerging web 2.0 social software: An enabling suite of sociable technologies in health and health care education. *Health Information and Libraries Journal*, *24*(1), 2–23. doi:10.1111/j.1471-1842.2007.00701.x PMID:17331140.

Bunt, G. G., Wittek, R. P., & Klepper, M. C. (2005). The evolution of intra-organizational trust networks. *International Sociological Association*, *20*(3), 339–369. doi:10.1177/0268580905055480.

Castilla, E. J. (2005). Social networks and employee performance in a call center. *American Journal of Sociology, 110*(5), 1243–1283.

Chang, C.-S., & Chang, H.-H. (2007). Effects of internal marketing on nurse job satisfaction and organizational commitment: Example of medical centers in southern Taiwan. *The Journal of Nursing Research, 15*(4), 265–274. doi:10.1097/01.JNR.0000387623.02931.a3 PMID:18080971.

Chin, W., Marcolin, B., & Newsted, P. (2003). A partial least squares latent variable modeling approach for measuring interaction effects: Results from a Monte Carlo simulation study and an electronic-mail emotion/adoption study. *Information Systems Research, 14*(2), 189–217. doi:10.1287/isre.14.2.189.16018.

Ciribelli, M. (2003). *Como realizar uma dissertação de mestrado através da pesquisa científica.* Rio de Janeiro, Brazil: Viveiros de Castro Editora.

Cook, J., & Wall, T. (1980). New work attitude measures of trust, organizational commitment, and personal need non-fulfillment. *Journal of Occupational Psychology, 53*(1), 39–52. doi:10.1111/j.2044-8325.1980.tb00005.x.

Dess, G., & Shaw, J. (2001). Voluntary turnover, social capital, and organizational performance. *Academy of Management Review, 26*(3), 446–456.

Donaldson, E. A., & Grant-Vallone, E. J. (2000). Longitudinal examination of mentoring relationships on organizational commitment and citizenship behavior. *Journal of Career Development, 26*(4), 233–248. doi:10.1177/089484530002600401.

Donavan, D., Brown, T., & Mowen, J. (2004). Internal benefits of service-worker customer orientation: job satisfaction, commitment, and organizational citizenship behaviors. *Journal of Marketing, 68*(1), 128–146. doi:10.1509/jmkg.68.1.128.24034.

Eker, M., Eker, S., & Pala, F. (2008). The effects of job satisfaction on organizational commitment among Turkish health care staff: an empirical study. *Journal of Academic Studies, 10*(36), 46–68.

Foster, M. K., Francescucci, A., & West, B. C. (2010). Why users participate in online social networks. *International Journal of e-Business Management, 4*(1), 3-19.

González, J., & Garazo, T. (2006). Structural relationships between organizational service orientation, contact employee job satisfaction and citizenship behavior. *International Journal of Service Industry Management, 17*(1), 23–50. doi:10.1108/09564230610651561.

Grabner-Kraeuter, S., & Waiguny, M. (2011). Why users stay in online social networks: Perceptions of value, trust, subjective norm and the moderating influence of duration of use. *American Marketing Association, 22*(1), 240-249.

Graham, J. (1991). An essay on organizational citizenship behavior. *Employee Responsibilities and Rights Journal, 4*(4), 249–270. doi:10.1007/BF01385031.

Hackman, R., & Oldham, G. (1975). Development of the job diagnostic survey. *The Journal of Applied Psychology, 60*(2), 150–170. doi:10.1037/h0076546.

Hackman, R., & Oldham, G. (1976). Motivation through the design of work: A test of a theory. *Organizational Behavior and Human Performance, 16*(2), 250–279. doi:10.1016/0030-5073(76)90016-7.

Hoang, H., & Antoncic, B. (2003). Network-based research in entrepreneurship: A critical review. *Journal of Business Venturing, 18*(2), 165–187. doi:10.1016/S0883-9026(02)00081-2.

Hurlbert, J. S. (2001). Social networks, social circles, and job satisfaction. *Work and Occupations*, *18*(4), 415–430. doi:10.1177/0730888491018004003.

Jones, M. (2006). Which is a better predictor of job performance: Job satisfaction or life satisfaction? *Journal of Behavioral and Applied Management*, *8*(1), 20–42.

Judge, T., Parker, S., Colbert, A., Heller, D., & Remus, I. (2001). Job satisfaction: A cross-cultural review. In Anderson, N., Ones, D., Sinangil, H., & Viswesvaran, C. (Eds.), *Handbook of Industrial, Work and Organizational Psychology* (*Vol. 2*, pp. 25–52). London: Sage Publications.

Katz, D., & Kahn, R. (1987). *Psicologia social das organizações* (3rd ed.). São Paulo, Brazil: Editora Atlas.

Konovsky, M., & Organ, D. (1996). Dispositional and contextual determinants of organizational citizenship behavior. *Journal of Organizational Behavior*, *17*(3), 253–266. doi:10.1002/(SICI)1099-1379(199605)17:3<253::AID-JOB747>3.0.CO;2-Q.

Lavelle, J., Brockner, J., Konovsky, M., Price, K., Henley, A., Taneja, A., & Vinekar, V. (2008). Commitment, procedural fairness, and organizational citizenship behavior: A multifoci analysis. *Journal of Organizational Behavior*, *30*(3), 337–357. doi:10.1002/job.518.

Lo, M.-C., & Ramayah, T. (2009). Dimensionality of organizational citizenship behavior (OCB) in a multicultural society: The case of Malaysia. *International Business Research*, *2*(1), 48–55.

Locke, E. (1968). *What is job satisfaction?* Washington, DC: American Psychological Association.

Locke, E., Latham, G., & Erez, M. (1988). The determinants of goal commitment. *Academy of Management Review*, *13*(1), 23–39.

Malik, M., Nawab, S., & Naeem, B. (2010). Job satisfaction and organizational commitment of university teachers in public sector of Pakistan. *International Journal of Business & Management*, *5*(6), 17–26.

Manso, J. (1996). *Estatística descritiva e previsão* (2nd ed.). Covilhã, Portugal: Universidade da Beira Interior.

Maroco, J. (2007). *Análise estatística com utilização do SPSS* (3rd ed.). Lisboa, Portugal: Edições Sílabo.

Maroco, J., & Garcia-Marques, T. (2006). Qual a fiabilidade do alfa de Cronbach? Questões antigas e soluções modernas? *Laboratório de Psicologia*, *4*(1), 65–90.

Marshall, B., Choi, J., El-Shinnaway, M. M., North, M., Svensson, L., & Wang, S. et al. (2009). Online and offline social ties of social network website users: An exploratory study in eleven societies. *Journal of Computer Information Systems*, *50*(1), 54–64.

Meyer, J., & Herscovitch, L. (2001). Commitment in the workplace: Toward a general model. *Human Resource Management Review*, *11*(3), 299–326. doi:10.1016/S1053-4822(00)00053-X.

Meyer, P., Stanley, D., Herscovitch, L., & Topolnytsky, L. (2002). Affective, continuance, and normative commitment to theorganization: A meta-analysis of antecedents, correlates, and consequences. *Journal of Vocational Behavior*, *61*(1), 20–52. doi:10.1006/jvbe.2001.1842.

Organ, D. (1977). A reappraisal and reinterpretation of the satisfaction-causes-performance hypothesis. *Academy of Management Review*, *2*(1), 46–53.

Organ, D., & Lingl, A. (1995). Personality, satisfaction and organizational citizenship behaviors. *The Journal of Social Psychology*, *135*(3), 339–250. doi:10.1080/00224545.1995.9713963.

Organ, D., & Moorman, R. (1993). Fairness and organizational citizenship behavior: What are the connections? *Social Justice Research*, *6*(1), 5–18. doi:10.1007/BF01048730.

Podsakoff, P., & MacKenzie, S., & Fetter. (1993). Citizenship behavior and fairness in organizations: Issues and directions for future research. *Employee Responsibilities and Rights Journal*, *6*(3), 257–269. doi:10.1007/BF01419449.

Podsakoff, P., & MacKenzie, S. (1997). Impact of organizational citizenship behavior on organizational performance: A review and suggestions for future research. *Human Performance*, *10*(2), 133–151. doi:10.1207/s15327043hup1002_5.

Podsakoff, P., MacKenzie, S., Paine, J., & Bachrach, D. (2000). Organizational citizenship behaviors: A critical review of the theoretical and empirical literature and suggestions for future research. *Journal of Management*, *26*(3), 513–563. doi:10.1177/014920630002600307.

Raykov, T., & Grayson, D. (2003). A test for change of composite reliability in scale development. *Multivariate Behavioral Research*, *38*(2), 143–159. doi:10.1207/S15327906MBR3802_1.

Rego, A. (2002). *Comportamentos de cidadania nas organizações*. Lisboa, Portugal: McGraw-Hill.

Rego, A., Ribeiro, N., & Cunha, M. (2010). Perceptions of organizational virtuousness and happiness as predictors of organizational citizenship behaviors. *Journal of Business Ethics*, *93*(1), 215–235. doi:10.1007/s10551-009-0197-7.

Saari, L., & Judge, T. (2004). Employee attitudes and job satisfaction. *Human Resource Management*, *43*(4), 395–407. doi:10.1002/hrm.20032.

Samad, S. (2005). Unraveling the organizational commitment and job performance relationship: Exploring the moderating effect of job satisfaction. *Business Review (Federal Reserve Bank of Philadelphia)*, *4*(2), 79–84.

Sledgianowski, D., & Kulviwat, S. (2009). Using social network sites: The effects of playfulness, critical mass and trust in a hedonic context. *Journal of Computer Information Systems*, *49*(4), 74–83.

Staw, B. (1986). Organizational psychology and the pursuit of the happy/productive worker. *California Management Review*, *28*(4), 40–53. doi:10.2307/41165214.

Ullrich, C., Tan, X., Borau, K., Shen, L., Luo, H., & Shen, R. (2008). Why web 2.0 is good for learning and for research: Principles and prototypes. In *Proceedings of the 17th International World Wide Web Conference*, (pp. 705-714). IEEE.

Vala, J., Monteiro, M., Lima, L., & Caetano, A. (1995). *Psicologia social das organizações: Estudos em empresas portuguesas*. Oeiras, Portugal: Celta Editora.

Van Dyne, L., Graham, J., & Dienesch, R. (1994). Organizational citizenship behavior: Construct redefinition, measurement and validation. *Academy of Management Journal*, *37*(4), 765–802. doi:10.2307/256600.

Viswesvaran, C. (2001). Assessment of individual job performance: A review of the past century and a look ahead. In Anderson, N., Ones, D., Sinangil, H., & Viswesvaran, C. (Eds.), *Handbook of Industrial, Work and Organizational Psychology* (*Vol. 1*, pp. 110–126). London: SAGE Publications. doi:10.4135/9781848608320.n7.

Williams, L., & Anderson, S. (1991). Job satisfaction and organizational commitment as predictors of organizational citizenship and in-role behaviors. *Journal of Management*, *17*(3), 601–617. doi:10.1177/014920639101700305.

Xiaowei, L. (2006). A test on the systematic fuzzy measures of the key degree for the core employees' performance traits. *Canadian Social Science*, *2*(5), 38–43.

Young, K. (2011). Social ties, social networks and the Facebook experience. *International Journal of Emerging Technologies and Society*, *9*(1), 20–34.

KEY-TERMS AND DEFINITIONS

Attitude: Describes an internal arrangement of the individual in relation to an element of the social world, which guides the conduct they adopt in the presence, real or symbolic, of that element.

Behaviour: It is the activity of an organism interacting with its environment.

Higher Education Institutions: Community service providers, specifically of transference and economic value increase of the scientific and technological knowledge, which have as main goals to facilitate environments in which people collaborate to create, share and advance knowledge.

Individual Performance: Defined as behaviours that can be evaluated, that is, behaviours that are identifiable only through operational measures.

Job Satisfaction: A positive emotional state—feelings and affective responses—or a generalized positive attitude towards work and the experiences that occur in the work environment, that depends on situational factors and/or on personality and personal factors, and that can be measured according to a global approach—based on the attitude towards work in general, not being a result of the sum of different aspects related to work, but depending on them—or to a multidimensional approach—satisfaction that reverses from a number of factors associated with work, being possible to measure satisfaction for each one of them.

Online Social Networks: They function as communication interfaces between millions of users, providing an efficient and user-friendly way to maintain social connections and to easily create and share information.

Organizational Citizenship Behaviours: Characterized as extra-role behaviours, that is, behaviours that arise as a way of acting beyond what is defined by work requirements (in-role behaviours), which means that the workers do non-mandatory tasks without expecting any rewards or recognition.

Organizational Commitment: It is a force of connection—a psychological or attitude stage—with the goals and values of the organization, which determines a direction at the level of the individual's behaviour towards the employer organization, with the aim of benefiting it.

Social Networks: They function as communication channels and allow the exchange of resources to several levels, as a form of spreading and sharing ideas. The social relationships established at work are an important tool for the understanding of the workers' outcomes in the organizations.

ENDNOTES

1 Indicators of the teaching staff of HEI in Portugal. http://www.ine.pt/xportal/xmain?xpid=INE&xpgid=ine_indicadores&indOcorrCod=0000887&contexto=pi&selTab=tab0.

Chapter 15
Innovation and Diversification Policies in the Banking Sector:
The Case of the Urban@ Program

Francisco J. Liébana-Cabanillas
University of Granada, Spain

Francisco Muñoz-Leiva
University of Granada, Spain

ABSTRACT

This chapter describes innovation and diversification policies (i + d) and analyzes the main drivers of innovation in financial institutions. In addition, recent examples of financial innovations and their effect on banking policies are discussed. Specifically, the Internet has been the key to enabling financial institutions to extend and optimize their business by improving the information and services they can offer to their customers and prospects. Due to innovations and changes, the banking sector now takes a new approach in the design of their offices ("bank branch 2.0") and Websites as a way to innovate and diversify business. This chapter explains the innovative strategies of the Urban@ program at the Caja Rural of Granada (Granada, Spain). The history and consolidation of the program, the internal institutional response, and the competition within the banking sector are described and analyzed. In general, the main strategies and achievements of this initiative are: (1) active customer listening, resulting in increased confidence and commitment from the staff; (2) use of up-sale strategies (cross-selling, reduced dropout rates, increased membership advantages), which increase both customer loyalty and customer satisfaction; and 3) a modern, more positive perception of the entity among the general public.

DOI: 10.4018/978-1-4666-4373-4.ch015

1. INTRODUCTION

1.1. The Importance of Technological Innovation in the Financial Sector

Innovation is "the generation, acceptance and implementation of new ideas, processes, products or services" (Kanter, 1983: 20). From an industrial point of view, innovation is "introducing a novelty in the production process, whatever its size and origin, to achieve more efficient economic objectives" (Inche, 1998: 9). Rogers (1983: 11) adds that innovation is "an idea, practice or object that is perceived as new by an individual or other unit of adoption."

Nowadays, specific Information and Communication Technology (ICT)-based innovations are shaping a new economic scenario, characterized by rapid technological change, increased competitiveness and reduced product life cycles. Companies are discovering the great potential of ICT to improve competitiveness and profitability in business (Lafuente, 2005: 29; Fujitsu, 2009; Torrent-Sellens et al., 2010: 53; Fundación Orange, 2010: 108). The increasing use of ICT represents a major challenge to the traditional modus operandi of trade relations, directly affecting company-customer relationships. While for many years, radio, television and the telephone were the tools used to market products and services efficiently, now newer, even more efficient means of communication such as the Internet, mobile phones and interactive television have produced interesting and innovative marketing results (Chaffey, 2000: 16; Heinonen and Strandvik, 2005; Heinonen, 2006; Zaidi, 2006; Masamila et al., 2010). These communication tools simultaneously serve as self-service delivery channels such as Internet banking (Heinonen, 2006).

In this context, technological innovation refers to both actions and decisions about the market as well as to products and services that make business management easier. Sometimes two or more innovations are presented together since they have, or are perceived to have a functional relationship, by potential adopters. Because of this, the concept of "technology clusters" or innovative packages consisting of one or more closely related technology components has appeared (Rogers, 1983: 143).

In an attempt to classify the different types of innovation in business, Mellor (2007: 38-39) distinguishes three types of innovation:

- **Invention Innovation:** Is the application of an invention or discovery. This type of innovation tends to be vertical and radical. However, most organizations are based on image and product (e.g. trademark protection) rather than new or radical advances in technology (patent protection).
- **Creative Innovation:** Is used as a tool to achieve competitive advantage in the market. The initial creation of a company or its business model is a form of creativity.
- **Diversity Innovation:** Regarded as a horizontal phenomenon (agent-to-agent or peer-to-peer) and incremental, this innovation includes conversations among peers with different knowledge bases or from other environments to offer solutions to a problem without requiring a significant degree of invention and / or creativity. Such innovation can add value and service to customers without having to "reinvent the wheel."

Figure 1 represents the three types of innovation described.

The formation of partnerships or strategic alliances between companies allows a degree of innovation in production, trade, or distribution. Kanter (1983: 21) adds that innovation involves creative use of original inventions as well.

But as a general rule, the most original innovations are less likely to be distributed, since products that are similar to existing ones require a lower degree of behavioural change in order to be used.

Figure 1. Types of innovation (source: Kanter, 1983 p. 21; Mellor, 2007, p. 36)

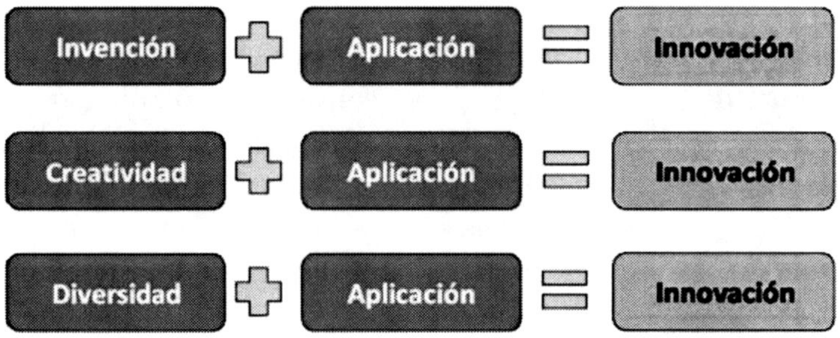

Innovation in financial institutions is of the utmost importance to meet the continuing needs of consumers and gain a competitive advantage over market rivals. But it is also an element that can be copied by others in the sector.

There are many reasons why financial institutions decide to innovate (based in Sánchez, 1997: 122-124):

- **Market Forces:** Financial institutions choose to innovate because they are interested in expanding the market or penetrating a new national or international market.
- **Profitability Ratios:** Typically, institutions innovate to improve yields and earn higher profits.
- **Corporate Image:** Companies innovate to create a stronger image in the market, ensuring optimal position in the consumer's mind and differentiation from the competition. In most cases a more modern, safer image emerges.
- **Technical Advantage:** Since financial products and services have ever-shorter life spans the continual development of new products or services is required in the maturity stage.

Broadly speaking, the banking sector is an information-intensive business in which ICTs are increasingly important in order to acquire, process and deliver information to users. This leads to general technological development, but in recent years the Internet in particular, has radically affected financial systems, overcoming geographical and time barriers.

Specifically, the Internet enables financial institutions to extend and optimize their business by improving the information and services they can offer to their customers and prospects. It is a medium that is transforming the traditional way of doing financial business. Therefore, it is necessary to know the potential of these new terms of trade, how to design an appropriate strategy for implementation in the organization and how to provide efficient, secure service that customers demand. Internet banking, coupled with the policy of diversification that some banks and savings banks follow, leads to innovations based on the World Wide Web.

Diversified growth makes perfect sense when good opportunities are available outside of existing businesses, provided that the company has the strengths needed for success. There are different types of diversification (Kotler, 2006: 52):

- **Concentric Diversification:** When the company develops new products that have technological or marketing synergies with existing product lines but are intended for a different consumer segment.
- **Horizontal Diversification:** When the company develops products that appeal to its customers and which are not technologically related to existing products.

- **Diversification in Conglomerate:** When the company seeks to develop new businesses that are not related to their current technology, products and markets.

1.2. The Importance of Electronic Services in the Financial Sector

The financial sector has undergone major changes in recent years due to technological innovations, increased competition, increased customer accessibility to services, increased social interaction between customers, the demand for lower transaction costs and the increased financial literacy of clients (Embid et al., 1998; Pereira, 2003; Calero et al., 2005; Momparler, 2008). One of the main responses to these changes was the development of electronic and online banking (hereinafter e-banking).

Since e-banking offers advantages to both institutions and customers, it has become an increasingly popular distribution channel, complimentary to traditional bank branches. E-banking's significant cost savings, improved transaction quality, comprehensiveness, transparency and comparison-shopping capabilities are highly valued advantages versus traditional channels. These advantages outweigh potential disadvantages such as errors and security concerns, which has led to increased use among customers. For these reasons, from the 1990's to the present e-banking has become one of the most important distribution channels for financial institutions (Karjaluoto et al., 2002, Torrent-Sellens, et al., 2010). The Urban@ program includes free access to computers to encourages customers to start using e-banking thereby reducing the number of transactions through traditional channels.

A 2010 study by the Orange Foundation highlights the importance of technological innovations that are taking place in the financial sector. This same study also verifies that e-banking in Spain is one of the most widely used online applications. According to this report, the percentage of electronic bankers in Spain is growing faster than the European Union (EU) average. In addition, a recent study published by the company comScore reveals that Spain is ranked eighth in the world for the highest number of online bankers after Canada, Holland, France, Sweden, United Kingdom, New Zealand, and Belgium, surpassing the United States and Australia.

Different entities, therefore, are redesigning their bank offices and Websites, and adding new services ("horizontal diversification") as a way to innovate and diversify their businesses. As a result of innovation policies, different pilot programs and innovative Websites are being developed to offer many new services simultaneously. These policies, and examples of them, are described in the following sections.

2. NEW INNOVATION POLICY AND DIVERSIFICATION (I + D) IN THE FINANCIAL SECTOR

In the world of financial services, where products are easily copied by competition, only two elements truly contribute to differentiation and competitive advantage: technological innovation and quality services (Embid et al., 1998: 34). Service quality has become an increasingly important factor for success and survival in the banking sector. High-quality service leads to customer satisfaction and its consequent brand loyalty and market share, attracts new customers, and improves financial performance, and profitability (Cui et al., 2003; Nadiri et al., 2009).

To achieve such differentiation and innovation, the banking sector now takes a new approach in the design of bank branches and Websites. Concepts such as transparency, flexibility, client proximity, innovation, and dynamism, previously unthinkable in the rigid world of finance, now occupy a central role in creation the customer relationships and branch models. There are many examples of such recent pilot projects. For example, at the Caja Navarra's 24-hour office (Spain) one can browse the Internet, read books or listen to concerts. The

Urban@ program at Caja Rural of Granada, offers a range of electronic products, trips, discounts at local businesses and other interesting information through its Website. Similar pilot programs are also present in other countries (see Figure 2), such as in Deutsche Bank Q110, located in Forchheim (Berlin), which serves as a test laboratory. This office sells cars and markets products from Deutsche Telecom through innovative ATMs that emerge from the ground. These profitable businesses, which generate 52% more business than a typical office, both in credit loans (35% more) and asset management (88% more) will continue to play an important role in the future. (Mendieta,

Figure 2. Examples of innovative branches and websites (Source: ING's, Deutsche Bank's, Caixa's LKXA, and Caja Navarra's CiberCan websites)

2007). Another original initiative is the 'Save Your Money Café' at ING Direct in major Canadian cities (Toronto, Montréal, Calgary, and Vancouver).

The examples above highlight the product diversification started several years ago by some banks. Another significant marketing change is the abandonment of a structural entity with marble facades and little windows in favour of large windows that show the bank's interior. Banks exploit these windows and interior spaces by installing billboards that showcase a variety of products and services thus setting up a new bank channel, called by some "the bank office 2.0" (Mendieta, 2007). The application of merchandising techniques used in other sectors has been adopted by entities such as Deutsche Bank and Caja Navarra, which advertise products (loans, credit cards, or savings accounts) in metal boxes placed in racks and on shelves in their establishments. These boxes contain information and applications to establish client relationships. The Deutsche Bank mega-office displays vehicles and technology inside to entice customers to come in. It also has a cafeteria at the back of the bank to talk with a financial advisor and a nursery for children to make bank visits easier, more productive, and more enjoyable for families.

Without a doubt, the Internet and its resources represent a major technological innovation, involving a wide range of new behaviours, products and services (Hoffman, 2000; Smith, 2005: 115). Consequently, the most innovative companies are using this medium to optimize their business by improving the information and services they can offer to their customers and prospects. To do this efficiently and securely, companies must design appropriate implementation strategies and understand the new terms of trade.

Associated with these initiatives, the Web has also led to the development of previously unknown business models called "virtual malls" (Delgado and Nieto, 2002), innovative enterprise applications or "applications of diversity" created from other business models and the Web. It contributes to the "incremental innovation", with primarily horizontal implementation. Small and medium businesses rarely develop inventions in a highly turbulent environment, so "innovation of diversity" has emerged as an important remedy to achieve flexibility in changing and competitive markets, especially (Mellor, 2007: 52) in those surrounding the financial sector.

Some examples (Figure 2) of such innovative Web spaces include Urban@'s innovative Website (http://www.urbancajarural.es), Caja Granada's "turestu" (http://www.tuerestu.es), The Caixa's LKXA (http://www.lkxa.es), BBVA's "blue joven" (http://soy.bluebbva.com), or Caja Navarra's CiberCan (http://www.cajanavarra.es). In addition to Internet banking services, these sites offer a variety of products and services (both commercial and informational).

One of the few initiatives that has been withdrawn from the market is the BBVA Bank program called Money Express. This service was started in 2005 in 130 bank offices to offer specific services to immigrants in Spain. Between 2008 and 2009, the BBVA was forced to reorganize its branch network and serve immigrants through other channels due to the changing economic environment and reduced business volume from this segment (Agencia EFE; Terra News, 2009).

The following sections describe the Urban@ program at Caja Rural of Granada including the history and consolidation of the program, and the institutional, market and sector reactions to the program.

3. THE CASE OF CAJA RURAL'S URBAN@ PROGRAM

3.1. The History of the Urban@ Program of Caja Rural of Granada

Caja Rural of Granada is a credit union that is part of Caja Rural Group with 203 offices (in the Andalusian provinces of Granada, Malaga,

Almeria and Madrid), total assets of 4,585,088 million euros, a profit of 20.1 million euros in 2010, and a network of 234 ATMs and a staff of 832 employees.

In April 2004, Caja Rural of Granada studied the introduction of a youth program in Andalusia in order to increase its presence among18-30 year olds, limiting the participation of those younger than 25 to 12% of the total. This initiative culminated in the Urban@ program, a new branch concept that opened to the public in October 2005. The Urban@ offices provide a groundbreaking business concept that combines banking with free Internet access, tourist services, a monthly magazine, the sale of electronic components and tickets for sporting events, concerts and other exciting benefits for their clients such as discounts at local stores. The Urban@ program has its own Website (http://www.urbancajarural.es) with information on these and other services (for example, university education, news releases and editorials) as well as links to the Caja Rural Website (Ruralvía).

To develop this innovative business model, a team at the Caja Rural analyzed the feasibility of such a program. The details of the action plan are outlined in the following stages:

3.1.1. Stage 1: Internal Competency and Viability Analysis

In February 2005, Caja Rural conducted a series of in depth interviews with 200 students at the University of Granada to understand their banking habits. The results of this preliminary study were:

- The university students maintained accounts primarily at the following entities: Caja Granada (35%, participants in its University Club Program), La Caixa (22%, participants in LKXA Program), BBVA (17%, participants in the Blue Youth Program), Santander (13%, participants in the Universia Program) and Caja Rural of Granada (13%).
- The features that young people wanted in a banking entity were technological innovation, agility, traditional services, close and no commissions.
- The terms that young people identified and associated with each of the competitor bank entities were:
  - **LKXA:** Technology, activity, speed, agility, and proximity...
  - **BBVA:** Independence, imagination, dreams, and gifts...

Figure 3. Classic and new Caja Rural's branches (source: Caja Rural)

    - **Santander:** Technology, international bank, quality education...
- Despite Caja Granada being the most heavily used bank among this segment, the most highly-valued institution was La Caixa (due to their Website, concert and theatre ticket offerings, proximity, and youthful image). Caja Granada was the next most highly valued bank (perceived as the traditional option for the region or the "life-long" bank); then Santander and BBVA (perceived as the "banks") and finally in last place, Caja Rural of Granada ("The Rural").

The following observations summarize the conclusions from this study: Young people did not identify with Caja Rural of Granada. The image of this entity did not attract young people. Young people did not realize that the entity could meet their financial needs. The needs of young people change very quickly and any institution targeting this segment should be prepared to adjust their pace to the speed of change.

After analyzing the small market share and the lack of positioning, the Granada bank designed a youth program to revitalize its image in the 18 to 30 year old segment. The program created a new brand and marketing formula for banking products and services for this segment. The entity expected no profit from the initiative in the short to medium term. Caja Rural designed a network of offices with a striking design and functionality, a mobile sales network to meet young people in places they frequent, a dynamic and groundbreaking Website to reinforce the young brand and improve the segment market share. Furthermore, the new program strived to address the needs of both financial and non-financial customers through Web technology and professional development for young people with a philosophy that was different from what the market was offering at that time. The Urban@ program is result of the bank's ambitious commitment to young people recognizing that they would the greatest future asset for the institution.

Some of the benefits that customers enjoy by joining the Urban@ Community, include:

- **Financial advantages:**
    - No management or maintenance fees on an Urban@ account.
    - Free debit card.
    - Free virtual card for secure Internet shopping.
    - Free online banking service.
    - Advances on scholarships.
    - Educational loans.
    - Preferential loans for purchases of computer equipment and vehicles.
    - Exclusive prices for car hires and motorcycle insurance.
- **Non-financial benefits:**
    - Free Internet access in Urban@ offices.
    - Discounts for their cardholders at more than 450 stores in the province including, clothing, accessories, hospitality, travel, leisure, adventure, and telephones.
    - Accommodation assistance.
    - Access to sporting and cultural events.
    - Class trip planning and funding assistance.

Figure 4. Claim (Source: Urban@'s old website)

Figure 5. Initial Urban@ website (Source: Urban@'s old website)

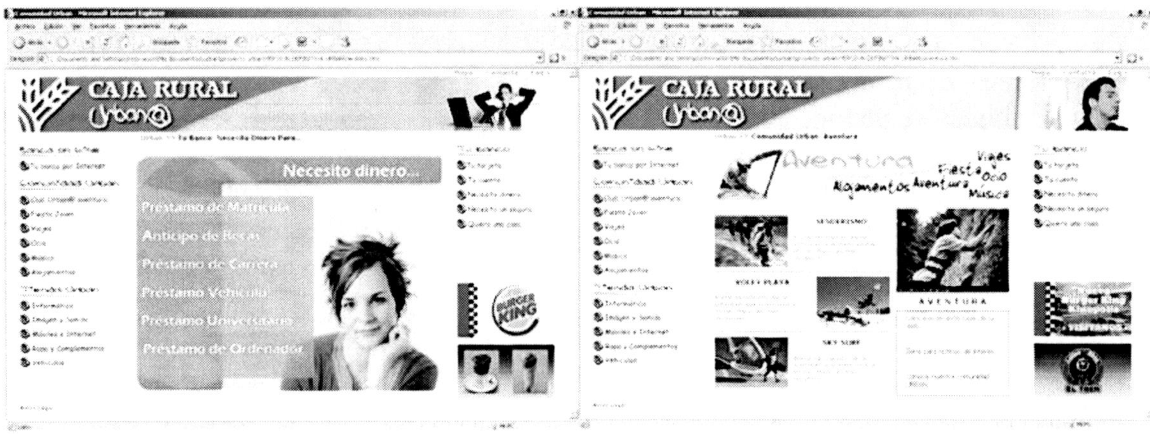

- Drawings for tickets for music, cultural and sporting events.

3.1.2. Stage 2: Program Launch

The launch of Urban@ took place in June 2005 and had two distinct stages:

Stage 2.1: "Creating a buzz" and brand launch took place from May to September 2005 using the claim "You can do it! JOIN" in Figure 4.
Simultaneously, a publicity campaign was run in newspapers, radio, billboards, buses and other channels advertising the launch of the first version of the Website www.urbancajarural.es (Figure 5) and a quarterly magazine was launched.

Stage 2.2: The opening of Urban@'s first office in October 2005 coincided with the start of the 2005-2006 academic year.
The design of this office is recognizable from a distance. The front shows the brand's corporate colours while contrasting tones blend in with the prevailing environment. The office has an easily recognizable bright orange band of windows around the outside of the premises that advertises recent promotions and core products. In the interior there are two clearly defined areas: a public area with various services and a private space offering only banking services at individual customer tables.
Notably, the public part has no doors except for the exterior door, which blurs the boundaries between outside and inside. This area offers a number of services such as soft drink vending machines, Internet access, a reading area, a rest area and information on student associations. The design of the office as a whole, including the layout, the furniture, the colours and the materials were chosen for functionality, dynamism, modernity and practicality that appeals to young people.
The brightly coloured office lighting changes depending on time of day, and contrasts with the black background to illuminate the walls. The modern and attractive lamps can be folded down to provide more light when needed. In addition, the banks hours are tailored to the needs of young people and, unlike most banks, the office is open from nine o'clock in the morning until eight o'clock in the evening (Figure 6). Clearly, this thoughtful design greatly differs from traditional bank offices (see prior Figure 3).

Figure 6. Interior and exterior of Urban@ (source: Urban@'s website)

3.1.3. Stage 3: Consolidation of the Program

After five years of operation the Urban@ program at Caja Rural of Granada has:

- Achieved favourable market share and brand recognition among young people in the provinces of Granada and Malaga.
- Attracted more than 15,000 customers with a conversion rate of over 90%, meaning that more than 13,000 customers are new to the organization.
- A regularly updated catalogue of products to attract young people.
- A higher number of office and Website visitors than initial estimates.

Figure 7. The evolution of the Urban@ website (Source: Urban's websites)

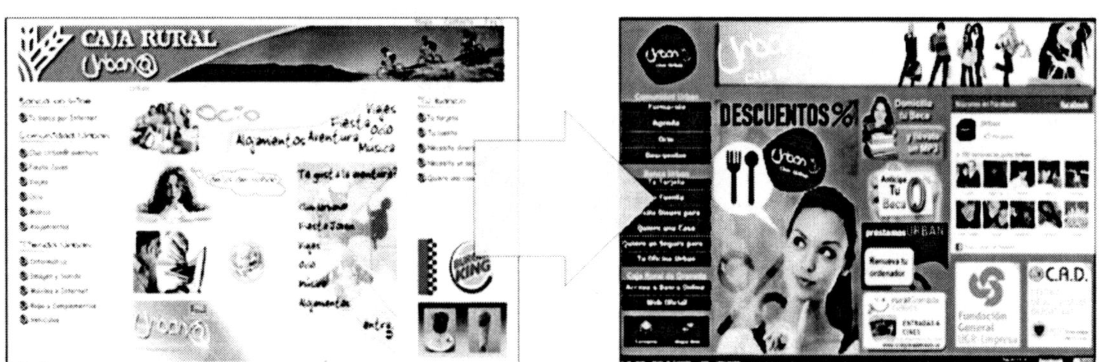

Since its inception, the program has evolved to make it more appealing and relevant to young people. The changes include:

- Web Adaptations. This main link between young clients and the entity has become a tool that is updated regularly to serve as a daily reference portal (see Figure 7).
- Elimination of the magazine due to its high production cost and low acceptance among young people. It was replaced by online news on the Website which generates more dynamism and connectivity.
- An increased number of businesses partnerships offering discounts to members the Urban@ community.
- Presence in social networking through Facebook, Twitter and Tuenti (a Spanish social networking site).
- Ticket sales for sporting and musical events through partnerships with the portal www.entradas.com.

3.2. Differentiating Elements of the Urban@ Program

The driving idea behind the Urban@ program design was the need to market this new service differently than other banks have traditionally done. The following distinguishing features used to meet the objectives of Caja Rural of Granada were:

- **Image:** The new brand had to promote the principles of youth, dynamism, proximity and adaptability.
- **Youth:** The managers and employees who designed the program initiatives had to be young enough to understand and to think like the target segment (unlike similar experiences, such as Hispano 20 from the former Central Hispano Bank, now Santander).
- **Website:** Innovative platforms for both processes and product sales through a dynamic Website.
- **Affiliated Discount Partnerships:** Education and entertainment elements that characterize the social life of young people were included in the program. In order to do this, discount agreements were made with more than 450 establishments. In addition, a partnership (the General Foundation of the University of Granada-Enterprise) was formed to facilitate the dissemination of training programs offered by the University.

3.3. Marketing Strategy Designed for the Urban@ Program

The **marketing strategy** established by the Caja Rural of Granada revolved around three main principles: communication with the younger generation, multi-channel contact points and a loyalty program.

1. The **strategic communication** focused on capturing as many young people as possible by driving customer traffic to the office and to retail outlets in the capital and thus improving the market share among young people.
2. The **multi-channel strategy** sought to establish systems to recruit young people through incentive campaigns to drive product purchases via channel integration (Urban@ office, mobile offices (see Figure 8), retail sales points, electronic banking, and mobile phones).
3. The **loyalty strategy** focused on developing communication between the bank and the youth segment so this group could define the incentives and actions that would achieve greater collective loyalty. The customers themselves and their decisions reinforced the effectiveness of many actions.

Figure 8. Urban@ mobile offices (source: Urban@ branch)

Figure 9. Objectives of the Urban@ program (Source: Caja Rural)

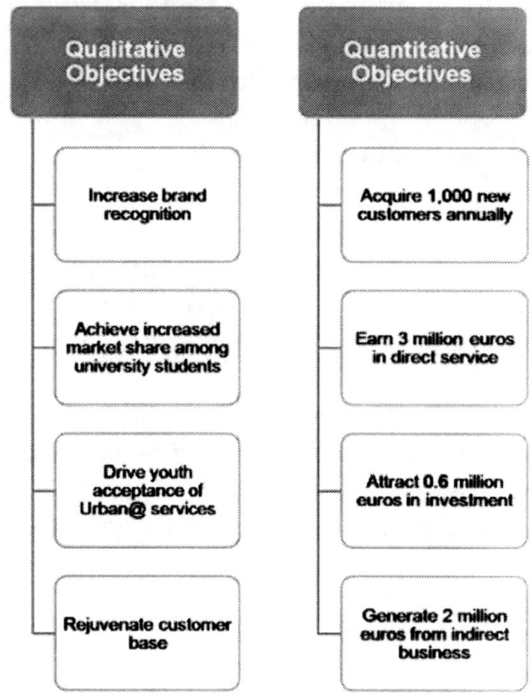

3.4. Objectives of the Urban@ Program

Prior to the conception of this program, Caja Rural of Granada needed a service that would promote its image to the youth segment. However, historically there were internal and external problems that precluded this. Therefore, once the entity's governing body decided to invest in the Urban@ program it was aware that there would be transition period before earning a profit, and that financial return would be generated in the mid-to-long-term.

Consequently, Caja Rural of Granada established a two pronged strategy of objectives: qualitative objectives, and perhaps, less significantly, in the initial years of the program, quantitative objectives.

The qualitative goals were: 1) Establish Urban@ brand recognition among young people and society in general, 2) capture a suitable college market share since the province of Granada has the largest number of university students in Spain, 3) achieve youth segment acceptance of the products and services designed for the Urban@ program, 4) rejuvenate the customer base, and 5) sponsor youth-related initiatives to improve the image of the institution and get closer to this segment.

The quantitative targets included: 1) attracting 1.000 new customers during each year of operation, 2) capturing a direct volume of 3 million euros and 0.6 million euros in investment, and 3) attract 2 million euros from indirect business (see Figure 9).

3.5. Market Reaction to the Urban@ Program

Caja Rural of Granada is the second most significant financial institution in the province of Granada after Caja Granada (now integrated into the structure of Mare Nostrum Bank). Since the two entities have 55% market share of client resources (Caja Rural of Granada has 22% and Caja Granada has 35%), it is clear that the main competitor in the province of Granada would have a competitive response (see Table 1).

As a result of the Caja Rural campaign and with the imminent opening of the office Urban@, in October 2005 Caja Granada decided to launch a new program to replace the then current "University Club Program." Caja Granada designed a new brand called "You are you" to compete with Caja Rural of Granada. Caja Granada developed a communications plan and redesigned an office located in close proximity to the Urban@ office.

3.6. Quantitative Results

In general, the quantitative results exceeded expectations. They are summarized below:

3.6.1. Number of Customers

As of the first quarter of 2011, the institution had contracted with over 16,000 customers in five years, representing an annual average acquisition rate of 3,200 new customers. Of the total clients, 76% are from the province of Granada and the rest are from various provinces in which Caja Rural had a presence (34%). The age distribution is represented in Figure 10.

3.6.2. Customer Loyalty

The customer loyalty of this segment is clearly above the bank average according to the information provided (40% higher) although this segment did not reach the minimum yield in relation to other segments of Caja Rural.

Some highlights of the customer business relationships during the first five years of the Urban@ program include a total of 600 credit operations for educational purposes (3.75% of total customer segment), more than 300 scholar-

Table 1. Similarities and differences between Urban@ and tuerestu program (source: present authors, based on website information)

Brand Characteristics	Urban@ CAJA RURAL	tuerestu.es (CAJA GRANADA)
Corporate Colours	Black and Orange	Black, Green, and Blue
Claim	You can do it! JOIN!	You are you
Website	www.urbancajarural.es	http://www.tuerestu.es
Differentiating Characteristic	Urban@ Community	Your Community
Affiliated Discount Partners	Yes	Yes
Preferential Loans	Yes	Yes
Identifying Office	Yes	Yes
Additional Services Offered in the Office	Yes	No
Mobile Offices	Yes	No
Branded Card	Yes	Yes
Event Calendar	Yes	Yes
Social Networking	Yes	Yes
Ticket Sales	Yes	No
Sponsors	Yes	Yes

ship advances (1.87% of total segment customers) and financing of more than 200 cars (1.25% of total customer segment). These figures are significantly higher than the average funding of other population segments.

3.6.3. Business Volume

According to Caja Rural information, the business volume in this segment of customers amounted to 13.5 million Euros from both loans and deposits. This represents an average volume of 843 Euros per customer, which is much higher than the initial expectations of Caja Rural.

3.7. Impact within Caja Rural and the Sector

The impact of the Urban@ program in Caja Rural of Granada marked a change in multiple dimensions: process innovation, customer focus, customer loyalty, and brand positioning.

The process innovation that took place concerned new ways of using existing products (Gomulka, 1990: 13) which are usually present in the financial sector but which were adapted to the youth segment generating a business line for recurring future revenue.

The main outcomes of this initiative are summarized as:

- A shift to younger customers as a source of current and future value for the institution through the role that the Urban@ program provides to customers (definition, participation, and implementation). Active listening, trust and commitment from the staff working with this segment were key factors in reaching these objectives.
- Loyalty as the ultimate goal of customer satisfaction was in line with expectations (Cardozo, 1965 and Howard and Sheth, 1969) for the Urban@ Program. To achieve these optimal levels of satisfaction, Caja

Figure 10. Number of clients by age (source: present authors using data from Caja Rural)

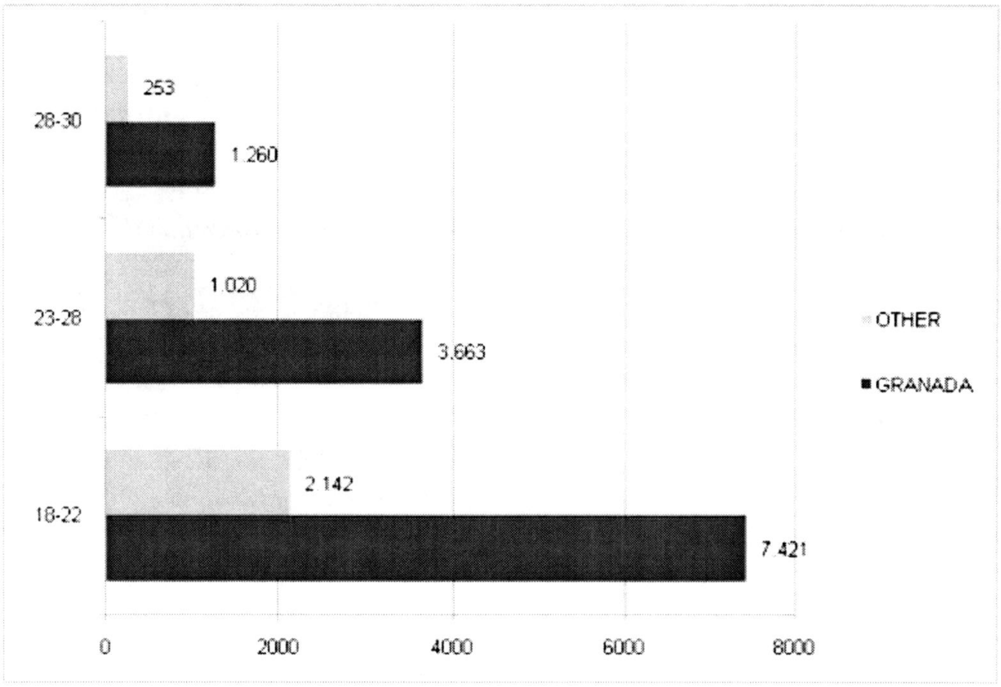

Rural of Granada used up-selling strategies, strategies for cross-selling products or services, turnover prevention programs, the creation of the Urban@ Community, and increased benefits with membership.

- Finally, the positioning of the Urban@ brand favoured the connection between the younger segment of customers and the entity that enhanced the image of modernity resulting in a sharp increase in the number of target clients.

4. CONCLUSION

Companies are discovering the great potential of new technologies for the development of their business, in terms of competitiveness and profitability. The increasing use of ICT represents a major challenge in the modus operandi that has traditionally been applied in commercial relationships. This directly affects relationships with customers.

Innovation in financial institutions is of the utmost importance to meet the continuing needs of consumers and gain a competitive advantage over the competition. Consequently, the concept of the "technology cluster" or innovation package consisting of one or more technological elements that are more or less related has appeared. Small- and medium-sized businesses rarely are able to develop inventions in highly turbulent environments, so "innovation of diversity" is an important remedy to achieve flexibility in changing and competitive markets, especially in the financial sector. Therefore, the establishment of partnerships or strategic alliances between companies is important to achieve innovation in the performance of business tasks.

The banking sector especially, uses a new approach in the design of its offices and Web sites as a way to innovate and diversify horizontally. Because of these innovation and diversification (i +d) programs, new pilot programs in many countries offer innovative Web sites including, the Spanish Caja Navarra's 24-hour offices, the Caja Rural of Granada's Urban@ office, the Deutsche Bank's Q110 office or the Canadian ING Direct's cafés. Concepts such as transparency, flexibility, client proximity, innovation and dynamism, previously unthinkable in the rigid world of finance, now occupy a central role in creation and cultivation of customer relationships and branch models.

Marble facades and little windows are being abandoned in favour of large windows that show bank interiors. In turn, banks are exploiting these windows and open spaces by installing billboards and using other merchandising techniques to showcase products and services. This has led to the creation of a new bank channel, known as "the branch bank 2.0."

In search of an appropriate implementation strategy in this new environment, the current article focuses on the Urban@ program that Caja Rural of Granada began in 2005. This office created an innovative business concept combining banking services with free Internet access, tourist services, a monthly newsletter, electronic component sales and exciting benefits for its customers.

After a period of internal and external analysis and feasibility studies, the first Urban@ office opened coinciding with the start of the 2005-2006 academic year. The design of the office as a whole, including the layout, the furniture, the colours and the materials were chosen for functionality, dynamism, modernity, and practicality to appeal to young people.

After the first five years of operation, the Urban@ program at the Caja Rural of Granada reached nearly all of its objectives. The driving idea at the inception of the program was to market this new service in a different manner than that of competing entities. To this end, Caja Rural defined distinguishing features to reach their objectives. The commercial strategy designed by the management of Caja Rural of Granada was established around three main principles: communication with the youth segment, multi-channel contacts, and a loyalty program.

Bank management established a two-pronged approach for the objectives: qualitative goals (including recognition of the new brand, positioning, acceptance, rejuvenation of the portfolio and sponsorship) and quantitative objectives (attracting new customers, direct and indirect resources).

The Urban@ program generated a series of competitive responses in the market. Most importantly, given the social impact caused by the campaign and the imminent opening of the Urban@ office, its main competitor decided to launch a new program to replace the one it had at that time.

As the five-year operation period demonstrates, the results have exceeded Caja Rural of Granada's expectations (with increases in the annual number of clients, educational loans, scholarship advances and car purchases). Additionally, the program introduced several significant marketing and operational changes for Caja Rural of Granada: process innovation, customer focus, customer loyalty programs and brand positioning.

ACKNOWLEDGMENT

The authors thank Caja Rural of Granada for its enriching contributions to this chapter.

REFERENCES

Agencia, E. F. E. (2009). BBVA cierra las sucursales de Dinero Express para unificar su negocio con inmigrantes. *Terra News*. Retrieved from http://noticias.terra.es/economia/2009/0519/actualidad/bbva-cierra-las-sucursales-de-dinero-express-para-unificar-su-negocio-con-inmigrantes.aspx

Calero, M. ª. R., Martinez, M., Ortega, J. M., & Román, Mª. V. (2005). Impacto de las nuevas tecnologías en los canales de distribución financieros. Madrid, Spain: Dykinson.

Cardozo, R. (1965). An experimental study of consumer effort, expectations and satisfaction. *JMR, Journal of Marketing Research*, *2*, 244–249. doi:10.2307/3150182.

Chaffey, D., Mayer, R., Johnston, K., & Ellis-Chadwich, F. (2000). *Internet marketing strategy, implementation and practice*. Harlow, MA: Prentice Hall.

Cui, C. C., Lewis, B. R., & Park, W. (2003). Service quality measurement in the banking sector in South Korea. *International Journal of Bank Marketing*, *21*(4), 191–201. doi:10.1108/02652320310479187.

Delgado, J., & Nieto, M. J. (2002). Incorporación de la tecnología de la información a la actividad bancaria en España: La banca por Internet. *Estabilidad Financiera*, *3*, 85–105.

Embid, P., Martín, M., & Zorrilla, V. (1998). *Marketing financiero*. Madrid, Spain: McGraw-Hill.

Fujitsu. (2009). *Soluciones para el sector bancario*. Fujitsu.

Fundación Orange. (2010). *eEspaña 2010: Informe anual sobre el desarrollo de la sociedad de la información en España*. Fundación Orange.

Gomulka, S. (1990). *Theory of technological change and economic growth*. Florence, Italy: Routledge. doi:10.4324/9780203013052.

Heinonen, K. (2006). Temporal and spatial e-service value. *International Journal of Service Industry Management*, *17*(4), 380–400. doi:10.1108/09564230610680677.

Heinonen, K., & Strandvick, T. (2005). Communication as an element of service value. *International Journal of Service Industry Management*, *16*(2), 186–198. doi:10.1108/09564230510592306.

Herrero, A. (2005). *El proceso de adopción de nuevos sistemas de venta: Aplicación al comercio electrónico entre particulares y empresas*. Cantabria, Spain: Departamento de Administración de Empresas, Universidad de Cantabria.

Hoffman, D. L. (2000). The revolution will not be televised: Introduction to the special issue on marketing science and the internet. *Marketing Science*, *19*(1), 1–3. doi:10.1287/mksc.19.1.1.15181.

Howard, J. A., & Sheth, J. N. (1969). *The theory of buyer behavior*. New York: Wiley.

Inche, J. L. (1998). Modelos de innovación tecnológica. *Industrial Data*, *1*(2), 9–16.

Kanter, R. M. (1983). *The change masters: Corporate enterpreneurs at work*. London: Routledge.

Karjaluoto, H., Mattila, M., & Pento, T. (2002). Factors underlying attitude formation toward online banking in Finland. *International Journal of Bank Marketing*, *20*(6), 261–272. doi:10.1108/02652320210446724.

Kotler, P., & Keller, K. L. (2006). *Dirección de marketing* (12th ed.). Madrid, Spain: Pearson Education.

Lafuente, R. (2005). *Los servicios financieros bancarios electrónicos*. Valencia, Spain: Tirant lo Blanch.

Masamila, B., Mtenzi, F., Said, J., & Tinabo, R. (2010). A secured mobile payment model for developing markets. *Communications in Computer and Information Science*, *87*(2), 175–182. doi:10.1007/978-3-642-14292-5_20.

Mellor, R. B. (2007). *Innovation nuclei in SMEs involved in Internet B2C e-commerce*. (Tesis doctoral). Retrieved from http://kurir.kingston.ac.uk/mellor2007.pdf

Mendieta, M. M. (2007). Llega la oficina bancaria 2.0. *Cinco días*.

Momparler, A. (2008). *El desarrollo de la banca electrónica en España: Un análisis comparativo entre entidades online y tradicionales en España y estados unidos*. (Doctoral Thesis). Department of Business Organization, Universidad Politécnica de Valencia, Valencia, Spain.

Nadiri, H., Kandampully, J., & Hussain, K. (2009). Zone of tolerance for banks: A diagnostic model of service quality. *Service Industries Journal*, *29*(11), 1547–1564. doi:10.1080/02642060902793425.

Pereira, P. F. (2003). *Comportamiento del consumidor bancario en internet*. (Doctoral Thesis). Department of Administration and Business Economics, University of Salamanca, Salamanca, Spain.

Rogers, E. M. (1983). *Difussion of innovations* (3rd ed.). New York: The Free Press.

Sánchez, J. R. (1997). *Marketing financiero: Principios y estrategias*. Madrid, Spain: Civitas.

Torrent-Sellens, J., Castillo, D., Gabaldón, P., Ruiz, E., & Sainz, J. (2010). *Hacia la banca multicanal*. Madrid, Spain: ESIC.

Zaidi, M. A. (2006). Is Google the best search engine marketing solution? *SearchMarketing-UK.com*. Retrieved from http://www.searchmarketing-uk.com

KEY TERMS AND DEFINITIONS

Credit Union: Is a member-owned financial cooperative that is democratically controlled by its members. The union operates by providing credit at competitive rates, promoting thrift and providing other financial services to its members. Many credit unions also provide other services to support community or/and sustainable development on a local or regional level.

Diversification: A strategy to increase profitability and client acquisiton through innovation and greater sales volumeachieved from new products and markets. This terms has also other meaning, as financial diversification that means reducing risk by investing in a variety of assets.

Innovation: Innovation means the generation, acceptance and implementation of new ideas, processes, products, services or technologies that are accepted by individuals, markets, goverments, and society in general. Innovation refers to the use of something considered new, whereas invention refers directly to the creation of something new.

Loyalty Strategy: A strategic plan focused on continual client retention and satisfaction through increased product offerings and service quality which results in increased profitability.

Marketing Strategy: Correct identification of the target market, provide products and services attractive to the specific segment which results in the best opportunity to achieve higher sales and sustain a competitive advantage.

Multi-Channel Marketing Strategy: Involves the utilization of several distribution channels to reach the target customers. Examples include: retail bank branches, mobile offices, a Web site, mail order catalogues or direct personal communication (by fax, telephone, email...). Some entities focus certain channels at target segments in different socio-economic strata.

Strategic Communication: This strategy develops a communication plan to provide consistent information within an organization and among customers. Furthermore, this plan identifies the target market, and creates a consistent messge, resulting in the achievement of qualitative and quantitative corporate goals. Equivalent business management terms are: organizational communication, integrated (marketing) communication, corporate communication or commercial communication.

Chapter 16
Internal Social Networks:
The Danger of Misleading Promises

Martin Heitmann
Berlin Institute of Technology, Germany

Monique Goepel
Berlin Institute of Technology, Germany

ABSTRACT

This chapter examines how the concept of social networks can be effectively transferred to a business context and why some of the promises associated with network use might be misleading. Special emphasis is given to the issue of co-determination within social networks in the light of networks' proposed benefits for modern companies. The chapter draws relevant insights from literature research and provides a comparison of social networks, user innovation communities, and company requirements. Findings are illustrated by three respective cases from the context of different networks, communities, as well as from network use in business contexts.

INTRODUCTION

Today's business is fast. Increased competition, dynamic environments as well as broad access to a global market pose challenges to business operations and organizations' internal coordinating mechanisms alike (Montoya-Weiss, Massey, & Song, 2001; Siggelkow & Rivkin, 2005). Hence, internal processes must meet the requirement of enabling the rapid flow of information to ensure well-informed decision making and successful coordination (Ericson, 2009; Lawrence & Lorsch, 1967; Milgrom & Roberts, 1995). As a result, the recent upsurge of social networks in different areas and these networks' seemingly superior potential for providing an efficient coordinating mechanism have come to the forefront of academic interest (Gloor, Paasivaara, Schoder, & Willems, 2008;

DOI: 10.4018/978-1-4666-4373-4.ch016

Hossain & Zhu, 2009). However, a question yet unanswered is whether these networks actually can help companies in establishing processes that meet the above mentioned requirement (Andriole, 2010). In this chapter, we propose that the fit of network activities and co-determination structures is an important aspect in order to answer this central question. Therefore, we ask if democratically structured networks are more suitable than meritocratically structured ones for companies to learn from.

Looking back, most companies used a hierarchical, top-down setup (Fayol, 1949). This setup had top management decide on strategic matters while management at lower levels of the firm dealt with more functional issues and front line employees were hardly involved in any kind of decision making. New organizational models have tried to reduce the rigidity of this original top-down model by setting up matrix-based structures, which cross-linked hierarchical lines with functional expertise (Galbraith, 1971). Until today, internal communication has continuously been revolutionized by establishing more internal communication channels to the point where finally any employee has the chance to contact and to be heard by upper management (Aldrich, 1979; Wyld, 2008). However, even in the research on these new organizational models the question of voting weight has largely been left unaddressed.

In parallel to this development a special kind of user network began a triumphal course – known today as social networks. Amongst other examples there are Facebook, MySpace, and Google+. To the huge surprise of many stakeholders, these networks rapidly developed into multi-billion user networks, in which members not only communicated daily issues, but also coordinated work related tasks, special events and much more content relevant to business contexts. As a consequence, these networks were quickly used as much by individuals as by companies (Dutta, 2010; Haislip, 2006; Wilson, Guinan, Parise, & Weinberg, 2011). Examples such as the role of Facebook in the Arab Spring demonstrated the unforeseen potential inherent to social networks (Benn, 2011), raising huge expectations about the advantage of their internal use in an organization. However, as companies have thus far merely learnt to use such networks externally (e.g., Schilling & Phelps, 2007), the question is how to most effectively internalize these coordination mechanisms into existing company structures, if this is possible at all. Moreover, in order to answer this question it is important to acknowledge that there are several different kinds of networks to learn from. Hence, a more comprehensive perspective on their types and their respective benefits is needed.

In the course of the development of open innovation the existence of user innovation communities became an observable phenomenon for management researchers. With it came another kind of organizational model, seemingly highly efficient and thus compelling for a direct comparison with its organizational counterparts (Lee & Cole, 2003). As such, user innovation communities can produce some valuable goods and services of a certain quality in astonishingly short time frames. One prominent example is the development of the Linux kernel, which is known for its high quality standards and rapid development. Such user innovation networks are usually driven by meritocratic mechanisms and outcome oriented objectives (O'Mahony & Ferraro, 2007). Given the fact that their membership is usually voluntary and their non-profit nature, most of them have a lot in common with social networks.

Pinpointing the superiority of user and social network coordination, management scholars such as Gary Hamel suggest that modern companies can benefit from a more democratic, Web-oriented setup (Hamel in Crainer & Birkinshaw, 2008). As such, companies could employ blogs, as they are used for information exchange on the Internet, in order to facilitate internal information and knowledge sharing (Lovejoy & Sinha, 2010). Further suggestions go beyond the aspect of tools for opinion sharing and propose that each company member has equal voting rights (Johnson, 2006), as seen in many social networks. But can this idea of basic democracy be the key to a comparable success of internal coordination and of company success in consequence? Insights from research on organizational design, for instance, reveal the advantages of hierarchical over consensus-based coordination methods (e.g. Mihm, Loch, Wilkinson, & Huberman, 2010).

Another argument is that one can observe very different kinds of user networks today, which differ not only in their coordination routines, but also in their objective settings. These networks provide valuable insights into how a company might best internalize user networks in order to remain effective. Open source software communities, for example, are driven by the ambition to create an IT product. In contrast, social networks such as Facebook have a narrow focus on information exchange and not so much on the creation of a common goal in terms of a product or service. Given the fact that most companies will have goals more similar to those of user innovation communities (e.g. open source software) than to those of social networks, it seems reasonable to compare their different coordination mechanisms respectively and to re-think the promises of network internalization.

For this purpose, we will take a deeper look into company-sided goal settings, user innovation communities, and social networks. We will show how the interaction in social networks is characterized by democratic values and social reputation, while user innovation communities can be marked by phase-dependent changes of meritocratic and democratic principles. Case studies will exemplify our argumentation and we will conclude the chapter with a matrix that includes managerial recommendations on a basis of Goal-to-Co-determination relations.

BACKGROUND

The most commonly accepted company objective is profit maximization (Bishop, 2004; Mankiw, 1998). Besides this, companies seem to increasingly seek growth, sustainability, and achievements in corporate social responsibility (McWilliams & Siegel, 2001, 2011; Pava & Krausz, 1996). Especially the goals of profit maximization and company growth require that companies are able to react adequately and, most importantly, rapidly to changing market conditions, and that they are able to adjust internally (Cohen & Levinthal, 1990). This requirement becomes even more important and also difficult when considering the evolution of so-called hypercompetitive industries today (Akhter, 2003). These industries are marked by a very strong competition and a highly dynamic company environment. Companies in such industries face the difficulty of adapting to very rapid and very complex environmental change. From a managerial perspective, the challenge is to quickly internalize external changes, to effectively process the data and to efficiently distribute it as information in the organization. This means that every affected unit should have access to all necessary information and that it must be able to coordinate the corresponding measures with other parts of the organization. Examples are market data, demographic change and the consequences of external shocks.

The usual approach for such information distribution would be to have a top down information flow hierarchy. That means that upper levels in the hierarchy decide which information is given to which unit. Also, in this approach upper levels will most likely coordinate the activities of units below. A more bottom-up approach is seen where lower hierarchical levels generate information and deliver them to the upper levels. However, the upper management would generally still coordinate the activities as a result of information analysis. It stands to reason that companies which experienced that they were too slow to react in time to external changes, have had these difficulties at least partially due to their use of either one of these approaches. So, the question remains what alternative coordination mechanism would facilitate this process, resulting in faster processing and reaction times.

A promising approach seems to be the use of social networks (Seokwoo, Nerur, & Teng, 2008). Social Networks recently have emerged especially on the Internet. These networks allow network members to share information on a digital platform. Their members were first primarily private customers and certain interest groups. Later commercial companies acknowledged their potential as a marketing platform and also joined these networks. One of the most impressing aspects of social networks is their tremendously fast success in acquiring a large member base (Hardy, Pomerantz, & Hill, 2010; Hempel & Kowitt, 2009; Moggridge, 2011). Today, after only a few years of their existence, billions of people inhabit this virtual space.

It seems that the use of social networks holds potential for companies in their attempt to cope with the above mentioned difficulties of excessive information processing time. Constituting a platform for real-time information exchange among a group of members, examples from political as well as from marketing contexts have shown that social networks enable users to react quickly to new information. On the political level, flash mobs and other kinds of crowds were able to change their movements according to the actions taken by their corresponding counterparts. This can be seen in many countries in the Arab spring (Attia, 2011; Hounshell, 2011), but also in other countries, where youth organizations from political parties organize their protest activities (Rosen, Kim, & Nam, 2010). On the marketing level, companies have successfully implemented social networks in order to leverage their distribution potential (Taylor, Lewin, & Strutton, 2011; Zeisser, 2010). However, these are only examples for the external use of social networks. The argument here is that companies could also use social networks to process information faster internally.

This requires focusing more narrowly on the information processing mechanism in social networks and how information can be translated into network-based action. Social networks usually display a rather informal hierarchy. Active and popular users are likely to have more followers and thus may receive more attention than other, less active network members (Boldi, Bonchi, Castillo, & Vigna, 2011). However, frequent contributors do not yet have any disciplinary power over the rest of the network and they do not have any hierarchical legitimization. If a certain topic is at the center of a network-wide discussion each network participant has the chance to express his or her opinion on the matter. Whether any kind of activity results in the end, depends upon the majority of opinions and the willingness of network members to take action instead of just expressing their agreement or rejection. Overall, this coordination mechanism can be described as a kind of democracy – including the possibility to democratically poll for a leading opinion without the necessity of subsequent action. However, it should be noted that this "social network democracy" is not rooted in any kind of constitutional declaration. Thus, it is an emergent pattern that can be observed in several different social networks.

Another aspect worth mentioning in the context of social networks is their goal system. Usually, social networks are used to exchange information (Coyle & Vaughn, 2008). The information that people share with each other is very diverse, ranging from scheduling shared events, discussions about certain topics, and polling trends to announcements and calling attention to other offerings on the Internet. Although these objectives can constitute a value adding function, they cannot be summarized as part of a general value adding function towards a certain product, service or state of an overarching process. This particular aspect of social networks is vital for the subsequent analysis, as the kind of coordination mechanism should not be investigated without the cross-comparison of goal systems.

As pointed out in the introduction we will compare the mechanisms of social networks with those of user innovation communities. For this purpose we will first take a look at what user innovation communities are, their main intentions, and how members can coordinate their activities.

User innovation communities have been in the focus of much academic research during recent decades (Heiskanen, Hyysalo, Kotro, & Repo, 2010; Hienerth, 2006; von Hippel, 2005). They are usually depicted as groups of customers or users who work in a collaborative process towards a certain goal. This process can be supported or even initiated by companies, but in countless occasions user innovation communities also work independently (Chanal & Caron-Fasan, 2010; Romero & Molina, 2011). The goals they pursue can take different shapes, ranging from offering a specific service to others up to the development of a whole product. Their ambition usually stems from an unavailability of the corresponding service or product, or from the unavailability of this service or product in the demanded quality, functional range or affordability (Jeppesen & Frederiksen, 2006; Ke & Zhang, 2009).

User innovation communities may differ widely in their organization's structural setup, cultural attitude or support systems. We will focus on a certain type of user innovation community that has received much attention in recent years, namely the peer-founded community in the open source software sector.

Open source communities consist of developers who collaboratively create and improve a software source code (Bretthauer, 2002). At this point, a noteworthy distinction has to be made between community members' individual motivation and the respective organizational goals. In this regard, previous studies have shown that some of the developers are driven by idealistic motives, while others mainly aim to signal their talent and skills to peers and potential employers, and yet some are paid developers who work for a software company (Benabou & Tirole, 2003; Bonaccorsi & Lamastra, 2003; Roberts, Hann, & Slaughter, 2006; Shah, 2005). Their unifying organization-wide goal is the development of certain software with a specific functionality (Raymond, 1999).

The coordination mechanism in open source communities is different from that of social networks. While some communities have been shown to use strictly hierarchical setups especially in the form of so-called onion models, others do not use any role-based differentiation of privileges or responsibilities (Crowston & Howison, 2006; Dahlander, Frederiksen, & Rullani, 2008; Franck & Jungwirth, 2003). But apart from the range of hierarchical setups, they also differ in coordination mechanisms in terms of co-determination. In their decisions about strategic developments of the code base, the choice of the software solution chosen and other community-related issues, decision-making processes can have different shapes, but are usually explicitly stated. Two models of co-determination are predominant – democratic and meritocratic (Carillo & Okoli, 2008; Hemetsberger & Reinhardt, 2009; O'Mahony, 2007; O'Mahony & Bechky, 2008). While the first is often used when general questions are discussed, the latter seems to dominate the more technically oriented and strategic matters.

Overall, most participants in social networks and user innovation communities share their voluntary engagement in a broader group of likeminded members. These differences will be at the heart of the subsequently formulated case-based arguments.

NETWORKS, COMMUNITIES, AND THE DANGER OF MISLEADING PROMISES

In the introduction we stated that the use of internal social networks may be due to misleading promises. A first step towards clarification of our argument here can be the investigation of the beginning of some of the most prominent examples today, namely Facebook, MySpace, and Twitter. These networks did not emerge by chance and neither was their success a random incident.

Most of the technologies which are now used by these networks already existed prior to the explosion-like growth of networks. Facebook enables its members to exchange messages and pictures. However, so did many other instant messenger and chat services before, e.g. ICQ or AIM or MySpace. On the other hand we have networks such as Twitter, which are also often named social networks, even if they have another intention, that is to enable microblogging. Again, Twitter and similar networks use a technology that has been around for quite a while. So what is different in these networks? And how can their success be a model for internal communication and coordination?

First, the major benefit for network members in these networks is that these networks work on an aggregate level. That means that singular functions are offered as a combined solution, and that previous peer-to-peer communication and coordination is now improved by many-to-many paths of communication. Network members can now more easily share their thoughts and experiences with all of their contacts or—if they want to—just a sub community. Additionally, they can use multiple functions in combination, e.g. general broadcasts, polls, and many more.

Similarly, microblogging networks enable their members to easily share their feelings, impressions, and thoughts with up to millions of other network members by entering a short message in a text field and then clicking on a submit button.

What these different kinds of networks have in common is that their success relates to their uncomplicated mode of communication and coordination. But before starting to exaggerate the benefits of this model, we have to consider what kind of communication is actually taking place and what kind of disadvantages, e.g. cluster thinking, can emerge through network settings. Usually, social networks are depicted as huge clusters of members, in which each of the nodes (network members) is related to a multiplicity of other nodes. In other words, one might easily get the impression that everyone knows everyone. It has been noted that this may be a misperception (Kossinets, Kleinberg, & Watts, 2008; Mislove, Marcon, Gummadi, Druschel, & Bhattacharjee, 2007). Most often these networks have some function that enables users to automatically follow the activities and statements of other users. Therefore, it is also important to consider who follows whom and for which reason. As stated above, the networks are primarily laid out to distribute information which usually consists of personal opinions or announcements. Therefore, it is not surprising that social networks include a variety of interest groups, each of them having a smaller or bigger number of followers. This in turn means two things: first, each of these clusters within a social network may be oriented towards a certain topic or even attitude, while the network as a whole may not be homogeneous or cohesive in terms of a common goal or interest. Second, communication and coordination of derivative activities within each of the clusters will tend to reinforce previous mental models. This means that the opportunity to create a diversity of perspectives may not be as fruitful as it could be.

A final note on the description of social network communication should address the source and characteristics of value-add within social networks. In social networks, added value emerges primarily from the distribution of information. This means that sub-communities of the network not necessarily derive activities from the previously discussed topics. Examples such as the Arab spring may seem to contradict this observation of ours, but under a more narrow focus it seems that the networks facilitated the revolutions, but they did not cause them. Again, it worked rather as an information platform distributing relevant information. Furthermore, the kind of information that was used in such cases was not very complex and it did not require a very sophisticated processing. Similarly, we can see how organizations use those networks for some events to lead network members to a certain location or to fulfill simple tasks, e.g. in a competition to win a price. But again, the information distribution in these networks is usually not associated with a complex process of information evaluation.

NETWORK USAGE IN BUSINESS CONTEXTS

How can such network settings now be fruitfully used within business contexts? And if internalized, how should communication be structured? To answer these questions, we will present case studies from the context of profit-seeking companies and open source communities, respectively. We have granted anonymity to all of our interview partners and their companies. Therefore, company names are fictive and interviewees will be referred to pointing to their organizational function instead of their actual names.

Keeping the difference in network setups in mind, the remaining question of this chapter thus is how network setups can effectively be internalized into business contexts as to enhance organizational efficiency and, ultimately, company performance. From a company perspective, three goals are paramount: efficiency gains, eliciting expertise by broadening the knowledge base, and the connection of members heretofore unconnected. From this we differentiate important side effects of internal network solutions which imply further benefits or risks to the company and should therefore be adequately accounted for. These include the flattening of hierarchical structures, free information flow between the parties involved both internal and external, as well as second order effects on intra- and inter-firm competition. Ways to deal with these issues will be presented in order to reap the benefits social networks can bring to organizational contexts.

In a business context, the use of social networks can be a source of efficiency gains that stems from three primary mechanisms: first, from the creation of a common knowledge base, e.g., Wikis or knowledge databases. Through members' collective and simultaneous contribution of specific content, high quality levels of information and codified knowledge can be created in short time frames spanning differences in time, place and hierarchical level:

One of our clients, a large corporation operating in the fast-moving consumer goods industry, had a sales problem in specific markets. The product was created in the US but did not sell well in some other markets such as Korea. As the corporation planned to introduce the product into the Chinese market shortly after, there was this huge theme among product managers as to why the product didn't sell in Korea when it did sell well in other countries such as England and the US. Through the platform, product managers finally were able to contact each other quickly and informally, while normally, in this company people would have had to ask their department head to ask the home country's country manager to contact the country manager of the other country to go down the hierarchical ladder in his department, as well, for asking the respective product manager why he thinks the product wouldn't sell. The problem turned out to be a very simple one, they simply had used the wrong colors, font or faces on the pictures, but network communication sped up the process and facilitated global discourse a lot. (CEO, Nettss)

As far as coordinating issues are concerned, simultaneous contributions visible to all participating members that have access to the platform reduce the level of bilateral emails and redundant information. Moreover, potentially emotion-laden discussions can gain in efficiency, with the object of discussion being focused on the content of the contribution only rather than getting distorted by situational dynamics:

We set up an internal polling platform with an organization that wanted to compile a complex proposal for the senate. During each of their sessions about 30 people got stuck in discussion, and they just never reached the point of compiling that proposal. We then delegated certain topics to certain people who each wrote a paragraph on a designated issue, these were digitalized and put on the platform, and every member of the committee had the right to vote for or against each of the paragraphs, free to leave a comment on each, as well. There was one final session where the article was printed out for each member, members voted on each single item, and everyone was able to prepare beforehand. (CEO, Commts)

This effect can be further enhanced when prioritizing or pre-structuration mechanisms such as coordination tools are deployed which automatically reconcile and consolidate the information contributed simultaneously by multiple parties.

Likewise, regional competition at the department or business unit level can be alleviated through supra-regional knowledge sharing and support, leading to greater performance at the level of the firm:

We worked with a large automotive company which is collaborating with several individual car dealers that are dispersed throughout entire country. The sales force selling their cars is not employed with the automotive manufacturer but with the car dealers that exclusively sell this manufacturer's cars. As sales staff was competing with each other for fringe benefits on a regional level based on their number of cars sold, sales staff wouldn't exchange ideas on enhanced sales strategies among each other, which in turn restrained company profits at the manufacturer's firm level. (…) A knowledge database on sales strategies for the sales staff was set up, with now 8,000 individual sales people exchanging ideas on how to sell more cars. (…) Roughly 40% of the sales force is now actively using this platform, exchanging ideas, rating others' ideas, and giving other sales staff positive ratings for very good ideas, and these ratings are part of that sales staff's incentive and compensation scheme, as well. (CEO, Nettss)

Finally, active participation can lead to greater commitment of participating parties, with debates being transparent to all participating members, therefore increasing trust in the company's decision-making and operative processes.

Through my name and the time of entry being visible to all others on the platform, my idea will inextricably be connected me and my person, and no one can take that away from me. This can surpass any hierarchical levels as anyone in the company will see my contribution. This is usually welcomed by people at the top of the company because they want the company to become more competitive or more innovative, e.g., leading to cost reduction, enhanced productivity, etc. While upper and middle management is usually rather afraid of this issue, lower management and front-line employees usually welcome this function again, as they hope this is a way for them to move up the hierarchical ladder. (…) In two cases we actually observed that two employees who appeared really fit to us in our meetings but who were very low within the company's hierarchy, climbed up the hierarchical ladder in very short time and emerged as opinion leaders on the social intranet. They induced several topics they found were worth discussing with loads of comments as a result, so that finally the general manager, who of course is always short on time and only looks at the most polemic issues, posted a comment on their contribution. It turned out that these two had either the guts or the brains to pinpoint to those issues that were hurting the company most. (CEO, Nettss)

However, special attention is to be paid if network structures transcend organizational boundaries, as in their use as a marketing- or distribution channel, as a platform for recruiting purposes, or as an interactive communication channel involving external parties. This way, unmanaged use of open and democratically organized platform settings can be associated with special pitfalls for company settings, as unmonitored posts of members may provoke negative reactions from outside parties that may do severe harm to a company:

The most prominent example happening this year was a short video spot on a game fare that a media company posted. The spot painted a very negative picture of the gamers participating in the fare. As a result, there was a tremendous negative reaction from the audience, with 50,000-60,000 comments and hundreds of people posting videos they made at home in order to complain about the discrediting tone of the spot. Even a children's-Website that was sponsored by that company was overloaded with comments of hatred and anger against the company's unfair treatment of the gaming industry. It literally flooded the company through all communication channels possible. (CEO, Nettss)

Moreover, network usage can only unfold its potential if accompanied by sound planning and support, both on the strategic as well as on the operative level, as the following case will illustrate:

We set up a platform with a budget gathered from several different departments. However, neither the upper management nor the board of directors were participating, and employees were afraid to participate because they felt if upper management was not participating this was not considered actual work and that they would be blamed for active participation. That way there was almost no activity except for one subarea that was closed but where there were very high levels of member activity. When we asked why people were using that subarea so heavily while not using others, people said „Apparently this is not considered work and we are afraid to lose our jobs when spending too much time in the open section where everyone is able to see, so we rather use the anonymous section internally." The platform was closed down shortly after. What is also happening a lot is that companies do really want to have these platforms but don't really know what they want to use it for, a me-too-attitude. There is no plan, no clear objective, no support, and no lead users who are really well taught to pioneer and form positive examples. (CEO, Netts)

Therefore, in order to reap the above mentioned benefits, companies should consider the following steps in order to avoid pitfalls:

- Strategic planning and review of the platform, as well as proper tracking in order to ensure the platform meets the strategic needs it was initiated for.
- Implementation of workflows where necessary.
- Introduction of closed subareas with limited access for designated members where necessary.
- Step-by-step introduction of the platform including the gradual amplification of platform functionalities and special training for lead users.
- Management support and active use, especially in the beginning, in order to convey to employees that active participation is worthwhile and welcomed. Incentives and rewards may be given for active participation.
- Monitoring of content before information is shared or visible to external parties through designated people, teams or departments such as legal, public relations or the works council.
- Community management where necessary, i.e. introduction of a code of conduct, active moderation of discussions and forums

and proper education of the workforce using the platform.

- Supplementary adjustments to the platform according to usage patterns

With sound alignment with company strategic goals, communication guidelines and active support, however, network settings offer several benefits to traditional company settings:

Of course there is potential loss of control associated with opening a forum or a Wiki and making people addressable directly. This primarily comes to companies' minds when information is about to be shared with external parties, as most often legal issues become relevant there.(...) Internally some departments feel that way, too. Employees can virtually exchange any information among each other once the platform is set up. (...) [And as a consequence], yes, companies become flatter. (...) Employees' are partly able to post information and knowledge on their own. And with the speed of information flow within these open organizations this of course leads to certain ivory towers or silos of information being opened out. (CEO, Commts)

The company cases have demonstrated that the main expectation for the use of internal social networks and especially social media is enhancing internal information and knowledge sharing. Besides, we could see that each of the aspects can, however, be associated with certain pitfalls. Therefore, companies should carefully plan their networking activities and make sure the strategic objective for setting up a network is clearly defined, that top management commitment is assured, and that employees have received proper guidance on network usage in order to fully benefit from the selected approach.

THE ISSUE OF CO-DETERMINATION

After having outlined different implementation goals and contexts from a company perspective, we will now turn to the question how these internal networks should best be structured internally. Therefore, we will take a closer look at the seemingly advantageous structures of output-oriented networks and, more specifically, at their respective coordinating mechanisms. To do so, we will focus on three cases on user innovation communities from the context of open source development. As each of the communities is driven by users, it serves well for a comparison with the social network settings described above.

A short overview over network size, age and focus of development is given in Table 1.

Although community members of all three cases differed in their individual motivation to participate in the respective network, community members of all three cases commonly shared an unifying organizational goal however, namely to create a new product or technology.

The communication was usually including all stakeholders, however differing in the public discussion of minor issues or a more closed evaluation of strategically important matters. A similar style occurred in the much related aspect of task coordination: While simple and more general issues were coordinated rather loosely, very important tasks were usually attended by core

Table 1. Sample of user innovation/open source communities

Community	Kind of Development	Community Size	Community Age
EmbeddedThinking	Operating systems	App. 60	> 5 years
FLOSSfire	Office applications	App. 550	> 10 years
CleanDesk	Desktop environments	App. 2000	> 15 years

developers. This two-tiered pattern of attendance, i.e. core- vs. peripherical developers, also covered the discussion of the kind of technological path to be followed. With regards to coordinating mechanism, within a project a rather democratic mode of opinion building was usually followed by a more meritocratic mode for getting things done, accompanied by a higher influence of a limited number of members.

Quotes:

It will change semantically from time to time. At the core it is basically a meritocracy. The more you do, the more power you accumulate. Also your opinion in the community will weigh more when you are a long-time contributor to the community. (Community manager, FLOSSfire)

In our community we have also a changing pattern of democracy and meritocracy depending on how long one has been a member. First, people will get judged on a meritocratic basis and later they may become part of the democratic voting system. (Marketing manager, FLOSSfire)

Who codes, decides. Whoever does good work, he decides. (Developer, CleanDesk)

The main difference compared to social networks and other kinds of social media is that these kinds of innovation communities do not merely want to exchange information. In social networks most members add content only to be heard, and rather few consider the added value which could arise from the re-use of their contributions. In user innovation communities on the other hand, are built around the concept of re-use of members' contributions. Hence, the goals of these two kinds of networks are fundamentally different from each other: Whilst the binding glue in a social network is rather based on the establishment of shared mental maps within certain clusters, the main goal within user innovation communities is the joint production of a specific output, which is usually overcoming a specific functional deficit.

I don't want to be found by a headhunter. I just want to see a wide distribution of my hacks. (Maintainer, EmbeddedThinking)

Motivations can vary a lot. Most people's goal is just to do something good. They are rewarded by knowing they are doing something good by giving all their experience and their skills to the benefit of the community or of the world ... if you want to see FLOSS as an asset for the whole world. (Community manager, FLOSSfire)

We want to develop code of a certain quality. And our review system where everybody can see the work of the others ensures this quality. No one wants to be blamed for bad coding. (Core developer, CleanDesk)

Overall, social networks and media and user innovation communities have many things in common, especially their nature of consisting of globally dispersed members and their virtual interaction. However, goal systems and co-determination seem to differ widely.

DISCUSSION, FUTURE RESEARCH DIRECTIONS, AND CONCLUSION

Companies on their quest to enable faster information processing have to consider in which situations the use of social networks, social media or user innovation communities may be most suitable. None of the community/network options appears to be a universally applicable approach. Given the experiences with these different structures we therefore highly stress the importance of the alignment between the network setting chosen and the company's specific objective. Likewise, network integration should be carefully prepared and intro-

Table 2. Goal-to-co-determination matrix

Primary Goal ↓		
Productive development	User innovation communities (project initiation phase)	User innovation communities (production phase)
Information exchange	Social networks (decentralized services)	Social media (centralized services, e.g. internal blogs)
Co-Determination →	Voting by all	Voting only by few important members

duced in order to make it an efficient supplement to existing company structures. Table 2 depicts our proposal of a Goal-to-Co-determination matrix, delineating the major differences of network setups along the dimensions of co-determination mechanisms prevalent in network settings.

The problem with this kind of managerial decision-making matrix is two-tiered. First, companies will have to consider which kind of goal system they pursue. Do they just want to incorporate the information from outside or do they also wish to quickly derive tasks from the processed information? Likewise, they have to consider ex ante in how far the top management wants to include all, most or only few organization members in the corresponding information exchange or decision-making processes. Ironically, a company that faces inertia in processing external change and information about it could be slowed down even more by widespread discussions among all organization members about the general course of the organization. At the same time, a company trying to exploit the benefits of internal user innovation communities could face reactance by its employees. A mainly production driven community approach could become counterproductive when people feel left out of important information flows and get the feeling to just be a cog in a machinery.

Second, companies that have considered the benefits but also the risks associated with network/community exploitation must deal with the difficulty of the corresponding setup. Exemplary remarks by members of both kinds of organizational structures have emphasized how much the members value the non-affiliation of their corresponding network/community with a company. It will therefore be a challenge for each company to design its network or community such that it is attractive to prospective members. Prominent examples like the internal communities at Microsoft and other companies have shown that it is insufficient to just prepare a certain technological basis and to wait for members to adapt it.

It has been shown that network settings can constitute a source of efficiency gains for companies through offering an alternative platform for communication and coordination. Future research is needed to focus more narrowly on the commonalities and differences between network and community structures. As both of these areas contain multiple multi-facetted phenomena of decision making as well as diverse people- and team-related social mechanisms, this field provides many opportunities for further elaboration. Moreover, subsequent works should take a closer look on how companies can implement network mechanisms into existing organizational structures in an attractive and easy manner and especially what is needed to keep them appealing to users over time.

In the long run, it seems also very appealing to investigate in how far organizations may change due to the use of networks and communities, e.g. in their communication patterns or hierarchical setups. It is already conceivable by now that value sets are likely to change and that daily working routines become more adapted to usual social network or community behavior. The investigation of whether or not such changes occur is another interesting road for future research. Finally, network effects offer huge potential for future research as companies that integrate network structures into their operations will be affected by the dynamic effects inherent in digital markets. Therefore, adequate coping strategies still deserve proper investigation.

Summing up, we have in this article briefly highlighted what kind of benefit internal social networks can bring to a company, but also what kind of misleading promise may be associated with it when not properly checked for compatibility with company goals and network setup.

REFERENCES

Akhter, S. H. (2003). Strategic planning, hypercompetition, and knowledge management. *Business Horizons*, *46*(1), 19. doi:10.1016/S0007-6813(02)00275-6.

Aldrich, H. E. (1979). *Organizations and environment*. Upper Saddle River, NJ: Prentice Hall.

Andriole, S. J. (2010). Business impact of web 2.0 technologies. *Communications of the ACM*, *53*(12), 67–79. doi:10.1145/1859204.1859225.

Attia, M. (2011). Arab spring from cyberspace to reality. *MultiLingual*, *22*(7), 36–39.

Benabou, R., & Tirole, J. (2003). Intrinsic and extrinsic motivation. *The Review of Economic Studies*, *70*(3), 489–520. doi:10.1111/1467-937X.00253.

Benn, T. (2011). The flowers of the Arab spring grow from buds of free information. *New Statesman (London, England)*, *140*(5048), 12.

Bishop, M. (2004). *Profit maximisation*. Economist Intelligence Unit.

Boldi, P., Bonchi, F., Castillo, C., & Vigna, S. (2011). Viscous democracy for social networks. *Communications of the ACM*, *54*(6), 129–137. doi:10.1145/1953122.1953154.

Bonaccorsi, A., & Lamastra, C. R. (2003). *Altruistic individuals, selfish firms? The structure of motivation in open source software*.

Bretthauer, D. (2002). Open source software: A history. *Information Technology and Libraries*, *21*(1), 3–11.

Carillo, K., & Okoli, C. (2008). The open source movement: A revolution in software development. *Journal of Computer Information Systems*, *49*(2), 1–9.

Chanal, V., & Caron-Fasan, M.-L. (2010). The difficulties involved in developing business models open to innovation communities: The case of a crowdsourcing platform. *M@n@gement*, *13*(4), 318-340.

Cohen, W. M., & Levinthal, D. A. (1990). Absorptive capacity: A new perspective on learning and innovation. *Administrative Science Quarterly*, *35*(1). doi:10.2307/2393553 PMID:10106582.

Coyle, C. L., & Vaughn, H. (2008). Social networking: Communication revolution or evolution? *Bell Labs Technical Journal*, *13*(2), 13–17. doi:10.1002/bltj.20298.

Crainer, S., & Birkinshaw, J. (2008). Who needs employees? *Business Strategy Review*, *19*(3), 18–21. doi:10.1111/j.1467-8616.2008.00547.x.

Crowston, K., & Howison, J. (2006). Hierarchy and centralization in free and open source software team communications. *Knowledge, Technology & Policy*, *18*, 65–85. doi:10.1007/s12130-006-1004-8.

Dahlander, L., Frederiksen, L., & Rullani, F. (2008). Online communities and open innovation: Governance and symbolic value creation. *Industry and Innovation*, *15*(2), 115–123. doi:10.1080/13662710801970076.

Dutta, S. (2010). What's your personal social media strategy? *Harvard Business Review*, *88*(11), 127–130. PMID:21049685.

Ericson, J. (2009). The real thing? *Information & Management, 19*(6), 14–19.

Fayol, H. (1949). *General and industrial management*. New York.

Franck, E., & Jungwirth, C. (2003). Reconciling investors and donators: The governance structure of open source. *Journal of Management and Governance, 7*, 401–421. doi:10.1023/A:1026261005092.

Galbraith, J. R. (1971). Matrix organization designs How to combine functional and project forms. *Business Horizons, 14*(1), 29–40. doi:10.1016/0007-6813(71)90037-1.

Gloor, P. A., Paasivaara, M., Schoder, D., & Willems, P. (2008). Finding collaborative innovation networks through correlating performance with social network structure. *International Journal of Production Research, 46*(5), 1357–1371. doi:10.1080/00207540701224582.

Haislip, A. (2006). Question of the day: What's your MySpace strategy? *Venture Capital Journal, 46*(9), 3–6.

Hardy, Q., Pomerantz, D., & Hill, K. (2010). In mark we trust. *Forbes, 186*(6), 80–86.

Heiskanen, E., Hyysalo, S., Kotro, T., & Repo, P. (2010). Constructing innovative users and user-inclusive innovation communities. *Technology Analysis and Strategic Management, 22*(4), 495–511. doi:10.1080/09537321003714568.

Hemetsberger, A., & Reinhardt, C. (2009). Collective development in open-source communities: An activity theoretical perspective on successful online collaboration. *Organization Studies, 30*(9), 987–1008. doi:10.1177/0170840609339241.

Hempel, J., & Kowitt, B. (2009). How Facebook is taking over our lives. *Fortune International, 159*(4), 34–41.

Hienerth, C. (2006). The commercialization of user innovations: The development of the rodeo kayak industry. *R & D Management, 36*(3), 273–294. doi:10.1111/j.1467-9310.2006.00430.x.

Hossain, L., & Zhu, D. (2009). Social networks and coordination performance of distributed software development teams. *The Journal of High Technology Management Research, 20*(1), 52–61. doi:10.1016/j.hitech.2009.02.007.

Hounshell, B. (2011). The revolution will be tweeted. *Foreign Policy*, (187): 20–21.

Jeppesen, L. B., & Frederiksen, L. (2006). Why do users contribute to firm-hosted user communities? The case of computer-controlled music instruments. *Organization Science, 17*(1), 45–63. doi:10.1287/orsc.1050.0156.

Johnson, P. (2006). Whence democracy? A review and critique of the conceptual dimensions and implications of the business case for organizational democracy. *Organization, 13*(2), 245–274. doi:10.1177/1350508406061676.

Ke, W., & Zhang, P. (2009). Motivations in open source software communities: The mediating role of effort intensity and goal commitment. *International Journal of Electronic Commerce, 13*(4), 39–66. doi:10.2753/JEC1086-4415130403.

Kossinets, G., Kleinberg, J., & Watts, D. (2008). The structure of information pathways in a social communication network. In *Proceeding of the 14th ACM SIGKDD International Conference on Knowledge Discovery and Data Mining*, (pp. 435–443). New York, NY: ACM. doi:10.1145/1401890.1401945

Lawrence, P. R., & Lorsch, J. W. (1967). *Organization and environment*. Boston: Harvard University Press.

Lee, G. K., & Cole, R. E. (2003). From a firm-based to a community-based model of knowledge creation: The case of the linux kernel development. *Organization Science*, *14*(6), 633–649. doi:10.1287/orsc.14.6.633.24866.

Lovejoy, W. S., & Sinha, A. (2010). Efficient structures for innovative social networks. *Management Science*, *56*(7), 1127–1145. doi:10.1287/mnsc.1100.1168.

Mankiw, N. G. (1998). *Microeconomics*. London: Elsevier.

McWilliams, A., & Siegel, D. (2001). Corporate social responsibility: A theory of the firm perspective. *Academy of Management Review*, *26*(1), 117–127. doi: doi:10.2307/259398.

McWilliams, A., & Siegel, D. S. (2011). Creating and capturing value. *Journal of Management*, *37*(5), 1480–1495. doi:10.1177/0149206310385696.

Mihm, J., Loch, C. H., Wilkinson, D., & Huberman, B. A. (2010). Hierarchical structure and search in complex organizations. *Management Science*, *56*(5), 831–848. doi:10.1287/mnsc.1100.1148.

Milgrom, P., & Roberts, J. (1995). Complementarities and fit strategy, structure, and organizational change in manufacturing. *Journal of Accounting and Economics*, *19*(2-3), 179–208. doi:10.1016/0165-4101(94)00382-F.

Mislove, A., Marcon, M., Gummadi, K. P., Druschel, P., & Bhattacharjee, B. (2007). Measurement and analysis of online social networks. In *Proceedings of the 7th ACM SIGCOMM Conference on Internet Measurement*, (pp. 29–42). New York, NY: ACM. doi:10.1145/1298306.1298311

Moggridge, C. (2011). The evolution of Facebook. *B&T Magazine, 61*(2734), 14.

Montoya-Weiss, M. M., Massey, A. P., & Song, M. (2001). Getting it together: Temporal coordination and conflict management in global virtual teams. *Academy of Management Journal*, 1251–1262. doi:10.2307/3069399.

O'Mahony, S. (2007). The governance of open source initiatives: What does it mean to be community managed? *Journal of Management and Governance*, *11*(2), 139–150. doi:10.1007/s10997-007-9024-7.

O'Mahony, S., & Bechky, B. A. (2008). Boundary organizations: Enabling collaboration among unexpected allies. *Administrative Science Quarterly*, *53*(3), 422–459. doi:10.2189/asqu.53.3.422.

O'Mahony, S., & Ferraro, F. (2007). The emergence of governance in an open source community. *Academy of Management Journal*, *50*(5), 1079–1106. doi:10.5465/AMJ.2007.27169153.

Pava, M. L., & Krausz, J. (1996). The association between corporate social-responsibility and financial performance: The paradox of social cost. *Journal of Business Ethics*, *15*, 321–357. doi:10.1007/BF00382958.

Raymond, E. (1999). The cathedral and the bazaar. *Knowledge, Technology & Policy*, *12*(3), 23–49. doi:10.1007/s12130-999-1026-0.

Roberts, J. A., Hann, I. H., & Slaughter, S. A. (2006). Understanding the motivations, participation, and performance of open source software developers: A longitudinal study of the Apache projects. *Management Science*, *52*(7), 984. doi:10.1287/mnsc.1060.0554.

Romero, D., & Molina, A. (2011). Collaborative networked organisations and customer communities: Value co-creation and co-innovation in the networking era. *Production Planning and Control*, *22*(5/6), 447–472. doi:10.1080/09537287.2010.536619.

Rosen, D., Kim, J. H., & Nam, Y. (2010). Birds of a feather protest together: Theorizing self-organizing political protests with flock theory. *Systemic Practice and Action Research, 23*(5), 419–441. doi:10.1007/s11213-010-9167-3.

Schilling, M. A., & Phelps, C. C. (2007). Interfirm collaboration networks: The impact of large-scale network structure on firm innovation. *Management Science, 53*(7), 1113–1126. doi:10.1287/mnsc.1060.0624.

Seokwoo, S., Nerur, S., & Teng, J. T. C. (2008). Understanding the influence of network positions and knowledge processing styles. *Communications of the ACM, 51*(10), 123–126. doi:10.1145/1400181.1400208.

Shah, S. K. (2005). Motivation, governance & the viability of hybrid forms in open source software development. *SSRN eLibrary*. Retrieved from http://papers.ssrn.com/sol3/papers.cfm?abstract_id=898247

Siggelkow, N., & Rivkin, J. W. (2005). Speed and search: Designing organizations for turbulence and complexity. *Organization Science*, 101–122. doi:10.1287/orsc.1050.0116.

Taylor, D. G., Lewin, J. E., & Strutton, D. (2011). Friends, fans, and followers: Do ads work on social networks? *Journal of Advertising Research, 51*(1), 258–275. doi:10.2501/JAR-51-1-258-275.

von Hippel, E. (2005). Democratizing innovation: The evolving phenomenon of user innovation. *Journal für Betriebswirtschaft, 55*(1), 63–78. doi:10.1007/s11301-004-0002-8.

Wilson, H. J., Guinan, P. J., Parise, S., & Weinberg, B. D. (2011). What's your social media strategy? *Harvard Business Review, 89*(7/8), 23–25.

Wyld, D. C. (2008). Management 2.0: A primer on blogging for executives. *Management Research News, 31*(6), 448–483. doi:10.1108/01409170810876044.

Zeisser, M. (2010). Unlocking the elusive potential of social networks. *The McKinsey Quarterly*, (3): 28–30.

KEY TERMS AND DEFINITIONS

Co-Determination: The configuration of co-determination permission. It is determining who is eligible to express his opinion, who is eligible to comment, who is eligible to decide, and who is eligible to receive certain privileges or responsibilities.

Codified Knowledge: Explicit and systematized knowledge.

Democratic: A system or determination principle characterized by the principle of equality for all.

Meritocratic: A system or determination principle characterized by advancement or decision right based on individual ability or achievement.

Social Media: Centralized media like blog services, which enable a small number of opinion leaders to express their thoughts and gives other participants limited writing access to a general debate about a given topic.

Social Network: Decentralized, digital communication channels that enable a multiplicity of participants to communicate to each other on pathways, which are not predetermined.

User Innovation Community: A community of people who work together on a project in order to achieve a common goal. Individual motivation can differ from the overall binding objective.

Compilation of References

A Wiki of Social Media Monitoring Solutions. (2011). *Monitoring solutions master list*. Retrieved from http://wiki.kenburbary.com

Abascal, J., & Civit, A. (2000). Mobile communication for older people: New oportunities for autonomous life. In *Proceedings of the Worshop on Universal Accessibility of Ubiquitous Computind: Providing for the Elderly* (pp. 255-268). Firenze, Italy: European Research Consortium for Informatics and Matematics.

Abecker, A., & Decker, S. (1998). Organizational memory: Knowledge acquisition, integration and retrieval issues. In *Proceedings of XPS-99* (LNAI), (vol. 1570, pp. 113-124). Berlin: Springer.

Acquisti, A. (2010). The economics of personal data and the economics of privacy. *WPISP-WPIE Roundtable*. Retrieved on November 3, 2011, from http://www.oecd.org/dataoecd/8/51/46968784.pdf

Actuate/BIRT. (2011). *BIRT open source*. Retrieved from http://www.actuate.com/

Adams, M., & Oleksak, M. (2010). *Intangible capital - Putting knowledge to work in the 21st-century organization*. Santa Barbara, CA: Praeger.

Adler, R. (2002). *The age wave meets the technology wave: Broadband and older americans*. Thousand Oaks, CA: Senior Net.

Afuah, A. (1998). *Innovation management*. New York: Harvard Press.

Agarwal, A., Shankar, R., & Tiwari, M. (2007). Modeling agility of supply chain. *Industrial Marketing Management*, *36*(4), 443–457. doi:10.1016/j.indmarman.2005.12.004.

Agarwal, R., & Prasad, J. (1999). Are individual differences germane to the acceptance of new information technologies. *Decision Sciences*, *30*(2), 361–391. doi:10.1111/j.1540-5915.1999.tb01614.x.

AGEMDI. (2011). *IV estudio sobre marketing y publicidad en medios interactivos*. Retrieved November, 20, 2010 from http://www. agemdi.es

Agencia, E. F. E. (2009). BBVA cierra las sucursales de Dinero Express para unificar su negocio con inmigrantes. *Terra News*. Retrieved from http://noticias.terra.es/economia/2009/0519/actualidad/bbva-cierra-las-sucursales-de-dinero-express-para-unificar-su-negocio-con-inmigrantes.aspx

Ahmad, M., & Bowman, I. (2011). Predicting system performance for multi-tenant database workloads. In *Proceedings of the Fourth International Workshop on Testing Database Systems* (pp. 6.1-6.6). ACM Press.

Ahrens, A., & Zaščerinska, J. (2011). Enterprise 3.0 in engineering education. In G. Noviks (Ed.), *Proceedings of the 15th International Student Scientific Practical Conference Human Environment. Technology* Rēzekne: Rēzeknes Augstskolas Izdevniecība.

Ahson, S. A., & Ilyas, M. (2011). *Near field communications handbook*. Boca Raton, FL: CRC Press. doi:10.1201/b11226.

Ajzen, I. (1991). The theory of planned behavior. *Organizational Behavior and Human Decision Processes*, *50*, 179–211. doi:10.1016/0749-5978(91)90020-T.

Akenti. (2009). *Amentia distributed access control*. Retrieved November 29, 2010, from http://dsd.lbl.gov/Akenti

Akhter, S. H. (2003). Strategic planning, hypercompetition, and knowledge management. *Business Horizons*, *46*(1), 19. doi:10.1016/S0007-6813(02)00275-6.

Akkermans, H., & Helder, K. (2002). Vicious and virtuous cycles in ERP implementation: A case study of interrelations between CSF. *European Journal of Information Systems*, *2*, 35–46. doi:10.1057/palgrave.ejis.3000418.

Aksu, A. A., & Tarcan, E. (2002). The internet and five-star hotels: A case study from the Antalya region in Turkey. *International Journal of Contemporary Hospitality Management*, *14*(2), 94–97. doi:10.1108/09596110210419282.

Al Mahmud, A., Mubin, O., Shaid, S., & Martens, J.-B. (2008). Desigining and evaluating the tabletop game experience for seniors citizens. In *Proceedings of the 5th Nordic Conference on Human-Computer Interaction: Building Bridges*. ACM.

Alavi, M., & Leidner, D. (2001). Knowledge management and knowledge management systems: Conceptual foundations and research issues. *Management Information Systems Quarterly*, *25*(1), 107–136. doi:10.2307/3250961.

Alba, J. W., & Hutchinson, J. W. (1987). Dimension of consumer expertise. *The Journal of Consumer Research*, *13*(4), 411–455. doi:10.1086/209080.

Albert, S., & Bradley, K. (1997). *Managing knowledge: Experts, agencies and organizations*. Cambridge, UK: Cambridge University Press. doi:10.1017/CBO9780511582486.

Alcobia, P. (2001). Atitudes e satisfação no trabalho. In Ferreira, J. M., Neves, J., & Caetano, A. (Eds.), *Manual de psicossociologia das organizações*. Lisboa, Portugal: McGraw-Hill.

Aldrich, H. E. (1979). *Organizations and environment*. Upper Saddle River, NJ: Prentice Hall.

Alee, V. (2003). *The future of knowledge: Increasing prosperity through value networks*. Burlington, MA: Elsevier Science.

Alee, V. (2008). Value network analysis and value conversion of tangible and intangible assets. *Journal of Intellectual Capital*, *9*(1).

Alexander, B. (2006). Web 2.0: A new wave of innovation for teaching and learning? *Educause Review*, *41*(2), 32-44. Retrieved May 28, 2011, from http://www.educause.edu/ir/library/pdf/erm0621.pdf

Alfiery, R. (2003). Managing dynamic user communities in a grid of autonomous resources. In *Proceedings of the Conference for Computing in High Energy and Nuclear Physics*. IEEE.

Algesheimer, R., Dholakia, U. M., & Herrmann, A. (2005). The social influence of brand community: Evidence from european car clubs. *Journal of Marketing*, *69*(3), 19–34. doi:10.1509/jmkg.69.3.19.66363.

Allee, V. (1997). *The knowledge evolution: expanding organizational intelligence*. Burlington, MA: Butterworth-Heinemann.

Allen, C., Jazayeri, D., Miranda, J., Biondich, P. G., Mamlin, B. W., & Wolfe, B. A. et al. (2007). Experience in implementing the OpenMRS medical record system to support HIV treatment in Rwanda. *Studies in Health Technology and Informatics*, *129*, 382–386. PMID:17911744.

Allen, N., & Meyer, P. (1990). Organizational socialization tactics: A longitudinal analysis of links to newcomers' commitment and role orientation. *Academy of Management Journal*, *33*(4), 1–18. doi:10.2307/256294.

Al-Mashari, M., Al-Mudimigh, A., & Zairi, M. (2003). Enterprise resource planning: Taxonomy of critical factors. *European Journal of Operational Research*, *146*(2), 352–364. doi:10.1016/S0377-2217(02)00554-4.

Al-Qawabah, M. (2012). *Assessing transformational leadership components as drivers in learning organisations*. (Doctor of Philosophy Dissertation). University of Technology, Sydney, Australia.

Alvesson, M. (2002). *Understanding organizational culture*. London: SAGE.

Alvesson, M. (2004). *Knowledge work and knowledge-intensive firms*. Oxford, UK: Oxford University Press.

AMA. (1985). AMA board aproves new marketing definition. *American Marketing Association News*, *19*(5).

AMA. (2007). *Definition of marketing*. Washington, DC: American Marketing Association.

Amabile, T. M. (1988). A model of creativity and innovation in organisations. *Research in Organizational Behavior, 19*, 123–167.

Amabile, T. M. (1996). *Creativity in context*. Boulder, CO: Westview Press.

Amariles, F., Paz, O. P., Russell, N., & Johnson, N. (2006). The impacts of community telecenters in rural Colombia. *Journal of Community Informatics, 2*(3).

Amoako-Gyampah, K., & Salam, A. F. (2004). An extension of the technology acceptance model in an ERP implementation environment. *Information & Management, 41*, 731–745. doi:10.1016/j.im.2003.08.010.

Anand, G., & Kodali, R. (2010). Development of a framework for implementation of lean manufacturing systems. *International Journal of Management Practice, 4*(1), 95–116. doi:10.1504/IJMP.2010.029705.

Anckar, B. (2008). Omena hotels: Technology towards operational efficiency. In Egger, R., & Buhalis, D. (Eds.), *eTourism: case studies* (pp. 37–47). Oxford, UK: Butterworth Heinemann - Elsevier.

Andersen, K. N., Henriksen, H. Z., Medaglia, R., Danziger, J. N., Sannarnes, M. K., & Enemarke, M. (2010). Fads and facts of e-government: A review of impacts of e-government (2003-2009). *International Journal of Public Administration, 33*(11), 564–579. doi:10.1080/01900692.2010.517724.

Anderson, L. (2004). *E-learning at Augsburg college*. Retrieved April 2011 from http://www.augsburg.edu/eteam/report.pdf

Anderson, L.W., & Krathwohl (Ed.). (2001). *A taxonomy for learning, teaching and assessing: A revision of Bloom's taxonomy of educational objectives*. New York: Longman.

Anderson, P. (2007). What is web 2.0? Ideas, technologies and implications for education. *JISC Technology and Standards Watch*, 2-64.

Anderson, A., McEwan, R., Bal, J., & Carletta, J. (2007). Virtual team meetings: An analysis of communication and context. *Computers in Human Behavior, 23*, 2558–2580. doi:10.1016/j.chb.2007.01.001.

Anderson, E. (2008). *The long tail: Why the future of business is selling less of more*. New York: Hyperion.

Anderson-Lehman, R., Watson, H. J., Wixom, B. H., & Hoffer, J. A. (2004). Continental airlines flies high with real-time business intelligence. *MIS Quarterly Executive, 3*(4), 163–176.

Andersson, S. (2008). Finnair: Innovating interactivity. In Egger, R., & Buhalis, D. (Eds.), *eTourism: Case studies* (pp. 293–303). Oxford, UK: Butterworth Heinemann - Elsevier.

Andreasen, A., Lee, N., & Rothschild, M. (2008). Further thoughts on the 2007 AMA definition of marketing and its implications for social marketing. *Social Marketing Quarterly, 14*(2), 101–104. doi:10.1080/15245000802103575.

Andrews, S. B. (1995). Structural holes: The social structure of competition by Ronald S. Burt. *Administrative Science Quarterly, 40*(3), 355–359. doi:10.2307/2393644.

Andriessen, J. H. E. (2003). *Working with groupware: Understanding and evaluating collaboration technology*. London: Springer-Verlag. doi:10.1007/978-1-4471-0067-6.

Andriole, S. J. (2010). Business impact of web 2.0 technologies. *Communications of the ACM, 53*(12), 67–79. doi:10.1145/1859204.1859225.

Andrus, D. (2005). The wiki and the blog: Toward a complex adaptive intelligence community. *Studies in Intelligence, 49*(3).

Anklam, P. (2007). *Net work - A practical guide to creating and sustaining networks at work and in the world*. Oxford, UK: Elsevier.

Anwer, S., & Ikram, N. (2006). Goal oriented requirement engineering: A critical study of techniques. In *Proceedings of the Software Engineering Conference* (pp. 121-130). IEEE Computer Society Press.

Apache. (n.d.). Retrieved from www.apache.org

Argyris, C. (1993). Education for leading-learning. *Organizational Dynamics*, *21*(3), 5–17. doi:10.1016/0090-2616(93)90067-B.

Argyris, C., & Schön, D. A. (1978). *Organisational learning: A theory of action perspective*. Philippines: Addison-Wesley Publishing Co..

Ariely, D. (2000). Controlling the information flow: Effects on consumers' decision making and preference. *The Journal of Consumer Research*, *27*(2), 233–248. doi:10.1086/314322.

Asunda, P. (2010). Productivity, social networks and net communities in the workplace. *Techniques: Connecting Education and Careers*, *85*(5), 38–41.

Attia, M. (2011). Arab spring from cyberspace to reality. *MultiLingual*, *22*(7), 36–39.

Azevedo, S., Carvalho, H., Cruz-Machado, V., & Grilo, F. (2010). The influence of agile and resilient practices on supply chain performance: An innovative conceptual model proposal. In Blecker, Kersten, & Luthje (Eds.), Innovative Process Optimization Methods in Logistics: Emerging trends, concepts and technologies, (pp. 265-281). Berlin: Erich Schmidt Verlag GmbH & Co. KG.

Azevedo, S. G., Carvalho, H., & Cruz-Machado, V. (2011). A proposal of LARG supply chain management practices and a performance measurement system. *International Journal of e-Education, e-Business, e-. Management Learning*, *1*(1), 7–14.

Azevedo, S. G., Machado, V., Barroso, A., & Cruz-Machado, V. (2008). Supply chain vulnerability: Environment changes and dependencies. *International Journal of Logistics and Transport*, *1*, 41–55.

Baggio, R. (2008). Province of Rimini: Communicating with the customer. In Egger, R., & Buhalis, D. (Eds.), *eTourism: Case studies* (pp. 213–223). Oxford, UK: Butterworth Heinemann - Elsevier.

Bagozzi, R. P., & Dholakia, U. M. (2006). Antecedents and purchase consequences of customer participation in small group brand communities. *International Journal of Research in Marketing*, *23*(1), 45–61. doi:10.1016/j.ijresmar.2006.01.005.

Bailey, A., & Ngwenyama, O. (2011). The challenge of e-participation in the digital city: Exploring generational influences among community telecentre users. *Telematics and Informatics*, *28*(3), 204–214. doi:10.1016/j.tele.2010.09.004.

Bajwa, I. S., Bordbar, B., & Lee, M. G. (2010). OCL constraints generation from natural language specification. In *Proceedings of the 14th IEEE International Enterprise Distributed Object Computing Conference* (pp. 204-213). New York: IEEE Press.

Baker, L., Rideout, J., Gertler, P., & Raube, K. (2005). Effect of an Internet-based system for doctor-patient communication on health care spending. *Journal of the American Medical Informatics Association*, *12*(5). doi:10.1197/jamia.M1778 PMID:15905484.

Balabanis, G., & Vassileiou, S. (1999). Some attitudinal predictors of home-shopping through the internet. *Journal of Marketing Management*, *15*, 361–385. doi:10.1362/026725799784870315.

Balasubramanian, S., & Mahajan, V. (2001). The economic leverage of the virtual community. *International Journal of Electronic Commerce*, *5*(3), 103–138.

Balieiro, M. A., Sousa, S. F. Jr, & Souza, C. D. (2008). Análise multidimensional de redes sociais de projetos de software livre. In *Proceedings of Simpósio Brasileiro de Sistemas Colaborativos* (pp. 23–33). Vitória, Brasil: IEEE.

Ball, S., Eckel, C., Grossman, P. J., & Zame, W. (2001). Status in markets. *The Quarterly Journal of Economics*, *116*(1), 161–188. doi:10.1162/003355301556374.

Baloglu, S., & Mangaloglu, M. (2001). Tourism destination images of Turkey, Egypt, Greece, and Italy as perceived by US-based tour operators and travel agents. *Tourism Management*, *22*, 1–9. doi:10.1016/S0261-5177(00)00030-3.

Baloglu, S., & Pekcan, Y. A. (2006). The website design and Internet site marketing practices of upscale and luxury hotels in Turkey. *Tourism Management*, *27*, 171–176. doi:10.1016/j.tourman.2004.07.003.

Bancroft, N., Seip, H., & Sprengel, A. (2001). *Implementing SAP R/3* (2nd ed.). Greenwich, CT: Manning Publications Co..

Bandopadhaya, S. K., Bhattacharyya, D., Mukherjee, S., Ganguly, D., & Das, P. (2008). Statistical approach for offline handwritten signature verification. *Journal of Computer Science*, *4*(3), 181–185. doi:10.3844/jcssp.2008.181.185.

Bandyo-Padhyay, N. (2002). *E-commerce: Context, concepts and consequences*. New York: McGraw-Hill.

Barabba, V. (2004). *Surviving transformation*. Oxford, UK: Oxford University Press.

Barão, A., & Rodrigues da Silva, A. (2011). A model to evaluate the relational capital of organizations (SNARE-RCO). In *Proceedings of Conference of Enterprise Information Systems* (Centeris'2011). Springer-Verlag.

Barão, A., & Silva, A. (2008). SNARE - Social network analysis and reengineering environment: Architecture overview. In *Proceedings of WEBIST - International Conference on Web Information Systems and Technologies*. Funchal, Portugal: WEBIST.

Barão, A., & Silva, A. R. (2010). The SNARE language overview. In *Proceedings of the 12th ICEIS - International Conference on Enterprise Systems, ICEIS'2010*. INSTICC.

Barão, A., & Silva, A. R. (2011). A model to evaluate the relational capital of organizations SNARE-RCO. In M. M. Crus-Cunha et al. (Eds.), *CENTERIS - Conference on Enterprise Information Systems*, (pp. 400-409). Berlin: Springer.

Barbeira, M. R., & Franco, M. J. (2009). Um sistema de gestão do conhecimento como fomentador de redes estratégicas interorganizacionais. *Revista Ibero-Americana de Estratégia*, *8*(2), 5–29.

Barnard, C. (1938). *The functions of the executive* (2nd ed.). Boston: Harvard University Press.

Barnatt, C. (2008). Higher education 2.0. *International Journal of Management Education*, *7*(3), 47–56. doi:10.3794/ijme.73.250.

Barrett, R., Maglio, P. P., & Kellem, D. C. (1997). How to personalize the web. In *Proceedings of Human Factors In Computing Systems*. New York: ACM Press.

Barrett, R., & Maurice Salles, M. (2006). *Social choice with fuzzy preferences. Center for Research in Economics and Management (CREM), University of Rennes 1*. University of Caen and CNRS.

Bass, B. M. (1985). *Leadership and performance beyond expectations*. New York: Free Press.

Bass, B. M. (1990). *Bass and Stogdill's handbook of leadership: Theory, research, and applications* (3rd ed.). New York: Free Press.

Bass, B. M., & Avolio, B. J. (1990). *Transformational leadership development: Manual for the multifactor leadership questionnaire*. Palo Alto, CA: Consulting Psychologists Press.

Bass, B. M., & Avolio, B. J. (1994). *Improving organisational effectiveness through transformational leadership*. Thousand Oaks, CA: Sage Publications.

Bassus, O., & Wolfgramm, K. (2009). The innovative entrepreneurship training program at Hochschule Wismar University of Technology, Business and Design. In Ahrens & Lange (Eds.), *First Asian Conference on e-Business and Telecommunications* (pp. 36-39). Berlin: Mensch & Buch.

Bassus, O., Ahrens, A., & Zaščerinska, J. (2011). Clustering for the development of engineering students' use of enterprise 3.0. In *Proceedings of the 4th International Conference of Engineering & Business Education and 1st SAFRI Journey to Excellence Conference* (pp. 373-383). Cape Town, South Africa: Cape Peninsula University of Technology.

Bassus, O., Zaščerinska, J., & Ahrens, A. (2011). From enterprise 2.0 to 3.0: Challenges in engineering and business education. In Bassus, , Ahrens, , & Lange, (Eds.), *Information and Communication Technologies in Engineering and Business* (pp. 79-96). Berlin, Germany: Mensch & Buch.

Batagelj, V. (2009). Social network analysis, large-scale. In Meyers, R. A. (Ed.), *Encyclopedia of Complexity and Systems Science* (pp. 8245–8265). Berlin: Springer. doi:10.1007/978-0-387-30440-3_489.

Batagelj, V., & Mrvar, A. (2003). Pajek analysis and visualization of large networks. *Science*, *2265*(19), 8–11.

Bateman, T., & Organ, D. (1983). Job satisfaction and the good soldier: The relationship between affect and employee 'citizenship'. *Academy of Management Journal, 26*(4), 587–595. doi:10.2307/255908.

Bates, D. W., & Wright, A. (2009). Evaluating eHealth: Undertaking robust international cross-cultural ehealth research. *PLoS Medicine, 6*(9), e10000105. doi:10.1371/journal.pmed.1000105 PMID:19753106.

Baumol, W. (2001). When is inter-firm co-ordination beneficial? *International Journal of Industrial Organization, 19*(5), 727–737. doi:10.1016/S0167-7187(00)00091-6.

Baumol, W. (2010). *The micro-theory of innovative entrepreneurship*. Princeton, NJ: Princeton University Press.

Bautista García-Vera, A. (2001). Desigualdades sociales, nuevas tecnologías y política educativa. In Area Moreira, M. (Ed.), *Educar en la sociedad de la información*. Bilbao, Spain: Desclée de Brower.

Beagrie, N. (2005). Plenty of room at the bottom? Personal digital libraries and collections. *D-Lib Magazine, 11*(6). Retrieved October 22, 2011, from http://www.dlib.org/dlib/june05/beagrie/06beagrie.html

Becker, M. Y., & Sewell, P. (2004). Cassandra: Distributed access control policies with tunable expressiveness. In *Proceedings of the Fifth IEEE International Workshop on Policies for Distributed Systems and Networks* (p. 159). Washington, DC: IEEE Computer Society.

Becker, J., Bergener, P., Niehaves, B., & Räckers, M. (2008). Social inclusiveness of electronic public service delivery in Germany: A quantitative analysis. *Information Systems Journal*.

BECTA. (2001). *The 'digital divide': A discussion paper*. BECTA.

Becta. (2008). *Harnessing technology: Next generation learning 2008-14: A summary*. Retrieved April 2011 from http://www.becta.org.uk

Bédard, F., & Louillet, M. C. (2008). BonjourQuebec.com: A vision, a strategy, a brand. In *R. Egger & D. Buhalis (2008). eTourism: Cases studies* (pp. 200–212). Oxford, UK: Ed. Butterworth Heinemann – Elsevier.

Beek, H. (1964). The influence of assembly line organization on output, quality, and morale. *Occupational Psychology, 38*(3/4), 161–172.

Been-Lirn Duh, H., Yi-Luen Do, E., Billinghurst, M., Quek, F., & Chen Hsueh-Hua, V. (2010). Senior-friendly technologies: Interaction design for seniors users. In *Proceedings of CHI*. Atlanta, GA: ACM.

Bel, R. (2010). *Leadership and innovation: Learning from the best*. Retrieved frm www.interscience.wiley.com

Belch, G. E. (1981). An examination of comparative and noncomparative television commercials: The effects of claim variation and repetition on cognitive response and message acceptance. *JMR, Journal of Marketing Research, 18*, 333–349. doi:10.2307/3150974.

Beldarrain, Y. (2006). Distance education trends: Integrating new technologies to foster student interaction and collaboration. *Distance Education, 27*(2), 139–153. doi:10.1080/01587910600789498.

Bell, M. (2008). *Service-oriented modeling: Service analysis, design, and architecture*. New York: John Wiley & Sons.

Bellotti, V., Dalal, B., Good, N., Flynn, P., Bobrow, D. G., & Ducheneaut, N. (2004). What a to-do: Studies of task management towards the design of a personal task list manager. In *Proceedings of the SIGCHI Conference on Human Factors in Computing Systems* (pp. 735-742). New York: ACM.

Benabou, R., & Tirole, J. (2003). Intrinsic and extrinsic motivation. *The Review of Economic Studies, 70*(3), 489–520. doi:10.1111/1467-937X.00253.

Ben-David, J., & Collins, R. (1966). Social factors in the origins of a new science: The case of psychology. *American Sociological Review, 31*(4), 451–465. doi:10.2307/2090769 PMID:5329541.

Benkler, Y. (2006). *The wealth of networks - How social production transforms markets and freedom*. New Haven, CT: Yale University Press.

Bennet, A. (2006). The learning organisation portfolio. *The Journal of information and Knowledge Management Systems, 36*(1).

Benn, T. (2011). The flowers of the Arab spring grow from buds of free information. *New Statesman (London, England), 140*(5048), 12.

Benson, V., Filippaios, F., & Morgan, S. (2010). Online social networks: changing the face of business education and career planning. *International Journal of e-Business Management, 4*(1), 20-33.

Benson-Armer, R., & Hsieh, T. (1997). Teamwork across time and space. *The McKinsey Quarterly, 4*, 18–27.

Bergeron, B. (2000). Regional business intelligence: The view from Canada. *Journal of Information Science, 26*(3), 153–160. doi:10.1177/016555150002600305.

Berkem, B. (2008). From the business motivation model (BMM) to service oriented architecture (SOA). *Journal of Object Technology, 7*(8), 57–70. doi:10.5381/jot.2008.7.8.c6.

Berkun, S. (2010). *The myths of innovation*. Cambridge, UK: O'Reilly Media.

Berling, R. J. (1993). The emerging approach to business strategy: Building a relationship advantage. *Business Horizons, 36*(4), 16. doi:10.1016/S0007-6813(05)80115-6.

Bernardino, J., & Ribeiro, P. (2011). Open source business intelligence: An alternative to proprietary tools. *International Journal of Electronic Business, 9*(3), 219–237. doi:10.1504/IJEB.2011.042543.

Berry, L. L. (1995). Relationship marketing of services - Growing interest, emerging perspectives. *Journal of the Academy of Marketing Science, 23*(4), 236–245. doi:10.1177/009207039502300402.

Berry, L. L. (2002). Relationship marketing of services - Perspectives from 1983 and 2000. *Journal of Relationship Marketing, 1*(1), 59–77. doi:10.1300/J366v01n01_05.

Bertino, E., Catania, B., Damiani, M. L., & Perlasca, P. (2005). GEO-RBAC: A spatially aware RBAC. In *Proceedings of the 11th ACM Symposium on Access Control Models and Technologies (SACMAT '06)* (pp. 29-37). New York: ACM.

Bertocci, V., Serack, G., & Baker, C. (2007). *Understanding Windows CardSpace: An introduction to the concepts and challenges of digital identities*. Reading, MA: Addison-Wesley.

Bertot, J. C., Jaeger, P. T., & Grimes, J. M. (2010). Using ICTs to create a culture of transparency: E-government and social media as openness and anti-corruption tools for societies. *Government Information Quarterly, 27*(3), 264–271. doi:10.1016/j.giq.2010.03.001.

Beyer, M. (2009a, February). Tutorial: Key roles for successful BI/DW delivery: Business intelligence solution architect. *Gartner*.

Beyer, M. (2009b, April). Fundamentals of data warehousing for the CIO. *Gartner*.

Beynon-Davies, P. (2002). *Information systems: An introduction to informatics in organizations*. New York: Palgrave.

Bhagwat, R., & Sharma, M. K. (2006). Management of information system in Indian SMEs: An exploratory study. *International Journal of Enterprise Network Management, 1*(1), 99–125. doi:10.1504/IJENM.2006.010068.

Bhargav-Spantzel, A., Squicciarini, A. C., & Bertino, E. (2007). Trust negotiation in identity management. *IEEE Security & Privacy, 5*(2), 55–63. doi:10.1109/MSP.2007.46.

Bhattacharya, C. B., Du, S., & Sen, S. (2010). Maximizing business returns to corporate social responsibility (CSR): The role of CSR communication. *International Journal of Management Reviews, 12*(1), 6–19.

Bhatti, R., Bertino, E., & Ghafoor, A. (2007). An integrated approach to federated identity and privilege management in open systems. *Communications of the ACM, 50*(2), 81–87. doi:10.1145/1216016.1216025.

Bianchi, G., Bonola, M., Falletta, V., Proto, F. S., & Teofili, S. (2008). The SPARTA pseudonym and authorization system. *Electronic Notes in Theoretical Computer Science, 197*(2), 57–71. doi:10.1016/j.entcs.2007.12.017.

Bian, Y. (1997). Bringing strong ties back In Indirect ties, network bridges, and job searches in China. *American Sociological Review*, *62*(3), 366–385. doi:10.2307/2657311.

Bierly, P., & Chakrabarti, A. (1996). Generic knowledge strategies in the U.S. pharmaceuticals industry. *Strategic Management Journal of Special Issue on Knowledge and the Firm*, *17*, 123–135.

Bin Husin, M. H., & Swatman, P. M. C. (2010). Removing the barriers to enterprise 2.0. In *Proceedings of the 2010 IEEE International Symposium on Technology and Society (ISTAS)* (pp. 275-283). IEEE.

Birt, J. L., Bilson, C. M., Smith, T., & Whaley, R. E. (2006). Ownership, competition, and financial disclosure. *Australian Journal of Management*, *31*(2), 235–263. doi:10.1177/031289620603100204.

Bishop, M. (2004). *Profit maximisation*. Economist Intelligence Unit.

Bitly. (2011). *Bitly: Shorten, share and track your links*. Retrieved November 15, 2011, from https://bitly.com/

Bizer, C., Lehmann, J., Kobilarov, G., Auer, S., Becker, C., & Cyganiak, R. et al. (2009). DBpedia-A crystallization point for the web of data. *Web Semantics: Science. Services and Agents on the World Wide Web*, *7*(3), 154–165. doi:10.1016/j.websem.2009.07.002.

Blau, P. M. (1964). *Exchange and power in social life*. New York, NY: Wiley.

Blaya, J. A., Gomez, W., Rodriguez, P., & Fraser, H. (2008). Cost and implementation analysis of a personal digital assistant system for laboratory data collection. *The International Journal of Tuberculosis and Lung Disease*, *12*(8), 921–927. PMID:18647452.

Blaze, M., Feigenbaum, J., & Lacy, J. (1996). Decentralized trust management. In *Proceedings of the 1996 IEEE Symposium on Security and Privacy* (pp. 164-173). IEEE Computer Society Press.

Blaze, M., Feigenbaum, J., Ioannidis, J., & Keromytis, A. D. (1999). *RFC-2704: The keynote trust management system version 2*. Geneva, Switzerland: Internet Engineering Task Force.

Blood, R. (2000). *Weblogs: A history and perspective*. Retrieved September 28, 2011, from http://www.rebeccablood.net/essays/Weblog_history.html

Bluma, D. (2008). Teacher education in the context of Bologna process. In Žogla, I. (Ed.), *Association for Teacher Education in Europe Spring University Conference Teacher of the 21st Century: Quality Education for Quality Teaching* (pp. 673–680). Riga, Latvia: University of Latvia.

Blumenstock, J. E. (2008). Size matters: Word count as a measure of quality on Wikipedia. In *Proceeding of the 17th International Conference on World Wide Web*. IEEE.

Blum, V., & Fallon, J. (2002). Welsh visitor attraction web sites: Multipurpose tools or technological tokenism? *Information Technology & Tourism*, *4*, 191–201. doi:10.3727/109830501108750985.

Boateng, R., Mbarika, V., & Thomas, C. (2010). When web 2.0 becomes an organizational learning tool: Evaluating web 2.0 tools. *Development and Learning in Organizations*, *24*(3), 17–20. doi:10.1108/14777281011037254.

Bobek, S., & Sternad, S. (2010). Management of ERP solutions. In Vaish, A. (Ed.), *Recent advances in management and information security* (pp. 31–47). New Delhi: Shree Publishers & Distributors.

Boehm, B., & Turner, R. (2003). *Balancing agility and discipline: A guide for the perplexed*. Boston: Pearson Education, Inc..

Boev, O. V., Kriushova, A. A., Kulyukina, E. S., Surygin, A. S., Freeston, I., Heitmann, G., & Chuchalin, A. I. (2011). *Guidelines on engineering curriculum design aligned with the European qualification framework and European standards for quality assurance of engineering education*. Tomsk: TPU Publishing House.

Bohus, D., & Rudnicky, A. I. (2009). The RavenClaw dialog management framework: Architecture and systems. *Computer Speech & Language*, *23*(3), 332–361. doi:10.1016/j.csl.2008.10.001.

Boisot, M. (1998). *Knowledge assets: Securing competitive advantage in the information economy*. New York: Oxford University Press.

Boldi, P., Bonchi, F., Castillo, C., & Vigna, S. (2011). Viscous democracy for social networks. *Communications of the ACM*, *54*(6), 129–137. doi:10.1145/1953122.1953154.

Bonaccorsi, A., & Lamastra, C. R. (2003). *Altruistic individuals, selfish firms? The structure of motivation in open source software.*

Bonacich, P. (1972). Factoring and weighting approaches to status scores and clique identification. *The Journal of Mathematical Sociology*, *2*(1), 113–120. doi:10.1080/0022250X.1972.9989806.

Bonsón, E., Torres, L., Royo, S., & Flores, F. (2011). *Local e-government 2.0: Social media and corporate transparency in municipalities.* Paper presented at XVI Congreso AECA. Granada, Spain.

Bonsón, E., Escobar, T., & Flores, F. (2006). Online transparency of the banking sector. *Online Information Review*, *30*(6), 714–730. doi:10.1108/14684520610716180.

Bonsón, E., Escobar, T., & Flores, F. (2008). Navigation quality as a key value for the web page of a financial entity. *Online Information Review*, *32*(5), 623–634. doi:10.1108/14684520810914007.

Bonsón, E., Escobar, T., & Martín, M. P. (2002). La mejora del sistema de información contable mediante la integración de tecnologías emergentes. *Revista de Contabilidad*, *3*(6), 21–48.

Bonsón, E., & Flores, F. (2011). Social media and corporate dialogue: The response of the global financial institutions. *Online Information Review*, *35*(1), 34–49. doi:10.1108/14684521111113579.

Bontis, N. (2001). Assessing knowledge assets: A review of the models used to measure intellectual capital. *International Journal of Management Reviews*, *3*(1). doi:10.1111/1468-2370.00053.

Bontis, N., Crossan, M., & Hulland, J. (2002). Managing an organisational learning system by aligning stocks and flows. *Journal of Management Studies*, *39*(4), 437–469. doi:10.1111/1467-6486.t01-1-00299.

Borgatti, S. P., & Cross, R. (2003). A relational view of information seeking and learning in social networks. *Management Science*, *49*, 432–446. doi:10.1287/mnsc.49.4.432.14428.

Borgatti, S. P., Mehra, A., Brass, D. J., & Labianca, G. (2009). Network analysis in the social sciences. *Science*, *323*(5916), 892–895. doi:10.1126/science.1165821 PMID:19213908.

Borgatti, S., & Foster, P. (2003). The network paradigm in organizational research: A review and typology. *Journal of Management*, *29*(6).

Borgman, C. (2003). Personal digital libraries: Creating individual spaces for innovation. *NSF/JISC Post Digital Library Futures Workshop*. Retrieved October 22, 2011, from http://www.sis.pitt.edu/~dlwkshop/paper_borgman.html

Boss, J. (2011). Les nouveaux visages du marketing. *Revue Française du Marketing*, (231), 61-74.

Bossio, J. F. (2006). *Social sustainability of telecenters from the viewpoint of operators: A case study from São Paulo.* (Unpublished doctoral dissertation). London School of Economics, London, UK.

Boudreau, M. C. (2002). Learning to use ERP technology: A causal model. In *Proceedings of the 36th Hawaii International Conference on System Sciences*. Retrieved July 7, 2008, from http://csdl2.computer.org/comp/proceedings/hicss/2003/1874/08/187480235b.pdf

Bouguessa, M., Wang, S., & Dumoulin, B. (2010). Discovering knowledge-sharing communities in question-answering forums. *Discovery*, *5*(1), 1–49.

Boulos, M. N., & Wheeler, S. (2007). The emerging web 2.0 social software: An enabling suite of sociable technologies in health and health care education. *Health Information and Libraries Journal*, *24*(1), 2–23. doi:10.1111/j.1471-1842.2007.00701.x PMID:17331140.

Bove'e, C. L., & Thill, J. V. (2000). *Business communication today* (6th ed.). Upper Saddle River, NJ: Prentice-Hall.

Bovi, A. M. (2003). Ethical guidelines for use of electronic mail between patients and physicians. *The American Journal of Bioethics*, *3*(3), 43–47. doi:10.1162/152651603322874771 PMID:12859845.

Bowers, D. (1964). Organizational control in insurance company. *Sociometry*, *27*(2), 230–244. doi:10.2307/2785719.

Bowers, D., & Seashore, S. (1966). Predicting organizational effectiveness with a four-factory theory of leadership. *Administrative Science Quarterly*, *11*(2), 238–263. doi:10.2307/2391247.

Box, S., & Cosgrove, S. (1968). The productivity of scientists in industrial research laboratories. *Sociology*, *11*(2), 163–172. doi:10.1177/003803856800200202.

Boyd, D. M., & Ellison, N. B. (2008). Social network sites: Definition, history, and schollarship. *Journal of Computer-Mediated Communication*, *13*, 210–230. doi:10.1111/j.1083-6101.2007.00393.x.

Brackett, L. K., & Carr, B. N. (2001). Cyberspace advertising vs. other media: Consumer vs. mature student attitudes. *Journal of Advertising Research*, *41*(5), 23–32.

Bradford, M. (2008). *Modern ERP—Select, implement & use today's advanced business systems*. Raleigh, NC: North Carolina State University, College of Management.

Bradford, M., & Florin, J. (2003). Examining the role of innovation diffusion factors on the implementation success of enterprise resource planning systems. *International Journal of Accounting Information Systems*, *4*(3), 205–225. doi:10.1016/S1467-0895(03)00026-5.

Bradley, J., & Lee, C. C. (2007). ERP training and user satisfaction: A case study. *International Journal of Enterprise Information Systems*, *3*(4), 33–55. doi:10.4018/jeis.2007100103.

Bradley, S. P., & Nolan, R. L. (1998). Capturing value in the network era. In Bradley, S. P., & Nolan, R. L. (Eds.), *Sense & Respond: Capturing Value in the Network Era*. Boston, MA: Harvard Business School Press.

Brandes, U. (2001). A faster algorithm for betweenness centrality. *The Journal of Mathematical Sociology*, *25*(2), 163–177. doi:10.1080/0022250X.2001.9990249.

Bremer, D., & Bryant, R. (2005). *A comparison of two learning management systems: Moodle vs Blackboard.* Paper presented at the 18th Annual Conference of the National Advisory Committee on Computing Qualifications. New York, NY.

Brescia, W., & Miller, M. (2006). What's it worth? The perceived benefits of instructional blogging. *Electronic Journal for the Integration of Technology in Education*, *5*, 44-52. Retrieved September 11, 2011, from http://ejite.isu.edu/Volume5/Brescia.pdf

Bretthauer, D. (2002). Open source software: A history. *Information Technology and Libraries*, *21*(1), 3–11.

Briggs, R., & Hollins, N. (1997). Advertising on the web: Is there response before click-through? *Journal of Advertising Research*, *37*(2), 33–45.

Brin, S., & Page, L. (2006). The anatomy of a large-scale hypertextual web search engine. *Search*, *30*(1-2), 5–10.

Brooks, R. G., & Menachemi, N. (2006). Physicians' use of email with patients: Factors influencing electronic communication and adherence to best practices. *Journal of Medical Internet Research*, *8*(1).

Brown, J., & Adler, R. (2008). *Minds of fire: Open education, the long tail and learning 2.0*. Retrieved May 2011 from http://net.educause.edu/ir/library/pdf/ERM0811.pdf

Brown, K., & Mitchell, T. (1991). A comparison of just-in-time and batch manufacturing: The role of performance obstacles. *Journal of the Academy of Management*, *34*(4), 906–917. doi:10.2307/256395.

Bruner, G. C. II, & Kumar, A. (2000). Web commercials and advertising hierarchy-of-effects. *Journal of Advertising Research*, *40*(1/2), 35–42.

Bryant, S. M., Albring, S. M., & Murthy, U. (2009). The effects of reward structure, media richness and gender on virtual teams. *International Journal of Accounting Information Systems*, *10*, 190–213. doi:10.1016/j.accinf.2009.09.002.

BT. (2004). *The digital divide in 2025*. BT.

Buchanan, F., & Huczynski, A. (2010). *Organizational behaviour*. Harlow, MA: Pearson.

Bucher, T., Gericke, A., & Sigg, S. (2009). Process-centric business intelligence. *Business Process Management Journal*, *15*(3), 408. doi:10.1108/14637150910960648.

Buckinx, W., Moons, W., Van Den Poel, D., & Wets, G. (2003). *Customer-adapted coupon targeting using feature selection*. Gent, Belgium: Universiteit Gent, Faculteit Economie En Bedrijfskunde.

Buckmaster, R. A. (2004). *English for specific purposes on-line course*. Retrieved March 15, 2005, from http://www.sisekaitse.ee/?id=831

Buczek, L. (2011). *The big failure of enterprise 2.0 social business*. Retrieved October 1, 2011, from http://www.lauriebuczek.com

Bueno, S., & Salmeron, J. L. (2008). TAM-based success modelling in ERP. *Interacting with Computers*, *20*(6), 515–523. doi:10.1016/j.intcom.2008.08.003.

Bueren, A., Schierholz, R., Kolbe, L., & Brenner, W. (2004). *Customer knowledge management - Improving performance of customer relationship management with knowledge management*. Paper presented at the 37th Hawaii International Conference on System Sciences. Hawaii, HI.

Bughin, J., & Manyika, J. (2007). *How businesses are using web 2.0: A McKinsey global survey*. Retrieved November 3, 2011, from http://www.mckinseyquarterly.com/article_page.aspx?ar=1913

Bughin, J., Chui, M., & Miller, A. (2009). McKinsey global survey results: How companies are benefitting from web 2.0. *The McKinsey Quarterly*. Retrieved September 3, 2009, from http://www.mckinseyquarterly.com

Bughin, J. (2008). The rise of enterprise 2.0. *Direct. Data and Digital Marketing Practice*, *9*(3), 251–259. doi:10.1057/palgrave.dddmp.4350100.

Bughin, J., & Chui, M. (2011). The rise of the networked enterprise: Web 2.0 finds its payday.[from http://www.mckinseyquarterly.com]. *The McKinsey Quarterly*, *22*, 2–9. Retrieved September 15, 2011

Buhalis, D. (1999). Limits of tourism development in peripheral destinations: problems and challenges. *Tourism Management*, *20*, 183–185.

Buhalis, D. (2000). Marketing the competitive destination of the future. *Tourism Management*, *21*, 97–116. doi:10.1016/S0261-5177(99)00095-3.

Buhalis, D. (2003). *eTourism: Information technologies for strategic tourism management*. Harlow, MA: Pearson Higher Education.

Buhalis, D., & Spada, A. (2000). DMS: Criteria for success – An exploratory research. *Information Technology and Tourism*, *3*(1), 41–58.

Bulik, B. (2000). Ad nauseum. *Business 2.0*, *12*, 112.

Bunt, G. G., Wittek, R. P., & Klepper, M. C. (2005). The evolution of intra-organizational trust networks. *International Sociological Association*, *20*(3), 339–369. doi:10.1177/0268580905055480.

Buono, A. F. (2003). *Enhancing inter-firm networks and interorganizational strategies*. Charlotte, NC: Information Age Publishing Inc..

Burnett, R., & Marshall, D. I. (2003). *Web theory: An introduction*. London: Routhledge.

Burns, J. M. (1978). *Leadership*. New York: Harper and Row.

Burt, R. S. (1992). *Structural holes: The social structure of competition*. Cambridge, MA: Harvard University Press.

Burt, R. S. (2004). Structural holes and good ideas. *American Journal of Sociology*, *110*(2), 349–399. doi:10.1086/421787.

Buttle, F. (2008). *Customer relationship management* (2nd ed.). Boston: Butterworth-Heinemann.

Byun, J.-W., Bertino, E., & Li, N. (2005). Purpose based access control of complex data for privacy protection. In *Proceedings of the 10th ACM Symposium on Access Control Models and Technologies (SACMAT 'O5)* (pp. 102-110). New York: ACM.

Cabot, J., Pau, R., & Raventós, R. (2010). From UML/OCL to SBVR specifications: A challenging transformation. *Information Systems*, *35*, 417–440. doi:10.1016/j.is.2008.12.002.

Cai, H., Reinwald, B., Wang, N., & Guo, C. (2011). SaaS multi-tenancy: Framework, technology, and case study. *International Journal of Cloud Applications and Computing*, *1*(1), 62–77. doi:10.4018/ijcac.2011010105.

Calero, M. ª. R., Martinez, M., Ortega, J. M., & Román, Mª. V. (2005). Impacto de las nuevas tecnologías en los canales de distribución financieros. Madrid, Spain: Dykinson.

Calisir, F., Gumussoy, C. A., & Bayram, A. (2009). Predicting the behavioural intention to use enterprise resource planning systems—An exploratory extension of the technology acceptance model. *Management Research News, 32*(7), 597–613. doi:10.1108/01409170910965215.

Calvo, S., & Reinares, P. (1999). *Comunicación en internet: Estrategias de comunicación y marketing interactivo*. Madrid: McGraw-Hill.

Camenisch, J., & Van Herreweghen, E. (2002). Design and implementation of the idemix anonymous credential system. In *Proceedings of the 9th ACM Conference on Computer and Communications Security (CCS '02)* (pp. 21-30). New York: ACM.

Camenisch, J., & Pfitzmann, B. (2007). Federated identity management. In Petkovic, M., & Jonker, W. (Eds.), *Security, Privacy, and Trust in Modern Data Management* (pp. 213–238). Berlin: Springer-Verlag. doi:10.1007/978-3-540-69861-6_15.

Cameron, K., & Quinn, R. (2005). *Changing organization culture*. New York: Wiley.

Cameron, K., & Whetten, D. (Eds.). (1982). *Organizational effectiveness: A comparison of multiple models*. New York: Academic Press.

Cameron, S., & Whetten, D. (1986). Effectiveness as paradox: Consensus and conflict in conceptions of organizational effectiveness. *Management Science, 32*(5), 539–553. doi:10.1287/mnsc.32.5.539.

Campanella, S., Dimauro, G., Ferrante, A., Impedovo, D., Impedovo, S., & Lucchese, M. G. et al. (2008). E-learning platforms in the Italian universities: The technological solutions at the University of Bari. *WSEAS Transactions on Advances in Engineering Education, 5*, 12–19.

Capozzi, M. (2007). Knowledge management architectures beyond technology. *First Monday, 12*(6). doi:10.5210/fm.v12i6.1871.

Carbone, F., Contreras, J., & Hernández, J. Z. (2010). Enterprise 2.0 and semantic technologies for open innovation support. *Lecture Notes in Computer Science, 6097*, 18–27. doi:10.1007/978-3-642-13025-0_3.

Cardoso, N. (2008). Rembrandt-reconhecimento de entidades mencionadas baseado em relações e análise detalhada do texto. *Encontro do Segundo HAREM, PROPOR 2008*.

Cardozo, R. (1965). An experimental study of consumer effort, expectations and satisfaction. *JMR, Journal of Marketing Research, 2*, 244–249. doi:10.2307/3150182.

Carillo, K., & Okoli, C. (2008). The open source movement: A revolution in software development. *Journal of Computer Information Systems, 49*(2), 1–9.

Carleial, L. (2001). *Redes industriais de subcontratação: Um enfoque de sistema nacional de inovação, um estudo das industrias eletrônica, metalmecânica e de confecções da Região Metropolitana de Curitiba*. São Paulo, Brazil: Hucitec.

Carley, K., Diesner, J., Reminga, J., & Tsvetovat, M. (2007). *Toward an interoperable dynamic network analysis toolkit*. Retrieved in January 2010, from https://community.bus.emory.edu/dept/ISOM/Shared%20Documents/Hightower%20Speaker%20Papers/KathleenCarley.pdf

Carlota, J., Silva, A. R., & Silva, P. (2009). The learning object pool and the BOA-GPI case study. In *Proceedings of the Iberoamerican Congress on Telematics (CITA-2009)*. CITA.

Carlson, A., Betteridge, J., Hruschka, E. R., Jr., & Mitchell, T. M. (2009). *Coupling semi-supervised learning of categories and relations*.

Carlsson, C., Fedrizzi, M., & Fuller, R. (2004). *Fuzzy logic in management*. Berlin: Springer. doi:10.1007/978-1-4419-8977-2.

Carroll, A. B., & Buchholtz, A. K. (2011). *Business and society: Ethics and stakeholder management*. South-Western Pub..

Carter, S. (2011). *Get social: Using social media to create a new type of social business*. Hoboken, NJ: IBM Press.

Casaló, L. V., Flavián, C., & Guinalíu, M. (2011). Understanding the intention to follow the advice obtained in an online travel community. *Computers in Human Behavior*, *27*, 622–633. doi:10.1016/j.chb.2010.04.013.

Casielles, R. V., Martín, A. M., & Vázquez, A. S. (2004). Cómo usan Internet las líneas aéreas para desarrollar relaciones estables con los clientes. *Universia Business Review*, *2*(2), 34–47.

Castañeda, J. A., Muñoz, F., Luque, T., & Alcántara, J. M. (2005). *Experience moderation effect on the relationship between usefulness, ease of use and website acceptance*. Paper presented at Network and Electronic Commerce Conference. Riva Del Garda, Italia.

Castells, M. (2001). *A galáxia Internet – Reflexões sobre internet, negócios e sociedade*. Lisbon, Portugal: Ed. Fundação Calouste Gulbenkian.

Castilla, E. J. (2005). Social networks and employee performance in a call center. *American Journal of Sociology*, *110*(5), 1243–1283.

Castro, J., Kolp, M., & Mylopoulos, J. (2002). Towards requirements-driven information systems engineering: The Tropos project. *Information Systems*, *27*(6), 365–389. doi:10.1016/S0306-4379(02)00012-1.

Cavaleri, S., Seivert, S., & Lee, W. L. (2005). *Knowledge leadership: The art and science of the knowledge-based organisation*. Alexandria, VA: KMCI Press.

Cavus, N., & Momani, A. (2009). Computer aided evaluation of learning management systems. *Procedia - Social and Behavioral Sciences*, *1*(1), 426-430.

Cechinel & Sicilia. (2011). Evaluating models for automated quality assessment of learning objects inside repositories. In *Proceedings of Laclo2011*. Laclo.

Cechinel, C., & Sánchez-Alonso, S. (2011). *Analyzing associations between the different ratings dimensions of the MERLOT repository*. Interdisciplinary Journal of E-Learning and Learning Objects.

Celaya, J., Vázquez, J. A., Saldaña, I., & García, Y. (2009). *Visibilidad de las ciudades en la web 2.0*. Grupo BPMO.

Cerf, V. (2007). An information avalanche. *IEEE Computer*, *40*(1).

Certo, S., & Certo, T. (2009). *Modern management*. New York: Pearson.

Chadwick, D., Zhao, G., Otenko, S., Laborde, R., Su, L., & Nguyen, T. A. (2008). PERMIS: A modular authorization infrastructure. *Concurrency and Computation*, *20*(11), 1341–1357. doi:10.1002/cpe.1313.

Chaffey, D., Mayer, R., Johnston, K., & Ellis-Chadwich, F. (2000). *Internet marketing strategy, implementation and practice*. Harlow, MA: Prentice Hall.

Chakravarthy, M. A., Ciravegna, P. F., & Lanfranchi, M. V. (2006). *Cross-media document annotation and enrichment*. Paper presented at the SAAW - 1st Semantic Authoring and Annotation Workshop. New York, NY.

Chan, J. O. (2005). Toward a unified view of customer relationship management. *Journal of American Academy of Business*.

Chan, A., Yung, E., Lam, P., Tam, C., & Cheung, S. (2001). Application of delphi method in selection of procurement systems for construction. *Construction Management and Economics*, *19*(7), 699–718. doi:10.1080/01446190110066128.

Chanal, V., & Caron-Fasan, M.-L. (2010). The difficulties involved in developing business models open to innovation communities: The case of a crowdsourcing platform. *M@n@gement*, *13*(4), 318-340.

Chandler, A. (1996). *Strategy and structure: Chapters in the history of the American industrial enterprise*. Cambridge, MA: MIT Press.

Chandon, P., Wansink, B., & Laurent, G. (2000). A benefit congruency framework of sales promotion effectiveness. *Journal of Marketing*, *64*(4), 65–81. doi:10.1509/jmkg.64.4.65.18071.

Chan, F., & Qi, H. (2003). An innovative performance measurement method for supply chain management. *Supply Chain Management*, *8*(3), 209–223. doi:10.1108/13598540310484618.

Chang, A. M., & Kannan, P. K. (2008). *Leveraging web 2.0 in government*. New York: IBM Center for The Business of Government.

Chang, C.-S., & Chang, H.-H. (2007). Effects of internal marketing on nurse job satisfaction and organizational commitment: Example of medical centers in southern Taiwan. *The Journal of Nursing Research, 15*(4), 265–274. doi:10.1097/01.JNR.0000387623.02931.a3 PMID:18080971.

Chang, S. C., & Lee, M. S. (2007). A study on relationship among leadership, organisational culture, the operation of learning organisation and employees' job satisfaction. *The Learning Organization, 14*(2), 155–185. doi:10.1108/09696470710727014.

Chan, K. W., & Li, S. Y. (2010). Understanding consumer-to-consumer interactions in virtual communities: The salience of reciprocity. *Journal of Business Research, 63*(9-10), 1033–1040. doi:10.1016/j.jbusres.2008.08.009.

Chatterjee, P., & McGinnis, J. (2010). Customized online promotions: Moderating effect of promotion type on deal value, perceived fairness, and purchase intent. *Journal of Applied Business Research, 26*(4), 13–19.

Chatterjee, R., & Eliashberg, J. (1990). The innovation diffusion process in a heterogeneous population: A micromodeling approach. *Management Science, 36*, 1057–1079. doi:10.1287/mnsc.36.9.1057.

Chaudhary, S. (2004). Management factors for strategic BI success. In *Business intelligence in digital economy: Opportunities, limitations and risks*. Hershey, PA: IDEA Group Publishing.

Chaudhary, S., Dayal, U., & Narasayya, V. (2011). An overview of business intelligence technology. *Communications of the ACM, 54*(8), 88–98. doi:10.1145/1978542.1978562.

Chen, T., Sun, F., & Lu, Y. (2007). Research on TPL-oriented fuzzy integrated evaluation method for supply chain. In *Proceedings of the Sixth Wuhan International Conference on E-Business*. Wuhan.

Chen, C.-T., Lin, C.-T., & Huang, S.-F. (2006). A fuzzy approach for supplier evaluation and selection in supply chain management. *International Journal of Production Economics, 102*, 289–301. doi:10.1016/j.ijpe.2005.03.009.

Cheng, B., & Atlee, J. (2007). Research directions in requirements engineering. In *Proceedings of the Future of Software Engineering Symposium* (pp. 285-303). IEEE Computer Society Press.

Chen, L., Soliman, K. S., Mao, E., & Frolick, M. N. (2000). Measuring user satisfaction with data warehouses: An exploratory study. *Information & Management*, 103–110. doi:10.1016/S0378-7206(99)00042-7.

Chen, S., & Bouvain, P. (2009). Is corporate responsibility converging? A comparison of corporate responsibility reporting in the USA, UK, Australia, and Germany. *Journal of Business Ethics, 90*(4), 523–536. doi:10.1007/s10551-010-0604-0.

Chen, Y. C. (2012). A framework for government 2.0 development and implementation. In Chen, Y.-C., & Chu, P.-Y. (Eds.), *Electronic Governance and Cross-Boundary Collaboration: Innovations and Advancing Tools* (pp. 350–368). Hershey, PA: IGI-Global.

Chesbrough, H. (2009). *Open innovation: The new imperative for creating and profiting from technology*. Boston: Harvard Business Press.

Cheung, C. M. K., Zhu, L., Kwong, T., Chan, G. W. W., & Limayem, M. (2003). *Online consumer behavior: A review and agenda for future research*. Paper presented at 16th Bled eCommerce Conference. Bled, Slovenia.

Chinowsky, P. S., & Rojas, E. M. (2003). Virtual teams: Guide to successful implementation. *Journal of Management Engineering, 19*(3), 98–106. doi:10.1061/(ASCE)0742-597X(2003)19:3(98).

Chin, W. W. (1998). Issues and opinions on structural equation modelling. *Management Information Systems Quarterly, 22*, 7–16.

Chin, W., Marcolin, B., & Newsted, P. (2003). A partial least squares latent variable modeling approach for measuring interaction effects: Results from a Monte Carlo simulation study and an electronic-mail emotion/adoption study. *Information Systems Research, 14*(2), 189–217. doi:10.1287/isre.14.2.189.16018.

Chou, D. C., Tan, X., & Yen, D. (2004). Web technology and supply chain management. *Information Management & Computer Security, 12*(4), 338–349. doi:10.1108/09685220410553550.

Christensen, P. H. (2007). Knowledge sharing: Moving away from the obsession with best practices. *Journal of Knowledge Management, 11*(1), 36–47. doi:10.1108/13673270710728222.

Christopher, M., & Peck, H. (2004). Building the resilient supply chain. *The International Journal of Logistics Management, 15*(2), 1–14. doi:10.1108/09574090410700275.

Christopher, M., & Towill, D. (2001). An integrated model for the design of agile supply chains. *International Journal of Physical Distribution & Logistics Management, 31*(4), 235–246. doi:10.1108/09600030110394914.

Chui, M., Miller, A., & Roberts, R. P. (2009). Six ways to make web 2.0 work.[from http://www.mckinseyquarterly.com]. *The McKinsey Quarterly*, 1–7. Retrieved April 24, 2009

Chung, T., & Law, R. (2003). Developing a performance indicator for hotel websites. *Hospital Management, 22*, 119–125. doi:10.1016/S0278-4319(02)00076-2.

Chu, R. (2001). What online Hong Kong travelers look for on airline/travel websites? *International Journal of Hospitality Management, 20*(1), 95–100. doi:10.1016/S0278-4319(00)00046-3.

Churchill, D. (2009). Educational applications of web 2.0: Using blogs to support teaching and learning. *British Journal of Educational Technology, 40*(1), 179–183. doi:10.1111/j.1467-8535.2008.00865.x.

Churchill, E., & Halverson, C. (2005). Social networks and social networking. *IEEE Internet Computing, 9*(5). doi:10.1109/MIC.2005.103.

Chu, S. K.-W. (2008). TWiki for knowledge building and management. *Online Information Review, 32*(6), 745–758. doi:10.1108/14684520810923917.

Ciribelli, M. (2003). *Como realizar uma dissertação de mestrado através da pesquisa científica*. Rio de Janeiro, Brazil: Viveiros de Castro Editora.

Clark, J., & Soliman, F. (1997). Application of scoring method for measuring the value of knowledge based systems to key employees. *Journal of Systems and Information Technology, 1*(2), 23–40. doi:10.1108/13287269780000736.

Clarkson, G., Jacobsen, T. E., & Batcheller, A. L. (2007). Information asymmetry and information sharing. *Government Information Quarterly, 24*(4), 827–839. doi:10.1016/j.giq.2007.08.001.

Coates, H., James, R., & Baldwin, G. (2005). A critical examination of the effects of learning management systems on university teaching and learning. *Tertiary Education and Management, 11*(1), 19–36. doi:10.1080/13583883.2005.9967137.

Coelli, T., Prasada Rao, S., O'Donnell, C., & Battese, G. (2005). *An introduction to efficiency and productivity analysis*. New York: Springer.

Coffee, S. (2011, November). *Freshly brewed tweets from Brad and Lee at Starbucks in Seattle, WA*. Retrieved from http://twitter.com/#!/starbucks

Cohen, L., & Manion, L. et al. (2003). *Research methods in education*. London: Routledge/Falmer Taylor & Francis Group.

Cohen, W. M., & Levinthal, D. A. (1990). Absorptive capacity: A new perspective on learning and innovation. *Administrative Science Quarterly, 35*(1). doi:10.2307/2393553 PMID:10106582.

Cohn, M. (2005). *Agile estimating and planning*. Upper Saddle River, NJ: Pearson Education, Inc..

Colclough, G., & Tinholt, D. (2009). *Smarter, faster, better e-government-8th benchmarking measurement*. Capgemini, RAND Europe, IDC, SOGETI and DTi

Cole, A. (2004). *Management*. London: Thomson.

Cole, M. (2007). The networked consumer: A critical review and assessment. *Journal of Customer Behaviour, 6*(1), 5–18. doi:10.1362/147539207X198347.

Coleman, J. S. (1990). *Foundations of social theory*. Cambridge, MA: Harvard University Press.

Coleman, J. S. (1998). Social capital in the creation of human capital. *American Journal of Sociology, 94*(Supplement), S95–S120. doi:10.1086/228943.

Coleman, J. S., Katz, E., & Menzel, H. (1966). *Medical innovation: A diffusion study*. Indianapolis, IN: The Boobs-Merrill Company.

Collins, J. (2001). *Why some companies make the leap ... and others don't*. Sydney, Australia: Random Books.

Collis, B., & Moonen, J. (2008). Web 2.0 tools and processes in higher education: Quality perspectives. *Educational Media International*, *45*(2), 93–106. doi:10.1080/09523980802107179.

Comisión de Mercado de las Telecomunicaciones. (2010). Retrieved from http://informeanual.cmt.es/informe-sector/comunicaciones-moviles

Commission of the European Communities. (2006). *Efficiency and equity in European education and training systems*. Retrieved December 3, 2011, from ec.europa.eu/education/policies/2010/doc/comm481_en.pdf

Company, T. N. (2011). *BlogPulse*. Retrieved September 28, 2011, from http://www.blogpulse.com/

Conger, J. A., & Kanungo, R. N. (1987). Toward a behavioural theory of charismatic leadership in organisational settings. *Academy of Management Review*, *12*, 637–647.

Connolly, T., Conlon, E., & Deutsch, S. (1980). Organizational effectiveness: A multiple-constituency approach. *Academy of Management Review*, *5*(2), 211–217.

Constantinides, E. (2006). The marketing mix revisited: Towards the 21st century marketing. *Journal of Marketing Management*, *22*(3-4), 407–438. doi:10.1362/026725706776861190.

Constantinides, E., Gómez, M., & Lorenzo, C. (2008). Social media: A new frontier for retailers? *Europea Retail Research*, *22*, 1–28.

Constanzo, H. (2009). Web 2.0: A simple concept, a complex solution. *Bank Technology News*, *22*(3), 24.

Conway, S., & Steward, F. (2009). *Managing and shaping innovation*. Oxford, UK: Oxford University Press.

Cook, J., & Wall, T. (1980). New work attitude measures of trust, organizational commitment, and personal need non-fulfillment. *Journal of Occupational Psychology*, *53*(1), 39–52. doi:10.1111/j.2044-8325.1980.tb00005.x.

Cook, N. (2008). *Enterprise 2.0: How social software will change the future of work*. Hampshire, UK: Gower Publishing Limited.

Cooper, C., Fletcher, J., Gilbert, D., & Wanhill, S. (1998). *Tourism: Principles and practice*. London: Prentice Hall.

Cooper, R. B., & Zmud, R. W. (1990). Information technology implementation research: A technological diffusion approach. *Management Science*, *36*(2), 123–139. doi:10.1287/mnsc.36.2.123.

Copper, W. (2008). *Amnesty looks to utilise social media in latest global campaign*. Retrieved October 25, 2011 from http://www.mad.co.uk/Main/Search/MadSearchResults/Articles/2bd0e47f9b3247719c112e0bf3968aaf/Amnesty-looks-to-utilise-social-media-in-latest-global-campaign.html

Corbett, P., & Ward, D. (2006). *Open source reporting solutions for institutional reporting: The BIRT approach. Australasian Association for Institutional Research*. AAIR.

Cordis. (n.d.). retrieved from cordis.europa.eu

Cormode, G., & Krishnamurthy, B. (2008). Key differences between web 1.0 and web 2.0. *First Monday*, *13*(6). doi:10.5210/fm.v13i6.2125.

Corso, M., Martini, A., Pellegrini, L., Massa, S., & Testa, S. (2006). Managing dispersed workers: The new challenge in knowledge management. *Technovation*, *26*, 583–594. doi:10.1016/j.technovation.2005.02.003.

Cossentino, M. (2007). *Open source software*. Retrieved from http://www.pa.icar.cnr.it/cossentino/ICT/ppt/S11%20-%20Open%20Source%20Software.pdf

Costantino, C. (1996). Using interest-based techniques to design conflict management systems. *Negotiation Journal*, *12*(3), 207–214. doi:10.1111/j.1571-9979.1996.tb00095.x.

Coyle, C. L., & Vaughn, H. (2008). Social networking: Communication revolution or evolution? *Bell Labs Technical Journal*, *13*(2), 13–17. doi:10.1002/bltj.20298.

Crainer, S., & Birkinshaw, J. (2008). Who needs employees? *Business Strategy Review*, *19*(3), 18–21. doi:10.1111/j.1467-8616.2008.00547.x.

Cramton, C. D. (1997). Information problems in dispersed teams. Academy of Management Proceedings, 298-302.

Cramton, C. D. (2001). The mutual knowledge problem and its consequences for dispersed collaboration. *Organization Science*, *12*, 346–371. doi:10.1287/orsc.12.3.346.10098.

Cramton, C. D. (2002). Finding common ground in dispersed collaboration. *Organizational Dynamics*, *30*(4), 354–367. doi:10.1016/S0090-2616(02)00063-3.

Cramton, C. D., & Orvis, K. L. (2003). Overcoming barriers to information sharing in virtual teams. In Gibson, C. B., & Cohen, S. G. (Eds.), *Virtual Teams that Work: Creating Conditions for Virtual Team Effectiveness*. San Francisco, CA: Jossey-Bass.

Cress, U., & Kimmerle, J. (2008). A systemic and cognitive view on collaborative knowledge building with wikis. *International Journal of Computer-Supported Collaborative Learning*, *3*(2), 105–122. doi:10.1007/s11412-007-9035-z.

Cristopher, M., Payne, A., & Ballantine, D. (1994). *Relationship marketing*. Boston: Butterworth-Heinemann, Ltd..

Croft, A. C. (2008). Emergence of new media moves PR agencies in new directions: Competitive pressure threatens agencies' livelihood. *Public Relations Quarterly*, *52*(1), 16–20.

Cross, R., & Parker, A. (2004). *The hidden power of social networks: Understand how work really gets done in organizations*. Boston: Harvard Business School Press.

Crowston, K., & Howison, J. (2006). Hierarchy and centralization in free and open source software team communications. *Knowledge, Technology & Policy*, *18*, 65–85. doi:10.1007/s12130-006-1004-8.

Cudanov, M., Jasko, O., & Jevtic, M. (2008). Influence of information and communication technologies on decentralization of organizational structure. *Computer Science and Information System*, *6*(1), 93–109. doi:10.2298/CSIS0901093C.

Cui, C. C., Lewis, B. R., & Park, W. (2003). Service quality measurement in the banking sector in South Korea. *International Journal of Bank Marketing*, *21*(4), 191–201. doi:10.1108/02652320310479187.

Cullen, R., & Morse, S. (2011). Who's contributing: Do personality traits influence the level and type of participation in online communities.[). IEEE.]. *Methodology*, *0*, 1–11.

Cunha, L. (2001). *Introdução ao turismo*. Lisbon, Portugal: Ed. Verbo.

Cunningham, B. (1977). Approaches to the evaluation of organizational effectiveness. *Academy of Management Review*, *2*(3), 463–474.

Cuppens, F., & Cuppens-Boulahia, N. (2008). Modeling contextual security policies. *International Journal of Information Security*, *7*(4), 285–305. doi:10.1007/s10207-007-0051-9.

Cusumano, M. (2010). Cloud computing and SaaS as new computing platforms. *Communications of the ACM*, *53*(4), 27–28. doi:10.1145/1721654.1721667.

Cutlip, S. M., Center, A. H., & Broom, G. M. (2000). *Effective public relations*. Englewood Cliffs, NJ: Prentice Hall.

Dabbagh, N., & Reo, R. (2010). Back to the future: Tracing the roots and learning: Affordances of social software. In Lee, M., & McLoughlin, C. (Eds.), *Web 2.0-Based E-Learning: Applying Social Informatics for Tertiary Teaching* (pp. 1–20). Academic Press. doi:10.4018/978-1-60566-294-7.ch001.

Dabbah, M. A., Woo, W. L., & Dlay, S. S. (2007). Secure authentication for face recognition. In *Proceedings of the IEEE Symposium on Computational Intelligence in Image and Signal Processing* (pp. 121 – 126). IEEE.

Daft, R. (2000). *Management*. Fort Worth, TX: The Dryden Press.

Daft, R. (2003). *Management*. Cincinnati, OH: South-Western College.

Daft, R. (2006). *Organization theory and design*. Cincinnati, OH: South Western College Publishing.

Daft, R. (2007). *Organization theory and design*. Cincinnati, OH: South-Western College.

Daft, R. (2009). *The new era of management*. Cincinnati, OH: South-Western College.

Daghfous, A. (2007). Absorptive capacity and innovative enterprise systems. *International Journal of Innovation and Learning*, *4*(1), 60–73. doi:10.1504/IJIL.2007.011475.

Dahlander, L., Frederiksen, L., & Rullani, F. (2008). Online communities and open innovation: Governance and symbolic value creation. *Industry and Innovation*, *15*(2), 115–123. doi:10.1080/13662710801970076.

Dahlen, M. (1998). *Controlling the uncontrollable: Towards the perfect web sample*. Paper presented at the Worldwide Internet Seminar. Amsterdam: Esomar Publications.

Dalkir, K. (2011). *Knowledge management in theory and practice* (2nd ed.). Cambridge, MA: The MIT Press.

Damacena, C., & Pedron, C. D. (2004). *Estratégia de CRM: O desafio da implantação*. Paper presented at the Congresso Anual de Tecnologia de Informação (CATI 2004). Aviero, Portugal.

Damiani, E., Frati, F., & Monteverdi, C. (2009). *Open source BI adoption*. Retrieved from http://www.ow2.org/xwiki/bin/download/BusinessIntelligence/Documents/OSBIadoption-v10.pdf

Dardenne, A., van Lamsweerde, A., & Fickas, S. (1993). Goal-directed requirements acquisition. *Science of Computer Programming*, *20*(1-2), 3–50. doi:10.1016/0167-6423(93)90021-G.

Davenport, T. (2008). Enterprise 2.0: The new, new knowledge management? *Harvard Business Review*.

Davenport, T. H., Harris, J. G., & Kohli, A. K. (2001). How do they know their customers so well? *MIT Sloan Management Review*, *42*(2), 63–73.

Davenport, T. H., & Short, J. E. (1990, Summer). The new industrial engineering: Information technology and business process redesign. *Sloan Management Review*, 11–27.

Davis, F. D. (1989). Perceived usefulness, perceived ease of use, and user acceptance of information technology. *Management Information Systems Quarterly*, *13*(3), 319–340. doi:10.2307/249008.

Davis, F. D., Bagozzi, R. P., & Warshaw, P. R. (1989). User acceptance of computer technology: A comparison of two theoretical models. *Management Science*, *35*(8), 982–1003. doi:10.1287/mnsc.35.8.982.

Davison, R. (2002). Distribution channel analysis for business travel. In Buhalis, D., & Eric, L. (Eds.), *Tourism distribution channels: Practices, issues and transformations* (pp. 73–86). New York: Continuum.

Dawley, H. (2007). *Coming at you and real soon, web 3.0*. Retrieved January 2011 from http://www.medialifemagazine.com/artman2/publish/New_media_23/Coming_at_you_and_real_soon_Web_3_0.asp

De Ascaniis, S., & Morasso, S. G. (2011). When tourists give their reasons on the web: The argumentative significance of tourism related UGC. In Law, R., Fuchs, M., & Ricci, F. (Eds.), *Information and Communication Technologies in Tourism 2011* (pp. 125–138). New York: Springer. doi:10.1007/978-3-7091-0503-0_11.

De Geus, A. (1988, March-April). Planning as learning. *Harvard Business Review*, 70–74.

De Hertogh, S., Viaene, S., & Dedene, G. (2011). Governing web 2.0. *Communications of the ACM*, *54*(3), 124–130. doi:10.1145/1897852.1897882.

De Pedro, X., Rieradevall, M., López, P., Sant, D., Piñol, J., Núñez, L., et al. (2006). *Writing documents collaboratively in higher education using traditional vs. wiki methodology: Qualitative results from a 2-year project study*. Paper presented at the 4th Internacional Congress of University Teaching and Innovation. New York, NY.

Deal, T., & Kennedy, A. (2000). *Corporate cultures*. Jackson, MI: Perseus Books Group.

Decree n. 6991, Oct 27, 2009. (2009). National Program to Support Digital inclusion in the communities - Telecentros. BR. DOU n. 206, Sec.1, pp. 3. Federative Republic of Brazil, Brasília, DF. Retrieved Nov 26, 2011, from http://www.in.gov.br/imprensa/visualiza/index.jsp?jornal=1&pagina=3&data=28/10/2009

del Arco Carabias, J., & San Segundo Encinar, J. M. (2010). *Los mayores ante las TIC: Accesibilidad y accesiquibilidad*. Fundacion Vodafone España.

Del Chiappa, G. (2011). Trustworthiness of web 2.0 applications and their influence on tourist behavior: An empirical investigation in Italy. In Law, R., Fuchs, M., & Ricci, F. (Eds.), *Information and Communication Technologies in Tourism 2011* (pp. 331–342). New York: Springer. doi:10.1007/978-3-7091-0503-0_27.

Delgado, J., & Nieto, M. J. (2002). Incorporación de la tecnología de la información a la actividad bancaria en España: La banca por Internet. *Estabilidad Financiera*, *3*, 85–105.

Dell. (2012). *Peace of mind! We've got covered!* Retrieved from http://www.dell.com/content/learnmore/learnmore.aspx?c=us&l=en&s=dhs&~id=serv_inspn&~line=notebooks&~lt=popup&~series=inspn&ref=CFG#tn2

DelVecchio, D., Henard, D. H., & Freling, T. H. (2006). The effect of sales promotion on post-promotion brand preference: A meta-analysis. *Journal of Retailing*, *82*(3), 203–213. doi:10.1016/j.jretai.2005.10.001.

Department of Digital inclusion - DDI. (2011). *Curso de formação de monitores do telecentros.BR. programa nacional de apoio à inclusão digital nas comunidades: Rede nacional de formação para inclusão digital*. Federative Republic of Brazil. [Documento orientador 2.0]. Brasília, DF: Ministério das Comunicações.

Deperlioglu, O., & Kose, U. (2010). The effectiveness and experiences of blended learning approaches to computer programming education. *Computer Applications in Engineering Education*.

Derby, E., & Larsen, D. (2006). *Agile retrospectives: Making good teams great*. New York: The Pragmatic Bookshelf.

Dess, G., & Shaw, J. (2001). Voluntary turnover, social capital, and organizational performance. *Academy of Management Review*, *26*(3), 446–456.

Devlin, B. P., & Murphy, P. T. (1988). An architecture for a business and information system. *IBM Systems Journal*, *7*(1), 60–80. doi:10.1147/sj.271.0060.

Dewever, B., Schellens, T., Valcke, M., & Vankeer, H. (2006). Content analysis schemes to analyze transcripts of online asynchronous discussion groups: A review. *Computers & Education*, *46*(1), 6–28. doi:10.1016/j.compedu.2005.04.005.

Dhar, R., & Wertenbroch, K. (2000). Consumer choice between hedonic and utilitarian goods. *JMR, Journal of Marketing Research*, *37*, 60–71. doi:10.1509/jmkr.37.1.60.18718.

Dholakia, R. R., & Kshetri, N. (2004). Factors impacting the adoption of the Internet among SMEs. *Small Business Economics*, *23*(4), 311–322. doi:10.1023/B:SBEJ.0000032036.90353.1f.

Dholakia, U. M., Bagozzi, R. P., & Pearo, L. K. (2004). A social influence model of consumer participation in network- and small-group-based virtual communities. *International Journal of Research in Marketing*, *21*(3), 241–263. doi:10.1016/j.ijresmar.2003.12.004.

Diamond, W., & Campbell, L. (1989). The framing of sales promotions: Effects on reference price change. *Advances in Consumer Research. Association for Consumer Research (U. S.)*, *16*, 241–247.

Dim Mock, N., Belokosztolszki, A., Eyers, D., Bacon, J., & Moody, K. (2004). Using trust and risk in role based access control policies. In *Proceedings of the 9th ACM Symposium on Access Control Models and Technologies* (pp. 156-162). New York: ACM.

Dinis, P., & Rodrigues da Silva, A. (2007). Design experiences with the learning objects board system. In *Proceedings of the 40th of Hawaii International Conference on System Sciences*. IEEE.

Dinis, P., & Rodrigues da Silva, A. (2009). Application scenarios for the learning objects pool. *Journal of Universal Computer Science*, *15*(7), 1455–1471.

Disney, S., Naim, M., & Towill, D. (1997). Dynamic simulation modeling for lean logistics. *International Journal of Physical Distribution & Logistics Management, 27*(3/4), 174–196. doi:10.1108/09600039710170566.

Divitini, M., Haugalokken, O., & Morken, E. M. (2005). *Blog to support learning in the field: Lessons learned from a fiasco.* Paper presented at the Fifth IEEE International Conference on Advanced Learning Technologies. New York, NY.

Dodds, P. S., Muhamad, R., & Watts, D. J. (2003). An experimental study of search in global social networks. *Science, 301*, 827–829. doi:10.1126/science.1081058.

Donaldson, E. A., & Grant-Vallone, E. J. (2000). Longitudinal examination of mentoring relationships on organizational commitment and citizenship behavior. *Journal of Career Development, 26*(4), 233–248. doi:10.1177/089484530002600401.

Donavan, D., Brown, T., & Mowen, J. (2004). Internal benefits of service-worker customer orientation: job satisfaction, commitment, and organizational citizenship behaviors. *Journal of Marketing, 68*(1), 128–146. doi:10.1509/jmkg.68.1.128.24034.

Dösinger, G., Stocker, A., Us, A., & Wagner, C. (2007). The three pillars of 'corporate web 2.0': A model for definition. In *Proceedings of I-MEDIA '07 and I-SEMANTICS '07*. Graz, Austria: IEEE.

Douglas, A., & Mills, J. E. (2004). Staying afloat in the tropics: Applying a structural equation model approach to evaluating national tourism organization websites in the Caribbean. *Journal of Travel & Tourism Marketing, 17*(2/3), 269–293. doi:10.1300/J073v17n02_20.

Dowling, G. R., & Uncles, M. (1997). Do customer loyalty programs really work? *Sloan Management Review, 38*(4), 71–82.

Doyle, S. (2002). Software review: Communication optimisation - The new mantra of database marketing: Fad or fact? *Journal of Database Marketing, 9*(2), 185–191. doi:10.1057/palgrave.jdm.3240074.

Dragoi, G., Draghici, A., Rosu, S. M., & Cotet, C. E. (2010). Virtual product development in university-enterprise partnership. *Information Resources Management Journal, 23*(3), 43–59. doi:10.4018/irmj.2010070104.

Drucker, P. (1946). *Concept of corporation.* New York: Harper and Row.

Drucker, P. (2007). *Management - Tasks, responsabilities and practices.* New Brunswick, NJ: Transaction Publishers.

Dubois, D., & Prade, H. (1987). The mean value of a fuzzy number. *Fuzzy Sets and Systems, 24*, 279–300. doi:10.1016/0165-0114(87)90028-5.

Dubois, D., Prade, H., & Ughetto, L. (1999). Fuzzy logic, control engineering and artificial intelligence. In Verbruggen, , Zimmermann, , & Babuska, (Eds.), *Fuzzy Algorithms for Control*, (pp. 17-57). Dordrecht, The Netherlands: Kluwer Academic Publishers. doi:10.1007/978-94-011-4405-6_2.

Dumas, M., van der Aalst, W. M. P., & ter Hofstede, A. H. M. (2005). *Process-aware information systems: Bridging people and software through process technology.* New York: Wiley. doi:10.1002/0471741442.

Dutta, S. (2010). What's your personal social media strategy? *Harvard Business Review, 88*(11), 127–130. PMID:21049685.

Duval, E. (2005). LearnRank: The real quality measure for learning materials. In Policy and Innovation in Education-Quality Criteria. European Schooet.

Dwyer, C., Hiltz, S., & Passerini, K. (2007). *Trust and privacy concern within social networking sites: A comparison of Facebook and MySpace.* Paper presented at the Americas Conference on Information Systems (AMCIS). New York, NY.

Dwyer, L., Edwards, D., Mistilis, N., Roman, C., & Scott, N. (2009). Destination and enterprise management for a tourism future. *Tourism Management, 30*(1), 63–74. doi:10.1016/j.tourman.2008.04.002.

Dyché, J. (2002). *The CRM handbook: A business guide to customer relationship management.* Reading, MA: Addison-Wesley Pearson Education.

Dyché, J., & Levy, E. (2006). *Customer data integration: Reaching a single version of the truth.* Hoboken, NJ: John Wiley & Sons, Inc..

e-Business W@tch. (2006). *ICT and e-business in the tourism industry.* Retrieved from http://www.ebusiness-watch.org/resources/tourism/SR08-2006 Tourism.pdf

Eclipse/BIRT. (2011). *BIRT project*. Retrieved from http://www.eclipse.org/birt

Editors of the American Heritage Dictionaries (EAHD). (2000). *The American heritage dictionary of the English language*. Boston: Houghton Mifflin.

Egan, J. (2011). *Relationship marketing* (4th ed.). Harlow, MA: Pearson Educational Limited.

Egbu, C., Botterill, K., & Bates, M. (2001). The influence of knowledge management and intellectual capital on organisational innovations. In *Proceedings of ARCOM Seventeenth Annual Conference*, (pp. 547-555). ARCOM.

Egger, R. (2010). Theorizing web 2.0 phenomena in tourism: A sociological signpost. *Information Technology & Tourism, 12*, 125–137. doi:10.3727/109830510X12887971002666.

Egger, R., & Buhalis, D. (2008). *eTourism: Case studies*. Oxford, UK: Ed. Butterworth Heinemann.

Egger, R., & Wörndl, L. (2008). Hotel Sallerhof: Innovations in interaction. In Egger, R., & Buhalis, D. (Eds.), *eTourism: Case studies* (pp. 56–64). Oxford, UK: Butterworth Heinemann - Elsevier.

Eginton, K. (1998). Knowledge management – Law firms can do it too! *Australian Law Librarian, 6*, 247–255.

Eker, M., Eker, S., & Pala, F. (2008). The effects of job satisfaction on organizational commitment among Turkish health care staff: an empirical study. *Journal of Academic Studies, 10*(36), 46–68.

Elgg. (2011). *Elgg - Open source social networking engine*. Retrieved October 4, 2011, from http://elgg.org/

Elia, G., Margherita, A., & Taurino, C. (2009). Enhancing managerial competencies through a wiki-learning space. *International Journal of Continuing Engineering Education and Lifelong Learning, 19*(2-3), 166–178. doi:10.1504/IJCEELL.2009.025025.

Ellison, L. (1999). *The internet changes everything and the CEO of Oracle is living proof.* Retrieved June 2011 from http://money.cnn.com/magazines/fortune/fortune_archive/1999/05/24/260276/index.htm

Ellison, C., Frantz, B., Lampson, B., Rivest, R., Thomas, B., & Ylonen, T. (1999). *RFC-2693: SPKI certificate theory*. Geneva, Switzerland: Internet Engineering Task Force.

Embarcadero Technologies. (2008). *Why data warehouse projects fail*. Retrieved from http://www.embarcadero.com/resources/technical_papers/Why-Data-Warehouse-Projects-Fail.pdf

Embid, P., Martín, M., & Zorrilla, V. (1998). *Marketing financiero*. Madrid, Spain: McGraw-Hill.

Emerson, R. (1962). Power-dependence relations. *American Sociological Review, 27*(1), 31–41. doi:10.2307/2089716.

Encyclopaedia Britannica. (2007). *Britannica concise encyclopedia*. London: Encyclopedia Britannica.

England, E., & Finney, A. (2007). *Managing interactive media: Project management for web and digital media*. Harlow, MA: Pearson Education, Inc..

Ericson, J. (2009). The real thing? *Information & Management, 19*(6), 14–19.

Erol, I., Sencer, S., & Sari, R. (2011). A new fuzzy multi-criteria framework for measuring sustainability performance of a supply chain. *Ecological Economics, 70*, 1088–1100. doi:10.1016/j.ecolecon.2011.01.001.

Estêvão, J. P., Carneiro, M. J., & Teixeira, L. (2011). Destination management systems: Improving the tourism experience by empowering visitors. In *Proceedings of the 4th Advances in Tourism Marketing Conference*. ATMC.

Ettredge, M., Richardson, V., & Scholz, S. (2001). The presentation of financial information at corporate web sites. *International Journal of Accounting Information Systems, 2*, 149–168. doi:10.1016/S1467-0895(00)00017-8.

Ettredge, M., Richardson, V., & Scholz, S. (2002). Dissemination of information for investors at corporate web sites. *Journal of Accounting and Public Policy, 21*, 357–389. doi:10.1016/S0278-4254(02)00066-2.

Etzioni, A. (1997). *Modern organizations*. London: Profile Books.

Europa. (n.d.). Retrieved from europa.eu

European Commission. (2010). *Communication from the commission to the European parliament, the council, the European economic and social committee and the committee of the regions: A Digital Agenda for Europe, L 245.* Brussels, Belgium: European Commission.

European Commission. (2010). *Communication from the commission to the European 2020: A strategy for smart, sustainable and inclusive growth.* Brussels, Belgium: European Commission.

European Opinion Research Group. (2011). *Attitudes on data protection and electronic identity in the European Union. Technical Report Special Eurobarometer 359.* Bruxelles, Belgium: European Commission.

European Parliament and Council. (1995). Directive 95/46/EC of the European parliament and of the council on the protection of individuals with regard to the processing of personal data and on the free movement of such data. *Official Journal of the European Communities, 281*, 31–50.

European Parliament and Council. (1999). Directive 99/93/EC of the European parliament and of the council on a community framework for electronic signatures. *Official Journal of the European Communities, 13*, 12.

European Parliament and Council. (2002). Directive 2002/58/EC of the European parliament and of the council concerning the processing of personal data and the protection of privacy in the electronic communications sector (directive on privacy and electronic communications). *Official Journal of the European Communities, 201*, 37–47.

European Parliament. (2011). *Consumer behavior in a digital environment.* Retrieved 20 November, 2010 from http://www.europarl.europa.eu/document/activities/cont/201108/20110825ATT25258/20110825ATT25258EN.pdf

European Union (EU). (2006). *Implementing the partnership for growth and jobs.* Brussels, Belgium: EU.

European Union. (2003). The new SME definition: User guide and model declaration. *Official Journal of the European Union, 124*, 36.

Eurostat. (2011). Retrieved from http://epp.eurostat.ec.europa.eu/portal/page/portal/eurostat/home/

Evans, D., & McKee, J. (2010). *Social media marketing: The next generation of business engagement.* New York: John Wiley & Sons, Inc..

Evan, W. (1976). Organizational theory and organizational effectiveness. *Organizational and Administrative Science, 7*, 15–28.

Evelson, B., & Hammond, J. S. (2010). *The Forrester Wave™: Open source business intelligence (BI), Q3 2010.* Forrester Research.

Eysenbach, G. (2001). What is e-health? *Journal of Medical Internet Research, 3*(2), e20. doi:10.2196/jmir.3.2.e20 PMID:11720962.

Facebook. (2011). *Statistics.* Retrieved November 15, 2011, from http://www.facebook.com/press/info.php?statistics

Fan, Z. P., Suo, W. L., Feng, B., & Liu, Y. (2011). Trust estimation in a virtual team: A decision support method. *Expert Systems with Applications, 38*(8), 10240–10251. doi:10.1016/j.eswa.2011.02.060.

FAO. (2010). *Organizational evaluation.* Retrieved in January 2010, from http://www.fao.org/docrep/w7510e/w7510e05.htm

Farah, R. M., & Arantes, R. P. (2010). *Novas tecnologias no envelhecimento..*

Fare, R., Grosskopf, S., & Fukuyama, H. (2004). *New directions: Efficiency and productivity.* Boston: Springer.

Faust, W., & Faust, K. (1994). *Social network analysis: Methods and applications: Structural analysis in the social sciences.* Cambridge, UK: Cambridge University Press.

Fayol, H. (1949). *General and industrial management.* New York.

Felder, R., & Soloman, B. (2011). *Learning styles and strategies.* Retrieved February 2011 from http://csu.edu/unity/lockers/users/f/felder/public/ILSdir/styles.htm

Felder, R. (1993). Reaching the second tier: learning and teaching styles in college science education. *Journal of College Science Teaching, 23*(5), 286–290.

Filev, A. (2007, September 29). *How do enterprise 2.0 technologies make companies more agile?* [Web log comment]. Retrieved from http://www.wrike.com/projectmanagement/09/29/2007/How-Do-Enterprise-2-0-Technologies-Make-Companies-More-Agile

Filev, A. (n.d.). *Project management 2.0: Blending bottom-up and top-down approaches*. Retrieved from http://www.wrike.com/apple_booklet_for_Web.pdf

Filipe, S., & Barbosa, M. (2012). The relationship markeitng under the perception of the client in the context of higher educaton: An exploratory study. *International Business and Economics Review, 3*.

Finkenzeller, K. (2010). *RFID handbook: Fundamentals and applications in contactless smart cards, radio frecuency identificacion and NFC*. New York: Wiley. doi:10.1002/9780470665121.

Fink, M., & Kraus, S. (Eds.). (2009). *The management of small and medium enterprises*. New York: Routledge.

Fishbein, M., & Ajzen, I. (1975). *Belief, attitude, intention, and behavior: An introduction to theory and research*. Reading, MA: Addison-Wesley Reading.

Flick, U. (2004). Design and process in qualitative research. In Flick, U., Von Kardoff, E., & Steine, I. (Eds.), *A Companion to Qualitative Research* (pp. 146–152). London: SAGE.

Flood, R. L. (2009). *Rethinking the fifth discipline: Learning within the unknowable*. London: Routledge.

Florida, R. (2002). *The rise of the creative class*. New York: Basic Books.

Flyvbjerg, B. (2006). Five misunderstandings about case-study research. *Qualitative Inquiry, 12*(2), 219–245. doi:10.1177/1077800405284363.

Foa, U. G. (1971). Interpersonal and economic resources. *Science, 29*, 345–351. doi:10.1126/science.171.3969.345.

Fonou-Dombeu, J. V., & Huisman, M. (2011). Combining ontology development methodologies and semantic web platforms for e-government domain ontology development. *International Journal of Web & Semantic Technology, 2*(2), 12–25. doi:10.5121/ijwest.2011.2202.

Ford, D. V., Jones, K. H., Verplancke, J. P., Lyons, R. A., John, G., & Brown, G. et al. (2009). The SAIL databank: Building a national architecture for e-health research and evaluation. *BMC Health Services Research, 9*, 157. doi:10.1186/1472-6963-9-157 PMID:19732426.

Fornell, C., & Larcker, D. F. (1981). Evaluating structural equation models with unobservable variables and measurement errors. *JMR, Journal of Marketing Research, 18*, 39–50. doi:10.2307/3151312.

Foster, M. K., Francescucci, A., & West, B. C. (2010). Why users participate in online social networks. *International Journal of e-Business Management, 4*(1), 3-19.

Fowler, M. (2003). *What is a bliki*. Retrieved October 6, 2011, from http://martinfowler.com/bliki/WhatIsaBliki.html

Fox, S. (2001). *pewInternet*. Retrieved from www.pewInternet.org

Foxall, G. R., Goldsmith, R. E., & Brown, S. (1998). *Consumer psychology for marketing* (2nd ed.). London: International Thomson Business Press.

FP6 IST Project PRIME (Privacy and Identity Management for Europe). (n.d.). Retrieved November 3, 2011, from https://www.prime-project.eu/

FP7 IST Project PrimeLife (Privacy and Identity Management in Europe for Life). (n.d.). Retrieved November 3, 2011, from http://www.primelife.eu/

Franck, E., & Jungwirth, C. (2003). Reconciling investors and donators: The governance structure of open source. *Journal of Management and Governance, 7*, 401–421. doi:10.1023/A:1026261005092.

Franklin, T., & Harmelen, M. V. (2007). *Web 2.0 for content for learning and teaching in higher education*.

Frappaolo, C. (2010). Implementing enterprise 2.0 within the European Union. *The 2.0 Adoption Council*. Retrieved September 1, 2011, from http://info.newsgator.com

Freeman, L. C. (1996). Some antecedents of social network analysis. *Connections, 19*(1), 39-42. Retrieved January 01, 2012, from http://www.insna.org/PDF/Connections/v19/1996_I-1-4.pdf

Freeman, L. C. (2004). *The development of social network analysis: A study in the sociology of science*. Canada: Empirical Press.

FreshMinds Research. (2010). *Turning conversations into insights: A comparison of social media monitoring tools*. Retrieved from http://shared.freshminds.co.uk/smm10/whitepaper.pdf

Friedkin, N. E. (2011). Spine segments in small world networks. *Social Networks*, *33*(1), 88–97. doi:10.1016/j.socnet.2010.11.004.

Friedkin, N. E., & Johnsen, E. C. (1997). Social positions in influence networks. *Social Networks*, *19*(3), 209–222. doi:10.1016/S0378-8733(96)00298-5.

Frissen, V., Millard, J., Huijboom, N., Iversen, J. S., Kool, L., & Kotterink, B. et al. (2007). *The future of eGovernment: An exploration of ICT-driven models of eGovernment for the EU in 2020*. European Comission Join Research Center.

Frondizi, R. (Ed.). (1992). *Qué son los valores? Introduccion a la axiología* (3rd ed.). Breviarios del Fondo de Cultura Económica.

Fujitsu. (2009). *Soluciones para el sector bancario*. Fujitsu.

Fukuyama, F. (1995). *Trust: The social virtues and the creation of prosperity*. New York, NY: Free Press.

Fundación Orange. (2010). *eEspaña 2010: Informe anual sobre el desarrollo de la sociedad de la información en España*. Fundación Orange.

Funk, W. (1992). *Word origins: An exploration and history of words and language*. Gravesend, NJ: Bell Publishing Company.

Furst, S. A., Blackburn, R. S., & Rosen, B. (1999). Virtual team effectiveness: A proposed research agenda. *Information Systems Journal*, *9*, 249–269. doi:10.1046/j.1365-2575.1999.00064.x.

Furst, S. A., Reeves, M., Rosen, B., & Blackburn, R. S. (2004). Managing the life cycle of virtual teams. *The Academy of Management Executive*, *18*(2), 6–20. doi:10.5465/AME.2004.13837468.

Gaffney, J. (2001). The battle over internet ads. *Business 2.0*. Retrieved from http://www.business2.com/articles/Web/0,1653,16546,00.html

Galaskiewicz, J., & Wasserman, S. (1993). Social network analysis: Concepts, methodology, and directions for the 1990s. *Sociological Methods & Research*, *22*(1), 3–22. doi:10.1177/0049124193022001001.

Galbraith, J. (2002). *Designing organizations*. New York: Wiley and Sons.

Galbraith, J. R. (1971). Matrix organization designs How to combine functional and project forms. *Business Horizons*, *14*(1), 29–40. doi:10.1016/0007-6813(71)90037-1.

Galbrait, J. (1995). *Designing organizations: An executive briefing on strategy, structure, and process*. San Francisco, CA: Jossey-Bass.

Gallagher, R. (2002). *The soul of an organization*. New York: Kaplan Business.

Gallaugher, J. (2010). Get S.M.A.R.T. – Social media awareness & response team. In *Information Systems: A Manager's Guide to Harnessing Technology* (pp. 125–134). Flat World Knowledge.

Gallup Organization. (2008). *Data protection in the European Union: Citizens' perceptions – Analytical report (flash eurobarometer 225)*. Retrieved November 3, 2011, http://ec.europa.eu/public_opinion/flash/fl_225_en.pdf

Gallupe, B. (2001). Knowledge management systems: Surveying the landscape. *International Journal of Management Reviews*, *3*(1), 61–77. doi:10.1111/1468-2370.00054.

Ganorkar, S. R., & Ghatol, A. A. (2007). Iris recognition: An emerging biometric technology. In *Proceedings of the 6th WSEAS International Conference on Signal Processing, Robotics and Automation* (pp. 91 – 96). WSEAS.

García Ponce, F. J. (2007). *Accesibilidad, TIC y educación. CNICE*. Centro Nacional de Información y Comunicación Educativa. Ministerio de Educación y Ciencia.

Gardner, W. L., & Avolio, B. A. (1998). The charismatic relationship: A dramaturgical perspective. *Academy of Management Review*, *23*, 32–58.

Gartner. (2011). *Gartner says enterprises that harness the power of collective behaviors will be the ultimate winners with social media*. Retrieved February 28, 2011, from http://www.gartner.com

Garvin, D. A. (1993). Building a learning organisation. *Harvard Business Review*, *71*, 78.

Garvin, D. A., Edmondson, A. C., & Gino, F. (2008). Is yours a learning organisation? *Harvard Business Review*, *86*(3), 109.

Gattiker, T. F., & CFPIM. (2002). Anatomy of an ERP implementation gone awry. *Production and Inventory Management Journal*, *43*, 96–105.

Gattiker, T. F., & Goodhue, D. L. (2005). What happens after ERP implementation: Understanding the impact of interdependence and differentiation on plant-level outcomes. *Management Information Systems Quarterly*, *29*(3), 559–585.

Gaved, M. B., & Mulholland, P. (2010). Networking communities from the bottom up: Grassroots approaches to overcoming the digital divide. *AI & Society*, *25*(3), 345–357. doi:10.1007/s00146-009-0259-5.

Gebert, H., Geib, M., Kolbe, L., & Brenner, W. (2003). Knowledge-enabled customer relationship management: Integrating customer relationship management and knowledge management concepts. *Journal of Knowledge Management*, *7*(5), 107–123. doi:10.1108/13673270310505421.

Gefen, D., Benbasat, I., & Pavlou, P. A. (2008). A research agenda for trust in online environments. *Journal of Management Information Systems*, *24*(4), 275–286. doi:10.2753/MIS0742-1222240411.

Gellman, R. (1996). Disintermediation and the internet. *Government Information Quarterly*, *1*, 1–8. doi:10.1016/S0740-624X(96)90002-7.

Getz, D. (1987). Tourism planning and research: Traditions, models and futures. In *Proceedings of the Australian Travel Workshop* (pp. 407-448). Bunbury, Australia: Australian Travel Workshop.

Ghorbel, M., & Mokhtari, M. (2005). Toward an assistive indoor/outdoor living environment for people with disabilities.[Boca Raton, FL: IOS Press.]. *Proceedings of ICOST*, *05*, 237–244.

Giaever, H. (1999). Collecting, storing and utilizing information about improvement opportunities: A discussion of the non-technological barriers to success. In *Proceedings of the 11th International Conference on Software Engineering & Knowledge Engineering*, (pp. 200-202). Kaiserslautern, Germany: IEEE.

Gigerenzer, G. (2004). Mindless statistics. *Journal of Socio-Economics*, *33*(5), 587–606. doi:10.1016/j.socec.2004.09.033.

Gilbert, D. C., Powell-Perry, J., & Widijoso, S. (1999). Approaches by hotels to the use of the Internet as a relationship marketing tool. *Journal of Marketing Practice: Applied Marketing Science*, *5*(1), 21–38. doi:10.1108/EUM0000000004549.

Gleanster. (2010). *Gleansight: Social media monitoring*. Gleanster, LLC

Gloor, P. A., Paasivaara, M., Schoder, D., & Willems, P. (2008). Finding collaborative innovation networks through correlating performance with social network structure. *International Journal of Production Research*, *46*(5), 1357–1371. doi:10.1080/00207540701224582.

Gluesing, J. C., & Riopelle, K. R. (2010). Correlating survey data and network data to understand performance in global virtual teams. *Procedia Social and Behavioral Sciences*, *2*, 6551–6560. doi:10.1016/j.sbspro.2010.04.065.

Goldman, J. et al. (1995). *Competitors and virtual organizations*. London: Van Nostrand Reinhold.

Goldsmith, R. E., & Lafferty, B. A. (2002). Consumer response to web sites and their influence on advertising effectiveness. *Internet Research*, *12*(4), 318–328. doi:10.1108/10662240210438407.

Goldstein, S. Z. (2006). Fast forward: Future trends in corporate communication: A checklist of top priorities for professionals in 2006. *Strategic Communication Management*, *10*(1), 14–17.

Gomez, R. (Ed.). (2012). *Libraries, telecenters, cybercafés and public access to ICT: International comparisons*. Hershey, PA: IGI Global.

Gomez, R., & Baron, L. F. (2011). Does public access computing really contribute to community development? Lessons from libraries, telecenters and cybercafés in Colombia. *Electronic Journal of Information Systems in Developing Countries*, *49*(2), 1–11.

Gomis, J. M. (2005). *Tourism, distribution and IT: Strategic approach to the effects of a new paradigm on intermediation*. (Doctoral Thesis). Universitat de Barcelona, Barcelona, Spain.

Gomulka, S. (1990). *Theory of technological change and economic growth*. Florence, Italy: Routledge. doi:10.4324/9780203013052.

Gonzales, M. L., & Wells, D. L. (2006). *BI strategy: How to create and document*. Austin, TX: HandsOn-BI, LLC.

González, J., & Garazo, T. (2006). Structural relationships between organizational service orientation, contact employee job satisfaction and citizenship behavior. *International Journal of Service Industry Management*, *17*(1), 23–50. doi:10.1108/09564230610651561.

Gonzalez, P., Sarkis, J., & Adenso-Diaz, B. (2008). Environmental management system certification and its influence on corporate practices: Evidence from the automotive industry. *International Journal of Operations & Production Management*, *28*(11), 1021–1041. doi:10.1108/01443570810910179.

Goodman, P., & Penningss, J. (Eds.). (1977). *New perspectives on organizational effectiveness*. San Francisco, CA: Jossey-Bass.

Goodman, R. (1970). Organizational preference in research and development. *Human Relations*, *23*(4), 279–298. doi:10.1177/001872677002300403.

Goodrich, K. (2011). Anarchy of effects? Exploring attention to online advertising and multiple outcomes. *Psychology and Marketing*, *28*, 417–440. doi:10.1002/mar.20371.

Goodwin, C. (2007). *Getting through*. Retrieved October 25, 2011 from www.directmag.com

Goodwin, J., Dolbear, C., & Hart, G. (2008). Geographical linked data: The administrative geography of great britain on the semantic web. *Transactions in GIS*, *12*, 19–30. doi:10.1111/j.1467-9671.2008.01133.x.

Gove, P. (Ed.). (2002). *Third new international dictionary of the English language*. Chicago: Merriam-Webster.

Govindarajan, V., & Trimple, C. (2010). *The other side of innovation*. Boston: Harvard Business Press.

Grabner-Kraeuter, S., & Waiguny, M. (2011). Why users stay in online social networks: Perceptions of value, trust, subjective norm and the moderating influence of duration of use. *American Marketing Association*, *22*(1), 240-249.

Grabova, O., Darmont, J., Chauchat, J.-H., & Zolotaryova, I. (2010). Business intelligence for small and middle-sized entreprises. *SIGMOD Record*, *39*(2), 39–50. doi:10.1145/1893173.1893180.

Grace, T. P. L. (2009). Wikis as a knowledge management tool. *Journal of Knowledge Management*, *13*(4), 64–74. doi:10.1108/13673270910971833.

Graham, J. (1991). An essay on organizational citizenship behavior. *Employee Responsibilities and Rights Journal*, *4*(4), 249–270. doi:10.1007/BF01385031.

Granovetter, M. (1973). The strength of weak ties. *American Journal of Sociology*, *78*(6), 1360–1380. doi:10.1086/225469.

Granovetter, M. (1983). The strength of weak ties: A network theory revisited. *Sociological Theory*, *1*, 201–233. doi:10.2307/202051.

Granovetter, M. S. (1973). The strength of weak ties. *American Journal of Sociology*, *83*, 1420–1443. doi:10.1086/226707.

Granovetter, M. S. (1982). The strength of weak ties: A network theory revisited. In Marsden, P. V., & Lin, N. (Eds.), *Social structure and network analysis* (pp. 105–130). Beverly Hills, CA: Sage Publications.

Granovetter, M. S. (1992). Problems of explanation in economic sociology. In Nohria, N., & Eccles, R. G. (Eds.), *Networks and organizations: Structure, form, and action* (pp. 25–56). Boston, MA: Harvard Business School Press.

Granqvist, M. (2005). Looking critically at ICT4Dev: The case of Lincos. *The Journal of Community Informatics, 2*(1).

Grant, R. (1996). Toward a knowledge-based theory of the firm. *Strategic Management Journal, 17*, 109–122.

Gray, K., Thompson, C., Clerehan, R., Sheard, J., & Hamilton, M. (2011). Web 2.0 authorship: Issues of referencing and citation for academic integrity. *The Internet and Higher Education*, 112–118.

Gray, P. H., Parise, S., & Iyer, B. (2011). Innovation impacts of using social bookmarking systems. *Management Information Systems Quarterly, 35*(3), 629–643.

Grebner, O., & Riss, U. (2008). Implicit metadata generation on the semantic desktop using task management as example. In *Proceedings of the Conference on Formal Ontologies Meet Industry* (pp. 33-44). Amsterdam: IOS Press.

Greenberg, G. (1998). Distance education technologies: Best practices for K-12 settings. *IEEE Technology and Society Magazine, 17*, 36–40. doi:10.1109/44.735862.

Greenberg, P. (2010). *CRM at the speed of light: Social CRM strategies, tools, and techniques for engaging your customers* (4th ed.). New York: The McGraw-Hill Companies.

Greene, D. (1999). *Measuring what matters: The paths of intangible value.* Paper presented at the Institute for International Research. San Diego, CA.

Greene, C. (2009). *Entrepreneurship: Ideas in action.* Mason, GA: South-Western.

Griffith, T. L., & Neale, M. (2001). Information processing in traditional, hybrid, and virtual teams: From nascent knowledge to transactive memory. *Research in Organizational Behavior, 23*, 379–421. doi:10.1016/S0191-3085(01)23009-3.

Griffith, T. L., Sawyer, J., & Neale, M. (2003). Virtualness and knowledge in teams: managing the love triangle of organizations, individuals, and information technology. *Management Information Systems Quarterly, 27*(2), 265–287.

Grönroos, C. (1980). Designing a long range marketing strategy for services. *Long Range Planning, 13*(2), 36–42. doi:10.1016/0024-6301(80)90030-8.

Grönroos, C. (1994). From marketing mix to relationship marketing: Towards a paradigm shift in marketing. *Management Decision, 32*(2), 4–20. doi:10.1108/00251749410054774.

Grönroos, C. (1997). Keynote paper: From marketing mix to relationship marketing - Towards a paradigm shift in marketing. *Management Decision, 35*(4), 322. doi:10.1108/00251749710169729.

Grönroos, C. (2006). On defining marketing: finding a new roadmap for marketing. *Marketing Theory, 6*(4), 395–417. doi:10.1177/1470593106069930.

Grossbart, S., Muehling, D., & Kangun, N. (1986). Verbal and visual references to competition in comparative advertising. *Journal of Advertising, 15*(1), 10–23. doi:10.1080/00913367.1986.10672984.

Grosseck, G. (2009). To use or not to use web 2.0 in higher education?. *Procedia - Social and Behavioral Sciences, 1*(1), 478-482.

Grosser, K. (1991). Human networks in organizational information processing. *Annual Review of Information Science & Technology, 26*, 349–402.

Gruban, B., Verčič, D., & Zavrl, F. (1997). *Pristop k odnosom z javnostmi.* Ljubljana, Slovenia: Pristop.

Gruber, T. (2008). Ontology. In Liu, L., & Ozsu, M. (Eds.), *Encyclopedia of Database Systems*. Berlin: Springer-Verlag.

Grunig, A. L., Grunig, E. J., & Dozier, M. D. (2002). *Inside the organization: Culture, structure, systems of internal communication, gender and diversity V: Excellent public relations and effective organizations.* Hoboken, NJ: Lawrence Erlbaum Associates, Inc..

Grunig, E. J., & Grunig, A. L. (2002). Implications of the IABC excellence study for PR education. *Journal of Communication Management, 7*(1), 34–42. doi:10.1108/13632540310807232.

Grusky, O. (1963). Managerial succession and organizational effectiveness. *American Journal of Sociology*, *69*(1), 21–31. doi:10.1086/223507.

Guarino, N. (Ed.). (1998). *Formal ontology in information systems: Proceedings of the first international conference (FOIS'98).* IOS.

Guenzi, P., Georges, L., & Pardo, C. (2009). The impact of strategic account managers' behaviors on relational outcomes: An empirical study. *Industrial Marketing Management*, *38*, 300–311. doi:10.1016/j.indmarman.2007.09.011.

Gummesson, E. (1987). The new marketing - Developing long-term interactive relationships. *Long Range Planning*, *20*(4), 10–20. doi:10.1016/0024-6301(87)90151-8.

Gummesson, E. (1997). Relationship marketing as a paradigm shift: Some conclusions from the 30R approach. *Management Decision*, *35*(4), 267. doi:10.1108/00251749710169648.

Gummesson, E. (1998). Implementation requires a relationship marketing paradigm. *Journal of the Academy of Marketing Science*, *26*(3), 242–249. doi:10.1177/0092070398263006.

Gummesson, E. (2008). *Total relationship marketing* (3rd ed.). Oxford, UK: Butterworth-Heinemann.

Gunasekaran, C., & Tirtiroglu, E. (2001). Performance measures and metrics in a supply chain environment. *International Journal of Operations & Production Management*, *21*(1/2), 71–87. doi:10.1108/01443570110358468.

Gunn, C. (1972). *Vacationscape: Designing tourist regions*. Austin, TX: University of Texas.

Gupta, J., & Sushil, S. (2004). *Creating knowledge based organizations.* Hershey, PA: Idea Group Publishing.

Gurumurthy, A., & Kodali, R. (2009). Application of benchmarking for assessing the lean manufacturing implementation. *Benchmarking: An International Journal*, *16*(2), 274–308. doi:10.1108/14635770910948268.

Guttentag, D. A. (2010). Virtual reality: Applications and implications for tourism. *Tourism Management*, *31*(5), 637–651. doi:10.1016/j.tourman.2009.07.003.

Guzzo, R. A., & Dickson, M. W. (1996). Teams in organizations: Recent research on performance and effectiveness. *Annual Review of Psychology*, *47*, 307–338. doi:10.1146/annurev.psych.47.1.307 PMID:15012484.

Hackman, R., & Oldham, G. (1975). Development of the job diagnostic survey. *The Journal of Applied Psychology*, *60*(2), 150–170. doi:10.1037/h0076546.

Hackman, R., & Oldham, G. (1976). Motivation through the design of work: A test of a theory. *Organizational Behavior and Human Performance*, *16*(2), 250–279. doi:10.1016/0030-5073(76)90016-7.

Haenlein, M., & Kaplan, A. (2010). Users of the world, unite! The challenges and opportunities of social media. *Business Horizons*, *53*(1), 59–68. doi:10.1016/j.bushor.2009.09.003.

Hagel, J., & Brown, J. S. (2010). *The enterprise value of social software.* Retrieved September 1, 2011, from http://blogs.hbr.org

Hagel, J. III, Brown, J. S., & Davidson, L. (2010). *The power of pull: How small moves, smartly made, can set big things in motion.* New York: Basic Books.

Haimes, Y. (2006). On the definition of vulnerabilities in measuring risks to infrastructures. *Risk Analysis: An Official Publication of the Society for Risk Analysis*, *26*(2), 293–296. doi:10.1111/j.1539-6924.2006.00755.x PMID:16573621.

Hair, J. F., Ringle, C. M., & Sarstedt, M. (2011). PLS-SEM: Indeed a silver bullet. *Journal of Marketing Theory and Practice*, *19*(2), 139–151. doi:10.2753/MTP1069-6679190202.

Haislip, A. (2006). Question of the day: What's your MySpace strategy? *Venture Capital Journal*, *46*(9), 3–6.

Halic, O., Lee, D., Paulus, T., & Spence, M. (2010). To blog or not to blog: Student perceptions of blog effectiveness for learning in a college-level course. *The Internet and Higher Education*, *13*(4), 206–213. doi:10.1016/j.iheduc.2010.04.001.

Hall, J., Nilsson, J., & Nivre, J. (n.d.). Single malt or blended? A study in multilingual parser optimization. *Trends in Parsing Technology*, (pp. 19-33). Academic Press.

Hall, C. M. (2000). *Tourism planning: Policies, processes and relationships*. Harlow, MA: Pearson Education.

Hall, R., & Clark, J. (1980). An ineffective effectiveness study and some suggestions for future research. *The Sociological Quarterly*, *21*, 119–134. doi:10.1111/j.1533-8525.1980.tb02203.x.

Hammond, K., Mcwilliam, G., & Narholz, A. (1998). Fun and work on the web: Differences in attitudes between novices and experienced users. *Advances in Consumer Research. Association for Consumer Research (U. S.)*, *25*, 372–378.

Ham, S., Kim, W. G., & Jeong, S. (2004). Effect of information technology on performance in upscale hotels. *International Journal of Hospitality Management*, *24*, 281–294. doi:10.1016/j.ijhm.2004.06.010.

Han, K. H., Yoon, D., & Cameron, G. T. (2001). *Web users' attitude and behavior toward online coupons*. Paper presented at 2001 Annual Conference of American Academy of Advertising. New York, NY.

Handy, C. (1995). Trust and the virtual organization. *Harvard Business Review*, *73*(3), 40–50.

Hanneman, R. A., & Riddle, M. (2005). Introduction to social network methods.[). IEEE.]. *Network*, *1*, 1–322.

Hansen, M. T., Nohria, N., & Tierney, T. (1999, March-April). What's your strategy for managing knowledge? *Harvard Business Review*, 106–116.

Hans, J. S., & Klischewski, R. (2007). E-government integration and interoperability: Framing the research agenda. *International Journal of Public Administration*, *30*(8-9), 889–920. doi:10.1080/01900690701402668.

Hanson, K. O. (2011). The long history of conscious capitalism: A response to James O'Toole and David Vogel's "Two and a half cheers for conscious capitalism". *California Management Review*, *53*(3), 77–83. doi:10.1525/cmr.2011.53.3.77.

Hao, W., Jhat, S., Livny, M., & McDaniel, P. D. (2004). Security policy reconciliation in distributed computing environments. In *Proceedings of the 5th IEEE International Workshop on Policies for Distributed Systems and Networks (POLICY'04)* (pp. 137-146). IEEE.

Hardy, Q., Pomerantz, D., & Hill, K. (2010). In mark we trust. *Forbes*, *186*(6), 80–86.

Harker, M. J. (1999). Relationship marketing defined? An examination of current relationship marketing definitions. *Marketing Intelligence & Planning*, *17*(1), 13–20. doi:10.1108/02634509910253768.

Harker, M. J., & Egan, J. (2006). The past, present and future of relationship marketing. *Journal of Marketing Management*, *22*(1-2), 215–242. doi:10.1362/026725706776022326.

Hars, A., & Qu, S. (2002). Working for free? Motivations for participating in open-source projects. *International Journal of Electronic Commerce*, *6*(3), 25.

Harvard Business Review Analytic Services. (2010). *The new conversation: Taking social media from talk to action*. Boston: Harvard Business School Publishing.

Harvey, M., Novicevic, M. M., & Garrison, G. (2004). Challenges to staffing global virtual teams. *Human Resource Management Review*, *14*, 275–294. doi:10.1016/j.hrmr.2004.06.005.

Harzing, A. W. (2007). *Publish or perish*. Retrieved from http://www.harzing.com/pop.htm

Hauser, C. H., Bakken, D. E., Dionysiou, I., Gjermundrod, H. K., Irava, V. S., Helkey, J., & Bose, A. (2008). Security, trust and QoS in next-generation control and communication for large power system. *International Journal of Critical Infrastructures*, *4*(1/2), 3–16. doi:10.1504/IJCIS.2008.016088.

Hay, R., & Gray, E. (1974). Social responsibilities of business managers. *Academy of Management Journal*, *17*(1), 135–143. doi:10.2307/254777.

Haythornthwaite, C. (2005). *Social network methods and measures for examining e-learning*. Graduate School of Library and Information Science.

Healey, J., & Prus, S. (2009). *Statistics: A tool for social research* (First Canadian Edition). Cengage Learning.

Hearn, G., Foth, M., & Gray, H. (2009). Applications and implementations of new media in corporate communications: An action research approach. *Corporate Communications*, *14*(1), 49–61. doi:10.1108/13563280910931072.

Hebert, R., & Link, A. (1989). In search of the meaning of entrepreneurship. *Small Business Economics, 1*(1), 39–49. doi:10.1007/BF00389915.

He, D. D., & Yang, J. (2009). Authorization control in collaborative healthcare systems. *Journal of Theoretical and Applied Electronic Commerce Research, 4*(2), 88–109.

Heeks, R., & León, K. L. (2009). *Remoteness, exclusion and telecentres in mountain regions: Analysing ICT-based information chains in Pazos, Peru.* Manchester, UK: Centre for Development Informatics. Retrieved November, 12, 2011, from http://www.sed.manchester.ac.uk/idpm/research/publications/wp/di/documents/di_wp38.pdf

Heiler, S. (1995). Semantic interoperability. *ACM Computing Surveys, 27*(2), 271–273. doi:10.1145/210376.210392.

Heinonen, K. (2006). Temporal and spatial e-service value. *International Journal of Service Industry Management, 17*(4), 380–400. doi:10.1108/09564230610680677.

Heinonen, K., & Strandvick, T. (2005). Communication as an element of service value. *International Journal of Service Industry Management, 16*(2), 186–198. doi:10.1108/09564230510592306.

Heiskanen, E., Hyysalo, S., Kotro, T., & Repo, P. (2010). Constructing innovative users and user-inclusive innovation communities. *Technology Analysis and Strategic Management, 22*(4), 495–511. doi:10.1080/09537321003714568.

Helms, R., & Buijsrogge, K. (2005). *Knowledge network analysis: A technique to analyze knowledge management bottlenecks in organizations.* Paper presented at the Sixteenth International Workshop on Database and Expert Systems Applications. New York, NY.

Hemetsberger, A., & Reinhardt, C. (2009). Collective development in open-source communities: An activity theoretical perspective on successful online collaboration. *Organization Studies, 30*(9), 987–1008. doi:10.1177/0170840609339241.

Hempel, J., & Kowitt, B. (2009). How Facebook is taking over our lives. *Fortune International, 159*(4), 34–41.

Henseler, J., Ringle, C. M., & Sinkovics, R. (2009). The use of partial least squares path modelling in international marketing. *Advances in International Marketing, 20*, 277–319. doi:10.1108/S1474-7979(2009)0000020014.

Herget, J., & Mader, I. (2009). Social software in external corporate communications - A conceptional approach towards measuring, assessment and optimization of web 2.0 activity. *Information-Wissenschaft und Praxis, 60*(4), 233–240.

Herrero, A. (2005). *El proceso de adopción de nuevos sistemas de venta: Aplicación al comercio electrónico entre particulares y empresas.* Cantabria, Spain: Departamento de Administración de Empresas, Universidad de Cantabria.

Hertel, G., Geister, S., & Konradt, U. (2005). Managing virtual teams: A review of current empirical research. *Human Resource Management Review, 15*, 69–95. doi:10.1016/j.hrmr.2005.01.002.

Hertel, G., Konradt, U., & Orlikowski, B. (2004). Managing distance by interdependence: Goal setting, task interdependence, and team-based rewards in virtual teams. *European Journal of Work and Organizational Psychology, 13*(1), 1–28. doi:10.1080/13594320344000228.

Hickson, D., Hinings, C., Lee, C., Schneck, R., & Pennings, J. (1971). A strategic contingencies' theory of interorganizational power. *Administrative Science Quarterly, 16*(3), 216–229. doi:10.2307/2391831.

Hienerth, C. (2006). The commercialization of user innovations: The development of the rodeo kayak industry. *R & D Management, 36*(3), 273–294. doi:10.1111/j.1467-9310.2006.00430.x.

Highsmith, J. (2004). *Agile project management: Creating innovative products.* Redwood City, CA: Addison Wesley Longman Publishing Co., Inc..

Hiltz, S. R., & Turoff, M. (1993). *The network nation* (Revised Ed.). Cambridge, MA: MIT Press.

Hinchcliffe, D. (2007). *The state of enterprise 2.0.* Retrieved September 1, 2011, from http://www.zdnet.com

Hinchcliffe, D. (2011). *Integration and connection to work are central to social business success.* Retrieved September 15, 2011, from http://www.ebizq.net

Hinds, D., & Lee, R. M. (2008). Social network structure as a critical success condition for virtual communities. In *Proceedings of the 41st Annual Hawaii International Conference on System Sciences (HICSS'08)*. Waikoloa, HI.

Hinton, P. R., Brownlow, C., McMurray, I., & Cozens, B. (2004). *SPSS explained.* London: Routledge Taylor & Francis Group.

Hirota, K., & Pedrycz, W. (1999). Fuzzy computing for data mining. *Proceedings of the IEEE, 87*(9), 1575–1600. doi:10.1109/5.784240.

Hirschman, E., & Holbrook, M. (1982). Hedonic consumption: Emerging concepts, methods and propositions. *Journal of Marketing, 46*(2), 92–101. doi:10.2307/1251707.

Hix, B. (2011). Seniors, mobile communication, and health care. Boca Raton, FL: 3CInteractive, LLC.

Ho, G., Lau, H., Chung, S., Fung, R., & Chan, T. (2008). Fuzzy rule sets for enhancing performance in a supply chain network. *Industrial Management + Data Systems, 108*(7), 947-972.

Hoang, H., & Antoncic, B. (2003). Network-based research in entrepreneurship: A critical review. *Journal of Business Venturing, 18*(2), 165–187. doi:10.1016/S0883-9026(02)00081-2.

Hobson, S., Anand, R., Yang, J., Lee, J., Campos, P., Graham, N., et al. (2011). Towards interoperability in municipal government: A study of information sharing practices. In Human-Computer Interaction – INTERACT 2011 (Vol. 6946, pp. 233-247). Springer. doi:10.1007/978-3-642-23774-4_21.

Hoek, V., Harrison, A., & Christopher, M. (2001). Measuring agile capabilities in the supply chain. *International Journal of Operations & Production Management, 21*(1/2), 126–148. doi:10.1108/01443570110358495.

Hoffman, D. L. (2000). The revolution will not be televised: Introduction to the special issue on marketing science and the internet. *Marketing Science, 19*(1), 1–3. doi:10.1287/mksc.19.1.1.15181.

Hoffman, D. L., & Novak, T. P. (1996). Marketing in hypermedia computer-mediated environments: Conceptual foundations. *Journal of Marketing, 60*(3), 50–69. doi:10.2307/1251841.

Hoffman, D. L., & Novak, T. P. (2000). How to acquire customers on the web. *Harvard Business Review, 78*(3), 179–188. PMID:11183979.

Hofstede, G., & Pedersen, P. (2004). *Cultures and organizations.* New York: McGraw-Hill.

Hogben, G. (2007). Security issues and recommendations for online social networks. ENISA European Network and Information Security Agency, 80211(1).

Ho, J. Y. C., & Dempsey, M. (2010). Viral marketing: Motivations to forward online content. *Journal of Business Research, 63*(9-10), 1000–1006. doi:10.1016/j.jbusres.2008.08.010.

Holbrook, M. B., & Gardner, M. P. (1993). An approach to investigating the emotional determinants of consumption duration, why do people consume what they consume for as long as they consume it? *Journal of Consumer Psychology, 2*(2), 123–142. doi:10.1016/S1057-7408(08)80021-6.

Holloway, J. C. (2002). *The business of tourism* (6th ed.). London: Prentice Hall.

Holt, D., & Ghobadian, A. (2009). An empirical study of green supply chain management practices amongst UK manufacturers. *Journal of Manufacturing Technology Management, 20*(7), 933–956. doi:10.1108/17410380910984212.

Holtz, S. (2002). *Public relations on the internet.* New York: Amazon.

Honeycutt, A., & Richards, B. (1989). An organizational transformation model: The road to renewal. *Educational Technology, 29*(10), 42–45.

Ho, S., Kauffman, R. J., & Liang, T. (2007). A growth theory perspective on B2C e-commerce growth in Europe: An exploratory study. *Electronic Commerce Research and Applications, 6*, 237–259. doi:10.1016/j.elerap.2006.06.003.

Hossain, L., & Zhu, D. (2009). Social networks and coordination performance of distributed software development teams. *The Journal of High Technology Management Research, 20*(1), 52–61. doi:10.1016/j.hitech.2009.02.007.

Houaiss, A., & Villar, M. S. (2001). *Dicionário houaiss de língua portuguesa.* Rio de Janeiro: Objetiva.

Hounshell, B. (2011). The revolution will be tweeted. *Foreign Policy*, (187): 20–21.

House, R. (1971). A path goal theory of leader effectiveness. *Administrative Science Quarterly*, *16*(3), 321–339. doi:10.2307/2391905.

House, R. (1980). *Evaluating with validity*. Beverly Hills, CA: Sage Publications.

House, R. J. (1977). A 1976 theory of charismatic leadership. In Hunt, J. G., & Larsons, L. L. (Eds.), *Leadership: The cutting edge* (pp. 189–207). Carbondale, IL: Southern Illinois University Press.

Howard, J. A., & Sheth, J. N. (1969). *The theory of buyer behavior*. New York: Wiley.

Howell, J. M., & Avolio, B. J. (1993). Transformational leadership, transactional leadership, locus of control, and support for innovation: Key predictors of consolidated-business-unit performance. *The Journal of Applied Psychology*, *78*(6), 891–911. doi:10.1037/0021-9010.78.6.891.

Hozjan, T. (2010). *Spletne skupnosti kot orodja odnosov z javnostmi*. Ljubljana, Slovenia: Fakulteta za družbene vede.

Hsieh, J. J. P. A., & Wang, W. (2007). Explaining employees' extended use of complex information systems. *European Journal of Information Systems*, *16*(3), 216–227. doi:10.1057/palgrave.ejis.3000663.

Hu, A., & Hsu, C. (2006). Empirical study in the critical factors of green supply chain management (GSCM), practice in the Taiwanese electrical and electronics industries. In *Proceeding of 2006 IEEE International Conference on Management of Innovation and Technology*. Singapore: IEEE.

Huang, R., Kahai, S., & Jestice, R. (2010). The contingent effects of leadership on team collaboration in virtual teams. *Computers in Human Behavior*, *26*, 1098–1110. doi:10.1016/j.chb.2010.03.014.

Huang, S.-L., & Yang, C.-W. (2009). Designing a semantic bliki system to support different types of knowledge and adaptive learning. *Computers & Education*, *53*(3), 701–712. doi:10.1016/j.compedu.2009.04.011.

Hubbard, D. W. (2010). *How to measure anything - Finding the value of intangibles in business* (2nd ed.). Hoboken, NJ: John Wiley & Sons, Inc..

Huber, J. T., Walsh, T. J., & Varman, B. (2005). Camp for all connection: A community health information outreach project. *Journal of the Medical Library Association*, *93*(3), 348–352. PMID:16059424.

Huffaker, D. (2005). The educated blogger: Using weblogs to promote literacy in the classroom. *AACE Journal*, *13*(2), 91–98.

Huisman, M., & van Duijn, M. A. J. (2003). Software for social network analysis. *Social Science Research*, *27*, 270–316.

Hull, R. (2008). Lecture Notes in Computer Science: *Vol. 5332. Artifact-centric business process models: Brief survey of research results and challenges* (pp. 1152–1163). Heidelberg: Springer. doi:10.1007/978-3-540-88873-4_17.

Hurlbert, J. S. (2001). Social networks, social circles, and job satisfaction. *Work and Occupations*, *18*(4), 415–430. doi:10.1177/0730888491018004003.

Huston, L., & Sakkab, N. (2006, March). Connect and develop: Inside Procter & Gamble's new model for innovation. *Harvard Business Review*, 1–9.

Hutley, R. (2009). *Social networking as a business tool*. Cisco Internet Business Solutions Group.

Hwang, H.-G., Ku, C.-Y., Yen, D. V., & Cheng, C.-C. (2004). Critical factors influencing the adoption of data warehouse technology: A study of the banking industry in Taiwan. *Decision Support Systems*, *37*(1), 1–21. doi:10.1016/S0167-9236(02)00191-4.

Hwang, J., Altman, J., & Kim, K. (2009). The structural evolution of the web 2.0 service network. *Online Information Review*, *33*(6), 1040–1057. doi:10.1108/14684520911010990.

Hwang, M. I., & Lin, J. W. (1999). Information dimension, information overload and decision quality. *Journal of Information Science*, *25*(3), 213–218. doi:10.1177/016555159902500305.

IAB. (2010). *Interactive advertising bureau*. Retrieved from www.iab.net

Iakovou, E., Vlachos, D., & Xanthopoulos, A. (2007). An analytical methodological framework for the optimal design of resilient supply chains. *International Journal of Logistics Economics and Globalisation*, *1*(1), 1–20. doi:10.1504/IJLEG.2007.014498.

IBM. (2006). *The global innovation outlook*. Armonk, NY: IBM.

IBM. (2009). *The new voice of the CIO*. Retrieved from http://www-935.ibm.com/services/us/cio/ciostudy/

Ihator, S. A. (2001). Communication style in the information age. *School of Journalism and Broadcasting*, *6*(4), 199–204.

Ilyinska, L. (2004). *English for science and technology: Course design, text analysis, research writing*. RTU Publishing House.

In Goldsmith, R. E., & Lafferty, B. A. (2002). Consumer response to web sites and their influence on advertising effectiveness. *Internet Research*, *12*(4), 318–328. doi:10.1108/10662240210438407.

Inche, J. L. (1998). Modelos de innovación tecnológica. *Industrial Data*, *1*(2), 9–16.

INE. (2010). *Encuesta de Tecnologías de la Información en los hogares 2010*. Retrieved from www.ine.es

Information Security Forum (ISF). (2007). *The standard of good practice for information security*. ISF.

Information Systems Security Association (ISSA). (2004). *Generally accepted information security principles*. GAISP.

Inmon, B. (2002). *Building the data warehouse* (3rd ed.). New York: Wiley and Sons.

Insiti, M. (2007). ERP end-users business productivity: A field study of SAP & Microsoft. *Keystone Strategy Research 2007*. Retrieved June 12, 2010, from http://download.microsoft.com

International Data Corporation (IDC). (2008). The hyperconnected: Here they come! A global look at the exploding 'culture of connectivity' and its impact on the enterprise. *Framingham USA/MA*. Retrieved February 9, 2012, from www.nortel.com/hyperconnectivity/idc/hyperconnectivity_idc.pdf

International Telecommunication Union. (2005). *Information technology – Open systems interconnection – The directory: Public-key and attribute certificate frameworks*. ITU-T Recommendation X.509. Retrieved November 29, 2010, from http://www.itu.int/rec/T-REC-X.509-200508-I

Internet World Stats. (2011). *Internet users in the world*. Retrieved from http://www.Internetworldstats.com/stats.htm

Ireland, R., & Hitt, M. (1997). Performance strategies for high growth entrepreneurial firms. *Frontiers of Entrepreneurship Research*, *9*(1), 101–104.

Iriana, R., & Buttle, F. (2005). *Strategic, operational and analytical customer relationship management: Attributes and measures (No. MGSM WP 2005-1)*. Macquarie Graduate School of Management.

Iriberri, A., & Leroy, G. (2009). A life-cycle perspective on online community success. *ACM Computing Surveys*, *41*(2). doi:10.1145/1459352.1459356.

Ismail, H. S., & Sharifi, H. (2006). A balanced approach to building agile supply chains. *International Journal of Physical Distribution & Logistics Management*, *36*(6), 431–444. doi:10.1108/09600030610677384.

ISO/IEC 27002. (2005). *Information technology - Security techniques - Code of practice for information security management*. ISO/IEC.

Israel, D. (2009). *Data analysis in business research: A step-by-step nonparametric approach*. Thousand Oaks, CA: Sage Publications Pvt. Ltd..

Itmazi, J., Megías, M. G., Paderewski, P., & Gutiérrez, F. L. (2005). *A comparison and evaluation of open source learning management systems*. Paper presented at the IADIS International Conference on Applied Computing. Retrieved September 21, 2011, from http://www.iadis.net/dl/final_uploads/200501C014.pdf

Ives, B., & Gersting, A. (1998, February/March). Implementing knowledge management – Lessons learned. *Knowledge Management*.

Jabbour, K. K. (2011). Web 2.0 tecnology tools for global education in Lebanon. *International Journal of Advanced Engineering Sciences and Technologies*, *7*(1), 151–168.

Jackson, B. (1985). Building customer relationships that last: How close can industrial markets get to their customers - And for how long? *Harvard Business Review*, *63*, 120.

Jain, A. K., Ross, A., & Pankanti, S. (2006). Biometrics: A tool for information security. *IEEE Transactions on Information Forensics and Security*, *1*(2), 125–144. doi:10.1109/TIFS.2006.873653.

Jankowski, N. W. (2009). Creating community with media: History, theories and scientific investigations. In Lievrouw, L. A., & Livingstone, S. M. (Eds.), *Handbook of new media: Social shaping and social consequences of ICT's* (pp. 55–74). Los Angeles, CA: Sage.

Jarvenpaa, S. L., & Leidner, D. E. (1999). Communication and trust in global virtual teams. *Organization Science*, *10*(6), 791–815. doi:10.1287/orsc.10.6.791.

Jarvis, J. (2012). *BuzzMachine*. Retrieved from http://buzzmachine.com/archives/cat_dell.html

Jaspersoft. (2011). *Jaspersoft*. Retrieved from http://www.jaspersoft.com/ Jedox/Palo. (2011). *Open source business intelligence*. Retrieved from http://www.jedox.com/

JavaHispano. (2011, November 15). *Tu lenguaje, tu comunidad*. Retrieved from http://javaHispano.org

Jennings, M. (2005). *Business: Its legal, ethical and global environment*. Brentford, UK: SW Pub..

Jeppesen, L. B., & Frederiksen, L. (2006). Why do users contribute to firm-hosted user communities? The case of computer-controlled music instruments. *Organization Science*, *17*(1), 45–63. doi:10.1287/orsc.1050.0156.

Jiang, Y., Raghupathi, V., & Raghupathi, W. (2009). Content and design of corporate governance web sites. *Information Systems Management*, *26*(1), 13–27. doi:10.1080/10580530802384704.

Jie, W., Arshad, J., Sinnott, R., Townend, P., & Lei, Z. (2011). A review of grid authentication and authorization technologies and support for federated access control. *ACM Computing Surveys*, *43*(2), 12:1-12:26.

Jin, Y., Matsuo, Y., & Ishizuka, M. (2007). Extracting social networks among various entities on the web. In E. Franconi, M. Kifer, & W. May (Eds.), *Proceedings of the Fourth European Semantic Web Conference* (Vol. 4519, pp. 251-266). Springer.

Johnson, E. J., Bellman, S., & Lohse, G. L. (2003). Cognitive lock-in and the power law of practice. *Journal of Marketing*, *67*, 62–75. doi:10.1509/jmkg.67.2.62.18615.

Johnson, P. (2006). Whence democracy? A review and critique of the conceptual dimensions and implications of the business case for organizational democracy. *Organization*, *13*(2), 245–274. doi:10.1177/1350508406061676.

Johnson, P., Heimann, V., & O'Neill, K. (2001). The wonderland of virtual teams. *Journal of Workplace Learning*, *13*(1), 24–29. doi:10.1108/13665620110364745.

Johnston, D., Pan, E., Walker, J., Bates, D. W., & Middleton, B. (2003). *The value of computerized provider order entry in ambulatory settings*. Wellesley, MA: Center for Information Technology Leadership.

Jones, J. (2008). An exploratory study on attitude persistence using sales promotion. *Journal of Managerial Issues*, *20*(3), 401–417.

Jones, M. (2006). Which is a better predictor of job performance: Job satisfaction or life satisfaction? *Journal of Behavioral and Applied Management*, *8*(1), 20–42.

Jordá, C. (2008). Impacto ambiental del transporte aéreo y de las infraestructuras aeroportuarias. *Ingeniería y Territorio*, *83*, 26–33.

Jordan, J., & Ellen, C. (2009). Business need, data and business intelligence. *Journal of Digital Asset Management*, *5*(1). doi:10.1057/dam.2008.53.

Joshi, J. B. D., Bertino, E., Latif, U., & Ghafoo, A. (2005). A generalized temporal role-based access control model. *Journal of IEEE Transactions on Knowledge and Data Engineering*, *15*, 4–23. doi:10.1109/TKDE.2005.1.

Joshi, K., & Curtis, M. (1999). Issues in building a successful data warehouse. *Information Strategy: The Executive's Journal*, *15*(2), 28–35.

Judge, T., Parker, S., Colbert, A., Heller, D., & Remus, I. (2001). Job satisfaction: A cross-cultural review. In Anderson, N., Ones, D., Sinangil, H., & Viswesvaran, C. (Eds.), *Handbook of Industrial, Work and Organizational Psychology* (*Vol. 2*, pp. 25–52). London: Sage Publications.

Junco, R., & Cotten, S. R. (2011). Perceived academic effects of instant messaging use. *Computers & Education*, *56*(2), 370–378. doi:10.1016/j.compedu.2010.08.020.

Jung, D. I., Chow, C., & Wu, A. (2003). The role of transformational leadership in enhancing organisational innovation: Hypotheses and some preliminary findings. *The Leadership Quarterly*, *14*, 525–544. doi:10.1016/S1048-9843(03)00050-X.

Jung, K., & Lee, B. Y. (2010). Online vs. offline coupon redemption behaviors. *International Business & Economics Research Journal*, *9*(12), 23–36.

JupiterResearch. (2011). *Jupiter research report 2006-2011*. Retrieved from www.jupiterresearch.com

Kahneman, D., & Tversky, A. (1984). Choices, values and frames. *The American Psychologist*, *39*, 341–350. doi:10.1037/0003-066X.39.4.341.

Kaldis, K., & Kaldis, E. (2008). Emmantina and Palmira beach hotels: Distribution for independent hotels. In Egger, R., & Buhalis, D. (Eds.), *eTourism: Case studies* (pp. 65–73). Oxford: Butterworth Heinemann - Elsevier.

Kalkan, V. D. (2008). An overall view of knowledge management challenges for global business. *Business Process Management Journal*, *14*(3), 390–400. doi:10.1108/14637150810876689.

Kalla, K. H. (2005). Integrated internal communications: a multidisciplinary perspective. *Corporate Communications: An International Journal*, *10*(4), 302–314. doi:10.1108/13563280510630106.

Kanigel, R. (1999). *The one best way: Frederick Winslow Taylor and the enigma of efficiency*. New York: Viking.

Kanter, R. M. (1983). *The change masters: Corporate enterpreneurs at work*. London: Routledge.

Kaplan, J., & Warren, A. (2009). *Patterns of entrepreneurship management*. New York: Wiley.

Kardoff, E. (2004). Qualitative evaluation research. In Flick, U., Von Kardoff, E., & Steinke, I. (Eds.), *A Companion to Qualitative Research* (pp. 137–142). London: SAGE.

Karjaluoto, H., Mattila, M., & Pento, T. (2002). Factors underlying attitude formation toward online banking in Finland. *International Journal of Bank Marketing*, *20*(6), 261–272. doi:10.1108/02652320210446724.

Kathleen, C. (2003). *Dynamic social network modeling and analysis: Workshop summary and papers*. Washington, DC: National Academy Press.

Katz, D., & Kahn, R. (1987). *Psicologia social das organizações* (3rd ed.). São Paulo, Brazil: Editora Atlas.

Katz, R. (Ed.). (2003). *The human side of managing technological innovation*. Oxford, UK: Oxford University Press.

Kaye, A. R. (1992). Collaborative learning through computer conferencing. In Kaye, A. (Ed.), *Computer Conference and Content Analysis* (pp. 117–136). Springer Verlag.

Kayworth, T. R., & Leidner, D. E. (2000). The global virtual manager: A prescription for success. *European Management Journal*, *18*(2), 183–194. doi:10.1016/S0263-2373(99)00090-0.

Kayworth, T. R., & Leidner, D. E. (2001). Leadership effectiveness in global virtual teams. *Journal of Management Information Systems*, *18*(3), 7–40.

Kear, K., Woodthorpe, J., Robertson, S., & Hutchison, M. (2010). From forums to wikis: Perspectives on tools for collaboration. *The Internet and Higher Education*, *13*(4), 218–225. doi:10.1016/j.iheduc.2010.05.004.

Keating, E., Nagai, E., Hadder, N., & Kowalsky, J. (2007). *The role of the mobile phone in the welfare of aged and disabled people*. Austin, TX: University of Texas / NTT DoCoMo, Inc..

Kekes, J. (1989). *Moral tradition and individuality*. Princeton, NJ: Princeton University Press.

Kelley, H. (2001). *Attributional analysis of computer self-efficacy*. (Unpublished doctoral dissertation). Richard Ivey School of Business, London, UK.

Kelley, D. (2009). Adaptation and organizational connectedness in corporate innovation programs. *Journal of Product Innovation Management*, *26*(5), 487–501. doi:10.1111/j.1540-5885.2009.00676.x.

Kelly, S. (1997). Data marts: The latest silver bullet. *Data Mart Review*, 12-16.

Kennedy, G. E., Judd, T. S., Churchward, A., Gray, K., & Krause, K. L. (2008). First year students' experiences with technology: Are they really digital natives? *Australasian Journal of Educational Technology*, *24*(1), 108–122.

Kermarrec, A.-M., Le Merrer, E., Sericola, B., & Trédan, G. (2011). Second order centrality: Distributed assessment of nodes criticity in complex networks. *Computer Communications*, *34*(5), 619–628. doi:10.1016/j.comcom.2010.06.007.

Kerzner, H. (2010). *Project management best practices: Achieving global excellence* (2nd ed.). Hoboken, NJ: John Wiley and Sons, Inc..

Ke, W., & Zhang, P. (2009). Motivations in open source software communities: The mediating role of effort intensity and goal commitment. *International Journal of Electronic Commerce*, *13*(4), 39–66. doi:10.2753/JEC1086-4415130403.

Khan, Z. H. (2010). *ICT and the changing face of higher education*. Paper presented at the International Conclave of Scientists on Regional Cooperation in Science & Technology: Opportunities and Challenges in the Context of Globalization. New Delhi, India.

Khan, A. (2002). *Implementing SAP with an ASAP methodology focus*. San Jose, CA: Writers Club Press.

Kimball, R., & Ross, M. (2002). *The data warehouse toolkit: The complete guide to dimensional modeling* (2nd ed.). New York: John Wiley and Sons.

Kim, D. H. (1993). The link between individual and organisational learning. *Sloan Management Review*, *35*(1), 37–50.

Kim, H. N. (2008). The phenomenon of blogs and theoretical model of blog use in educational contexts. *Computers & Education*, *51*(3), 1342–1352. doi:10.1016/j.compedu.2007.12.005.

Kim, S.-Y., Jung, T.-S., Suh, E.-H., & Hwang, H.-S. (2006). Customer segmentation and strategy development based on customer lifetime value: A case study. *Expert Systems with Applications*, *31*, 101–107. doi:10.1016/j.eswa.2005.09.004.

King, M. F., & Balasubramanian, S. K. (1994). The effects of expertise, end goal, and product type on adoption of preference formation strategy. *Journal of the Academy of Marketing Science*, *22*(2), 146–159. doi:10.1177/0092070394222004.

Kirkman, B. L., & Mathieu, J. E. (2005). The dimensions and antecedents of team virtuality. *Journal of Management*, *31*(5), 700–718. doi:10.1177/0149206305279113.

Kirkman, B. L., & Rosen, B. (2000). Powering up teams. *Organizational Dynamics*, *28*(3), 48–66. doi:10.1016/S0090-2616(00)88449-1.

Kirkman, B. L., Rosen, B., Gibson, C. B., Tesluk, P. E., & McPherson, S. O. (2002). Five challenges to virtual success: Lessons from Sabre, Inc. *The Academy of Management Executive*, *16*(3), 67–79. doi:10.5465/AME.2002.8540322.

Kirkman, B. L., Rosen, B., Tesluk, P. E., & Gibson, C. B. (2004). The impact of team empowerment on virtual team performance: The moderating role of face-to-face interaction. *Academy of Management Journal*, *47*(2), 175–192. doi:10.2307/20159571.

Kitchen, P. (1997). *Public relations: Principles and practice*. London: International Thomson Business Press.

Kitsak, M., Gallos, L. K., Havlin, S., Liljeros, F., Muchnik, L., Stanley, H. E., & Makse, H. A. (2010). Identification of influential spreaders in complex networks. *Nature Physics*, *6*(11), 888–893. doi:10.1038/nphys1746.

Kleinberg, J. M. (1999). Hubs, authorities, and communities. *ACM Computing Surveys*, *31*(4), 5. doi:10.1145/345966.345982.

Klein, S., Köhne, F., & Öörni, A. (2004). Barriers to online booking of scheduled airline tickets. *Journal of Travel & Tourism Marketing*, *17*(2/3), 27–29. doi:10.1300/J073v17n02_03.

Knight, M. (2011). *BI growth to buck economic trends*. Retrieved July 14, 2011, from http://www.itpro.co.uk/183480/bi-growth-to-buckeconomic-trends

Koch, C. (2003). *Open source - Your open source plan*. Retrieved from http://www.cio.com/article/31768/Open_Source_Your_Opensource_Plan

Koch, M., & Richter, A. (2008). Functions of social networking services. In *Proceedings of COOP '08: the 8th International Conference on the Design of Cooperative Systems*. COOP.

Kojima, S., & Kaplinsky, R. (2004). The use of a lean production index in explaining the transition to global competitiveness: The auto components sector in South Africa. *Technovation*, *24*(3), 199–206. doi:10.1016/S0166-4972(03)00142-1.

Konovsky, M., & Organ, D. (1996). Dispositional and contextual determinants of organizational citizenship behavior. *Journal of Organizational Behavior*, *17*(3), 253–266. doi:10.1002/(SICI)1099-1379(199605)17:3<253::AID-JOB747>3.0.CO;2-Q.

Korten, D. (2009). *Agenda for a new economy*. San Francisco, CA: Berrett-Koehler.

Kositanuri, B., Nqwenyama, O., & Osei-Bryson, K. M. (2006). An exploration of factors that impact individual performance in an ERP environment: An analysis using multiple analytical techniques. *European Journal of Information Systems*, *15*, 556–568. doi:10.1057/palgrave.ejis.3000654.

Kossinets, G., Kleinberg, J., & Watts, D. (2008). The structure of information pathways in a social communication network. In *Proceeding of the 14th ACM SIGKDD International Conference on Knowledge Discovery and Data Mining*, (pp. 435–443). New York, NY: ACM. doi:10.1145/1401890.1401945

Kotler, P., Armstrong, G., Saunders, J., & Wong, V. (1999). *Principles of marketing*. London: Prentice Hall.

Kotler, P., Armstrong, G., Wong, V., & Sauders, J. (2008). *Principles of marketing* (5th ed.). London: Prentice Hall.

Kotler, P., Bowen, J. T., & Makens, J. C. (2003). *Marketing for hospitality and tourism* (3rd ed.). Upper Saddle River, NJ: Pearson Prentice Hall.

Kotler, P., & Keller, K. L. (2006). *Dirección de marketing* (12th ed.). Madrid, Spain: Pearson Education.

Kotler, P., & Keller, K. L. (2009). *Marketing management* (13th ed.). Upper Saddle River, NJ: Pearson Education International.

Kotler, P., & Lee, N. (2004). *Corporate social responsibility: Doing the most good for your company and your cause*. Hoboken, NJ: Wiley.

Koufaris, M., Kambil, A., & Labarbera, P. A. (2002). Consumer behavior in web-based commerce: An empirical study. *International Journal of Electronic Commerce*, *6*(2), 115–138.

Kouwenhoven, T. (1998). Reengineering for learning. *SIGGROUP Bulletin*, *19*(1), 39–45.

Krackhardt, D. (1987). Cognitive social structures. *Social Networks*, *9*(2), 109–134. doi:10.1016/0378-8733(87)90009-8.

Krackhardt, D. (1992). The strength of strong ties: The importance of philos in organizations. In Nohria, N., & Eccles, R. G. (Eds.), *Networks and organizations: Structure, form, and action* (pp. 216–239). Boston, MA: Harvard Business School Press.

Krackhardt, D. (2000). Modeling structures of organizations. In Ilgen, D. R., & Hulin, C. L. (Eds.), *Computational Modeling of Behavior in Organizations: The Third Scientific Discipline*. American Psychological Association.

Krackhardt, D., & Hanson, J. R. (1993). Informal networks: The company behind the chart. *Harvard Business Review*, *71*(4), 104–111. PMID:10127036.

Krebs, V. (2000). Working in the connected world. *IHRIM Journal*, *4*(2), 89–91.

Krebs, V. (2007). Managing the 21st century organization. *IHRIM Journal*, *9*(4), 2–8.

Krogh, G. (1998). Care in knowledge creation. *California Management Review*, *40*(3), 133–153. doi:10.2307/41165947.

Kumaran, S., Liu, R., & Wu, F. Y. (2008). On the duality of information-centric and activity-centric models of business processes. *Lecture Notes in Computer Science*, *5074*, 32–47. doi:10.1007/978-3-540-69534-9_3.

Kumar, N., & Idris, K. (2006). An examination of educational institutions' knowledge performance: Analysis, implications and outlines for future research. *The Learning Organization, 13*(1), 96–116. doi:10.1108/09696470610639158.

Kumar, R., & Best, M. L. (2006). Social impact and diffusion of telecenter use: A study from the sustainable access in rural India project. *Journal of Community Informatics, 2*(3), 328–349.

Kumar, V., & Reinartz, W. J. (2006). *Customer relationship management: A databased approach.* New York: Wiley.

Kummervold, P. E., Chronaki, C. E., Lausen, B., Prokosch, H. U., Rasmussen, J., & Santana, S. et al. (2008). eHealth trends in Europe 2005-2007: A population-based survey. *Journal of Medical Internet Research, 10*(4), e42. doi:10.2196/jmir.1023 PMID:19017584.

Künzle, V., & Reichert, M. (2009). Towards object-aware process management systems: Issues, challenges, benefits. *Lecture Notes in Business Information Processing, 29,* 197–210. doi:10.1007/978-3-642-01862-6_17.

Kupp, M., & Anderson, J. (2007). Zopa: Web 2.0 meets retail banking. *Business Strategy Review, 18*(3), 15–17. doi:10.1111/j.1467-8616.2007.00478.x.

Kuratko, D. (2008). *Entrepreneurship: Theory, process, and practice.* Cincinnati, OH: South-Western College.

Kurniawan, S. (2007). mobile phone design for older persons. *Design for Seniors: Innovations for Graying Tmes, 14*(4), 24–25.

Küster, J. M., Ryndina, K., & Gall, H. (2007). Generation of business process models for object life cycle compliance. *Lecture Notes in Computer Science, 4714,* 165–181. doi:10.1007/978-3-540-75183-0_13.

Kwahk, K. Y., & Lee, J. N. (2008). The role of readiness for change in ERP implementation: Theoretical bases and empirical validation. *Information & Management, 45*(7), 474–481. doi:10.1016/j.im.2008.07.002.

Kwan, M., & Ramachandran, D. (2009). Trust and online reputation systems. In *Computing with Social Trust* (pp. 287–311). Berlin: Springer-Verlag. doi:10.1007/978-1-84800-356-9_11.

Kwon, T. H., & Zmud, R. W. (1987). Unifying the fragmented models of information systems implementation. In Boland, R. J., & Hirschheim, R. A. (Eds.), *Critical Issues in Information Systems Research.* New York: John Wiley & Sons.

Lafley, A., & Johnson, M. (2010). *Seizing the white space: Business model innovation for growth and renewal.* Boston: Harvard Business Press.

Lafollette, H. (Ed.). (2005). *The Oxford handbook of practical ethics.* Oxford, UK: Oxford University Press. doi:10.1093/oxfordhb/9780199284238.001.0001.

Lafuente, R. (2005). *Los servicios financieros bancarios electrónicos.* Valencia, Spain: Tirant lo Blanch.

Lai, Y. C., & Ng, E. M. W. (2011). Using wikis to develop student teachers' learning, teaching, and assessment capabilities. *The Internet and Higher Education, 14*(1), 15–26. doi:10.1016/j.iheduc.2010.06.001.

Lakatos, I., & Musgrave, A. (Eds.). (1970). *Criticism and the growth of knowledge.* Cambridge, UK: Cambridge University Press.

Lambercy, V. (2010). Preaching for aviation 2.0. *PlasticPilot.* Retrieved February 9, 2012, from http://www.plasticpilot.net/blog/2010/11/14/preaching-for-aviation-2-0/

Lambert, D. M., & Cooper, M. C. (2000). Issues in supply chain management. *Industrial Marketing Management, 29,* 65–83. doi:10.1016/S0019-8501(99)00113-3.

Lambert, D. M., Stock, J. R., & Ellram, L. M. (1998). *Fundamentals of logistics management.* Burr Ridge, IL: Irwin/McGraw-Hill.

Langenwalter, G. (2000). *Enterprise resources planning and beyond: Integrating your entire organization.* Boca Raton, FL: St. Lucie Press.

Larrán, M., & Giner, B. (2002). The use of the internet for corporate reporting by Spanish companies. *The International Journal of Digital Accounting Research, 2*(1), 53–82.

Laster, J. (2010). Seton Hill to offer iPads to full-time students. *The Chronic of Higher Education.* Retrieved February 2012 from chronicle.com/blogs/wiredcampus/seton-hill-to-offer-ipads-to-full-time-students/22153

Lau, H., Pang, W., & Wong, C. (2002). Methodology for monitoring supply chain performance: A fuzzy logic approach. *Journal of Enterprise Information Management*, *15*(4), 271–280.

Lau, K. (2011). Benchmarking green logistics performance with a composite index. *Benchmarking*, *18*(6), 873–896. doi:10.1108/14635771111180743.

Lavelle, J., Brockner, J., Konovsky, M., Price, K., Henley, A., Taneja, A., & Vinekar, V. (2008). Commitment, procedural fairness, and organizational citizenship behavior: A multifoci analysis. *Journal of Organizational Behavior*, *30*(3), 337–357. doi:10.1002/job.518.

Lawler, E., Worley, C., & Porras, J. (2006). *Built to change: How to achieve sustained organizational effectiveness*. San Francisco, CA: Jossey-Bass.

Law, R., & Hsu, C. H. C. (2005). Customers' perceptions on the importance of hotel web site dimensions and attributes. *International Journal of Contemporary Hospitality Management*, *17*(6), 493–503. doi:10.1108/09596110510612130.

Law, R., Leung, K., & Wong, R. J. (2004). The impact of the Internet on travel agencies. *International Journal of Contemporary Hospitality Management*, *16*(2), 100–107. doi:10.1108/09596110410519982.

Law, R., & Leung, R. (2000). A study of airlines' online reservation services on the Internet. *Journal of Travel Research*, *39*, 202–211. doi:10.1177/004728750003900210.

Lawrence, A., & Weber, J. (2007). *Business and society*. New York: McGraw-Hill.

Lawrence, P. R., & Lorsch, J. W. (1967). *Organization and environment*. Boston: Harvard University Press.

Lawrence, P., & Lorsch, J. (1967). Differentiation and integration in complex organizations. *Administrative Science Quarterly*, *12*(1), 1–30. doi:10.2307/2391211.

Lawton, G. (2009). Users take a close look at visual analytics. *IEEE Computer*, *42*(2), 19–22. doi:10.1109/MC.2009.61.

Lebacqz, K. (1986). *Six theories of justice: Perspectives from philosophical and theological ethics*. Augsburg, Germany: Augsburg Books.

Lee, A. J., & Yu, T. (2009). Towards a dynamic and composable model of trust. In *Proceedings of the 14th ACM symposium on Access Control Models and Technologies (SACMAT '09)* (pp. 217-226). New York: ACM.

Lee, D. H., Lee, S. M., Olson, D. L., & Chung, S. H. (2010). The effect of organizational support on ERP implementation. *Industrial Management & Data Systems*, *110*(1-2), 269–283. doi:10.1108/02635571011020340.

Lee, G. K., & Cole, R. E. (2003). From a firm-based to a community-based model of knowledge creation: The case of the linux kernel development. *Organization Science*, *14*(6), 633–649. doi:10.1287/orsc.14.6.633.24866.

Lee-Kelley, L., & Sankey, T. (2008). Global virtual teams for value creation and project success: A case study. *International Journal of Project Management*, *26*(1), 51–62. doi:10.1016/j.ijproman.2007.08.010.

Lee, M. R. (2009). E-ethical leadership for virtual project teams. *International Journal of Project Management*, *27*, 456–463. doi:10.1016/j.ijproman.2008.05.012.

Lee, M. R., & Lan, Y. (2007). From web 2.0 to conversational knowledge management: Towards collaborative intelligence. *Journal of Entrepreneurship Research*, *2*(2), 47–62.

Lefebvre, L., Harvey, J., & Lefebvre, E. (1991). Technological experience and the technology adoption decisions in small manufacturing firms. *R & D Management*, *21*(3), 241–249. doi:10.1111/j.1467-9310.1991.tb00761.x.

Leganza, G. (2010). *The top 15 technology trends EA should watch: 2011 To 2013*. Forrester Research, Inc.

Legoinha, P., Pais, J., & Fernandes, J. (2006). *O Moodle e as comunidades virtuais de aprendizagem*. Paper presented at the VII Congresso Nacional de Geologia. New York, NY.

Leighninger, M. (2011). Citizenship and governance in a wild, wired world: How should citizens and public managers use online tools to improve democracy? *National Civic Review*, *100*(2), 20–29. doi:10.1002/ncr.20056.

Leiper, N. (1990). *Tourism systems: An interdisciplinary perspective*. Palmerston North, New Zealand: Massey University Printery.

Lemieux, V., & Ouimet, M. (2004). L'analyse structurale des réseaux sociaux. *Recherches Sociographiques, 47*(1), 179–182.

Lerner, J. (2009). *Boulevard of broken dreams: Why public efforts to boost entrepreneurship and venture capital have failed and what to do about it.* Princeton, NJ: Princeton University Press.

Lerner, J., & Tirole, J. (2002). Some simple economics of open source. *The Journal of Industrial Economics, 50*(2), 197–234. doi:10.1111/1467-6451.00174.

Leroy, G. A., & Iriberri, A. (2007). *Natural language processing and e-government: Extracting reusable crime report information.* Paper presented at the IRI - Information Reuse and Integration. New York, NY.

Lester, K., & Piore, M. (2004). *Innovation - The missing dimension.* Cambridge, MA: Harvard Business Press.

Leung, H., Lee, A., & Law, R. (2011). Adopting web 2.0 technologies on chain and independent hotel websites: A case tudy of hotels in Hong Kong. In Law, R., Fuchs, M., & Ricci, F. (Eds.), *Information and Communication Technologies in Tourism 2011* (pp. 331–342). New York: Springer. doi:10.1007/978-3-7091-0503-0_19.

Levy, M., & Powell, P. (1998). SME flexibility and the role of information systems. *Small Business Economics, 11*(2), 183–196. doi:10.1023/A:1007912714741.

Levy, M., Powell, P., & Yetton, P. (2002). The dynamics of SME information systems. *Small Business Economics, 19*(4), 341–354. doi:10.1023/A:1019654030019.

Lewis, R. (1998). Membership and management of a 'virtual' team: The perspectives of a research manager. *R & D Management, 28,* 5–13. doi:10.1111/1467-9310.00076.

Leydesdorff, L. (2006). *The knowledge-based economy.* Boca Raton, FL: Universal Publishers.

Li, N., & Mitchell, J. C. (2003). Datalog with constraints: A foundation for trust management languages. In *Proceedings of the 5th International Symposium on Practical Aspects of Declarative Languages* (pp. 58-73). IEEE.

Li, N., Mitchell, J. C., & Winsborough, W. H. (2002). Design of a role-based trust management framework. In *Proceedings of the 2002 IEEE Symposium on Security and Privacy* (pp. 114-130). IEEE.

Li, N., Winsborough, W. H., & Mitchell, J. C. (2001). Distributed credential chain discovery in trust management: Extended abstract. In *Proceedings of the 8th ACM Conference on Computer and Communications Security (CCS '01)* (pp. 156-165). New York: ACM.

Liang, T. P., & Huang, J. S. (1998). An empirical study on consumer acceptance of products in electronic markets: A transaction cost model. *Decision Support Systems, 24,* 29–43. doi:10.1016/S0167-9236(98)00061-X.

Liao, S. (2006). The effects of nonmonetary sales promotions on consumer preferences: The contingent role of product category. *The Journal of American Academy of Business, 8*(2), 196–203.

Lim, S., Matolcsy, Z., & Chow, D. (2007). The association between board composition and different types of voluntary disclosure. *European Accounting Review, 16,* 555–583. doi:10.1080/09638180701507155.

Lin, T. C., Lee, C. K., & Lin, J. C. C. (2010). Determinants of enterprise 2.0 adoption: A value-based adoption model approach. In *Proceedings of the 2010 International Conference on Information Society (i-Society)* (pp. 12-18). i-Society.

Lin, W.-J., Liu, Y.-L., Kakusho, K., Yueh, H.-P., Murakami, M., & Minoh, M. (2006). *Blog as a tool to develop e-learning experience in an international distance course.* Paper presented at the Sixth International Conference on Advanced Learning Technologies. New York, NY.

Lindholm, C., & Keinonen, T. (2003). *Mobile usability: How Nokia changed the FACE of the mobile phone.* New York: McGraw Hill.

Lin, N. (2001). *Social capital: A theory of social structure and action.* Cambridge, UK: Cambridge University Press. doi:10.1017/CBO9780511815447.

Lin, N., Cook, K., & Burt, R. (2001). Social capital: Theory and research. *Contemporary Sociology, 31,* 333.

Lin, N., Fu, Y., & Hsung, R. M. (2001). *The position generator: Measurement techniques for investigations of social capital. Social Capital Theory and Research.* Aldine de Gruyter.

Linstone, H. A., & Turoff, M. (Eds.). (1975). *The delphi method: Techniques and applications.* Reading, MA: Addison-Wesley.

Lioudakis, G. V., Gaudino, F., Boschi, E., Bianchi, G., Kaklamani, D. I., & Venieris, I. S. (2010). Legislation-aware privacy protection in passive network monitoring. In Portela, I. M., & Cruz-Cunha, M. M. (Eds.), *Information Communication Technology Law, Protection and Access Rights: Global Approaches and Issues*. Hershey, PA: IGI Global. doi:10.4018/978-1-61520-975-0.ch022.

Lippert, S., & Spagnolo, G. (2008). Internet peering as a network of relations. *Telecommunications Policy*, *32*(1), 33–49. doi:10.1016/j.telpol.2007.11.004.

Liu, L., & Ma, Q. (2006). Perceived system performance: A test of an extended technology acceptance model. *Journal of Organizational and End User Computing*, *18*(3), 1–24.

Li, X., & Wang, Y. (2010). Evaluating the effectiveness of destination marketing organisations' websites: Evidence from China. *International Journal of Tourism Research*, *12*, 536–549.

Locke, E. (1968). *What is job satisfaction?* Washington, DC: American Psychological Association.

Locke, E., Latham, G., & Erez, M. (1988). The determinants of goal commitment. *Academy of Management Review*, *13*(1), 23–39.

Lodahl, T., & Porter, L. (1961). Psychometric score patterns, social characteristics, and productivity of small industrial work groups. *The Journal of Applied Psychology*, *45*(2), 73–79. doi:10.1037/h0043379.

Lo, M.-C., & Ramayah, T. (2009). Dimensionality of organizational citizenship behavior (OCB) in a multicultural society: The case of Malaysia. *International Business Research*, *2*(1), 48–55.

López, S. P., Montes Peón, J. M., & Ordás, C. J. V. (2006). Human resources management as a determining factor in organisational learning. *Management Learning*, (37): 215–239. doi:10.1177/1350507606063443.

Lorincz, B., Tinholt, D., Linden, N. V. d., Colclough, G., Cave, J., Schindler, R., et al. (2010). *Digitizing public services in Europe: Putting ambition into action - 9th Benchmark Measurement*. Capgemini, RAND Europe, IDC, SOGETI and DTi.

Lovejoy, W. S., & Sinha, A. (2010). Efficient structures for innovative social networks. *Management Science*, *56*(7), 1127–1145. doi:10.1287/mnsc.1100.1168.

Lubbe, B. (2008). Kulula.com: Low-cost carrier and ICTs. In Egger, R., & Buhalis, D. (Eds.), *eTourism: Case studies* (pp. 282–292). Oxford, UK: Butterworth Heinemann – Elsevier.

Lu, J., Chun-Sheng, Y., Liu, C., & Yao, J. E. (2003). Technology acceptance model for wireless Internet. *Internet Research: Electronic Networking Applications and Policy*, *13*(3), 206–222. doi:10.1108/10662240310478222.

Lūka, I. (2008). Development of students' ESP competence and educator's professional activity in tertiary level tourism studies. In Žogla, I. (Ed.), *Association for Teacher Education in Europe Spring University Conference Teacher of the 21st Century: Quality Education for Quality Teaching* (pp. 689–697). Riga, Latvia: University of Latvia.

Luo, L. (2009). Web 2.0 integration in information literacy instruction: An overview. *Journal of Academic Librarianship*, *36*(1), 32–40. doi:10.1016/j.acalib.2009.11.004.

Lu, R., Sadiq, S., & Governatori, G. (2009). On managing business processes variants. *Data & Knowledge Engineering*, *68*(7), 642–664. doi:10.1016/j.datak.2009.02.009.

Lybaert, N. (1998). The information use in a SME: Its importance and some elements of influence. *Small Business Economics*, *10*(2), 171–191. doi:10.1023/A:1007967721235.

Lymbix. (2011). *Add sentiment intelligence to your applications*. Retrieved from http://www.lymbix.com/

Lynn, G. S., Lipp, S., Akgün, A. E., & Cortez, A. Jr. (2002). Factors impacting the adoption and effectiveness of the world wide web in marketing. *Industrial Marketing Management*, *31*, 35–49. doi:10.1016/S0019-8501(00)00104-8.

Lyons, B., & Henderson, K. (2005). Opinion leadership in a computer-mediated environment. *Journal of Consumer Behaviour*, *4*(5), 319–329. doi:10.1002/cb.22.

Machado, M., & Tao, E. (2007). *Blackboard vs. Moodle: Comparing user experience of learning management systems*. Paper presented at the 37th ASEE/IEEE Frontiers in Education Conference. New York, NY.

Macías, A. G. (2002). *Redes sociales y clusters empresariales*. Revista Hispana para el análisis de redes sociais, (v. 1, n. 6). Retrieved Dec 01, 2011, from http://revista-redes.rediris.es/html-vol1/vol1_6.htm

MacIntosh, R. W., & Goeldner, C. R. (1986). *Tourism principles, practices, philosophies*. New York: John Wiley & Sons INC.

Mackeviciute, A., & Iacubiţchi, S. (2010). *The impact of enterprise 2.0 tools on innovation processes: The case study of incentive at IBS*. (Master Thesis). Jönköping International Business School, Jönköping, Sweden.

Madon, S., Reinhard, N., Roode, D., & Walsham, G. (2009). Digital inclusion projects in developing countries: Processes of institutionalization. *Information Technology for Development*, *15*(2), 95–107. doi:10.1002/itdj.20108.

Magretta, J. (1999). *Managing in the new economy*. Boston: Harvard Business School.

Magretta, J. (2002, May). Why business models matter. *Harvard Business Review*, 86–92. PMID:12024761.

Mahmoud, S. S. (2008). *A proposed model for distributing e-courses content through mobile technology architectures*. Paper presented at the word academy of science, engineering and technology. New York, NY.

Malik, M., Nawab, S., & Naeem, B. (2010). Job satisfaction and organizational commitment of university teachers in public sector of Pakistan. *International Journal of Business & Management*, *5*(6), 17–26.

Mangleburg, T. F., Doney, P. M., & Bristol, T. (2004). Shopping with friends and teens' susceptibility to peer influence. *Journal of Retailing*, *80*(2), 101–116. doi:10.1016/j.jretai.2004.04.005.

Mankiw, N. G. (1998). *Microeconomics*. London: Elsevier.

Manso, J. (1996). *Estatística descritiva e previsão* (2nd ed.). Covilhã, Portugal: Universidade da Beira Interior.

Maqsood, T., Walker, D., & Finegan, A. (2007). Extending the knowledge advantage: Creating learning chains. *The Learning Organization*, *14*(2), 123–141. doi:10.1108/09696470710726998.

March, J. G., & Olsen, J. P. (1975). The uncertainty of the past, organisational ambiguous learning. *European Journal of Political Research*, *3*, 147–171. doi:10.1111/j.1475-6765.1975.tb00521.x.

Margaryan, A., Littlejohn, A., & Vojt, G. (2011). Are digital natives a myth or reality? University students' use of digital technologies. *Computers & Education*, *56*(2), 429–440. doi:10.1016/j.compedu.2010.09.004.

Marimin, M., Hatono, I., & Tamura, H. (1998). Linguistic labels for expressing fuzzy preference relations in fuzzy group decision making. *IEEE Transactions on Systems, Man, and Cybernetics. Part B, Cybernetics*, *28*(2), 205–218. doi:10.1109/3477.662760 PMID:18255937.

Marjanovic, O., & Freeze, R. D. (2011). Knowledge intensive business processes: Theoretical foundations and research challenges. In *Proceedings of the IEEE 44th Hawaii International Conference on System Sciences*. New York: IEEE Press.

Mark, G., Grudin, J., & Poltrock, S. (1999). Meeting at the desktop: An empirical study of virtually collocated teams. In *Proceedings of ECSCW'99, the 6th European Conference on Computer Supported Cooperative Work*, (pp. 159-178). ECSCW.

Markkula, M. (1999). Knowledge management in software engineering projects. In *Proceedings of the 11th International Conference on Software Engineering & Knowledge Engineering*, (pp. 20-27). Kaiserslautern, Germany: IEEE.

Marks, O., & Patel, S. (2010). *Accelerating business performance*. Retrieved from http:///www.e2conf.com/downloads/whitepapers/ent2-10_TWwhitepaper.pdf

Marks, O., & Patel, S. (2010). Enterprise 2.0 white paper: Accelerating business performance. *Sovos Group*. Retrieved September 1, 2011, from http://sovosgroup.com

Maroco, J. (2007). *Análise estatística com utilização do SPSS* (3rd ed.). Lisboa, Portugal: Edições Sílabo.

Maroco, J., & Garcia-Marques, T. (2006). Qual a fiabilidade do alfa de Cronbach? Questões antigas e soluções modernas? *Laboratório de Psicologia*, *4*(1), 65–90.

Marshall, B., Choi, J., El-Shinnaway, M. M., North, M., Svensson, L., & Wang, S. et al. (2009). Online and offline social ties of social network website users: An exploratory study in eleven societies. *Journal of Computer Information Systems*, *50*(1), 54–64.

Martin, D., Alzua, A., & Lamsfus (2011). A contextual geofencing mobile tourisdm service. In R. Law, M. Fuchs, & F. Ricci (Eds.), *Information and Communication Technologies in Tourism 2011* (pp. 331-342). New York: Springer.

Martin, R. (2009). *Opposable mind: Winning through integrative thinking*. Boston: Harvard Business Press.

Martins, L., Gilson, L., & Maynard, M. (2004). Virtual teams: What do we know and where do we go from here? *Journal of Management*, *30*(6), 805–835. doi:10.1016/j.jm.2004.05.002.

Masamila, B., Mtenzi, F., Said, J., & Tinabo, R. (2010). A secured mobile payment model for developing markets. *Communications in Computer and Information Science*, *87*(2), 175–182. doi:10.1007/978-3-642-14292-5_20.

Maslo, E. (2007). Transformative learning space for life-long foreign languages learning. In D. Cunningham, D. Markus, J. Valdmanis, et al. (Eds.), *International Nordic-Baltic Region Conference of FIPLV Innovations in Language Teaching and Learning in the Multicultural Context* (pp. 38-46). Rīga: SIA Izglītības Soļi.

Masoumzadeh, A., & Joshi, J. B. D. (2008). PuRBAC: Purpose-aware role-based access control. In *Proceedings of the On the Move to Meaningful Internet Systems: OTM 2008* (LNCS), (vol. 5332). Berlin, Germany: Springer Berlin / Heidelberg.

Matheus, R., Ribeiro, M. M., Vaz, J. C., & De Souza, C. A. (2010). Internet use for social control and participation: What are local governments doing in Latin America? In *Proceedings of the 4th International Conference on Theory and Practice of Electronic Governance* (pp. 333–338). ACM.

Mathews, A. W. (2000). Advertisers find many web sites too tasteless.

Mathies, C., & Weiermair, K. (2003). *Technological change in the accommodation industry - Enhancing and constraining factors of the IT adaptation*. Paper presented at the Biennal Conference: Leisure, Change and Diversity. Sydney, Australia.

Mayring, P. (2004). Qualitative content analysis. In Flick, , von Kardoff, , & Steinke, (Eds.), *A Companion to Qualitative Research* (pp. 266-269). London: SAGE.

Mayring, P. (2007). On generalization in qualitatively oriented research. *Forum Qualitative Sozial Forschung*, *8*(3), 1–8.

Maznevski, M. L., Gomez, C. B., Noorderhaven, N. G., & Wu, P. (1997). *The cultural orientations framework and international management research*. Paper presented at the Academy of International Business Annual Meeting. Monterrey, Mexico.

Maznevski, M. L., & Chudoba, K. M. (2000). Bridging space over time: Global virtual team dynamics and effectiveness. *Organization Science*, *11*(5), 473–492. doi:10.1287/orsc.11.5.473.15200.

Mazur, A., Doran, C., & Doran, P. R. (2010). The use of social network analysis software to analyze communication patterns and interaction in online collaborative environments. In J. Baralt, N. Callaos, W. Lesso, A. Tremante, & F. Welsch (Eds.), Teacher (p. 447). International Institute of Information and Systemics.

McAfee, A. (2006, May 27). *Enterprise 2.0, version 2.0*. [Web log comment]. Retrieved from http://andrewmcafee.org/2006/05/enterprise_20_version_20/

McAfee, A. (2011). *Data from the edge*. Retrieved September 15, 2011, from http://andrewmcafee.org

McAfee, A. (2011). *Putting enterprise 2.0 into context*. Retrieved September 15, 2011, from http://andrewmcafee.org

McAfee, A. (2006). Enterprise 2.0: The dawn of emergent collaboration. *MIT Sloan Management Review*, *47*(3), 21–28.

McAfee, A. (2006). Enterprise 2.0: The dawn of emergent collaboration. *Sloan Management Review*.

McAfee, A. (2009). *Enterprise 2.0: New collaborative tools for your organization's toughest challenges*. Boston, MA: Harvard Business Press.

McAfee, A. P. (2006). Evangelizing in the empty quarter. In *The Business Impact of IT*. New York: Wordpress.

McAfee, A. P. (2008). Some questions you might get asked. In *The Business Impact of IT*. New York: Wordpress.

McAfee, A. P. (2009). *Enterprise 2.0: New collaborative tools for your organization's toughest challenges*. Boston: Harvard Business Press.

McAtamney, G., & Parker, C. (2006). An examination of the effects of a wearable display on informal face-to-face communication. In *Proceedings of the SIGCHI Conference on Human Factors in Computing Systems*. Montréal, Canada: ACM.

McAuley, J., Duberley, J., & Johnson, P. (2007). *Organization theory: Challenges and perspectives*. Harlow, MA: Pearson.

McGrath, C., Blythe, J., & Krackhardt, D. (1997). The effect of spatial arrangement on judgments and errors in interpreting graphs. *Social Networks, 19*(3), 223–242. doi:10.1016/S0378-8733(96)00299-7.

McGraw-Hill Company. (1989). *McGraw-Hill encyclopedia of science and technology*. New York: McGraw-Hill Company.

McGregor, J. (2006, April 24). The world's most innovative companies. *BusinessWeek*, 63-74.

McKnight, D. H., Cummings, L. L., & Chervany, N. L. (1998). Initial trust formation in new organizational relationships. *Academy of Management Review, 23*(3), 473–490.

McLoughlin, C., & Lee, M. J. W. (2007). *Social software and participatory learning: Pedagogical choices with technology affordances in the web 2.0 era*. Paper presented at the Ascilite. Singapore.

McWilliams, A., & Siegel, D. (2001). Corporate social responsibility: A theory of the firm perspective. *Academy of Management Review, 26*(1), 117–127. doi: doi:10.2307/259398.

McWilliams, A., & Siegel, D. S. (2011). Creating and capturing value. *Journal of Management, 37*(5), 1480–1495. doi:10.1177/0149206310385696.

Meder. (1999) Didaktische ontologien: Globalisierung und wissensorganisation: Neue aspekkte fur wissen. *Wissenschaft und Informationsysteme,* 401-416.

Mehrez, A. (2010). *The role of quality gaps in assessing the performance of management programs*. (Ph.D. thesis). University of Newcastle, Newcastle, Australia.

Mehrtens, J., Cragg, P. B., & Mills, A. M. (2001). A model of internet adoption by SMEs. *Information & Management, 39*(3), 165–176. doi:10.1016/S0378-7206(01)00086-6.

Mellor, R. B. (2007). *Innovation nuclei in SMEs involved in Internet B2C e-commerce.* (Tesis doctoral). Retrieved from http://kurir.kingston.ac.uk/mellor2007.pdf

Mellow, P. (2005). *The media generation: Maximise learning by getting mobile*. Retrieved May 27, 2011, from http://www.ascilite.org.au/conferences/brisbane05/blogs/proceedings/53_Mellow.pdf

Mena Tobar, L., Latorre Andrés, P., & Lafuente Lapena, E. (2009). WebA mobile (web analysis mobile), assistance tool for the design and evaluation of website for mobile devices. In *New Trends on Human-Computer Interaction. Research, Development, New Tools and Methods*. London: Springer. doi:10.1007/978-1-84882-352-5_13.

Mendieta, M. M. (2007). Llega la oficina bancaria 2.0. *Cinco días*.

Mentzer, J. T., De Witt, W., Keebler, J. S., Min, S., Nix, N. W., Smith, C. D., & Zacharia, Z. G. (2001). Defining supply chain management. *Journal of Business Logistics, 22*(2), 1–25. doi:10.1002/j.2158-1592.2001.tb00001.x.

Meta Group. (2001). *Integration: Critical issues for implementation of CRM solutions*. Stanford, CA: Meta Group Inc..

Meyer, M., Hannappel, A., Rensing, C., & Steinmetz, R. (2007). Automatic classificaion of didactic functions of e-learning resources. In *Proceedings of 15th International Conference on Multimedia* (pp. 513-516). Augsburg, Germany: ACM.

Meyer, J., & Herscovitch, L. (2001). Commitment in the workplace: Toward a general model. *Human Resource Management Review, 11*(3), 299–326. doi:10.1016/S1053-4822(00)00053-X.

Meyer, K. A. (2010). A comparison of web 2.0 tools in a doctoral course. *The Internet and Higher Education, 13*(4), 226–232. doi:10.1016/j.iheduc.2010.02.002.

Meyer, P., Stanley, D., Herscovitch, L., & Topolnytsky, L. (2002). Affective, continuance, and normative commitment to theorganization: A meta-analysis of antecedents, correlates, and consequences. *Journal of Vocational Behavior, 61*(1), 20–52. doi:10.1006/jvbe.2001.1842.

Middleware Architecture Committee for Education (MACE). (2001). *Shibboleth system.* Retrieved November 3, 2011, from http://shibboleth.Internet2.edu/

Mihm, J., Loch, C. H., Wilkinson, D., & Huberman, B. A. (2010). Hierarchical structure and search in complex organizations. *Management Science, 56*(5), 831–848. doi:10.1287/mnsc.1100.1148.

Milgrom, P., & Roberts, J. (1995). Complementarities and fit strategy, structure, and organizational change in manufacturing. *Journal of Accounting and Economics, 19*(2-3), 179–208. doi:10.1016/0165-4101(94)00382-F.

Miller, M. (2012). *East Stroudsburg University suspends professor for Facebook posts.* Retrieved February 2012 from chronicle.com/blogs/wiredcampus/east-stroudsburg-u-suspends-professor-for-facebook-posts/21498

Miller, M., Marks, A., & DeCoulode, M. (2011). Social software for business performance. *The Deloitte Center for the Edge.* Retrieved February 23, 2011, from http://www.deloitte.com/

Miller, S. S. (1998). *ASAP—Implementation at the speed of business.* New York: McGraw-Hill.

Mill, R. C., & Morrison, A. M. (1998). *The tourism system: An introductory text* (3rd ed.). Dubuque, IA: Kendall/Hunt.

Mill, S. (2002). *Utilitarianism.* Indianapolis, IN: Hackett Pub..

Milojicic, D. (2008). Interview with Rich Friedrich, Dave Cohen, and Alex Dreiling. *IEEE Internet Computing, 12*(1), 10–13. doi:10.1109/MIC.2008.15.

Mimno, P. (2002). *How to avoid data mart chaos using hybrid methodology.* TDWI Flash point column.

Mislove, A., Marcon, M., Gummadi, K. P., Druschel, P., & Bhattacharjee, B. (2007). Measurement and analysis of online social networks. In *Proceedings of the 7th ACM SIGCOMM Conference on Internet Measurement,* (pp. 29–42). New York, NY: ACM. doi:10.1145/1298306.1298311

Misuraca, G. C. (2009). e-Government 2015: Exploring m-government scenarios, between ICT-driven experiments and citizen-centric implications. *Technology Analysis and Strategic Management, 21*(3), 407–424. doi:10.1080/09537320902750871.

Mitchell, V. W., & Vassos, V. (1997). Perceived risk and risk reduction in holiday purchases: A cross-cultural and gender analysis. *Journal of Euromarketing, 6*(3), 47–79. doi:10.1300/J037v06n03_03.

Mittal, M., & Sethi, P. (2011). The effectiveness of sales promotions tools among Indian consumers: An empirical study. *Journal of Promotion Management, 17,* 165–182. doi:10.1080/10496491.2011.580693.

Miyazoe, T. (2008). *LMS-based EFL blended learning: Blackboard vs. Moodle.* Paper presented at the JALT2007. New York, NY.

Mobile Web Best Practices Working Group. (n.d.). Retrieved from http://www.w3.org/2005/MWI/BPWG/

MobileOk Checker. (n.d.). Retrieved from http://www.w3.org/2005/MWI/BPWG/Group/TaskForces/Checker/

Moggridge, C. (2011). The evolution of Facebook. *B&T Magazine, 61*(2734), 14.

Mohamed, F. Z. M., Saravanan, S., Muthaiyah, O., & Arman, K. (2011). TM: A development technique for e-government 2.0 portals. *WSEAS Transactions on Information Science and Applications, 8*(2), 96–108.

Moisil, I., & Jitaru, E. (2006). E-health progresses in Romania. *International Journal of Medical Informatics, 75,* 315–321. doi:10.1016/j.ijmedinf.2005.08.013 PMID:16275159.

Molina, J. L. (1999). El organigrama informal en las organizaciones: Una aproximación desde el análisis de redes sociales. *Redes Revista Hispana para el Análisis de Redes Sociales.* Retrieved from http://revista-redes.rediris.es/Webredes/textos/organizaciones.doc

Momparler, A. (2008). *El desarrollo de la banca electrónica en España: Un análisis comparativo entre entidades online y tradicionales en España y estados unidos.* (Doctoral Thesis). Department of Business Organization, Universidad Politécnica de Valencia, Valencia, Spain.

Monge, P. R., & Contractor, N. S. (2001). Emergence of communication networks. In Jablin, F. M., & Putnam, L. L. (Eds.), *Handbook of Organizational Communication* (pp. 440–502). Thousand Oaks, CA: Sage.

Montoya, E. V. (2007). Telecentros comunitarios: Un espacio para la participación y formación ciudadana: La experiencia de Manizales, Colombia. *Journal of Community Informatics, 3*(3).

Montoya-Weiss, M. M., Massey, A. P., & Song, M. (2001). Getting it together: Temporal coordination and conflict management in global virtual teams. *Academy of Management Journal*, 1251–1262. doi:10.2307/3069399.

Moodle. (2011). *Moodle*. Retrieved June 2, 2011, from http://moodle.org/

Moody, J., & White, D. R. (2003). Structural cohesion and embeddedness: A hierarchical concept of social groups. *American Sociological Review, 68*(1), 103–127. doi:10.2307/3088904.

Moore, M., & Kearsley, G. (2005). *Distance education: A systems view* (2nd ed.). Belmont, CA: Wadsworth Publishing Company.

Moreira, M. A. (1998). *Desigualdades, educación y nuevas tecnologias.* Quaderns Digitals.

Morgan, J. P. (2011). *Annual report forecasting trend.* Retrieved from http://www.jpmorgan.com

Morgan, G. (1986). *Images of organization.* Beverly Hills, CA: SAGE.

Mori, C. K., & Assumpção, R. O. (2007). Brazilian digital inclusion public policy: Achievements and challenges. *Journal of Community Informatics, 3*(3). Retrieved September 30, 2011 from http://ci-journal.net/index.php/ciej/article/view/424

Morris, M. G., & Venkatesh, V. (2000). Age differences in technology adoption decisions: Implications for a changing work force. *Personnel Psychology, 53*(2), 375–404. doi:10.1111/j.1744-6570.2000.tb00206.x.

Motiwalla, L. F., & Thompson, J. (2009). *Enterprise systems for management.* Upper Saddle River, NJ: Pearson Education, Inc..

Moura, R., & Bernardino, J. (2010). Um modelo para a integração de serviços: Moodle e sistemas de gestão Académica. *RISTI- Revista Ibérica de Sistemas e Tecnologias de Informação,* (5), 31-44.

Moura, A., & Carvalho, A. A. (2009). Mobile learning: two experiments on teaching and learning with mobile phone. In Hijón-Neira, R. (Ed.), *Advanced Learning* (pp. 89–100). Academic Press. doi:10.5772/8105.

Mowery, D., Oxley, J., & Silverman, B. (1996). Strategic alliances and interfirm knowledge transfer. *Strategic Management Journal, 17*, 77–91.

Mulej, M. (2000). *The dialectical systems theory.* Maribor, Slovenia: FEB.

Mulej, M., & Kajzer, S. (1998). Ethics of interdependence and the law of requisite holism. In M. Rebernik & M. Mulej (Eds.), *Proceedings of STIQE 1998* (pp. 24-34). Maribor, Slovenia: FEB.

Mulej, M., et al. (2000). *Dialectical and other soft systems theories.* Maribor, Portugal: FEB.

Mulej, M., et al. (2008). *Management of innovation processes.* Maribor, Slovenia: FEB.

Mulej, M. (1974). Dialectical systems theory. *Our Economy, 21*(3-4), 207–212.

Mulej, M. et al. (2012). *Dialectical systems thinking and the law of requisite holism.* Phoenix, AZ: ISCE Publishing.

Mullins, R., Duan, Y., Hamblin, D., Burrell, P., Jin, H., Jerzy, G., … Aleksander, B. (2007). A web based intelligent training system for SMEs. *The Electronic Journal of e-Learning, 5*, 39-48.

Mullins, L. (2006). *Essentials of organizational behavior.* Harlow, MA: Prentice Hall.

Mullins, L. (2010). *Management and organizational behaviour.* New York: Prentice Hall.

Mullins, N. C. (1972). The development of a scientific specialty: The phage group and the origins of molecular biology. *Minerva, 10*(1), 51–82. doi:10.1007/BF01881390.

Muniz, A. M., & O'Guinn, T. (2001). Brand community. *The Journal of Consumer Research*, *27*, 412–432. doi:10.1086/319618.

Munkvold, B. (2003). *Implementing collaboration technologies in industry: Case examples and lessons learned*. London: Springer-Verlag. doi:10.1007/978-1-4471-0073-7.

Munkvold, B., & Zigurs, I. (2007). Process and technology challenges in swift-starting virtual teams. *Information & Management*, *44*, 287–299. doi:10.1016/j.im.2007.01.002.

Murata, T. (1989). Petri nets: Properties, analysis and applications. *Proceedings of the IEEE*, *77*(4), 541–580. doi:10.1109/5.24143.

Murphy, J., Forrest, E. J., Wotring, C. E., & Bryman, R. A. (1996, June). Hotel management and marketing on the internet. *The Cornell Hotel and Restaurant Administration Quarterly*, 70–82. doi:10.1177/001088049603700322.

Musaji, Y. F. (2003). *Integrated auditing of ERP systems*. New York: John Wiley & Sons, Inc..

Mutch, A. (1998). Using information technology. In Thomas, R. (Ed.), *The management of small tourism and hospitality firms* (pp. 92–206). London: Cassell.

My Starbucks Idea. (2011, November). *Share. Vote. Discuss. See. Share your ideas, tell us what you think of other people's ideas and join discussion*. Retrieved from http://mystarbucksidea.force.com/

MySQL. (n.d.). Retrieved from www.mysql.com

Nadhan, E. G. (2008). *Forecast for the next generation enterprise 3.0*. Paper presented at the EDS Distinguished SE Open Group Enterprise Architecture Practitioners Conference. Chicago, IL.

Nadiri, H., Kandampully, J., & Hussain, K. (2009). Zone of tolerance for banks: A diagnostic model of service quality. *Service Industries Journal*, *29*(11), 1547–1564. doi:10.1080/02642060902793425.

Nahapiet, J., & Ghoshal, S. (1998). Social capital, intellectual capital, and the organizational advantage. *Academy of Management Review*, *23*(2), 242–266.

Nah, F. F., Tan, X., & Teh, S. H. (2004). An empirical investigation on end-users' acceptance of enterprise systems. *Information Resources Management Journal*, *17*(3), 32–53. doi:10.4018/irmj.2004070103.

Nazalek, M. (2008). Orbis on line: Internet distribution strategies for a regional hotel group. In Egger, R., & Buhalis, D. (Eds.), *eTourism: Case studies* (pp. 74–82). Oxford, UK: Butterworth Heinemann - Elsevier.

Ndou, V., & Petti, C. (2007). DMS business models design and destination configurations: Choice and implementation issues. *Information Technology and Tourism*, *9*, 3–14. doi:10.3727/109830507779637602.

Neil, Y., Shih, Chao, & Jin. (2010). Ranking metrics and search guidance for learning object repository. *IEEE Transactions on Learning Technologies, 3*, 250-264.

Nelson, M. R., & Otnes, C. C. (2005). Exploring cross-cultural ambivalence: A netnography of intercultural wedding message boards. *Journal of Business Research*, *58*(1), 89–95. doi:10.1016/S0148-2963(02)00477-0.

Nevin, J. R. (1995). Relationship marketing and distribution channels: Exploring fundamental issues. *Journal of the Academy of Marketing Science*, *23*(4), 327–334. doi:10.1177/009207039502300413.

Newman, A. C., & Thomas, J. G. (2009). *Enterprise 2.0 implementation*. New York: McGraw Hill.

Newman, M. E. J., & Girvan, M. (2003). Finding and evaluating community structure in networks. *Physical Review E: Statistical, Nonlinear, and Soft Matter Physics*, *69*(2 Pt 2), 16.

Newsroom, S. (2011, January). *Starbucks support of the troops/military*. Retrieved from http://news.starbucks.com/about+starbucks/myths+facts/militarydonations.htm

Ngai, E. W. T., Law, C. C. H., & Wat, F. K. T. (2007). Examining the critical success factors in the adoption of enterprise resource planning. *Computers in Industry*, *59*, 548–564. doi:10.1016/j.compind.2007.12.001.

Nielsen. (2008). *Trends in online shopping*. Retrieved January 01, 2009 from http://www.nielsen.com

Nielsen, J. (1993). *Usability engineering*. Academic Press.

Ni, Q., Bertino, E., Lobo, J., Brodie, C., Karat, C. M., Karat, J., & Trombetta, A. (2010). Privacy-aware role-based access control. *Journal of ACM Transactions Information System Security*, *13*(3), 1–31. doi:10.1145/1805974.1805980.

Nonaka, I. (1991). The knowledge creating company. *Harvard Business Review*, *69*(6), 96–104.

Nonaka, I., & Konno, N. (1998). The concept of ba: Building a foundation for knowledge creation. *California Management Review*, *40*(3), 40–55. doi:10.2307/41165942.

Nonaka, I., & Takeuchi, H. (1995). *The knowledge creating company: How Japanese companies create the dynamics of innovation*. New York: Oxford University Press.

Nonaka, I., & Takeushi, H. (1991). The knowledge creating company. *Harvard Business Review*.

Nonaka, I., Toyama, R., & Konno, N. (2000). SECI, ba and leadership: A unified model of dynamic knowledge creation. *Long Range Planning*, *33*, 5–34. doi:10.1016/S0024-6301(99)00115-6.

Nurcan, S. (2008). A survey on the flexibility requirements related to business processes and modeling artifacts. In *Proceedings of the IEEE 41st Hawaii International Conference on System Sciences*. New York: IEEE Press.

Nussbaum, B., Berner, R., & Brady, D. (2005, August 15). Special report. *Business Week*, 51-68.

O'Connor, P. (2008). InterContinental hotel group: Dealing with online intermediaries. In Egger, R., & Buhalis, D. (Eds.), *eTourism: Case studies* (pp. 15–22). Oxford, UK: Butterworth Heinemann - Elsevier.

O'Mahony, S. (2007). The governance of open source initiatives: What does it mean to be community managed? *Journal of Management and Governance*, *11*(2), 139–150. doi:10.1007/s10997-007-9024-7.

O'Mahony, S., & Bechky, B. A. (2008). Boundary organizations: Enabling collaboration among unexpected allies. *Administrative Science Quarterly*, *53*(3), 422–459. doi:10.2189/asqu.53.3.422.

O'Mahony, S., & Ferraro, F. (2007). The emergence of governance in an open source community. *Academy of Management Journal*, *50*(5), 1079–1106. doi:10.5465/AMJ.2007.27169153.

O'Reilly, T. (2005). What is web 2.0: Design patterns and business models for the next generation of software. *O'Reilly*. Retrieved October 22, 2011, from http://oreilly.com/Web2/archive/what-is-Web-20.html

O'Reilly, T., & Battelle. (2009). Web squared: Web 2.0 five years on. *Web 2.0 Summit*. Retrieved from http://assets.en.oreilly.com/1/event/28/Web2009_Websquared-whitepaper.pdf

O'Reilly, T. (2007). What is web 2.0: Design patterns and business models for the next generation of software. *International Journal of Digital Economics*, *65*, 17–37.

Ochoa, X. (2011). Intercambio social y recomendación de material educativo. *Tutorial LACLO 2011*. Retrieved from www.slideshare.net/xaoch

Ochoa, X., & Duval, E. (2006). Quality metrics for learning object metada. In *Proceedings of World Conference on Educational Multimedia, Hypermedia and Telecommunications 2006* (pp. 1004-1011). IEEE.

Ochoa, X., & Duval, E. (2008). Relevance ranking metrics for learning objects. *IEEE Transactions on Learning Technologies*, *1*(1), 34–48. doi:10.1109/TLT.2008.1.

OECD. (2005). *Modernising government: The way forward*. OECD.

Oganisjana, K., & Koke, T. (2008). Developing students' enterprise. In Maslo, Kiegelmann, & Huber (Ed.), Qualitative Psychology in the Changing Academic Context (pp. 218-233). Tübingen, Germany: Academic Press.

Ohdar, R., & Ray, P. (2004). Performance measurement and evaluation of suppliers in supply chain: An evolutionary fuzzy-based approach. *Journal of Manufacturing Technology Management*, *15*(8), 723–734. doi:10.1108/17410380410565311.

Oliveira, J., & Fazendeiro, P. (2003). On the achievement of both accurate and interpretable fuzzy systems using data-driven design processes. In Casillas, J. et al. (Eds.), *Accuracy Improvements in Linguistic Fuzzy Modeling*. Physica-Verlag.

Oliver, S. (1997). *Corporate communication: Principles, techniques and strategies*. London: Kogan Page.

Olson, G. M., & Olson, J. S. (2003). Groupware and computer-supported cooperative work. In Jacko, J. A., & Sears, A. (Eds.), *The Human-Computer Interaction Handbook*. London: Lawrence Erlbaum Associates.

Olszak, C. M., & Ziemba, E. (2006). Business intelligence systems in the holistic infrastructure development supporting decision-making in organizations. *Interdisciplinary Journal of Information. Knowledge and Management*, *1*, 47–58.

Olugu, E., & Wong, Y. (2009). Supply chain performance evaluation: Trends and challenges. *American Journal of Engineering and Applied Sciences*, *2*(1), 202–211. doi:10.3844/ajeas.2009.202.211.

OMG. (2010). Retrieved in January 2010, from www.uml.org

OMG-BPMN. (2011). *Business process model and notation*. Retrieved October 14, 2011, from http://www.omg.org/spec/BPMN/

OMG-OCL. (2010). *Object constraint language*. Retrieved October 14, 2011, from http://www.omg.org/spec/OCL/

OMG-SBVR. (2008). *Semantics of business vocabulary and business rules*. Retrieved October 14, 2011, from http://www.omg.org/spec/SBVR/

OMG-UML. (2011). *Unified modeling language: Superstructure*. Retrieved October 14, 2011, from http://www.omg.org/spec/UML/

ONTSI. (2011). *La sociedad en red 2010*. Retrieved January 01, 2011 from http://www.ontsi.red.es/estudios-informes

Öörni, A. (2004). Consumer objectives and the amount of search in electronic travel and tourism markets. *Journal of Travel & Tourism Marketing*, *17*(2/3), 3–14. doi:10.1300/J073v17n02_01.

Open, I. (2011). *Open intelligence*. Retrieved from http://www.openi.org/

Open Source. (n.d.). Retrieved from www.opensource.org

OpenSourceInitiative. (2011). Retrieved from http://www.opensource.org/

O'Reilly, T. (2005). *What is web 2.0: Design patterns and business models for the next generation of software*. Retrieved May 18, 2011, from http://oreilly.com/Web2/archive/what-is-Web-20.html

O'Reilly, T. (2006). *Web 2.0 compact definition: Trying again*. Retrieved May 18, 2011, from http://radar.oreilly.com/archives/2006/12/Web-20-compact.html

Organ, D. (1977). A reappraisal and reinterpretation of the satisfaction-causes-performance hypothesis. *Academy of Management Review*, *2*(1), 46–53.

Organ, D., & Lingl, A. (1995). Personality, satisfaction and organizational citizenship behaviors. *The Journal of Social Psychology*, *135*(3), 339–250. doi:10.1080/00224545.1995.9713963.

Organ, D., & Moorman, R. (1993). Fairness and organizational citizenship behavior: What are the connections? *Social Justice Research*, *6*(1), 5–18. doi:10.1007/BF01048730.

Organización Mundial del Turismo. (1998). *Introducción al turismo*. Madrid, Spain: Organización Mundial del Turismo.

Organization for Economic Co-Operation and Development (OECD). (1980). *Guidelines on the protection of privacy and transborder flows of personal data*. Retrieved November 3, 2011, from http://www.oecd.org/document/18/0,3343,en_2649_34255_1815186_1_1_1_1,00.html

Organization for Economic Co-Operation and Development (OECD). (2011). *The evolving privacy landscape: 30 years after the OECD privacy guidelines*. Retrieved November 3, 2011, from http://dx.doi.org/10.1787/5kgf09z90c31-en

Organization for the Advancement of Structured Information Standards (OASIS). (2004). *OASIS eXtensible access control markup language (XACML) TC*. Retrieved November 3, 2011, from http://www.oasis-open.org/committees/xacml/

Organization for the Advancement of Structured Information Standards (OASIS). (2005). *Security assertion markup language (SAML) v2.0*. Retrieved November 3, 2011, from http://docs.oasis-open.org/security/saml/v2.0/saml-2.0-os.zip

Ortenbald, A. (2004). The learning organisation: Towards an integrated model. *The Learning Organization, 11*(2/3), 129. doi:10.1108/09696470410521592.

Ortiz-Rodriguez, F., Palma, R., & Villazón-Terrazas, B. (2007). *EgoIR: Ontology-based information retrieval intended for eGovernment.* Paper presented at the 2nd International Applications of Semantic Technologies (AST) Workshop - Informatik 2007.

Osarenkhoe, A. (2006). Customer-centric strategy: A longitudinal study of implementation of a customer relationship management solution. *International Journal of Technology Marketing, 1*(2), 115–144.

Osimo, D. (2008). Web 2.0 in government: Why and how. *Institute for Prospectice Technological Studies (IPTS), JRC, European Commission, EUR, 23358.*

Osterle, H. (1995). *Business in the information age: Heading for new processes.* Berlin: Springer.

Ostroff, C., & Schmitt, N. (1993). Configurations of organizational effectiveness and efficiency. *Academy of Management Journal, 36*(6), 1345–1361. doi:10.2307/256814.

Otte, E., & Rousseau, R. (2002). Social network analysis: A powerful strategy, also for the information sciences. *Journal of Information Science, 28*(6), 441–453. doi:10.1177/016555150202800601.

Oyelere, P., Laswad, F., & Fisher, R. (2003). Determinants of internet financial reporting by New Zealand companies. *Journal of International Financial. Management and Accounting, 14*(1), 26–63.

Page, L., Brin, S., Motwani, R., & Winograd, T. (1999). *The Pagerank citation ranking: Bringing order to the web.* Technical Report. Stanford InfoLab. Retrieved Dec 20, 2011, from http://ilpubs.stanford.edu:8090/422/1/1999-66.pdf

Page, S. J. (1999). *Transport and tourism.* Harlow, MA: Addison Wesley Longman.

Page, S. J., & Hall, C. M. (2003). *Managing urban tourism.* Harlow, MA: Prentice Hall.

Pagliari, C. (2007). Design and evaluation in eHealth: Challenges and implications for an interdisciplinary field. *Journal of Medical Internet Research, 9*(2), e15. doi:10.2196/jmir.9.2.e15 PMID:17537718.

Paiva Dias, G. (2011). *Local e-government information and service delivery: A survey of municipal websites in Portugal.* Paper presented at the CISTI 6ª Conferência Ibérica de Sistemas e Tecnologias de Informação. Aviero, Portugal.

Palazon, M., & Delgado-Ballester, E. (2009). Effectiveness of price discounts and premium promotions. *Psychology and Marketing, 26,* 1108–1129. doi:10.1002/mar.20315.

Pape, W. (1997). The book of virtuals. *INC Technology, 4*(19), 7–26.

Parkinson, S. (2005). *Telecentres, access and development: Experience and lessons from Uganda and South Africa.* Kampala, Uganda: Fountain Publishers.

Parkinson, S., & Lauzon, A. (2008). The impact of the internet on local social equity: A study of a telecenter in Aguablanca, Colombia. *Information Technologies and International Development, 4*(3), 21–38. doi:10.1162/itid.2008.00015.

Parkinson, S., & Ramirez, R. (2006). Using a sustainable livelihoods approach to assessing the impact of ICTs in development. *Journal of Community Informatics, 2*(3).

Park, Y., & Gretzel, U. (2006). Evaluation of emerging technologies in tourism: The case of travel search engines. In Hitz, M., Sigala, M., & Murphy, J. (Eds.), *Information and communication technologies in tourism 2006* (pp. 371–382). Vienna, Austria: Springer Verlag. doi:10.1007/3-211-32710-X_51.

Parolini, C. (1999). *The value net: A tool for competitive advantages.* Chichester, UK: Wiley.

Parra-López, E., Bulchand-Gidumal, J., Gutierrez-Taño, D., & Díaz-Armas, R. (2011). Intentions to use social media in organizing and taking vacation trips. *Computers in Human Behavior, 27,* 640–654. doi:10.1016/j.chb.2010.05.022.

Parra-Luna, F. (2000). *The performance of social systems.* New York: Kluwer Academic / Plenum Publishers. doi:10.1007/978-1-4615-4251-3.

Parra-Luna, F. (2003). *Elementos para un teoria formal del sistema socia: Una orientacion critica.* Madrid, Spain: Universidad Complutense.

Parveen, M., & Rao, T. (2009). An integrated approach to design and analysis of lean manufacturing system: A perspective of Lean supply chain. *International Journal of Services and Operations Management*, *5*(2), 175–208. doi:10.1504/IJSOM.2009.023232.

Pather, S., & Gomez, R. (2010). Public access ICT: A south-south comparative analysis of libraries, telecentres and cybercafés in South Africa and Brazil. In *Proceedings of AMCIS 2010*. AMCIS.

Paulraj, A. (2009). Environmental motivations: A classification scheme and its impact on environmental strategies and practices. *Business Strategy and the Environment*, *18*(7), 453–468. doi:10.1002/bse.612.

Paulsen, M. (2003). Experiences with learning management systems in 113 European institutions. *Journal of Educational Technology & Society*, *6*(4), 134–148.

Paulus, T. M., Payne, R., & Jahns, L. (2009). Am I making sense here? What blogging reveals about undergraduate student understanding. *Journal of Interactive Online Learning*, *8*(1).

Pava, M. L., & Krausz, J. (1996). The association between corporate social-responsibility and financial performance: The paradox of social cost. *Journal of Business Ethics*, *15*, 321–357. doi:10.1007/BF00382958.

Pavon, F., & Casanova, J. (2006). Telefonía móvil y personas mayores: La accesibilidad como derecho. *Latinoamericana de Tecnología Educativa*, *5*(2), 385–395.

Payne, A. (2005). *Handbook of CRM: Achieving excellence through customer managemen*. Boston: Butterworth-Heinemann.

Payne, A., Ballantyne, D., & Christopher, M. (2005). A stakeholder approach to relationship marketing strategy: The development and use of the six markets model. *European Journal of Marketing*, *39*(7/8), 855–871. doi:10.1108/03090560510601806.

Payne, A., Christopher, M., Clark, M., & Peck, H. (1997). *Relationship marketing for competitive advantage*. Oxford, UK: Butterworth-Heinemann.

Pedersen, P. E., & Nysveen, H. (2003). *Search mode and purchase intention in online shopping behavior*. Retrieved March 10, 2004 from http://citeseer.ist.psu.edu/article/pedersen03search.html

Pedron, C. D., & Caldeira, M. (2005). *Objectivos da adopção do CRM: Um estudo de caso em uma empresa brasileira de telecomunicações*. Paper presented at the 6ª Conferência da Associação Portuguesa de Sistemas de Informação. Aviero, Portugal.

Peixoto, S. (2010). *Web trends - 10 cases made in web 2.0. Gaia*. Comunicarte Publishing.

Pelkonen, T. (2008). Value creation patterns and current trends in digital media service creation: A case study of the Finnish digital media industry. In Bruck, P. A., & Boumans, J. M. (Eds.), *High Performance Multimedia: A Reader on the Technological, Cultural and Economic Dynamics of Multimedia* (pp. 23–65). Amsterdam: IOS Press.

Pennings, J. (1975). The relevance of the structural-contingency model for organizational effectiveness. *Administrative Science Quarterly*, *20*(3), 393–410. doi:10.2307/2391999.

Pentaho Community. (2011). *Pentaho community home*. Retrieved from http://community.pentaho.com/

Pentaho. (2011). *Pentaho open source BI*. Retrieved from http://www.pentaho.com/

People, N. C. (n.d.). *ICT and older people in Ireland: Evidence from a study by the national council on ageing and older people*. Dublin, Ireland: Author.

Peppers, D., & Rogers, M. (2004). *Managing customer relationships: A strategic framework*. Hoboken, NJ: John Wiley & Sons, Inc..

Pereira, P. F. (2003). *Comportamiento del consumidor bancario en internet*. (Doctoral Thesis). Department of Administration and Business Economics, University of Salamanca, Salamanca, Spain.

Perrow, C. (1961). The analysis of goals in complex organizations. *American Sociological Review*, *26*(6), 854–866. doi:10.2307/2090570.

Petersen, C., & Plenborg, T. (2006). Voluntary disclosure and information asymmetry in Denmark. *Journal of International Accounting, Auditing & Taxation, 15*, 127–149. doi:10.1016/j.intaccaudtax.2006.08.004.

Pettinger, R. (2007). *Introduction to management*. Chicago: Palgrave MacMillan.

Pfeffer, J., & Salancik, G. (1978). *The external control of organizations*. New York: Harper & Row.

Philippou, S. (2005). The problem of the European dimension in education: A principled reconstruction of the Greek Cypriot curriculum. *European Educational Research Journal, 4*(4), 343–367. doi:10.2304/eerj.2005.4.4.2.

PHP. (n.d.). Retrieved from www.php.net

Pick, J. B., & Gollakota, K. (2010). Technology for rural telecenters in India: A model and exploratory study of diffusion of information for telecenter use and sustainability. In *Proceedings of AMCIS 2010*. AMCIS.

Pijpers, G. G. M., & Montfort, K. (2006). An investigation of factors that influence senior executives to accept innovations in information technology. *International Journal of Management, 23*(1), 11–23.

Pilevari, N., Hosseini, S., & Jassbi, J. (2008). Fuzzy logic supply chain agility assessment methodology. *IEEE International Conference on Industrial Engineering and Engineering Management*, 1113-1117.

Pinelle, D., & Gutwin, C. (2000). A review of groupware evaluations. In *Proceedings of 9th IEEE WETICE 2000 - Workshop on Enabling Technologies: Infrastructures for Collaborative Enterprises*. WETICE.

Podsakoff, P., & MacKenzie, S. (1997). Impact of organizational citizenship behavior on organizational performance: A review and suggestions for future research. *Human Performance, 10*(2), 133–151. doi:10.1207/s15327043hup1002_5.

Podsakoff, P., & MacKenzie, S., & Fetter. (1993). Citizenship behavior and fairness in organizations: Issues and directions for future research. *Employee Responsibilities and Rights Journal, 6*(3), 257–269. doi:10.1007/BF01419449.

Podsakoff, P., MacKenzie, S., Paine, J., & Bachrach, D. (2000). Organizational citizenship behaviors: A critical review of the theoretical and empirical literature and suggestions for future research. *Journal of Management, 26*(3), 513–563. doi:10.1177/014920630002600307.

Politis, J. D. (2001). *The relationship between self-management leader behaviour, self-leadership worker behaviour and job-related attitudes and perceptions*. (PhD dissertation). University of Technology, Sydney, Australia.

Polk, W. T., Hastings, N. E., & Malpani, A. (2003). Public key infrastructures that satisfy security goals. *IEEE Internet Computing, 7*(4), 60–67. doi:10.1109/MIC.2003.1215661.

Pollock, A. (1995). The impact of information technology on destination marketing. *EU Travel and Tourism Analyst, 3*, 66–83.

Portelli, J. P., & Vilbert, A. B. (2002). A curriculum of life. *Education Canada, 42*(2), 36–39.

Portelli, J. P., & Vilbert, A. B. (2002). Standards, equity, and the curriculum of life. *Analytic Teaching, 22*(1), 4–19.

Porter, M. (1980). *Competitive strategy*. New York: Free Press.

Porter, M. (1998). *Competitive advantage of nations*. New York: Free Press.

Portes, A. (1998). Social capital: Its origins and applications in modern sociology. *Annual Review of Sociology, 22*, 1–24. doi:10.1146/annurev.soc.24.1.1.

Portes, A., & Sensenbrenner, J. (1993). Embeddedness and immigration: Notes on the social determinants of economic action. *American Journal of Sociology, 98*(6), 1320–1350. doi:10.1086/230191.

Potocan, V. (2003). Transition from ethics of independence to ethics of interdependence as a factor of sustainable development. In *Proceedings of the 10th Interdisciplinary Information Management Talks*, (pp. 123-130). Linz, Austria: Universitätsverlag Trauner.

Potocan, V. (2004). *Operations management*. Maribor, Portugal: FEB.

Potocan, V. (2008). Why we need trust in organization?. *Issues in GRBE*, 102-115.

Potocan, V., & Mulej, M. (2007). *From an institutional transition to a real one.* Maribor, Slovenia: FEB.

Potocan, V., & Mulej, M. (2010). *From an institutional transition to a real one into an innovative enterprise.* Maribor, Slovenia: FEB.

Potocan, V., & Rebernik, M. (2002). Achieving synergy of business system via anticipatory system. In *Proceedings of the AIP Conference,* (pp. 441-447). AIP.

Potocan, V. (2005). Efficiency or effectiveness? *Organization, 38*(10), 570–576.

Potocan, V. (2006). Business operations between efficiency and effectiveness. *Journal of Information and Organizational Sciences, 30*(2), 251–262.

Potocan, V. (2009). What culture do we need for economic development? *Business Review (Federal Reserve Bank of Philadelphia), 12*(1), 102–107.

Potocan, V., & Kuralt, B. (2007). Synergy in business: Some new suggestions. *The Journal of American Academy of Business, 12*(1), 199–204.

Potocan, V., Mulej, K., & Kajzer, S. (2005). Business cybernetics: A provocative suggestion. *Kybernetes, 34*(9/10), 1496–1516. doi:10.1108/03684920510614786.

Potocan, V., & Mulej, M. (2006). Ethics of a sustainable enterprise. *Systemic Practice and Action Research, 19*(6), 35–47.

Potter, R. E., & Balthazard, P. A. (2002). Understanding human interaction and performance in the virtual team. *Journal of Information Technology Theory and Application, 4*, 1–23.

Power, D. J. (2007). A brief history of decision support systems, version 4.0. *DSSResources.com.* Retrieved from http://DSSResources.COM/history/dsshistory.html

Prabhakar, S., Pankanti, S., & Jain, A. K. (2003). Biometric recognition: Security and privacy concerns. *IEEE Security & Privacy, 1*(2), 33–42. doi:10.1109/MSECP.2003.1193209.

Prado, P. (2009). *Bridging digital poverty: Adoption of information and communication technologies at community technology centers in the Dominican Republic.* (Doctoral dissertation). University of Miami, Coral Gables, Florida.

Prado, P., Câmara, M. A., & Figueiredo, M. A. (2011). Evaluating ICT adoption in rural Brazil: A quantitative analysis of telecenters as agents of social change. *The Journal of Community Informatics, 7*(1&2).

Prensky, M. (2001). Digital natives, digital immigrants: Do they really think differently? *Horizon, 9*(5), 1–6. doi:10.1108/10748120110424816.

Presenza, A., Sheehan, L., & Ritchie, B. J. (2005). Towards a model of the roles and activities of destination management organizations. *Journal of Hospitality, Tourism and Leisure Science.*

Price, D. J. D. S. (1986). *Little science, big science-- and beyond.* New York: Columbia University Press.

Price, J. (1972). The study of organizational effectiveness. *The Sociological Quarterly, 13*(4), 3–15. doi:10.1111/j.1533-8525.1972.tb02100.x.

Price, L. L., Feick, L. F., & Guskey, A. (1995). Everyday market helping behavior. *Journal of Public Policy & Marketing, 14*(2), 255–266.

Przeclawski, K. (1990). *Le tourisme et le monde de l'unité dans la pluralité. Cahiers du Tourisme (139, Série C).* Aix-en-Provence: Centre des Hautes Etudes Touristiques.

Purvanova, R. K., & Bono, J. E. (2009). Transformational leadership in context: Face-to-face and virtual teams. *The Leadership Quarterly, 20*, 343–357. doi:10.1016/j.leaqua.2009.03.004.

Putnam, R. D. (2000). *Bowling alone: The collapse and revival of american community.* New York, NY: Simon & Schuster. doi:10.1145/358916.361990.

Pyka, A., & Scharnhorst, A. (2009). *Innovation networks.* Berlin: Springer. doi:10.1007/978-3-540-92267-4.

Quick, D., & Nelson, J. (2009). *Principles of organization behavior: Realities and challenges.* Cincinnati, OH: South-Western College.

Quinn, J. B. (1992). *Intelligent enterprise: A knowledge and service based paradigm for industry*. New York: The Free Press.

Quinn, J. B., Anderson, P. Y., & Filkenstein, S. (1996, March-April). Managing professional intellect: Making the most of the best. *Harvard Business Review*, 71–80.

Quinn, R., & Rohrbaugh, J. (1983). A spatial model of effectiveness criteria: Toward a competing values approach to organizational analysis. *Management Science*, *29*(3), 363–377. doi:10.1287/mnsc.29.3.363.

Quintarelli, E. (2011). *Socializing the extended value chain*. Retrieved September 30, 2011, from http://www.socialenterprise.it

Quivy, R., & Campenhoudt, L. (2008). *Manual de investigação em ciências sociais* (5th ed.). Lisboa, Portugal: Gradiva.

Rabassa, B. (1987). *Promoción de ventas: Cómo se prepara una campaña*. Madrid, Spain: Editorial Pirámide.

Rajib, P., Tiwari, D., & Srivastava, G. (2002). Design and development of an integrated supply chain management system in an Internet environment. *Journal of Service Research*, *2*(1), 22–43.

Raju, P. S. (1980). Optimum stimulation level: Its relationship to personality, demographics and exploratory behavior. *The Journal of Consumer Research*, *7*, 272–282. doi:10.1086/208815.

Ramanathan, J., Ramnath, R., Singh, N., Xu, Z., & Xu, Y. (2011). Sense-respond cloud mediator architecture for services evolution. In *Proceedings of the 2011 ACM Symposium on Applied Computing - SAC '11*, (pp. 162-169). ACM Press.

Rao, P., & Holt, D. (2005). Do green supply chains lead to competitiveness and economic performance? *International Journal of Operations & Production Management*, *25*(9), 898–916. doi:10.1108/01443570510613956.

Rasmusson, L., & Janson, S. (1996). *Simulated social control for secure internet commerce*. New York: ACM Press. doi:10.1145/304851.304857.

Ratnasingam, P. (2005). Trust in inter-organizational exchanges: A case study in business to business electronic commerce. *Decision Support Systems*, *39*(3), 525–544. doi:10.1016/j.dss.2003.12.005.

Ravari, A. N., Jafarian, J. H., Amini, M., & Jalili, R. (2010). GTHBAC: A generalized temporal history based access control model. *Journal of Telecommunication Systems*, *45*(2), 111–125. doi:10.1007/s11235-009-9239-9.

Rawls, J. (1971). *A theory of justice*. Cambridge, MA: Harvard University Press.

Raykov, T., & Grayson, D. (2003). A test for change of composite reliability in scale development. *Multivariate Behavioral Research*, *38*(2), 143–159. doi:10.1207/S15327906MBR3802_1.

Raymond, E. (1999). The cathedral and the bazaar. *Knowledge, Technology & Policy*, *12*(3), 23–49. doi:10.1007/s12130-999-1026-0.

Rebelo, T. M., & Gomes, A. D. (2008). Organisational learning and the learning organisation. *The Learning Organization*, *15*(4), 294–308. doi:10.1108/09696470810879556.

Recordon, D., & Reed, D. (2006). OpenID 2.0: A platform for user-centric identity management. In *Proceedings of the 2nd ACM Workshop on Digital Identity Management (DIM'06)* (pp. 11-16). New York: ACM.

Reddick, C. G. (2005). Citizen interaction with e-government: From the streets to servers? *Government Information Quarterly*, *22*(1), 38–57. doi:10.1016/j.giq.2004.10.003.

Rego, A. (2002). *Comportamentos de cidadania nas organizações*. Lisboa, Portugal: McGraw-Hill.

Rego, A., Ribeiro, N., & Cunha, M. (2010). Perceptions of organizational virtuousness and happiness as predictors of organizational citizenship behaviors. *Journal of Business Ethics*, *93*(1), 215–235. doi:10.1007/s10551-009-0197-7.

Reich, K. (2005). *Systemisch-konstruktivistische pädagogik*. Weinheim: Beltz.

Reisenwitz, T., Iyer, R., Kuhlmeier, D., & Eastman, J. (2007). The elderly's internet usage: An updated look. *Journal of Consumer Marketing*, *24*(7), 406–418. doi:10.1108/07363760710834825.

Report, S. M. (2010). *Lightspeed research and the internet advertising bureau UK*. Retrieved from http://www.iabuk.net/en/1/socialmedialanding.html

Rethlefsen, M. L. (2007). Social networking. *Medical Reference Services Quarterly, 26*(supl), 117-141.

Rezabakhsh, B., Bornemann, D., Hansen, U., & Schrader, U. (2006). Consumer power: A comparison of the old economy and the Internet economy. *Journal of Consumer Policy, 29*(1), 3–36. doi:10.1007/s10603-005-3307-7.

Rezgui, Y. (2007). Exploring virtual team-working effectiveness in the construction sector. *Interacting with Computers, 19*(1), 96–112. doi:10.1016/j.intcom.2006.07.002.

Rhinesmith, S. (1999). *A manager's guide to globalization*. Chicago: Erwin.

Rice Doran, P., Doran, C., & Mazur, A. (2011). Social network analysis as a method for analyzing interaction in collaborative online learning environments. *Journal of Systemics Cybernetics and Informatics.*

Rice, J., & Caniato, F. (2003). Building a secure and resilient supply network. *Supply Chain Management Review, 7*(5), 22–31.

Rico, D. et al. (2009). *The business value of agile software methods: Maximizing ROI with just-in-time processes and documentation*. Fort Lauderdale, FL: J. Ross Publishing.

Ringle, C. M., & Will, A. (2005). *SmartPLS 2.0 (M3)*. Retrieved June 1, 2009, from http://www.smartpls.de

Riss, U. V., Rickayzen, A., Maus, H., & van der Aalst, W. M. P. (2005). Challenges for business process and task management. *Journal of Universal Knowledge Management, 2*, 77–100.

Rist, R. (1997). Challenges faced by the data warehousing pioneers. *Journal of Data Warehousing, 2*(1).

Roberts, J. A., Hann, I. H., & Slaughter, S. A. (2006). Understanding the motivations, participation, and performance of open source software developers: A longitudinal study of the Apache projects. *Management Science, 52*(7), 984. doi:10.1287/mnsc.1060.0554.

Roberts, J. H., & Urban, G. L. (1988). Modeling multiattribute utility, risk and belief dynamics for new consumer durable brand choice. *Management Science, 34*, 167–185. doi:10.1287/mnsc.34.2.167.

Robertson, S. (1998). Telecenters in Mexico: Learning the hard way. *The Journal of Development Communication, 9*(2).

Rocha, C. C. (2003). *Relaciones estratégicas entre pymes: Contraste de hipótesis empresariales mediante ARS*. Revista Hispana para el análisis de redes sociais (v. 4, n. 4, jun. 2003). Retrieved Nov 21, 2011, from http://revista-redes.rediris.es

Rodgers, W., Negash, S., & Suk, K. (2005). The moderating effect of on-line experience on the antecedents and consequences of online satisfaction. *Psychology and Marketing, 22*(4), 313–331. doi:10.1002/mar.20061.

Rodrigues, M., Dias, G. P., & Teixeira, A. (2010). *Human language technologies for e-gov*. Paper presented at the WEBIST. Valencia, Spain.

Roebuck, K. (2011). *Near field communication (NFC), hight-impact strategies - What you need to know: Definition, adoptions, impact, benefits, maturity, vendors*. Emereo Pty Limited.

Roehm, M. L., Pullins, E. B., & Roehm, H. A. Jr. (2002). Designing loyalty-building programs for packaged goods brands. *JMR, Journal of Marketing Research, 39*(2), 202–213. doi:10.1509/jmkr.39.2.202.19085.

Rogers, E. M. (1983). *Difussion of innovations* (3rd ed.). New York: The Free Press.

Rogers, E. M. (2003). *Diffusion of innovations* (5th ed.). New York, NY: The Free Press.

Rogers, E. M., & Kincaid, D. L. (1981). *Communication networks: Toward a new paradigm for research*. New York: The Free Press.

Romero, D., & Molina, A. (2011). Collaborative networked organisations and customer communities: Value co-creation and co-innovation in the networking era. *Production Planning and Control, 22*(5/6), 447–472. doi:10.1080/09537287.2010.536619.

Rosen, A. (2006). *Technology trends: E-learning 2.0 learning solutions*. Retrieved March 2011 from http://www.readygo.com/e-learning-2.0.pdf

Rosen, D., Kim, J. H., & Nam, Y. (2010). Birds of a feather protest together: Theorizing self-organizing political protests with flock theory. *Systemic Practice and Action Research*, *23*(5), 419–441. doi:10.1007/s11213-010-9167-3.

Rosen, D., & Nelson, C. (2008). Web 2.0: A new generation of learners and education. *Computers in the Schools*, *25*(3-4), 211–225. doi:10.1080/07380560802370997.

Ross, J. W., Vitale, M. R., & Willcocks, L. P. (2003). The continuing ERP revolution: Sustainable lessons, new modes of delivery. In Shanks, G., Seddon, P. B., & Willcocks, L. P. (Eds.), *Second-wave enterprise resource planning systems—Implementing for effectiveness* (pp. 102–132). Cambridge, UK: Cambridge University Press. doi:10.1017/CBO9780511815072.005.

Rosu, S. M., Guran, M., & Mateescu, L. M. (2007). E-learning sites development using open source software support in the enterprise. In *Proceedings of the 4th Balkan Region Conference on Engineering Education & MSE* (pp. 98-103). Sibiu, Romania: MSE.

Rosu, S. M., & Dragoi, G. (2011). VPN solutions and network monitoring to support virtual teams work in virtual enterprises. *Computer Science and Information System*, *8*(1), 1–26. doi:10.2298/CSIS100127033R.

Rosu, S. M., Dragoi, G., Rosu, L., & Guran, M. (2010). Virtual enterprise network solutions to support e-learning sites development. In Katalinic, B. (Ed.), *DAAAM International Scientific Book 2010* (pp. 725–742). Vienna, Austria: DAAAM International. doi:10.2507/daaam.scibook.2010.63.

Rotman, J. (2010). *Unite breaks guitars – Case study*. Toronto, Canada: School of Management, University of Toronto.

Rowe, G., & Wright, G. (1999). The delphi technique as a forecasting tool: Issues and analysis. *International Journal of Forecasting*, *15*(4), 353–375. doi:10.1016/S0169-2070(99)00018-7.

Rudman, R. J., & Steenkamp, L. P. (2009). Potential influence of web 2.0 usage and security practices of online users on information management. *South African Journal of Information Management*, *11*(2).

Rudra, A., & Yeo, E. (1999). Key issues in achieving data quality and consistency in data warehousing among large organizations in Australia. In *Proceedings of the 32nd Hawaii International Conference on System Sciences*, (pp. 7012-7019). IEEE.

Rugimbana, R. O., & Iversen, P. (1994). Perceived attributes of innovations. *International Journal of Bank Marketing*, *12*(2), 30–35. doi:10.1108/02652329410052955.

Rusman, E., van Bruggen, J., Sloep, P., & Koper, R. (2010). Fostering trust in virtual project teams: Towards a design framework grounded in a trustworthiness antecedents (TWAN) schema. *International Journal of Human-Computer Studies*, *68*(11), 834–850. doi:10.1016/j.ijhcs.2010.07.003.

Russ-Eft, D., & Preskill, H. (2001). *Evaluation in organizations: A systemic approach to enhancing learning, performance, and change*. Cambridge, MA: MIT Press.

Russell, N., ter Hofstede, A. H. M., Edmond, D., & van der Aalst, W. M. P. (2005). Workflow data patterns: Identification, representation and tool support. *Lecture Notes in Computer Science*, *3716*, 353–368. doi:10.1007/11568322_23.

Ryan, M. (2003). Public relations and the web: Organizational problems, gender and institutional type. *Public Relations Review*, *29*(3), 335–349. doi:10.1016/S0363-8111(03)00040-7.

Rybski, D., Buldyrev, S. V., Havlin, S., Liljeros, F., & Makse, H. A. (2009). Scaling laws of human interaction activity. *Proceedings of the National Academy of Sciences of the United States of America*, *106*(31), 12640–12645. doi:10.1073/pnas.0902667106 PMID:19617555.

Saari, L., & Judge, T. (2004). Employee attitudes and job satisfaction. *Human Resource Management*, *43*(4), 395–407. doi:10.1002/hrm.20032.

Saaty, T. L. (1980). *The analytic hierarchy process*. New York: McGraw Hill Publications.

Saaty, T. L. (1996). *Decision making with dependence and feedback: The analytic network process*. Pittsburgh, PA: RWS Publications.

Sadik, A. (2009). Improving pre-service teachers' visual literacy through flickr. *Procedia - Social and Behavioral Sciences, 1*(1), 91-100.

Salancik, G., & Pfeffer, J. (1974). The bases and uses of power in organizational decision making: The case of a university. *Administrative Science Quarterly, 19*(4), 453–473. doi:10.2307/2391803.

Salvetti, F., & Srinivasan, S. (2005). Local flow betweenness centrality for clustering community graphs. *Internet and Network Economics*, 531–544.

Samad, S. (2005). Unraveling the organizational commitment and job performance relationship: Exploring the moderating effect of job satisfaction. *Business Review (Federal Reserve Bank of Philadelphia), 4*(2), 79–84.

Sánchez, J. R. (1997). *Marketing financiero: Principios y estrategias*. Madrid, Spain: Civitas.

Sánchez, M. J., & Villarejo, A. F. (2004). La calidad del servicio electrónico: Un análisis de los efectos moderadores del comportamiento de uso de la web. *Cuadernos de Economía y Dirección de la Empresa, 21*, 121–152.

Sandoval-Almaz, R. (2007). Digital literacy: Problems faced by telecenter users in Mexico. *Information Systems Journal, 13*(3), 217–232.

Santo, C. D., Colace, F., Santo, M. D., & Vento, M. (2003). *Evaluating on-line learning platforms: A case study.* Paper presented at the 36th Hawaii International Conference on System Sciences. Hawaii, HI.

Santoro, F. M., Borges, M. R. S., & Santos, N. (2006). Patterns for designing planning mechanisms. *International Journal of Computer Applications in Technology, 25*(2/3), 102–115. doi:10.1504/IJCAT.2006.009066.

Santos, A. (2010). *Robust and adaptable platforms of dynamic educational environment content: Contribution to the Portuguese education success in the secondary level*. (Unpublished master dissertation). Open University, Aviero, Portugal.

Santos, M. B., & Souza, C. D. (2008). Visualização temporal de redes sociais com o OSSNetwork. In *Proceedings of WIVA - Workshop on Information Visualization and Analysis in Social Networks,* (pp. 79-88). Campinas, Brasil: WIVA.

Sanz Rodriguez, J. (2010). *Evaluación apriorística de la reusabilidad de los objetos de aprendizaje*. Retrieved from http://dbspace.uah.es/dbspace/handle/10017/8715

Sanz, J., Dodero, J. M., & Sanchez-Alonso, S. (2009). A preliminary analysis of software engineering metrics-based criteria for the evaluation of learning objects reusability. *International Journal of Emerging Technologies in Learning, 4.*

Sashkin, M. (1988). The visionary leader. In Conger, J. A., & Kanungo, R. N. (Eds.), *Charismatic leadership: The elusive factor in organisational effectiveness*. San Francisco, CA: Jossey-Bass.

Saxenian, A. (1994). *Regional advantage: Culture and competition in silicon valley and route 128*. Boston: Harvard University Press.

Sbarcea, K. (1998, March 6). Know what, know how, know why: Implementing a knowledge management system – The Phillips Fox experience. *Australian Law Librarian*, 4-8.

Schegg, R., Liebrich, A., Scaglione, M., & Ahmad, S. F. S. (2008). An exploratory field study of web 2.0 in tourism. In O'Connor, P., Höpken, W., & Gretzel, U. (Eds.), *Information and Communication Technologies in Tourism 2008* (pp. 209–219). New York: Springer. doi:10.1007/978-3-211-77280-5_14.

Schein, E. (1992). *Organizational culture and leadership: A dynamic view*. San Francisco, CA: Jossey-Bass.

Schein, E. (2004). *Organization culture and leadership*. New York: Wiley.

Schermerhorn, J. (2009). *Management*. New York: Wiley-Blackwell.

Schilling, M. A., & Phelps, C. C. (2007). Interfirm collaboration networks: The impact of large-scale network structure on firm innovation. *Management Science, 53*(7), 1113–1126. doi:10.1287/mnsc.1060.0624.

Schmid, H. (1994). *Probabilistic part-of-speech tagging using decision trees.*

Schultz, W. (2001). *The moral conditions of economic efficiency.* Cambridge, UK: Cambridge University Press. doi:10.1017/CBO9780511549649.

Schumpeter, J. (1934). *The theory of economic development.* Cambridge, MA: Harvard University Press.

Schwaber, K. (2004). *Agile project management with scrum (Vol. 7).* Redmond, WA: Microsoft Press.

Schwartz, J. (2006). *The magic of thinking big.* London: Simon & Schuster.

Schwarz, A. (2003). *Defining information technology acceptance: A human-centred, management-oriented perspective.* (Unpublished doctoral dissertation). University of Houston, Houston, TX.

Scott, J. (2000). Social network analysis. *American Ethnologist, 24*(1), 219–220.

Scott, J. E., & Walczak, S. (2009). Cognitive engagement with a multimedia ERP training tool: Assessing computer self-efficacy and technology acceptance. *Information & Management, 46*(4), 221–232. doi:10.1016/j.im.2008.10.003.

Sears, N. (2009). Measures should be taken to provide granular control over each social networking site. *Engineering & Technology, 6*, 6.

Seashore, S., & Yuchtman, E. (1967). Factorial analysis of organizational performance. *Administrative Science Quarterly, 12*(3), 377–395. doi:10.2307/2391311.

Seddon, P., Shanks, G., & Willcocks, L. P. (2003). Introduction: ERP—The quiet revolution? In Shanks, G., Seddon, P. B., & Willcocks, L. P. (Eds.), *Second-wave enterprise resource planning systems—Implementing for effectiveness* (pp. 1–19). Cambridge, UK: Cambridge University Press. doi:10.1017/CBO9780511815072.001.

Semple, E. (2007). *Survey proves 90% of managers are clueless.* Retrieved September 1, 2011, from http://www.fastforwardblog.com

Senge, P. M. (1990). *The fifth discipline: The art and practice of the learning organisation.* New York: Doubleday.

Seokwoo, S., Nerur, S., & Teng, J. T. C. (2008). Understanding the influence of network positions and knowledge processing styles. *Communications of the ACM, 51*(10), 123–126. doi:10.1145/1400181.1400208.

Serrano, C., Fuertes, , & Gutiérrez, B. (2007). Online reporting by banks: A structural modelling approach. *Online Information Review, 31*(3), 310–332. doi:10.1108/14684520710764096.

Serusi, M. (2011). Customer service 2.0: Top 10 airlines and airports performing customer service through social media. *SimpliFlying.* Retrieved February 9, 2012, from http://simpliflying.com/2011/customer-service-2-0-top-10-airlines-and-airports- performing-customer-service-through-social-media/

Seyedhoseini, S., Jassbi, J., & Pilevari, N. (2010). Application of adaptive neuro fuzzy inference system in measurement of supply chain agility: Real case study of a manufacturing company. *African Journal of Business Management, 4*(1), 83–96.

Shachaf, P. (2008). Cultural diversity and information and communication technology impacts on global virtual teams: An exploratory study. *Information & Management, 45*(1), 131–142. doi:10.1016/j.im.2007.12.003.

Shadbolt, N. (2006). *Problemas sociales, eticos y legales: ¿Cómo afecta el aumento al acceso al conocimiento a nuestra sociedad?* Paper presented at Memories for Life: The Future of our Pasts. London, UK.

Shah, S. K. (2005). Motivation, governance & the viability of hybrid forms in open source software development. *SSRN eLibrary.* Retrieved from http://papers.ssrn.com/sol3/papers.cfm?abstract_id=898247

Shane, S. (2008). *The handbook of technology and innovation management.* New York: Wiley-Blackwell.

Shankar, C., & Bellefroid, V. (2011). *Microsoft dynamics sure step 2010: The smart guide to the successful delivery of Microsoft dynamics business solutions.* Birmingham, UK: Packt Publishing.

Shapiro, D. L., Furst, S. A., Spreitzer, G. M., & Von Glinow, M. A. (2002). Transnational teams in the electronic age: Are team identity and high performance at risk? *Journal of Organizational Behavior*, *23*, 455–467. doi:10.1002/job.149.

Sherman, K. (1998, November 1). Let the seller beware. *CIO Magazine, 1*.

Sheshimski, E., Strom, R., & Baumol, W. (2007). *Entrepreneurship, innovation, and the growth mechanism of the free-enterprise economies*. Princeton, NJ: Princeton University Press.

Sheth, J. N., & Parvatiyar, A. (1995). Relationship marketing in consumer markets: Antecedents and consequences. *Journal of the Academy of Marketing Science*, *23*(4), 255–271. doi:10.1177/009207039502300405.

Sheth, J. N., & Parvatiyar, A. (2002). Evolving relationship marketing into a discipline. *Journal of Relationship Marketing*, *1*(1), 3–16. doi:10.1300/J366v01n01_02.

Shi, D., Zhu, S., & Liu, L. (2007). Clustering coefficients of growing networks. *Physica A: Statistical Mechanics and its Applications, 381*, 515-524.

Shiels, M. (2011). Twitter co-founder Jack Dorsey rejoins company. *BBC News*. Retrieved from http://www.bbc.co.uk/news/business-12889048

Shih, Y. Y., & Huang, S. S. (2009). The actual usage of ERP systems: An extended technology acceptance perspective. *Journal of Research and Practice in Information Technology*, *41*(3), 263–276.

Shimp, T. A., & Bearden, W. O. (1982). The use of extrinsic cues to facilitate product adoption. *JMR, Journal of Marketing Research*, *19*(2), 229–240. doi:10.2307/3151623.

Shim, S. S. Y., Bhalla, G., & Pendyala, V. (2005). Federated identity management. *IEEE Computer*, *38*(12), 120–122. doi:10.1109/MC.2005.408.

Shin, Y. (2005). Conflict resolution in virtual teams. *Organizational Dynamics*, *34*(4), 331–345. doi:10.1016/j.orgdyn.2005.08.002.

Shivers-Blackwell, S. L., & Charles, A. C. (2006). Ready, set, go: Examining student readiness to use ERP technology. *Journal of Management Development*, *25*(8), 795–805. doi:10.1108/02621710610684268.

Shi, Y. Z., Cheung, K. M., & Prendergast, G. (2005). *The effectiveness of sales promotion tools: A Hong Kong study*. Hong Kong: Hong Kong Baptist University.

Shum, S. B., Motta, E., & Domingue, J. (2000). ScholOnto: An ontologybased digital library server for research documents and discourse. *International Journal on Digital Libraries*, *3*(3), 237–248. doi:10.1007/s007990000034.

Shu, W., & Chuang, Y.-H. (2011). Why people share knowledge in virtual communities? *Social and Personality*, *39*(5), 671–690. doi:10.2224/sbp.2011.39.5.671.

Sicilia, M., Ruiz, S., & Munuera, J. L. (2005). Effects of interactivity in a web site: The moderating effect of need for cognition. *Journal of Advertising*, *34*(3), 31–45. doi:10.1080/00913367.2005.10639202.

Siegel, J., & Shim, J. (2000). *Accounting handbook*. New York: Barron.

Sigala, M. (2002). Modelling e-marketing strategies: Internet presence and exploitation of Greek hotels. *Journal of Travel & Tourism Marketing*, *11*(2), 83–103.

Sigala, M. (2008). Web 2.0, social marketing strategies and distribution channels for city destinations: Enhancing the participatory role of travelers and exploiting their collective intelligence. In Gascó-Hernández, M., & Torres-Coronas, T. (Eds.), *Information Communications Technologies and City Marketing*. Hershey, PA: Information Science Publishing.

Sigala, M. (2011). Preface – Special issue on web 2.0 in travel and tourism: Empowering and changing the role of travelers. *Computers in Human Behavior*, *27*, 607–608. doi:10.1016/j.chb.2010.04.005.

Sigala, M., & Marianidis, D. (2010). DMOs, e-democracy and collaborative destination management: An implementation framework. In Gretzel, U., Law, R., & Fuchs, M. (Eds.), *Information and Communication Technologies in Tourism 2010* (pp. 235–246). New York: Springer. doi:10.1007/978-3-211-99407-8_20.

Siggelkow, N., & Rivkin, J. W. (2005). Speed and search: Designing organizations for turbulence and complexity. *Organization Science*, 101–122. doi:10.1287/orsc.1050.0116.

Siika, A. M., Rotich, J. K., Simiyu, C. J., Kigotho, E. M., Smith, F. E., & Sidle, J. E. et al. (2005). An electronic medical record system for ambulatory care of HIV-infected patients in Kenya. *International Journal of Medical Informatics*, *74*(5), 345–355. doi:10.1016/j.ijmedinf.2005.03.002 PMID:15893257.

Silva, A., & Gardesani, R. (2005). *Impactos do CRM no relacionamento da empresa com clientes*. Paper presented at the Congresso Anual de Tecnologia da Informação. Aviero, Portugal.

Silva, P., & Silva, A. (2007). Design experiences with the learning objects board system. In *Proceedings of the Hawaii International Conference on System Sciences (HICSS-40)*. IEEE Computer Society.

Silva, P., & Silva, A. R. (2009). Application scenarios for the learning objects pool. *Journal of Universal Computer Science*, *15*(7).

Simões, D. (2010). *Enterprise data warehouses: A conceptual framework for a successful implementation*. Paper presented at the Canadian Council for Small Business & Entrepreneurship Annual Conference (CCSBE 2010). Calgary, Canada.

Simões, D., & Soares, A. L. (2003). *Redes organizacionais e desenvolvimento de sistemas de informação*. Paper presented at the 4ª Conferência da Associação Portuguesa de Sistemas de Informação (CAPSI'03). Porto, Portugal.

Simões, D., Ferreira, H., & Soares, A. L. (2007). *Ontology engineering in virtual breeding environments*. Paper presented at the 8th IFIP Working Conference on Virtual Enterprises (PRO-VE'07). New York, NY.

Simões, D., & Soares, A. L. (2007). Knowledge communities and inter-organizational networks. In Putnik, G. D., & Cunha, M. M. (Eds.), *Encyclopedia of Networked and Virtual Organizations*. Hershey, PA: Information Science Reference.

Simon, C. J., & Warner, J. T. (1992). Matchmaker, matchmaker: The effect of old boy networks on job match quality, earnings, and tenure. *Journal of Labor Economics*, *10*(3), 306–330. doi:10.1086/298289.

Simon, H. (1976). *Administrative behavior: A study of decision-making processes in administrative organizations*. New York: Free Press.

Simon, S. J., & Paper, D. (2007). User acceptance of voice recognition technology: An empirical extension of the technology acceptance model. *Journal of Organizational and End User Computing*, *19*(1), 24–50. doi:10.4018/joeuc.2007010102.

Singer, P. (1999). *Practical ethics*. Oxford, UK: Oxford University Press.

Sirin, E., & Parsia, B. (2004). *Pellet: An owl dl reasoner*.

SITA. (2007). *Airline ICT trends survey 2007 executive summary*. Retrieved from http://www.sita.aero/NR/rdonlyres/2C464901-6574-4AA0-B4E317199B9B8D45/0/AirlineIT07Booklet.pdf

Sittig, D. F., King, S., & Hazlehurst, B. L. (2001). A survey of patient-provider e-mail communication: What do patients think? *International Journal of Medical Informatics*, *61*(1), 71–80. doi:10.1016/S1386-5056(00)00134-9 PMID:11248604.

Skarzynski, P., & Gibson, R. (2008). *Innovation to the core*. Boston: Harvard Business Press.

Skoog, R., Von Lehmen, A., Clapp, G., Gannett, J. W., Kobrinski, H., & Poudyal, V. (2004). Metro network design methodologies that build a next-generation network infrastructure based on this generation's services and demands. *Journal of Lightwave Technology*, *22*(11), 2680–2692. doi:10.1109/JLT.2004.836748.

Skrt, R. (2007). *Spletne socialne mreže*. Retrieved October 25, 2011, from http://www.mojmikro.si/preziveti/kar_tako/spletne_socialne_mrezenavidezna_indija_koromandija

Sledgianowski, D., & Kulviwat, S. (2009). Using social network sites: The effects of playfulness, critical mass and trust in a hedonic context. *Journal of Computer Information Systems*, *49*(4), 74–83.

Sliger, M., & Broderick, S. (2008). *The software project manager's bridge to agility*. Boston: Pearson Education, Inc..

Small, G. (2009). *El cerebro digital*. Barcelona, Spain: Ediciones Urano.

Smith, A., & Peck, B. (2010). The teacher as the `digital perpetrator': Implementing web 2.0 technology activity as assessment practice for higher education innovation or imposition?. *Procedia - Social and Behavioral Sciences, 2*(2), 4800-4804.

Snowden, D., & Boone, M. (2007). A leader's framework for decision making. *Harvard Business Review, 85*(11), 68–76. PMID:18159787.

Social Business Systems. (2011). *Success factors for enterprise 2.0 applications*. Retrieved October 30, 2011, from http://www.aiim.org

Soliman, F., Innes, C., & Spooner, K. (1999). Managing the human resources' knowledge. In *Proceedings of the Seventh Annual Conference of the International Employment Relations Association*, (pp. 497-510). Christchurch, New Zealand: Lincoln University.

Soliman, F. (2009). Modelling the appraisal of quality management programs. *The Employment Relations Record, 9*(2), 73–83.

Soliman, F. (2010). Role of human resources management as a CoP match-maker. *The International Employment Relations Review, 16*(1), 69–81.

Soliman, F. (2011). Could one transformational leader convert the organisation from knowledge based into learning organisation, then into innovation? *Journal of Modern Accounting and Auditing, 7*(12), 1352–1361.

Soliman, F. (2011). Globalisation as driver for transforming organisations from knowledge to learning and then to innovation. In Srivastava, R., Pandy, T., Kumar, N., & Singhal, R. (Eds.), *Business Competitiveness in the 21st Century* (pp. 42–52). New Delhi: MacMillan Publishers India Ltd..

Soliman, F. (2011). Modelling the role of HRM in the innovation chain. *The Employment Relations Record, 11*(2), 1–20.

Soliman, F., & Spooner, K. (2000). Strategies for implementing knowledge management: Role of human resources management. *Journal of Knowledge Management, 4*(4), 337–345. doi:10.1108/13673270010379894.

Soliman, F., & Youssef, M. (2003). The role of critical information in enterprise knowledge management. *Industrial Management & Data Systems, 103*(7), 484–490. doi:10.1108/02635570310489188.

Solomon, C. M. (1995). Global teams: The ultimate collaboration. *The Personnel Journal, 74*(9), 49–53.

Solomon, C. M. (2001). Managing virtual teams. *Workforce, 80*(6), 60–64.

Solove, D. J. (2006). A brief history of information privacy law. In Wolf, C. (Ed.), *Proskauer on Privacy: A Guide to Privacy and Data Security Law in the Information Age* (pp. 1–46). New York, NY: Practising Law Institute.

Somers, M. T., Nelson, K., & Karimi, J. (2003). Confirmatory factor analysis of the end-user computing satisfaction instrument: Replication within an ERP domain. *Decision Sciences, 34*(3), 595–621. doi:10.1111/j.1540-5414.2003.02428.x.

Somers, T. M., & Neslon, K. G. (2004). A taxonomy of players and activities across the ERP project life cycle. *Information & Management, 41*(3), 257–278. doi:10.1016/S0378-7206(03)00023-5.

Sood & Adams. (1984). Model of management learning styles or predictor of export behavior and performance. *Journal of Business Research, 12*, 169–182. doi:10.1016/0148-2963(84)90004-3.

Sorj, B. (2003). *Brasil@povo.com: A luta contra a desigualdade na sociedade da informação*. Brasilia, Brazil: Unesco.

Soule, A. (2010). *Fighting the social media wildfire: How crisis communication must adapt to prevent from fanning the flames*. (Thesis). University of North Carolina at Chapel Hill, Chapel Hill, NC.

Sousa, L., & Gomes, R. (2010). Strategy 2.0 to a teaching and learning process in higher education. In *Proceedings of the 2010 International Conference on E-Education, E-Business, E-Management and E-Learning: Ic4e 2010*, (pp. 484-489). Los Alamitos, CA: IEEE Computer Soc.

So, W. C. M., Wong, T. N. D., & Sculli, D. (2005). Factors affecting intentions to purchase via the internet. *Industrial Management & Data Systems, 105*(9), 1225–1244. doi:10.1108/02635570510633275.

Spago, B. I. (2011). *Spago business intelligence*. Retrieved from http://www.spagoworld.org/

Spivack, N. (2007). *How the WebOS evolves?* Retrieved February 2011 from http://novaspivack.typepad.com/nova_spivacks_Weblog/2007/02/steps_towards_a.html

Splichal, S. (1997). *Javno mnenje: Teoretski razvoj in spori v XX*. Ljubljana, Slovenia: Fakulteta za družbene vede.

Spruit, M., & Abdat, N. (2012). The pricing strategy guideline framework for SaaS vendors. *International Journal of Strategic Information Technology and Applications*, *3*(1), 38–53. doi:10.4018/jsita.2012010103.

Srivastava, S. (2007). Green supply-chain management: A state-of-the-art literature review. *International Journal of Management Reviews*, *9*(1), 53–80. doi:10.1111/j.1468-2370.2007.00202.x.

Stanforth, N. F., Lennon, S. J., & Moore, S. (2000). *Perceived risk and purchase intent associated with television shopping*. Paper presented at Frontiers in Direct and Interactive Marketing Research. New York, NY.

Starbucks (Producer). (2011, October 28). *The create jobs for USA fund* [informative video]. Retrieved November 15, 2011, from http://www.youtube.com/user/Starbucks

Starbucks. (2011). *LinkedIn*. Retrieved November 15, 2011, from http://www.linkedin.com/company/starbucks

Starbucks. (2011). *Facebook*. Retrieved November 15, 2011, from http://www.facebook.com/Starbucks

Stata, R. (1989). Organisational learning-the key to management innovation. *Sloan Management Review*, *30*(3), 63–74.

Staw, B. (1986). Organizational psychology and the pursuit of the happy/productive worker. *California Management Review*, *28*(4), 40–53. doi:10.2307/41165214.

Steckle, N., & Fondas, N. (1995). Building team leader effectiveness: A diagnostic tool. *Organizational Dynamics*, *23*(3), 20. doi:10.1016/0090-2616(95)90023-3.

Steenkamp, J. E. M., & Baumgartner, H. (1992). The role of optimum stimulation level in exploratory consumer behavior. *The Journal of Consumer Research*, *19*, 434–448. doi:10.1086/209313.

Steers, R. (1975). Problems in the measurement of organizational effectiveness. *Administrative Science Quarterly*, *20*(4), 546–558. doi:10.2307/2392022.

Steers, R. (1977). *Organizational effectiveness: A behavioral view*. Santa Monica, CA: Goodyear.

Steffen, A. (2006). *Worldchanging: A user's guide for the 21st century*. New York: Harry N. Abrams.

Stepper, J. (2011). *Don't retweet the revolution*. Retrieved October 1, 2011, from http://johnstepper.com

Sterne, J. (2010). *Social media metrics: How to measure and optimize your marketing investment*. New York: John Wiley & Sons, Inc..

Stevenson, J. S., Bruner, G. C. II, & Kumar, A. (2000). Webpage background and viewer attitudes. *Journal of Advertising Research*, (January): 29–34.

Stewart, D., & Grout, J. (2001). The human side of mistake-proofing. *Production and Operations Management*, *10*(4), 440–459. doi:10.1111/j.1937-5956.2001.tb00086.x.

Stoitsev, T., Scheidl, S., & Spahn, M. (2007). A framework for light-weight composition and management of ad-hoc business processes. *Lecture Notes in Business Information Processing*, *4849*, 213–226.

Strange, K. F. T. (2009). *Making BI and data warehousing strategic: The key issues, LE-19-4691*. Gartner Group.

Strasses, S., Eveland, J., Cummins, G., Deniston, L., & Romani, J. (1981). Conceptualizing the goal and systems models of organizational effectiveness – Implications for comparative evaluation research. *Journal of Management Studies*, *18*(3), 321–340. doi:10.1111/j.1467-6486.1981.tb00105.x.

Straub, D. (1989). Validating instruments in MIS research. *Management Information Systems Quarterly*, *13*(2), 147–169. doi:10.2307/248922.

Student, K. (1968). Supervisory influence and work group performance. *The Journal of Applied Psychology*, *52*(3), 188–194. doi:10.1037/h0025886 PMID:5659502.

Suchanek, F. M., Ifrim, G., & Weikum, G. (2006). *LEILA: Learning to extract information by linguistic analysis*.

Su, F., & Beaumont, C. (2010). Evaluating the use of a wiki for collaborative learning. *Innovations in Education and Teaching International*, *47*(4), 417–431. doi:10.1080/14703297.2010.518428.

Sum, S. M. (2008). *Internet technology and social capital: how the Internet affects seniors' social capital and wellbeing*. Sydney, Australia: University of Sydney.

Sung, Y., Kim, Y., Kwon, O., & Moon, J. (2010). An explorative study of korean consumer participation in virtual brand communities in social network sites. *Journal of Global Marketing*, *23*(5), 430–445. doi:10.1080/08911762.2010.521115.

Sun, P. Y. T., & Scott, J. L. (2003). Exploring the divide-organisational learning and learning organisation. *The Learning Organization*, *10*(4), 202–215. doi:10.1108/09696470310476972.

Sun, Y., Bhattacherjee, A., & Ma, Q. (2009). Extending technology usage to work settings: The role of perceived work compatibility in ERP implementation. *Information & Management*, *46*, 351–356. doi:10.1016/j.im.2009.06.003.

Sun, Y., & Chen, C. (2011). Towards coequal authorization for dynamic collaboration.[LNCS]. *Proceedings of Active Media Technology*, *6890*, 229–240. doi:10.1007/978-3-642-23620-4_26.

Sveiby, K.-E. (2010). *Methods for measuring intangible assets*. Retrieved in July 2010, from www.sveiby.com/articles/IntangibleMethods.htm

Swafford, P., Ghosh, S., & Murthy, N. (2008). Achieving supply chain agility through IT integration and flexibility. *International Journal of Production Economics*, *116*(2), 288–297. doi:10.1016/j.ijpe.2008.09.002.

Swanson, M., & Guttman, B. (1996). Generally accepted principles and practices for securing information technology systems. Washington, DC: National Institute of Standards and Technology (NIST).

Tamashiro, R. (2002). *Pros and cons of online learning: Conflicting perceptions among teacher education students*. Retrieved January 2011 from http://www.hiceducation.org/edu_proceedings/Roy Tamashiro.pdf

Tang, C. S. (2006). Robust strategies for mitigating supply chain disruptions. *International Journal of Logistics: Research and Applications*, *9*(1), 33–45. doi:10.1080/13675560500405584.

Tan, S. T. (1999). Strategies for reducing consumers' risk aversion in internet shopping. *Journal of Consumer Marketing*, *16*(2), 163–180. doi:10.1108/07363769910260515.

Taylor, D. G., Lewin, J. E., & Strutton, D. (2011). Friends, fans, and followers: Do ads work on social networks? *Journal of Advertising Research*, *51*(1), 258–275. doi:10.2501/JAR-51-1-258-275.

Teichmann, K., & Zins, A. (2008). Information elements on DMO-Web sites: Alternative approaches for measuring perceived utility. In O'Connor, P., Höpken, W., & Gretzel, U. (Eds.), *Information and Communication Technologies in Tourism 2008* (pp. 209–219). New York: Springer. doi:10.1007/978-3-211-77280-5_19.

Tenenhaus, M., Vinzi, V. E., Chatelin, Y. M., & Lauro, C. (2005). PLS path modelling. *Computational Statistics & Data Analysis*, *48*, 159–205. doi:10.1016/j.csda.2004.03.005.

The Liberty Alliance Project. (2005). *Liberty alliance identity federation 1.2 (ID-FF 1.2) specifications*. Retrieved November 3, 2011, from http://www.projectliberty.org/liberty/resource_center/specifications/liberty_alliance_id_ff_1_2_specifications/

Themistocleous, M., & Chen, H. (2004). Investigating the integration of SMEs' information systems: An exploratory case study. *International Journal of Information Technology and Management*, *3*(2-4), 208–234. doi:10.1504/IJITM.2004.005033.

This WeekIn Startups (Producer). (2011, January 4). *This week in startups - Frank Speiser, founder of SocialFlow.com* [informative video]. Retrieved November 15, 2011, from http://thisweekin.com/thisweekin-startups/this-week-in-startups-105-frank-speiser-founder-of-socialflow-com/

Thompson, L., & Cupples, J. (2008). Seen and not heard? Text messagind and digital sociality. *Social & Cultural Geography*, *9*(1), 95–108. doi:10.1080/14649360701789634.

Thompson, R., Compeau, D., & Higgins, C. (2006). Intentions to use information technologies: An integrative model. *Journal of Organizational and End User Computing, 18*(3), 25–46. doi:10.4018/joeuc.2006070102.

Thorbjornsen, H., & Supphellen, M. (2004). The impact of brand loyalty on website usage. *Journal of Brand Management, 11*(3), 199–208. doi:10.1057/palgrave.bm.2540166.

Tidd, J., & Bessant, J. (2009). *Managing innovation: Integrating technological, market and organizational change*. Chichester, UK: Wiley.

Top, E., Yukselturk, E., & Inan, F. A. (2010). Reconsidering usage of blogging in preservice teacher education courses. *The Internet and Higher Education, 13*(4), 214–217. doi:10.1016/j.iheduc.2010.05.003.

Torrent-Sellens, J., Castillo, D., Gabaldón, P., Ruiz, E., & Sainz, J. (2010). *Hacia la banca multicanal*. Madrid, Spain: ESIC.

Townsend, A., DeMarie, S., & Hendrickson, A. (1998). Virtual teams: Technology and the workplace of the future. *The Academy of Management Executive, 12*(3), 17–29.

Treville, S., & Antonakis, J. (2006). Could lean production job design, be intrinsically motivating? Contextual, configurational, and levels-of-analysis issues. *Journal of Operations Management, 24*(2), 99–123. doi:10.1016/j.jom.2005.04.001.

Trevino, L., & Nelson, K. (2006). *Managing business ethics: Straight talk about how to do it right*. New York: Wiley.

Tsui, A. (1990). A multiple-constituency model of effectiveness: An empirical examination at the human resource subunit level. *Administrative Science Quarterly, 35*(3), 458–483. doi:10.2307/2393313.

Turban, E. Aronson, Liang, & Sharda, R. (2007). Decision support and business intelligence systems (8th Ed.). Englewood Cliffs, NJ: Prentice Hall.

Turban, E., King, D., Lee, J. K., & Viehland, D. (2004). *Electronic commerce 2004: A managerial perspective* (3rd ed.). Englewood Cliffs, NJ: Prentice Hall.

Turban, E., Sharda, S., Aronson, J. E., & King, D. (2008). *Business intelligence: A managerial approach*. Upper Saddle River, NJ: Pearson Prentice Hall.

Tversky, A., Sattath, S., & Slovic, P. (1988). Contingent weighting in judgement and choice. *Psychological Review, 95*, 371–384. doi:10.1037/0033-295X.95.3.371.

Twidale, M., Randall, D., & Bentley, R. (1994). Situated evaluation for cooperative systems. In *Proceedings of Computer-Supported Cooperative Work Conference – CSCW'94*. Chapel Hill, NC: CSCW.

Ullrich, C., Tan, X., Borau, K., Shen, L., Luo, H., & Shen, R. (2008). Why web 2.0 is good for learning and for research: Principles and prototypes. In *Proceedings of the 17th International World Wide Web Conference*, (pp. 705-714). IEEE.

Umble, E. J., Haft, R. R., & Umble, M. M. (2002). Enterprise resource planning: Implementation procedures and CSF. *European Journal of Operational Research, 146*(2), 241–257. doi:10.1016/S0377-2217(02)00547-7.

UN. (2010). *Government survey 2010 leveraging e-government at a time of financial and economic crisis*. New York: UN.

Universal McCann. (2010). *The socialisation of brands – Social media tracker wave 5*. Retrieved December 01, 2011 from www.mccannworldgroup.com/

Usluel, Y. K., & Mazman, S. G. (2009). Adoption of web 2.0 tools in distance education. *Procedia - Social and Behavioral Sciences, 1*(1), 818-823.

Uysal, M., Chen, J. S., & Williams, D. R. (2000). Increasing state market share through a regional positioning. *Tourism Management, 21*, 89–96. doi:10.1016/S0261-5177(99)00082-5.

Uzoka, F. M. E., Abiola, R. O., & Nyangeresi, R. (2008). Influence of product and organizational constructs on ERP acquisition using an extended technology acceptance model. *International Journal of Enterprise Information Systems, 4*(2), 67–83. doi:10.4018/jeis.2008040105.

Uzzi, B., & Schwartz, M. (1993). Structural holes - The social-structure of competition. In R. S. Burt (Ed.), Contemporary Sociologya Journal of Reviews, 22(2), 155-157. doi:doi:10.2307/2075713 doi:10.2307/2075713.

Vala, J., Monteiro, M., Lima, L., & Caetano, A. (1995). *Psicologia social das organizações: Estudos em empresas portuguesas*. Oeiras, Portugal: Celta Editora.

ValueNetworks. (2010). *What is value network analysis (VNA)?* Retrieved in December 2010, from www.valuenetworks.com

Van den Bulte, C., & Stremersch, S. (2004). Social contagion and income heterogeneity in new product diffusion: A meta-analytic test. *Marketing Science*, *23*(4), 530–544. doi:10.1287/mksc.1040.0054.

Van Den Bulte, C., & Wuyts, S. (2007). *Social networks and marketing*. Cambridge, MA: Marketing Science Institute.

van der Aalst, W. M. P., Pesic, M., & Schonenberg, H. (2009). Declarative workflows: Balancing between flexibility and support. *Computer Science -. Research for Development*, *23*(2), 99–113.

van der Aalst, W. M. P., Weske, M., & Grünbauer, D. (2005). Case handling: A new paradigm for business process support. *Data & Knowledge Engineering*, *53*(2), 129–162. doi:10.1016/j.datak.2004.07.003.

Van der Merwe, L. F., Pitt, L.P., & Abratt, R. (2005, Spring). Stakeholder strength: PR survival strategies in the internet age. *Public Relations Quarterly*, 39-48.

Van Dyne, L., Graham, J., & Dienesch, R. (1994). Organizational citizenship behavior: Construct redefinition, measurement and validation. *Academy of Management Journal*, *37*(4), 765–802. doi:10.2307/256600.

Vanilla. (2011). *True open source BI platform*. Retrieved from http://www.bpm-conseil.com/

Varadharajan, V. (2009). A note on trust-enhanced security. *IEEE Security & Privacy*, *7*(3), 57–59. doi:10.1109/MSP.2009.59.

Varian, H. R. (2002). Market structure in the network age. In Brynjolfsson, E., & Kahin, B. (Eds.), *Understanding the digital economy: Data, tools, and research*. Cambridge, MA: MIT Press.

Varner, P. E. (1999). *The economics of open source software*. Retrieved from http://www.cs.virginia.edu/~pev5b/writing/econ_oss/

Vázquez, J. A., Saldaña, I., & Celaya, J. (2009). La visibilidad de los museos en la web 2.0. *Portal Cultural Dosdoce.com*. Retrieved October 17, 2011, from http://www.dosdoce.com/articulo/estudios/3071/la-visibilidad-de-los-museos-en-la-Web-2-0/

Venkatesh, V. (1998). *User acceptance of information technology: A unified view*. (Unpublished doctoral dissertation). University of Minnesota, Minneapolis, MN.

Venkatesh, V., & Bala, H. (2008). Technology acceptance model 3 and a research agenda on interventions. *Decision Sciences*, *39*(2), 273–315. doi:10.1111/j.1540-5915.2008.00192.x.

Venkatesh, V., & Davis, F. D. (2000). A theoretical extension of the technology acceptance model: Four longitudinal field studies. *Management Science*, *46*(2), 186–205. doi:10.1287/mnsc.46.2.186.11926.

Venkatesh, V., Morris, M. G., Davis, G. B., & Davis, F. D. (2003). User acceptance of information technology: Toward a unified view. *Management Information Systems Quarterly*, *27*(3), 425–445.

Virkus, S. (2008). Use of web 2.0 technologies in LIS education: Experiences at Tallinn University, Estonia. Program: Electronic Library and Information Systems, 42(3), 262 - 274.

Virtuoso, O. (2010). *Universal server platform for the real-time enterprise*. Retrieved from http://virtuoso.openlinksw.com/

Viswesvaran, C. (2001). Assessment of individual job performance: A review of the past century and a look ahead. In Anderson, N., Ones, D., Sinangil, H., & Viswesvaran, C. (Eds.), *Handbook of Industrial, Work and Organizational Psychology* (*Vol. 1*, pp. 110–126). London: SAGE Publications. doi:10.4135/9781848608320.n7.

von Hippel, E. (2005). Democratizing innovation: The evolving phenomenon of user innovation. *Journal für Betriebswirtschaft*, *55*(1), 63–78. doi:10.1007/s11301-004-0002-8.

Vossen, G. (2009). Web 2.0: A buzzword, a serious development, just fun, or what? In J. Filipe, D. A. Marca, B. Shishkov, M. van Sinderen (Eds.), *ICE-B 2009 - Proceedings of the International Conference on e-Business*, (pp. 33-40). Milan, Italy: INSTICC Press.

Vygotsky, L. S. (1978). *Mind in society: The development of higher psychological processes*. Cambridge, MA: Harvard University Press.

Wagner, J., & Schneider, B. (1987). Legal regulation and the constraint of constituency satisfaction. *Journal of Management Studies*, *24*(2), 189–200. doi:10.1111/j.1467-6486.1987.tb00943.x.

Walsh, J. P., & Ungson, G. R. (1991). Organizational memory. *Academy of Management Review*, *16*, 57–91.

Wang, C., Xiong, M., Zhou, Q., & Yu, Y. (2007). Panto: A portable natural language interface to ontologies. *The Semantic Web: Research and Applications*, 473-487.

Wang, P., Zheng, J., Fu, L., Patton, E., Lebo, T., Ding, L., et al. (2011). A semantic portal for next generation monitoring systems. In *Proceedings of the Semantic Web – ISWC 2011* (Vol. 7032, pp. 253-268). Springer.

Wang, X. H., Zhang, D. Q., Gu, T., & Pung, H. K. (2004). *Ontology based context modeling and reasoning using OWL*.

Wang, H., Song, Y., Hamilton, A., & Curwell, S. (2007). Urban information integration for advanced e-planning in Europe. *Government Information Quarterly*, *24*(4), 736–754. doi:10.1016/j.giq.2007.04.002.

Wan, L., & Zhao, C. (2007). Construction of a knowledge management framework based on web 2.0. *Wireless Communications. Networking and Mobile Computing*, *12*, 5341–5344.

Warner, M., & Witzel, M. (2004). *Managing in virtual organizations*. London: Thomson.

Wasko, M. M., & Faraj, S. (2005). Why should I share? Examining social capital and knowledge contribution in electronic networks of practice. *Management Information Systems Quarterly*, *29*(1), 35–57.

Wasserman, S., & Faust, K. (1994). *Social network analysis: Methods and applications*. Cambridge, MA: Cambridge University Press. doi:10.1017/CBO9780511815478.

Wasserman, S., & Galaskiewicz, J. (1994). *Advances in social network analysis: Research in the social and behavioural sciences*. Thousand Oaks, CA: Sage Publications.

Watch, S. (2002). *Older people and information society technology: A comparative analysis of the current situation in the European Union and of future trends*. Academic Press.

Waterman, R., & Peters, T. (1982). *In search of excellence*. New York: Harper Collins.

Watson, H. J. (2009). Tutorial: Business intelligence –Past, present, and future. *Communications of the Association for Information Systems*, *25*(39).

Watson, H. J., Gerard, J. G., Gonzalez, L. E., Haywood, M. E., & Fenton, D. (1999). Data warehousing failures: Case studies and findings. *Journal of Data Warehousing*, 44–55.

Watson, H. J., & Wixom, B. H. (2007). The current state of business intelligence. *IEEE Computer*, *40*(9), 96–99. doi:10.1109/MC.2007.331.

Watts, D. J. (1999). Networks, dynamics, and the small-world phenomenon. *American Journal of Sociology*, *105*, 493–527. doi:10.1086/210318.

Weber, M. (1968). *Economy and society*. Totowa, NJ: Bedminster Press.

Webster Dictionary (WD). (1928). *An American dictionary of the English language*. Retrieved September 16, 2011 from http://www.cbtministries.org/resources/Webster1828.htm

Webster, F. E. Jr. (1992). The changing role of marketing in the corporation. *Journal of Marketing*, *56*(4), 1–17. doi:10.2307/1251983.

Weeks, S. (2001). Understanding trust management systems. In *Proceedings of the 2001 IEEE Symposium on Security and Privacy* (p. 94). Washington, DC: IEEE Computer Society.

Wei, S., Ruys, F., van Hoof, H. B., & Combrink, T. (2001). Uses of the internet in the global hotel industry. *Journal of Business Research*, *54*, 235–241. doi:10.1016/S0148-2963(00)00117-X.

Wellman, B., & Berkowitz, S. D. (1988). Social structures: A network approach. *PsycCRITIQUES*, *2*, 513.

Welti, N. (1999). *Successful SAP R/3 implementation—Practical management of ERP project*. Boston: Addison-Wesley Longman Publishing Co..

Were, M. C., Sutherland, J. M., Bwana, M., Ssali, J., Emenyonu, N., & Tierney, W. M. (2008). Patterns of care in two HIV continuity clinics in Uganda, Africa: A time-motion study. *AIDS Care*, *20*(6), 677–682. doi:10.1080/09540120701687067 PMID:18576169.

Werther, W., & Chandler, D. (2005). *Strategic corporate social responsibility: Stakeholders in a global environment*. London: SAGE.

Werthner, H., & Klein, S. (1999). *Information technology and tourism – A challenging relationship*. New York: Springer Verlag. doi:10.1007/978-3-7091-6363-4.

Werthner, H., & Klein, S. (2000). ICT and the changing landscape of global tourism distribution. *EM-Electronic Markets*, *9*(4), 256–262.

Weske, M. (2007). *Business process management - Concepts, languages, architectures*. Berlin: Springer.

What Is, R. S. S. (n.d.). *RSS explained*. Retrieved October 14, 2011, from http://www.whatisrss.com/

White, J. (2005). *Contemporary moral problems*. Surrey, UK: Wadsworth.

Wikström, S., Carlell, C., & Frostling-Henningsson, M. (2002). From real world to mirror world representation. *Journal of Business Research*, *55*(8), 647–654. doi:10.1016/S0148-2963(00)00205-8.

Wiley, D. (2000). *Connecting learning objects to instructional design theory: A definition, a metaphor, and a taxonomy*. Retrieved from http://reusability.org/read/chapters/williams.doc

Wiley, D. (2001). Peer-to-peer and learning objects: The new potential for collaborative constructivist learning online.[ICALT.]. *Proceedings of ICALT*, *2001*, 494–498.

Williams, J. B., & Jacobs, J. (2004). Exploring the use of blogs as learning spaces in the higher education sector. *Australasian Journal of Educational Technology, 20*(2), 232-247. Retrieved September 28, 2011, from http://www.ascilite.org.au/ajet/ajet20/williams.html

Williams, K. T. (2009). Case study: Dell hell: The impact of social media on corporate communication. Hoboken, NJ: CorpCommCollab.

Williams, L., & Anderson, S. (1991). Job satisfaction and organizational commitment as predictors of organizational citizenship and in-role behaviors. *Journal of Management*, *17*(3), 601–617. doi:10.1177/014920639101700305.

Wilson, S. (2008). Public key superstructure it's PKI Jim, but not as we know it! In *Proceedings of the 7th Symposium on Identity and Trust on the Internet (IDtrust '08)* (pp. 72-88). New York: ACM.

Wilson, H. J., Guinan, P. J., Parise, S., & Weinberg, B. D. (2011). What's your social media strategy? *Harvard Business Review*, *89*(7/8), 23–25.

Wixom, B., & Watson, H. J. (2001). An empirical investigation of the factors affecting data warehousing success. *Management Information Systems Quarterly*, *25*(1), 17–41. doi:10.2307/3250957.

Wold, H. (1982). Soft modelling: The basic design and some extensions. *Systems Under Indirect Observations*, 1–52.

Wolfinbarger, M., & Gilly, M. (2001). Shopping online for freedom, control, and fun. *California Management Review*, *43*(2), 34–55. doi:10.2307/41166074.

Wollan, R., Smith, N., & Zhou, C. (2011). *The social media management handbook: Everything you need to know to get social media working in your business*. New York: John Wiley & Sons, Inc..

Womack, J., Jones, D., & Roos, D. (1991). *The machine that change the world*. New York: HarperCollins Publishers.

Woodman, R. W., Sawyer, J. E., & Griffin, R. W. (1993). Toward a theory of organisational creativity. *Academy of Management Review*, *18*, 293–321.

World Bank. (2009). Retrieved from http://go.worldbank.org/M1JHE0Z280

World Tourism Organization Business Council. (1999). Introduction. In *Marketing tourism destinations online: Strategies for the information age*. Madrid, Spain: World Tourism Organization.

World Tourism Organization. (2001). *E-business for tourism – Practical guidelines for tourism destinations and businesses*. Madrid, Spain: World Tourism Organization.

Wren, D. (2004). *The history of management thought*. New York: Wiley.

Wyld, D. C. (2008). Management 2.0: A primer on blogging for executives. *Management Research News*, *31*(6), 448–483. doi:10.1108/01409170810876044.

Xiaowei, L. (2006). A test on the systematic fuzzy measures of the key degree for the core employees' performance traits. *Canadian Social Science*, *2*(5), 38–43.

Xie, G., Yang, Y., Liu, S., Qiu, Z., Pan, Y., & Zhou, X. (2007). EIAW: Towards a business-friendly data warehouse using semantic web technologies. In K. Aberer, et al. (Eds.), *ISWC/ASWC '07: Proceedings of the 6th International Semantic Web Conference and 2nd Asian Semantic Web Conference* (LNCS), (vol. 4825, pp. 851-904). Berlin: Springer Verlag.

Xinyi, H., Yang, X., Chonka, A., Jianying, Z., & Deng, R. H. (2011). A generic framework for three-factor authentication: Preserving security and privacy in distributed systems. *IEEE Transactions on Parallel and Distributed Systems*, *22*(8), 1390–1397. doi:10.1109/TPDS.2010.206.

Yammarino, F. J., Spangler, W. D., & Bass, B. M. (1993). Transformational leadership and performance: A longitudinal investigation. *The Leadership Quarterly*, *4*, 81–102. doi:10.1016/1048-9843(93)90005-E.

Yang, H., Lim, S., King, J., & Helal, A. (2006). Open issues in nomadic pervasive computing. In *Proceedings of UbiSys'06 (LNCS)*. Berlin: Springer.

Yang, T., & Lai, H. (2006). Comparison of product bundling strategies on different online shopping behaviours. *Electronic Commerce Research and Applications*, *5*, 295–304. doi:10.1016/j.elerap.2006.04.006.

Yao, Y. (2006). Three perspectives of granular computing. *Journal of Nanchang Institute of Technology*, *25*(2), 16–21.

Yau, S., & Chen, Z. (2008). *Security policy integration and conflict reconciliation for collaborations among organizations in ubiquitous computing environments. Ubiquitous Intelligence and Computing (LNCS)* (*Vol. 5061*, pp. 3–19). Berlin: Springer.

Yaxley, H. (2008). *How PR practitioners should engage with social networking*. Retrieved October, 25, 2011 from http://greenbanana.wordpress.com/2008/02/28/how-pr-practitioners-should-engage-with-social-networking/

Yelmo García, J. C., San Miguel González, B., & Martín García, Y. S. (2007). *Análisis del potencial de las comunicaciones móviles para la mejora de los servicios proporcionados por la administración pública a las personas con discapacidad*. Retrieved from http://www.tecnimap.es

Ye, Q., Law, R., Gu, B., & Chen, W. (2011). The influence of user-generated content on traveler behavior: An empirical investigation on the effects of e-word-of-mouth to hotel online bookings. *Computers in Human Behavior*, *27*, 634–639. doi:10.1016/j.chb.2010.04.014.

Yeung, J., Chan, A., Chan, D., & Li, L. K. (2007). Development of a partnering performance index (PPI) for construction projects in Hong Kong: A Delphi study. *Construction Management and Economics*, *25*(12), 1219–1237. doi:10.1080/01446190701598673.

Yeung, T. A., & Law, R. (2004). Extending the modified heuristic usability evaluation technique to chain and independent hotel websites. *Hospital Management*, *23*, 307–313. doi:10.1016/j.ijhm.2003.03.001.

Yi, Y. M., Fiedler, K. D., & Park, J. S. (2006). Understanding the role of individual innovativeness in the acceptance of IT-based innovativeness: Comparative analyses of models and measures. *Decision Sciences*, *37*(3), 393–426. doi:10.1111/j.1540-5414.2006.00132.x.

Yongchareon, S., & Liu, C. (2010). Lecture Notes in Computer Science: *Vol. 6426*. *A process view framework for artifact-centric business processes* (pp. 26–43). Heidelberg: Springer. doi:10.1007/978-3-642-16934-2_6.

Yoo, K. H., & Gretzel, U. (2008). Understanding differences between online travel review writers and non-writers. In T. Hara (Ed.), *Proceedings of the 13th Annual Graduate Education and Student Research* (pp. 21-29). Orlando, FL: GESR.

Yoo, K. H., & Gretzel, U. (2010). Antecedents and impacts of trust in travel-related consumer-generated media. *Information Technology and Tourism*, *12*, 139–152. doi:10.3727/109830510X12887971002701.

Yoo, K. H., Lee, Y., Gretzel, U., & Fesenmaier, D. R. (2009). Trust in travel-related consumer generated media. In Höpken, W., Gretzel, U., & Law, R. (Eds.), *Information and Communication Technologies in Tourism 2009* (pp. 49–59). New York: Springer. doi:10.1007/978-3-211-93971-0_5.

Young, J. (2012). *College 2.0: Teachers without technologies strikes back*. Retrieved February 2012 from chronicle.com/article/College-20-Teachers-Without/123891/

Youngberg, E., Olsen, D., & Hauser, K. (2009). Determinants of professionally autonomous end user acceptance in an enterprise resource planning system environment. *International Journal of Information Management, 29*, 138–144. doi:10.1016/j.ijinfomgt.2008.06.001.

Young, K. (2011). Social ties, social networks and the Facebook experience. *International Journal of Emerging Technologies and Society, 9*(1), 20–34.

Youssef, H., Sait, S. M., & Khan, S. A. (2002). Topology design of switched enterprise networks using a fuzzy simulated evolution algorithm. *Engineering Applications of Artificial Intelligence, 15*, 327–340. doi:10.1016/S0952-1976(02)00066-0.

Yu, A. Y., Tian, S. W., Vogel, D., & Chi-Wai Kwok, R. (2010). Can learning be virtually boosted? An investigation of online social networking impacts. *Computers & Education, 55*(4), 1494–1503. doi:10.1016/j.compedu.2010.06.015.

Yu, C. S. (2005). Causes influencing the effectiveness of the post-implementation ERP system. *Industrial Management & Data Systems, 105*(1/2), 115–132. doi:10.1108/02635570510575225.

Yuchtman, E., & Seashore, S. (1967). A system resource approach to organizational effectiveness. *American Sociological Review, 32*(6), 891–903. doi:10.2307/2092843.

Yuki, G., & Howell, J. M. (1999). Organisational and contextual influences on the emergence and effectiveness of charismatic leadership. *The Leadership Quarterly, 10*(2), 257–283. doi:10.1016/S1048-9843(99)00014-4.

Yun, T. W., & Lee, W. (2001). *Psychological antecedents of amount of attention to web sites – An exploratory study*. Paper presented at 20th Annual Advertising and Consumer Psychology Conference, Online Consumer Psychology: Understanding and Influencing Consumer Behavior in the Virtual World. Seattle, WA.

Zablah, A. R., Bellenger, D. N., & Johnston, W. J. (2004). An evaluation of divergent perspectives on customer relationship management: Towards a common understanding of an emerging phenomenon. *Industrial Marketing Management, 33*, 475–489. doi:10.1016/j.indmarman.2004.01.006.

Zaccaro, S., & Bader, P. (2003). E-leadership and the challenges of leading e-teams: Minimizing the bad and maximizing the good. *Organizational Dynamics, 31*(4), 377–387. doi:10.1016/S0090-2616(02)00129-8.

Zack, M. H. (1999). Developing a knowledge strategy. *California Management Review, 41*(3), 125–145. doi:10.2307/41166000.

Zadeh, L. (1976). The concept of linguistic variable and its application to approximate reasoning. *Information Sciences, 8*, 199–249, 301–357. doi:10.1016/0020-0255(75)90036-5.

Zadeh, L. (1997). Toward a theory of fuzzy information granulation and its centrality in human reasoning and fuzzy logic. *Fuzzy Sets and Systems, 90*, 111–127. doi:10.1016/S0165-0114(97)00077-8.

Zadjabbari, B., Wongthongtham, P., & Hussain, F. K. (2008). Towards an ontological intellectual capital based model in sustainable business performance. In *Proceedings of CIMCA*. IEEE.

Zafiropoulos, C., Vrana, V., & Paschaloudis, D. (2006). The Internet practices of hotel companies: An analysis from Greece. *International Journal of Contemporary Hospitality Management, 18*(2), 156–163. doi:10.1108/09596110610646709.

Zaidi, M. A. (2006). Is Google the best search engine marketing solution? *SearchMarketing-UK.com*. Retrieved from http://www.searchmarketing-uk.com

Zammuto, R. (1982). *Assessing organizational effectiveness: Systems change, adaptation and strategy*. Albany, NY: SUNY Press.

Zammuto, R. (1984). A comparison of multiple constituency models of organizational effectiveness. *Academy of Management Review*, *9*(4), 606–618.

Zaščerinska, J. (2010). Conditions, criteria, indicators and levels of forming communicative competence. In *Proceedings of International Scientifical Conference Society, Integration, Education of Rezekne Higher Education Institution*. Rēzekne, Latvia: Rēzeknes Augstskolas Izdevniecība.

Zaščerinska, J. (2010). *Efficiency of English for academic purposes activity in student language education: developing the system of the external and internal perspectives*. Paper presented at the European Conference on Educational Research Education and Cultural Change. Helsinki, Finland. Retrieved December 3, 2011, from http://www.eera-ecer.eu/ecer-programmes/conference/ecer-2010/contribution/465-2/?no_cache=1&cHash=3b88f1a563

Zaščerinska, J., & Ahrens, A. (2011). *Components of languaging in tertiary studies*. Paper presented at the European Conference on Educational Research 2011 Urban Education. Berlin, Germany.

Zaščerinska J. (2009). Designing teaching/learning activities to promote e-learning. In AhrensLange (Eds.), First Asian Conference on e-Business and Telecommunications (pp. 22-35). Berlin, Germany: Mensch & Buch.

Zaščerinska, J. (2011). Social dimension of web 3.0 in engineering education. In Bassus, , & Ahrens, , & Lange (Eds.), *Information and Communication Technologies in Engineering and Business* (pp. 101-130). Berlin, Germany: Mensch & Buch.

Zaščerinska, J. (2011). How to teach content: Existing concepts and prospects for development. *Changing Education in a Changing Society*, *1*, 134–149.

Zaščerinska, J., Ahrens, A., & Bassus, O. (2011). Enterprise 2.0 and 3.0 in education: Engineering and business students' view. In Cruz-Cunha, M. M., Putnik, G. D., Lopes, N., Gonçalves, P., & Miranda, E. (Eds.), *Business Social Networking: Organizational, Managerial, and Technological Dimensions* (pp. 472–494). Hershey, PA: IGI Global. doi:10.4018/978-1-61350-168-9.ch025.

Žbogar, D. (2010). *Vpliv družbenih medijev na prakso odnosov z javnostmi*. Ljubljana, Slovenia: Fakulteta za družbene vede.

Zeinstejer, R. (2008). The wiki revolution: A challenge to traditional education. *TESL-EJ*, *11*(4). Retrieved September 28, 2011, from https://tesl-ej.org/~teslejor/ej44/m1.html

Zeisser, M. (2010). Unlocking the elusive potential of social networks. *The McKinsey Quarterly*, (3): 28–30.

Zenko, Z., Mulej, M., & Marn, J. (2004). Innovation before entry into the EU: The case of Slovenia. *Post Communist Economies*, *16*(2), 169–189. doi:10.1080/1463137042000223877.

Zhang, C. (2008). The institutional framework of the United Nations development programme--Ministry of science and technology (UNDP--most) telecenter project in rural china. *Information Technologies and International Development*, *4*(3).

Zhang, X., Song, M., & Huang, G. Q. (2009). Tourism supply chain management: A new research agenda. *Tourism Management*, *30*, 345–358. doi:10.1016/j.tourman.2008.12.010.

Zhou, S.-M., & Gan, J. (2008). Low-level interpretability and high-level interpretability: A unified view of data-driven interpretable fuzzy system modelling. *Fuzzy Sets and Systems*, *159*, 3091–3131. doi:10.1016/j.fss.2008.05.016.

Zigurs, I. (2003). Leadership in virtual teams: Oxymoron or opportunity? *Organizational Dynamics*, *31*(4), 339–351. doi:10.1016/S0090-2616(02)00132-8.

Zolin, R., Hinds, P., Fruchter, R., & Levitt, R. (2004). Interpersonal trust in cross-functional, geographically distributed work: A longitudinal study. *Information and Organization*, *14*(1), 1–26. doi:10.1016/j.infoandorg.2003.09.002.

zur Muehlen, M., & Indulska, M. (2010). Modeling languages for business processes and business rules: A representational analysis. *Information Systems*, *35*, 379–390. doi:10.1016/j.is.2009.02.006.

About the Contributors

Maria Manuela Cruz-Cunha is currently an Associate Professor in the School of Technology at the Polytechnic Institute of Cavado and Ave, Portugal. She holds a Dipl. Eng. in the field of Systems and Informatics Engineering, an M.Sci. in the field of Computer Integrated Manufacturing and a Dr.Sci in the field of Production Systems Engineering. She teaches subjects related with Information Systems, Information Technologies, and Organizational Models to undergraduate and post-graduate studies. She supervises several PhD projects in the domain of Virtual Enterprises and Information Systems and Technologies. She regularly publishes in international peer-reviewed journals and participates on international scientific conferences. She serves as a member of Editorial Board and Associate Editor for several International Journals and for several Scientific Committees of International Conferences. She has authored and edited several books and her work appears in more than 120 papers published in journals, book chapters and conference proceedings. She is the co-founder and co-chair of several international conferences: CENTERIS – Conference on ENTERprise Information Systems and ViNOrg – International Conference on Virtual and Networked Organizations: Emergent Technologies and Tools. She is editor-in-chief of the *International Journal of Web Portals*.

Fernando Moreira graduated in Computer Science (1992), M.Sc. in Electronic Engineering (1997), and Ph.D. in Electronic Engineering (2003), both at the Faculdade de Engenharia da Universidade do Porto. He is a member of the Dep. Informatics at Universidade Portucalense since 1992, currently as Associate Professor. He is a (co-)author of several scientific publications with peer-review on national and international conferences. He has already regularly serves as a member of the Programme and Organizing Committees of national and international workshops and conferences, namely CAPSI, ISEIS, CISTI, and CENTRIS. He conducts his research activities in Communication Networks, Quality of Services, eLearning, and m-Learning. He is the coordinator of the M.Sc. of Informatics. He is associated with NSTICC, ACM, and IEEE.

João Eduardo Varajão is a professor of Information Systems Management, Project Management and Software Engineering at the University of Trás-os-Montes e Alto Douro and a visiting professor at the University of Porto Business School. He is also a researcher of the Centro Algoritmi at the University of Minho. Born and raised in Portugal, he attended the University of Minho, earning his Undergraduate (1995), Masters (1997), and Doctorate (2003) degrees in Technologies and Information Systems. In 2012, he received his Habilitation degree from the University of Trás-os-Montes e Alto Douro. His current main research interests are in Information Systems Management and Project Management. Before joining academia, he worked as an IT/IS consultant, project manager, information systems analyst, and software developer, for private companies and public institutions. He has supervised more than 50 Masters and Doctoral dissertations in the Information Systems field. He has published over 250 works, including refereed publications, authored books, edited books, book chapters, and communications at international conferences. He serves as editor-in-chief, associate editor, and member of the editorial board for international journals and has served in numerous committees of international conferences and workshops. He is co-founder of CENTERIS – Conference on ENTERprise Information Systems and other events.

* * *

Andreas Ahrens was born in Wismar, Germany, in January 1971. He received the Dipl.-Ing. degree in electrical engineering from the University of Rostock in 1996. From 1996 to 2008, he was with the Institute of Communications Engineering of the University of Rostock, from which he received the Dr.-Ing. and Dr.-Ing. habil. degree in 2000 and 2003, respectively. In 2008, he became a Professor for Signal and System theory at the Hochschule Wismar, University of Technology, Business, and Design, Germany. His main field of interest includes error correcting codes, multiple-input multiple-output systems, iterative detection for both wireline and wireless communication as well as social computing.

Ana Margarida Almeida holds a PhD in Sciences and Technologies of Communication and is an Assistant Professor at the Department of Communication and Arts, University of Aveiro, Portugal. She is also the first cycle degree Director (New Communication Technologies Degree) and member of the Cetac.media research unit direction board. Her present research interests are related to multimedia projects management, communication, and health and digital inclusion.

Helena Alvelos graduated in Electronics and Telecommunications Engineering, received a MSc degree in Management (MBA) and a PhD in Engineering Sciences. She is currently an Assistant Professor in the Department of Economics, Management, and Industrial Engineering at the University of Aveiro and teaches subjects in the fields of Applied Statistics and Quality. She has published in several conferences and journals, and currently she is a researcher at the Governance, Competitiveness, and Public Politics (GOVCOPP), and her current research interests include data analysis, quality management, and statistical quality control.

Anna Antonakopoulou is a PhD candidate of the Intelligent Communications and Broadband Networks Laboratory (ICBNet) of the National Technical University of Athens (NTUA), Greece. She received her diploma in Electrical and Computer Engineering from the University of Patras in 2006. As a research fellow of the NTUA since 2007, she has participated in several European and national research projects. Her research interests include Internet Technologies, Information Security & Privacy, Semantic Web, Object-oriented software design and development, QoS in IP networks, Transport and control protocols; she has eight publications related to these fields.

Susana Garrido Azevedo (Ph.D in Management) is Assistant Professor of Logistics and Management at University of Beira Interior (UBI) – Portugal. She is member of the Research Unit UNIDEMI. Her research interests include: logistics, ICT in logistics (RFID), and supply chain management. She has published in several international journals and has published books in Operations Management, Logistics and Competitiveness areas. Also, she has collaborated as reviewer with many journals and also international conferences. She has published in several international journals and is also associate editor of The *International Journal of Management Science and Information Technology* (IJMSIT) and member of the editorial board of the *International Journal of Business Performance and Supply Chain Modelling* (IJBPSCM).

Zélia Baptista is a Portuguese and French language teacher and is currently the head of the Portuguese language department at the Macau Portuguese School. She received her degree in Romanic Languages from the University of Coimbra in 1979. Since 1976 until 1995, Zélia worked as a teacher for the public educational system in Portugal where she held several coordination positions in different schools. Afterwards, she moved to the Special Administrative Region of Macau where she has been teaching for the past two decades both Portuguese curricula and Portuguese as a foreign language (UMAC, IPM, IPOR). Zélia has worked at the Macau Portuguese School since its very beginning and has devoted much of her late career to translational pedagogy using the territory's unique characteristics as a learning platform. Zélia co-authored three trilingual publications with her students and is currently a Master in Education student at the University of Saint Joseph.

Alexandre Humberto dos Santos Barão is teacher of Portuguese Education Ministry and researcher of Instituto de Engenharia de Sistemas e Computadores - Investigação e Desenvolvimento (INESC-ID) Lisboa. As a teacher, he was responsible for several disciplines such as: object oriented programming, Web development, algorithms and data structures, and information systems modeling. He is the Social Network Analysis and Reengineering Environment (SNARE) operational coordinator. SNARE is a research project developed at the Information System Group, INESC-ID. He has interests in the following areas: Modeling and Metamodeling, Oriented Objects Programming, Hypermedia, Social Computing and Organizational Knowledge Management, Learning Objects, Social Software, and Collaborative Learning Platforms.

Salvador Del Barrio-García has a Ph.D. in Business Administration from University of Granada (Spain). He is an Associate Professor of Marketing and Market Research Department at this University. His area of specialization are the Integrated Marketing Communication (IMC), Online Consumer Behaviour, and Marketing for Higher Education. He has published several books as author and co-author on these matters. He has also published various peer-reviewed papers in prestigious journals such as *European Journal of Marketing, Cities, EURE, Public Relations Review, Industry and Higher Education, Journal of Marketing Trends, European Marketing Academy, Spanish Journal of Marketing Research.* He has directed research projects with businesses and the public administration and has taught master and doctoral studies in various universities. He is referee for several international journals: *European Journal of Marketing, CyberPsychology and Behavior, Cornell Hospitality Quarterly, Innovar Journal, Journal Research Science Teaching, European Marketing Academy.*

Olaf Bassus was born in Wolfsburg, Germany, in January 1956. He received the Dipl.-Oec. degree in Business Administration from the University of Economics, Berlin, in 1981. From 1981 to 1985, he was with the Institute of Business Administration of the University of Economics, Berlin, from which he received the Dr. Oec. degree in 1985. From 1986 to 1990, he worked as the Head of the Operative Planning Division and Deputy Head of the Finance Division in the machine building company NILES in Berlin. From 1990 to 1994, he worked as an assistant scientific director of the Institute of Financing, Taxation, and Auditing at the University of Technology and Economics in Berlin, and as freelance lecturer and management consultant in Berlin and Brandenburg. In 1994, he became a Professor for Accountancy and Auditing at the Hochschule Wismar, University of Technology, Business, and Design, Germany.

Roberto Berjón (PhD.). Received a PhD. in Computer Science from the Universidad de Deusto in 2006. At present, he is Professor at the Universidad Pontificia de Salamanca (España). He obtained a degree in Engineering in Computer Sciences at the Universidad de Deusto in 1993. He has been a member of the organizing and scientific committee of several international symposiums such as IWAAPAMS, SPEDECE, etc., and has co-authored papers published in a number of recognized journals, workshops, and symposiums. He is currently developing applications for mobile environments, focusing his work on Android.

Jorge Bernardino is Coordinator Professor at ISEC (Instituto Superior de Engenharia de Coimbra) of Polytechnic of Coimbra, Portugal. He received his MsC degree in Systems and Technologies of Information and PhD Degree in Computer Engineering from University of Coimbra, in 1994 and 2002, respectively. He was President of Scientific Council of ISEC during 2003–2005 and President of ISEC from 2005–2010. He is member of Software and Systems Engineering (SSE) group of Centre for Informatics and Systems of the University of Coimbra (CISUC) research centre. His research interests are in the areas of data warehousing, business intelligence, database knowledge management, e-business, and e-learning.

Samo Bobek is a professor of Information Systems at the Faculty of Economics and Business at University of Maribor. He teaches courses in undergraduate level (Introduction to Information Systems, Information Systems in Finance and Banking), Master of Science program (Information Systems Management, Management Information Systems, Information Systems in Service Organizations), and MBA program (Information Management). Professor Bobek's research areas are Strategic Information Systems Planning, Information management, and Banking technology. He has published several books in Slovene language. His bibliography includes more than 200 articles, conference papers, research reports etc. Professor Bobek is head of Information and organization systems department. Professor Bobek also acts as consultant to several corporations, banks, and insurance firms in Slovenia.

Silvana Rossy de Brito, Cyberspace Institute, Federal Rural University of Amazônia (UFRA), Brazil. Silvana R. Brito received the BS degree in computer science from the Federal University of Pará (1993), and she is a doctoral student in the same university. Her current research is focused on monitoring and evaluating training programs for large-scale digital inclusion.

Giorgio Bruno is an Associate Professor at Politecnico di Torino, where he teaches courses on software engineering and object-oriented programming. His current interests concern the operational modeling of business processes and collaborative services, and the design of information systems and workflow systems. He has authored two books and over 140 technical papers on the above-mentioned subjects.

María del Mar Sánchez Cañadas, Doctorate in Accounting and Professor of the Department of Business Administration and Management at the University of Almería. She teaches subjects related to the area of Financial Economics and Accounting at the Master and Doctorate. She is member of the research group New Approaches in Finance and Business Information Systems as well as several research projects with public funding. She has published articles in national and foreign magazines and has presented conference papers both nationally and internationally, as Congress of AEDEM, AECA, ASEPUC, etc.

Vera Silva Carlos graduated in Work and Organizational Psychology and took a Master's degree in Marketing. Currently, she is a Ph.D. Student in Business at the University of Beira Interior (Portugal) and she is teaching 'Marketing' and 'Electronic Commerce and Web Marketing' in this university. She is also a researcher at the Research Centre on Enterprise Science (NECE – Núcleo de Estudos em Ciências Empresariais). Her research interests are mainly focused on Internal marketing, Online social networks and Quality management, specifically on their influence on the individual's attitudes and behaviours at work. She is now investing in publishing her research papers in international journals and in books.

Maria João Carneiro is Assistant Professor of Tourism at the University of Aveiro (UA) (in Portugal) and researcher at the Governance, Competitiveness, and Public Policy (GOVCOPP) research unit at this University. She holds a Degree in Tourism Management and Planning from UA, an MBA from New University of Lisbon and a PhD in Tourism from UA. She is the Director of the degree program (licenciatura) in Tourism of the UA. She has published papers in several journals and conference proceedings, and has also presented several works in conferences and seminars. Her research interests are competitiveness of tourism destinations, consumer behaviour in tourism and destination marketing.

Maébh Coleman (MeBus, BSc) is a researcher in the College of Engineering and Informatics at the National University of Ireland, Galway. Her current research interests include green innovation and enterprise, open innovation, e-business, and technology transfer. Maébh has over ten years' international experience in the areas of ICT, project management, marketing and communications, and high-tech procurement.

Kathryn Cormican (Ph.D.) is a lecturer in the College of Engineering and Informatics at the National University of Ireland Galway. Her research interests lies in the areas of enterprise integration and analysis and technology innovation management. Kathryn leads a number of research projects in this area. She has published over 70 papers at international conferences and peer reviewed journals. Kathryn works closely with many leading organisations and SMEs helping them to diagnose, develop, and deploy new processes and systems.

Carolina Costa graduated in Teaching of Mathematics and in Applied Mathematics and Computation and received a MSc degree in Information Management. Currently she is pursuing a PhD in the Information Systems area from University of Aveiro. She has worked in technology applied to the teaching and learning process. During her studies, she has published in several conferences.

João Crisóstomo Weyl Albuquerque Costa, Applied Electromagnetism Laboratory, Federal University of Pará (LEA-UFPA), Brazil. João C. W. A. Costa received the B.Sc. (Elect.) degree from the Federal University of Pará (UFPA), the M.Sc. degree from the Catholic University of Rio de Janeiro in 1981, and 1990, respectively. He received the Doctor Degree in Electric Engineering in 1994 from the State University of Campinas, São Paulo. He is a researcher of the Brazilian National Research Council (CNPq) since 1994.

Esmeralda Crespo-Almendros has a Ph.D. in Business Administration from University of Granada (Spain). She is an Assistant Professor of Marketing and Market Research Department at this University. Their areas of specialization are the Marketing Communication, Online Consumer Behaviour and Marketing Online. She has published peer-reviewed papers in prestigious Spanish journals such as Revista Europea de Dirección y Economía de la Empresa and she has participated in prestigious congress such as EMAC, American Marketing (AM), ICORIA, ICMC.

V. Cruz-Machado Ph.D. in Industrial Engineering in CIM (Cranfield University, UK). He is an Associate Professor of Industrial Engineering at Faculdade de Ciências e Tecnologia, Universidade Nova de Lisboa, Portugal. He coordinates Postgraduate programmes in industrial engineering, project, and lean management. He teaches operations and production management and has published more than 150 papers in scientific journals and conferences, in addition to having supervised 50 MSc and PhD students. His main scientific activities are directed to the design of lean supply chains. He is the President of UNIDEMI (R&D Unit in Mechanical and Industrial Engineering) and the President of the IIE Portugal Chapter.

José C. Delgado is an Associate Professor at the Computer Science and Engineering Department of the Instituto Superior Técnico (Lisbon Technical University), in Lisbon, Portugal, where he earned the Ph.D. degree in 1988. He lectures courses in the areas of Computer Architecture, Information Technology, and Service Engineering. He has performed several management roles in his faculty, namely Director of the Taguspark campus, near Lisbon, and Coordinator of the B.Sc. and M.Sc. in Computer Science and Engineering at that campus. He has been the coordinator of and researcher in several research projects, both national and European. As an author, his publications include one book, several book chapters, and more than 40 papers in international refereed conferences and journals.

Gonçalo Paiva Dias holds a PhD in Computer Engineering from the University of Aveiro. He is currently the Director of the School of Technology and Management of Águeda of the University of Aveiro and researcher at the Research Unit for Governance, Competitiveness, and Public Policies (GOVCOPP) of the same University. He is a member of the International Editorial Review Board of the *International Journal of Electronic Government Research* (IJEGR), the Scientific Committee of the *Iberian Journal of Systems and Information Technology* (RISTI), and the Coordinating Committee of the Iberian Conference on Information Systems and Technologies (CISTI). He has more than thirty internationally published papers in the areas of electronic government, information society and systems and information technology.

George Dragoi received the B.S. in Electronics & Telecommunications and Dr. Eng. degrees and in Industrial Informatics from University "Polytechnica" of Bucharest, Romania, in 1982 and 1994, respectively. From 1982-1986, he was an Associate Researcher of the Romanian National Research Center in Telecommunication of Bucharest. From 1986 to 1990, he was a Research Assistant, from 1990 to 1993 lecturer, from 1993 to 1998 associate professor, and from 2006 to present, professor at the "Politehnica" University of Bucharest. He has been active in the fields of the industrial robots control, industrial informatics, computer-integrated enterprise, computer networks and telecommunications, virtual enterprise, and collaborative design systems. Since 1998, he has been associated with the Institute National Polytechnic at Grenoble, France, as Associate and Visiting Professor. He received the Romanian Academy Award "Aurel Vlaicu" in 1993, and it has served as a member of the National Council for Technological Education and Innovation after 1999.

João Vaz Estêvão is a researcher in the area of tourism studies. He completed his BA in Tour Operating Management at the Estoril Higher Institute for Hotel and Tourism Studies, in Portugal. In 2004, João Estêvão completed his MSc in Local Tourism Destination's Management at the University of Barcelona, Spain. João Estêvão is currently undertaking a PhD in Tourism at the University of Aveiro, Portugal. His PhD research subject is the adoption of Information Technologies by tourism destinations. Regarding his current professional activity, João Estêvão is a Professor at the School of Tourism and Hospitality Management of the Polytechnic Institute of Guarda, in Portugal, where he lectures subjects in the areas of tour operations, tourism planning, and development and Information Technologies in Tourism. He has presented papers in more than ten national and international conferences and workshops.

Paulo Fazendeiro received the Ph.D. in Computer Science and Engineering (2010), the equivalence of M.S. degree in Computer Science (2001), and the B.S. degree in Mathematics and Informatics (1995, with honors) all from the University of Beira Interior, Portugal. Currently, he is an Assistant Professor at the Informatics Department of the University of Beira Interior. His research interests encompass Computational Intelligence and Granular Computing including the application of fuzzy set theory and fuzzy systems, knowledge discovery and data mining, evolutionary algorithms and their parallelization, multi-objective optimization and clustering techniques with applications to image processing. Dr. Fazendeiro is member of the Pattern and Image Analysis group of the Portuguese Telecommunications Institute and is also a member of the Informatics Laboratory of the University of Algarve.

Carlos Figueroa was born in San Juan, Puerto Rico in 1959. He received the B.S. degree in computer science in 1981, and Master's degree from Jackson State University, USA, in 1991. He is currently Associate Professor of Information Systems at University of Turabo. His research interests are in database design, object business applications and social media influence in society. He is a freelance system analyst and has imparted many different courses and seminars in various topics to the public and private sector.

Sandra Filipe is an Invited Assistant Professor at the Higher Institute of Accounting and Administration of Aveiro University (ISCA-UA), Portugal, since 1999. She teaches Management and Marketing to undergraduate and postgraduate courses. She obtained her Master's Degree in Management by Business School of Lisbon University Institute (ISCTE–IUL), Portugal, in February 2000, and is a doctoral student of Marketing since 2009 at the same school (ISCTE-IUL). Currently, she is a researcher at the Research Unit of Governance, Competitiveness and Public Policy (GOVCOPP) of Aveiro University. Her main research interests are digital marketing, corporate social responsibility, relational marketing, consumer behavior, and marketing research. She has published in scholarly journals.

Juan A. Fraile is a PhD. in computer science from the University of Salamanca, Spain. He obtained the Engineering in Computer Sciences degree at the Pontifical University of Salamanca in 2000. He has been involved in the development of automated systems in the Everis Group company and the Data Processing Centre (Pontifical University of Salamanca). He has also been a co-author of papers published in recognized journals, workshops, and symposiums.

Carlos Renato Lisboa Francês, Laboratory of High Performance Networks Planning, Federal University of Pará (UFPA), Brazil. Carlos R. L. Francês received the BS degree in Computer Science from the Federal University of Pará (1995), master's degree in Computer Science from the University of São Paulo (1998), and Ph.D. in Computer Science and Computational Mathematics at the University of São Paulo (2001). Has experience in Computer Science, acting on the following subjects: Last mile networks, performance models (Markovian and simulation), and Bayesian networks. He is currently a professor of Computer Engineering at the Federal University of Pará and a researcher of the Brazilian National Research Council (CNPq).

Monique Goepel, M.A. in International Business Studies, is a research assistant at the Chair of Strategic Leadership and Global Management at the Berlin Institute of Technology. Her current research interests include innovation management and effective decision making in adaptive organizations. Previous engagements include Ernst & Young Australia and Audible GmbH.

Fotios Gogoulos is a PhD candidate of the Intelligent Communications and Broadband Networks Laboratory (ICBNet) of the National Technical University of Athens (NTUA), Greece. He received his diploma in Electrical and Computer Engineering from the NTUA in 2007. As a research fellow of the NTUA since 2007, he has participated in several European and national research projects. His research interests include Information Security and Privacy, Semantic Web, IPTV, Service Discovery Protocols, System Modelling and Simulation, P2P Networks; he has seven publications related to these fields.

Jacqueline Gladys Guzmán Sequeira is a Student Mastery of Computer Engineering in the Information Systems area. The studies and research have been performed in the Engineering Faculty of the Republic,Uruguay. She is member of the research group Semantic Information Systems of the University. She is interested in the following areas: Modeling, Semantic Web, Ontology, and problems related with interoperability and integration. In the last years she has worked in e-Learning. She has experience in teaching, she has been teaching in presential courses as well as in distance courses, and she has coordinated teaching areas.

Martin Heitmann is a research assistant at the Chair of Strategic Leadership and Global Management at the Berlin Institute of Technology. His main research interests are business development and company-community interaction in the software industry. Previous engagements of his include Deutsche Städte Medien-GmbH and Deutsche and Deutsche Telekom Laboratories.

Damjana Jerman received a Ph.D. in Marketing in 2008 from the Faculty of Economics at the University of Ljubljana. She is an Assistant Professor of Marketing at the International Business School Ljubljana. She also worked as an Assistant Professor at Faculty of Tourism Studies University of Primorska. In addition to teaching and researching, she is primary responsible for public relations and managing marketing communications programs in the logistical company Intereuropa Ltd. Co. where she oversees the management of public relations and marketing communications. Her research interests include empirical and theoretical issues in business-to-business marketing communications, public relations, consumer behavior and marketing communication strategy and implementation. She has published articles in domestic and international journals.

Dimitra I. Kaklamani is a Professor at the School of Electrical and Computer Engineering (SECE) of the National Technical University of Athens (NTUA). She has received the Diploma and Ph.D. degrees from the SECE, NTUA. She has published over 150 journal and conference papers and led and participated in several EU and national research projects. Her research interests span across different fields and include the use of Object-Oriented methodologies and middleware technologies for the development of distributed systems and privacy-aware infrastructures, and the development of visualisation and real-time simulation techniques for solving complex, large scale modelling problems of microwave engineering and information transmission systems.

Francisco J. Liébana-Cabanillas is an Assistant Professor in the Marketing and Market Research Department at the University of Granada (Spain) and holds a Ph.D. Business Sciences in this university. He has a degree in Business and Administration Science and a Master in Marketing and Consumer behavior, from the University of Granada. His main area of research and interest the field is the effectiveness of the mobile and online banking, the results of which are reflected in various papers, which have been presented at the AEMARK, JORNADAS HISPANOLUSAS. He is currently working on different research projects in Internet social networks, Internet ad effectiveness, and new technologies acceptance.

Georgios V. Lioudakis is a senior research associate of the Intelligent Communications and Broadband Networks Laboratory (ICBNet) of the National Technical University of Athens (NTUA), Greece. He received his Dr.-Ing. degree in Electrical and Computer Engineering from the NTUA in 2008. As a research fellow of the NTUA since 2000, he has participated in several European and national research projects. His research interests include privacy protection, mobile networks and services, software engineering, middleware and distributed technologies; he has several publications related to these fields. Since 2009, George is also an adjunct lecturer at the Department of Telecommunications Science and Technology, University of Peloponnese, Greece.

Dalton Lopes Martins, University of Sao Paulo (USP), Brazil. Dalton L. Martins received the B.Sc. (Elect.) degree from the State University of Campinas (2002), master degree in Computer Engineering from the State University of Campinas (2004) and he is a doctoral student in the Information Science from the University of São Paulo. Her current research is focused on Social Network Analysis (SNA).

Francisco Vitorino Martins is Economist Ph.D. in Management Science by University of Paris IX-Dauphine. Professor of Faculty of Economics of the University of Porto from 1981, and, of the Research Centre CEPESE-Management Studies. He is Professor and Researcher on Econometrics, Applied Statistics, Forecasting Methods, and Marketing Research. Author of the book *Econometrics* (1997, McGraw-Hill).

Montserrat Mateos (PhD.) at the present is a Professor at the Pontifical University of Salamanca, Spain. She received a Phd (with distinction) in Computer Science and Languages and Systems from the University of Salamanca in 2006. She obtained a degree in Engineering in Computer Sciences at the University of Salamanca in 2001. She has participated in several research projects related to Mobile and NFC technology, in some of them as main researcher; also she has published in a number international conference proceedings and has co-authored of papers in several recognized scientific journals. She currently is researching and developing applications for mobile environments, focusing her work on smartcards and NFC.

Sandra Morley is a quality engineer and holds a Masters Degree in Operations and Quality Management from the National University of Ireland Galway. She has worked for a large multinational medical device organisation in Galway in various roles over the last 15 years. In her current role of Senior Quality Systems Engineer, she has been involved in a large number of multi-site, multi-discipline teams. This involvement has prompted an interest in the theory of 'virtual teaming' and in the desire to understand how the work of these dispersed teams can be better supported and more appropriately structured.

Regina Motz holds a PhD in Computer Science from the Technische Universität Darmstadt, Germany (2004) and a Master in Computer Science from Universidade Federal Pernambuco, Brazil (1990). She obtained her degree on Computing Engineer Systems at the University of the Republic Uruguay (1988). She currently serves as Full Professor at Institute of Computing Faculty of Engineering of the University of the Republic, Uruguay.

Matjaz Mulej was born on Jan. 1941, in Maribor, Slovenia. Living in Maribor, Slovenia. Retired from University of Maribor, Faculty of Economics & Business, Maribor, as Professor Emeritus of Systems and Innovation Theory. He has published +1,500 publications in +40 countries. Visiting professor abroad for 15 semesters. Author of the *Dialectical Systems Theory* (see: François, 2004, International Encyclopedia) and Innovative Business Paradigm for catching-up countries. Member of New York Academy of Sciences (1996), European Academy of sciences and Humanities, Paris (2004), president of IFSR (International Federation for Systems Research with 37 member associations). M.A. in Development Economics, Doctorates in Systems Theory and in Management.

Francisco Muñoz-Leiva is Associate Professor in Marketing and Market Research at the University of Granada (Spain). He has a first-cycle degree in Statistics from the University of Jaén, a second-cycle degree in Research and Market Techniques and holds a Ph.D. in Business Sciences from the University of Granada. Although his main research interest is Internet consumer behavior and e-banking acceptance, he has also published papers other topics. His recent works have appeared in *Information & Management, Online Information Review, Cities, Quality & Quantity, The Service Industries Journal, Computers in Human Behavior, Defense and Peace Economics, International Journal of Internet Marketing & Advertising*, and communications in international conferences.

Zlatko Nedelko, born 1983, is an Assistant Professor at the Faculty of Economics and Business, Department of Organization and Informatics, University of Maribor (Slovenia). He has published over 40 texts, many of them abroad. The fields of his research interests include organization and management. Recently, he was involved in researching managerial values. He is also a member of many scientific committees at several international conferences.

João Negreiros took his Computer Science licentiate degree in Lisbon, Portugal (1989), MBA in San Diego, CA (1993), PhD in Lisbon, Portugal (2004), and Post-Doc in Almeria, Spain (2009). He worked for several Portuguese and American institutions during his stay in those previous countries while he published over fifty articles for conferences and research magazines worldwide and seven books regarding Geographical Information Systems (GIS), UNIX, and Processing of Digital Image by several publishers. Currently, he is an Associate Professor at Saint Joseph University, Macau, China.

Abraham Otero was born in Orense, Spain in 1978. He received the B.S. degree in physics in 2000 (with honors), and Ph.D degree from the University of Santiago de Compostela, in 2006. He is currently an Associate Professor of Computer Science and Artificial Intelligence at University San Pablo CEU. His research interests include fuzzy temporal knowledge representation and reasoning, biosignal processing, fuzzy constraint satisfaction problems, patient supervision, and the impact of social media. He is author of over 50 scientific papers in these fields.

Carmen Caba Pérez, Doctorate in Accounting and Professor of the Department of Business Administration and Management at the University of Almería. She teaches subjects related to the area of Financial Economics and Accounting at the Master and Doctorate. She is currently Deputy Dean of the

Faculty of Economics and Business Administration. She has published numerous articles in magazines including American and European ISI as well as in national magazines. She has published chapters in books published in North America and has presented papers at national and international conferences, such as the InterAmerican Accounting Conference, AEDEM, AECA, ASEPUC, European Association Accounting, CIGAR, etc. She is responsible for a research group and director of research projects with public funding.

Vojko Potocan, born 1962, is a Full Professor of organization and management on the Faculty of Economics and Business (FEB), Department of Organization and Informatics, University of Maribor, Slovenia. He teaches (on the graduate level, on the undergraduate level, and in doctoral program) in three universities in Slovenia and in three universities abroad (Germany, Croatia, and Czech Republic). He is also the head of postgraduate study of Management and Organization in FEB. He takes part in different foreign scientific conferences and realized a number of study visits on abroad. He was 10 times a visiting professor abroad and gave about eight further seminars at foreign universities. He has published +450 texts (+350 in foreign languages in 32 countries), including 8 books, and edited proceedings and textbooks. His research interests include Management, Organization, and Business Ethics.

Cláudio Alex Jorge da Rocha, Laboratory of High Performance Networks Planning, Federal University of Pará (UFPA), and University of Amazônia (UNAMA), Brazil. Cláudio A. J. da Rocha is graduated in Data Processing from the University of Amazônia (1991), masters in Computer Science and Computational Mathematics at the University of São Paulo (2001) and Doctor Degree in Electric Engineering from the Federal University of Pará (2009). He is currently a professor of Computer Science (University of Amazônia) and professor of Postgraduate Electrical Engineering (Federal University of Pará).

Mário Jorge Ferreira Rodrigues is a Teaching Assistant at the School of Technology and Management of Águeda of the University of Aveiro. He received his BSc degree in Applied Mathematics in 2000, from the University of Porto, and his MSc degree in Electronics and Telecommunications Engineering in 2004, from the University of Aveiro Electronics Telecommunications and Informatics Department. Currently, he is a PhD student in Computer Engineering in the same department. His current research interests include Human Language Technologies, namely Natural Language Processing and Knowledge Representation, and Electronic Government. He has been involved in European and national funded research projects.

Ricardo Gouveia Rodrigues has a Ph.D. in Business and teaches Marketing Research, Entrepreneurial Marketing and Data Analysis to undergraduate, master and doctoral students at the University of Beira Interior, Portugal. He is also a researcher at the Research Centre on Enterprise Science (NECE – Núcleo de Estudos em Ciências Empresariais). His main research interests are Entrepreneurial Marketing and Entrepreneurship Education, but he is also interested in studying the impact of marketing efforts on themes such as physical activity, children behaviour, online gaming addiction, and happiness. Ricardo Gouveia Rodrigues has published several books and book chapters, as well as peer-reviewed papers in international journals.

Arturo Haro de Rosario, research fellow in the department of Business Administration and Management at the University of Almería. He teaches subjects related to the area of Financial Economics and Accounting. He is member of the research group New Approaches in Finance and Business Information Systems as well as several research projects with public funding. He has published articles in national and foreign magazines such as the Spanish Venture Capital Journal and the Accounting and administration Journal. He has presented conference papers both nationally and internationally, as Congress of AEDEM, AECA, ASEPUC, Conferences Hispanic Lusas Scientific Management, etc.

Sebastian Marius Roşu received the B.E. in Aerospace Construction and in Informatics from University "Polytechnica" of Bucharest, in 2000 and University "Dunărea de Jos" of Galaţi in 2002, respectively. In 2009 obtained doctoral degree in Automatics from University "Polytechnica" of Bucharest. From 2001-2004, he was a Researcher in Machines and Thermal Equipment at the GRUP ROMET Buzău. Since 2004, he was Quality Surveillance Receiving Inspector and Pressure Test Supervisor at the Nuclear Power Plant Unit Two Site of Cernavodă. Since as 2006 he is telecommunications engineer at the Romanian Special Telecommunications Service. He has been active in the fields of the thermodynamic, design, nuclear systems, quality control, industrial informatics, computers, computer integrated enterprise, computer networks, radio communications network and collaborative design systems. Since 2005, he has been associated with the PREMINV Research Laboratory at the Polytechnic University of Bucharest, as PhD Student.

Miguel A. Sánchez (PhD.) Associate Professor at the Pontifical University of Salamanca (Spain). At present he is Director of the "Máster en Informática Móvil y Tarjetas Inteligentes" (MIMO – www.upsa.es/mimo) and Director of Innovation Projects based on Mobile Technology. He received a PhD. in Computer Science from the Pontifical University of Salamanca (Madrid campus) in 2007. He obtained an Information Technology degree at the Pontifical University of Salamanca (Madrid campus) in 1999 and an Engineering in Computer Sciences degree at the Pontifical University of Salamanca in 1993. He has been member of the organizing and scientific committee of international symposiums such as SPDECE, IWPAAMS, and IWANN, and co-author of more than 20 papers published in recognized journals, workshops and symposiums. He has worked on several Artificial Intelligence (AI) and Mobility Research projects sponsored by Spanish public and private Institutions, in 3 of them as main researcher.

Neide Santos earned a Master of Education degree from the Federal University of Rio de Janeiro (Brazil) in 1989 and a DSc degree in Engineering of Production at the same university in 1994. Since 1999, she is an associate professor in the Department of Computer Science at the State University of Rio de Janeiro. Currently, she is the assistant coordinator of graduate studies in Computer Science. She published nearly 30 papers in international journals and more than 50 papers in international and Brazilian conference proceedings. In addition, her main areas of interest are Knowledge Representation, Ontologies and Semantic Web, Computer-Supported Cooperative Work, Computer-Supported Cooperative Learning, Artificial Intelligence and Education, and Web-Based Education.

Alberto Manuel Rodrigues da Silva is Associate Professor of Information Systems at the Computer and Information Systems Department at the Technical University of Lisbon (Instituto Superior Técnico – IST/UTL) Lisbon, Portugal. He is also a senior researcher at INESC-ID Lisboa, and a partner at the SIQuant – Engenharia do Território e Sistemas de Informação company. He has interests in the following areas: Modeling and Metamodeling, Model Driven Engineering, Requirement Engineering, Social Computing and Organizational Knowledge Management with a particular emphasis on Software Engineering, Social Software, Learning and Cultural application domains. He is the author or co-author of 5 technical books and more than 150 peer-reviewed scientific communications and he has served on program committees of several international conferences and workshops. He is member of the ACM, PMI, and the Portuguese Ordem dos Engenheiros.

Aleksandra do Socorro da Silva, Cyberspace Institute, Federal Rural University of Amazônia (UFRA), Brazil. Aleksandra S. da Silva received the BS degree in computer science from the Federal University of Pará (1994) and she is a doctoral student in the same university. Her current research is focused on metrics to social network analysis to extract indicators from interaction networks and their correlation with indicators of participation in learning environments.

Ana Silva is currently responsible for Digital Marketing and Social Media at a large international manufacturing group, following a vast experience in the area of Competitive Intelligence and also of Collaboration Management. She holds a Management degree from the University of Porto (Portugal) and post-graduation studies in the areas of Marketing and Information Management and Marketing Intelligence. She teaches Enterprise 2.0 at the Porto Business School and is particularly interested in the future trends affecting work and the workplace. Ana is also involved in the organization of conferences that discuss the impact of social tools and platforms, and also of new concepts such as crowdsourcing or mass collaboration, in businesses, citizenship and society as a whole.

Marisa Silva graduated from Superior Institute Miguel Torga in Social Work. She has also a Master Degree in Family and Social Systems from the same Institute and has a PhD, with mention of European Doctor from the University of Salamanca. Presently she is teaching at The Polytechnic Institute of Viseu – School of Technology and Management of Lamego (ESTGL). She is the scientific coordinator of the Postgraduate studies in Centre Management and Social Services and one of the directors of GAADS – Office of Social Development and Monitoring. She collaborated on the project "Support to Education via Internet," held at ESTGL.

Dora Simões received her PhD in Informatics Engineering from the Faculty of Engineering of Porto University (FEUP-UP), Portugal, in 2008. She is Adjunct Professor, in informatics area, at the Higher Institute of Accounting and Administration of Aveiro University (ISCA-UA). Portugal. She is member of the Advisor Board of the *Journal Studies of ISCA-UA*. Currently, she is researcher at the Research Unit of Governance, Competitiveness, and Public Policy (GOVCOPP) of Aveiro University. As part of her doctoral work, she worked as a invited researcher at the Institute of Engineering and Computer Systems of Porto (INESC Porto), between 2003 and 2008. Her current research interests include information and knowledge management, organizational information systems (CRM – Customer Relationship Management), and collaborative virtual networks. She has published in various conferences and journals, nationals and internationals.

Fawzy Soliman graduated with a PhD degree and Master of Engineering Science degree from the University of New South Wales, Australia, and a Bachelor of Engineering degree from the University of Sydney. Published in international journals in excess of twenty-six papers, six book chapters, and three books, and in excess of fifty-two conference proceeding papers. Former editor of *Journal of Knowledge Management*. Guest editor of *Journal of Knowledge Management and Journal Operations Management*. His publication citations is in excess of 593 with an author impact h-index of 9 and I10-index of 9. Supervised 9 PhD graduates. Convenor of Australia's first conference on Knowledge Management KNOW'99 held on 26-27 November 1999. Taught in a number of international business schools in Australia and overseas. Invited speaker in a number of prestigious conferences. Prior to joining academia, he has held various positions in large Australian organisations.

Ana Filipa Sousa is a communication designer from Aveiro, Portugal. She has a bachelor's degree in New Communication Technologies and a master's degree in Multimedia Communication (Interactive Multimedia Specialization) both by University of Aveiro. During her academic journey, she developed projects within a variety of technological and social fields and became an enthusiast for project management. Besides previous research works in agile management, she has also explored the online education thematic. Furthermore, Filipa has undergone a specialized training in drawing and illustration and currently works as a freelance professional developing Web and graphic design projects.

Simona Sternad is senior lecturer of Information Systems at the Faculty of Economics and Business at University of Maribor. She has a PhD in the field of management information science. Her research areas are Business process reengineering, ERP solutions and e-business solutions, implementation of ERP solutions and maintenance of ERP solutions. Her bibliography includes more than 70 articles, conference papers, research reports, etc. She collaborates in several courses in undergraduate level (E-business, Introduction to Information Systems, E-Finance and E-Banking, Enterprise Resource Planning Solutions, E-Business Information Systems) and several courses in master of science program (Business Information Solutions, Strategic Management Issues in E-Business). Simona Sternad also cooperates with some companies in Slovenia as a consultant.

António Joaquim da Silva Teixeira is Assistant Professor at University of Aveiro Electronics Telecommunications and Informatics Department. He received his BSc and Master in Electronics and Telecommunications Engineering in 1991 and 1993, and his PhD in Electronics Engineering in 2000, all from the University of Aveiro. He is Chair of the Special Interest Group on Iberian Languages of the International Speech Communication Association (ISCA) and the Director of the Master in Speech and Hearing Sciences. His main research activity is in the area of Speech Processing and Multimodal Human-Machine Interaction. He is involved in several national funded research (LUL, AAL4ALL, Smartphones for Smart Seniors) and in a starting European project (AAL Paelife), has supervised 4 concluded PhDs and more than 35 Masters, supervises more than 10 PhD projects and co-authored more than one hundred publications (books, book chapters, international journals, and proceedings of international conferences).

Leonor Teixeira graduated in Management and Industrial Engineering, received an MSc degree in Information Management and a PhD in Health Information Systems area. She is currently an Assistant Professor with the Department of Economics, Management, and Industrial Engineering at the University of Aveiro and teaching in Technology and Information Systems areas. She has published in several conferences and journals, and currently she is researcher at the Governance, Competitiveness, and Public Politics (GOVCOPP) and of the Institute of Electronics and Telematics Engineering (IEETA) of Aveiro research units.

Ana Torres is a Ph.D. candidate at the Faculty of Economics of University of Porto, and recently finished her thesis. She holds a Master of Science in Management Science from the Faculty of Economics of University of Porto, in 2003. She was assistant Professor of Marketing at the University of Aveiro, and presently she teaches at University Portucalense, Portugal. Her previous work experience was in market research and marketing consultancy, having worked with several industries and services. She has published and presented several papers at the international conferences on Internet and leading technologies. Her current research interests are in digital economy, networks analysis, e-marketing strategy, e-commerce, consumer behavior, and quantitative marketing models. Her research is empirical in nature and makes extensive use of structural equation modeling.

Iakovos S. Venieris is a professor at the School of Electrical and Computer Engineering of the National Technical University of Athens since 1994. He received the Dipl.-Ing. degree from the University of Patras, Greece, in 1988, and the Ph.D. degree from the National Technical University of Athens, in 1990, all in Electrical and Computer Engineering. His research interests are in the fields of distributed systems, service engineering, agent technology, multimedia, mobile communications, and Intelligent Networks, Internetworking, signalling, resource scheduling, and allocation for network management, modelling, performance evaluation, and queuing theory. He has over 150 publications in the above areas. Prof. Venieris has received several national and international awards for academic achievement. He is a member of the IEEE and the Technical Chamber of Greece.

Jeļena Zaščerinska received the diploma in Russian Philology in 1994 from the Daugavpils University, Daugavpils, Latvia, Master Degree in English Philology in 2002 from the University of Latvia, Riga, Latvia. In 2011, she was awarded Dr. paed. Degree for her promotion thesis "Development of Students' Communicative Competence in English studies for Academic Purposes." In February 2012, Jeļena Zaščerinska was awarded expert rights in pedagogy by the Latvian Council of Science, Riga, Latvia. Jeļena Zaščerinska worked for a number of years at the interface of pedagogy and philology, and is now a senior researcher at the Centre for Education and Innovation Research, Riga, Latvia. She is a founding member and the Chair of the Board of the Centre for Education and Innovation Research, Riga, Latvia. She is author or co-author of some 40 contributions on teacher, engineer, and language education.

Bruno Završnik is a Professor of Marketing in the Faculty of Economics and Business. He received his PhD in Marketing from the same Faculty. He teaches a variety of courses at the undergraduate and graduate levels at Faculty of Economics and Business. His research interests include empirical and theoretical issues in B2B marketing communications, effectiveness of purchasing, retailing strategy, and implementation. He has published articles in domestic and international journals.

Index

P

R

S

T

U

V

W

Z

CPSIA information can be obtained at www.ICGtesting.com
Printed in the USA
BVOW06*1633021214

377175BV00001B/2/P